FIELDING'S
WORLDWIDE
CRUISES
FIFTH REVISED EDITION

FIELDING'S BERMUDA AND THE BAHAMAS 1991
FIELDING'S BUDGET EUROPE 1991
FIELDING'S CARIBBEAN 1991
FIELDING'S EUROPE 1991
FIELDING'S HAWAII 1991
FIELDING'S ITALY 1991
FIELDING'S MEXICO 1991
FIELDING'S PEOPLE'S REPUBLIC OF CHINA 1991
FIELDING'S SELECTIVE SHOPPING GUIDE TO EUROPE 1991

FIELDING'S ALASKA AND THE YUKON
FIELDING'S BUDGET ASIA and Southeast Asia and the Far East
FIELDING'S FAMILY VACATIONS USA
FIELDING'S FAR EAST 2nd revised edition
FIELDING'S HAVENS AND HIDEAWAYS USA
FIELDING'S LEWIS AND CLARK TRAIL
FIELDING'S LITERARY AFRICA
FIELDING'S TRAVELER'S MEDICAL COMPANION
FIELDING'S WORLDWISE CRUISES 5th revised edition

FIELDING'S WORLDWIDE CRUISES

FIFTH REVISED EDITION

BY
ANTOINETTE DELAND

FIELDING TRAVEL BOOKS
c/o WILLIAM MORROW & COMPANY, INC.
105 Madison Avenue, New York, N.Y. 10016

Text design by Marsha Cohen/Parallelogram

to

THOMAS KILLIP II, M.D.
(1903 to 1961)

always in grace with the sea . . .

Antoinette DeLand has been an observer, reporter and critic of the cruise industry for over a decade and finds each year to be just a little more volatile than the last! She has been among those present on several historic occasions—aboard the first western passenger vessel to call in China since 1948, at a christening by the late Princess Grace of Monaco in New York harbor, a launching or two, inaugural sailings and several reentries to service by various cruise ships.

Ms. DeLand studied Greek and Art History at Bryn Mawr College, the University of California at Berkeley, the University of Florence and Sophia University in Tokyo. She has worked as a journalist on London's Fleet Street as well as in Tokyo, Hong Kong and New York. She now works for herself—the only way to live—writing travel guides and articles and creating and producing travel films. She is the author of *Fielding's Far East* and a guide to Bermuda—now in its tenth successful year.

Antoinette Deland is married to Stephen Carter, an architect and photographer. They live in Connecticut and New York with two devoted Pekes—Mr. Ying and Genghis. Her only regret is that the Pekes are not invited to accompany her on cruises!

CONTENTS

FOREWORD

As this 5th revised edition of Fielding's Worldwide Cruises goes to press, I am aboard the new and spectacular *Crystal Harmony*—cruising through Alaska's dramatic Inside Passage. The 'Crystal Age' has begun and the product can now speak for itself. What a fine product it is! *Crystal Harmony* is a beautiful vessel with spacious public areas and decks. In fact, the ship boasts the highest passenger space ratio of any afloat at this time—just slightly over that of *Royal Viking Sun*. What places *Crystal Harmony* above other large vessels in the same category is the food service, which certainly deserves a five-plus star rating and is supervised by Michel Blanchet (chef/owner of the famed L'Hermitage restaurant in Los Angeles). The Crystal Dining Room (open seating at luncheon but two seatings each at breakfast and dinner) is among the most elegant restaurants at sea, with its lovely table settings, service and menus. Although large, the dining room has intimate table placings and the most comfortable chairs! Food service on Lido deck is also above reproach (under the direction of my friend from NAC, Cosmo, who is also responsible for the two specialty restaurants onboard—Kyoto for Oriental cuisine and Prego for popular pastas and other Italian dishes). Cosmo orchestrated an Italian Buffet one afternoon in the Trident pool area that featured at least a dozen different types of pasta—but never mind, the Crystal Spa is one deck above and very well-appointed!

Did Crystal Cruises revolutionize a 'return to luxury' in cruising as its advertisements proclaim? Very little has been overlooked in the appointments and amenities onboard *Crystal Harmony*. The staterooms are spacious and service is impeccable—a different set of chocolates appeared every night! However, storage is a real problem and the bathroom is very poorly designed (the tub is a mere 44″ long—not exactly made for Westerners!) For a top-quality ship, these oversights in passengers' comfort are very disappointing. Nonetheless, we wish *Crystal Harmony* great success and look forward to additions of the Crystal fleet!

There have been so many new cruise ships in the past two years that some of the older vessels have lost their luster—not because of service, itineraries of food, but because their owners have not kept up with the times. Passengers have become accustomed to fresh furnishings, spas, top-rated entertainment, unique designs like *Crown Princess* and *Regal Princess,* fancy toiletries and bedtime chocolates. And passengers do not want to be nickel and dimed to death—a cruise is presumed to be all-inclusive. When Sun Line sells 'eskimo pies' for 75 cents on its Amazon River cruise, when NCL adds a $2 plus 15% gratuity on room service, and when Club Med I charges $4 for a chicken sandwich in the cabin, these are petty charges and the antithesis of what cruising is all about. Tips to cabin and dining room personnel are a tradition and have always been part of the cruise experience and I don't mind having a 15% gratuity added to wine, bar, and beauty salon bills (it saves the embarrassment of having to figure it out yourself)! And have you noticed the Lotto booths now prevalent on several cruise ships? Bingo and the Casino are, at the very least, social sports with lots of interaction but Lotto seems to be just a device to raise shipboard revenue at the expense of the passengers (and crew). Pity.

The new vessels are glamorous, indeed, and the differences between 4, 4-plus and 5 stars have become very slight—cabin size and amenities, attention to detail in the public areas, and food service. The standards of cruise food are certainly being upgraded on some lines through better caterers or the services of notables as chef/restaurateur Michel Roux of London consulting with Celebrity Cruises' new *Horizon* and *Meridian,* and Paul Bocuse for *Royal Viking Sun.* Let us hope that as the quality of food increases on the mass market vessels, the overabundance of same decreases. We will be the better for it!

While the large ships afloat serve their purpose—there is never a dull moment onboard—the small or 'boutique' type vessels have become an important element in cruising and their numbers are growing rapidly. Some consider their higher-priced lifestyle as 'seeing how the other half lives', while many passengers prefer their low-key ambience and unusual itineraries. They are also the only true 'luxury' vessels— with their all-suite accommodations and high ratio of crew to passenger, their refrigerators stocked with brew to your liking, their fabulous 'nouvelle' food and 'un-assigned tables' in the restaurant. *Sea Goddess I* and *II* are pioneers, so to speak, and have been joined by *Seabourn Pride* and *Seabourn Spirit, Renaissance I—VIII, Song of Flower,* and *Oceanic Grace.* Less elegant but great favorites are *Wind Star, Wind Song* and *Wind Spirit, Nantucket,* and *Yorktown Clipper,* and coming along are *Star Clipper* and *Star Flyer.*

Expedition-type vessels are also increasing in popularity. The legendary Lars-Eric Lindblad is no longer the adventurous force that he was, but several others have taken his place. His son operates three small vessels that follow the fauna around the world. Salen Lindblad (no relation) operates the former *North Star,* now *Caledonian Star,* and markets the new *Frontier Spirit.* Society Expeditions has two older vessels plus two new elegant expedition ships to entice its loyal following.

Exploring the wonders of land and sea is a wonderful way to 'cruise' for these expeditions, combining the joy of shipboard life with knowledge and sensitivity about the oceans that surround Mother Earth. Like the 'boutique' set above, expedition ship prices are high, but itineraries are often unique and comraderie of fellow passengers and staff is unforgettable!

As always, there is plenty of choice in cruise ships and their itineraries as vacations at sea are still are the most complete possible. Just being aboard is exciting and some readers inform me that they never even leave the ship in port! Well, it is nice to have the place to oneself—when everyone is off touring—and I confess to also enjoying such respite from time to time! For the cruise vessel is the focal point—and ports of call a fantastic bonus of being at sea.

As we go to press again, I wish to thank all who have helped me with information and humor—especially my husband, Stephen Carter, and our two Pekingese. We have moved our city pied a terre down to Battery Park City and I enjoy seeing 'my ships' coming into port under the Verrazzano Bridge, past the Statue of Liberty, and upriver to the passenger terminal. I also enjoy my views of the Moran tugboats that are so active in the harbor. Occasionally, I run over to my friend Mary (just around the corner) whose condominium seems to hang right over the river and we discuss the verifications of the vessels that pass so closely under her window. It's a wonderful place to live, and when the cruise ships are not entertaining me, the Staten Island ferries are always active and every morning I salute the Miss Liberty boat as she begins her rounds back and forth between Battery Park and the beloved statue. A very popular ride from the numbers I see onboard!

I can never finish this guide without the assistance and support of my editor Randy Ladenheim-Gil, with whom I have worked for many happy years. I would also like to mention our new associate editor, Curtis March, who has brought a high degree of professionalism to the position and it is most appreciated.

Until the next edition, Happy Cruising. Be sure to write and share your good times (I always hear about the not so good) so others can follow in your 'wake' as the sailors say!

Antoinette DeLand
August 1990

FIELDING'S
WORLDWIDE
CRUISES
FIFTH REVISED EDITION

CRUISING—THE MOST COMPLETE VACATION POSSIBLE

In *The European Discovery of America,* Samuel Eliot Morison described what he considered the first pleasure cruise in American history. It took place around 1536 when a London leather merchant named Richard Hoare chartered two vessels to sail to Newfoundland for the double purpose of catching some codfish and enjoying the cruise. Sixty persons are said to have signed on (including thirty "gentlemen"), but the excursion was hardly a success. The first ship was lost soon after setting sail, and although the second did reach Newfoundland the voyagers found nothing but misery there and had to eat each other to keep alive. When this ship eventually returned to England, there were few survivors—and one could say the tourist trade was set back several centuries!

In fact, it was well over three hundred years before people went down to the sea for the sheer joy of sailing, and several more decades passed before life aboard was at all comfortable. One inveterate traveler and recorder was our beloved Mark Twain, who left us with *Life on the Mississippi* and *The Innocents Abroad.* The latter described a year-long "great Pleasure Excursion to Europe and the Holy Land" in 1867, which he called "a picnic on a gigantic scale." The passage cost $1250, and five dollars per day in gold was recommended for shore excursions. Although his expectations that the excursionists would be "filling the ship with shouts and laughter" received some setbacks, he was grateful that at the end of the year he was still on speaking terms with many of his fellow passengers and had even made some friends. Above all, he recommended that people undertake such cruises "regularly," because his shore excursions had taught him that "travel is fatal to prejudice, bigotry, and narrow-mindedness."

This was also the time when Thomas Cook purported to organize

1

the first "world cruise," which involved rail travel in addition to four ships. Begun with a transatlantic crossing from Liverpool to New York in 1872, this tour had been abandoned by many of its participants by the time it reached Cairo 220 days later. Fifty years later Cunard offered the first official world cruise—a four-month voyage on the *Laconia* from New York to New York. The 1922–23 itinerary included Honolulu, Shanghai, Hong Kong, Cairo, Naples, and other ports of call still popular today.

Today's global voyages average over 100 days, cover the world faster than ever before, and offer passengers not only the old haunts of the 1920s but also a goodly number of ports never before visited. These modern circumnavigations are popular with the idle rich, of course, who book the best suites and have seen it all before, as well as less wealthy and more adventurous souls who stay as long as they can afford to and have a jolly good time of it. Companies still offering annual around-the-world cruises are Cunard *(Sagafjord, Vistafjord,* or *Queen Elizabeth 2),* Royal Viking Line, Costa, and P & O. However, ship lines do change their schedules and offer long winter cruises that do not exactly circumnavigate the world. Holland America dropped all long sailings from its gameplan due to worldwide political situations as well as the thought from management that the global voyage market was "drying up." Management is rethinking this decision and we can expect more longer sailings of the *Rotterdam* and *Westerdam* in the 1990s.

Among the prestigious and historic ship lines still in existence, the Peninsular and Orient Steam Navigation Company (P & O) boasts over a century of service worldwide. One of its most lucrative and popular passenger routes was between Britain and Egypt or India, long before the advent of the airplane. Sailing roundtrip on this route precipitated the advent of a very special word in the English language—POSH—which, stamped on steamship tickets, indicated the passenger had bought Port Out and Starboard Home, the coolest and therefore most expensive cabins. Frankly, a reader or two has disputed this story but I stand by it—doesn't it sound romantic?

According to company correspondence, P & O Line had such a fine reputation in the Victorian 19th century that even its shipwrecks were considered the best of any passenger fleet! In a letter dated 1863, from a Mrs. Dulcimer to her friend, Laura, the writer advises, "If you are ever shipwrecked, do contrive to get the catastrophe conducted by the Peninsular and Orient Company. I believe other companies drown you sometimes, and drowning is a very prosaic arrangement fit only for seafaring people and second class passengers. I have just been shipwrecked under the auspices of P & O, and I assure you that it is the pleasantest thing imaginable. It has its little hardships, to be sure, but so have a picnic; and the wreck was one of the most agreeable picnics you can imagine." Didn't they have fun during the 19th century!

Cruises as we know them today began more or less in the 1920s, although on a grand scale and for a small segment of society. Transatlantic sailings and sea tours of the Mediterranean or South America were on three-class ships (four classes when there were immigrants). These cruises assumed the importance that a global voyage does today. Staterooms, as large as drawing rooms, sported heavy, hand-carved furniture. In first class, especially, you traveled with trunks of evening clothes and dinner jewels, servants who cared for them and you (and who slept somewhere below deck), and pets who stayed above. Except that ladies and gentlemen often separated after the evening meal for their own pleasures, life aboard was usually not much different from today. Some rules were never broken. If a young woman alone wished the pleasure of a charming steward for the night, she would most likely not acknowledge his presence the next morning because, good heavens, they had not yet been properly introduced!

It is always so delightful to recapture the glamour of transatlantic crossings in their heyday. The old Fred Astaire movies become more wonderful each year, and Danielle Steele's *Crossings* captures the essence of the grand life that once was aboard the *Normandie*. True ship buffs can either read histories of the old liners by friends Frank Braynard and Bill Miller, plan to spend some days at sea aboard such famous vessels as Swedish American Line's *Gripsholm* (now *Regent Sea*) or *Kungsholm* (now *Sea Princess*) or even visit the *Queen Mary,* now a hotel in Long Beach (California), where those who once served aboard stop by from time to time to reminisce.

Weekend party cruises were popular in the 1920s—from the East Coast to Havana, Bermuda, the Bahamas, and to Nowhere! Ships became floating speakeasies during Prohibition when liquor was legal (and very cheap) on the high seas. The low cost and steady flow of alcohol on cruises is still a lure, but most of us take to the sea for romance and adventure and for the temporary dream world that exists the minute we step aboard. The cruise vessel is a floating capsule of contentment as it transports us from one exotic port to another. And as we follow the progress of the ship on the navigation chart posted near the purser's office (and even place a dollar in the daily pool), the world looks so large and this voyage so small. Life at sea is such a fantasy of time and place that the glow lasts long after the cruise is over.

Weekend party cruises are still popular—perhaps more than ever because the liquor is still cheap, the gambling very heady, and there are facilities for the whole family. These include sailings that actually do stop at one or more ports from South Florida or southern California as well as Cruises to Nowhere, which seem to fill in schedules that have a hole here and there. From South Florida, for example, Chandris offers champagne cruises to Nowhere from spring through fall while New York Harbor features the *QE2* from time to time. These sailings out to Ambrose Lighthouse are always a sell-out, as they are the perfect way to get away from it all—if only for 60 hours.

Sailing today is certainly safer and far more comfortable than it ever was before, despite the pint-sized staterooms and lack of ladies' maids and gentlemen's valets. Ships are better maintained, and passengers have far more consideration than a few decades ago. We have stabilizers to cut down the roll, air conditioning to keep out the heat, and plenty of ice in every bar. In addition to all passengers on board being equal (except on *QE2* where SuperClass has its own two grill rooms), the run of the ship means more facilities, more food and drinks, more entertainment, and generally more people than anyone can appreciate fully in just five, seven, or 14 days. There is no doubt that today's travelers are offered more for their money aboard a ship than anywhere else on earth and 90% is paid for in advance. If the advantage of just one rate for everything and no hidden extras (except what you intend to spend for shopping, drinks, and tipping) appeals to you, you may also enjoy the fact that all the many details of when, where, and what time things happen each day have already been solved by the ship lines. You not only leave the driving to them, but the food and entertainment decisions as well. They have even eliminated any language problem. You just sit on deck and relax.

Perhaps you are nervous that a cruise is too slow a pace for you, that it doesn't allow enough time in ports, or that there is too much group activity. Cruising is not an individual experience, and that is precisely why so many people enjoy it. If you are traveling alone, you can have instant companionship whenever you wish. Couples can be by themselves or seek others for conversation or cards. Children, no matter what age, make instant friends and become purveyors of all the news within this floating world. And if you're worried about being bored, there are so many different types of cruises available (see ''Choosing the Right Cruise'') that you can ship hop the rest of your life and never be satiated with the excitement of being at sea.

If you demand a place in the sun, then the Caribbean is your natural habitat, with its potpourri of colors and people and splendid tropical climate (and should you ever tire, Hawaii or the South Seas might entice your senses). If you're looking for adventure and wildlife, you'll love the Galapagos and Antarctica, the Amazon, or watching the whales off Baja. If majestic scenery fills your soul with wonder, then you should sail through the southern tip of South America, Alaska's Inside Passage, along the Saguenay River, or in and out of Norway's saw-toothed fjords. Serious scuba divers will love the Mexican Riviera on sailings from either the West Coast or Florida; and our own eastern seaboard can be explored all the way from Ft. Myers, Florida to the rocky coastal islands of Maine. If you wish to stretch your mind as well as your legs in every port, the whole world is waiting for you, but you will especially enjoy cruises to Greece and Turkey, Israel and Egypt, the northern capitals, the British Isles, around South America, through the Indonesian archipelago, and the Far East. And if it's river life you like, try the small boats on the waterways of Europe, the paddle-wheelers on the Mississippi and Ohio rivers, cruises along the historic Hudson, and the barges along the Nile. You can be as enriched and fulfilled as you desire, or pursue each day at a snail's pace. This is the perfection of a cruise.

CHOOSING YOUR CRUISE

Thirty million Americans can't be wrong! That is the approximate number of vacationers who took cruises in the 1980s, and this figure is expected to double and triple during the current decade. At least, CLIA (Cruise Line International Association—whose membership totals some 35 or so ship lines to date) hopes so, considering the fact that some 40 new ships (representing over 31,000 new berths) over 30 made their debut between 1980 and 1990—10 of them in 1988 and another six in 1989! And these figures do not include the over 40 existing vessels that have been refurbished extensively—some even receiving new names.

There is no doubt that the cruise industry is healthy and wealthy, representing an investment of multibillions of dollars (primarily by foreign banks and shipyards) and offering the most exciting floating resorts cum transportation ever imagined! Never, in my craziest dreams, did I envision a ship like the spanking new 2300-passenger *Sovereign of the Seas* with its 360-degree Viking Crown lounge and a seven-story atrium through which two glass elevators zip up and down with the greatest of glee. And, I suspect, this is only the beginning of the future.

While *Sovereign* is a ship ahead of its time, most modern vessels do blend the most up-to-date facilities, high-tech control centers, and comfortable amenities with itineraries that aim to please. Those who prefer more traditional ships, where wood is wood and not a plastic laminate, will find plenty still alive and afloat—albeit with new names and more upbeat decor.

In the world of cruises today, there are so many choices of ships and destinations that the first-time passenger is quite overwhelmed and the experienced passenger (anyone who has taken a cruise) is challenged to continue the adventure on other sailings and never repeat an itinerary. The phrase "right cruise" or "right ship" means just about anything afloat. Ship-board life on the majority of vessels is so diverse that anyone's style and interest can be satisfied—no matter what age group and budget.

TRENDS While the Caribbean Sea continues to feature 70% of all cruise sailings (followed by Alaska, Mexican Riviera, Far East/South Pacific, Europe, and South America), private islands and exclusive resorts (such as Royal Caribbean's Labadee on the north coast of Haiti) add luster to itineraries with too many familiar and overcrowded ports of call (on a slow day, St. Thomas plays host to only a half dozen ships; on a busy day, the number is doubled).

Because the port of Miami (Dodge Island) is bursting with cruise vessels, Fort Lauderdale is the easier and more relaxing south Florida embarkation point. However, San Juan has become the true cruise capital of the Caribbean because it is *in* the Caribbean and it is a U.S. territory. Passengers find the airport easy to maneuver, and the port is just a short walk from the old and historic part of town. As an added bonus, the natives are friendly, the dollar is legal tender, and everyone speaks the same language (American). From San Juan, seven-day cruises can capture the essence of the lower Caribbean area and ships can call on as many as seven different islands in one week.

The Caribbean and Alaska are comfortable and secure destinations when other cruise areas are experiencing political difficulties. Since the hijackings in Greece and Egypt (1985 and '86), a tidal wave of fear and uncertainty kept Americans from cruising in the Mediterranean/Aegean, although they have returned the past few seasons. Also during this period, cruises to the Baltic (especially Helsinki and Leningrad) and the Black Sea became popular once again as relations between the USA and USSR seemed to enter a warmer climate—there is nothing like a summit to spur tourism.

Meanwhile, the Far East/South Pacific have been slowly gaining momentum for cruise popularity. While *Ocean Pearl* (formerly *Pearl of Scandinavia*) continues her year-round sailings in this area, she has company in vessels from Royal, Royal Viking, Princess, and Cunard— but China is very much *out* and will be for the next few years. South America is still a difficult destination for cruises, primarily because even experienced travelers are timid when one mentions this vast continent. Visas are a problem and one has to be a political animal to understand which country is staging a coup.

Another interesting trend: The decreasing value of the US dollar abroad increases the appeal of a cruise vacation to Americans as well as foreign travelers. To our foreign friends, such destinations as the Caribbean, Bermuda, and Alaska are travel bargains; while Americans can pay upfront and relax while visiting European or Far Eastern ports. Ship lines with interests in the Mediterranean, Baltic, and North Cape have been advertising that European cruises offered better value than land-based vacations. Land-based vacations throughout Europe have, indeed, doubled in price because of the exchange rate while most cruise rates had risen less than 10 percent.

SHORT CRUISES Time and money are the primary considerations when contemplating a cruise. As my cocktail napkins say, "It does not cost any more to travel First Class—you just can't stay so long!" Short cruises are perfect for getting those important sea legs, and a satisfying respite from the hurly-burly of everyday. Even in the two- to five-night market, the choices are overwhelming! On the west coast, Admiral Cruises' *Azure Seas* is now joined by Norwegian Cruise Line's *Southward* on Monday and Friday sailings to Catalina Island and Ensenada (San Diego is another port call on Monday departures), and there is always talk of additional ships in this arena. Other vessels from California occasionally offer short Party Cruises, in between their longer sailings.

From southern Florida, departing every Monday and Friday for the Bahama Islands are four different vessels: *Carnivale, Dolphin IV, Emerald Seas,* Carnival's brand-new *Fantasy* and Royal Caribbean's new *Nordic Empress,* and *Sunward II* from Miami, while Carnival's *Mardi Gras* sails on Thursday and Sunday from Port Everglades year-round. All but the Carnival ships call at Nassau and an Out Island; the Carnival ships feature Nassau and a day at sea on the three-day cruises, Nassau and Freeport on the four-day sailings. Premier Cruise Line's StarShip *Atlantic* and StarShip *Oceanic* call at Nassau and an Out Island on Monday and Friday sailings while StarShip *Majestic* sails to a number of small "family" Bahamian islands on Thursday and Sunday departures and offer the addition of Walt Disney World, EPCOT Center, MGM Studios, and a tour of the Kennedy Space Center for a full one-week holiday.

Crown Cruises offers two- and five-night sailings from Palm Beach. Three- and four-night cruises from Piraeus to the Greek Islands and Turkey are a perfect way to see the ancient monuments, especially when the political climate is favorable. Three and four nights are enough time to enjoy a taste of the Nile River, the Rhine, the waterways of France and England, or to develop the confidence to swim with a sea lion in the Galapagos Islands. During the summer season in Alaska, cruises of less than one week are just fine for catching a glimpse of the glaciers and can always be combined with a few extra days in our 49th state.

ONE-WEEK CRUISES are the most prevalent these days and offer excellent value in time and money. A seven-day holiday at sea provides plenty of relaxation, interesting ports of call, and enough shopping opportunities to keep the creditors in business. One week is also enough time to make lasting friendships with others onboard. Since people of all ages have difficulty sneaking away for more than five weekdays, these cruises are popular with everyone—young singles, professional couples, families at school break, retired folk—I have even encountered a few nuns on board having the time of their lives! It is a joy to see such a diversity of passengers on the one-week sailings taking advantage of seven days at sea.

In just one week, passengers aboard *Cunard Countess* or *Amerikanis* from San Juan year-round visit as many as six different Caribbean Islands or make just three port calls aboard the *Celebration* from Miami. Seven days from Piraeus aboard a Sun Line or Epirotiki vessel features both Greek Islands and historic sites in Turkey; you can sail from New York to Bermuda and spend three full days in port. One-week cruises between Vancouver and Whittier/Anchorage offer even more glacial spectacles than the popular roundtrips from Vancouver. Both coasts of Mexico can be covered nicely on a seven-day cruise; so can the beauty and history of the Northeast/Canada between New York and Montreal. And some of the most diverse weekly cruises can be found aboard *Ocean Islander* and *Stella Maris* between Nice and Venice or *Wind Star* roundtrip from Monte Carlo.

The possibilities are endless—especially in our own backyard. Clipper Cruise Line offers one-week cruises around the beautiful Virgin Islands from St. Thomas during the winter season as well as seven-day sailings along the eastern seaboard from spring through fall, featuring both southern hospitality and Yankee tradition. One week among the Hawaiian Islands is a lovely respite, available on American Hawaii's two different American-flag ships, and seven days from Papeete (Tahiti) around French Polynesia is the *in* thing (if you can stand the flight out and back). Wind Star Sail Cruises, despite all odds of doing business in the area, is very successful and a delightful experience. Meanwhile, Regency offers a partial transit of the Panama Canal in a week (from Montego Bay) and *Ocean Islander* will transport you up the Orinoco River from Barbados (and return) in just seven days.

LONGER CRUISES   The world of longer cruises is fast diminishing, and even 14-day sailings are now available as two seven-day segments. More popular with passengers are the 10- and 11-day sailings, which can be combined to make a three-week cruise and not repeat a port call. Although 10- to 13-day programs (including a two-night land package) seem to be popular, the full two weeks is often necessary to enjoy a destination in full. For example, *Vistafjord* from Hamburg takes 14 splendid days to sail to Spitzbergen (Top of the World) and back on North Cape cruises. When China was in fashion, it was a definite two-week voyage, plus whatever additional time passengers wished to take in the area. The South Pacific is also a definite two-week cruise plus travel to and fro, and Sun Line's 10- and 14-day cruises up the Amazon River are not to be missed. While two full weeks is the traditional and more leisurely way to transit the Panama Canal, most ship lines have cut the time to 10 and 11 days (Royal Cruise Line and Princess Cruises) by using Acapulco as the turnaround port. Two weeks or so is also a good length for any South American sojourn by sea, especially when you consider the long flights to and from this land below the equator. Ten to 14 days is necessary to circumnavigate the British Isles or visit the Northern capitals along the Baltic Sea, cruise down our eastern seaboard from New England to Florida through the Intracoastal Waterway, or take that once-in-a-lifetime trip up the Mississippi from New Orleans to St. Paul.

VERY, VERY LONG CRUISES   There are people who can and will spend 100 or more days on the same vessel as they circumnavigate the world, although one might think that they would have to be "un-glued" on day of final disembarkation. The *Royal Viking Sun*'s 1990 world cruise was a total of 109 days round trip from Port Everglades, with the option of two extra bonus days in either Los Angeles or Fort Lauderdale. Quite a long time to be out of the office! The vessel sailed from Florida through the Panama Canal, to Hawaii and through the islands of the South Pacific to Australia, up through ports in the Far East and then to Bombay, through the Red Sea and Suez Canal to the Mediterranean and across the South Atlantic to Florida. The full cruise called at 36 ports in Australia, Africa, Asia, and Europe, not to forget all the great oceans and seas and the two spectacular canals transitted. Overland tours to such world monuments as the temples of Luxor and the Taj Mahal were available, as were shorter cruise segments ranging from 12 to 21 days—all including air fare.

Cunard's flagship, *Queen Elizabeth 2*, scheduled a 94-day circumnavigation of the globe in 1991—the first time in a few years that this venerable vessel has done do. Her itinerary includes ports in the Mediterranean for the first time in seven years, which shows how certain areas of the world wax and wane in passenger favor—for purely political reasons. Maiden voyages and overnight stays in 11 different ports are part of the agenda, as well as shorter cruise segments from 14 to 60 days—with air fare included, of course!

AIR-SEA PACKAGES   are here to stay and one of the reasons why the cruise industry is booming. One must remember, however, that unless the flight has been chartered by the ship line (Concorde or subsonic) that air-sea passengers are at the mercy of the mess airlines and airports have made over the past decade. That means crowds, delayed flights, lost luggage, and the like. The only good news is that your cruise will wait (if there are sufficient numbers of passengers delayed) and the ship line will join the search for anything lost.

When you sit down with your travel counselor to consider a cruise, measure carefully the advantages of all-inclusive air-sea packages. These feature cruise rate, reduced air fare, transfers from airport to ship, and often port taxes, all at less than the cost of each component individually. This is certainly a worry-free way to travel, for you are met at the airport and transferred to the cruise vessel without even having to claim your own baggage (it is transferred separately by the ship's personnel). You don't have to live in a major metropolis to qualify. Every ship line today must offer convenient air-sea programs to enable anyone living anywhere to come aboard. It is one of the ironies of the travel industry that airplanes once put transatlantic liners out of business—yet today the two forces have joined to bring passengers to and from ports of embarkation. Air fare is often included in the passage, especially in the higher cabin categories; if it is not, the ship line will offer a reasonable "add-on." You do not have to accept either the included air fare or the add-on, as ship lines make every effort to be fair and offer rebates for those making their own travel arrangements.

SHIP PERSONALITIES Whether you choose a fun-and-sun cruise, an adventure or cultural cruise, or a sailing with special scenery, you should pay particular attention to the type of vessel that suits you best. If you're not fussy as long as the vessel sails for your destination, you have a choice of ships of varying size, shape, and nationality. A ship really does have a personality, which is a mesh of many factors—crew, size, ports, and the people who sail aboard. Costa promotes cruising "Italian style" and so it is, with friendly and fun-loving Italian crew who make a point of keeping the single ladies happy. Sitmar also has Italian atmosphere and both feature lots of homemade pasta, pizzerias, and plenty of sparkle. If you speak German, you will enjoy the top-rated *Europa* and *Vistafjord,* which both cater to large German clientele. Cunard has the traditionally British *QE2* and the two baby vessels, *Countess* and *Princess,* which offer a combination of British officers and international crew. The Greek lines have all-Greek officers and crew, with an international clientele and plenty of feta cheese on the menu! Royal Cruise and Sun Line are the top rated of the Greek vessels, with the most interesting itineraries worldwide.

The Miami-based shiplines—Carnival, Commodore, Norwegian Cruise Line (note: Norwegian Caribbean Lines is now called Norwegian Cruise Line), and Royal Caribbean—promote happy and fun ships with plenty of activities on board. Carnival's emphasis is on gambling, and its Caribbean itineraries all include a stop at the line's own casinos in Nassau. Royal Caribbean is known for attention to detail in the public rooms, so passengers do not notice their tiny cabins. Norwegian Cruise Line has the *Norway*—and the best entertainment afloat. Although Carnival, NCL, and RCCL have been committed to the Caribbean since their beginnings in south Florida, they are all spreading their sails around North America and the world. Carnival, which has bought Holland America Cruises and WindStar Sail Cruises (previously owned by Holland America), now has worldwide representation and an impressive presence in Alaska. Kloster Cruises, the parent company of Norwegian Cruise Line, also owns Royal Viking Line and recently purchased Royal Cruise Line. Both are not only far more upscale companies than NCL but they also cover the globe. Royal Caribbean Cruise Line, which fought off a takeover attempt a few years ago, is now committed to send at least one of its vessels to Europe during the summer—watch for more as additional *Sovereign of the Seas* vessels are launched for the Caribbean market.

Cunard/NAC, Seabourn Cruise Line, Renaissance Cruises, and Royal Viking Line appeal to the upscale traveler, who enjoys dressing for dinner and leisurely, single-seating meals in elegant surroundings. Holland America/Westours has retained its Dutch officers and atmosphere, with a charming Indonesian crew known for its eagerness to please the passengers.

Princess Cruises' officers wear shorts and knee socks (just like on the popular TV series "Love Boat") on the P & O vessels, but not on the ships acquired from Sitmar last year, which still retain Italian officers, but the line boasts Italians in the kitchen. The new WindStar Sail Cruises offer smaller vessels and a Club Med ambience of "do your own thing." Nothing new lasts forever, and a real Club Med ship has joined the sail cruiser fleet (with a total of six masts and built in the same yard as WindStar!). No doubt the authentic Club Med atmosphere and "gentle organizers" (also known as GOs) will make passengers who already know the product feel right at home.

Ships built for discerning passengers where per diem is not discussed include *Sea Goddess I* and *II*, *Seabourn Pride* and *Seabourn Spirit*, and *Renaissance I* through *VIII* in the small vessel category, and *Royal Viking Sun*, which carries 740 passengers. Sea Goddess Cruises were among the first in the 1980s to offer a top-of-the-line yachtlike experience with regular sailings, and Seabourn Cruise Line improved greatly upon the concept. Renaissance Cruises—the newest game in town—offers luxury on destination-oriented vessels. The *Royal Viking Sun* represents the new glitz at sea for a medium-sized vessel and rave reviews from loyal RVL passengers.

Unfortunately, cruise vessels flying the stars and stripes at their stern did not fare well during the past few years. The refurbished *Monterey* (Aloha Pacific Cruises) arrived in Hawaii and was declared bankrupt within months. Also bankrupt are Exploration Cruise Lines of Seattle, WA, with its innovative itineraries, and American Cruise Lines of Haddam, CT. All told, over a dozen ships laid up, although a few have already been recycled, including the *Sea Lion* for Special Expeditions.

Still sailing strongly are the Clipper Cruise Line fleet—*Newport, Nantucket,* and *Yorktown Clipper*—as well as the famous Delta Queen Steamboat Company—*Delta* and *Mississippi Queen.* American Canadian Caribbean Line offers casual cruises in the Bahamas, Caribbean, and Belize areas during the winter season aboard the cozy and homey *Caribbean Prince* and *New Shoreham II* and then repositions both small vessels to New England and the Great Lakes. ACCL is already planning its 1992 itineraries in the Caribbean—in the footsteps (wake) of Christopher Columbus!

Big ships have different personalities from the smaller ones. In this age of megavessels, size has more bearing than ever on your cruise experience. While the *QE2* and *Norway* are each in a class by herself—one a floating city, the other a movable resort—most of the new ships being built today are programmed to carry between 1350 and 2000 passengers! Just walking the length of the vessel is more activity than most people expect. And, while the public rooms may be bigger and bigger, many of the cabin sizes get smaller and smaller. RCCL's *Sovereign of the Seas* is a perfect example of the new breed of megavessels. With 2300 passengers, the ship is the largest afloat today and likely to cause waves in the industry for some time. *Sovereign* will offer a challenge to design and construct a cruise ship of this size that actually feels like a ship—and not a floating Hyatt Regency Hotel. *Sovereign* has less tonnage than *Queen Elizabeth* and *Queen Mary,* and less length than the 25 longest transatlantic liners built since 1945.

Megavessels have arrived, and Royal Caribbean Cruise Line has ordered *Sovereign of the Seas II* and *III,* while Carnival is expecting its *Sensation* and *Ecstacy* within the next few years to join *Fantasy*—the largest and fanciest vessel on the three- and four-day run to the Bahamas from Miami! And Knut Kloster, who founded Norwegian Caribbean Lines (now Norwegian Cruise Line), bought and refurbished the *Norway* (ex-*France*), and bought Royal Viking Line (the company now owns Royal Cruise Line as well), is still talking about his Phoenix Project—a vessel with high-rise accommodations that will carry 5000 passengers and synthetic beaches. Sounds crazy, but it just may happen!

FRESHWATER CRUISES are expanding with every season along the rivers, lakes, and canals of the world—from the Hudson to the Yangtze. Rhine Cruise Agency represents the river vessels that ply Germany's most historic waterway, and you can set foot in four different countries sailing through the heartland of Europe in a few days. Floating Through Europe, French Horizons of Duxbury, MA, French Cruise Lines, Esplanade Tours, Abercrombie and Kent, Barge About France, Afloat in France, and Raymond & Whitcomb all offer lovely excursions, with gourmet wine and food, bicycles, and pastoral scenes in France, Holland, England, Ireland, Germany-Austria-Hungary, and Belgium from early spring through late fall. As you glide slowly past small towns and villages, your captain and host delivers wonderful meals as well as participation in learning about the food and wines of each region. Never mind such temptations—you can walk or bike off all the sumptuous courses while visiting local markets and historic sites—even guiding your hotel barge through the many locks.

The Mississippi has been a favored waterway for years (even a president vacationed there while in office). Less well known to cruise passengers are the historic Hudson, where so much of the Revolution was fought, the beautiful Saguenay off the St. Lawrence, and the spectacular rivers on the West Coast. Special Expeditions, which upgraded and renamed the former Great River Explorer *Sea Lion,* has some marvelous river trips for the outdoor set that combine scenery with adventure. The St. Lawrence Seaway should not just be considered a cargo route, and Great Lakes cruises offer a wonderful opportunity to appreciate an area of the country that mankind has not yet polluted so much as others I might mention.

The waterways of Europe are a special treat; the pace is leisurely and the ability to integrate with each locality enhances the experience. Seeing Europe via these waterways offers an appreciation of how life was managed centuries ago; the townfolk may drive automobiles (although most still use the trusty bicycle) and use computers, but they continue traditions begun Before Christ and still valid in modern society. Give me the backroads and the watery byways any day! This is the way to absorb European and Western culture.

SPECIAL-INTEREST CRUISES   come in all guises. Parquet French Cruises was famous for its classical music cruises aboard the *Mermoz* and *Renaissance*—one in the Mediterranean, the other in the Caribbean. Paquet is back in business and promises its Festival at Sea aboard the *Mermoz* in the Mediterranean as well as courses in the French language on transatlantic crossings. Other ship lines have occasionally continued this fine tradition. Music of all types is a natural for ''theme'' or special-interest cruises because passengers have plenty of opportunity to socialize with the artists, attend rehearsals, and dine with them. Jazz, big bands, country and western, pop and everything else one can think of are frequently featured by ship lines today—offering the best of both worlds to their passengers.

Wildlife fans will especially enjoy the fine Galapagos Island cruises, which offer a unique experience among the birds and sea lions in these uninhabited Pacific islands, where Darwin did much of his work. Sven Olof Lindblad, son of Lars-Eric, has a special interest in the marine life of the West Coast and offers expeditions around Baja California to watch what is happening in the Sea of Cortez during the winter months. He also takes small groups into Alaskan waters at migration time for a cruise that none of the other lines can touch. Father Lindblad was known for his fascinating sailings to the Arctic and Antarctica, but this area is now the domain of Society Expeditions and Salen Lindblad, who also carry onward to New Guinea and all those exotic islands of the Pacific. Those seeking the unusual may also find cruises to Iceland/Greenland during the summer, or North and West Africa as well as from the Seychelles to the Red Sea during the winter months.

If it's China that beckons, only Abercrombie & Kent now offer cruise programs on the deluxe Bashan Riverboat on the Yangtze River since both Lindblad Travel and Hemphill Harris (although Hemphill Harris is trying a comeback) have closed their doors and declared bankruptcy—blaming much of their troubles on the dwindling China market. In fact, none of the popular lines—Royal Viking, Princess, Royal—are offering China cruises at this time. Only *Ocean Pearl* (the former *Pearl of Scandinavia*) is going back on a preliminary basis. Most of the other lines have changed their course to offer Far East sailings or cruises across the South Pacific to Australia, New Zealand, and romantic islands.

If you have a particular interest in archaeological sites, historic preservation, Egyptian monuments along the Nile, etc., no doubt you have already received tempting brochures from companies that specialize in cultural cruises. Many of these cruises are sold only through museum memberships, college alumni associations, or cultural associations. I receive literature from the Smithsonian Museum, the National History Museum, the National Trust for Historic Preservation, and the Metropolitan Museum of Art for wonderful-sounding cruises from the Indonesian Archipelago to little-known ports along the Turkish coastline. Classical Cruises, Abercrombie and Kent, Raymond and Whitcomb and Swan Hellenic Cruises can all guarantee an enriching and stimulating experience aboard ship, as they hire knowledgeable speakers and plan the shore excursions with great care. In general, the vessels employed are not the most luxurious afloat, but any lack of superfluous amenities is more than compensated for by the mind-stretching lectures and interesting fellow passengers.

Not all special interest/theme cruises are "highbrow," and there is something to entice just about everybody on board. If you are a mystery buff, love trivial and other pursuits, wish to play bridge or backgammon with the experts, play along with the Miami Dolphins and other athletic stars, want to enjoy Oktoberfest in the Caribbean, theater and movie stars, or the wines of the world, chances are there is a cruise in your future. Some of these sailings are purposefully scheduled at "shoulder periods." That is, between seasons or on repositioning cruises. So, instead of paying more for this extra enjoyment, you are most likely paying less. RCCL calls itself the ship line of the PGA, but Royal Viking Line has excellent golf cruises as well. The elegant new *Royal Viking Sun* has all of the above plus a croquet court with experts often on board. Norwegian Cruise Line has been successful in bringing aboard the *Norway* and its other vessels athletic stars for Sports and SuperSport Cruises that have become very popular with their passengers. The ship line is also promoting a new sport theme for the 1990s—Ski Cruises— which offer instruction, lectures, workshops, fashion shows,. and more, well in advance of the snow bunny season! Check with your travel agent for upcoming special-interest cruises that might appeal to you. In addition to the ports of call and usual shipboard experience, you will have the opportunity to meet many people who share your interests.

YOUR FELLOW PASSENGERS   are going to surprise you. A few years ago I suggested that you would be choosing your cruise companions by the ship you take. No more! On a recent *CostaRiviera* sailing, I was impressed by the diversity of passengers, who mixed well together and had a good time from day one. The ages ranged from babes in arms to senior citizens, but in between were plenty of youthful faces. My colleague and I sat at a table for six and it was such a pleasure to anticipate dinner! Our companions were an elegant couple from Paris, who arrived via Concorde and loved cruising the Caribbean. We were joined by two amusing and attractive working gals in their late twenties from Texas on their first cruise. Why did they choose this particular ship? The itinerary. Conversation centered on "amore." Carol and Wendy were having a wonderful time every evening in the disco—dancing up a storm with all the attentive Italian officers. We all became very friendly, and I can't wait to get to Paris because Jacques and Monica promised dinner at Maxim's!

I spoke recently with a very elegant, retired gentleman who said he has just sailed aboard the *Sunward II* (he won the cruise in a charity raffle). He had a wonderful time and did not feel out of place with all the rah-rah and emphasis on watersports. In fact, he said there were many older people aboard from large American companies who received the cruise as a reward for good service. Incentive groups, as they are called, are now very prevalent aboard ships and they comprise interesting personalities who contribute greatly to the passenger complement.

The "yuppie" generation is also discovering cruises, as ship lines have decided that romance at sea is very important. Note: the number of double-, queen-, and king-size beds has risen dramatically in the past few years. Carnival Cruise Lines, which puts tremendous emphasis on fun and gambling, claims that every cabin on the new ships has "convertible" king-size beds. (Well, you can convert them yourself—as my husband and I have done on numerous occasions.) Premier Cruise Lines has added 167 double beds to the StarShip *Oceanic,* and the *Costa-Riviera* has 86 queen-size beds. In fact, most ships designed or refurbished during the 1980s boast a choice of sleeping arrangements in beds that convert from twin to queen or king. It is wise to specify your choice when booking a cabin.

Working people prefer Saturday departures and returns home, because they need that Sunday to "rest up" before the office. Honeymooners have discovered that Sunday departures suit them well because it allows time to "rest up" after the wedding and get to the port of embarkation unhassled. The three- and four-day cruises are popular with vacationers who also wish to spend some time in Florida or California. Both Carnival and Premier offer Thursday and Sunday departures on their Bahamian cruises from, respectively, Port Everglades and Port Canaveral—which can be combined with land packages at Disney World/ Epcot, etc.

Singles looking for action are almost certain to find it at sea on a wide variety of cruise vessels. High-density passenger list ships are best for the singles scene, since these vessels carry more people in smaller than usual spaces and offer a better opportunity for being "thrown together in a storm." Try Royal Caribbean Cruise Line among the others that sail from Miami, and the Norwegian Cruise Line's seven-day ships for starters. Singles might also consider cruise ships with one thousand passengers or more, like the *Norway* or Carnival fleet, that have a reputation for continual social activities: deck games, parlor games, gambling, calisthenics, singles' parties, and don't forget those Italian officers!

The longer the cruise, the older the passengers. This is a general rule, but it works and makes sense. How many young couples can afford the time and money to sail around the world, or even a continent? Many retired couples take to the sea and discover a wonderful new realm that is both relaxing and stimulating; so they take longer and longer sailings, and some seem to stay aboard forever. However, even the *Royal Viking Sun*'s 109-day saga of 1990 to 36 ports on six continents was divided into so many shorter segments that even the busiest of professionals could have embarked for some part of the voyage. Let the older passengers enjoy themselves and introduce the shorter cruisers into the ship-board scenario from time to time. This is the joy of being aboard one of life's great adventures.

Cruises are perfect for families who wish to vacation together, especially when both parents have careers and wish to spend leisure time with their children. Most ship lines offer very good discounts for third, fourth, and fifth passengers in the same cabin—but watch that these are "little" passengers or the cabin may be crowded! All ship lines also offer good facilities for children, from the very small through teenagers, who have their own video/disco room where they can meet others aboard. Parents can relax during the day while their offspring enjoy many pleasant activities. With an adequate cabin, the whole family can enjoy a cruise, and the little ones add to the pleasure of everyone on board—from crew to captain.

Cruises are also perfect for the handicapped, for even those in wheelchairs can join in the daily program. There is a problem if the ship anchors in port, but who cares? Many ambulatory passengers never bother with port calls—they just love being aboard. CLIA (Cruise Lines International Association), with a membership of 35 ship lines, publishes a very fine guide to their member lines that welcome wheelchair travelers. Write to CLIA, 500 Fifth Ave., Suite 1407, New York, NY 10110 and check with your travel agent for those lines not listed.

Geographic distribution might also determine your cruise companions. A few years ago geographic distribution of passengers was determined by ship lines' ports of embarkation. No more. Even the west-coast companies now draw passengers from all over the world. While the Miami-based lines have a strong draw from the Midwest, and the California lines still have many west-coasters aboard, the passenger complement is very diversified. Aboard the *Stella Solaris* on a Christmas/New Year's cruise up the Amazon, we met people from Barcelona, Mexico City, Monte Carlo, Genoa, Chicago, Washington, DC, and many points in between. Wonderful!

HOW MUCH WILL IT COST? With all the discounting in the cruise marketplace these days, the cost of a cruise is undeterminable, although CLIA claims that the average cost of a seven-day cruise is less than $1500 per person—but most travelers "trade up." Prices do vary with vessel, itinerary, and season, but the best advice is to watch your Sunday travel sections for the latest in what is available and what is being offered. Discounts up to $1000 per person are advertised frequently through local travel agencies or travel sections in newspapers. So, if a cruise never appealed before—the time is *now* to try one. You will soon be hooked. I overheard a first-time cruise passenger recently, who said to his wife, "I am never taking another vacation unless there is a Jacuzzi and a rudder. I am hooked!"

The very top-rated vessels will have very top-rated prices, although some of these ships try to keep a few cabins at more reasonable rates. But discounting the published prices is here to stay, and it's a buyers' (passengers') market with excellent values for all. Pricing and what you can afford to pay is best arranged in the office of a cruise-only specialist who knows all the ship lines, and probably has very close relations with the key personnel and what is best when. There are good bargains available on Chandris, Bermuda Star, and Commodore year-round, as well as seasonal discounts on practically every vessel on your wish list. There are excellent values on Regency, which travel agents have extolled for fine itineraries and good service/food on board.

There are many criteria for cost: quality of service, food and facilities; age and size of the vessel; management of company and how much debt it has incurred and at what rates. Companies that keep themselves "lean and mean"—Holland America Line and Regency Cruises—at home can afford to offer their passengers better service, food, and itineraries than is to be expected at their rates.

On the other hand, some ships are prided on their high rates. Sea Goddess Cruises, which my colleague George Devol, founder of the World Ocean & Cruise Liner Society, calls "ultimate deluxe" in his ratings, has a per diem (daily rate per person) that runs the gamut from $325 to over $1000, plus air fare! However, this does include all the champagne and caviar you can consume and a no-tipping policy. Seabourn Cruise Line boasts rates around $650 per day (more for the Regal Suites), which includes a strict no-tipping policy, and service on board is superb and most sincere. Both lines do offer a most sybaritic experience and homogenous vessels on which everyone (except in a few larger suites) has the same accommodations.

There are so many fares, options, this and that available these days that it is best to calculate several different cruise options, consider add-ons (air fare, port taxes, tipping requirements, cost of shore excursions that sound interesting, etc.) and divide the cost by number of nights you will be aboard ship. It is impossible to dispute the number of nights you spend in a cabin; however, many ship lines delude the public by insisting that a 7-night cruise is an 8-day cruise (the truth is: How many breakfasts were you offered?).

We all have tastes that do not quite match our pocketbook, but the fun and adventure of travel is to start at a reasonable level and work oneself up. With few exceptions, passengers in the lower category cabins have just as much fun and full run of the ship and service as those in the highest-priced suites. Even on the QE2, where you dine according to your cabin category, the captain divides his time between the first-class Columbia and economy-class Mauretania restaurants—and, no doubt, has a better time in the latter.

There has been considerable talk about the differences between cruise rates and land-based resort rates, some of which is valid. The entire cruise package is a better value because there are no surprises, such as high tax and service charges, and prices of extras on board (drinks, shopping, photography, beauty shop, massage, skeet shooting) are less than at resorts. There is also that extra element on which one can not put a price tag—a cruise means a decisionless vacation; there is never a question of where to eat and how much it will cost. The dining room is there, in addition to room service/poolside buffets/midnight snacks, and the cost is all-inclusive. Your cruise should cost exactly what you wish to budget, especially in this climate of so many new berths every month. You can plan a "dream cruise" a year in advance, or decide at the last moment to catch a sailing that appeals (and a cabin not yet sold). The whole realm of vacation planning has changed, with later decisions for shorter but more frequent vacations.

TIPPING   is like dust—it just never goes away. According to the hotel manager aboard *QE2*, a *TIP* derives from the habit of British businessmen To Insure Promptness when giving letters to stagecoach drivers for delivery at the next stop. Today, it is also considered a gratuity and offered as a thank you for services rendered. Some lines, like Holland America/Westours, have a No Tipping Required policy, but passengers do tip for the delightful service rendered. On many of the new and higher-priced ships (Sea Goddess, WindStar, and Seabourn Cruise Line), a no-tipping policy (as mentioned above) is in effect. However, on almost all cruise ships, tipping is expected, so add gratuities to your cruise budget well in advance. The good news is that many ship lines will accept credit cards (even personal checks) for tips. This is especially true on the Greek vessels, because it is mandatory to tip in bulk at the end of the cruise. The entire amount is then distributed to all members of the crew—including those behind the scenes.

Gratuities should be rendered to the cabin stewards or stewardesses, dining room stewards, wine steward, and bar. For wine and drinks, the usual 15% is acceptable. If you make arrangements to charge your wine and drinks, the ship line will often add the gratuity for you—a saving grace. For the cabin and dining room personnel, the cruise director will offer a suggested per passenger daily amount, which will average around $10 per day during the early 90s.

With a total of $7 to $9 per day, you are offering your cabin and dining room stewards about $3 each and the busboy between $1 and $1.50. Some ships suggest more, some less. It depends very much upon the ambience aboard and the nationality of the service crew. These amounts have not risen much in the past few years—more good news!

Some instances demand much more. For example, if you are in *super class* aboard the *Queen Elizabeth 2* and eating in the Queen's or Princess grills, where you can order the moon and several stars for dinner every night, you will be expected to offer more. The grill manager deserves a gratuity (a minimum $30 per couple per week) as well as your head waiter (a minimum $50 per couple per week). Then, of course, there is your personal waiter (a minimum $5 per person, per day) and the wine steward, who expects the usual 15% of your total bill. Cunard suggests that passengers in Columbia restaurant (first class) pay a minimum $4 per person per day to each steward and those in

Mauretania (transatlantic class) restaurant offer a minimum $3. With the slightest breath of inflation, the above is subject to change—upward, of course.

Although ship lines pay their service crew a pittance and expect the passengers to make up the rest, I consider tipping a very personal matter and wait until the final day to make any decision about amounts. It depends primarily on how efficient the service was, how genuine, and how much I prevailed on special favors (breakfast in bed, ice, clean towels more than usual, etc.). However, there are some ships where I know the service will be superb and I am always prepared for tipping generously. There is a problem with tips that cruise lines have yet to address. No matter how much of your hard-earned money has been rendered, do not expect the same courtesy and smiling faces coming into port to which you had become accustomed during your cruise. Something happens when cabin and dining-room stewards receive their tips—they tend to dismiss the passenger(s) as already disembarked and are thinking about the next lot of envelopes. It is a terrible, terrible situation; I have observed it in every category of ship-board life and I always blame the hotel manager, captain, and ship-line executives for not ensuring that passengers enjoy every last minute of their cruise as much as the first.

Consider gratuities to the crew as money well spent if you have enjoyed yourself and are disembarking with many happy memories. Above all, do not offer tips to officers or cruise directors. They have done their job only if your cruise was the best vacation ever. If you feel they have acted beyond the call of duty, commend them by letter to the ship line. Perhaps you will find your favorite first officer as a captain someday!

BEFORE YOU BOOK

WHAT TO WEAR   With visions of seascapes and sunsets and dreamy days spent at the rail watching flying fish—not to mention dancing on the moonlit deck—you may wonder if you will need a new wardrobe for your cruise. Unless your closet has nothing but designer jeans, you can probably pack right now and not purchase one new item for ship-board life. Cruise clothes are simply resort clothes, and you'll need the same basic outfits that you wear at home when casual by day and off to cocktails and dinner in the evening. Some cruise vessels require more clothes than others, due to more activities on board and on shore and a greater number of port calls and climate changes. A more formal atmosphere prevails on Royal Viking Line's elegant new *Sun,* Cunard's *Sagafjord, Vistafjord, Sea Goddess I* and *II,* and *Seabourn Pride* and *Seabourn Spirit,* among others. On the other hand, life aboard the Swan Hellenic vessels and other specialty cruises like Society Expeditions hardly dictate black tie or elegant jewels.

A problem that ship lines have still not solved is informing passengers exactly what the dress code is each evening, so they can pack accordingly. The brochures are of little help; perusing the latest offering from Windstar Sail Cruises, most pictures of the ships are devoid of people! There is not even a hint that passengers may dress as they like and do not even have to pack a tie or dress shirt. The *Sea Goddess Life* shows nothing but formal evening dress—in the restaurant, bar and casino, on the beach—as well as a few sexy bathing suits when the sun is shining—so the wise traveler would forgo packing anything to wear in between!

For most cruises, you will want very casual and colorful wear during the day. This means slacks and T-shirts for both men and women, with low-heel and comfortable shoes. One swimsuit and a coverup (for walking through the public rooms and having buffet luncheon on deck), along with a pair of rubber flip-flops, are fine for a week's cruise. A pair of sneakers and espadrilles are perfect for walking on deck and sightseeing. (I never take expensive shoes for daytime wear, because many of the interesting sites are dusty and the old winding streets in port can be dirty and slippery.) Short shorts for everyone who looks good in them are perfect for lazy days at sea but are known to offend many inhabitants of host ports (especially in Haiti and the Dominican Republic). In general, you should dress moderately on shore and save the strutting, the open shirts, and the gold chains for the pleasure of your fellow passengers.

Many ship lines request that male passengers wear a coat and tie in public rooms after 6 p.m., so if this is not your style you should find another cruise vessel (or go to Club Med). For women, the evening is time for high heels, silk blouses, and romantic long skirts. Being on a cruise means getting dressed up almost every night. The first and last evenings spent on board are always casual—the first because you are probably tired from traveling, and the last because your suitcase is usually already packed and you dine in your onward-bound clothes. On a seven-day cruise, four nights will be called ''formal,'' and on a fourteen-day sailing seven nights will require party clothes. Just how formal you wish to be depends upon your taste, the ambience on board your vessel, and the itinerary. Many cruise line spokespeople say that the night life in the Caribbean demands black tie at the Captain's parties, but only a dark suit in some other areas. The reason: with many more days at sea in the Caribbean, passengers have plenty of time to primp; when islands are very close together, everyone is just too exhausted from visiting a port (and sometimes two) every day.

Your ship-board clothing should be fun to wear and should more or less take care of itself. Few vessels offer dry cleaning services, but many now include launderettes and self-service pressing facilities on board. (Salt air can cause many lovely fabrics to become limp and lifeless on board.) Silk or synthetic blouses are best, with a variety of pants and skirts to mix and match. You may want a simple but colorful gown for the captain's party and the traditional photo of your meeting with the master of the vessel. For a seven-day cruise, I take four outfits for the evening (which is far too many, but I like the feeling of choice).

No matter what sunny part of the world your ship is sailing, always pack enough sweaters and wraps for the air conditioning on board, the breezy evenings on deck, and the early arrivals in port. You just never know, and it's terrible to be clothed in nothing but filmy see-throughs. Along with an extra pullover, bring some inexpensive and lightweight rain gear (jacket and folding umbrella). Spring and fall are unpredictable the world over, and my closet is full of umbrellas bought on vacations because I forgot to pack one. When you arrive in port, the purser will announce the weather forecast as well as the present temperature. However, a comfortable-sounding temperature can be either warm or cool, depending upon wind and clouds, and your tour bus may be air-conditioned, so always take an extra sweater.

The best way to decide what to wear is to study the cruise news, the daily activity sheet slipped under your door during the night. It will suggest proper dress for shore excursions as well as for the evening. If you're just beach-bound, you'll know what to wear; but you may need a Windbreaker for an open boat ride across the bay.

SHIP-BOARD FACILITIES   Cruise ships have truly become floating resorts, as more and more facilities are added to keep passengers healthy and happy. No more shall you be contented with just a small dipping pool and some lounge chairs. Indeed, there are minigyms with the latest in pulling and pushing equipment, glamorous spas at sea that would cost thousands per week on land, aerobics and other dance exercise, jacuzzis, saunas, and massage. In addition to the traditional shuffleboard and skeet shooting, there is table and platform tennis and often a golf driving range. The *Royal Viking Sun* boasts a "proper" croquet court! And if you can't live without a weekly game of golf or tennis, don't leave your kit behind because the ship line can arrange a game in port.

Joggers should also be aware that they are not forgotten. One cannot run a marathon at sea, but several miles are possible. Most vessels make it easy for runners and post the number of times around deck make a mile. However, joggers are requested to refrain from running until a reasonable hour, because there may be fellow passengers asleep underneath that thump, thump, thump. If you prefer running in port, visit the local tourist office for a map and a good route. Running has become so popular all over the world, you will undoubtedly be in good company wherever the ship docks.

Water and underwater activities are very popular on cruises in the Bahamas, Caribbean, Hawaii, South Pacific, Bermuda during the season, and along both Mexican coastlines. Indeed, the beaches on some islands surpass any other attraction and passengers can delight in this fantastic underwater world along specified trails or on their own. All ships are well equipped but first-timers are encouraged to attend classes in the ship's pool with a qualified instructor before they're allowed to take out the gear. The Caribbean is perfect throughout for snorkeling, but if you're a real addict and want to dive in every port, be sure your cruise ship calls at St. Thomas, St. Croix, the Cayman Islands, Barbados, Cozumel, Nassau and Freeport, or even in Atlantic-bound Bermuda. You can also rent Sunfish in most of these (and other) ports, have a quick turn around the bay on water skis, and do a little fishing.

The new and smaller vessels now carry their beaches and watersports with them. For example, WindStar, Sea Goddess, and Seabourn Cruise Line all boast aft platforms that descend into the sea so passengers can swim, waterski, windsurf, snorkel, and the like from the safety of the ship. There is always someone on duty to watch over you, and plenty of companions with whom to swim or snorkel. It's the closest thing to being a turtle, i.e., carrying your house and toys with you, that I have yet experienced!

Parasailing has become another addiction along beautiful beaches— although it is not for everyone. On a recent Acapulco stop, however, the price was reasonable and well worth the experience! Alternatively, passengers who feel more comfortable in fresh-water pools may always head for a famous resort in port, and have lunch and a dip. Cruise passengers have the best of both worlds!

Cruises can also be a family affair, so bring the young ones along— especially if the price is right. Many ship lines specialize in youthful passengers, especially during the summer months and holidays, by adding counselors to the staff to keep the young crowd entertained. There are computer classes, video games, and all kinds of fun gatherings available daily, so you can relax and enjoy your own colleagues. Some ships even have recreation rooms and soda fountains, while the *QE2* hires proper nannies for the wee ones and cribs and playpens. On a cruise ship, it is possible to park your offspring from after breakfast until dinnertime and everyone seems the happier for it!

On the other hand, there are some pleasant quiet areas aboard every cruise ship. The library is a good place to start, both for browsing through periodicals or for finding some light reading matter. If you wish to catch up on your correspondence, there is generally a good writing room (the Princess Grace room on the *Constitution* is perfectly lovely and a tasteful memorial). Look for the Computer Center if you wish to improve your skills, or just figure out what your secretary does all day. Bridge and backgammon aficionados will want to find the card room as quickly as possible, and the social hostess will set up some good competition. Check out the public areas and dining room for nonsmoking areas, which are increasingly demanded by health-conscious passengers.

The list of activities on board can tire even the hardiest souls! Lectures abound all day long: financial advice, photography tips, graphoanalysis, fashion parades, wine tastings, cooking demonstrations, navigator talks and so it goes. Bingo, masquerade parties, handicraft clinics, feature films, horse racing, grandmothers' teas (bring photos of the little ones), Rotary, AA and other organizations as well as religious services are all featured on the weekly programs.

However, if you intend to do nothing of the above but find a nice bar stool— that is also fine. There are plenty of watering holes aboard a cruise ship and you will discover a favorite spot in no time. If you are a serious gambler, be sure your vessel has a full casino or you will be frustrated by a few slot machines tucked away in a dark corner. Some ship lines, like Carnival Cruise Lines, emphasize gambling and gambling-type entertainment although I noticed that even a tiny establishment, as on *Wind-Song,* was good fun with good company.

SHIP SANITATION is a pain in the neck, but it is here to stay—especially for newspaper editors who have never been to sea! Since July, 1975, after some serious intestinal outbreaks aboard cruise vessels, the Atlanta-based Centers for Disease Control (known affectionately as CDC) instituted a federally funded program to ensure periodic inspections of all cruise ships calling in U.S. ports. A biweekly summary of these sanitation inspections is released and copies sent to anyone who wishes to read the results. Although ships are now "graded" (86 is passing) and many do not make the required amount, any score within the 80s should be considered adequate. There are some *very* low scores on the list, which I would tend to worry about.

The inspection program has served a good purpose, as outbreaks of any intestinal disorders due to contaminated food or water are rare these days. In fact, any unusual incidence of illness aboard ship must be reported within 24 hours of arrival at U.S. ports. Everyone is aware of the necessity of sanitation these days, and the kitchens of many vessels look like operating rooms. Anyone handling food or drink wears a cap, a white uniform that began the day spotless, and plastic throwaway gloves. Even on deck, at breakfast and luncheon buffets, these plastic gloves are worn by servers.

The official CDC Vessel Sanitation Program cost the U.S. government about $300,000 annually, so it was eliminated from the budget in May 1986 and ship lines were requested to "police" themselves. It was revived in March 1987 and, a year later, continued with a private firm conducting the semiannual inspections, paid for by the ship lines themselves. CDC awarded contracts in three separate North American regions, and then assessed each line to cover expenses. A summary of recent inspections is available from: Chief, Vessel Sanitation Program, 1015 North America Way, Room 107, Miami, FL 33132.

BOOKING YOUR CABIN Alas, the days are gone when you can study a deck plan and decide exactly which cabin you desire. Ship lines today will only guarantee a cabin in the category you choose—unless you insist upon the top suite and will settle for nothing less. The good news is: No matter what category your purse can handle, you and all other cruise passengers will enjoy the same facilities, food, activities, entertainment and get the same photo taken with the Captain. There may be some difference in cabin service—this is especially true on the *QE2*—but most cruise vessels have crew that serve all passengers equally and with the same happy face.

If you plan to use your cabin only to sleep and change your clothes, or share it with another single traveler (the ship will assign a cabin mate), then by all means choose the lowest category and spend all your time out on the decks. However, if you and your spouse or companion plan to frequent the cabin or expect to entertain new-found friends, then spend a little more and book a larger, outside cabin that you will enjoy every minute. Request a cabin midships where the ride is certainly smoother if you're prone to motion sickness. It's also better to be midway between the upper and lower deck, especially on transatlantic crossings that may be stormy. The deluxe outside cabins will have larger windows, while the rest of the outside categories may still feature the standard porthole seen on the late-late show, although designers of the new ships afloat have taken some healthy liberties with cabin windows. Whatever the aperture, never open it at sea, because it's very dangerous and because the ship is fully air-conditioned. With the advent of air conditioning, inside cabins became comparable to those with a sea view (except for knowing what the weather is like).

The category you choose to book will probably determine the layout of your cabin—upper and lower berths, two parallel lower berths (with uppers in the wall), two lower berths in "L" shape, or a double/queen/king bed. Deluxe suites with a separate sitting area (even another room) may also have a sofa-bed to accommodate additional passengers (if they are small). But whatever your category, unless you have booked the lovely suites aboard *QE2, Sagafjord, Vistafjord, Seabourn Pride* and *Seabourn Spirit,* and Royal Viking Line, expect to be shocked at the size. Lack of spaciousness in most cabins seems to have come full circle since the days of Charles Dickens. Dickens sailed to Boston in 1842 aboard the *Britannia* and was surprised to find his deluxe stateroom for three only a little larger than a closet. As the voyage progressed, however, Dickens and his cabin mates agreed that their accommodation was indeed quite spacious, especially if they all turned around in unison!

When choosing a cabin, no matter what category, consider your habits. If you are in bed by 9 p.m., stay away from the disco (which doesn't begin popping until 10:30 every night). If walking is a problem, select a cabin near one of the elevators. Do you need a bathtub? Will a shower do just as well? Some showers are so small that if you drop the soap you've had it. Do you need extra space to work; does the cabin have a telephone; do you wish to have a great deal of privacy? I have noted elsewhere that connecting cabins should be avoided unless you're purchasing both parts, because the so-called connecting panel is a conduit for conversations from both sides. Unless the connecting cabins have a proper, water-tight door between them, book a higher or lower category. Another common error, booking a deluxe cabin on Promenade Deck, allows everyone to watch you as they pass by. Passengers in these cabins on many vessels complain mightily, and some even try to transfer to a lower deck. You should also be aware that some *(Vistafjord, Norway)* deluxe cabins have wonderful views of lifeboats and little else. Discuss this and all the other nuances of cabin selection with your travel agent; then decide what category and its placement on the ship suits you.

Many of the older vessels in fleets—Regency Cruises, Chandris Fantasy Cruises, BSL (Bermuda Star Line)—do have spacious cabins in even lower categories, and Carnival's standardized cabins are bigger than most. However, even the lock-knee cabins (travel with someone friendly, I always say) on the Royal Caribbean Cruise Line vessels do not diminish the fun, as these vessels have won Ship of the Year consistently in the World Ocean & Cruise Liner Society passenger polls. The cruise experience does not necessarily depend upon the size of your cabin, only if you insist upon it. I heard about a Norwegian family of four in a standard *Sovereign of the Seas* cabin (minuscule), and they were having a wonderful time! Even on *Sea Goddess I* and *II,* the cabin size does not equal the per diem, hence Cunard's decision to offer suite-suites for those who wish to pay double for greater comfort. Seabourn's all-suite accommodations are *most* comfortable for a new vessel—as are the spacious staterooms aboard Renaissance Cruises.

In addition to beds (one to four), you can expect to find a dresser/vanity, a wardrobe, a chair or two, and a small table (for the champagne bucket and breakfast tray) in your cabin. On some of the newer vessels, the beds will convert to sofas by day (and may even fold into the wall). More good news: the number of double-, queen- and king-size beds has boomed on board ships recently as lines try to entice honeymooners and younger couples traveling without children. Double beds have been placed in many inside or lower category cabins to make them more saleable. The newer vessels boast twin beds that make easily into king in most cabins—so passengers can even make their own choice during the course of the cruise!

Some of the nicest cabins I have ever encountered are aboard the WindStar Sail cruisers. They are spacious in their design, with plenty of wardrobe space and even a small safe for money and jewelry. The bathrooms are beautifully constructed, with every amenity ever needed and a state of the art shower (that took me three days to figure out)! These are cozy cabins in which the twin beds make into a queen—and perfect for honeymooners and other loving couples.

Specify the sleeping arrangements you and your traveling companion desire when booking the cruise. Do not wait until aboard or you may be disappointed. When your tickets arrive check cabin assignment on the deck plan to confirm that your choice has been honored. As your travel agent will say, solve all discrepancies before you embark—so there will be nothing to do but relax and enjoy!

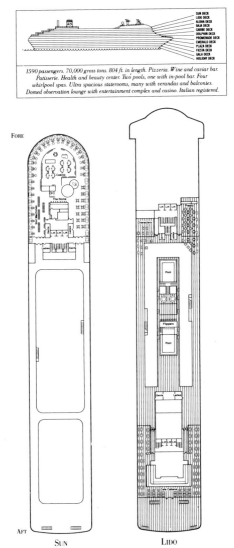

SUN DECK
LIDO DECK
ALOHA DECK
BAJA DECK
CARIBE DECK
DOLPHIN DECK
PROMENADE DECK
EMERALD DECK
PLAZA DECK
FIESTA DECK
GALA DECK
HOLIDAY DECK

*1590 passengers. 70,000 gross tons. 804 ft. in length. Pizzeria. Wine and caviar bar.
Patisserie. Health and beauty center. Two pools, one with in-pool bar. Four
whirlpool spas. Ultra spacious staterooms, many with verandas and balconies.
Domed observation lounge with entertainment complex and casino. Italian registered.*

FORE

AFT

SUN

LIDO

Princess Cruises
Crown Princess

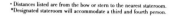
· Distances listed are from the bow or stern to the nearest stateroom.
*Designated stateroom will accommodate a third and fourth person.

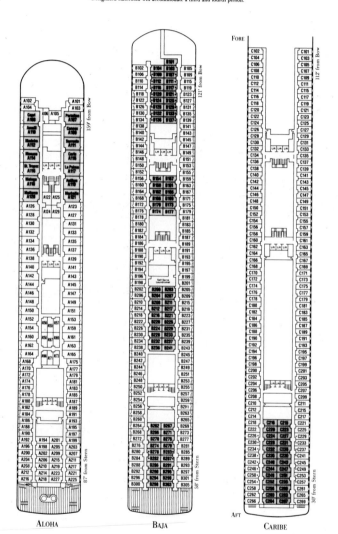

ALOHA   BAJA   CARIBE

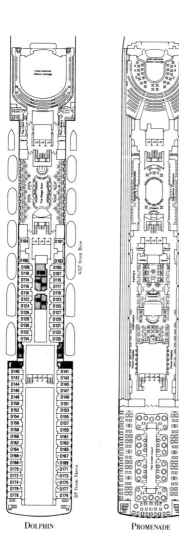

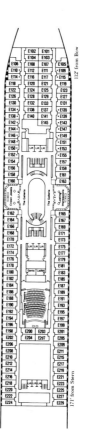

DOLPHIN

PROMENADE

EMERALD

ANCHORS AWAY!

When the cruise tickets arrive in the mail, you know you're on the way! It's a nice feeling just to grasp them and consider lazy days at sea, lunch on deck, adventuresome foods, personalized service, new ports, and new friends. Not to disturb the reverie, but while tickets are in hand, check the boxes and make sure the date and point of embarkation are correct. Since most ship lines no longer assign cabins when you book but instead guarantee a certain category (and rate), check to see that the cabin number on your ticket coincides with the category you paid for (occasionally, it will even be a grade higher). Also make sure the name of the ship is correct. Norwegian Cruise Line officials claim that the majority of passengers who arrive for embarkation in Miami are not even aware which vessel they have booked, so don't laugh at this suggestion.

You might also read the passage contract carefully, for it details the ship owner's liability and cancellation charges. If you cannot use the ticket and do not give notice to the company within sixty days of departure, charges are levied (unless the space is immediately sold). If you decide not to sail less than five days before embarkation, the total fare may be forfeit unless the ship line is sympathetic to the calamitous happenings that prevent your traveling. However, once you embark and begin your cruise (and then get sick or whatever), there is no recompense. (If the ship line must cancel a cruise, however, you will probably receive a full refund.) This contract also states the cruise fare (with all inclusions), procedures describing how to settle your account for any purchases on board, luggage restrictions (if any), policy regarding cabin changes, instructions to safeguard valuables, and a caution against carrying goods of a dangerous nature. These items are all detailed on, or along with, your ticket, in hope that no misunderstanding between passenger and ship operator will cause a future problem.

Baggage tags will accompany your tickets, and you should transfer the information on your ticket to that required on the tags. Some lines, like Royal Cruise, have color-coded tags so porters will immediately recognize on which section of the ship your bags should be placed. If you're traveling on an air-sea program and are met at the airport for transfer to the vessel, you will probably be requested to tag your bags with the ship's labels before you check them at the airport. This enables the ship line personnel to claim your bags upon your flight's arrival and transport them to the ship. (Most companies send all baggage in bond straight to the ship, eliminating customs' inspection.) If you neglect to follow these instructions, your cruise wardrobe may just sit in the baggage claim area until you begin to wonder why your cabin is so empty. Alternatively, if you fly into the city of embarkation on your own and did not follow the instructions sent to you (and tagged your bags too soon), your cruise wardrobe will be sent straight to the ship—while you run around the airport with visions of sailing away naked. Of course, bags do become authentically lost. If this happens to you, inform both the airline and the ship line at once; and don't leave the airport without filing a claim form and leaving your cruise itinerary (ports of call in order of appearance). I have known luggage to miraculously appear in the rightful cabin midway in a cruise, especially if the passenger is part of an air-sea program.

LUGGAGE Luggage can easily become a problem, if you're not careful. Few of us can afford to rent the cabin next door just for our bags! One average-size suitcase and one carry-on bag is quite sufficient for the normal seven-day cruise, especially if you plan to be casual by day. Pack your feathers and other fancies first, and put the casual clothes around them. If your spouse or companion prefers a fold-over bag, all the better; you can sneak in a few dresses or suits. Ships were once famous for the huge amounts of baggage they could accommodate. No longer. Space is at a premium on most of today's cruise vessels (unless you have booked a fabulous suite complete with walk-in closets and butler-maid to aid in the unpacking). So just bring along what you can comfortably put in your cabin, either under the beds or in the wardrobe areas, because you don't want to fall over a suitcase every time you open the door. On ships offering longer cruises (more than a month or so), a proper baggage room for storage may exist. If you no longer have your wardrobe trunk from school or camp days, some companies will still come to your home, pack your clothing in a stand-up carton, and deliver it aboard your cruise vessel. At the end of the voyage, they will transport your wardrobe back to its proper home. All for a fine fee, of course (check with your travel agent or ship line for the most reputable and efficient firms).

IMMUNIZATION AND DOCUMENTS If your cruise is confined to Caribbean or European waters, you probably will not need any immunizations. But if you are sailing for the Far East, be aware of requirements—for smallpox, cholera, typhoid, tetanus, hepatitis, and even yellow fever—imposed by some of the countries your ship will visit. If you cruise within the Galapagos Islands and certain other parts of South

America or along the African coastline, your doctor may advise that you take malaria-prevention medicine before and after your journey. Double-check each country's requirement *before* you sail so that your own doctor can administer the immunization and your arms will return to normal before embarkation.

You do not need a passport or visas for Caribbean cruises, but you must carry some proof of citizenship (voter's registration or birth certificate will do). However, if you do not carry a passport and must clear customs in major airports like New York, you will also have to pass through Immigration—which is a bore! (The lines are very, very long and air officials have not studied the fine art of etiquette, as a general rule.) Elsewhere, you certainly must bring an up-to-date passport along.

The ship line should advise you of any visas necessary for the ports of call, and your travel agent will help you obtain them from the appropriate consulates. For China cruises, the ship line receives a blanket visa for all passengers aboard who plan to disembark and take tours handled by Luxingshe (China International Travel Service). If, however, your ship is calling at ports in the USSR and Poland, you may be requested to obtain your own visa, especially if you do not intend to take an organized shore excursion. (You also have to obtain your own visa for other countries.) When you board your vessel bound for these wonderful and exotic places, the purser will require you to surrender your passport. This enables the local immigration and customs officials to clear the ship as soon as possible upon arrival in a port. You may not see or need your passport again (except in certain countries, such as USSR and Brazil) until your voyage ends. If you return to the same port of embarkation, you will receive your documents the evening before arrival. If the port of disembarkation is in a different country whence you departed, the ship line will keep your passport for clearance and return it to you directly.

MONEY All cruise lines today accept credit cards as well as cash/traveler's checks for final payment of on-board expenses. In fact, most cruises are now considered "cashless," and you will be asked to sign for everything, so you must have your credit card imprinted at the purser's office upon embarkation. Your on-board expenses include wine, drinks, masseuse, casino loans (some lines allow $100 a day to be charged to the cabin), shore excursions, and possibly boutique purchases. The beauty shop usually insists upon separate payment, and tips must be rendered in cash (except on certain Greek-flag vessels where a lump sum from every passenger is placed in the "pot" for distribution by the Chief Steward). The purser's office often will convert your dollars into local currency at certain hours if the supply on board is adequate. But this is not a bank, and the purser and his staff cannot reconvert your local currency into dollars (so don't ask, they often get mad). If the port officials are friendly and obliging, they will frequently allow a representative of a local bank to come aboard for several hours to handle passengers' monetary transactions. This helpful courtesy saves so much valuable time in port, be properly grateful when it occurs.

ELECTRICAL APPLIANCES   At this time you may also want to check if your hair dryer, electric shaver, and foot warmer will work properly in the cabin. Most ship lines have the correct electrical fixture in the bathroom for these items; however, hair dryers may not function properly on the older vessels and travel irons should definitely be left at home. If you travel with children, many vessels now have self-laundry/ironing rooms by popular demand. Although all ships offer laundry and pressing services, it is nice to know one can press out a crease quickly, if necessary. The newer vessels also offer drycleaning services at reasonable prices.

EMBARKING   When it's embarkation time and you know that your cruise ship will be returning to the same terminal, be observant. The departure is usually a blur and the returning a hassle, but if you have memorized the terminal's layout and know where you parked your car or where the nearest taxi service is you will feel better. (See "Ports of Embarkation.") For a 4:30 sailing, most ships begin embarkation around 1:30 p.m. If you embark on your own, do it early so you can relax and enjoy the getting underway. Local stevedores will carry your baggage onto the vessel and you will not see it again until it appears in the cabin. (In some of the smaller ports, you and your baggage will never part company, which can be more comforting.) If you carry expensive camera equipment or a great deal of jewelry, stop by the customs office in port and declare your valuables prior to leaving the country. This saves considerable time and embarrassment upon return.

Once up the gangplank, you will meet a steward who will show you the location of your cabin and introduce you to the cabin attendant. If you are expecting visitors and wish to have a small Bon Voyage party, the cabin attendant will bring ice and glasses, and deliver any flowers, champagne, or fruit that arrives in your name. Hors d'oeuvres or petits fours are a nice addition, and your room steward will try to oblige, but most ship lines require prior notification. Any special services at embarkation should be arranged for in advance, because the crew is so busy at this time. If your ship line allows visitors, it will enclose some guest passes (usually two per passenger) along with your tickets. It may also enclose an order form for possible embarkation requests, as Holland America does, and the cost will be charged to your shipboard account for payment at the end of the cruise. Some of the ship's watering holes will be open in port, and tea is often served at embarkation. If bon voyage parties are possible, you may bring along your own beverages for the privacy of the cabin only. It is certainly frowned upon to carry your own spirits into public areas and, frankly, more fun to join fellow passengers in one of the lounges. You may also bring along your own party treats, but keep them to a minimum. Remind your well-meaning friends that you are embarking on a *cruise* and suggest they send the overloaded hampers off to someone who won't be served so many courses in the next several days. In any event, most Bon Voyage parties are less than two hours (visitors must disembark at least thirty minutes prior to sailing), so how much do you really need?

If you wish to have a large reception catered by the ship line, arrange the details through your travel agent. The line will handle refreshments and set aside enough space for you in one of the lounges. It is increasingly popular and convenient to have postnuptial parties on board your own personal "love boat." You may even plan an on-board ceremony, but you must bring along your own officiate since captains are no longer allowed to perform marriages, even at sea. For a full-blown wedding reception featuring a many-tiered cake, champagne, open bar, sandwiches, coffee, and live music for dancing, the ship's hotel manager will prepare one of the lounges for you, and your guests may board as early as noon. I met a charming young couple recently who were married aboard the *Britanis* in New York harbor and then treated their guests to an all-day Cruise to Nowhere complete with champagne reception, luncheon, cake and casino!

Embark early enough to explore your new home, check out the pool area and deck chair situation, even plot which side of the ship is better for a tan. It's also a good idea to look in the boutiques (for future indulgences) and find the drugstore or gift shop, just in case the sun lotion or film supply runs low. And don't forget to locate your life jacket—usually under the bed or on the top shelf of the wardrobe—and study the deck plans on the back of your cabin door. Instructions for your lifeboat station and drill information also should be on the door. A drill will occur soon after sailing, or early the next morning if the first day of your cruise is spent at sea. When you hear the alarm, put on your life jacket and quickly walk up to your station on Boat Deck. Some ship lines take attendance, so don't fool around. The ship's photographer (whom you no doubt met upon embarkation) will record the event for posterity. You haven't been on a cruise until you have been immortalized in a life jacket!

A FEW WARNINGS   Basically, if you consider your cruise vessel a floating resort that transports you from one wonderful port to another as an added bonus, everything will be placed in proper perspective. For example, if you feel naked without your diamonds and emeralds (or wads of cash in your hip pocket) then bring them along, but place all valuables in a safe deposit box provided by the ship line (the very same boxes a hotel would provide) or in the small safe in the privacy of your cabin when not wearing or carrying them. I have rarely heard of a shipboard theft, but why offer the temptation?

If you plan to sun, take it easy; protect yourself with plenty of lotion. Many passengers forget that tropical sun is more intense than that found in most parts of North America. Too much sun for passengers on the *Norway* was such a problem a few years ago, that Norwegian Cruise Line wisely transposed the port calls; the beach party at Little San Salvador now takes place after the shopping spree in St. Thomas. If your cruise takes you to new and exotic parts of the world, you might want to discuss the itinerary with your doctor or druggist, who might recommend an effective sun screen. Hats are mandatory if you are out touring along the equator all day, for a scalp burn is just as dangerous as any other.

Another danger may be to your camera, if you decide to bring it. The sea spray can damage lenses, and sand is "the end." The best advice is to visit your favorite camera shop with itinerary in hand and find out what lens, filters, film speed and type, and covers to use. Having the proper equipment is important if you're to enjoy taking your vacation photographs, especially at sea when so many elements are working together (and some against you) at the same time—and you're moving besides!

Speaking of moving, there is such a thing as *mal de mer*—simply, motion sickness—which must be addressed immediately because the source is the ship's rock and roll. There are many remedies available (pills, shots, patches, bracelets, etc.), but the best is experience—being rewarded with one's sea legs. Most ship lines will dispense Dramamine (the old-fashioned remedy) along with aspirin and Alka-Seltzer from the on-board bars free of charge; however, they do charge for a better remedy (Bonine or Antivert), which costs about 25 cents a tablet and does not make you sleepy. If you do not wish to take pills, my friend Toby Scholz recommends powdered ginger capsules—a natural remedy that works if you believe in it.

For serious cases, the ship-board doctor will administer a shot or suppository that sedates the nervous system and somehow makes one feel terrific again (my husband swore by shots until he received his "sea legs"). The transderm patch, available through druggists, is popular but not terribly efficient as most victims do not follow the instructions properly. The patch must be applied behind the ear *before* you even step aboard, and it is effective for just 72 hours; then, it must be removed and a new one applied. Although you can eat or drink anything while wearing the patch, it is considered an appetite depressant and can cause both dryness of the mouth and blurred vision. With the shot, you should not drink coffee.

New on the market are the natural, non-drug Sea Bands or acupressure bracelets that alleviate nausea within minutes, as tested by both the Royal British Navy and Australian Yacht Club. These are wrist bands into which a button is sewn, whose gentle pressure at a specific point on the wrist controls nausea. As no medication is involved, there are no side effects, so Sea Bands are safe for older passengers as well as pregnant women, and do not have to be employed until nausea occurs.

Sea Bands are available aboard American Hawaii Cruises' vessels, or by contacting Travel Accessories (P.O. Box 391162, Solon, OH 44139. Phone numbers: (800) 229–8432; in Ohio (216) 248–8432. The cost is $9.95 a pair (one for each wrist), plus $2 shipping; evening Glitter Bands also available at $12.50 a pair. Visa/MC accepted on phone orders. Please note: I am not promoting Sea Bands, but appreciate anything that does not involve drugs.

Since I dislike anything stronger than a Vitamin C pill, my own cure for queasiness is a nice hot cup of consomme (usually available on deck at about 11 a.m.), some crackers (saltines are best), and deep breaths of sea air. One ship-line executive also said: the best antidote for *mal de mer* is preoccupation. Joining in the many onboard activities is the best way to forget about the roll of the ship. In fact, that queasy feeling will most likely disappear, forever!

However, if you feel you must have something stronger, there is a concoction called ''the stabilizer'' to which I was introduced aboard the *Sagafjord* by Kurt the morning I looked a bit pale. I had boarded the vessel in the nice calm waters of Acapulco, but the sea was a bit rough that morning as we sailed toward the Pacific side of the canal. I took Kurt's advice and drank the potion he mixed before me—half brandy and half port wine—in three gulps. It tasted pretty awful and it was a little early in the morning to be imbibing, but it worked wonders in just minutes. Whatever bothered me left immediately, and I now swear by stabilizers. An Irish friend said later that she remembers her grandmother mixing this potion for upset stomachs. The old remedies sometimes work the best!

A final warning on board ship is to treat the vessel with respect. Those railings are meant to keep you from falling overboard, but not if you are careless about safety. Children should not be allowed to play near the railings under any circumstances, and adults should not be foolish enough to sit on them. A recent case of a passenger who decided to sit on the railing after several drinks resulted in his going overboard. He was lucky enough to be picked up immediately by a fishing trawler and was eventually returned to the vessel. But not for long; the captain requested he disembark at the next port because his foolishness endangered the lives of all aboard.

SECURITY AT SEA is here to stay, and all precautions undertaken are to passengers' benefit. Many ship lines no longer allow visitors at

Anchors Away, and X-ray machines are a normal sight now on every pier. Both plain clothes and uniformed security are aboard every vessel whether you realize it or not. On many cruises, ID cards are issued to passengers for their own protection and must be shown to the gangway guard in ports of call. The best advice: Be aware of security yourself and if you become suspicious of a person or situation, report immediately to the purser's office. We live in a world in which our senses must be activated at all times.

ON BOARD

Getting underway never fails to make my skin tingle, my eyes mist slightly, and my knees a bit weak as I lift a glass of the bubbly in salute. Casting off and feeling the ship pull away from the pier is, indeed, one of the most exciting parts of being aboard. And the exhilaration exists whether you are sailing under the Golden Gate, past the Statue of Liberty, away from Dodge Island, or into the bustling harbor of Piraeus. As familiar landmarks disappear and the sun dips into the horizon, you know that adventure lies ahead. To fully enjoy the sailing away, I always like to have unpacked and treated myself to a quick tour of the public areas, so I can be out on deck, glass in hand, to toast the leave-taking. Whatever port of departure, it is always festive, with lots of streamers, music, and waving to those on the pier below. Some memorable leave-takings have been in the port of Piraeus at sunset, Nice at midday, Port Everglades in the early evening, New York past the famous Statue of Liberty, Honolulu at night, and Miami in the afternoon. Indeed, the flotilla departing Miami is quite a sight; the decks are generally a sea of orange life vests as passengers prepare for their mandatory life boat drill!

The modern cruise ship is a self-contained city. It has its own government and staff, communications, housing, recreation, food service, protection and fire department, water supply, and garbage disposal. Coming aboard is like moving to a new town; you think you know how it will be, but the unexpected always happens! It takes some time to become accustomed to your new surroundings, which must be why some passengers request the same cabin and dining-room assignment year after year. (I have even heard of some loyal passengers who become upset over a new decor in their favorite stateroom). And some sweet old things, who come aboard for world cruises or longer, are even allowed to bring their own bedspreads and other familiar accouterments.

RESERVING A TABLE   Before you really settle in, be sure to take care of your table assignment and meal hour preference, if you have not already done so. (Most ship lines handle this on shore and notify you by mail or by card in your cabin.) At sailing time, the maitre d' (or someone on his staff) will be receiving passenger requests outside the dining room or in one of the public lounges, so seek him out speedily if you want a good choice of tables. Unfortunately, most ship lines have two seatings for all meals in the dining room (exceptions include Royal Viking, Cunard/NAC, *QE2* and *Stella Maris,* which have assigned tables; on Sea Goddess, Windstar, ACCL, Seabourn, Renaissance, Classical, Special Expeditions, Clipper, etc., there is open seating at all meals), which means that your stomach is fed either earlier than it is accustomed to or later than satisfactory. Meal hours vary somewhat among the lines, but the main seating is around 7:30 a.m. (breakfast), noon (luncheon), and 6:30 p.m. (dinner). Second or late seating hours are generally around 8:45 a.m., 1:30 p.m., and 8:30 p.m. Since you may avoid these schedules by having breakfast in bed or out on deck and partaking of the luncheon buffet that is usually served around the pool, dinner hour is your only real decision. If you have young children, you will be encouraged to consider the earlier time period. The later seating is more fashionable, of course, and more suited to couples and swinging singles.

On most ships you may request, and be very firm about, a table for two. (I have always found this the most satisfactory, as my husband and I enjoy our quiet conversations at sea.) If this is not possible, however, ask for a table for six or eight, because at a table for four you may get stuck with a completely incompatible couple. Many ship lines claim that they are experts at putting people together in the dining room. I don't believe for one moment that any maitre d' or his staff can look at seven hundred different passengers in the space of an hour or two and match them perfectly. It's simply dumb luck, and if your luck doesn't hold and you find your table companions to be not your type, then take your case back to the maitre d'. In most instances he will be obliging, but his hands may be tied if the ship is fully booked. If you are traveling alone or in a group of singles, you will want the largest table possible. Explain this in a gentle way to the maitre d' and he will do his best. After all, he wants everyone happy (and many a romance has begun at the table).

EATING ABOARD More has been written about food on board cruise vessels than about itinerary, ambience, service, size of cabins, or anything else. Because at least five meals are served daily, you can have a "pig out" (as my husband calls it) from early morning to late at night. For starters, you can rise early (good heavens!) and have coffee on deck at 6:30 a.m. This may stimulate your appetite for the three choices of full breakfast available on most ships. You may return to your cabin for everything from the dainty Continental breakfast to kippers, assorted cheeses, and hot chocolate. If you want the proper sit-down service that you paid for, head for the dining room where your waiter will keep the java hot and you may have everything on the menu. Or, you may have a pleasant buffet breakfast out on deck; although lighter than what is available in the dining room, this may include scrambled eggs, bacon and sausage, English muffins, toast, fresh Danish pastries, juice, fruit, and coffee/tea. Hours for this repast will be posted in your daily program. For the real sleepyheads, coffee and Danish may be served in one of the lounges until about 11 a.m. Deck service is now the norm on cruising vessels, and any repast in the open air is what cruises are all about, if you don't mind plastic service—it's a safety feature.

Not many ships continue the tradition of bouillon at 11 a.m., a hangover from the grand old days of transatlantic travel. Bouillon, always good for warming the insides as you sat under a steamer rug on a deck chair in the misty air, was also an excellent antidote for queasy stomachs. In the Caribbean you will probably not be served bouillon (instead you head for a cool, refreshing drink from the bar), but if you are cruising in the colder waters of Alaska, the Baltic, around the North Cape, or across the Atlantic, you can count on it (and it may be a lifesaver). American Hawaii Cruises features orange sherbet at 11 a.m. and it is very refreshing indeed.

Before you have digested those waffles with whipped butter and rasher of bacon, lunch is being served. At sea (or in port) on pleasant days, a cold buffet is usually served near a swimming pool (and you may fill your plate while bikini-clad). Some ships also have hamburgers and hot dogs sizzling on a nearby grill. I always avoid the dining room at lunchtime, if possible, and love these outdoor buffets. Even if the weather is on the cool side, it's refreshing to sit on deck and inhale the sea breezes. Aboard the *Stella Solaris* one spring, we sat on deck with some fruit and cheese from the cold buffet, shared a bottle of local wine with new-found friends, and thought life was certainly splendid as the ship sailed away from Dikili and the ruins of Pergamum. Such a feeling would have been entirely lost in a packed dining room.

However, if you must have a hot lunch, the dining room readies a complete range of dishes for your palate. Soups, salads, and entrees change daily, and the chef prepares a special. I always ask the waiter what he advises before making a final decision. After all, he's been in the kitchen and knows what looks good. After a day or so, a wise waiter will know your preferences and begin to recommend dishes before you even pop the question. Every ship line features some sort of specialty that you will soon not be able to live without. Ships with Italian kitchens have their wonderful pasta, and Sitmar started the pizzeria boom— so tempting! Norwegian-staffed vessels feature lots of herring, and the *Sagafjord* serves more fresh seafood than anyone ever dreamed of eating. The small American vessels make sure that their menus follow the coastline, and American Hawaii offers lots of pineapple and papaya. Black olives (a handful a day are good for the skin), pounds and pounds of feta cheese, and wonderful grain breads can be enjoyed on Greek-flag vessels.

Food takes top priority at sea for excellent reasons: It's included in the fare; and you are obliged to do nothing but read the menu, order, and enjoy being served! If you wish to try a little bit of this and that, in addition to what you order—no problem! Ship lines enjoy satisfied passengers, so if food is your yellow brick road to happiness—all the better.

Food is, however, a very personal taste, and what one passenger considers flavorable—another will not. Although some cruise food is far better than others, the quality of meals even on value cruises (i.e., Chandris) has risen considerably over the past decade as Americans themselves demand a better diet and more sophisticated selection. In deference to more exciting dining, Cunard has (finally) introduced the International Food Bazaar on selected nights in its transatlantic-class Mauretania Restaurant, and all class of passengers may partake. The Bazaar features four theme buffet tables as well as four theme bars offering appropriate regional drinks. Dinner dancing on occasional evenings has also returned to sea, especially in the *QE2*'s Columbia and Mauretania restaurants and aboard *CostaRiviera* and Seabourn Cruise Line. This is a splendid and festive touch and, hopefully, will be offered on all ships.

The care and feeding of a shipload of passengers is no mean task, especially when two seatings are involved. The 1700-passenger *Canberra* serves an average of 7500 meals a day, not to forget the printing of some 1374 menus. The *QE2* employs 239 waiters, 139 kitchen personnel, 50 beverage personnel, 14 bartenders, 16 bakers, and 18 wine stewards. The ice cream stocked for one transatlantic crossing would make 24,000 single-dip cones, and the caviar consumed (mainly in the Grills) is about 150 pounds. When the *Sovereign of the Seas* sails from Miami every week, 1500 bottles of champagne, 50 pounds of caviar, and 200 pounds of smoked salmon are stocked. Other impressive items on the grocery list are 2400 lobster tails, 2000 filet mignons, 1750 pounds of shrimp and 600 gallons of ice cream in 14 flavors.

Should you have the slightest feeling of hunger by late afternoon, full tea service in one of the lounges will feature sandwiches, pastries, and little cakes. Royal Caribbean serves ice cream sundaes at 4 p.m. in the pool cafe. Ice cream parlors (for the purchase of gooey concoctions), found on the *Norway* and the *Independence,* are popular gathering places throughout the day.

Finally, you hightail it to the dining room as the first note of chimes is struck for your dinner seating. (Most cruise ships request that you enter the dining room not more than fifteen minutes after the meal has been announced when there are two seatings. This is a courtesy both to the kitchen and your table companions.) Most of these floating restaurants assume a new and enjoyable personality in the evening. The stewards are usually in a good mood because dinner is their favorite meal to serve, and their day is almost over. If the lights are low enough to hide your wrinkles but still find your plate, all the better!

Aside from the first and final evenings on board, which are casual and often awkward, your evenings in the dining room will be very special. You can expect a Captain's Welcome Dinner as well as a Captain's Farewell Dinner plus any number of other galas. Often featured are Spanish Night, Italian Night, French Night, Caribbean Night, Greek Night, American Night, Hawaiian Night, Norwegian Night, and two or three galas depending upon the nationality of your crew and the length of your cruise. If you are aboard a Greek-flag vessel, you will certainly enjoy the menu on Greek Night. For appetizers, the list reads: dolmadakia, taramosalata, tzatziki, amphissa olives, bourekakia, fried baby squashes, and ouzo special. The soup specialty is Augolemono, consisting of chicken broth, egg, and lemon—all delicious! This is followed by: shrimps Microlimano style, baby lamb Roumeli style or veal liver, roast potatoes and buttered artichokes, Greek salad (cucumbers, tomatoes, feta cheese, onions, black olives, oil and vinegar), assorted Greek cheeses, and for dessert a choice of baklava, kataifi, galaktoboureko, or kaimaki ice cream (or all four). And by the end of the meal, the sommelier has recommended a number of Greek wines.

And this is just one special evening! Royal Caribbean claims that you have a choice of some 1500 separate items on its weekly menus (but I suspect this includes all three meals). On some of the more elegant cruise vessels, you may order off the menu and have a steak every night if you wish. Settle any special diet needs before you book your cruise, because some lines will not cater to individuals but do carry enough different types of foodstuffs so that you may work around the problem. Passengers on salt-free diets will find plenty from which to choose on the menu, and many ship lines (including Royal Cruise Line and Royal Caribbean Cruise Lines) follow suggestions from the American Heart Association at every meal. Strictly speaking, I would say that the food on most cruise ships is good, and it's difficult not to overeat (especially when those luscious desserts come rolling in). Steaks, prime ribs, and fresh fish of all varieties are the best selections at sea. The presentation of salads and vegetables somehow misses at sea, except on the top-rated vessels. And don't expect mounds of caviar anymore (unless you are Super Class on the *QE2* or floating around in sybaritic splendor aboard *Sea Goddess I* or *II* or lucky enough to be aboard *Seabourn Pride* and *Spirit*), because it is just too expensive for everyone's taste! Anyway, a little dab here and there is enough to make you feel like royalty—especially if it does happen to be the best variety.

On the other hand, many fine and memorable dishes will keep you from becoming bored at sea. How about reindeer meat with juniper berries, real Russian borscht and piroshki, rack of lamb a la *QE2*, freshly grilled Alaskan salmon, grilled baby calves' liver, duck a l'orange, and uncountable numbers of "omelette surprise" (baked Alaska) and special gateau! It's difficult not to indulge, so it's best to diet beforehand. Then, by the end of your cruise, you cannot complain that the sea air shrank your wardrobe.

In case you just can't make it to bed without another little snack, the midnight buffet begins about 11:30 p.m. and lasts until 1 a.m. or so. Here you will find deviled eggs, cold meats, cheeses, salads, lobster and shrimp, fresh fruit, and tempting little pastries. Some ships pay particular attention to this final meal of the day, especially in the Caribbean (Carnival Cruise Lines claims to have three different buffets on every vessel). If you happen to be sailing in Europe, you may not be honored with a buffet, or you may find only a simple table of cheeses, bread, and cold meats (such as Royal Viking arranges in its Sky Deck lounges, where I rarely saw anyone with nerve enough to partake, because the dinners on board were all so splendid).

DRINKING ABOARD   A captain of the *Dolphin,* a cozy vessel that cruises out of Miami twice weekly to the Bahamas, used to say the amount of alcohol consumed per day per passenger is directly related to the length of the cruise. He claimed that three- and four-day passengers drink more in each 24-hour period than do passengers on longer cruises. Well, for the getting underway, nothing beats those bubbles up your nose. It's traditional, and popping that cork is good for the soul! Norwegian American Cruises believed in this tradition so much that every one of its cabins included a complimentary bottle of champagne for the sailing. Cunard/NAC carries on the tradition, but it's not quite the same. Beware of the California bubbly on the *Sagafjord*—I'm still looking for the plastic cork that zoomed out of one bottle! (No wonder there is a warning to aim it away from the face when opening.) Now, where to enjoy your champagne . . . if you have a large cabin with terrace, you know where. Otherwise, out on deck to enhance every bittersweet moment of departure.

Most cruise vessels have several lounges with bars. Outstanding are the RCCL (Royal Caribbean Cruise Line) trademark Viking Crown Lounge, ten stories up and cantilevered from the smokestack, and the *Norway's* Club International, the most elegant lounge afloat and a lovely hangover from French Line days. Once the vessel is underway and you have time to explore, you'll be surprised how many little nooks are tucked around where you have a preprandial cocktail, waker-upper, or putter-to-sleeper. With the exception of the Club International (which concentrates solely upon itself), I always venture toward the best view and find my spot for the duration of the cruise (a true creature of habit).

Most vessels have some type of glass-enclosed lounge located on a high deck, so that you can be on top of (yet a part of) the sea below. On the *Stella Solaris,* the glassed-in Piano Bar has a panoramic view and the *Mississippi Queen*'s two-story, glass-enclosed Paddlewheel Lounge is among the most dramatic. On the Princess vessels, the view is best from the Starlight lounges. Royal Viking has its Discovery, Windjammer, or Stella Polaris room up on Sky Deck (by whichever name, the view is the same and always splendid). And so on. Every vessel has at least one spectacular public area, a quiet bar, and plenty of spots where the action congregates.

Drinks on board ship, no longer so inexpensive as they were, are still less than on dry land. There are plenty of juices, sodas, and designer waters in the $1 plus range, as well as beer in the can, bottle, or on tap for a $1.50 or so. It has become very popular now to obtain a variety of wines by the glass at the bar, and mixed drinks range from $3.50 and upwards. Daily "specials," bloody Marys, Cuba libres, screwdrivers, etc., are posted around the pool. There are also special concoctions in glasses you take with you for $6 and up (if you can decipher what you are drinking). The types of drinks served depend upon the cruise ship and where you are sailing; few passengers begin the day with a rum punch aboard *Vistafjord*'s North Cape cruise!

If you enjoy wine with your dinner, you'll love being at sea. The wine list is usually interesting, especially if you're aboard a Greek- or Italian-flag vessel and wish to try the many local brands at reasonable prices. Greek white wines might be retsina, Robola, Santa Elena, Hymettos, Santa Laura, Demestica; red wines of the same type are Chevalier de Rhodes, Naoussa, Monte Nero, Santa Laura, Demestica, and Lava. On Italian vessels, Soave Bolla seems to be the popular brand, along with Verdicchio, Frascati, and the straw-covered Chiantis. The more expensive French white and red burgundies, Beaujolais, California names, and even blue Nun are on most wine lists, plus champagnes from sparkling German wines to vintage french. The *QE2* boasts a "cellar" of some 20,000 bottles ranging from prize-winning vintages to vin ordinaire. And if you prefer domestic American wines, many brands from California and Washington have found their way on cruise-ship lists. Wine prices have escalated greatly in the past few years aboard cruise ships. No longer is that fun bottle of Greek or Italian nectar to be enjoyed for just a few dollars! Expect prices just barely below a good restaurant. Ship lines are using liquor and wine sales as serious sources of on-board revenue these days—as an antidote to the drastic discounting occurring in the marketplace.

If you wish to order wine, advise your dining room steward as soon as you are seated, for the sommelier can become very busy as the evening progresses and may not have time to chill or uncork the bottle properly. He knows the "cellar" and can offer worthy suggestions if you catch him before he is beckoned away and you have to wait forever for your choice. Most cruise vessels post the menus in advance and allow you to order your dinner wine early for more efficiency—a fine idea.

SHIP'S PERSONNEL AND SERVICES The most important people in your personal shipboard life are your cabin attendants and the dining room staff assigned to your section. The names of your cabin attendants should be posted and visible as you enter your cabin for the first time, and in fact, he/she or they should be waiting to greet you and offer any assistance. These stewards or stewardesses are your link with the rest of the cruise vessel, for they know what time meals are and what to do about laundry, pressing, ice, or extra glasses for cocktail parties. They will clean your cabin when you depart in the morning and should have a sixth sense about what you might want upon your return from a long day in port or up at the pool. If you enjoy breakfast in bed, your cabin steward or stewardess will collect your order in the late evening and bring the tray at the appointed time the following morning. If there is a small service you wish to have performed each day (like tea at 4:00 or the ice bucket filled at 5:00), inform him or her as you get settled (and a small tip then may help). Your cabin attendants are chosen for their cheerful attitude and willingness to serve. If you find them the contrary and it threatens to ruin your cruise, discuss the situation with the chief purser. If there is space elsewhere on the ship, the chief purser may move you to another cabin. If there is not, you may have to settle for his reprimanding the proper person. My husband and I have had excellent cabin attendants and a rare few less excellent. If you have strong feelings about your cabin service either way, reflect it in your tips (good service should be rewarded well).

The same goes for the dining room personnel. If the maitre d' has placed you at a table of stimulating people, the sommelier has suggested the most perfect wines each evening, and the stewards have been attentive and gracious at every meal, they should all be tipped appropriately. And don't forget how many times you have requested additional favors, like an extra dessert, a birthday cake for your husband, or farewell champagne for the table. You will have found your own favorite barman who, within a few hours of sailing, remembers your favorite brand and how much ice to add. If he also remembers your names, you belong to an exclusive club, indeed. And don't be surprised if your favorite steward or stewardess serves at other functions, like the luncheon buffet around the pool, afternoon tea in the lounge, or a private cocktail party. A good waiter is in demand throughout the vessel.

Other service personnel you may wish to know are the deck steward, the pool attendants (indoors or out), the gymnasium attendant, and any children's counselors. On deck, you may need assistance with setting up the chaises (some ships, like the *QE2,* still charge for them), getting proper towels for swimming, and the accouterments of deck games such as shuffleboard or table tennis. If you use the indoor pool, another set of attendants will service that area as well as the sauna and gymnasium equipment. An expert in physical fitness will be on board to instruct you in the use of the Nautilus or other machinery and to offer classes in yoga, aerobics, and muscle toning several times daily. Staying in shape has become such an integral part of the cruise experience these days, you can continue your daily regime of jogging, dancersize, or swimming without interruption. Cunard raised the joy of fitness to the highest level by offering the Golden Door Spa at Sea aboard its five deluxe vessels. As a result, other lines have upgraded their own facilities with specified jogging tracks and soothing Jacuzzis—so pack your gear and feel right at home continuing your favorite fitness regime, or try something new. The Spa at Sea and Spa Cuisine on the dining room menu are very *in.*

If you are sailing with the children, you will be delighted to know that they are entertained in their own part of the ship and you may not see them from breakfast to dinner time (after that, it's your responsibility). Many ships have separate children's playrooms and also add a set of young counselors to their service personnel during school vacation periods and the summer months. Young passengers have their own games, are tended while swimming, get their favorite junk food for lunch (hamburgers, hot dogs, french fries, and sodas), watch movies geared to their age, and even have their own tea parties. Children love shipboard life and they are a pleasure to watch at play. On many ships the young people have their own video arcade (the grown-ups' video is now known as a Computer Center and available widely at sea). A Christmas/New Year's sailing up the Amazon aboard the *Stella Solaris* had a substantial children complement and it contributed greatly to the festive atmosphere. Because children are so well cared for during the day, families will enjoy the evening meal with them, and it is suggested that they dine at the early sitting. Afterward if parents wish to enjoy the late hours, arrangements with the purser and cabin stewards to baby-sit are always acceptable (for the usual sitting fee, of course).

If you wish to use the beauty/barber shop and spa facilities found on most cruise ships, make your appointments well in advance and make several of them to be sure (you can always cancel later). Beauticians and barbers on board have excellent reputations and will give you a new hairstyle for less than it costs at home (haircuts are especially reasonable for men). Most of these shops also offer pedicure/manicure treatments on availability. Make appointments especially early for evenings that feature a gala, because space in these shops is limited. The same goes for sauna or massage appointments. The price of such pampering is not included in the cruise fare, so you may wish to consider whether you really need a massage. Since the answer is usually "yes," book early for a mid-or late-cruise treatment. Directly after a strenuous port tour is the best time, and it will make you feel like a new person.

After you have learned the ropes of wining, dining, exercising, and pampering yourself with a manicure and massage, you may either collapse in a deck chair for the rest of the voyage or attend marathon activities. Foremost in your schedule should be the Captain's Welcome Aboard Cocktail and Dinner Gala on the evening of your first full day at sea. This is the most formal event of the cruise, and just how dressy you should be will depend upon your particular ship line. If you enjoy "dressing for dinner," you will love these special gala evenings. On a seven-day cruise, there will be just one, since the farewell dinner is a little less formal. If you are on longer sailings, there will be many more formal evenings that dictate black-tie and long gowns. It all depends upon your own comfort and the type of ship you have chosen. Expect more formality aboard Royal Viking, Cunard/NAC, Cunard Sea Goddess, and Seabourn Cruise Line. Aboard American Hawaii's two vessels, the Captain's Welcome dinner is very dressy but the farewell evening dictates aloha shirts and muumuus! Your travel agent should be able to advise the type of evening clothes suitable. If you enjoy wearing black tie and long gowns, bring them along; if you prefer dark suits and short dresses—be as comfortable as you wish. This is your vacation.

At the captain's Welcome Aboard evening, the cruise director (or directrice) will ask your name and then introduce you to the chief purser and the captain. It's easy to tell which one is the *captain,* or master of the vessel, because he wears the most gold on either shoulder (usually four wide bars). The *chief purser,* who deals with the day-to-day running of the cruise and is general information officer, wears three gold (sometimes silver) bars on either shoulder and an insignia that looks like a clover. After you have been introduced to these two men and photographed by the ship's professional shutterbug (the photos will be on display and sale later), you are offered a drink (martini, Manhattan, juice, champagne) and an hors d'oeuvre or two. When all the passengers have been received, the captain introduces the rest of his staff. This will consist of the *chief engineer* (four stripes and a propeller) who makes everything work properly, the *chief radio operator* (three stripes and a radio signal), the *chief electrician* (three stripes and some electrical current), and the *doctor* (three stripes with red or three strips and a caduceus). And then the *cruise director* will introduce his or her staff, and you are invited to the dining room for a splendid seven-course meal. On some ships, champagne, caviar, and baked Alaska are still part of the traditional welcome dinner.

The cruise director is a very special being and the range in personalities and talent is quite incredible. Some of the more impressive beings we have encountered lately have been Fernando de Oliveira of Royal

Cruise Line and John Butts of Cunard—all professionals and among the hardest working individuals at sea. The cruise staff is generally dressed alike, so it is impossible to miss them around the ship. They handle all the activities on board and must always be upbeat when dealing with any problems, complaints, etc. Frankly, the staff assigned to the young people have the best jobs—it's like being the pied piper as so many small devotees follow around all day long!

The person responsible for that lovely meal—in fact, the entire hotel function of your cruise vessel—is the *hotel manager.* He also wears four gold bars, although they are just a little less elegant than the captain's stripes. The hotel manager is a fairly new position aboard ship (it is thought that Holland America started it about ten years ago), but his responsibility is enormous. On his shoulders are all the cabins, all the stewards, all the food and drink and even the entertainment. Some, like Ingvar Torstensson on the *Sagafjord,* are the most popular of all the shipboard personnel because they manage to keep everyone happy at the same time. It takes a special personality to be a good hotel manager as well as a strong dose of humor and patience.

The chief purser and the cruise director report directly to the hotel manager, and are your most evident contact with what is happening behind the scenes. The chief purser and his staff handle all money transactions, stamps, and stationery; clear you through customs at ports of call; and provide general information. Whatever you need to know about the vessel and any scheduling you will find at the purser's office, which is open daily from about 9:00 a.m. and usually situated in the middle of the main public deck. Should you need the doctor, you will find his hours posted as well, and you will be advised what numbers to call in case of emergency. If you need to send a message or make a ship-to-shore phone call, the radio room is open to passengers at certain hours (but always closed by law in port). Communication with office or home is very expensive, so be prepared to pay plenty for the privilege. Most communication is excellent and swift, so there is nothing to fear about being way out at sea, and many cruise ships now advertise their use of satellites for telephone calls, placed in the privacy of your cabin. (It's called Progress when you can't even get away from it all on a cruise!)

If you plan to cruise aboard *Sovereign of the Seas,* you can do most of the above with your fingertips, via an interactive state-of-the-art television system called Cruise Control. This video-viewing system enables you to preview on-board activities, review bar tabs, order room service and even wine with dinner from the privacy of your cabin. It sounds truly modern, but what happened to the interaction with other persons, which is what a cruise is all about?

ACTIVITIES   Your cruise director, responsible for the daily passenger activity list, will invite everyone to the main lounge on the morning of the first full day at sea to explain the myriad of happenings that is called a cruise. He will run down the basics—like the library, card room, and writing room (for books, bridge, and backgammon)—and offer the outdoor crowd such sports as shuffleboard, golf driving range, table or deck tennis, badminton, and volleyball (although not every ship offers every sport). He will also explain rules around the pool areas: what to do about towels, how to get and keep a deck chair, how to get beverage service. Then he will probably begin to check off the more sophisticated entertainment, like skeet shooting, wine tasting parties, ice carving lessons, dance lessons, trap shooting, lectures, and concerts. And we must not forget bingo, which is still everyone's favorite pastime—and the stakes can become very high! Just remember that bingo—like slot machines and the casino—would not be offered if the ship line did not make a bundle from the operations.

Entertainment at sea these days is quite overwhelming and, like the food, almost too much to digest in a short time. Many ship lines advertise Big-Name Talent, which is marvelous for those that remember them when they *were* big. I often think—good heavens, is he or she still around? Frankly, the Big Names are usually a bust—whether they have written books or made millions in show business. I prefer the average-size (even the small) names; they try harder and are much more personable around the ship. Nonetheless, there is some sort of evening entertainment for everyone, and if you find the spectacle in one lounge too noisy, there is always an alternative. High-brow, low-brow, middle-brow—entertainment is very personal taste and mood, but cruise ships offer good variety and many different venues.

Cunard started its Festival of Life series over a decade ago; Royal Viking Line has its Enrichment Lectures; the cruise cup runneth over with daytime offerings. Now that we are once again at peace from Halley's Comet, ship lines are busy creating other wonderful reasons for you to enjoy a cruise and an event. So, in between worldwide celebrations of centennials and natural phenomena, ship lines are inviting you aboard to participate in a real-life mystery play. Intrigue is *in*—so is chili, photography, music, wine, eclipse of the sun, graphology, amusing psychiatrists, and behind-the-scenes lectures on just about anything. Forget financial experts (if they really knew what they pretend, they would own their own yachts by now), fashion coordinators, hypnotists, and the like. Languages are sometimes offered and great fun to learn. Music is always soothing—from jazz to classical—and passengers are always welcome at informal rehearsals.

Unless you are aboard one of the very serious and intellectually stimulating cruises, your shipboard life will also feature elaborate evening entertainment and gambling. The latter ranges from a few slot machines to a full casino, complete with "bunny club" type croupiers. Here you can play roulette, 21, and blackjack to your heart's content, and some of these casinos are open from twelve to fourteen hours per day. (Just keep in mind that the "house" usually wins more than you do.) Slot machines are the more casual form of tempting Lady Luck, and some vessels also go in for "horse racing" (using films in one of the lounges and accepting big bets on who will win). The jackpot does overflow from time to time, so if you're in the mood for a little gambling you will not be disappointed. Carnival prides itself on the biggest and splashiest casinos afloat, which the ship line manages and operates. Most companies franchise their casinos and take a pre-determined piece of the action. Crystal Cruises has a "deal" with Caesar's Palace of Las Vegas—whom do you think will win the most?

Aside from the races and travel shorts, you can also find full-length feature films that are first-rate. Times and titles are posted in the bulletin daily; if you have a cabin with TV you can watch the film in privacy while relaxing or dressing for dinner. Many ship lines also offer news broadcasts via satellite, and Crystal has an arrangement with the prestigious Cable News Network. Cabin VCRs are also popular in the top-rated cabins on many vessels as well as on the newer ships, and video lending is available in the library or purser's office. (On the WindStar fleet, the cassette is charged to your account until returned; on *Sea Goddess I* and *II*, the honor system prevails.) Cruise ships have excellent theaters—although some of them are way, way down below—and religious services are held here as well. The *Rotterdam* theater is known for weddings from time to time! *Norway*'s Saga Theatre is famous for its broadway productions, live concerts with "stars," and a Las Vegas–style revue spectacular that even the most jaded enjoy.

A little less spectacular, but equally enthusiastic, entertainment is offered in the largest lounge after the evening meal. This is one of the day's big events and a wonderful way to wind down. The shows are always energetic and some are topnotch (so enjoyable that you would even pay to see them). The best evening entertainment can be usually found aboard the ships cruising in the Caribbean, for passengers here are discerning and receptive to good acts. And you are soon aware if a ship line pays particular attention to its entertainment. For example, Royal Caribbean boasts that you never see the same act twice, as it shuttles groups between ports and its vast fleet. But however good a professional group can be, I always prefer the traditional cruise staff talent show to anything (probably because the faces are familiar). This is where the Norwegians, Greeks, and other nationalities distinguish themselves in native dances, colorful costumes, a little clowning, and some singing. You may also have to endure a passenger talent show (less polish but always fun) and, without fail, the great masquerade party. If you enjoy dressing up and being someone else for a few hours, bring along a splendid costume and be the show stopper (I think you also win a bottle of something that goes by the name of champagne).

Late in the evening the main lounge continues to keep some passengers contented with soft music and dancing, while others scatter around the ship. This is the time I choose a quiet moonlit nightcap and my cabin. Elsewhere the action continues in a discotheque and doesn't even break while the midnight buffet is served. After all, the hours fly by, and A Club Called Dazzles aboard the *Norway* actually advertises a closing at 3 a.m. Oh well, that leaves just enough time for a short rest before early bird coffee at 6 and then the fun begins all over again!

GLOSSARY OF NAUTICAL TERMS

No one wants to sound like an Old Salt, as they say, but learning some of the language of the sea will make you feel like an experienced sailor—especially if this is your first cruise. Study a few of the nautical terms listed below, and you'll be surprised at how quickly you will begin to say port and starboard without giving it another thought. Port, of course, is the left side of your ship (both words have four letters so that's easy to remember) and starboard is the right side.

ABEAM—anything perpendicular to the structure of the ship; off the side.
ACCOMMODATION LADDER—a lightweight ladder made of wooden slats or aluminum, that is slung from the ship to a dock or small boat. Pilots and other officials use this ladder to come aboard while at sea. Passengers use this ladder at some ports as well, when the vessel is anchored out and tenders are the only available transportation between ship and shore.
AFT—toward the rear of the vessel, or to the stern.
ALLEYWAY—any passageway or narrow corridor of a ship. Sailors also use this term ashore to describe the narrow street behind port.
AMIDSHIPS—in the middle of the vessel; halfway between bow and stern.
AWNING—the same term as on land. Any canvas covering strung over an open deck area for protection from sun and rain.
ASTERN—behind the rear or stern of the ship; often refers to something in the wake.
ATHWART—across the width of the ship.
BALLAST—weight placed in the ship to keep her on an even keel when empty. Calle Cristo, Old San Juan's most famous street, is paved with adoquines—bluish-tint bricks formerly used for ballast in Spanish ships.
BAR—sandbar, caused by current or tide near the shore.

BEAM—width of ship at her widest point.

BEARING—compass direction, expressed in degrees.

BELOW—under the deck or on a subsequent deck farther down in the ship. Can also mean "at rest" or "off duty" for crew member.

BELLS—sounding of the ship's time, at half-hour intervals, from one to eight, beginning at 4:30, 8:30, and 12:30 anew.

BERTH—nautical term for bed, means where vessel docks in port as well as the beds in your cabin.

BON VOYAGE—French expression for Happy Voyage or Journey. When you tell your friends you are taking a cruise, they will say Bon Voyage!

BOW—the forward, or foremost, part of the ship.

BRIDGE—ship's command center, where all navigation and navigational decisions are made. It is located above and forward of the passenger areas, much like the cockpit of a 747 aircraft. This is the domain of the captain and his officers; passengers are admitted only by special invitation.

BULKHEAD—wall-like construction inside a vessel for subdividing space or strengthening the structure; partition wall.

BUNKERS—a large bin or receptacle for storing fuel. Also refers to the fuel itself.

CABIN—your bedroom or sleeping accommodation aboard ship. Also called a stateroom, depending upon size and situation.

CABLE—the heavy iron chain used for the ship's anchor.

CLASS—first, cabin, and tourist were the three classes passengers booked across the Atlantic for years. Under my definition, Cunard Line has the three-class system on the *Queen Elizabeth 2* transatlantic run (although they only admit to having two classes).

COLORS—refers to the national flag or emblem flown by the ship.

COMPANIONWAY—interior stairway leading from deck to deck.

COURSE—ship's heading—laid down by pencil. Even though computers do most of the work now, the navigator is responsible for whether the ship is on course.

CROW'S NEST—the lookout cage high up on the foremast.

DAVIT—the apparatus that secures the lifeboats at sea and from which they are launched. (Pronounced day-vit.)

DECK—each floor of a ship.

DISEMBARK—to go out from a ship. Opposite of embark.

DOCK—where the ship ties up. Also called pier, wharf, quay.

DRAFT OR DRAUGHT—the amount of water a ship draws or needs to keep out of trouble. The draft is calculated from the lowest point of the ship to the waterline.

DRILL—any exercise ordered by the master of the ship, like the lifeboat drill the first day out.

EMBARK—to board a ship. Opposite of disembark.

FATHOM—a measure of six feet; used in determining the depth of water by soundings. This term is familiar to all Americans, because Mark Twain, the pen name of Samuel Clemens (who spent his youth as a pilot on the Mississippi River), means "two fathoms sounded."

FIX—to obtain a position by any method (sextant, radar, satellite navigator).

FLAGS—ships talk to each other with flags in an international code of signals that all nations understand. While the flag hoisted on a private yacht might say "Come over for a drink," the signals on a large ship leaving port will show if a pilot is aboard, whether a medical doctor is in attendance, and what type of cargo is carried. Signal flags are never flown at sea, except when a vessel is in distress. The ship's country of registry is flown from the stern in port; on the gaff from the mast at sea. The company flag is on the foremost. A courtesy ensign is flown on the starboard side of available halyards when ship is approaching a port. This ensign can be at a height equal to (but no higher) than the ship's national flag.

FREEBOARD—the outer part of a ship's hull between the waterline and main deck.

FREE PORT—a port not included in customs territory, or free from import taxes. For example, St. Thomas in the U.S. Virgin Islands is a free port and a favorite stop for Caribbean cruise shoppers.

FUNNEL—the smokestack, or chimney, of the ship.

GALLEY—the kitchen.

GANGWAY—a portable accommodation for entry/exit from the ship. Used to be known as a gangplank.

GMT—standard of time as designated at the Observatory in Greenwich, England. Used in England and as a basis of calculation elsewhere.

GROSS REGISTER TON—a measure of the size of a ship. One hundred cubic feet equals one gross register ton.

HATCHWAY—wide openings on deck allowing access to the holds.

HAWSER—a rope of sufficient size and strength to tow or secure a ship.

HEAD—toilet.

HELM—the entire steering apparatus of the ship. The expression "at helm" means whoever has charge of the ship's course at that time.

HOLD—the area below deck where cargo is stored.

HOUSE FLAG—the company flag or symbol flown from the mast, or a design on the funnel that designates who owns the ship.

HULL—also called hulk, the body of the ship.

ISTHMUS—a narrow strip of land bordered on both sides by water.

JACOB'S LADDER—a rope ladder usually with wooden rungs.

JONES ACT—the Jones Act of 1886, designed to protect American shipping interests, forbids foreign-registered ships from carrying passengers between U.S. ports. It is often strictly enforced by the U.S. Bureau of Customs. Puerto Rico and the U.S. Virgin Islands and some others are exempted.

KEEL—the backbone of the vessel. To be ''on even keel'' means to be in balance, or steady.

KEELHAULED—seamen's expression for giving someone a good ''telling off.''

KNOT—a unit of speed for a ship. One knot is equal to one nautical mile (6080.2 feet), or approximately 1.15 statute (land) miles per hour. The speed of a ship is measured in knots.

LATITUDE—angular distance measured in degrees north and south of the Equator. One degree equals about 60 nautical miles.

LEAGUE—a unit of distance. In English-speaking countries, a league is approximately 3.45 nautical miles.

LEEWARD—the direction toward which the wind blows.

LETTING THE CAT OUT OF THE BAG—has nothing to do with secrets or gossip. Meant impending punishment, as seamen were whipped with something called ''a cat and nine tails.''

LIFEBOAT—a small launch designed to carry passengers in an emergency. Lifeboat stations are noted in every cabin. Lifeboat drills, mandatory on all vessels, require passengers and crew to don their life vests and proceed to their boat stations (listed on back of cabin door).

LOG—the daily record in which details of navigation, weather, engine performance, and other aspects of ship's progress are kept. The log is also a device for measuring speed.

LONGITUDE—angular distance measured east and west of Greenwich, England. One degree varies according to the earth's curvature.

MANIFEST—list of ship's passengers, crew, and cargo.

MASTER—the captain of the ship.

NAUTICAL MILE—6080.2 feet (land mile is 5280 feet).

NOON—when sun reaches its highest point.

PITCH—the rise and fall of the ship in rough seas, as opposed to the ''roll'' or rocking motion from side to side. Pitch is also the angle of the propeller blade.

PORT—the left side of the ship looking forward, also indicated by red navigational light; harbor.

PORTHOLE—the round window in your cabin. Deluxe cabins have large, rectangular windows.

PROW—another word for bow or front of the ship.

QUAY—dock, berth, pier. (Pronounced ''key.'')

RAILING—something to keep you from falling off the ship; good to lean on in the moonlight or to watch flying fish.

REGISTRY—certificate of ownership. The country of registry is denoted by the national flag flown at the stern of the vessel. The port of registry is written on the stern of the ship.

ROLL—the sideways motion of the ship, as opposed to the "pitch" or up and down motion.

RUNNING LIGHTS—the colored lights required on all vessels at night to indicate her direction or course.

SAFETY AT SEA LAWS—according to the International Convention for the Safety of Life at Sea of 1960, all ships embarking passengers in U.S. ports must comply with the strict standards set forth at this convention.

SHE—yes, ships are always considered members of the female gender. It's an old tradition that even feminists have to accept. Longtime men at sea have their own reasons . . . but here are two. "It's not the initial expense that breaks you, it's the upkeep." "Because she shows her topsides, hides her bottom, and when coming into port, heads straight for the buoys."

SHIP TO SHORE—communications with land by radio telephone. Some ships now use a telephone link by satellite, which is faster.

SHIP'S TOTE—want to spend a dollar? Guess how many nautical miles the ship has steamed in a given time. The cruise staff announces the daily tote.

SKIPPER—slang for captain. This term is not used on cruise ships, as the more formal "master" is generally employed.

SPLICING THE MAIN BRACE—any sailor who ran up to splice or repair the main brace in the heat of battle received an extra tot of rum!

STABILIZER—a retractable fin extending into the water on either side of the vessel to ensure smooth sailing in rough seas. Most vessels are now equipped with stabilizers of the Denny Brown type from England.

STACK—funnel or chimney of the vessel.

STAGE—a walkway protruding from the front of a "steamboat," that can be raised while cruising or lowered to embark passengers and/ or supplies.

SOUNDING—see fathom.

STARBOARD—the right side of the ship looking forward, also indicated by a green navigational light.

STATEROOM—a sleeping accommodation aboard ship.

STERN—the aft, or extreme rear section of the ship.

SUPERSTRUCTURE—the structural part of the ship above the main deck.

TENDER—a smaller vessel, sometimes a lifeboat, used to carry passengers from ship to shore and vice versa.

TIME AT SEA—nautical time is like Navy time, based on the 24-hour clock. Hence, 8 a.m. is 0800 and 8 p.m. is 2000 hours.

UNCHARTED—anything (rock, reef, canyon) that does not appear on a chart of the area.

UNDER WAY—indicates the ship is set to sail, the anchor has been brought up, and the lines let go.

WAKE—the trail a ship leaves behind in the water, the foam churned up by the propellers.

WATERLINE—the painted line dividing the ship between the portion that should remain above water and the section that is below.

WEIGH ANCHOR—to raise the anchor and prepare to get under way, a command given from the bridge.

WINCH—power-operated machine used to work the ship's cranes and/or davit.

WINDWARD—the direction from which the wind is blowing.

WINDLASS—a device for raising the anchor.

YARDARM—either outer arm of the yard (beam) of a square sail. The expression "when the sun is over the yardarm" now means that cocktail time is approaching. However, the sun is over the yardarm in the morning.

YAW—to deviate from the ship's course, usually caused by high seas.

ABBREVIATIONS

MS—Motor Ship
MTS—Motor Turbine Ship
MV—Motor Vessel
TSS—Turbine Steamship
SS—Steamship
USS—United States Ship

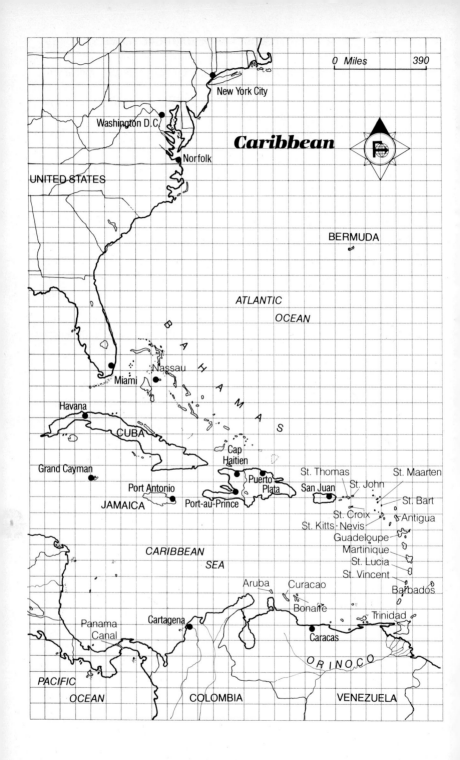

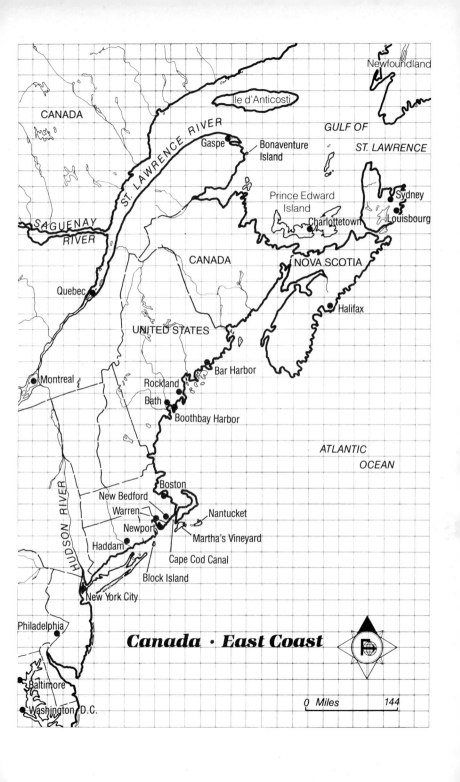

Canada · East Coast

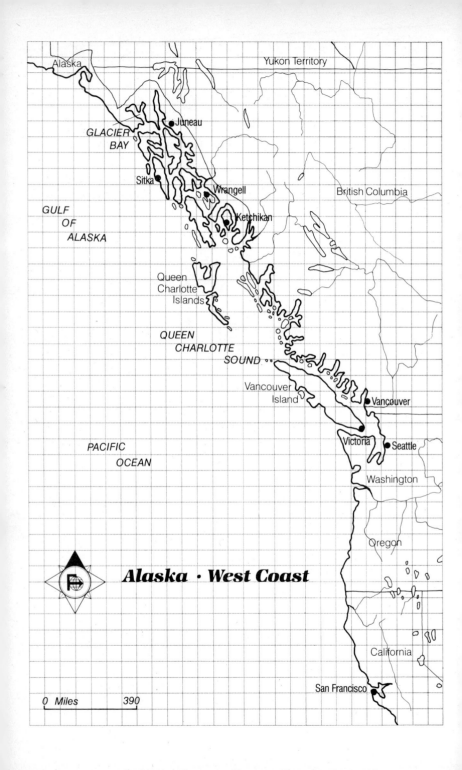

Alaska

Yukon Territory

Juneau

GLACIER
BAY

Sitka

Wrangell

British Columbia

Ketchikan

GULF
OF
ALASKA

Queen
Charlotte
Islands

QUEEN
CHARLOTTE
SOUND

Vancouver
Island

Vancouver

PACIFIC
OCEAN

Victoria

Seattle

Washington

Oregon

Alaska · West Coast

California

San Francisco

0   Miles   390

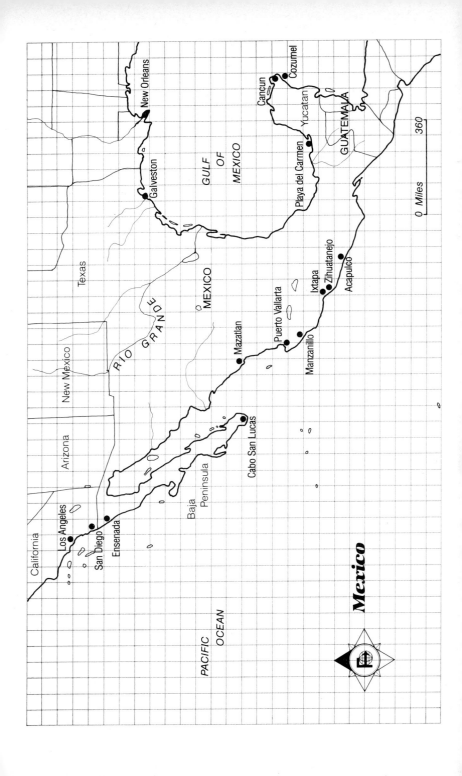

Mexico

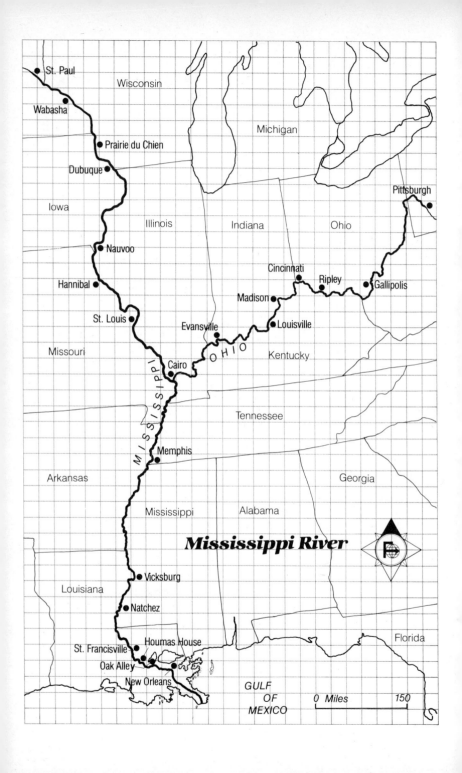

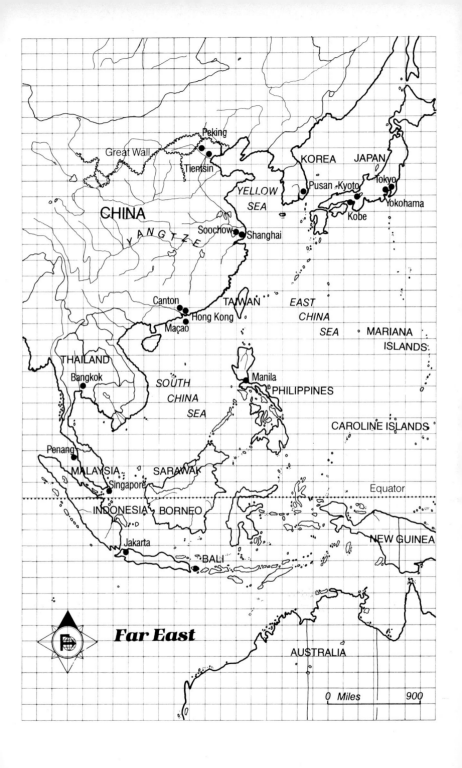

Far East

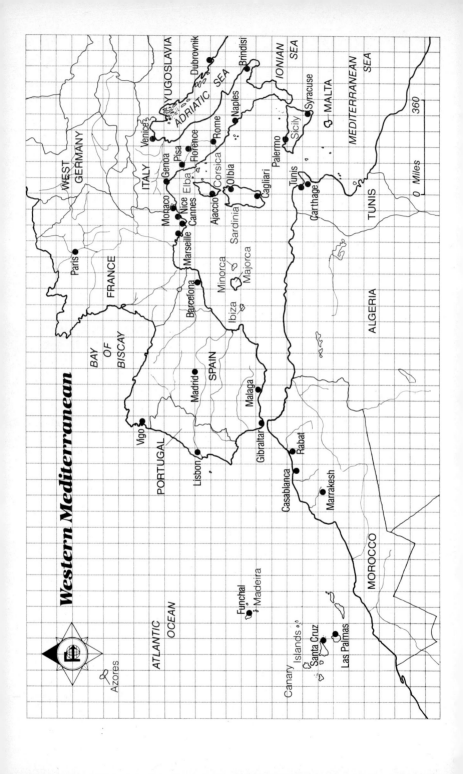

Western Mediterranean

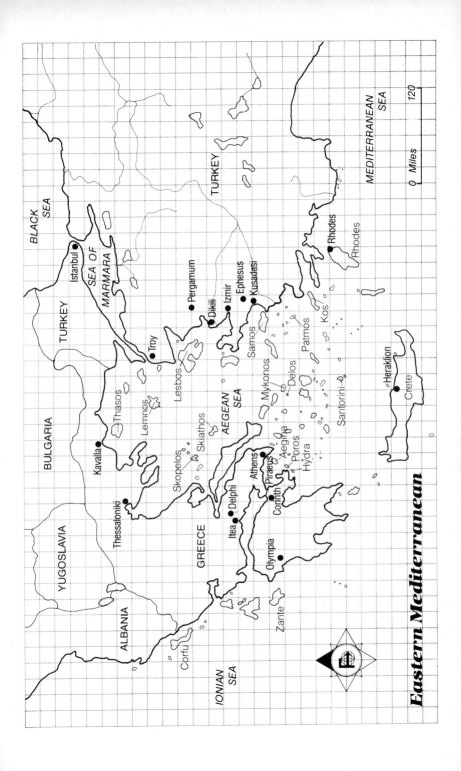

Eastern Mediterranean

BLACK SEA

BULGARIA

YUGOSLAVIA

ALBANIA

TURKEY

Istanbul

SEA OF MARMARA

TURKEY

Kavalla

Thessaloniki

GREECE

Corfu

IONIAN SEA

Zante

Olympia

Itea ● Delphi

Athens

Corinth

Piraeus

Aegina

Poros

Hydra

Skopelos

Skiathos

Lemnos

Thasos

Lesbos

Troy

Pergamum

Dikili

Izmir

Ephesus

Kusadasi

Samos

Mykonos

AEGEAN SEA

Delos

Patmos

Santorini

Kos

Rhodes

Rhodes

Heraklion

Crete

MEDITERRANEAN SEA

0 Miles 120

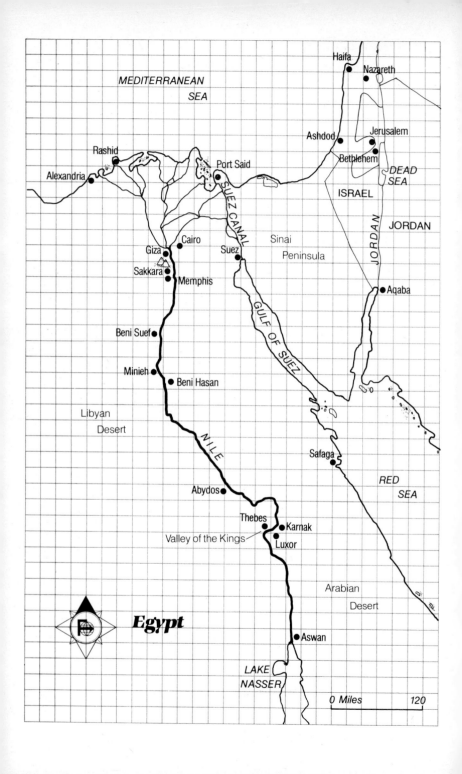

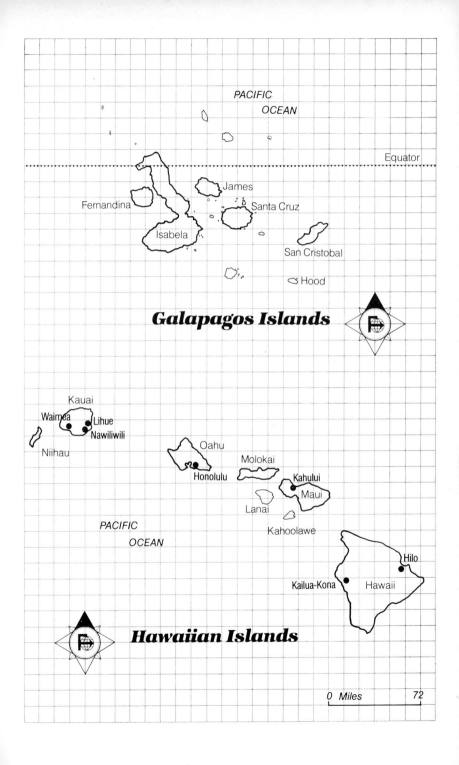

PACIFIC

OCEAN

Equator

James

Fernandina   Santa Cruz

Isabela

San Cristobal

Hood

Galapagos Islands

Kauai

Waimea   Lihue
                Nawiliwili
Niihau   Oahu

                    Molokai
                Honolulu   Kahului

                    Lanai   Maui

PACIFIC   Kahoolawe

OCEAN

Hilo

Kailua-Kona   Hawaii

Hawaiian Islands

0   Miles   72

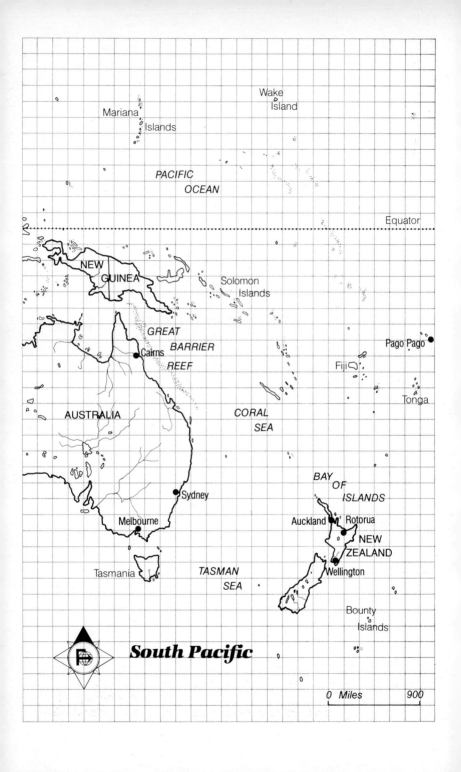

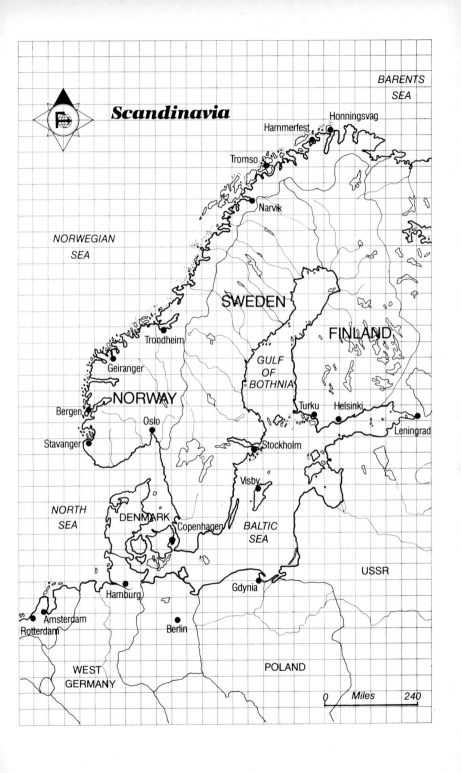

PORTS OF CALL

BAHAMAS AND BERMUDA

THE BAHAMA ISLANDS

Christopher Columbus was the first tourist to this lovely archipelago that begins just fifty miles off the coast of Florida and stretches in a great south-easterly arc to within fifty miles of eastern Cuba and Haiti. Columbus arrived in 1492 on an island he named San Salvador. However, the Spanish never quite got around to settling these islands (seven hundred strong) that are scattered across some 100,000 square miles of the Atlantic Ocean. The British arrived in 1629 and ruled for about three hundred years, leaving behind a legacy in language, architecture, law, and some lovely manners. The Bahamas became self-governing in 1964 and independent in 1973, although they still belong to the Commonwealth and Queen Elizabeth II continues as head of state.

Ever since Columbus' visit, tourism has played an important role in the growth of these islands. Ponce de Leon came looking for his Fountain of Youth, and when George Washington stopped by in the eighteenth century he called them "Isles of Perpetual June." For cruise vessels, the center of tourism is Nassau, the main port and capital city on the island of New Providence. Nassau has retained some charming colonial overtones, although its Bay Street area looks like any mid-American town with all the fast-food chains. Strolling along, there are some nice shops with prices for British goods not duty free but possibly better than you would find back home. The street is fronted by the

74

British Colonial Hotel, (now a Sheraton), and one of the prettiest and most historic places in The Bahamas. But it's an easy town to explore from your vessel docked at Prince George Wharf. The government buildings are all around Rawson Square, which has a high-priced straw market in the middle. Try not to miss the statue of Queen Victoria and the 1797 octagonal structure that was once a prison but is now a public library. You might also want to have a look at Christopher Columbus, who stands in front of government house. If you like forts, three are within easy reach: 1790 Fort Charlotte, named after the wife of King George III; 1741 Fort Montagu, built to guard the eastern entrance of the harbor; and Fort Fincastle. Nearby is the so-called Queen's Staircase, a 102-foot-high set of limestone steps that number the sixty-five years of Victoria's reign. If you take a city tour you will also visit the Ardastra Gardens to see trained flamingos, and the Seafloor Aquarium to see dolphins perform. Or, you can take a three-hour catamaran cruise around the harbor, have a rum punch, and swim off one of the island's lovely beaches.

Just a hop, a skip, and a few dollars' taxi ride from Prince George Wharf is Paradise Island, an exquisite crescent-shaped beach famous for bathing beauties, nightclub entertainment, and gambling. Here are also some beautiful gardens and a fourteenth-century cloister, but no doubt you will want to take Lady Luck straight into the casino at the Britannia Beach Hotel and then enjoy the Las Vegas-style review in Le Cabaret.

In the past few years, Cable Beach has grown into *the* place to visit, especially if you are a passenger on Carnival Cruise Lines, which manages the casino and entertainment in conjunction with the Bahamian government. Carnival pushes the Cable Beach Casino and Supper Club, where Les Fantastiques offer Las Vegas–type revues. Just remember that the money you lose goes into someone's pocket!

Gambling is also the most interesting distraction in **Freeport,** on Grand Bahama Island, the second most popular cruise call in the archipelago. Here, El Casino is reputed to be the largest gambling den on this side of the Atlantic, and it certainly is the most frequented, especially by those on the four-day cruises from Miami. When you've had enough of the chips, browse around the International Bazaar for one of those famous T-shirts (my favorite is the one in French), that say "It's Better in The Bahamas."

The Bahama Out Islands should not be overlooked either. More and more cruise vessels are calling among these little pieces of paradise. To accommodate the 1800-passenger *Norway,* Norwegian Caribbean Lines bought an island in the southeast called Little San Salvador. The line's other vessels also call at the Berry Islands for beach parties, snorkeling, and Sunfishing. Other islands that some of the smaller cruise vessels visit are Abacos in the north, long and skinny Eleuthera, and the Exumas. Most of the three- and four-day crowd from Miami have followed

Norwegian Cruise Line's lead, and offer their passengers an Out Island as well as Nassau and Freeport. The *Dolphin IV* and *SeaBreeze* of Dolphin Cruise Line call at Blue Lagoon Island. Premier Cruise Lines uses Salt Cay on three- and four-day cruises from Port Canaveral aboard StarShip *Oceanic* and *Atlantic,* while the *Majestic* concentrates on what is known as the "family" islands of the Bahamas series.

No matter where you happen to go in the Bahamas you will be welcome. Many of the cruise vessels have excellent People to People programs in which Bahamian couples come on board to exchange experiences. Several islands have popular programs in which travelers can visit a Bahamian home. Often these visits make for enduring friendships.

BERMUDA

Britain's oldest colony sits out in the Atlantic Ocean some 600 miles due east of Savannah, Georgia, and approximately 775 miles (forty hours) southeast of New York, from where you will most likely sail. Since the late nineteenth century this tiny coral island with pastel-colored houses and quaint British customs has been a popular watering hole for cruise passengers. Mild winters used to attract the wealthy, who arrived with steamer trunks and servants for a long stay.

Bermuda is booming as a cruise destination lately because it is a clean, safe haven where the natives are friendly. Local prices for accommodations and food tend to be outrageous, so cruises make sense for pleasure-seekers and their pocketbook! The traditional Saturday to Saturday sailings are still in the picture, but Sunday and midweek departures are now available on one-week cruises.

Many cruise vessels dock at the pier on Front Street in downtown **Hamilton,** Bermuda's only city and its capital. Other ships dock in St. George's and spend a day or two at the other end of the island. Hamilton, a nice, clean place, has interesting shops where, despite a few good buys, most British goods now unfortunately sell for exorbitant prices. If you're interested in pullovers and other woolens, check prices at home before you leave to see how they compare with Hamilton stores. My favorite shop is Bluck's, at the corner of Front Street and Bermudiana Road, where the beautiful and expensive china, crystal, silver, and antiques will knock your eyes out.

If you don't take the shore excursions and feel confident on the road, rent a motorbike the minute you disembark. It's the best way to get around as no rental cars are allowed and buses are poky. Remember to follow the rules of the road—drive on the left and always wear your helmet.

Exploring this 21-square-mile piece of land that geologists say lies on top of a submerged mountain is loads of fun, especially if you opt to do it with a friend instead of a crowd. Since your ship will stay three full nights in port if you're on the seven-day cruise, you'll have time to see everything. The Visitors Bureau (left as you leave the pier) has terrific maps and pamphlets and will answer any questions. When you go on your jaunts, be sure to take a swimsuit, because you will be tempted by many beautiful beaches. My favorites are the public beaches along the South Shore, especially Jobson Cove or Warwick Long Bay, where you can spend the whole day among cliffs, rocks, and sparkling sand. At the large supermarket along the way (if you're coming from Hamilton, it's just past St. Paul's Lane on the left) you can stock up on cold drinks and snacks. (Don't be shocked by the prices. Food is very expensive on this island.)

Try not to miss the Blue Grotto Dolphin Show in Harrington Sound (just before the causeway), the Crystal or Leamington caves, where stalagmites and stalactites form a forestlike maze, and Gibbs Hill Lighthouse. This is the oldest cast-iron lighthouse in the world. Built in the 1850s, the view of the entire island from the top of its 185 steps is fantastic. Gibbs Hill Lighthouse is off the South Shore Road, just behind the fanciful highrise Southampton Princess Hotel. It's open from 9 a.m. to 4:30 p.m. daily, and admission is about fifty cents. What a bargain!

Save an entire day for **St. George's,** the island's original capital and in 1609 the landing spot for the 150 passengers of the shipwrecked *Sea Venture*. St. George's, my favorite place for browsing, has loads of charm and history. Even if you don't like churches, you'll enjoy St. Peter's, which dates from 1713. The head stones in the graveyard read like *Who's Who* (some Americans lie there). Across the street is the Confederate Museum and King's Square, where you can be photographed in the pillory and stocks. The Print Shop houses a working model of a seventeenth-century press, and the hostess at President Henry Tucker house will entice you with some interesting history and gossip about the days of the American Revolution. Catty-corner to this house is the Carriage Museum, chock full of the custom-built carriages that were used until the advent of automobiles on the island in 1945. The St. George's restoration project at Somers' Wharf is wonderful, and you can dine in old warehouses and shop in the less-crowded branches of the well-known Hamilton stores. There are plenty of nice beaches in the St. George's area, as well as restaurants (Tom Moore's Tavern) and the fabulous Marriott at Castle Harbour. Chandris Celebrity Cruises, which began service in the spring of 1990, has made a long-time commitment to Bermuda—weekly Saturday cruises during the season from New York to both St. George's and Hamilton aboard the new $175-million *Horizon* and Sunday departures from New York to Somerset aboard the refurbished *Meridian* (former *Galileo*). Other ships sailing to Bermuda from New York on weekly schedules are *Royal Viking Star* and the *Nordic Prince*.

THE BLACK SEA

BULGARIA

Varna is Bulgaria's largest seaport and the jumping-off point for visiting nearby resorts, such as Zlatni Pyassutsi (or Golden Sands) some eleven miles up the coast, renowned for the silky beaches that stretch some five hundred feet into the sea. Midway between the two towns is the coastal resort of Drouzhba, with its eighteenth-century monastery. South of Varna lies Bulgaria's largest and most popular resort, Slunchev Bryag, or Sunny Beach. A few miles inland the sixth-century Aladja Monastery is built right into the rocks. You can find traces of Bulgarian history all along the coast. Life here began in the seventh century when Finno-Tartar tribes mingled with Slavic settlers and held their own against the Greek and Byzantine empires in the south.

ROMANIA

The seaside resort of **Constanta** was built on the ruins of an old Greek colony called Tomis, where the poet Ovid is said to have spent his last years. The country actually was founded by the Roman emperor, Trajan, who conquered Dacia in A.D. 106 and called it Romania. Constanta (also spelled Constanza) today is a modern city with narrow streets and mosques left over from the days of the Ottoman Empire. Nearby resort towns along the coast are famous, year-round health spas for the treatment of nervous disorders and skin diseases. Pay special attention to the Romanians enjoying their beaches, for they are among the most independent and interesting of all the Eastern Bloc peoples.

Some even say that their Latin heritage has never been stronger nor more apparent than now. The tourist shops offer romantic, richly embroidered scarves and blouses, peasant skirts, rugs, ceramics, and charming handcrafts. Shore excursions in Constanta are lively and the local scenery is very interesting. Following a visit to the local museum, a drive to the countryside through farmland and vineyards features a visit to a state-owned winery where tastings are in order as well as ample samplings of grainy breads and full-bodied cheeses. The wines are light and refreshing, and glasses stamped with the winery seal are presented to all visitors. Guides are friendly and a good time is enjoyed by all!

USSR

Yalta, the most famous of all Black Sea resorts, was a favorite with nineteenth-century Russian princes, who built many beautiful palaces along its shores. Originally a Greek colony, Yalta passed through the hands of Romans, Genoese, and Turks before becoming Russian at the end of the eighteenth century. Fifty years later, Yalta was a major battleground in the Crimean War. Today this large seaport and spa backs up on Livadia, where the 1945 Yalta Conference took place. Livadia Palace, the White Palace, where the conference was held, was built in 1911 for Tsar Nicholas II in Italian Renaissance style. Every window looks out on a different view. Opposite the entrance is a marble column, which was a gift from the Shah of Persia to the tsar. This palace, like so many others in the area, is now a sanatorium. Yalta is the most interesting of all Black Sea resorts, especially for Americans. Franklin D. Roosevelt Street, one of Yalta's oldest avenues, leads straight into town, linking with Lenin Promenade. Monuments are everywhere—to Lenin, to Gorky, and to playwright Chekhov, who lived on Kirov Street from 1898 until his death in 1904 (his house is now a museum). The Alexander Nevsky Cathedral, built in the old Russian style in 1902, is open to visitors daily, but other churches are generally closed or have been turned into museums. In Alupka, the farthest town on the Yalta coastline, is a palace built by Count Vorontsov, a confirmed Anglophile and a favorite of both Alexandra and Nicholas. Vorontsov's palace (built between 1828 and 1846) was designed by an English architect who used Indian styles. An Arabic inscription repeated tenfold says, "There is no happiness but that which comes from Allah." This palace is now a museum of European and Russian paintings, with a bust of Vorontsov himself and a bust of British statesman William Pitt the Younger in the winter garden. The area has many other lovely palaces that can be viewed only from the outside, plus beautiful but crowded beaches. Alas, the local populace is very unfriendly to visitors from the west, and the place is full of suspicion. This is a one-time experience, and you can only feel compassion for the situation in which these people live.

Odessa, the third largest city in the Ukraine, is home port of the Black Sea Shipping Company, whose cruise ships sail all over the world but not from North America. One would hardly call Odessa "the jewel of the Russian Riviera," as one ship brochure does, but it is certainly a city of note and history. A fascinating period was 1803 to 1814, when the Duke Richelieu was mayor and the city prospered from all the customs duties he collected. By the end of the nineteenth century Odessa was Russia's largest port and third most important city, after Moscow and St. Petersburg (Leningrad). Today Odessa is an industrial, educational, and tourist center that claims to have inspired poets and prides itself on its revolutionary past. Among many fine monuments cruise passengers can visit is another palace built by Prince Vorontsov in 1826, this time in the classical Russian style. The lighthouse in port also bears his name. A few of the famous old churches are open for services and tours, including the five-domed Uspensky Cathedral. An archaeological museum has a large collection of artifacts from ancient Greek settlements along the Black Sea coasts. But the most striking monument of all is to the Russian poet Pushkin from the citizens of Odessa, a tribute to the four years (1820 to 1824) the writer was forced to live here in exile. Unfortunately, this port is another unfriendly and depressing place—perhaps the climate will change with "glasnost," but these people have suffered so many decades of oppression that it will be difficult to put smiles on their faces.

THE CARIBBEAN

BARBADOS

One of the most British of all the Caribbean islands, Barbados lived under the Union Jack from 1625 to 1966. The island took its name from the Portuguese who arrived in 1536 and thought the hanging roots of the banyan trees looked like beards, hence "barbados." Capital and main port of the island is **Bridgetown,** whose harbor police still wear the uniforms of Nelson's sailors. A statue of Lord Nelson stands in the town's Trafalgar Square, and is said to be some seventeen years older than its counterpart in London.

Exploring Bridgetown is easily done on foot at a leisurely pace. Begin with the activity-filled Careenage, or Inner Harbor, and the Pelican Village craft center, then head to Trafalgar Square for a look at old Nelson. St. Michael's Cathedral was first built in 1665, but the present structure dates from 1831. Too bad, because if George Washington really came to Barbados (along with his half-brother Lawrence) for a health cure, he worshiped on the site but not in this building. A house on Upper Bay Street is where he may have lived for a while, and one story says he even caught smallpox. Wander through other interesting lanes for local color before you take a taxi to the Barbados Museum at Garrison, about a mile out of town. If you've opted for an organized tour, you will most likely stop at another Great House, Villa Nova, the former home of British diplomat Sir Anthony Eden. Beautifully renovated and furnished with Barbadian antiques of local mahogany, it once dominated a large sugar cane plantation.

Barbados has some lovely beaches, especially those adjoining elegant resort hotels. If you are discreet, no one minds if you find a little hideaway from your cruise ship for the day. Taxis are abundant at Deep Water pier, but barter a little before you hop in, as most of the drivers are minor bandits. I have always enjoyed the beach at Sandy Lane, but others have opted for the long ride out to Sam Lord's Castle, which caters to the American palate. Have a peek in the nineteenth-century mansion built by the legendary Sam Lord, still one of the more famous sites in the Caribbean.

Barbados is the most British and the most stable of all Caribbean islands. The Queen of Great Britain is also the Queen of Barbados, which may explain why she knighted the island's number one "all-rounder" for his contribution to the game of cricket—the Bajan national sport. Cricket is a wonderful game to watch when visiting the islands, and Barbados is no exception; in fact, you will find the best cricket here in the whole West Indies. Another local pastime is the Bajan delicacy "flying fish," which are so popular they have become a national symbol of what to eat when on the island. Flying fish are small fish that skim acrosss the top of the water—as if flying. They can be found all day long in boats and stalls along the Careenage as well as in dishes from beachside sandwiches to gourmet concoctions. The Bajan say you have not been to Barbados until you have enjoyed a flying fish sandwich!

~~~~~~

BRITISH LEEWARD ISLANDS

Lying north of Barbados, between Anegada and Guadeloupe passages, the Leewards consist of Antigua, Barbuda, Montserrat, St. Kitts, and Nevis. Of the group, Antigua is the most popular for cruise ship calls, although St. Kitts and Nevis are coming into their own.

Antigua: This 108-square-mile island was discovered in 1493 by Columbus, who named it after Santa Maria la Antigua of Seville. The British colonized the island around 1623. Its capital and main port is St. John's, where you can see rum made and buy a barbecue pot, but the real attraction of the island is Lord Nelson's Dockyard in **English Harbour.** The romance and history of the harbor recall the days when the 25-year-old Horatio Nelson was senior captain of the Leeward Islands Squadron in 1784. He rose to commander-in-chief and was married on nearby Nevis in 1787, with the future King William IV as his best man. A residence built for the king when he was still the Duke of Clarence can be visited when the present governor is not using it. Nelson House, now a museum of Nelson and naval memorabilia, as well as the Master Shipwright's House, Sew Pit Shed, Mast House, Joiner's Loft, and Sail Loft are all part of this fascinating area. And don't forget the charming Admiral's Inn, where you can enjoy a rum punch before the drive back to the capital via Swetes Village and Fig Tree Hill. Or, you can skip all the sightseeing and take a tour of Buccaneer Cove for lunch and swimming. If you still want to be cruising, try the fantastic West Coast and a stop in Emerald Bay for swimming. Some shore excursions feature the island of Montserrat—fifteen minutes away by air—for a tour of the capital, Plymouth, and the smoking crater Soufriere, as well as a bit of the Irish who colonized this emerald isle in 1632.

English Harbour is the be-all for visiting Antigua and if you are in a group, you may wish to head straight there in a taxi (rates are standardized and published) and forget the rest of the tour. Shopping can be confined to the cruise shed where locals lay out objects made of shells. The little birds are adorable and can usually be bought for $1. There is an art gallery in English Harbor, however, which also will frame your purchases while you have lunch at one of the inns in the complex.

St. Kitts: Nearby St. Kitts was also discovered by Columbus in 1493. He named it after his patron saint, St. Christopher, who had carried him safely on a voyage to the New World. Often called the Mother Colony of the British West Indies, St. Kitts was first settled in 1623. From here people set out to colonize the other islands. The English fought over St. Kitts with the French for many years. In 1783 the Treaty of Versailles ceded it to the British at last. The island became an associated state of the British Commonwealth in 1967, but French influences are still intact in names like **Basseterre,** the capital and main harbor. Basseterre means ''low land,'' and the harbor it describes has an Old World charm, with lovely colonial structures like Government House and the Old Court House. If you have four hours, you can drive around all of St. Kitts and stop at the 1694 Brimstone Hill Fortress at Sandy Point for a view of the nearby island of St. Eustatius.

Nevis: Otherwise, you might as well carry on to the 35-square-mile **Nevis,** just two miles south. Surrounded by coral reefs, Nevis has at its center three high peaks that usually have halos of white clouds. Columbus thought this was similar to the snow-covered Pyrenees, so named the place Las Nievas. Shore excursions here stop at Fig Tree Church, where Admiral Nelson was married to the wealthy young widow, 22-year-old Fanny Nisbet. Other sites include the house in Charlestown where Alexander Hamilton was born in 1757, the 200-year-old thermal baths, and St. Thomas Church and its ancient tombstones.

BRITISH WINDWARD ISLANDS

St. Lucia, St. Vincent, and Grenada are the most popular cruise stops in the British Windwards (which also include Dominica and the Grenadines).

St. Lucia: The second largest island in this chain, St. Lucia features Mt. Soufriere, the only ''drive-in'' active volcano in the world. You can drive up to the lip of the crater, cook an egg in the steam, and visit the sulfur baths. St. Lucia is believed to have been discovered by Columbus on St. Lucia's Day, June 15, 1502, although some scholars claim the Spanish arrived later. Early settlers had to contend with the Caribs, who were determined to keep the white man away. In the mid-seventeenth century the French arrived, and from then until the turn of the nineteenth century they fought with the British over possession of this island. Although the British finally won in 1802, everyone involved suffered a split personality. The French-sounding **Castries** is the island's capital and main harbor. Unfortunately, nothing colonial or interesting remains. A fire in 1948 completely destroyed the old town. Apart from the volcano excursion, you can take a tour across the causeway to

Pigeon Island, now a national park, where British Admiral Rodney once kept pigeons. If you wish to bypass the Soufriere shore excursion (it's not worth the time and energy necessary), grab a local cab and pop over to Cunard's La Toc Hotel & Suites for lunch and a walk on the beach. All types of watersports are available—for a fee, of course!

St. Vincent: This island, eighteen miles by eleven miles, was named by Columbus when he arrived on St. Vincent's Day in 1498. Another piece of property that the Caribs hung onto for as long as possible, St. Vincent was declared neutral during the fighting between the French and the English in 1748, but it went to the British in the latter part of the eighteenth century. After the British Captain Bligh brought breadfruit here from Tahiti, it was nicknamed Breadfruit Island, and breadfruit is still a major product. This is another split-personality island with French names and British overtones. And it has *its* own volcano called Mt. Soufriere, but this one is semi-dormant. You can climb to its 4000-foot rim for a view of the crater lake below. Capital and main port of the island is **Kingstown,** which has some attractive nineteenth-century dwellings as well as a 200-year-old botanical garden. The Mesopotamia Valley has twenty-eight miles of rural beauty. If boat tours are offered to any of the Grenadines, hop aboard, especially if you like to snorkel in crystal-clear waters or swim at sparkling beaches.

Grenada: Originally named Concepcion by Columbus, who first saw it on August 15, 1498, this island is nicknamed the Spice Island. Again, the Caribs kept their 133 square miles of volcanic mountains, green valleys, and beautiful beaches as long as they were able. The British and the French fought over this small piece of real estate, but the British assumed possession in 1783. Grenada became a crown colony in 1877 and was granted its independence in 1974. Its capital and main port, **St. George,** is one of the most picturesque harbors in the Caribbean. On a protected harbor and blue inner lagoon, the town has pastel warehouses and gabled dwellings. A good walking tour takes about two hours, and you can enjoy such sights as Old Fort George, which has French origins, the Market Place, and Marryshow House. There are plenty of local arts-and-crafts exhibits, and you can fill your pockets with cinnamon, nutmeg, ginger, vanilla, bay leaf (laurel), and clove. Organized excursions feature a bus tour or a catamaran cruise to Grand Anse Beach for sunning and snorkeling. The bus goes through the Mt. Parnassus Valley by the famous nutmeg trees, stops for a panoramic view of the harbor from Richmond Hill, and drives on to Morne Jalous and the charming fishing village of Woburn. You meet your fellow passengers from the catamaran at Grand Anse Beach.

The inland tours of Grenada are tortuous because, although the island is lush and beautiful, the roads are up-down and very, very bumpy.

Add to this vans that have no springs or cushions and you will appreciate why it is more fun to remain in the St. George's harbor/Grand Anse Beach area. Both offer a colorful lifestyle and plenty of entertainment as well as food and drink. And never are you very far from aggressive ladies offering fragrant spices, or young men with guitar and song. You can have a custom-made hat for a few dollars, a potent rum punch, or refreshing local beer from vendors who seem to appear from everywhere!

CAYMAN ISLANDS

These are known by locals as the Alligator Islands, because reptiles were once plentiful. Before that, our friend Columbus, who discovered them in 1503 on his fourth voyage, called them Las Tortugas for the many turtles. The islands are also famous for their ring of coral, which has been the nemesis of more than three hundred ships whose hulls and buried treasures keep the intrigue level high. Life on Grand Cayman, twenty-two miles long and eight miles wide, is slow and casual, with the emphasis for cruise passengers on relaxation and beach parties. The small capital and main port of **George Town** is quiet, and its tax-haven status interests many visitors (Grand Cayman may yet become the Monaco of the Caribbean). There is free-port shopping, and you can purchase a gift package of frozen green-turtle steaks.

There are two primary reasons for stopping by Grand Cayman. The British arrive to stay in their legal (sort of) residences and visit their money (since off-shore banking is the island's number-one business). The Americans fall off cruise ships and head straight for Seven Mile (also known as West Bay) Beach, along which many a high-rise resort has been built where aficionados can rent diving equipment and other watersports paraphernalia. On the other hand, these beach-front resorts are good for coming in from the heat and enjoying a libation at the low-rise bars.

DOMINICAN REPUBLIC

After Columbus discovered this island, he installed his brother Bartolome as governor. Bartolome founded Santo Domingo, the oldest city in the New World, which drew the influential and adventurous in the first half of the sixteenth century. The independent Dominican Republic was established in 1844. Its capital and chief port is **Santo Domingo,** which boasts the oldest cathedral in the Americas, dating from 1514. Other sights are the Alcazar of Diego Columbus (built in 1510 and restored in 1957), the sixteenth-century Casa del Cordon, the National Museum, and the Palace of Fine Arts. Also here are a national theater, a national library, and the Museo del Hombre Dominicano on the Plaza de la Cultura.

Santo Domingo, on the south coast, is considered by some experienced cruise passengers to be their favorite port of call in the entire Caribbean. True, port facilities have been improved and the pier is close to the sights of the old city, but be sure to take an organized shore excursion as English is not spoken here with the fluency one finds on other Spanish-heritage islands.

Puerto Plata is situated on the north or so-called Amber Coast of the Dominican Republic, and a more frequent cruise call than Santo Domingo, although the port is not all that attractive. Frankly, neither is the town and there is not much to see. So either take the bus tour and be bored until you end up at the beach for a quick swim, or hop into a taxi with some friends and head straight for one of the familiar hotels at Playa Dorado.

DUTCH WINDWARD ISLANDS

Of these three small dots—Sint Maarten, Saba, and Sint Eustatius (also known as Statia)—Sint Maarten is the most popular for cruise calls.

Sint Maarten: Columbus was here, too, on St. Martin's Day, apparently in 1493, but records say that he never went ashore. The island is divided, and only the Dutch side is called Sint Maarten. The larger French section is called St. Martin and is a member of the French West Indies. On the Dutch side, the capital and chief port, **Philipsburg,** has little to offer but a few narrow streets. St. Martin, the French section of the island, is where the shops carry Parisien imports and the restaurants serve up a bit of la belle France in the Caribbean. Some vessels now dock at Marigot, the port for St. Martin, as this section of the island is becoming more and more popular as a cruise call—despite the obvious problems that accompany an increased influx of tourists. Other than the seventeenth-century Fort Amsterdam, now very crumbly, the island has few historical sites. Beautiful scenery and interesting people are the main attractions. You can take a catamaran cruise aboard the

Maison Maru to some spectacular beaches (bring your bathing suit) and caves that are not accessible from the road.

~~~~~~

FRENCH WEST INDIES

Largest and northernmost of the French West Indies is Martinique, called the Pearl of the Antilles. Cruise ships also dock at Guadeloupe, and occasionally at Iles des Saintes and St. Barthelemy (or St. Barts, which used to be one of the best-kept secrets in the Caribbean).

Martinique: The capital and main seaport of Martinique is **Fort-de-France,** a city 100,000 strong that will remind you of New Orleans with its iron-grillwork–studded buildings. Although Columbus is said to have landed on the western coast of this twenty-by-fifty-mile island, he did not stay long enough to think of a name. So the naming was left to the French, who arrived in 1635 and used the Carib name, "Island of Flowers." In 1848 the islanders were granted full French citizenship, and in 1946 Martinique became a *departement* of France, governed by a prefect appointed through the French Minister of the Interior.

Organized shore excursions take you north to **St.-Pierre,** once considered a little Paris but destroyed in 1902 by Mt. Pelee, the 4500-foot volcano. You can visit the museum that chronicles the terrible eruption. Then your drive goes almost to the base of the volcano and through forests of giant fern to Balata for a visit to the church that looks like a small replica of Sacre Coeur in Paris. Martinique was the birthplace of Napoleon's wife Josephine, and a museum in the village of Trois Ilets tells of the local beauty who became Empress of France. Other tours might include Absalon, a thermal resort, and Carbet, said to be where Columbus landed, or the restored eighteenth-century De Leyritz Plantation. A Kon Tiki tour, in a catamaran, features a Calypso steel band and complimentary rum punch. But you may just prefer to explore the bustling port of Fort-de-France on your own—graceful women in colorful native dress, side streets redolent of Creole cookery, a library, a cathedral, Fort St.-Louis overhanging the bay, and a statue of Josephine looking out toward her native village.

Everyone talks about shopping in Martinique, but the only shop worth visiting, Roger Albert, is jammed with your fellow cruise passengers. Nonetheless, perfume prices here are said to be among the best in the world, and Hermes ties are well priced. The shop has an annex where leather goods and fancy pens are sold, but not necessarily at bargain rates. There are a few other shops in the area selling French imports at fairly decent prices; look for specials if you are so inclined. After your shopping excursion, head for the ferry pier and cross the bay to the Meridien Trois Islets Hotel, which has a lovely french-style buffet and a beautiful beach, Pointe du Bout. If you prefer more casual beach life, catch any ferry across the bay from Fort de France.

Guadeloupe: This island is in two parts, like a butterfly with spread wings. Columbus discovered it in 1493 and named it in honor of Our Lady of Guadeloupe of Estremadura. The French settled here in 1635, but the English interfered for almost two centuries. The Treaty of Paris in 1815 finally made the island French, and in 1946 it was made a *departement* with the same status as Martinique. Guadeloupe consists of Grande-Terre and Basse-Terre, divided by the Riviere Salee. Capital is **Pointe-a-Pitre,** a busy seaport that was a pirate haven in the eighteenth century (pirate spirits are said to still hover over the city) and that has quaint streets and European-style buildings.

Tours from Pointe-a-Pitre will take you across the bridge of the Riviere Salee to Guadeloupe's verdant rain forest and Parc Naturel, a botanist's paradise. A stop is made at Fort Fleur d'Epee, with interesting underground passages and dungeons. This was the keystone of French defense during the long battle against the British, and the view of the sea and other islands from here is spectacular. Other historic sites include Sainte-Marie, where Columbus is said to have landed, and Trois-Rivieres, where relics and rocks bear inscriptions by the Carib Indians. Guadeloupe also has a La Soufriere volcano—which is only sleeping—with extraordinary views from the top (but watch out for the hot-lava bogs).

Iles des Saintes: This cluster of eight islands off the southern coast of Guadeloupe includes **Terre-de-Haut,** an occasional cruise call. Here, you can explore the peaceful and charming harbor of Bourg and enjoy some of the best snorkeling that exists anywhere.

You may also climb up to Fort Napoleon, which dates from the eighteenth century and is noted for its fine walls. Here, you can visit a small museum of island history and such and hear that the "free French" were encased within this compound during World War II because the Vichy government took over the town below. Afterward, you can walk through the island and enjoy some great body surfing on the opposite beach (but watch out for the stiff undertow).

St. Barthelemy: Dependent upon Guadeloupe but 140 miles north, St. Barths is considered by a loyal following to be the most chic island in the Caribbean. Its 2500 inhabitants are mostly of French-Norman and Swedish background. Its capital is **Gustavia,** known for fabulous French food and charming atmosphere, but don't let on where you heard this. Some of the smaller cruise vessels now stop in the harbor. *Zut alors!*

HAITI

This country of black magic and primitive paintings was discovered by Columbus in 1492. He named it Hispaniola, but the native Arawak Indians already called it Hayti, the mountainous country. Hispaniola still refers to the entire island, of which Haiti occupies one-third and the Spanish-speaking Dominican Republic the rest. The Spanish ceded the Haitian portion of Hispaniola to the French in 1697 and it was called Saint-Dominique until 1791 when the country reverted to the original Indian name. The history of Haiti has been turbulent. Often called the world's first black republic, it has been independent, more or less, since approximately 1806, although the U.S. assumed control between 1915 and 1924. The terror reign of "Papa Doc" Duvalier (1957–71) raised some dust that has now settled somewhat. "Baby Doc" Duvalier was forced out of Haiti in late 1985, and there is hope that poverty will be less of a problem and some sort of democracy may reign.

The jury is still out regarding Haiti; meanwhile, the entire cruise industry (with one exception) has bypassed this country until further notice. The exception is Royal Caribbean Cruise Line, which has developed its own 260-acre secluded port—called Labadee—on the northwest coast. Located in the Pointe Honora area, Labadee features dining facilities, shopping, snorkeling, sunbathing, nature walks, an enclosed artist and native crafts marketplace, local entertainment, and a flea market (for Haitian souvenirs). RCCL is also restoring historic sites in the area—Nellie's Place, Fort Belli, and the original Bell Tower. Port calls at Labadee (which can accommodate up to 3000 cruise passengers) are cancelled, however, during times of Haitian unrest.

Capital of Haiti and main cruise port is **Port-au-Prince,** a city of incongruities and squalor. Its French, African, and West Indian cultural mix makes it exotic and colorful. With landmark buildings and the famous Iron Market, you can sightsee and barter over the bargains all day. Haitian art is well known now; primitive painting and sculpture is on every street corner, but you may wish to visit the Arts Center first, the Museum of Haitian Art, and a few local galleries before you purchase anything. Other tourist attractions in the capital are the voodoo relics in the Ethnographical Museum, the tomb of the late President Duvalier in Fort Dimanche, and Habitation Leclerc, a luxury resort hotel that was the renowned mansion of Pauline Bonaparte, Napoleon's sister. Tours out of town take you to Petionville, the Land of Perpetual Spring, and the 3500-foot-high lookout called Boutillier, from which you can enjoy a panorama of the bay, city, and distant mountains. Your excursion may also include a local rum distillery that offers complimentary tastings and samplings.

About two hundred miles north of the capital is **Cap Hatien,** a more popular cruise port because of San Souci Palace and La Citadelle La Ferriere. Once the rich capital of Sainte-Dominique, "Le Cap" is Haiti's most historic town—and the least offensive to tourists. The two famous monuments built in the early part of the nineteenth century by the black emperor Henri Christophe—who controlled the northern part of Haiti—are about a twenty-mile drive from the port. Sans Souci Palace, which is similar to Versailles, was the most splendid structure in the New World and even the roofless ruins of the reception rooms, ballrooms, and royal compartments never fail to impress me. The Citadelle, which some call the Eighth Wonder of the World, was built by some 200,000 slaves and finished in 1817. Its walls, 140 feet high and twelve feet thick, house a garrison designed to hold 15,000 men and a suite of forty rooms for the emperor. The climb to the top is long and arduous, even by horse or mule, but it is well worth the effort for both the tour of this fortress and the view beyond.

JAMAICA

Another mountainous island, Jamaica has four peaks surpassing six thousand feet. Discovered by Columbus in 1494 and colonized by his son Diego, this lovely isle of streams and forests (Xamayca, the Arawaks called it) was under Spanish domain only until the mid-seventeenth century. The British seized it in 1655 and allowed it to become a pirate base. One of the greatest pirates of all, Henry Morgan, later became lieutenant governor of Jamaica. The island, independent for almost two decades, depends heavily upon tourism. Cruise vessels concentrate on the northern shore. **Port Antonio,** one of the cruise calls, is a beautiful little harbor with the majestic Blue Mountains (where that wonderful coffee comes from) as a backdrop. With little of interest to passengers, the port's biggest attraction is river rafting on the Rio Grande. The bamboo rafts are about thirty feet long and can accommodate three people—two is more comfortable—plus a raftsman. It's a relaxing three-hour journey down the river, with time out for a rest in the shade or a dip in the cool, clear, fresh waters. Bathing suits are a must for this one.

The beach resort of **Ocho Rios** has been built around a pleasant, natural harbor. If your cruise vessel arrives in the late afternoon, don't miss the performance of local dances on the beach, complete with stars overhead and torchlights all around you. By day you can visit Dunn's River Falls, where the sparkling water rushes straight from the mountain to the beach below. It's fun to explore these beautiful falls, and you can even climb them if you are properly dressed—bathing suit and sneakers will do the trick. If you wish to get away from the water, an interesting plantation tour takes you to the 1200-acre Prospect Estate, where spices and cattle are big business.

Montego Bay, or Mo'Bay as everyone calls it, is the largest of these three Jamaican ports. Once the favorite of the international set, Mo'Bay's glitter is now long gone. Restored Rose Hall, once among the grandest of eighteenth-century plantation homes in the West Indies, attracts many visitors. The house, which has had two novels written about it, has enjoyed a notorious past. Its second mistress allegedly murdered three spouses and a lover and then was mysteriously done in herself. For a different kind of intrigue—a la James Bond (his creator had a house here)—catch a glimpse of the crocodiles and alligators in nearby swamplands. Some of these beasts, kept by a fearless young man, will do tricks for you as they did in the James Bond film *Live and Let Die.*

Jamaica is an island on which cruise passengers should take the suggested tours or travel in groups. There are rental cars and some wonderful places to tour on your own, such as Noel Coward's former hideaway—now open to the public at appointed hours—or the monuments around Kingston. However, it is best to do some homework before you set out as distances can be quite long and you will want to be "home" again before dark. And watch another problem prevalent in Jamaica— Say NO to Drugs!

NETHERLAND ANTILLES

Aruba, Bonaire, and Curacao (The "ABC islands") are popular pieces of Holland not only for their Dutch manner but also for their business acumen. These islands have long offered substantial tax credits to companies incorporated here, and one of the world's largest oil refineries is on Curacao. So, while you explore the delights of Dutch treats in the sunshine, your cruise vessel may be refueling at an economical price. Lying off the Venezuelan coast, all three of these islands were settled by the Spanish.

Curacao: **Willemstad,** the capital, might just be the most photographed port in the whole Caribbean; its narrow, eighteenth-century gabled houses are painted in every color. The island, discovered by the Spanish explorer Alonzo de Ojeda in 1499, greeted the first Spanish settlers three decades later. They didn't have long to get comfortable, however, because the Dutch arrived, established a colony, and named Peter Stuyvesant governor not long after, in 1643. It was here that Stuyvesant supposedly lost his right leg in an excursion against Sint Maarten. As you wander around this charming port, notice the many Dutch-ingrained influences—in the little canals, the colorful floating market, and the old-style dwellings. Take a walk across the famous Queen Emma Pontoon Bridge, which swings open to let ships pass in and out of the harbor. Also interesting are Fort Amsterdam (now a seat of government), the 1769 Old Dutch Reformed Church, and the 1732 Mikve Israel—Emmanuel Synagogue, which claims to be the oldest in the Western Hemisphere (but then, so do several others). If you fancy refineries, you'll love the one operated by Shell. Another local concern, Curacao orange-flavored liqueur, offers a free sip at the Chobolobo Mansion (you can also buy some to take home in pretty Delft jugs).

Aruba: Alonzo de Ojeda claimed Aruba for Spain in 1499, at the same time he discovered Curacao, but the Dutch moved in here, also, in 1634. Aruba, much smaller and less prosperous than Curacao (although it has a huge oil refinery), is only fifteen miles from the Venezuelan coastline and twelve degrees from the Equator. Its capital and main port, **Oranjestad,** is another delightfully Dutch harbor with old-style houses whose red-tiled roofs sparkle in the sunshine. Take a walk over to the schooner harbor and open market, then on to Wilhelmina Park and the nearby street lined with typical early Aruban buildings.

If you take an organized shore excursion, it may feature such tourist attractions as Frenchmen's Pass (where Indians allegedly fought the French), the natural bridge, and the rock formation garden of Casibari. In the tiny village of Noord an interesting church, St. Anna's, has an oak altar handcarved in Holland in 1850 by well-known Dutch artist Van Geld. Some rather fascinating caves and grottos with hieroglyphics show evidence of Arawak Indian habitation. Aruba also has its own Palm Beach, complete with fancy resort hotels and gambling facilities, if you like that sort of thing.

Bonaire: Noted for flamingos and excellent scuba diving, Bonaire was discovered by a band of men under Amerigo Vespucci in 1496. Second largest of this ABC group, it seems small and very quiet in contrast to its two sisters. The main port, **Kralendijk,** is storybook pretty, with its tiny harbor and pink fish market. Take a wonderful drive out to the Washington National Park, a game preserve and the first of its kind in this area. And if you aren't watching the lovely flamingos, you will want to be underwater watching the myriad colors of the world below. Visibility supposedly reaches to 65 feet below the surface, and all kinds of equipment can be rented.

PUERTO RICO

On any Saturday during the winter season as many as nine cruise ships may be making "turn arounds" in **San Juan,** the most popular port for seven-day cruises in the lower Caribbean. From early morning to late afternoon and early evening, these ships will be resting gently in their berths waiting to take on passengers for sailings to La Guaira, Barbados, St. Lucia, and the like. But San Juan holds her own as a port of call and is well worth an extra day or two to explore, either before or after your cruise.

It's not hard to see why Ponce de Leon exclaimed "puerto rico!" (rich port) when he arrived in the harbor in 1508 to establish a European settlement. Columbus discovered the island on November 19, 1493, during his second voyage to the New World, and the Indian inhabitants received him cordially. When Ponce de Leon arrived fifteen years later to colonize the island for Spain, the chief of the Taino Indians greeted him and, following Indian custom for friendship, the two men exchanged names. Ponce de Leon became the first governor of Puerto Rico and moved the early settlement to the present site of Old San Juan in 1521. A 24-foot-square frame house was built for him here as a reward for his services, but he never lived to occupy it. However, the Ponce descendants inhabited the house, Casa Blanca, for 250 years. It is now a museum that illustrates Puerto Rican life of the sixteenth and seventeenth centuries. The former Spanish colony was ceded to the United States in 1898 as a result of the Spanish-American War, and Puerto Ricans have been U.S. citizens since the Jones Act of 1917. Spanish is still the primary language, although English is the tourist tongue. Old San Juan, which includes the seven-block-square quarter once enclosed by a city wall and the forts El Morro and San Cristobal, celebrated its 465th birthday in 1986—no small feat. This old section has tremendous charm, and the colonial architecture and ambience are being conserved. Lovely wrought-iron balconies and heavy, carved wooden doors and shutters decorate the whitewashed houses. Inside, the ceilings are supported by beams in such a way that each room is a work of art.

Walking is the most practical way to get around Old San Juan. You can easily design your own tour with a copy of *Que Pasa,* the tourism publication, in hand. (Get a copy at the Visitors Center in the square near Pier Number One.) El Morro, the sixteenth- to eighteenth-century fort built 140 feet above the sea, is the perfect place to begin. Stop next at the Plaza de San Jose, dominated by the statue of Juan Ponce de Leon that was made from a British cannon after an unsuccessful attempt on the city in 1797. This large square also houses San Jose Church, a former Dominican convent that is now the Institute of Puerto Rican Culture, and several renovated buildings that are now museums. On the right side of the square are a small Museum of Santos (small, wooden, religious statues that are a great part of the island's history and folklore) and the Pablo Casals Museum, which has the Maestro's cello. Calle Cristo, Old San Juan's most famous street, runs from the Plaza de San Jose to the harbor wall and is paved with bluish-tint bricks, *adoquines,* which were used for ballast in Spanish ships. Cristo Street runs down past the Cathedral of San Juan and El Convento Hotel (superb buffet is served in the courtyard of this seventeenth-century former convent) and dead ends at Cristo Chapel, built to honor a miracle that occurred on the spot in 1753. Adjacent is Pigeon Park, which overlooks the harbor and La Princesa Jail. Backtrack a bit and pay a visit to La Fortaleza, the governor's mansion, which is the longest continually occupied executive house in this hemisphere. (Museum times in San Juan are a trial, to say the least. If the guidebook says they're open at certain times—and they're not—try to convince the attendants. Manana is the common word here.)

Shopping in Old San Juan is fun, especially if you're not in the mood for anything too grand. Some very expensive-looking jewelry stores may tempt you, but for straw items, hammocks, and inexpensive beachwear, the place is great. Take advantage of the factory shirt outlet that sells Hathaway, Dior, and other name brands at terrific bargains, as well as the Ralph Lauren outlet store next door (prices are still outrageous even at discount)! I generally stay away from places such as Barrachina that send advertisements to the ships to entice you the day before your flight leaves. Compare prices before you buy anything—even a quart of rum. Remember, there's always an angle when you are offered something for nothing.

Save metropolitan San Juan and the excellent resort hotels on Condado and Isla Verde for a longer stay; life there is glamorous and exciting in the birthplace of the Pina Colada! If you feel like a visit to where the famous rum (Bacardi) is made—bypass the expensive shore excursion offered on board and catch the local ferry from Pier 2 to the Bacardi distillery (round trip from San Juan is less than $5 a person). The tour is free! With the money saved, you can purchase and tuck a bottle or two of the duty-free brew under your arms.

ST. VINCENT AND THE GRENADINES

In a search for new and untapped island calls, many of the smaller vessels are now concentrating on the Grenadines, a string of islands between St. Vincent and Grenada that (including St. Vincent) have been independent from Great Britain since 1979. Including Mayreau, Bequia, Mustique, Palm Island, and Tobago Cays, they are among the most beautiful and least "discovered" islands of the Caribbean, as they are accessible only by water (or very small seaplane).

Snorkeling and other watersports are perfect on **Bequia,** where your small cruise vessel or private yacht lolls in Port Elizabeth harbor. The beaches boast sand like confectioner's sugar, but you if are aboard *Sea goddess I* or *WindStar,* you can water ski, snorkel, and swim from the mechanized sports platform aft of the vessel.

Tiny **Mayreau** is so peaceful and picture perfect, it is even a shame to mention it in public! However, if your small ship calls here—consider yourselves gone to heaven, if only for the day. **Mustique,** on the other hand, has become just "too too" as it is privately owned by a British lord as well as home and hideaway to such loyal subjects as Princess Margaret and rock stars Mick Jagger and David Bowie (not an unlikely combination as neighbors). There is one fabulous resort on the island, called the Cotton House, or you can have a peek at Les Jolie Eaux (the house of Margaret) and even make plans to rent it when she is not in residence.

The 110-acre **Palm Island** is also privately owned and a delightful stop on many cruise itineraries for a beach and rum punch party/barbecue complete with steel band. The island is not spectacular, like the others, but quiet and attractive and you can walk all around it, swim or eat to your heart's content before sailing into the sunset aboard your comfortable cruise vessel.

TRINIDAD AND TOBAGO

Most southerly of the West Indian groups, Trinidad is the island on which government and commerce are located, while Tobago is the weekend resort, getaway spot. Columbus discovered Trinidad in 1498 on his third voyage to the New World and named it La Trinidad for the three hills around the bay where he anchored. The Spanish settled here a century later, but many battles with the British followed. The island was finally ceded to Britain by the Treaty of Amiens in 1802. Both islands ended their link with the monarchy in 1976 and became a republic.

Trinidad: From the capital and main port, **Port of Spain,** Calypso and steel bands originated and spread throughout the Caribbean. For people watching and a walk through the sights and sounds of this exciting place, begin at Queen's Wharf and walk north to Independence Square, Frederick Street, Queen Street, and the Red House (seat of government). You may also want to pay a visit to the Angostura Bitters factory and then continue to the 200-acre Queen's Park Savannah area, with its racecourse, cricket fields, and diverse architecture. The park's lovely Botanical Gardens, laid out in 1820 on a 63-acre plot, provide licensed guides who will show you around and be happy to explain the flora. Built on a peak over a thousand feet above Port of Spain is the 1803 Fort George, which offers the most wonderful view all around, including the mountains of Venezuela.

The people of Trinidad are well educated and prosperous and it is a delight to visit their lovely island. Shore excursions take you over to the Atlantic side, with some spectacular beaches. You may want to pack a towel and swimsuit if you feel comfortable in an ominous-looking undertow.

Tobago: From Trinidad to Tobago, which some claim was Robinson Crusoe's island, the flight takes fifteen minutes. Tobago is completely unspoiled, and the weather is often better than on Trinidad. Here you'll find some exotic bird life, and the main town of Scarborough has a colorful market.

Cruise ships anchor off Pigeon Point and tender their passengers into the palm-fringed beaches for an afternoon of sunbathing and watersports complemented by calypso music and rum punches. Optional shore excursions feature a glass-bottom boat ride to Buccoo Reef or a drive around the island—which fellow travelers aboard *Ocean Islander* said was the best ever! Tobago is the antithesis of Trinidad's kinetic energy and a good place to enjoy the beaches and relax.

U.S. VIRGIN ISLANDS

Lying forty miles due east of Puerto Rico, the USVI were discovered by Columbus in 1493 during his second voyage to the New World. He christened them Las Virgenes, in honor of St. Ursula's legendary eleven thousand martyred virgins. On the island he called Santa Cruz (now St. Croix) he searched for fresh water but was chased off by the Carib Indians and sailed away. The Caribs kept the islands off limits for seafarers until 1555, when Spain claimed the territory. Throughout most of the century, however, the islands were contested by England, France, Holland, and Denmark. The Danish won and kept the islands until 1916 when they sold them to the United States for $25 million. This probably makes the U.S. the only governing power in the Caribbean that ever paid for anything! The package included St. Thomas, St. Croix, and St. John as well as several lesser land masses in the area.

St. Thomas: **Charlotte Amalie,** capital of St. Thomas, is the most important port in the USVI, not only for its charm and beauty—the town is named for a Danish queen—but also for all the duty-free shopping available to American cruise passengers. In this little town with cobblestone streets and quaint shops displaying gold watches and cases of liquor, Americans can purchase and bring back duty-free twice the amount allowed elsewhere. No wonder more than a dozen cruise vessels dock in this harbor at one time.

If you don't wish (God forbid) to shop, you won't be bored. You can take a tour of this lovely 30-square-mile island, passing famous landmarks such as Bluebeard's Castle and lookout tower where the pirate could spot unsuspecting galleons. Continue your drive up Mafolie Hill and have a look at Louisenhoj Castle before catching the view from Drake's Seat of Magens Bay Beach, reportedly one of the ten most splendid beaches in the world. St. Thomas also has a magnificent underwater observatory, and a visit here is not soon forgotten. Called the Coral World Underwater Observation Tower, and located on a lush tropical peninsula on the northeastern shore of the island, the observatory/tower's three stories rise from the sea some one hundred feet from shore. On the lowest level hundreds of tropical fish, coral formations, and beautiful deep-water flowers are visible. On the second level you will be surrounded by sharks, stingrays, barracudas, and huge sea turtles. The top level of the tower is an extraordinary geodesic dome with a spectacular view of St. John's and the British Virgin Islands.

St. John's: Another highlight is the excursion to St. John's, a ten-minute ride by motor launch across Pilgrim Bay (don't sit at the rail unless you are prepared to be drenched). At Cruz Bay you board a motorized surrey—complete with the fringe on the top—for the short but spectacular ride to Trunk Bay, which is often mentioned as one of the world's most beautiful beaches. Trunk Bay has pristine white sands and coral green seas, and is wonderful for snorkeling. A short underwater trail leads to the best look at colorful tropical fish and coral. Don't touch the coral because it's sharp, and don't take souvenirs because that's against the law. You may also go to Coki Point under the auspices of the Virgin Islands Diving Schools, which will teach you how to approach this underwater world and then give you a diploma testifying to your accomplishments. For enjoying the coral reefs with much less effort, join the Kon Tiki raft party, which includes rum punches, a steel band, and swimming on the beaches of Honeymoon Bay.

St. Croix: As the largest and most southerly of the main islands in the U.S. Virgin Islands group, St. Croix has become not only a popular port of call but a departure point for many of the smaller cruise vessels. **Christiansted** on the northern coast is the capital and largest town, while Frederiksted on the western coast boasts the advantage of a deepwater harbor. Both have Danish overtones in architecture and place names as well as left-hand traffic.

Right on the harbor in Christiansted is Fort Christiansvaern, built of bricks brought from Denmark as ballast in the sailing vessels. It was completed in 1774 and held troops until 1878. The Old Danish Customs House is situated to the west of the fort. Now an art gallery, it dates from the early 19th century. Goods were weighed and checked at the only slightly younger Scale House. The oldest section of Government House on King Street dates from 1747. Nearby is the colorful Outdoor Market, the former Warehouse of the Dutch West Indies Company, and Steeple Building—originally built as a Lutheran church in 1753.

Buck Island, a short boat trip from Christiansted, is now a national park with a reef nature trail for underwater sports enthusiasts. It is a strictly controlled nature reserve, so nothing can be collected of what you may discover along the reef.

Frederiksted has a population of about 4000 and generally livens up a bit when cruise ships come to call. Just north of the pier is the former Fort Frederick, which dates from 1755 and where the abolition of slavery in Danish possessions was proclaimed in 1848. It is now a small museum. Other points of interest in town are the Old Danish School (c. 1830) and Market Square (1751). Along Strand Street from the pier are the old Customs House and Victoria House. Most of the old Danish buildings in Frederiksted were destroyed by fire in 1848.

Outside the town are some former plantation houses, a botanical garden and a good golf course. The St. Croix airport is not far from Frederiksted.

BRITISH VIRGIN ISLANDS

Columbus stopped by the British Virgin Islands in 1493 and they remained in Spanish hands until the arrival of Sir Francis Drake in 1595.

Drake sailed through the channel south of Tortola, which now bears his name. Britain annexed Tortola in 1672, but many of the neighboring islands were pirate haunts which inspired Robert Louis Stevenson to write *Treasure Island*. Today, the more than 50 islands and inlets as well as 12,000 people are subjects of the Crown and Queen Elizabeth II is represented by a local governor and other officials. Vehicles travel on the left side of the road, but the local currency is the U.S. dollar!

As largest of the British Virgin Islands, **Tortola** is 25 square miles and has a population of about 9000. Its capital and main port is Road Town, which has an excellent deep-water harbor. The Sir Francis Drake Channel separates Tortola from the smaller BVIs—**Norman, Peter, Salt, Cooper,** and **Ginger.** Sailing, fishing, scuba diving and snorkeling are the main pastimes here. The beaches are beautiful and the land is lush with tropical fruits and breezes.

Mount Sage National Park is in the southwest of the island, and Frenchman's Cays lies offshore. To the northwest of Tortola are the even more spectacular beaches of **Jost van Dyke,** an island originally settled by Quakers.

Although smaller than Tortola, the eight square mile **Virgin Gorda** is the principal island in the BVI group for vacationers. Spanish Town is the center of its 1000 population, sheltered as it is by a barrier reef. Virgin Gorda boasts the renowned Little Dix Bay Hotel as well as some beautiful beaches on North Sound.

CENTRAL AND NORTH AMERICA

ALASKA AND THE INSIDE PASSAGE

The 1000-mile-long sea corridor that skirts the west coast of British Columbia and Alaska, known as the **Inside Passage,** is a busy waterway from May to September. During this popular season as many as a dozen cruise vessels sail through what one might call the Last Frontier, our rugged forty-ninth state. The scenery compares favorably with the Norwegian fjords, both with sheer-rock cliffs, massive glaciers, and snowcapped mountains. Nature's more somber colors prevail in this spectacular setting. Be forewarned; the weather can be tricky—the locals say it's a *good* day when it's only drizzling! Hence, choose such cruises carefully—forget sunbathing and shopping and concentrate on shore excursions and equal time for absorbing the majestic scenery.

The longer cruises through the Inside Passage depart from San Francisco, while the shorter, seven- to 11-day sailings originate in **Vancouver.** This delightful seaport is considered Canada's gem of the Pacific for its fine weather, prosperity, rich cultural life, and interesting sights. Modern high-rises of steel and glass sit beside Victorian structures in a beautiful setting between mountains and sea. The city, founded in the 1860s, has a wonderful historic section, Gastown, which is a renovated gaslight district. Two other areas of interest are Chinatown, second in size only to San Francisco's in North America, and Robsonstrasse, with chic European shops and restaurants.

Vancouver built a fabulous new cruise pier for its International Expo a few years ago, which is a city in itself with convention facilities, shops, restaurants, and hotels. It is well worth exploring—especially to appreciate what can be done when local government gets its act together.

You can head straight for 1000-acre Stanley Park on the northern edge of Vancouver, where you can swim in pools or from the beach, visit a zoo and aquarium, see century-old totem poles, or just stroll among the more than 100,000 trees. (By the way, hockey's Stanley Cup and this park were both named after the same man, Lord Stanley, Governor General of Canada in 1889.) If there is time, drive over the Lions Gate Bridge to see the lovely homes and the symbol of Vancouver, two mountain peaks known as the Lions.

Some fortunate cruise passengers aboard ships on the Alaska run will call at the charming city of **Victoria,** capital of British Columbia, on Vancouver Island. Named after Britain's favorite (non-living) queen, Victoria has a milder climate than Vancouver, a delightful colonial atmosphere as well as a beautiful natural setting. A favorite attraction is Butchart Gardens, a good half-day excursion. Midtown has horse and buggies, Parliament Square full of Victorian structures, a fabulous museum combining anthropology with natural history, and the landmark Canadian Pacific Empress Hotel, where one can enjoy proper tea in the lobby and the accommodations are certainly a reminder of the past. It's fun to stay here—as I once did—and listen to the plumbing fixtures conversing all night long!

On board and underway, it's time to wrap yourself in a warm blanket, settle into a deck chair, and watch the view as the sunshine (you hope) warms the crisp air. Your first sight will undoubtedly be Lynn Canal, where fjords, fishing villages, and foothills will keep your camera busy. This is the beginning of the famous 1000-mile Inside Passage.

It's beautiful and rugged and somber, and it's easy to relax up here and slip into a slower pace. First port of call for many ships is **Ketchikan,** a city of some ten thousand or so that claims to be both the salmon capital of the world and totemland. Hence a tour of the city includes a salmon hatchery and Totem Park, where these handcarved poles portray legendary chiefs, mythical birds, and even Abraham Lincoln. Totem Bight State Park, a fifteen-minute drive north of Ketchikan, which has plenty more of these tall poles as well as a handcarved Ceremonial House, is the center of early Alaskan Indian culture.

Juneau, capital of Alaska, is a product of the 1880 gold rush. For the forty-ninth state, Juneau is considered sophisticated, and suburbanites live in modern, low-slung houses with beautiful views of mountains, glaciers, and the sea. One of the most impressive of several tours features Mendenhall Glacier, which is about one and a half miles wide by one mile long. It has been retreating at the rate of approximately fifty feet per year (you stand where the glacier ended around 1940). If you prefer to save your glaciers for later, don't miss the good performances of Tlingit and Haida tribal dances and snacks of fresh, fire-baked Alaskan salmon. For a more adventurous (and costly—about eighty dollars per person) salmon bake, catch one of the seaplanes parked along the waterfront for the half-hour ride to Taku Lodge. This forest-surrounded, log-cabin lodge offers a hearty lunch of salmon, homemade biscuits, beer chilled by glacial ice, baked beans, potato salad, coffee, and cookies—and there is time to walk it off before the flight back to Juneau.

Highlight of every Inside Passage cruise is **Glacier Bay National Monument,** about forty miles northwest of Juneau, accessible only by plane or boat. The scenery here is some of Alaska's most spectacular, and park rangers will board your vessel in the morning to comment on the history and habits of glaciers as you cruise along. The better part of a day is spent cruising slowly through Glacier Bay while you relax on board watching the ice floes pass by, occasionally hearing a glacier calve, or crack off, and learning about the rare wildlife that inhabit the area. Perhaps the sun will be brilliant this day, and your stewards will serve a wonderful buffet luncheon on deck.

Final port of call on most seven-day roundtrip Inside Passage routes is the former Russian settlement of **Sitka,** a town that lives in the past for the sake of its many tourists. On the site of an ancient Tlingit village, Sitka was founded by Aleksandr Baranof when he transferred the headquarters of the Russian-American Company here. On October 18, the 1867 ceremony in which the American flag replaced the Imperial Russian one is reenacted. Sites to visit in the area include the 54-acre Sitka Historical National Park, where Tlingit tribes made their last stand against the Russians and where Indian craftsmen now demonstrate their carving techniques. (The carvings for sale in town are rather pricey, I feel.) You can tour the onion-domed Russian church. It was rebuilt in 1966 after a disastrous fire, but the icons are original. The Alaska Pioneers' Home, the Russian cemetery, and a fine museum of local history and artifacts that span two centuries are also interesting. During the summer months a group of Sitka women perform typical Russian folk dances.

Even more popular these days are Inside Passage cruises that either begin or end in Whittier or Anchorage, with transportation via vintage glass-domed railcars the other way. These itineraries offer a more in-depth view of this spectacular scenery, including Hubbard Glacier, through Valdez Arm into Columbia Glacier (Alaska's most active). Also featured sights on this route are a cruise through Prince William Sound and an arrival in College Fjord, where as many as a baker's dozen of glaciers cascade down the mountain at once, with such awe-inspiring names as Harvard, Yale, Radcliffe, and Smith. The route also includes Kings Bay, Port Nellie Juan, and Seward—gateway to Kenai Fjords National Monument. Whether or not all of the above can be enjoyed on your cruise, the *in* way to go these days is by sea one way and rail the other *or* a one-week cruise with additional days amidst the beauty of our 49th state.

COSTA RICA

Tiny Costa Rica is about the size of West Virginia, sandwiched between Nicaragua to the north and Panama to the south, not the most peaceful neighbors in the world. However, Costa Rica refuses to join the Central American struggles; it even abolished the military and boasts a true democracy and the highest literacy rate in the area. With coastlines on both the Atlantic and Pacific oceans, it is a natural for cruise calls. Many cruise vessels transiting the Panama Canal call at Puerto Caldera, transporting passengers from the capital, San Jose, by antique train through jungle terrain, while others call at Puerto Moin and uses the excellent road-tour bus system for shore excursions.

This tiny country is a paradise for naturalists because eight percent of the land has been designated to the national park system. The tropical forests are home to one-tenth of the world's known bird species and up to 2000 different varieties of orchids are estimated to grow wild throughout the land. As it is the national flower, collecting orchids is forbidden except by government permit.

The capital, **San Jose,** has a beautiful National Theater, built between 1890 and 1897 with money raised by coffee growers, a national museum located in the former army barracks, wonderful wooden souvenirs from Sarachi, and pounds and pounds of flavorful coffee sold for a song.

INTRACOASTAL WATERWAY

Exploring the beauty and history of our own southeast coastline is gaining in popularity for yachtlike vessels, especially those operated by American Canadian Caribbean Line (ACCL) of Rhode Island and Clipper Cruise Line of St. Louis. The Intracoastal Waterway (ICW) joins random rivers, bays, and sounds for some 1085 miles between Norfolk, Virginia and Miami, Florida and provides vessels of all sizes a sheltered passage along this route. The idea dates from the time of the Revolution, but wasn't completed until the turn of this century. The waterway was actually meant for commercial vessels, but whoever dreamed that container ships would be constructed as big as several city blocks? So, today this protected 1000-plus-mile coast is full of pleasure boats and their passengers, who revel in sailing leisurely from one historic town to another. In many of the small ports, shore excursions are led by the local inhabitants in their own vehicles, and the whole experience offers the epitome of American-style hospitality!

The major cruising area along this waterway is between Baltimore, Maryland and Savannah, Georgia—either on full two-week sailings between the two ports or as one-week round-trip sailings from each port. **Baltimore,** gateway to the Chesapeake Bay area, has long lived in the shadow of our nation's capital as a rather poor and unsightly cousin. However, an impressive revitalization of the city's Inner Harbor with the renovation of old warehouses and a year-round marketplace, in addition to such tourist attractions as the National Aquarium, has made this the place to be. The restoration has also brought new cultural and leisure activities to the area. In short, Baltimore is definitely worth a visit and a linger—before or after the cruise.

Sailing from Baltimore harbor, where American lawyer Francis Scott Key wrote "The Star Spangled Banner" from the deck of a battleship, your vessel enters famed Chesapeake Bay—known not only for its scenic beauty but also for the succulent seafood found in its waters. First call is most likely **Oxford,** on the eastern shore of Maryland and a port of entry since 1694. Oxford has retained much of its early charm, when the town prospered on the exportation of tobacco and the importation of rope and other ships' supplies. Passengers are encouraged to take their own walking tours through the residential and shopping areas, or catch a ride on Tred Avon Ferry, which is said to be the oldest continuously operating car ferry in the country. St. Michaels, Cambridge, Salisbury, and Crisfield are other old port towns on Maryland's eastern shore that might be visited.

Yorktown, Virginia is located at the mouth of the York River, and not much changed since its heyday in the eighteenth century, when the exportation of tobacco made it rich and famous. Today, the port is noted for the Battle of Yorktown in 1781, which is credited with ending the American Revolution. You may explore the silent battlefields on foot, and perhaps feel the ghost of General Cornwallis, who surrendered to the commander of the Continental Army—George Washington. Yorktown is just a short distance from colonial **Williamsburg,** located on a peninsula between the James and York rivers and home of our nation's second oldest university (William and Mary, founded 1693). Williamsburg needs no introduction as a tourist attraction, and the 173-acre historic area contains more than 100 gardens and greens and the largest restoration of eighteenth century public buildings and houses in the world.

Leaving Yorktown and entering Chesapeake Bay once again, passengers will be able to spot Mile Marker No. 1, which marks the beginning of the Intracoastal Waterway south. If your cruise calls at **Norfolk,** home of the U.S. naval fleets patrolling the Atlantic and Mediterranean, you can tour some interesting monuments. The port was founded by decree of King Charles II in 1682, but most of the colonial structures remaining date from the eighteenth century. However, you should not miss the General Douglas MacArthur Memorial or the Chrysler Museum. St. Paul's Church, built in 1739, still has a cannonball imbedded in one wall—courtesy of a British bombardment in 1776.

Cruising along the Cape Fear River and Myrtle Grove Sound, your vessel arrives at the port of **Wrightsville Beach,** which is just a hop from the Atlantic Ocean. Wrightsville Beach is a short drive from the lovely town of **Wilmington,** North Carolina, itself a leading port since the eighteenth century and full of restored antebellum homes. After a half day on the beach, your vessel will sail for Morehead City, N.C. for a tour of **Beaufort** located across the Newport River. This historic town was founded in 1709, and boasts some 25 homes dating from the Revolutionary War period as well as over 100 from the Civil War era. In Beaufort, passengers are treated to an escorted tour by members of the local historical society. Of special interest are Bell House (1876), the Third Courthouse and Apothecary (1796), and the Cemetery (1714).

Along the coast of South Carolina, your cruise may call first at **Bucksport** on the Waccamaw River. The town was founded by a Captain Henry Buck, a shipbuilder from Bucksport, Maine. The stretch from here through the Cape Romain National Wildlife Refuge is considered one of the most beautiful of the Intracoastal Waterway. Note, especially, the live oak trees covered in mistletoe along the Waccamaw River.

An entire day in elegant **Charleston** features a three-hour tour of the 780-acre historic district and includes visits to the 1809 Nathaniel

Russell House, Rainbow Row, the oldest theater in America (so they say), and the East and South Batterys along the waterfront. Charleston was settled by the English in 1670 and named in honor of Charles II. Before the Revolution, it was the largest and wealthiest port south of Philadelphia, but its magnificent public buildings and homes suffered greatly during the Civil War. Today, however, it is again the most famous and visited city in the south and proud of the eighteenth- and nineteenth-century structures that have been so lovingly restored by their owners. There are many, many beautiful homes open year-round to visitors, even more during the Festival of Houses in the spring (mid-March to mid-April), and the annual House and Garden tours held for three weeks in October.

South Carolina also has its **Beaufort,** first settled around 1562 by French Huguenots, but not officially founded until 1710. Beaufort is located at the end of a day's cruise along the Stono and Edisto rivers, St. Helena Sound, and through the Coosaw and Ashepoo rivers. Picturesque and beautifully preserved, the entire downtown area of Beaufort is listed on the National Historic Register and has been designated a National Historic Landmark. A three-hour tour of the area is available, highlighting the town's history and the fortunes made here in rice and indigo and the production of Sea Island cotton from the early eighteenth to mid-nineteenth centuries.

Leaving Beaufort via Port Royal Sound and Skull Creek, your vessel will dock at Hilton Head Plantation on **Hilton Head Island,** off the South Carolina coast. Here, you can explore one of the country's most famous resorts, home of the Heritage Golf Classic at the Harbor Town Golf Course. Check out the posh boutiques in Harbor Town Village, or catch a nearby taxi for a tour of the entire island.

From Hilton Head, your vessel will cruise across Caliboque Sound and up the Savannah River to historic **Savannah,** Georgia's oldest and most sophisticated city. Founded in 1733 on a high bluff overlooking the river, Savannah profited from astute urban planning as early as the eighteenth century. In the Central Historic District, more than 1000 structures have been restored in the past twenty-five years, including fine Georgian, Federal, Greek Revival, and Gothic Revival buildings. A Victorian Historic District, primarily residential, is now receiving the same care and attention. Self-guided tours of both areas are suggested by the local Visitors Center, and the Historic Savannah Foundation offers other tours featuring sights on the outskirts of the town. If your cruise begins or ends in Savannah, you will no doubt find yourself at the Rousakis Riverfront Plaza, but be sure to save some time for this lovely city.

Following the Georgian coastline south, cruise passengers can not miss the port of Brunswick and two of the so-called Golden Isles— Jekyll Island and St. Simons Island. **Brunswick** was a rival of Savannah during the nineteenth century, but has matured to just a quiet place with Victorian architecture, the gateway city to the two Golden Isles. **Jekyll Island** is famous for its Millionaires' Village, located between Riverview Drive and Old Village Boulevard. This was a chic colony of some of America's industrialist rich during the late nineteenth century. Most of those who bought land here for their private retreat are well-known in history books: the Rockefellers, McCormicks, Goodyears, Pulitzers, etc. The spacious homes were closed during World War II and later bought by the state of Georgia as a tourist attraction. The "cottages" can be seen on guided tours and are interesting for their social history, but hardly for their architectural style. **St. Simons Island** was a strategic spot during colonial times, as Fort Frederica protected English settlers along the Georgia coast. It is now a national monument and open to visitors. St. Simons Lighthouse and keeper's building are also interesting, as the latter now houses a Museum of Coastal History.

Fernandina Beach, on Amelia Island off Florida's Atlantic coast, is one of the first calls in the state of Florida, and a favorite for its colorful history. The beach is strategically located at the entrance to St. Mary's River and Cumberland Sound, and the flags of eight nations have flown here since the eighteenth century. During the Civil War, the beach was under Union control, and it flourished afterward. Many of the fine Queen Anne and Italianate residences in the historic district date from this period. Fernandina is just north of **Jacksonville,** one of the state's largest and most industrious cities. Located on the St. Johns river, the town was first called Cowford under British rule, but was renamed for Andrew Jackson when it became a U.S. possession. Jacksonville has Fort Caroline National Memorial, which dates from 1564–5, and an excellent Museum of Arts and Sciences.

Everyone loves **St. Augustine,** the oldest continuously occupied city in the United States. A permanent settlement was founded here in 1565 by Don Pedro Menendez de Aviles, on instructions from King Philip II, and existed under Spanish domination until 1821. Much of the center city is an historic district and a National Historic Landmark. At the end of the nineteenth century, St. Augustine became a winter resort, thanks to the labors of industrialist Henry Flagler, who built two large hostelries here and then bought a railroad to transport his guests to and from winter climes. Both luxury properties have been reborn: the former Hotel Ponce de Leon (1888) as Flagler College; and the former Alcazar Hotel (1889) as the Lightner Museum. Don't miss St. Augustine Cathedral (1797) and the Castillo de San Marcos National Monument (1672–96) and the city's oldest house.

Port Canaveral is famous for its proximity to the Kennedy Space Center, Disney World, and the new Epcot Center, and a two-day layover here certainly does the area justice. You can be a kid again or step into the twenty-first century and watch man against the moon all in the same breath.

From Stuart, you will cruise across the **Okeechobee Waterway** to Ft. Meyers on the Gulf of Mexico. Through this inland passage from the Atlantic Ocean, you will have an intimate view of south-central Florida and the people who work the cattle ranches, the citrus groves, and the sugar plantations. You'll pass through a number of quiet little towns as well as the St. Lucie Lock and Canal, across Lake Okeechobee (Seminole Indian for ''plenty big water'') and into the Caloosahatchee River at Moore Haven. At least, this is the route that American Cruise Lines offers. Once in **Ft. Meyers,** you can visit the Thomas A. Edison Museum, Sanibel and Captiva Islands (South Seas Plantation), and the Darling Wildlife Sanctuary. Whether Ft. Meyers is the beginning or the end of your cruise, linger a while and enjoy some of its fine attractions.

MEXICO

Our neighbors south-of-the-border extend their arms in welcome to *norteamericano* cruise passengers who come for a taste of the continual feast of colors, sights, and beautiful beaches. Mexico's western coastline is one of the most popular of all cruise destinations, especially for ships originating from southern California. The so-called Mexican Riviera stretches from Mazatlan to Acapulco and includes Puerto Vallarta and Zihuatanejo. If you don't delude yourself into expecting Puerto Vallarta to have the crazy chic of St. Tropez, or Acapulco to be as sophisticated and glamorous as Monte Carlo, then you will enjoy what this Riviera has to offer.

Sailing directly south from San Pedro, California, the port for Los Angeles, many cruise vessels call first at **Ensenada,** a peaceful little community just sixty-seven miles south of the California border, in Baja California (the lower peninsula that belongs to Mexico). Juan Rodriguez Cabrillo founded Ensenada in 1542. However, neither he nor Fray Junipero Serra (who founded San Diego) stayed, because they couldn't find fresh water in this beautiful, natural harbor. Today fresh water is found in underground wells, but this is still a frontier town with spectacular beaches and not much else—a pleasant but uninspiring cruise stop.

At the tip of Baja California are San Jose del Cabo and **Cabo San Lucas,** the latter more famous because the waters of the Sea of Cortes and the Pacific Ocean meet here. Sea lions frolic under nearby Los Arcos, natural rock arcades that are best viewed from small boats. Small cruise vessels simply sail by Cabo San Lucas and consider it seen, but others stop for a few hours for the small boat excursion to Los Arcos and a drink on the terrace of the Hyatt Hotel, which overlooks the Bay of Chileno. If you care to return someday, the fishing is considered some of the best in the world.

Mazatlan, one of the best harbors on Mexico's Pacific coastline, is noted for its shrimp industry, which feeds much of the U.S. market. Fishing here is also good, and marlin can be caught year-round. The fishing and the continual sunshine make Mazatlan a popular tourist town. Your shore tour will take you along the Olas Atlas section to the cathedral, Indian market, and outdoor cafes. You can watch high cliff-divers at Glorieta's Rocky Promontory, but it's more rewarding to shop for Indian handcrafts and Mexican silver. Or you can find your way to Las Gaviotas Beach and pay a visit to the new hotels that have grown up alongside this lovely stretch of the city. This is the perfect place for swimming and sunning.

Some people I know bought houses in a sleepy, slightly seedy little fishing village named **Puerto Vallarta** before it became fashionable; or shall I say "popular," since it's debatable whether or not this town has ever been "fashionable." Nonetheless, cruise brochures love to call it an "exquisite, picturesque seaside village." Don't expect too much, for aside from a few beaches and an area now known as "Gringo Gulch," Puerto Vallarta does not have a great deal to offer the quick visitor. There are some nice beaches in Puerto Vallarta, so plan to spend your time browsing, people-watching (both the swells and the indigents congregate in this town), and sunning. I thought the city tour was not worth my while or money, so don't feel guilty about passing it up. This is one of the many port calls you can do on your own and be the better for it.

While **Manzanillo** and its beautiful beaches are often the next port of call, **Zihuatanejo** is more interesting for its beaches and its similarity (although smaller) to Acapulco. As a town, it doesn't have much to offer except its five splendid beaches and a few nice restaurants. Shore excursions will take you to Ixtapa's sixteen-mile beach. The Mexican government has invested heavily in Ixtapa's future as a tourist attraction. The Palma Real Golf Club and some new hotels welcome you and help you relax in resort style. Other than that, what can one say but enjoy the scenery.

At last, **Acapulco.** A true resort. A port worthy of your time and a city with real bite to it. Acapulco is where even jetsetters take their honeymoons, not to mention brief getaway weekends. It has eternal sunshine, bikinis, no ties, siestas, nonlunches on the beach—whatever you like any time of the year. Although the official season runs from mid-December to the end of April, even Frank Sinatra has visited in the summer. And both the J. F. Kennedys and the Henry Kissingers spent their honeymoons here (albeit in private villas). If there is any real Riviera on the Mexican Pacific coast, this is it. One can play high or low here, either walking casually along "hotel row" or taking a tour to La Quebrada to watch divers plunge from a cliff 136 feet high into the sinister, swirling waters below. Acapulco is an exciting place with too many high-rise hotels, too-crowded beaches, too-expensive shops, and never a moment to spare for anyone.

If you go on an organized shore excursion, you will see the city and, perhaps, the only historic monument around, Fort San Diego, which was originally built in 1616 and rebuilt in the late eighteenth century after it was destroyed by an earthquake in 1776. Also here are a beautiful yacht club (where some 1968 Olympic events took place), a cathedral built in the 1930s, the west or older section of town that should become fashionable someday, a new convention/cultural center, and a public market. One sight not to miss is Las Brisas, overlooking Acapulco Bay, one of the world's most imaginative hotels. (You will most likely see the hotel jeeps, complete with fringed tops, buzzing all over town.) Some shore tours take you way out of town to the Acapulco Princess/Pierre Marques Hotel complex for lunch and swimming on the beach. This has become *the* place in town, and when you see the others you will understand why. The Princess/Pierre Marques has several restaurants and is full of action. It is very near the airport, so if you are planning your last few hours in Acapulco, remember this! Acapulco by night is exciting, as are most resort towns, but in my experience the taxi drivers here are experts in the art of *bandido*.

If your cruise ship spends two full days at port in Acapulco, you may be offered the opportunity to visit **Taxco,** the city of silver. Taxco is 145 miles straight up from Acapulco, along a narrow highway that might make you exceedingly nervous (it does everyone), but your attention will be diverted from time to time by the children along the side selling iguanas. It's all worth it, though, for Taxco is charming. Reportedly explored by Cortes (who noted the silver-mining potential), this cobblestoned, colonial town sits atop some rich silver mines, although more than two hundred shops furnish the town with approximately ninety percent of its income. Take a look at the Church of Santa Prisca and Casa Figueroa, the local art gallery and museum. There are also some interesting and vast caves in the area, Las Grutas de Cachuamilpa. Be certain to pack extra sweaters for the excursion to the caves; Taxco is 5700 feet above sea level, and the average temperature ranges only from sixty-six to seventy-six degrees.

The **Yucatan Peninsula** on the Atlantic coast of Mexico is a major tourist haven, for both its abundance of comfortable tourist facilities and its historical interest. This is the land of Mayan splendors. The best known and most remarkable ruin is **Chichen Itza.** For cruise passengers it's a three-hour drive from the port of **Cancun.** Chichen Itza is the chosen city of Kukulcan, the "Plumed Serpent," the incarnation of God who founded Mayapan as the civil center of the peninsula (while Chichen

Itza remained the religious center). Hundreds of structures here dot the more than six-square-mile complex that straddles the highway, the earliest buildings dating from the fifth century, and additional ruins (some not yet excavated) extend deep into the surrounding jungle. Most impressive is El Castillo, or the Pyramid of Kukulcan, which the Spanish used as a fortress. One of the many fascinations of this pyramid is the solar phenomenon that occurs during the vernal and autumnal equinoxes—the sun creates a shadowy serpent up its northeast side. Other points of interest in Chichen Itza include the ball court, the Temple of the Warriors, and the Well of Sacrifices. A tour to this ancient site makes for a long day (about eleven hours), but it is worth the effort.

If you prefer to visit an ancient Mayan city closer to the seashore, you will want to see **Tulum,** a short drive from Cancun. This walled fortress by the sea was first viewed in 1518 and rediscovered only in the mid-nineteenth century. Tulum is one of the most ancient cities in Mexico, but all that remains now is the tower (or Castillo) of Tulum, a pyramidal structure sitting atop a forty-foot bluff. Down below lies the crystal-blue Caribbean. You may just wish to enjoy the beautiful sea from one of the empty, sweeping beaches of Cancun, a resort that some say is the best in Mexico. Both the flora and fauna are lovely here, and the water is so shallow that you can walk out ''forever'' before you reach any noticeable undertow. The Caribbean's newest spa, Cancun means ''pot of gold'' in one of the many Mayan dialects. So true.

Two other Mexican calls in the Caribbean are **Cozumel** and **Playa del Carmen,** both popular for their fine beaches, excellent underwater diving opportunities, and resort atmosphere, not to mention terrific beach parties.

THE MISSISSIPPI RIVER

As the principal waterway in the United States, the Mississippi River has touched the lives of all Americans at one time or another. ''Ole Man River'' is one of our nation's most moving folk tunes. Tom Sawyer and Huck Finn of Hannibal are a part of every child's vocabulary early on. And many of us stumbled over the stinger ''Mississippi'' at some school spelling bee and then learned how to say it fast—backward. The river flows south some 2470 miles from northern Minnesota to the Gulf of Mexico, offering a historic venue for cruises and an unparalleled view for passengers of a way of life that has endured along its banks—sleepy river towns that are slightly behind the times, plantations that show us what wealth there was in the land, and cities that have become industrial centers but still retain the charm of yesteryear.

Thanks to the Delta Queen Steamboat Company, Mississippi River cruises are now available year-round on your choice of the only two overnight paddlewheel steamboats left in America. You can choose the venerable old lady named *Delta Queen,* who is listed in the Register of Historic Places, or her baby sister, the *Mississippi River,* launched in 1975 but already a legend. Most of the cruises originate from **New Orleans,** that romantic, much-fought-over city founded by the French in 1718 on the first high ground above the Mississippi Passes, about ninety-five miles upriver from the Gulf. New Orleans was poverty stricken and sparsely populated in 1811 when the first steamboat, named the *City of New Orleans,* was built in Pittsburgh and launched on her first trip downriver.

By 1840, some 100,000 people lived in New Orleans, and it was the second largest port in America. Just before the Civil War the number of steamboats at her miles-long terminus numbered at least a hundred. Today the city is still a busy and colorful port, famous for Mardi Gras, Bourbon Street jazz, the French Quarter, Garden District, and the new Superdome. Time is well spent here either before or after your steamboat cruise. Other major ports of embarkation on the Mississippi are Memphis, St. Louis, and St. Paul.

Cruising upriver on the lower half of the Mississippi, your first steamboat landing is **Nottoway Plantation,** built in 1859 by John Hampton Randolph. Renowned as the largest plantation home in the South, Nottoway has sixty-four rooms and boasts twenty-two enormous columns enhancing its Greek Revival and Italianate architecture! Steamboat passengers may tour the grounds and mansion from the docking at water's edge, enjoying views of the river and century-old live oak trees from the largest of Nottoway's two hundred windows.

At the river's 153-mile mark is **Oak Alley Plantation,** first settled in the early 1700s by a Frenchman who had the foresight to plant two rows of oak trees from the house to the river. When the steamboat ties up at the water's edge, you walk to the Greek Revival mansion, built in 1837, beneath an alley of 250-year-old oaks with Spanish moss dripping from their solid boughs. It's a truly wonderful experience, and if you close your eyes and breathe deeply, hoop-skirted Southern belles with velvet ribbons around their necks are stepping daintily down to greet you.

Another restored, antebellum-style plantation complex open to visitors is **Houmas House,** which is also approached from the river. (Perhaps you will recognize this house, for it has been in many television films and was the setting for *Hush, Hush, Sweet Charlotte.*) Named after an Indian tribe that once inhabited this spot, Houmas House commands a river view of several miles in both directions. The Greek Revival mansion dates from 1840, and from that year until the Civil War this 20,000-acre plantation was the foremost sugar producer in America.

Houmas was spared the ravages of famine and fighting during the war because its Irish owner declared British immunity—a ploy that worked! Under new ownership and management in the 1880s, the plantation flourished again, reaching a record production of twenty million tons of sugar in one year. But success was short-lived. By the end of the century, the land was parceled off and the house stood in disrepair. It was purchased by a New Orleans doctor in 1940, who devoted the last twenty-five years of his life to planting formal gardens and to restoring the house and furnishing it with museum-quality early Louisiana craftsmanship. A tour of this house and grounds is a real treat.

Baton Rouge, capital of Louisiana, is situated at the 230-mile mark of the lower Mississippi and named for the red post that once divided two Indian nations here. Founded in 1719, the city was the site of a Revolutionary War battle that did not even involve a colonist—it was strictly between the British and the Spanish (who had possession of this territory). Today this gracious Southern metropolis has wide avenues lined with former plantation homes, like the 1791 Magnolia Mound, now a museum of Federal-period furniture. Baton Rouge is also known for Louisiana State University, whose Rural Life Museum is a reconstructed plantation settlement, and the Old State Capitol that overlooks the river from a bluff. The original 1849 Gothic structure that stood here was burned by Union troops during the Civil War (accidentally, they say) and reconstructed in 1882.

The next call for the Delta Queen Steamboat Company is the sleepy river town of **St. Francisville,** Louisiana, which boasted half the millionaires in America during the cotton boom of the 1850s. Today, the luxury and splendor this region knew is recalled only in the restoration of once-thriving plantations, foremost of which are Rosedown and The Myrtles. Rosedown Home and Gardens were built in 1835 by a wealthy cotton planter and his wife, who spared neither money nor means to create a magnificent setting in the style of seventeenth-century France. The Myrtles was built in the early 1830s, and locals believe that the ghost of a former resident still roams the house. In the restoration, special care was given to the iron grillwork that surrounds a 100-foot veranda. Both these plantations are near Audubon state park and on the steamboat tour.

Natchez, Mississippi, lies at the 363-mile mark in the heart of the fertile Mississippi River delta. The antebellum homes here also reflect the wealth of early cotton planters who often used European architects and craftsmen. Many of the fine places here can still be visited because General Ulysses S. Grant spared Natchez Over The Hill (as it was called then) in his thrust south during the Civil War. Semiannual events in this gracious river town, founded in 1716, are the spring and fall Natchez Pilgrimage Cruises that bring passengers to view some of the more than 200 antebellum properties in the best seasons. Some of the highlights of these tours are Stanton Hall, occupying an entire block and patterned after an Irish ancestral home; Connelly's Tavern where the first American flag in Mississippi was raised in 1797; a lovely Georgian home named Rosalie; Longwood, looking just as the workers left it when war broke out; and D'Evereux, where the most elaborate balls in Natchez were said to have taken place.

Just seventy-three miles upriver is **Vicksburg,** site of the siege of 1863. To this day the citizens of Vicksburg refuse to celebrate the fourth of July, for on that day their ancestors surrendered to the Union Army that had surrounded the city for three solid months. This peaceful town has many memories, war memorials, and cemeteries. The Old Court House Museum, former headquarters of the Confederates, has touching memorabilia from the period—receipts from the sale of slaves, Confederate money and clothing, and photographs of Mississippi River steamboats. A few of the local homes that survived are also worth visiting, especially Cedar Grove with a cannonball still lodged in the parlor wall. For a change of pace, your tour may take you to a scale model of the entire Mississippi River system at the Waterways Experiment Station (operated by the U.S. Army Corps of Engineers).

Memphis, Tennessee, at the 736-mile mark on the lower Mississippi, was planned in 1818 and named after the ancient city on the Nile. Hernando DeSoto supposedly came through here in 1541, stopping only long enough to build some barges to cross the river. Memphis became an important port and agricultural center in the 1800s, and the world's largest cotton market was established here in 1873. Located on Cotton Row, the Memphis Cotton Exchange is still active and handles more than four million bales each year. Tours in Memphis include a visit to the Exchange and, when weather permits, to a cotton field and working cotton gin. It's also fun to visit the old Beale Street haunts of famous blues musicians W. C. Handy, Elvis Presley's mansion "Graceland," Schwab's famous Five and Dime, and the Chucalissa Indian Village and Museum.

At the mouth of the upper Mississippi is the quiet town of **Cairo,** Illinois, whose prosperity was tied to the steamboat trade. Cairo's dreams of a future more exciting than Chicago's were dashed by the southern extension of the Illinois Central Railroad in 1855. However, memories of a glorious past linger, with landmarks like the restored Magnolia Manor and Holiday Park to give us an indication of once-abundant wealth.

St. Louis, Missouri, at the 180-mile mark on the upper Mississippi, was second only to New Orleans in the days of steamboat packets; and as the historic Gateway to the West, St. Louis played host to thousands of famous and infamous settlers, traders, and trappers. Wagon trains bound for the west crowded the riverfront as pioneers formed some unusual alliances in their battle against the elements of the new frontier. Among enterprising Americans who made their homes in St.

Louis, at least for a while, were Abraham Lincoln and Charles Lindbergh, who christened his plane "The Spirit of St. Louis" in honor of the city whose business leaders believed in him. St. Louis has interesting buildings in all styles—from the much-photographed Gateway Arch on the riverfront to WPA projects and historic structures. The Old Courthouse was the scene of the notorious Dred Scott case, and the Anheuser-Busch Brewery is the largest in the world. The Jefferson Memorial has original documents relating to the Louisiana Purchase as well as some of Lindbergh's trophies commemorating his New York to Paris flight.

Everyone's favorite river town is still **Hannibal** (at the 308-mile mark on the upper Mississippi), where Tom Sawyer, Huck Finn, and Becky Thatcher played their pranks. The author of these escapades (Samuel Clemens) was born in nearby Florida, Missouri, but grew up in Hannibal, where the arrival of the steamboat was about the only event to raise the dust (or a few waves) on a somnolent summer's day. While still in his teens Clemens boarded a paddlewheeler en route to New Orleans, and a combined career of river pilot/writer—and Mark Twain was born. Shortly after he left, the railroad came to save Hannibal from extinction when riverboat traffic diminished after the Civil War. Any visit to Hannibal is strictly a do-it-yourself tour about the town, wandering along the street with the whitewashed fence, the Pilaster House with law office and drugstore, and the birthplace of Margaret Tobin (also known as the "Unsinkable" Molly Brown).

Nauvoo, Illinois, at the 375-mile mark on the upper Mississippi, was founded in 1839 by Joseph Smith and followers of the Church of the Latter-Day Saints (Mormons). But Smith and his disciples fled for their lives seven years later over a series of disputes with the non-Mormon community. However, they left behind some interesting Mormon-style buildings that have been restored by descendants of the original pilgrims. Nauvoo is also known for its fruit harvests, especially the vineyards that produce abundant native wine. And to enjoy with the wine, try some domestic "blue cheese."

As the Mississippi continues and your riverboat cruises upstream, **Dubuque,** Iowa, lies at the 579-mile mark, a commercial city in America's heartland. An air-conditioned motorcoach from the docking site takes passengers to visit the quiet backwater of **Galena,** known for its quaint atmosphere and its nineteenth-century architecture. The tour features a walk through the town's antique and specialty shops and the former home of Ulysses S. Grant, our eighteenth president.

Prairie Du Chien, Wisconsin, is near the meeting of the Mississippi and Wisconsin rivers, where Indians are believed to have lived for some ten thousand years. The many tribes included the Woodland, Fox, Sauk, and Winnebago, and the Hopewell culture built huge burial mounds about two thousand years ago. The settlers built a fort on top of one of the mounds in 1812. It was burned and replaced by Fort Crawford in 1816, which still remains. Prairie du Chien was a thriving frontier settlement in 1826 when Hercules Dousman arrived as a confidential agent for John Jacob Astor, the American Fur Company millionaire. The Dousman family became rich from fur trading and built an enormous mansion named Villa Louis on one of the Indian burial mounds. This restored villa is a showplace of Victorian architecture and furnishings. You can also visit the original Astor Fur Warehouse and restored Fort Crawford, complete with hospital.

At one time, **LaCrosse,** Wisconsin, claimed the largest transportation organization on the upper Mississippi—with two hundred steamboats landing a month. Three rivers meet here: the Mississippi, the Black, and the La Crosse. A stop at Grandad Bluff, 675 feet above the city, offers a view of three states: Wisconsin, Minnesota, and Iowa.

At **Wabasha,** Minnesota, in unspoiled wilderness, the two *Queens* dock at Read's Landing. Steamboats brought supplies up to this logging and fur-trading center in the early 1800s and took log rafts back down the Mississippi. The Wabasha Country Museum chronicles the regional history of steamboats and rafts, and if you're interested in a view of Sitting Bull's peace pipe, pay a visit to the Suilman Antique Museum. Visitors can enjoy a tour of the Anderson House Hotel as well, which opened in 1856 and to this day warms guests' beds with hot bricks. Wabasha is also the home of the Nelson Cheese Factory, where sampling is part of the tour.

Minneapolis/St. Paul, the twin cities on the upper Mississippi, mark the 839th mile and the final point of navigation on the river and the end of your steamboat cruise. In the old days, ox carts provided transit from this point northward, with as many as five hundred wagons per caravan shuttling between the steamboat landing and Fort Garry, which is now Winnipeg, Manitoba. The city of St. Paul grew up around the landing while Minneapolis blossomed next door. Twin City attractions include the Guthrie Theatre; a 36-foot-high onyx Indian statue; Fort Snelling, established in 1825 by the U.S. cavalry; the home of the Betty Crocker testing kitchens; the Walker Art Center; and Minnehaha Falls.

THE NORTHEAST PASSAGE

From New York to Montreal, summer cruises are popular along the northeast coastline and through the passage of the St. Lawrence and Saguenay rivers. This is the so-called Northeast Passage, through which you will enjoy a wealth of historical sights. A special charm penetrates cruises in this section of North America—the beauty of the scenery and the flavor of these seafaring people. Along the way you will sail by centuries of our maritime heritage, from New York's South Street Seaport to Mystic, Connecticut, where America's last wooden whaleship, the *Charles W. Morgan,* lies in state. You may also see old sea captain's houses in Stonington, Connecticut, and the Bath Marine Museum, built along the broad waters of the Kennebec River of Maine.

One of the first islands to view after leaving New York is **Martha's Vineyard,** Massachusetts, which was settled in 1642 by Thomas Mayhew (who bought it for forty pounds). Edgartown, the Vineyard's first port and a major whaling center in the eighteenth and nineteenth centuries, still boasts many fine old mansions built by wealthy sea captains and ship owners. Whaling was also important to the development of nearby **Nantucket,** called affectionately by locals the "Little Gray Lady." Nantucketers caught their first whale in 1672, and the Whaling Museum on Broad Street declares this island was once the center of the world's whaling industry. Few cruise vessels stop here, so it is a treat if you can explore the town's cobblestone streets and old dwellings that remain much as they were 150 years ago. The island is a testimonial to historic preservation, and many of the finely restored buildings are open to the public. Herman Melville's whaling novel, *Moby Dick,* devotes an entire chapter to the island and its inhabitants.

Newport, Rhode Island, renowned as the playground of the ostentatious rich in the late nineteenth century, was once the most prosperous seaport on the eastern coastline. Now it is the yachting capital of the Atlantic, with some of the most prestigious races either starting or ending there, including the Newport to Bermuda (even years) and the Annapolis to Newport (odd years). It was also home of the famous America's Cup until Dennis Connor recaptured the trophy from Australia and will have nothing to do with Newport since he feels the Eastern Establishment snubbed him. Aside from the glittering mansions and the beautiful boats, Newport is noted for some fine eighteenth-century public buildings and its more than 100 colonial homes that have been refurbished and made available for rental. Cruise passengers should not miss the superb 1726 Trinity Church (called a matchless reminder of Colonial America), and the 1763 Touro Synagogue (the country's first), commissioned by Sephardic Jews from Portugal and designed in Georgian style by local architect Peter Harrison. The glamorous mansions of the formerly filthy rich along Bellevue Avenue are now open to the public and worth a visit, as is the distinctive Newport Casino, which houses the Tennis Hall of Fame. If you are lucky, you may be able to catch a tennis or croquet tournament on its lovely grass courts.

To call at **Boston** Harbor and Massachusetts Bay is to follow the route of the early European explorers to the New World. The first European settlement here was at Weymouth in 1623. In addition to the many interesting and historic places within the old city, Boston's waterfront has undergone an impressive revitalization and should be the starting point of your walking tour. And ferry boats will take you from Long Wharf to some of the more than thirty islands that dot the harbor. If you like sailing ships, don't forget "Old Ironsides," the *USS Constitution,* that was built in Boston between 1794 and 1797. The restored version graces the waterfront near the museum. There is something for everyone in Boston—excellent eateries, museums, universities, and historic sites. The one-and-a-half-mile Freedom Trail links landmarks to capture the essence of early American history. This and other well-known walks make it impossible to be blase about America, at least when in Boston.

Bar Harbor lies on the east coast of Mount Desert Island, off the rockbound coast of Maine. During the mid-nineteenth century Bar Harbor was an enclave of the very wealthy, and despite a devastating fire after World War II, some of the elegant summer cottages still exist. One prime example, the former wood and stone mansion of the late Nelson Rockefeller, was sold a few years ago for about one million dollars to a member of the Ford Motor Company family. However, Bar Harbor is no Newport; today the island is known more for Acadia National Park, with views from Cadillac Mountain. The island's succulent lobsters and clams often find their way into local bakes.

Halifax is Nova Scotia's capital and the largest city in the Maritime Provinces. Lord Cornwallis founded the city in 1749 and built the Citadel to guard against the French on Cape Breton Island at Louisburg. Once the mightiest fortress in British North America, the Citadel still dominates the capital but is now a park with military, marine, and provincial museums. The only shots fired from the Citadel these days are from the cannon at noontime, a well-preserved tradition. Halifax has a spectacular harbor, and water tours aboard the *Bluenose II* are available (but the best overall view is still from the fortress). A large redevelopment plan to save the city's lovely eighteenth- and nineteenth-century structures from destruction began in the early 1960s. Even the eighteen-acre Public Gardens on Spring Garden Road (originally laid out in 1753) have been preserved. Another interesting park is Point Pleasant, the only spot in North America where Scottish heather grows wild. Apparently the seeds were spread when British sailors shook their mattresses out long ago.

Off the coasts of Nova Scotia and New Brunswick, in the Gulf of the St. Lawrence, is **Prince Edward Island,** a garden province that explorer Jacques Cartier in 1534 called "the fairest land 'tis possible to see." Its capital, a popular cruise call, is **Charlottetown,** named after the consort of England's King George III. Charlottetown has great charm and an atmosphere reminiscent of Victoria, a city on Canada's western coast. In fact, Victoria Park overlooks Charlottetown's harbor and is the site of Fort Edward, whose six-gun battery protects the harbor's entrance. Province House sheltered the Fathers of Confederation when they met in 1864 to plan the union of British North America and Canada. Visit the more contemporary home of Green Gables in Cavendish (on the island's north shore), which was the setting for the novel *Anne of Green Gables,* and stop at the post office nearby, the most popular on Prince Edward Island.

Gaspe Peninsula reaches out into the Gulf of the St. Lawrence at the southeast extremity of the Province of Quebec. When Champlain landed here, it was called Gachepe or Land's End by the local Indian tribe, the Micmacs. Gaspe is a rugged peninsula, with centuries-old, twelve-foot fir trees and streams filled with Atlantic salmon that have been spawning here for thousands of years. Take an excursion to nearby **Perce,** known for its incredible natural beauty, and for Perce Rock where explorer Cartier anchored his three small ships in 1534. A small boat will take you out two miles to Bonaventure Island, a wildlife sanctuary where you can tour bird colonies with a naturalist and see thousands of gannets, gulls, puffins, and kittiwakes nestling in the cliffs.

The *piece de resistance*—the **Saguenay River,** sinuous arm of the St. Lawrence, flows 450 miles from Lake Saint John and boasts sheer granite gorges that rise to 1500 feet. This is one of the most spectacular waterways in the world. You won't forget the sight of whales feeding here, where the Saguenay and St. Lawrence rivers come together. From May through November, they surge upon this spot and often stay on the surface long enough for good photographs. A sail along the fjordlike Saguenay River will give you some feeling for what fur traders, explorers, and missionaries experienced centuries before.

Quebec City, perched high above the majestic St. Lawrence, is often called the Gibraltar of North America; its place in history was forged by its natural assets. The city, founded in 1608 by Samuel de Champlain, is situated along an eight-mile plateau atop solid rock. The highest point, some 360 feet above the river, is Cap Diamant, site of the famed Citadel. The only walled city in North America, Quebec has never lost its French heritage and lifestyle. It is a popular tourist center that is best explored on foot or by *caleches,* colorful horse-drawn carriages. Romance and drama come to life in this delightful old town whose seventeenth- and eighteenth-century buildings have been lovingly restored. Take a look at Place d'Armes, where settlers and Indian traders used to meet. And don't miss Le Chateau Frontenac facing the square—a beautiful old hotel where Roosevelt, Churchill, and Mac-Kenzie King met to discuss strategy during World War II. Off Place d'Armes are streets lined with historic houses, and the sites of the first girls' school in North America and the first Anglican cathedral constructed outside the British Isles. You can also see the Continent's oldest house of worship—Notre Dame des Victoires, built in 1688. Recapture even more history from Dufferin Terrace, two hundred feet above the waterway, where Champlain built his fort in 1620; the views are spectacular on a clear day.

Quebec is divided into an upper and lower town. Dufferin Terrace is part of the upper town, the historic center for administration and defense. The old town, along the waterfront, functioned primarily as a post for fur trading and other commercial enterprises. Quebec's heart is crowded with so many restored historic dwellings, museums, shops, and fine restaurants that even experienced travelers are surprised and delighted.

Montreal, Canada's chief port and richest cultural center, is located around an island at the junction of three bodies of water. This was such a natural point of interchange that when Cartier came upon it in 1535 he found a community of some 3500 Indians living there. These Indians were soon scattered by French settlers, explorers, and missionaries who were determined to make this site their Gateway to the West. Doubtless they would be very pleased to know that they founded the second largest French-speaking city in the world. Montreal's oldest landmark, Place Royale, is said to have been named by Champlain. The foundations of the city laid here in 1642 were given the name Ville Marie. The old section also boasts a Place d'Armes, rich with history and memories and with beautiful old streets leading away from it. In the eastern part of the old city are lovely homes, open squares, and an 1834 hotel where Charles Dickens once stayed. Many of these eighteenth-century dwellings have had French, English, and American occupants during the city's varied history.

Modern Montreal is just as much fun to explore. The heart of the city, Centre Town, has shopping streets, business districts, cafes and restaurants, and fine hotels. Montreal's underground system is also worthy of attention—a city in itself. Fascinating tours around the island take you to the former Olympic village and along the banks of the St. Lawrence. Of special note is a view of St. Lambert Lock of the St. Lawrence Seaway, a 9500-mile network of navigable waters extending into the body of this continent.

THE OHIO RIVER

The Ohio River flows almost one thousand miles from its source in Pittsburgh, Pennsylvania, to its confluence with the Mississippi River at Cairo, Illinois. Like the Mississippi, the Ohio River was discovered and explored by the French, and many of its early settlers came from the not-so-distant east. The Ohio has played its role in the story of America: the last battle of the Revolutionary War was fought on its banks in Wheeling, West Virginia, and Ulysses S. Grant, general and president, was born near the shore in Point Pleasant, Ohio. The first steamboat, built in 1811 in Pittsburgh and named the *City of New Orleans,* paddled the entire length of the Ohio River.

Evansville and **New Harmony,** Indiana, are located near the 795-mile mark on the Ohio River. Evansville was established in 1812 when Hugh McCarey crossed the river so his wife could visit her family. The landing grew into a large shipping center for coal, oil, and lumber. In the late 1800s this area became known as Lincoln Land, and a Lincoln Heritage Trail winds through Kentucky, Indiana, and Illinois, tracing the life of our sixteenth president. Nearby New Harmony was settled in 1814 by a group of dissident Lutherans hoping to build a perfectly planned community. Your tour will take you to some restored communal Harmony houses as well as the Labyrinth, an elaborate shrubbery maze that leads to a small temple symbolizing harmony.

The home of beautiful women, bluegrass, the Kentucky Derby, and the best bourbon in the south—**Louisville,** Kentucky—is at the 603-mile mark on the Ohio River. The city is at its best during Derby Week, the first part of May, when the southern belles come out and Churchill Downs is filled with spectators watching the famous "Run for the Roses." A special cruise is offered the first week in May, but if you miss it, some of the excitement and atmosphere can be found in the Churchill Downs Museum. Other sights include the Thomas Jefferson-style Manor House, built around 1810, which stands as the only example of his design west of the Alleghenies, and Bakery Square where an inner-city restoration now holds thirty shops.

Madison, Indiana, is considered the finest example of a typical American town. The town was laid out in 1810, and by the middle 1800s was the largest city in Indiana. Jenny Lind performed in the local pork house (which apparently surprised her). The town today is interesting; the many restored buildings reflect the Federal era, the Regency period, the classic Revival style, and the Americanized Italian villa. Many of the restored and furnished homes are open to the public for a do-it-yourself tour.

Located on the 470-mile mark of the Ohio River, **Cincinnati,** Ohio, is home to the Delta Queen Steamboat Company and a major industrial center of the Midwest. Located here are steel mills, machine-tool plants, and the bases of many leading consumer products as well as the Taft Museum, a well-known zoo, and the Cincinnati Reds. The first suspension bridge to span the Ohio River, completed in 1867, connects Cincinnati with Covington, Kentucky.

Ripley, Ohio, was a major station on the Underground Railroad for four decades prior to the Civil War, although it was considered primarily a quiet river town noted for the breeding of fine draft horses. Ripley citizens now breed Arabian horses for distinguished sportsmen. Visitors to Rankin House learn that the Reverend John Rankin sheltered more than two thousand escaped slaves and helped them find routes north. You will follow in the footsteps of Harriet Beecher Stowe who visited Rankin in 1851. Upon hearing the story of Eliza Hariss' midnight river crossing on ice floes, Stowe wrote the book that inflamed the nation, *Uncle Tom's Cabin.*

Gallipolis, Ohio, is located at the 270-mile mark on the Ohio River. The town was settled by a group of Frenchmen, almost five hundred strong, who crossed the Atlantic in 1789 for this very purpose. Much of the town's French heritage remains. The Gallipolis City Park houses the first log cabins built here. Ouc House Tavern, now restored, was the center of village social life and boasted a visit by the Marquis de Lafayette in 1825. Crafts passed down by the French settlers are still taught in the schools, and your city tour includes a visit to Bob Evans Farm, which covers over one thousand acres near Rio Grande and offers outdoor recreation activities.

Pittsburgh, Pennsylvania, is located at the junction of the Monongahela, Allegheny, and Ohio rivers and became important as early as 1758 as a strategic spot for exploration of the West. Fort Pitt was built by the British in 1764 and named for William Pitt, then prime minister. Pittsburgh flourished and steamboats were familiar sights here for transporting wheat, rye, barley, flour, and whiskey to other river ports as far south as New Orleans.

Today's Pittsburgh is no longer the smoky, polluted city it was, due to an ambitious urban renewal program during the last three decades. Visitors will enjoy touring the Fort Pitt Blockhouse, the Fort Pitt Museum, the Carnegie Museum, the Duquesne Incline, and many arts events. Left off of the itineraries of the Delta Queen Steamboat Company for a few years, Pittsburgh seems to have returned to favor.

THE PANAMA CANAL

The approximately eight-hour transit of the Panama Canal is a cruise highlight for passengers sailing between Pacific and Atlantic ports. In addition to lush tropical scenery and exciting historical commentary by a shipboard lecturer, the passage of this fifty-mile "big ditch" will take you through one of the largest man-made bodies of water in the world, the island-studded 166-square-mile Gatun Lake. The Panama Canal was opened to commercial ship traffic in 1914, just ten years after the United States began serious construction of the canal, and almost four centuries after King Charles V of Spain ordered a survey (in 1524) to determine a possible canal route. The 51.2-mile waterway is a commercial enterprise although it was not structured to actually turn a profit—just break even. Tolls are based on vessel size and cargo, and revenues are sensitive to the world economy. For the past few years, the running of the canal has been somewhat of a mess and many cruise lines have stayed away, but the prognosis for Panama's political future has improved and so has the popularity of canal transits. One result of the recent ordeal with Noriega is that few (if any) cruise vessels still fly the Panamanian flag—the Bahamas have become the country of registry most preferred.

Building the canal was a great human achievement that involved more than just American engineering genius and administrative skill. The problems with sanitation brought about the solution to some monumental public health problems stemming from foul water and causing the rapid spread of malaria. If your vessel passes from the Atlantic or Caribbean side into the Pacific, you will enter the channel at **Limon Bay** at Cristobal breakwater, just before the Gatun locks and lake. One of the most interesting portions of the trip is **Gaillard Cut,** an eight-mile channel through solid rock that got its present name from the engineer in charge. It is often said that Gaillard Cut, more than any other section of the canal, gives the impression of an enormous man-made ditch. Which is just what it is. At the south end of Gaillard Cut are the Miguel and Miraflores locks, the Canal Zone city of **Balboa,** and the Pacific Ocean. Of course, if your ship is traveling from north to south, you will have to read this article backward, but either way, passage of the Panama Canal is an exciting experience. It is possible to experience the transit of the Panama Canal in less than a two-week cruise. And a partial transit is just as exciting, according to the success of *Regent Star* and *Regent Sun* from Montego Bay. The vessels enter Gatun Lock in the morning while on-board lecturers describe the history of the canal. Following a cruise around Gatun Lake, the ships transit through the lock again and return to the Atlantic side.

THE FAR EAST

CHINA

That the world's most populous and intriguing country has been a favored destination for cruise vessels and their passengers is not difficult to understand. The first cruise passengers to visit China in recent times were aboard the *France* in 1974, but the ship docked in Hong Kong harbor, and passengers took the train from Kowloon to Canton for a three-day visit. Two years later groups from both the *Rotterdam* and *Queen Elizabeth 2* followed the same route.

China cruises, aboard such comfortable vessels as those in the Royal Viking, Royal Cruise, and Princess fleets, and Ocean Pearl were very popular when this book was last revised, but everything changed after June 1989 and the sad events in Tien' An Men Square. Perhaps the "Chinese showdown" was just an excuse for the ship lines as passengers were dwindling anyway; vessels were diverted quickly from their published itineraries and sent to other exotic places around the Far East. Of the companies mentioned above, only Ocean Pearl is returning to Chinese ports in 1990; others feel the climate is still a bit uncertain and have no plans for China cruises until perhaps late 1991.

In February 1977, I was aboard the Greek vessel *Danae* as she made cruiseship history by sailing up the Pearl River in the dead of night to dock in Whampoa, the port of **Guangzhou** (Canton). The *Danae* was the first Western passenger ship in twenty-seven years to dock at a People's Republic of China port. Today, in addition to frequent cruise calls, there is twice-daily hydrofoil service from Hong Kong to the port of Whampoa, about a forty-five-minute dusty but fascinating ride from Guangzhou.

At first glance, Guangzhou, with its 3 million inhabitants, looked like a drab, gray version of neighboring Hong Kong. As my initial reaction faded, a sense of the city's character began to appear. This old city, dating from about the third century B.C., has been a center for foreign commerce for more than 2000 years. The Portuguese, the first foreigners to appear in this area, arrived in 1514. By 1557 they had received permission to settle Macau—a province they still occupy (although the Chinese have managed the politics for some years). By the 1860s foreign traders controlled Guangzhou from the Shamian island on the Pearl River in the heart of the city, and remained there until 1949. You will pass by this rather forlorn-looking island many times in your travels about the city. Its once-bulging warehouses and churches have been converted to factories.

Tours of Guangzhou are rather standard and under the control of Luxingshe (China International Travel Service or C.I.T.S.). Visits will be made to the zoo, the largest in China, to see the giant pandas and the aviary, and to Yuexia Park with its artificial lakes and Zhenhai Tower. The tower, constructed in 1380, has a fine view of the city and houses a pottery museum. It is also a good spot to observe the local residents. You will also visit a factory or two, sip tea with the approved spokesperson, and be expected to ask questions about production, birth control, and life in China. Lastly, you will be allowed to peer through the iron gate at the Dr. Sun Yat-sen Memorial, dedicated to the "father of the Chinese revolution in 1911." He was born in Guangzhou and founded the Kuomintang or Nationalist party there in 1923.

If you are spending a few days in Guangzhou, you will most likely be accommodated at one of the glamorous new hotels—no longer at the Tung Fang (Dongfang) Hotel, which has huge, old-fashioned rooms, broad red-carpeted stairways, and lumpy beds that have mosquito-netting drawn about them each evening. The Tung Fang also has a cavernous dining room where Welcoming Banquets are often held. The Tung Fang is across from a theater, where Chinese opera and acrobatics are performed, and the Canton Trade Fair exhibition halls. If your visit coincides with one of the semiannual fairs (mid-April to mid-May and mid-October to mid-November), by all means request permission of your guides to visit. The fair is China's impressive display to the world of her more than 40,000 products—rooms and rooms of bicycles with the brand name Flying Cloud, sewing machines, sneakers lining four walls, machinery, natural resources, synthetics, and silks. Unfortunately, as a tourist, you cannot buy at the fair. Your shopping must be done either at the local Friendship Store or department store. Guangzhou also has a nice antique shop, but the guides again must be persuaded to let you stop here. While many of the items are what I would call "antiqued" rather than antique, the shop has some charming mementos.

The most famous restaurant for tourists in Guangzhou is the Ban Xi (also spelled Pan Hsi), a series of old tea houses connected by zigzagging bridges around and across an ornamental lake. Ban Xi is known for its *dim sum*, or little dumplings, and seems to serve an endless variety. One guide told me gleefully of a Japanese who dined there every day for a week and still did not exhaust the menu. If you think China is a classless society, your thoughts will fly away at the Ban Xi. The pavilions cater to different clientele—workers in one area, party members in another, while foreigners are served in a new, two-story pavilion overlooking a lake. As in all Chinese banquets, a sweet and a fiery wine for toasts, beer, and orange soda are the refreshments, followed by tea. But the desserts here are the best—especially the little cakes filled with chestnut puree and dusted with sesame seeds. A takeout service is just to the side of the entry hall.

Everything that has ever been written about **Shanghai** must be true, for this is one of the world's most fascinating cities. While today's Shanghai is a far cry from the notorious, bad old days of the 1930s and 1940s when sailors were "shanghaied," China's largest city and port has lost none of her excitement. Her eleven million or so inhabitants (who own and ride some two million bicycles) spread themselves out along the Huangpu, or Yellow River, while the mighty Yangtze is just twelve miles upstream. Shanghai is still the center of China's trade and industry—a role that began with the Treaty of Nanking, which granted the British certain territorial trading rights in 1840. From then until the 1940s, the foreign communities lived in large mansions encircled and protected by their concessions (Shanghai International Settlement). So it is not surprising that the Chinese Communist party was founded in Shanghai in 1921 by, among others, a young student named Mao Tse-tung.

Because Shanghai has seen ships come from all over the world with goods and people, it has always been China's most cosmopolitan city. Shops are full of pretty things. Young girls wear colored ribbons in their hair and flowered blouses beneath their Mao jackets (which are really Sun Yat-sen suits). Couples hold hands in public and smile as you pass by. Your cruise vessel docks within sight of the Bund, that wide boulevard along the water's edge with handsome European-style buildings. From the deck of your ship you will recognize the former Palace Hotel (now called Peace) with its bronze-green roof and pointed tower. Once the most palatial hotel in the East (and owned by a prominent British family), it carries on as a survivor of the past, with old-fashioned rooms and atmosphere. Pay this place a visit if only to look at the sign that says "Ping Pong Room" (next to the Barber Shop). The coffee shop serves real coffee and cakes plus some fantastic-looking and intriguingly named cocktails that I did not try. The eighth-floor dining room has a great view of the harbor. Peek in next door at the banquet rooms, where high-level meetings are held.

Other buildings along the Bund once housed foreign banks and trading companies. The Bank of China now has the large building next to the Peace Hotel, and farther down is the Customs House whose 100-foot clock tower chimes "East is Red" at least every hour. Behind the Bund is the real Shanghai, with narrow, winding alleys lined with low houses—tile roofs curving up at the corners—built around mysterious-looking courtyards. This is the Shanghai to explore, and you're perfectly safe to do so at all hours (although the city locks up early in the evening). Your ship is so convenient to the city that you can walk up to the Bund in a few minutes or call a taxi from the guard house (if you know where you are going and can speak a little Chinese). Walk along the Bund in the early morning when thousands gather to do their Tai-chi exercises. In the evening musical instruments and singing can be heard floating over the river. My favorite memories of Shanghai are of just standing along the Bund embankment, surrounded by curious but friendly Chinese, watching the parade of boats in the harbor.

Your organized tour of Shanghai will include a factory or two, a school or Children's Palace, and the Yu Yuan (Mandarin's Garden), which was built from 1559 to 1577 for Pan Yuntuan, an official of the Ming Dynasty. Although always very crowded, the garden is worth your time and is a preview of the wonderful imperial gardens you will probably visit in Suzhou (Soochow). At the restored Temple of the Jade

Buddha, or Yu Fo Si, you will encounter large groups of devout Overseas Chinese (Chinese who do not live in mainland China). Shopping
in Shanghai is, to me, the most fun of any city in China not only because of the variety of tempting and inexpensive gifts but also because
the clerks are so friendly and helpful. The best place to shop is the
Number One Department Store, the largest in the country, just around
the corner from the Guoji or International Hotel. This store has floors
and floors of jade, jewelry, bamboo flutes, sandalwood fans, and other
Oriental treasures. On the ground floor, among household items of the
cheapest quality, I found some wonderful, cream-filled vanilla cookies
for a few cents a pound. At a store next to the Friendship Hotel a dozen
hand-embroidered linen handkerchiefs cost but a few dollars. A friend
bought some lovely chopsticks, but we had to draw pictures of rice
bowls and the like to get our point across. And, down on the Bund
where the British Embassy used to be is the state-managed Friendship
Store, with glorious items from expensive rugs to T-shirts with the simple character that says "Shanghai."

The **Yangtze River** has become one of China's major tourist attractions, so Abercrombie & Kent have chartered the 68-passenger *Bashan* (formerly under exclusive Lindblad Travel contract) for five-night
cruises between Chongqing and Yichang, which can be booked on a
cruise-only basis or as part of an 18-day comprehensive A&K China
Tour. The *Bashan* was constructed in 1985 for the deluxe market.

The upstream voyage begins in Shanghai, along the Huangpu River
to **Wusong,** where the Yangtze River begins. The first night and following day are spent at **Zhenjiang** in Jiangsu Province, where ancient temples are located on islands in the river or up on hills overlooking them.
Opposite Zhenjiang on the north bank is the delightful city of **Yang-
zhou,** full of gardens and temples as well as some of China's most
famous handicraft and art workshops. A full day of sightseeing is scheduled for the city of **Nanjing,** famous for its Dr. Sun Yat-sen Mausoleum, the Nanjing Museum, and the Yangtze River Bridge. Nearby,
you can visit Ming Tombs whose sacred ways are lined with huge stone
statues of animals.

An entire day is spent cruising through Anhui Province, enjoying
the peace and quiet of the vessel and the passing scenery of small towns
and bustling markets. A late afternoon arrival at **Jiujiang** allows time
for a stroll. The following morning means a drive to Guling at the top
of **Mt. Lushan,** one of China's most renowned resort areas. Here, you
can visit the Lushan Botanical Garden, the Immortal's Grotto, Floral
Path, and generally absorb the mountain scenery.

Wuhan, one of China's most important shipping hubs, lies at the
confluence of the Yangtze and its largest tributary, the Han River.

Sightseeing tours are scheduled for each of the city's three sectors: Wuchang, Hanyang, and Hankou. In contrast, **Yueyang** is celebrated for its lovely Dongting Lake, which has been the subject of numerous Chinese poems and paintings. Following a day visiting **Shashi** and **Jingzhou,** your vessel arrives early the next morning at **Yichang.** Here, you will see the mammoth Gezhouba hydroelectric power dam and ancient sites around the city, before the *piece de resistance* of the Yangtze River. This is the spectacular cruise through Three Gorges, one of the most memorable stretches of river scenery in the world.

After a short tour of **Wanxi** in Sichuan Province the next morning, the vessel sails for **Shibao Block** and another highlight of the cruise. This tiny rural town has narrow streets and very friendly folk. You can visit the nine-story pavilion in the center, before climbing up to the ancient temple at the top of a sheer cliff for a view of the Yangtze and surrounding region.

Chongqing is located on a rocky promontory at the confluence of the Yangtze and Jialing rivers. With its traditional atmosphere of a Chinese city, it is a fitting finale to this wonderful cruise up the Yangtze River. (Note: the one-week sailings transport you between Wuhan and Chongqing, considered the most scenic stretch.)

Guilin (formerly Kweilin) is located in the southwestern section of China, and many travelers consider it one of the most beautiful spots in the world. A bit off the beaten track, it is situated in a valley on the Li River and reachable from the major gateways by air—although misty weather often means delayed flights. However, if you have time for a two-day stopover it may be the highlight of your China tour as the scenery is spectacular. It is rather like a gentle cruise through an ancient Chinese painting.

Xian has become another side trip worthy of effort, for it is here that a vast imperial tomb was discovered in 1974 to contain a veritable army of terra cotta soldiers and horses that had lain buried for at least 2000 years. It is known as the longest graveyard in the world, although only about 6000 of the estimated 65,000 figures have been unearthed to date. Picture taking is forbidden, alas, but there are plenty of publications on the subject available back home.

Tianjin (Tientsin) is China's third largest city—after Peking and Shanghai—and like them is under direct control of the central government. The city possesses a fine harbor, built during the Japanese occupation of 1937 to 1945, which is often the getaway for cruise passengers to the North China Plain.

An important industrial center, the city is home of the famous Tientsin carpet, said to have originated in 200 B.C. Some eight major factories produce about 150,000 square yards of carpet each per year, and no foreign visitor departs this city without a tour of the Number One Carpet factory, employing more than 1400 people. This is the most interesting factory tour in China, for it allows you to follow the production of a carpet from beginning to end and justifies the price all the more. (If you plan to buy a carpet here, advise your guide. You may be able to purchase one at the factory, or you may be directed to a Friendship Store.) Tianjin also has a fine zoo, an antique shop (highly overpriced), several new and very comfortable western-style hotels. The seventy-four-mile trip to Peking takes about one and a half hours on the train. The trip is a great adventure, especially if you are required to set your alarm for 4 a.m. and 5 a.m., as I was, to make the connection.

The center of **Beijing** (Peking) is Tien' An Men Square, an area that covers almost one hundred acres and accommodates as many as a million people for the May Day festivities. Chances are your first view of Beijing will be from this square, which has the Monument to the People's Heroes in the center. Standing in this vast area, one senses the continuity of China through all her warring periods and revolution. Bounding the northern end of the square is Tien' An Men, or the Gate of Heavenly Peace, whose five passages lead across five marble bridges to five gateways and the Imperial or Old Forbidden City. On the western side is the Great Hall of the People, where the National People's Congress meets and visiting dignitaries are honored in the 5000-seat banqueting hall. On the east end is a large building housing the Museum of the Revolution (in the left wing) and the Museum of Chinese Hichay (in the right wing). But the most impressive structure is the Chairman Mao Tse-tung Memorial Hall, completed in November 1977 after only ten months' construction time. If you are in luck, the Memorial Hall may be open and the Chairman able to receive visitors—leave all belongings on the tour bus and file silently by.

All touring in Beijing is, of course, under the direction of the C.I.T.S., which has taken Chinese interests into consideration when planning your activities. Fortunately, excursions are confined to exciting historical monuments and you are free from the obligations of visiting hospitals, schools, factories, and the like. A half-day is set aside for touring the Temple of Heaven (Tien Tan) and the Forbidden City, where you can easily get lost for several hours. Another half-day will be spent driving to the Summer Palace, about forty-five minutes from the center of Beijing. Since the twelfth century the Imperial Court transported itself to this area during the summer to avoid the city heat, and the Summer Palace (Yiheyuan) grew into a sumptuous playground for the aristocracy. The 650-acre area has an enormous man-made lake for boating, pavilions with such names as Orderly Clouds, Joy and Longevity, Virtue and Harmony, and the famous Marble Boat that the Empress Dowager Tzu Hsi commissioned in 1890 with funds intended to expand the Chinese navy.

The highlight of any visit to China is a climb on the **Great Wall, Wan Li Chang Chen,** or the Long Wall of Ten Thousand Li (about 3000 miles). A comfortable tourist train or motorcoach whisks you from Beijing Station to Badaling, just over two hours away, with tea going and lunch returning. The scenery is spectacular as the train winds up into the Yian Mountain chain, and soon you see sections of the ancient wall undulating along the crests, between flowering trees in the foreground and snow-capped peaks in the distance. Just before Badaling the train stops (for quick leg stretchers and photographs) and then backs into the station. After a brisk twenty-minute walk from the station to the reconstructed section of the wall, the stiff climb begins, in the company of thousands of others from all over China and the world. The right-hand section (as you face the wall) is less steep and therefore more popular with first-time visitors. And when you arrive at the top tower you'll know it, for a sign tells you (in Russian, Chinese, and English) not to go any farther. Indeed, the unreconstructed part of the wall is exceedingly dangerous. (The wall is slippery, so flat shoes with a tread are recommended. It can also be very windy, so hats, scarves, and Windbreakers should be worn and taken off as you warm up. Layers of clothing are very important here.)

Some tours combine the **Ming Tombs** with the Great Wall. This makes for a long and arduous day, but it's better than to miss something. The Ming Tombs are in the foothills of Beijing, where the wind and water (Feng Shui) were considered favorable to enjoying the hereafter. This beautiful and peaceful area adjoins a huge reservoir that Chairman Mao is said to have helped build (as he also supervised the restoration of the Forbidden City, Summer Palace, and parts of the Great Wall). Entrance to the tombs is through the Avenue of the Animals, perhaps the most photographed stone carvings in China. The tomb generally visited is Ting Ling, or Tomb of Emperor Wan Li (1573–1620). The tomb itself is rather a disappointment, but the setting—especially the large square red tower and landscaping—is impressive. And do not miss the two small museums flanking the tower, which portrays a chronology of the excavations of the tomb as well as some of the treasures found—delicately beaten gold objects, silk brocades, and money.

No one leaves Beijing without a visit to the three-tiered Friendship Store and a sumptuous meal of the renowned Peking Duck. The Friendship Store on Chang An Jie caters to foreigners and thus has Mao suits, silk pajamas, dresses, and T-shirts in all sizes. It also sells such items as Happy Brain Pills, Flying Pigeon bicycles, hand-painted silk fans (for twenty-five cents apiece), rugs, furniture, food, and liquor. Not far from the Beijing Hotel, on Wangfujing, is a good handcrafts store, a fur shop, and a bookstore with revolutionary posters. Good antique shops line Liu Li Chang, or Glazed Tile Works Street, but again, be sure you differentiate between what is antique and what has been antiqued.

Beijing can also boast a bevy of new hotels, including The Great Wall Hotel, Fragrant Hill (designed by Chinese-American architect I. M. Pei) and others that will remind you of Hyatt, Sheraton, and Hilton, for good reasons. Accommodations will never be as comfortable or "homelike" as the ship on which you are cruising, but you will have an adventure—which is what travel is all about! If you wish, you may even attempt the new Maxim's de Paris in Beijing—and the growing list of discos that seem to be sprouting like crazy!

The most popular Peking Duck restaurant (and the one you will most likely visit) is known as the Big Duck by locals—as opposed to another called the "Sick Duck," because it is near a hospital. The feast here seems to go on forever, even before one comes to the platters of crisp, sliced duck served with green onions, brown sauce, sesame buns, or pancakes. For dessert come platters of sizzling apple fritters and bowls of cold water. To consume the delicacy, dip the hot fritter into the cold water and then immediately pop it into your mouth. It's perfectly wonderful!

It is easy to get around Beijing on your own, provided your guide is obliging and you have the time to explore or to visit friends. There are tourist buses at Beijing Station, a subway system, taxis for hire at the large hotels, and your own reliable feet—or you can do as the local inhabitants (both Chinese and foreign) do and hire a bicycle. But it's best to discuss any personal plans with your guide. The Chinese are easily offended by our abrupt Western ways, and prefer to lead a harmonious group in which everyone does and sees the same thing.

The appropriate clothing for a China tour is just the opposite of what you would wear on board ship. You may need two wardrobes. As there are no formal evenings, long dresses and jewelry should be left on board. Casual, washable slacks, skirts and sweaters, or jackets and blouses are best for daytime wear, with something a bit nicer for evening. If you're staying in hotels in China, the laundry facilities are good for men but I wouldn't use them for most ladies' wear. As you will be walking a great deal, as well as climbing on and off buses and trains, daytime shoes should be low-heeled and comfortable—again with something a tiny bit fancier for the evening. And then there's the climate. Beijing is bitter cold in the winter, rainy and cold in the spring, and hot as Hades in the summer. Autumn is pleasant. At any time, dress in layers that can be increased or decreased as the temperatures change.

China is a photographer's paradise. If you intend to take many pictures, discuss your trip with a good camera shop. Because of frequent indoor shooting, and many fascinating subjects seen from moving buses and trains, you may have best results with high-speed film (400 ASA) for both prints and slides. If you want to draw a crowd quickly, take along a Polaroid-type camera. It's the best device yet for making fast friends anywhere in the world!

HONG KONG

I envy everyone the adventure ahead of sailing into **Hong Kong,** Jewel of the Orient, that 403-square-mile British Crown Colony sitting on the southern coast of China. Hong Kong is a dazzling collage of modern skyscrapers lining the waterfront and winding their way up the Peak in Victoria; typhoon shelters where untold thousands live out their whole existence on small boats; and nonstop harbor traffic from all over the world. A bustling, dirty city on the sea, it is home to over five million (no one knows the exact count) people. The majority are Chinese (including more than a million refugees), but just about every nationality is represented here.

Hong Kong has been the brightest jewel in the British crown since 1841; but relations with China, which completely surrounds it, have not always been good. During the years of the Bamboo Curtain, China used the colony as a money exchange (the Bank of China, with its two enormous lion statues, is a landmark). When times were tense, China could have cut off Hong Kong's supply of fresh water and pork. Relations now are friendly, as British Prime Minister Margaret Thatcher has settled the great question that haunted both the Crown and the Colony for a century—who will get Hong Kong at the expiration of the lease in 1997? Well, China won the draw and, after the initial shock, life is quite the same in Hong Kong as there is plenty of time to organize an orderly succession of government and social strata in the ensuing decade.

Passenger ships dock at the Ocean Terminal complex in the Tsimshatsui section of Kowloon. The clean, well-kept terminal houses a grand bazaar of shops, restaurants, banks, tourist facilities, the Harbour Village with traditional Chinese products, and whatever else one desires. One need never leave this three-story building that spills onto the Hong Kong Hotel, but there is much, much more outside. Hong Kong is a walking city, so put on your comfortable shoes the minute you arrive. Five minutes on foot from your cruise ship is Nathan Road, once a famous shopping street, flanked by the fabulous Peninsula Hotel and the Sheraton, the New World Centre, and the elegant Regent Hotel. When your feet are tired, God forbid, have a cup of tea in the lobby of the Peninsula where, as the saying goes, you'll see the world pass by and probably everyone you know if you sit long enough.

Two minutes from the terminal is the Star Ferry Building, easily found by its clock tower, where a cross-harbor ferry to Hong Kong Island leaves every few minutes. (Be sure to buy a first-class or upper-deck ticket so you can enjoy the scenery—it costs only pennies.) Victoria is the capital of Hong Kong Island, and Central District is its busiest section—deluxe hotels, office buildings, and elegant shops. Just behind the Hilton Hotel, another longtime landmark, is the Peak Tram station. The ride up this funny, wooden, cog railway is a must for the lovely residences along the way and the view from the top. Since the 1880s, foreigners and wealthy Chinese have made this former mountain wilderness *the* place to live, even though it's often fogged in and thoroughly uncomfortable.

At the fishing port of Aberdeen you can eat fresh fish aboard a floating restaurant; or you can take a ferry from Central District (a few minutes' walk from the Star terminal) to other islands like Lan Tao or Cheung Chau. Another popular tour is to the New Territories, Hong Kong's only rural countryside (held under that 99-year lease from China that expires in 1997). Most of the land out there is rocky, hilly, or swampy, but you can get a view of the mainland from a lookout point called Lok Ma Chau.

Although Hong Kong is often called the world's number one shopper's paradise, dining out is also continually exciting. Numerous continental restaurants exist, of course, but for Chinese cuisine Hong Kong is the closest thing to heaven. In my opinion, the dishes here are more interesting and tastier than in China because the ingredients are more suited to the Western palate. One of the best restaurants, right near Ocean Terminal, is the Jade Garden in Star House, which seats several hundred hungry customers in a series of rooms. It's especially popular on Sunday afternoons, when whole families eat merrily around tables set up for ten or more. In Hong Kong you can pick any Cantonese, Hunan, Szechuan, and other types of Chinese restaurants by just letting your nose lead the way. If your taste buds shout for Continental food, my choices always include Gaddi's at the Peninsula, Plume at the Hong Kong Regent (nouvelle cuisine and best view in town), Pierrot at the Mandarin (complete with Picasso prints) and Lalique with champagne bar at the Royal Garden. If you're in the mood for a view of the whole colony, go to the top of one of the luxury hotels, all of which have nice cocktail lounges and restaurants (especially the Eagle's Nest at the Hong Kong Hilton).

As many cruises embark or disembark in Hong Kong, it is definitely worth your while to spend a few days here—especially if the ship-line package is reasonable and offers a good hotel. Hong Kong has been building hotels like crazy the past decade, but it is still almost impossible to book acccommodation as clothing manufacturers, trade groups, journalists and financiers fly in and out of the colony with regularity. Well, why not? There is just no other place like it in the world!

INDONESIAN ARCHIPELAGO

Bali is that paradisiacal island off the eastern tip of Java that you've always wanted to visit—and once you have visited, you can't wait to return. It's been called the Morning of the World, but it's not even of this world—it's too peaceful, too perfect. To be on Bali is to be content. Local women walk barebreasted in the street, temple bells tinkle in the breezes, and everyday is a Hindu holiday. Life in Bali means a simple sarong, a motorbike, and some fruit. It hasn't always been so idyllic. Bali is a Hindu island in a Moslem archipelago, the 13,662 lesser islands and six large ones that make up Indonesia. Ruled by Dutch colonists for 300 years and occupied by the Japanese during World War II, Indonesia announced her independence in 1945. Twenty years of flirtation with Communism under Sukarno ended with one of the worst bloodbaths in modern history—some 300,000 Indonesian communists were killed, and whole villages (including some on Bali) were burned to the ground.

The capital of Bali's three million inhabitants is **Denpasar,** a scruffy, touristy town that has no relation to the rest of the island. It does have an art museum and a large market, and large resort hotels are centered on Sanur Beach, a few minutes from town. Despite the influx of Western comforts and customs, the Balinese are adamant about preserving their beautiful island—no building can be higher than a palm tree!

Ubud, about fifteen miles from Denpasar, has long been an artist's colony for both native and foreign craftsmen. Here you can visit the studios of painters who will be delighted that you came to call. The nearby village of **Mas** is famous for the finest woodcarvers in Indonesia. Their sophisticated and stylized figures of polished teak and dark ebony are quite different from the mass productions found in Denpasar. Balinese artisans also make wonderful hand puppets of buffalo parchment for a popular form of entertainment—shadow plays, where mythical princes and princesses come to life on a screen while the storyteller chants dialogue from familiar tales.

Entertainment in Bali comes from the temples, so intertwined are religion and theater. Dancing is everywhere and taught by imitation. Although the dances you see are staged for tourists, the impact is not lessened. Two of the most popular are the classical, feminine Legong, the dance of three divine nymphs, and the Ketjak, which features a male chorus of 150, who chant in place of the ever-present gamelon (an Indonesian musical instrument), and who become an army of chattering monkeys at the finale. You will not witness either of these two dances without feeling something of that special spirit that hovers tightly about this island.

Bali is also beautiful mountains and terraced rice fields, and Pura Besakih, the sacred temple on the slopes of **Mt. Agung.** The Balinese consider this mountain the navel of the world. It's an active volcano that frets and fumes and last erupted in 1963 (killing several thousand people who were told the gods would take care of them). But wherever you go on Bali, you must leave your cares behind. As a young Balinese once said to me, as he was planning the next day's adventure, "Now leave your sensitive American stomach behind, and we'll have a good time!"

Butung is a small island across the strait from Sulawesi, which once had a reputation for piracy. In fact, the old pirate haunt of Wasuemba can still be see along the south coast. The inhabitants of Butung are mainly Muslim, who do interesting weavings and copperwork. The capital, **Bau Bau,** is known mainly for the Sultan's residence, built in 1942, which contains some artifacts of the area (skulls, weaponry, china pieces). A nearby mosque was the first built on the island, and it offers a fine view of the sea. Cruise passengers are also treated to some local dances here, and are forewarned that the mode of transportation may be rather primitive. All available vehicles are used, including *bemos* (trucks with benches), antiquated cars, and minibuses.

The 200-mile-long mountainous island of **Flores** is inhabited by a population of Malay, Papuan, and Portuguese, who have developed their own distinctive cultures. Some two-thirds practice Catholicism, but animism is deeply entrenched, and head-hunting was legal until recently. Villagers dance to celebrate plantings and harvests, weddings and burials. They also make scarecrows to keep away evil spirits. Passengers wishing to enter a village must endure first a welcome ceremony, including a speech and some sort of food and drink. When concluded, visitors may wander around traditional village dwellings.

Larantuka is the administrative center of the eastern end of Flores and a port city in the Portuguese tradition. Here, you will find stone and stucco houses that need a good paint job, and a colorful market. Behind the town is Ile Mandiri, a semi-active volcano that boasts the proud village of Lewoleba on its shoulder. You can buy wonderful hand-woven materials here, with designs indigenous to the various clans. Finished products are for sale following weaving demonstrations (and bargaining is certainly expected). Note: Cruise passengers may have to walk up to 50 minutes to the village, if the narrow road is wet and impassable by vehicles.

Komodo is possibly the only island in the world where dragons are said to outnumber people! Indeed, the tiny wildlife island of Komodo is actually a national park and sanctuary for its 3000-strong dragon population. It sounds like an overwhelming number, but their very existence is threatened because only about 300 of the 1500 adult animals are female and they don't mate very often. The Komoda dragon is thought to be a survivor of the prehistoric dinosaurs that once ruled the earth. Up to twelve feet long and 350 pounds in weight, the Komodo is carnivorous, sharp-eyed, and keen-nosed. A good hunter, the beast can devour an entire water buffalo without chewing (honest!), and eat its own weight in just seventeen minutes.

In order to view this giant lizard, the creature must be lured from the coziness of its cave by placing a goat (killed the night before) on a stake in a clearing. Before too long (and hopefully as cruise passengers arrive), the Komodo will appear for a snack at the appointed dragon-watching site. However, passengers should be warned that not only is there a "wet landing" (into the shore from small boats with shoes and camera equipment held overhead), but there is about a 45-minute walk to the viewing area. Hence, passengers should protect themselves from tropical sun or a sudden rain shower and be sure their expensive equipment is covered in plastic during these times. Well, how often do you get to see a real dragon? And even if one does not deign to appear, Komodo itself has a dramatic landscape with 2000-foot mountain peaks and golden green lontor palms. So, the discomfort of visiting the island is not a total loss.

The island of **Java** is the fifth largest in the Indonesian archipelago (after Kalimantan, Sumatra, Irian Java, and Sulawesi), yet has always been the most dynamic force in the Republic in terms of commerce and culture. About 80 million people live on Java, some 5 million of them in the capital city of Jakarta. They consist primarily of Javanese, but a good number of Sudanese live in the western part and some Madurese in the eastern section. **Jakarta,** once called Batavia by the Dutch traders who arrived in 1619 and stayed around for almost 325 years, is the seamy capital and usually only graced with a half-day tour by most cruise passengers. You will pass by the Bridge of Sighs in the restored port section *(Taman Fatahilla)* as well as the remains of the Kasteel or fortress. A must visit is made to the Wayang Museum, housed in an old Dutch house, and perhaps there will be a demonstration of the *kulit* (shadow play) or *golek* (puppets in the round) show in the courtyard. A drive through the Medan Medeka area, with Sukarno's self-styled tributes, and to the Istiqlal Mosque complete the city tour. The mosque, said to be the largest in Southeast Asia, has a celestial white dome and most unusual minaret.

If you plan to stay in Jakarta, the two top hotels are the Hilton and Mandarin, and there are some excellent restaurants around the city. Shopping is also terrific here, especially at the showroom of Iwan Tirta and at the handicraft center. Pasar Baru has fabrics at a song and Pasar Barung is famous for birdcages. Watch out for "antiques," as many may only be "antiqued" while the authentic may not be exported.

Some cruise vessels stop in the port of **Semarang** for a two-day optional excursion to the cultural capital of Java as well as two of its most famous religious monuments. **Yogyakarta** is a small city of approximately 400,000 that lies at the foot of an active volcano. Some Javanese believe that it lies in the "realm of the dead" because of its location. Yogyakarta is famous for its handicrafts, especially batik, and many artisans have congregated here to work and live together. They have truly elevated the making of batik to a national art, and you can find not only lovely saronglike fabrics but one-of-a-kind batik "paintings." These are meant to be framed in wood and lit from behind; obviously, they make a wonderful gift or souvenir.

However, the cultural and political life of "Jogja" (as knowledgeables pronounce it) is the palace of the Sultan. Begun in 1797, it is a maze of courtyards and apartments that now feature handicraft workshops, schools for dance, two museums, and a population of about 25,000 people. Visitors are welcome to see the Golden Pavilion, finished in 1792, with its solid teak pillars, and the Glass Pavilion, with its Hindu motifs and Buddhist lotus flowers and writings from the Koran. The Glass Pavilion is furnished European-style, but also houses a collection of royal palanquins, sedan chairs, and antique gamelan instruments.

Jogja is definitely the home of Wayang Kulit puppets, which are used to tell tales from the Ramayana. A *dalang,* or puppeteer, sits behind a lighted screen, and the shadowy puppets move across to carry along the tale. *Wayang* means shadow, and the origins of these puppets is traced to animistic beliefs that shadows are the manifestations of ancestral spirits.

The Hindu temple of **Prambanan** stands in a village just outside Jogja. It was completed around A.D. 900 in classic Indian architectural style, but was deserted about 100 years later and collapsed in ruins around 1600. Restoration of the central temple, the masterpiece dedicated to Siva (known as the slender virgin), began in 1918 and was completed in 1953. In addition to having a glorious symmetry and grace, Prambanan is known for its wealth of sculptural detail—especially on the base of the main terrace. Here, a menagerie of charming creatures, groups of singers and dancers and Ramayana episodes all enchant the onlooker.

One of the world's great Buddhist monuments and the largest ancient structure in Southeast Asia is **Borobudur,** about a forty-five minute drive from Yogyakarta. Borobudur was begun at the beginning of the eighth century A.D., under the direction of a ruler of the Sailendra dynasty. Completed about a century later, the monument took the labor of 10,000 men and an estimated 2 million cubic feet of stone; the building was supervised by priests of the Vajrayana sect to which the shrine is a testament. Indeed, every aspect of the structure is full of religious symbolism. Forgotten for nearly 1000 years, it was found by a local prince at the turn of the nineteenth century. In 1815 Sir Thomas Stamford Raffles inspected the site, had it cleared of the jungle, and properly surveyed. Proper restoration began only in 1973, partly under the auspices of UNESCO, but more importantly, with aid from business concerns around the world. IBM, among them, offered computers on which each stone was programmed and able to be replaced in exactly the correct spot.

Surabaya is Java's second port/city and is often called "The City of Heroes," for its role in the Indonesian struggle for independence. Otherwise, the city is known for some traditional arts and as a port of entry for shore excursions to Yogyakarta or the island of Madura. Just across the strait, **Madura** is the home of the *kerapan sapi,* or bull races. These unusual events can be attended throughout the months of August and September in Pamekasan (the capital of the island) and nearby Sampang. For those that like that sort of thing.

Pare Pare is a seaport and the second largest town on the island of **Sulawesi,** and a cruise call for overnight shore excursions to the village of Tana Toradja. About a hundred bumpy miles north of the port, **Tana Toradja** rises to some 5000 feet above sea level in one of the most beautiful landscapes in all of Indonesia. The village is inhabited by descendents of an ancient race of Proto Malayan stock, who believe they are all children of the king of gods and one huge family. (*Tana Toradja* means "Land of Heavenly Kings.")

The Toradjas are a study in primitive culture and their ways have long fascinated travelers. Despite the narrow, treacherous mountain route to the village, you will not leave disappointed unless you run out of film. The dwellings lend much to photography, for they look like richly ornamented ships afloat on seas of ripening rice. They are great arklike structures with geometrical designs, and a life-size wood carving of a buffalo (symbol of fertility) at every door. They are built facing north, and in such a way that they can be moved in one piece from place to place. Always on stilts (the cool underneath area is for animals), only wood, rattan, and bamboo materials may be used.

These villagers also believe in eternal life, and they make much of funerals—or festivals of joy, as they call them. Funerals are postponed until sufficient opulent ceremonies can be staged, with several buffalo slaughtered. Final burial takes place in caves or "hanging graves" chiseled from the volcanic cliffs. Life-size wooden effigies are placed at the graves, which make for an eerie sight. About half the Toradjas adhere to the ancestral Aluk Todolo animist religion, while the others are either Christians or Muslims. All in all, this is an overnight excursion that only the most adventurous would appreciate!

Sumatra is Indonesia's largest island and stretches more than one thousand miles from the Andaman Sea to the Sunda Strait. In the northern end of the island, the main port of entry is Belawan, just off the

Malacca Strait. This port is easily accessible to **Medan,** the capital city, which has very little to offer the tourist. Rather, most visitors head straight for **Lake Toba** for an overnight in Parapat. Attractions around this beautiful lake in the highlands include Samosir Island and the Batak Toba villages. If your cruise vessel sails around to **Padang,** the main port for West Sumatra, you will have a lovely drive down and some interesting views of the Indonesian Ocean—perhaps even a swim on the beach.

JAPAN

Your cruise ship will come alongside Osambashi, or South Pier, in **Yokohama;** if it's a clear day (and you're very lucky), you may be able to see Mt. Fuji in the distance—Japan's highest and most sacred mountain. Fuji-san, as the Japanese call it, is considered one of the two most beautiful conical volcanoes in the world (the other is Mt. Cotopaxi in Ecuador). But the volcano has not been active for more than 200 years, and Mt. Fuji has served as the favorite subject matter of poets and artists throughout Japan.

As a gateway for visitors to Tokyo and northern Honshu, Yokohama is a cosmopolitan port, although only opened to foreign trade since 1859. Twice devastated in this century (the 1923 earthquake and the 1945 air raids), it is now a city of 3 million inhabitants, including a large foreign community who add character from their homes up on The Bluff, their boutiques on Motomachi, and their bargain shops in Isezaki-cho. This is the shopping center of Yokohama, where the prices are less and the stores even more swinging than on Tokyo's Ginza.

A short cruise call, alas, cannot do justice to this Land of the Rising Sun. You will, though, enjoy a small but delectable taste of what it means to say "We Japanese." This nation flowered as early as the sixth century, when Prince Shotoku made his Constitution of Seventeen Articles and encouraged culture and education. Chronicles of the seventh and eighth centuries are still around, as well as the Manyoshu, a collection of some 4500 poems. Todaiji, a temple in Nara, has a repository holding some 9000 art treasures made by Japanese craftsmen or brought from around the world. Each subsequent century, in this floating world that was Old Japan, was more fruitful than the last. During the late sixteenth century, or Momoyama Period, Japanese arts flourished as never before, and these are the very arts you see and buy today. The tea ceremony, or *chanoyu,* was raised to the dignity of a national art. *Kabuki, Noh, Bunraku,* and other theater forms developed. Flower arranging became a national pastime, and paintings on scrolls and screens reached new grandeur. Today Japan is industrialized and computerized but, with all the changes, traditional arts are just as important to everyday life as they became during the Momoyama Period.

Tokyo has been the administrative capital of Japan since 1603, as Edo. But because of natural and man-made disasters, the only thing remaining from this time is an iron post in the center of Nihonbashi, which was used as a highway measure up until World War II. This sprawling, bustling metropolis has a daytime population of about 20 million. (Avoid train and subway stations during the morning and evening rush hours. "Pushers" on the train platforms pack the cars with commuters, and it's not very comfortable, to say the least. And never try to walk against the flow of traffic in a train station or you'll be knocked flat.) Many visitors to Tokyo are a little afraid of the city and find it cold and impersonal. But, aside from the gray older buildings like the Imperial Diet and Library, Tokyo is just a series of small towns linked together. Many areas have not changed much in character since the turn of the century.

One of my favorite monuments in Japan is Meiji Shrine, a place of pilgrimage for the Japanese because it honors Emperor Meiji (and his empress), who opened Japan to the rest of the world in 1869 and encouraged Western ideas and social and land reforms. This Shinto shrine, destroyed in World War II but rebuilt in the 1950s, has beautiful gardens where you can enjoy every type of Japanese tree and flower. In the spring the *sakura* (cherry blossoms) are overwhelming; in summer a large iris garden boasts a hundred different varieties; and autumn brings pots and pots of *kiku* (chrysanthemums) along the paths. Even in winter the Meiji Shrine is not a bad place, for the days are sunny and bright and all the trees have been wrapped in burlap against the cold. You'll see many young couples spending the day at the shrine. You will also find couples and families enjoying Ueno Park, once the estate of a Daimyo and now a huge complex of museums, gardens, temples, a zoo, a pond, and even a pagoda. Nearby is the popular Asakusa Kannon Temple, founded in the seventh century by three fishermen, and now surrounded by one of Tokyo's many entertainment areas—the path to the temple is lined with souvenir shops.

Save some energy and money for the crowded Ginza, the famous silver street, lined with shops (where sweet-faced girls with white gloves bow and welcome you to each floor) and billboards. Stop in at the Sony Building and see what the latest invention is. If you're interested in Kabuki, the Kabukiza is just off the Ginza, and you may wander in for an hour or so and then leave. Everyone does, especially in the afternoon (the best actors play in the evening). Don't miss the Imperial Palace plaza, where swans float in the moats. You cannot visit the Imperial Palace, because the emperor and empress live there, but the grounds are open to the public on January 2 (New Year's) and April 29 (the emperor's birthday and a national holiday). You may enjoy day trips to Nikko, a national park in the mountains north of Tokyo that is famous for Toshogu Shrine, and to Hakone in the west, another national park with hot springs, where the views of Mt. Fuji are the best.

Gateway to the western part of Japan and situated on the edge of the beautiful Inland Sea, **Kobe** has been an important port since Chinese and Korean cultural emissaries arrived in the fourth century. Kobe is a delight, has a sister-city relationship with Marseilles and Seattle, and is famous for Kobe beef and the choice Nada sake (Japanese rice wine). Kobe is the starting point for luxury steamers that ply the Inland Sea, carrying sightseers to such interesting places as Beppu (a famous hot spring), Takamatsu, Shikoku, Shodo, and Awaji islands. The area is dominated by Mt. Rokko, which you can ascend by cable car for a lovely view of the bay and sea.

But Kobe is also known as a cruise port for the new breed of two-week China/Korea sailings that embark or disembark here. Not far by train or car are the historic sites of Nara and Kyoto. **Nara,** capital of Japan from 710 to 784, is noted for beautiful temples and shrines. The most famous is Kofukuji, or Happiness-Producing Temple, which boasted 175 buildings at the height of its prosperity. All that remains is the reconstructed Kondo, or Main Hall, with a wooden image of Sakya-muni, now registered as an Important Cultural Property. The Five-Story Pagoda is another National Treasure (first built in 730 and rebuilt in 1426). My favorite spot is Kasuga Shrine, built in 768 by a member of the Fujiwara family, the most powerful in Japan (because, among other things, they supplied wives for the emperors), it consists of four small shrines—painted in vermilion and built in the Kasuga style of architec-ture—in a serene wooded setting. Don't leave Nara without feeding the deer that roam under the Japanese cedar, oak, and wisteria. And walk over to nearby Sarusawa Pond, where the Five-Story Pagoda is often reflected in the still water. Japan's oldest existing temple is Horyuji, built in 607 just outside Nara. Horyuji, regarded as the fountainhead of Japanese art and culture, is headquarters for the Shotoku sect of Bud-dhism, named in honor of the progressive Prince Shotoku (574–622). Horyuji consists of several large buildings: Nandaimon (Great South Gate), Kondo (Main Hall), Shoryoin (Sacred Spirit Hall), Yumedono (Hall of Dreams), and a Five-Story Pagoda considered one of the oldest buildings in the world.

Temples and more will entice you to **Kyoto,** where the spirit of old Japan prevails. From Kyoto (cultural capital since 794), the coun-try's arts flowed for more than ten centuries. Although it is Japan's fifth largest city and an important industrial center, Kyoto still exudes so much charm that visitors consider the city the culmination of their entire Japanese experience. Birthplace of most Japanese arts and crafts, it is also the center of the silk industry, and its Gion, or Pleasure Quarter, has worldwide fame. The Gion section, near the Kamo River, where dyed silks were once a common sight drying on the banks, is enchanting by day and night. The quarter is lined with wonderful restaurants offering traditional Japanese dishes as well as many different noodle shops. Gion is also the home of the Geisha, or Art Lady, who has trained since childhood in the subtle and refined ways of entertainment. The Geisha house is a very respectable place to be seen, although the cost of being so well taken care of for a few hours is almost prohibitive (and always was so, even in ancient Japan). If you are lucky enough to attend a Geisha party (Western women are welcome), it's a delightful experience. During the presentation of the meal, the Geisha and her Maiko (young assistant) will attend to your every wish, filling your tiny cup of sake over and over, even helping you manage the *o hashi* (chopsticks). All the while, you may admire her elegant kimono, powdered neck and face, sparkling white *tabi* (socks with one toe), and symbolic, ornamented wig. When the meal is finished, the Geisha and her assistant will sing, play the *koto,* and dance. The real fun begins as they entice guests to join in dances both nice and naughty. There is the Tankobushi (coal miner's dance), the Bon dance, the very naughty Ykuyuken (wading dance), and the Japanese baseball dance. It's all orchestrated to break the ice, so to speak, rather like charades or word games at a formal dinner. When the party is over, the Geisha will bow you gracefully from the room and return to her private quarters to await the next assignment or perhaps have a private visit with her patron.

Kyoto was laid out in checkerboard fashion—a plan taken from the Chinese—and originally called Heian-kyo (peaceful, tranquil capital), but the name was appropriately changed to Kyoto (capital city) because there was constant infighting in ancient Japan between church (the many Buddhist sects) and state (the imperial court). None of the temples was destroyed during World War II, because the Allied forces agreed to save the irreplaceable culture from the ravages of war. Kiyomizudera, or waterfall temple, is everyone's favorite and most closely spans the history of the city itself. It was never aligned with any one sect and survived by managing to remain on friendly terms with all. Approached by a long series of shop-lined steps, the temple has a superb view of the city from the top. For centuries the Japanese have made pilgrimages here and even bathe in the falling waters *(brrrh)*. If you are a gardener, Kyoto will enchant you with wonderful gardens, each evoking its own particular mood, within which are endless variations according to the weather, the season, and the number of visitors treading its path. If you linger long enough, a garden will change its mood as a bird flies in to perch, a pine needle falls, or a few rain drops alter the pattern raked in sand and bounce on the lily-strewn pond.

The gardens in Kyoto are often more memorable than the temples they adjoin. The garden at Ryoanji is famous for its rock symbolizing mountains, islands, and fierce animals. The garden of Ginkakuji (silver pavilion temple) epitomizes the spirit of Zen. The garden at Nijo Castle was designed without trees, so the shogun would not be saddened by the sight of passing seasons. Nijo, in the center of Kyoto, on part of the site of the original Imperial Palace, was built in the sixteenth century (so it is not even old by Japanese standards) for the Tokugawa shoguns, and its wooden pavilions have exceptionally beautiful carvings and paintings of the period. What I like best are the squeaky floors, intended to warn the shogun of anyone approaching.

Kyoto is memorable any time of the year—spring cherry blossoms at the Heian Shrine; willow trees in summer at Uji Bridge; fall chrysanthemums; and snowflakes dusting the swans on Shinsen-en pond.

MALAYSIA

Penang is a relaxing, charming resort city with beautiful beaches and the blend of four cultures—Malay, Indian, Chinese, and Thai—with British overtones in its white, colonial architecture and civic monuments. It's an island-city where life hasn't moved along that fast since the turn of the century. Once you disembark, there is no need to rush about, because the tourist attractions are few. Hire a trishaw (a rickshaw that is peddled) and drive along Campbell and Carnarvon streets, where you can find goods from all over Asia. This is a so-called Free Port, which means the prices should be low, but compare before you buy. Above all, enjoy the local color of street hawkers, beautiful women in saris with their children, and old men falling asleep on the curbside. Indeed, one wonders how anything ever gets done in Penang since half the population seems to be having a snooze.

Fort Cornwallis is a pleasant spot in town and great for photographs, along with another colonial landmark, the Eastern and Oriental Hotel, where you can have a cool drink in the palm-fringed lobby or out on the lawn overlooking the harbor. For a view of the colonial side of Penang, take a drive through the old residential area where lovely, large homes were built long ago for British military and civil servants.

Penang has many Chinese temples (including a Snake Temple), Buddhist statues, and other religious monuments. My favorite outing is the funicular up Penang Hill for the lush view and a cool drink on the lawn of the restaurant/hotel. Penang Hill is one of the mountain retreats founded by the British in Malaysia and frequented during the oppressive summer heat. If you prefer beautiful beaches, tell the taxi driver to take you to ''Batu Ferringhi'' (Foreigner Mile), about twenty minutes out of town. Here you'll find lovely white sand, swaying palms, and casual, family-style hotels where Americans seek solace from the oil fields of Indonesia.

Port Kelang is the point of entry off the Straits of Malacca for Malaysia's beautiful capital city, **Kuala Lumpur.** The Klang River connects the two, but no doubt your ship will rest in port while you drive into K.L., as everyone calls it. This is one of the greenest and most charming cities in all of Southeast Asia, and may God please keep the developers away! Here you can view local tigers in the National Zoo, the Selangor Turf Club with its fabulous race course, the National Mosque, the Moorish-style railway station and other structures built under British rule in the late nineteenth century, and the *Padang* in front of the Selangor Club. Many sections of K.L. still have a colonial ambience, but there are enough Rolls-Royces on the roads to bring you back to modern times (the country is rather oil rich). A day spent in K.L. is pure pleasure!

PHILIPPINES

The Philippines stretch some 1100 miles on a staggering 7107 islands, although 94% of the land area and population occupy only eleven islands. This nation of great natural resources and as yet unrealized industrial potential has too much disparity between rich and poor, understandable social unrest, and a potboiler political situation. Nonetheless, **Manila** is a romantic and historic capital edging a beautiful bay, an exotic mix of Malay, Spanish, and American influences. The Philippines were discovered, more or less, by Magellan in 1521, and after colonization by the Spanish in 1571 were named for Philip II. For over three hundred years Spanish rule influenced culture, architecture, and religion. Then, following the Spanish-American War, the islands were ceded to the United States in 1898. After Japanese occupation during World War II, the Republic of the Philippines was proclaimed on July 4, 1946. Americans added a legacy of English to Spanish and Tagalog (the local dialect) and the idea of democracy as a way of life.

Port calls to the Philippines will increase as the political situation stabilizes. It's a wonderful country and its people are warm and friendly. They deserve a new lease on life and, hopefully, the new regime will allow them that.

The Filipinos have given us two lifetime joys—terrific dance bands and the *barong Tagalog,* a loose-fitting, long-sleeved shirt that Filipinos wear from morning to night to keep cool in this hot climate. The more elegant variety is perfectly acceptable in place of coat and tie at the best restaurants and nightclubs. Leave your heavies behind on the ship when you dock in Manila, and head for the nearest shop—the styles have been modified to include pants suits and shirtwaist dresses for women, too.

Your first view of Manila will probably be from the Rizal Monument in the Luneta, a large park along the water. Rizal, a national hero and pride of the Malay people, was executed here in 1896, becoming the first Asian martyr to have opposed Western colonization. The Luneta faces Roxas Boulevard, the city's most famous street, and to the south you will see the pride of former first lady Imelda Marcos—a new complex built on reclaimed land featuring cultural, design, theater, and convention centers. To the north is the renovated Manila Hotel, built at the turn of the century and once home to General MacArthur. (It's possible to book the suite of rooms he occupied, but the price is about U.S. $2000 a night!)

Unfortunately, most of the fine old Spanish structures in Manila, including the seventeenth-century Manila Cathedral, were destroyed during World War II. However, St. Augustine Church, second oldest in the country, survived and is the most important landmark. Founder of the city, Miguel Lopez de Legazpe, is buried here; the British left some fine woodcarvings during an invasion from 1762–64; the Spanish surrender of the Philippines to the Americans occurred here in 1898. St. Augustine's is located inside the former Walled City, or Intramuros Section, whose broad and impregnable walls were built by the Spanish in the sixteenth century to discourage potential invaders as well as to control a large Chinese community that lived outside.

Excursions from Manila include a hydrofoil ride to Corregidor, the island at the entrance of Manila Bay, where Americans and Filipinos fought so hard in 1942, and a trip to Bataan Peninsula. Far more refreshing to the spirit is the drive south one hour to Tagaytay Ridge, where the air is cool at 2000 feet, and you can see a volcano within a volcano at Taal Lake. Farther south by one more hour is the most exciting excursion of all—shooting the rapids in a *banca* (canoe) at Pagsanjan Falls. The scenery is spectacular and the thrill is something to talk about for years!

SINGAPORE

About the only thing exotic about Singapore these days is the name, Singapura, which means "Lion City" in Malay. Billed as "Instant Asia," this city-island-state at the tip of Malaysia is renowned as a multiracial melting pot. Living and working together in more or less perfect harmony are more than two million citizens who enjoy the highest standard of living in Southeast Asia. The majority are Chinese, of course, but they are joined by Malays, Indians, Pakistanis, Ceylonese, Indonesians, Europeans, and Eurasians.

Two men whose names are synonymous with Singapore are Stamford Raffles, an Englishman who founded a trading post of the East India Company here in 1819 because he predicted the island would become a crossroads of the East, and Prime Minister Lee Kuan Yew, a Cambridge-educated Chinese who decided in the 1950s that his people should not be the "pawn and plaything of foreign powers" and set about putting the British back in their place. Some call his sixteen-year rule ruthless (he threatened to close down all British clubs that did not accept Chinese members), but his vision and vigor have made modern Singapore successful. What you see is what it is: clean streets (there is a stiff fine for discarding cigarettes); an uncorrupted police force; plenty of parks and housing projects; nonstop automobiles driven by affluent, hard-working people; and high-rises everywhere. You also see the old (buildings) coming down with a fury, and the new going up. Singapore is in a constant leap forward, but some of us yearn for a little familiarity—for a little dirt and intrigue to remain as well!

Sailing into Singapore harbor is impressive. The busiest port in Southeast Asia and the third largest in the world, it harbors some three hundred vessels unloading raw materials or loading up with rubber, tin, and "Made in Singapore" products. The city itself is small and easy to explore on your own from your landing at Clifford Pier on Colliers Quay. While the downtown business district is becoming a monument to modern architecture, like the multimillion dollar projects designed by I. M. Pei and John Portman for Raffles City and Marina Centre, there are still some pure Asian sights.

My first and most important stop is always Raffles Hotel. I sit under one of the whirling overhead fans in this charming bastion of colonialism, sip a cool drink, and dream of the romantic Far East of long ago. Somerset Maugham, Noel Coward, and Rudyard Kipling all wrote about Raffles, which began life as a tiffin house (an Anglo-Indian expression for lunch place) in the 1800s and was the birthplace of the Singapore (Gin) Sling in the 1920s. The hotel's colorful history parallels that of Singapore itself, and there is an encouraging sense of continuity under these fans—note: Raffles is reopening soon with a modern tower behind it.

I also love the Botanical Gardens, one of the best and most beautiful in the world, with exotic plants as well as a well-planned oasis of lily ponds, happy swans, orchard pavilions, and herbarium on eighty lush acres. If you like garish art, stop at the Tiger Balm Gardens, a place I have fortunately resisted on every visit. Save some time for shopping. The prices are on a par with Hong Kong, with almost the variety in merchandise. At night Singapore is a different city. Although the government has moved much of the street life to a more sanitized location behind the Singapore Tourist Promotion Board (STPB), there are still some wonderful festivities to enjoy behind the main thorough-fares. Don't look for Bugis Street, however, because the government never approved of transvestites and closed down their parade ground. What the government has done is build gigantic hotel/office cities within the city. Raffles City and Marina Centre are the two most recent—and, alas, the real Singapore of today.

SOUTH KOREA

The Republic of South Korea's principal port and historical gate-way from Japan and the Western world is **Pusan.** This city of 2-million-plus inhabitants once sequestered another million or so refugees, as the only major area never to fall into Communist hands during the Korean Conflict. Situated on the southern tip of the peninsula and becoming a popular port of call for cruise vessels on the China circuit between Hong Kong and Kobe, its name *Pusan* derives from the Koryo Dynasty period (936 to 1392). Pusan refers to the mountain peaks that rise 2500 feet behind the port and make the city around the harbor resemble something of a cauldron, or steaming pot.

The occupying-Japanese opened the port of Pusan to outside trade in 1876 and began construction of a railway northward in 1904. Al-though always considered a commercial and industrial center, the city is also now enjoyed as the main tourist center in the South. It boasts a splendid beach, a milder climate than most other places in both summer and winter, and some not-so-bad attractions. Optional shore excursions of the city offered by Pearl Cruises feature the Fish Market, the famous United Nations' Cemetery, and a panoramic view from the 387-foot Pusan Observation Tower. In proper weather, Haeundae Beach and neighboring resort hotel are both perfect for a few hours' relaxation.

Less than one hour along the excellent Pusan–Seoul Expressway is one of the country's largest and most interesting temples. This is the thirty-five-structure-plus Tongdo-sa, built in 647 (during the reign of Queen Sondok) by the Priest Chajang. This priest, who studied in China and was considered a *taeguksa* or Great National Priest, founded many temples around the land; but this one is considered to be his most pres-tigious legacy. The Zen-sect *Tongdo-sa* means "To Save the World by Mastering the Truth," and its uniquely-different main hall *(Taeung-jon)* has been designated as National Treasure No. 144. Up in the hills around the temple are a dozen or so small hermitages where the resident priests retreat for enlightenment.

Another hour along the super-highway is Korea's *piece de resistance*—the museum without walls that dates from the great Silla Dynasty (57 B.C. to A.D. 935). This is **Kyongju,** which still boasts royal tombs, temple sites, Buddhist reliefs, and fortress ruins in impressive states of preservation. It is a full-day (seven and a half hours) tour to this cradle of Korea's ancient culture, and worth every moment. Here you will see many recent findings in the National Museum, visit several recently excavated Silla tombs, marvel at the beaten gold crowns and girdles, see the oldest observatory in the world, and wonder at other ancient sites. Kyongju offers inspiration to all of us, and the Korean government is paying considerable attention to the area as one of the country's most impressive tourist attractions. A special Korean luncheon at one of the new resort hotels on Bodrum Lake is also included in the tour.

If your vessel calls at **Inchon,** a booming harbor and Korea's fourth largest city, you are fortunate in being a short distance from **Seoul**—South Korea's capital and center of commerce and culture. En route to Seoul, most likely, you will hear the story of dawn on September 15, 1950, when Gen. Douglas MacArthur directed a brilliant amphibious landing of U.S. forces that turned the bitter Korean struggle in favor of the south and its allies.

Seoul is one of the world's most fascinating metropoli and is, indeed, the pulse of this country. Life never seems to rest here, and the ancient world of the capital coexists quite peacefully with some of the most modern buildings and facilities in all of Asia.

NamSan (South Mountain) is focal point of the city, and two of the original nine gates that surrounded Seoul still exist—Namdaemun (Great South Gate) and Tongdaemun (Great East Gate)—as subtle reminders of a 10-mile-around ancient wall of stone erected some 500 years ago. There are many historic monuments to visit in Seoul, in between shopping forays and rest stops at sophisticated new hotels. Kyongbok (Shining Happiness) Palace is a good place to begin, as its grounds also include the National Museum and National Folk Museum. Changdok (Illustrious Virtue) Palace dates from the year 1405 and still has vestiges of the royal family living in it; however, its secret garden (Piwon) is now a public park. On the grounds of Toksu (Virtuous Longevity) Palace are a statue of the great 15th-century King Sejong, who commissioned scholars to develop a distinctive Korean writing system, and the National Museum of Modern Art. As most of the sights of Seoul mean a great deal of walking out of doors, be sure to pray for good weather!

In addition to the above, Seoul now boasts a number of new structures built for the 1988 Summer Olympiad, which, no doubt, guides will insist upon showing all visitors. Tell them to hurry through because Kimchee and Bulgogki—the national dishes of pickled cucumbers and grilled garlic/sesame-coated beef chunks—are awaiting!

SRI LANKA

Sri Lanka means Resplendent Land. It also means curry and rice, swimming in the Indian Ocean, graceful women in saris, men in dhotis, and serene monks. A favorite memory is of a monk walking down a road, barefoot and alone, oblivious to a sudden summer rain. Sri Lanka is both the ancient and contemporary name of this beautiful island that has been called Ceylon; it lies just thirty-one miles from the southern tip of India, and fifty-five miles (ten degrees) north of the equator.

Sri Lanka's first inhabitants came from northern India in the sixth century B.C. and their descendents were converted to Buddhism in the third century B.C. Indeed, we are told the religion was brought to Sri Lanka by a missionary son of India's famous Emperor Ashoka. The island seems to have been on an important trading route, for the Arabs appeared in the twelfth century. When the Portuguese occupied the coastal areas in the sixteenth century they called the island Celaio (Ceylon), a name that stuck for 450 years. The Dutch took over from 1658 to 1795, when they deferred to the British. In 1802, Ceylon became a British Crown Colony (except for the kingdom of Kandy, which did not submit until 1815). She gained her independence from Britain in 1948 and reassumed the name Sri Lanka in 1972.

The best way to approach **Colombo** is by sea, the way the early visitors came, because the capital has a superb harbor (made even better by the British). The city is a hodgepodge of British colonial architecture, Oriental bazaars, and industrial suburbs. Your ship will dock in front of the Fort, the scene of many a battle but today a commercial hub with large banks, shipping offices, jewelry shops, and kiosks. The western fringes of the Fort dissolve into *pettah* (outer fort), which gives the appearance of an Oriental bazaar—a rabbit warren of streets and nonstop haggling for just about anything in the world. Among other items, Sri Lanka is renowned for gems—rubies, amethysts, emeralds, aquamarines, garnets, topazes, and moonstones. South of the Fort is another complex, in the Galle Face section of the seventy-two-mile Galle Road.

You'll want to see Victoria Park, now called Vihara Maha Devi, the Colombo Museum with its throne of the last king of Kandy, the performing elephants at Dehiwela Zoo, the President's Palace and

Clocktower, and the sun setting over the Indian Ocean from the Mount Lavinia Hotel. Or you can cross the Victoria Bridge for a visit to Kelaniya and the 2000-year-old sacred shrine, where Buddha is said to have bathed in the river. The temple is called Raja Maha Vihare, and is one of the three most sacred places in Sri Lanka.

During a recent visit to Sri Lanka, my charming guide, Constance Perera, told me that some cruise ships now call at **Trincomalee,** a major east-coast city whose harbor is considered to be one of the best sheltered in the world. "Trinco," as aficionados call it, was home base for the Allied fleet during World War II and a major Royal Navy base thereafter. Today, it is known mainly for some of the most unspoiled beaches in the world, and for whale-watching off its shores. If your vessel calls at Trinco and then Colombo, you will have the best of all worlds—including a three-day overland journey to **Ratnapura,** city of gems, **Kandy** and the verdant hill country where tea and spices grow in abundance, and a peek at the cultural triangle. This latter area features the ancient cities of **Anuradhapura,** the ruins at **Polonnaruwa,** and the citadel at **Sigiriya.** Accommodations are excellent throughout Sri Lanka, to compensate for the lousy roads.

THAILAND

Bangkok is the most exhilarating and exasperating city in all of Southeast Asia. To say it is a city of contrasts is putting it mildly. It's hot and humid all the time, noisy, dirty from traffic fumes, and dotted with tawdry bars and shops (left over from the Vietnam War, when this was a favorite R & R)—yet the city has the most charming people on earth, beautiful traditions, and exquisite temples and houses. A curious melange of the old and new, with 4 million inhabitants, Bangkok has been the capital of Thailand only since 1780, when a General Chao P'ya Chakri became King Rama I and moved his court from Thon Buri, across the Chao Phya River. Today's Thailand (the former Kingdom of Siam) is still a monarchy, albeit modified, and the present King Bhumibol Adulyadej (Rama IX) and his lovely Queen Sirikit (he calls her his "smile") live in the Royal Palace in the center of town. They are much loved by their people, although it is no secret that some stern generals behind the throne really control things.

This is the city of *klongs* (canals) and *wat* (temples), and between the two you'll be well-occupied. Some say there are more than three hundred wat in Bangkok—which isn't too difficult to believe. These religious structures are a mixture of Indian, Chinese, and Khmer (Cambodian) influences, with the addition of Thai fancy in their colorful, multitiered roofs and curved gables. Adding even more local color is the endless stream of barefoot monks who wander about, their rice bowls extended for contribution while their saffron robes sway gently in the warm breezes.

The best place to begin a tour of Bangkok is the Royal Palace complex, a fascinating mixture of European and Thai architectural styles. In the compound is the most famous wat in the country, the Chapel of the Emerald Buddha (Wat Phrakaeo), a 31-inch statue sitting on a high altar. (Men are requested to wear coat and tie and ladies a skirt and appropriate shoes on the Royal Palace tour. And Thais remove their shoes when entering temples.) The Temple of the Reclining Buddha (Wat Po), close to the Royal Palace, houses a 160-foot statue of the Reclining Buddha, symbolizing the passing of Lord Buddha into Nirvana. In the courtyard of this temple is a bodhi tree, said to have sprung from a branch of the very tree under which the Buddha once rested. Another impressive temple is Wat Trimitr, the Temple of the Golden Buddha, with its five-and-one-half-ton seated Buddha of gold. My favorite landmark in Bangkok is Wat Arun, or Temple of the Dawn, on the banks of the Chao Phya River. Near it is the collection of the king's barges, ornately carved and gilded for ceremonial occasions. When you have had enough of wat, it's time for the klongs, where you will see another side of life. On these canals that wind through Bangkok are long, narrow boats loaded with fruits, flowers, vegetables, and handmade wooden products. See them early in the morning (6:30 a.m.) when the floating markets are in full force, and you will also observe the many families living along the banks as they rise for the day. (A guided tour is best for this excursion, but you can also bargain for your own boat.)

Thailand's National Museum is one of the most interesting in Southeast Asia. For a view of more personal treasures, visit Jim Thompson's House (open weekday mornings) or the charming Suan Pakkard Palace, former home of the Queen Mother. Both are good examples of typical Thai houses, which are actually exquisitely carved teak pavilions pieced together. Don't forget to look for the "spirit house" on the grounds. This interesting birdhouselike object on a pole is kept filled with fresh flowers, food, and incense to appease the spirits who first inhabited the land.

If you can make it through the smog and traffic, and the noise of the three-wheeled cycles that act as cheap taxis, see the beautiful Thai dances on the lawn of the Oriental Hotel. Here, in the somewhat cooler breezes of the Chao Phya River, you will be treated to tales of the Ramayana, the Monkey King, and such, danced by local beauties wearing rich Thai silk costumes. It's worth the effort to get across town, and if you take taxis on your own, be sure you know how much to pay. The Thais haggle over everything, taxis included. You must set a price with the driver, and then disregard what the meter says as it ticks merrily on all the time. And remember, traffic jams are endemic in Bangkok, so leave for appointments early and be patient.

If your vessel calls at the beach resort of **Pattaya** on the Eastern Gulf, you may opt for an air-conditioned bus tour of Bangkok or just taxi a few minutes into town to see what all the shouting is about. Pattaya was a sleepy little fishing village until the early 1960s, when American servicemen arrived in force and turned the place into a boomtown. Since then, the natives have never looked back. Pattaya is Atlantic City, Miami Beach, and Waikiki with Thai overtones. Good times is the name of the game here, and there is plenty of sun and surf to make anything happen. There are some good hotels and good seafood restaurants, but take care not to overpay. The place LIVES on tourists, most of whom are one-time visitors. Pattaya is not a place for serious sightseeing or shopping; it is strictly for relaxing (R & R, the soldiers call it) and people-watching.

THE MEDITERRANEAN

EGYPT AND THE NILE RIVER

While many cruise vessels call at Port Said, then pack their passengers onto a bus for the three-hour ride through the desert to Cairo, the real gateway to Egypt and the Valley of the Kings is **Alexandria,** the country's second largest city. Founded by Alexander the Great almost by chance—he was enroute elsewhere but liked the fine harbor—Alexandria was an important trading and commercial center for the ancient world. Its lighthouse on the Isle of Pharos shone for centuries and was considered one of the Seven Wonders of the ancient world. Culturally, the city was also prominent, and its library had only one close rival—Ephesus. Politically, Alexandria was the base for Egypt's rulers—Ptolemy I and his son Ptolemy II, as well as Cleopatra, who lived here with her lovers Julius Caesar and later Mark Antony.

Poets have always loved Alexandria for its romance and color; Lawrence Durrell even dedicated his *Alexandria Quartet* to the place.

However, in the present metropolis you will have to look around corners and through shabby exteriors to imagine the glories of yesteryear. Pay a visit to the Greco-Roman Museum with its busts of Alexander and various Roman emperors to realize that this was, indeed, a classical town; the Roman amphitheater; the catacombs used when Christianity tried to take hold; and the many mosques established after the Muslims conquered the land in the seventh century. A pillar once attributed to Pompey is now thought to be a victory column dedicated to the Roman Emperor Diocletian by his troops.

Outside of Alexandria—only ten miles—is a former residence of the royal family known as Montaza Palace. Here King Faruk abdicated on July 26, 1952 (a calendar with the date still hangs on the wall). The palace is as gaudy and overdecorated as Faruk and his family left it, but the lovely grounds have landscaped gardens and a small beach where you can swim. About an hour from Alexandria is the town of Rashid, where the Rosetta stone was discovered in 1799, which is worth a visit for those with time to spare.

But all roads lead to **Cairo,** the capital of Egypt and a city of mansions and squalor, peace initiatives (Americans are now treated well) and hostile looks (Muslims are sometimes insulted by the way we dress, so leave your skin back on the ship, please), and *baksheesh* (tips) every time you turn around! If your time is limited, and it is for most cruise passengers, the best deal in town is the Egyptian Museum, one of those rare museums that even those who usually don't like museums seem to agree is beyond description. But there are other museums of interest: the Islamic; the Coptic; the Center for Art and Life; the Papyrus Institute; and the Cotton Museum. Within Cairo you can also tour the early Christian churches in the Old City, an abundance of mosques, and a shop for every kind of souvenir possible—even have a caftan made while you wait. If you are adventurous, try an outrageously priced camel ride or an economical and thoroughly enjoyable sail on the Nile in the age-old, much-photographed, high-masted boat called a *felucca.*

But, no doubt, the Sphinx and pyramids are what you came to see, and your tour will take you to nearby Giza, actually considered a suburb of Cairo. Of the nine pyramids in the Giza complex, the Great Pyramid of Cheops is the most impressive and well known, and you may wish to visit only this one. Long ranked among the wonders of the ancient world, it was constructed about 2500 B.C. to ensure the Pharaoh Cheops of a trouble-free afterlife. (The Egyptians prepared themselves richly for what happened with death, while the Greeks were in love with being alive.) The pyramid took twenty years to build, and several thousand slaves moved more than two million blocks of stone. (Herodotus, the Greek historian, claimed that it took 100,000 men per year to do the job, but later historians say this is a slight exaggeration!) If this is the only pyramid that you desire to tour, you will find it the best example of what these luxurious resting places were all about. You may go inside all three of the Great Pyramids, but if you are tempted to climb them be forewarned that the stones have weathered over thousands of years and are very crumbly (and I certainly wouldn't want to lose you at this point). Alas, more than one tourist has fallen to his demise. Six smaller pyramids and many lesser tombs are in this area, as well as the Solar Boat (which may not be open to the public) used to ferry the body of the pharaoh from his palace in Memphis to this final resting place. Below the valley of the pyramids sits the majestic Sphinx, with the head of the Pharaoh Chephren (owner of the second pyramid) and the body of a lion. It measures some 240 feet long by 66 feet high but seems much smaller than you had imagined. Between its paws is an inscription that tells of a young prince who rested in its shadow, and was promised the double crown of Egypt if he would remove the sand from its paws. Of course he did, and that prince became the Pharaoh Tuthmose IV (whose reign lasted from about 1425 to 1417 B.C.), who had the inscription carved.

One-day tours will not include **Memphis** and Saqqara. If you have the time, though, go to this ancient city and its necropolis on the west bank of the Nile not more than a dozen miles south of Cairo. Memphis, capital of ancient Egypt during the Old Kingdom and part of the Middle Kingdom periods (from approximately 2700 to 1800 B.C.), was reputed to have matched the splendor of Babylon. Not much is left to see of all this past glory but a few statues and a lovely site covered by palm trees! Out in the desert lies the necropolis of **Saqqara,** the city of the dead. Here you will see a large complex of pyramids and tombs of the important personages of Memphis (try to visit in the early morning, afternoon heat can be intense). The most famous is the step pyramid of Zoser, the first pharaoh in whose name a pyramid was constructed. As he lived a very long time, what began as an elaborate tomb became a continually expanded stepped pyramid.

Sailing slowly on the **Nile River** in a small, air-conditioned ship is one of the highlights of worldwide cruising—for here are all the names of ancient monuments you have read about and always wanted to see. You pass by six thousand years of civilization, magnificent scenery, and ancient, unspoiled villages. A view of life on any river, and especially the Nile, is an unparalleled experience. In the company of your fellow passengers and guides you will understand why Herodotus wrote some 2500 years ago, "Egypt is the gift of the Nile."

The cruise ships vary from small, almost private yachts that carry not more than twenty passengers to larger, more luxurious vessels that hold about eighty passengers and come with swimming pools and on-board boutiques. You have a choice of from three days with stops of just the most popular sites to two full weeks on some six hundred miles of the river. Most of the vessels feature their own hand-picked Egyptologists who ensure that your mind is busy and not too muddled by all the dynasties, kingdoms, and gods and goddesses of ancient Egypt. (If you are especially keen on Egypt, choose one of the longer Nile cruises operated by Swan Hellenic of London or Abercrombie and Kent of Chicago. They are more expensive but worth every penny for the excellent lecturers and tours.)

A few of the more famous monuments that you will visit on your Nile cruise are the temples and tombs at Abydos, among the most ancient in all Egypt; the temple of Hathor (the cow-headed goddess) at Dendera; the temples of Karnak and Luxor commemorating the victories that made Egypt a great power in the ancient world; Thebes and the Valley of the Kings (as well as the Valley of the Queens); Aswan with Elephantine Island; and the great temple of Rameses II at Abu Simbel. In addition, you will see something of rural Egypt and the forty million people who live along the banks of the Nile in the very footsteps of their ancestors. All this adds to the appreciation of how vital this river was to the ancient world, and why the Egyptians believed that even their gods traveled upon these waters. Who knows—perhaps they did.

FRANCE

One of my most favorite cruise discoveries of the past year is **Bordeaux,** that wine capital that lies on a graceful curve of the Garonne River in the southwest corner of France. Bordeaux, sixty miles upriver from the Atlantic Ocean, is one of France's major ports and most historic areas. The city is famous for the great quantities of wine produced in the surrounding area and shipped down the Gironde to England and northern Europe. Indeed, according to the late Alexis Lichine in his excellent *Guide to the Wines and Vineyards of France,* the equivalent of 1 million of today's cases was recorded shipped in the year 1350! Considering the adult population of Europe at the time, that 1 million figure is even more astounding.

My first view of the Bordeaux area was from the deck of the *Vistafjord,* as we sailed slowly up the Gironde and then Garonne rivers to dock right in the center of the town's medieval structures. It was early September, just a few weeks before harvest, and the perfect time to see the famous chateaux with last year's wine lying peacefully in barrels in the cool *chais* (Bordelaise for *caves*), and the plump grapes on the rows and rows of vines just waiting for that special moment of picking. The Bordeaux countryside is varied and two days in port do not do it justice, but it certainly beats just sailing by!

Shore excursions in the Bordeaux region feature wine tours and tastings at the various chateaux as well as some superb meals. If you are very lucky, you may visit Chateau Lafite-Rothschild and Chateau Mouton Rothschild with its fine wine museum (the two properties are side by side but the proprietors do not speak 'unless absolutely necessary). You may also see Chateau de Beychevelle, the very elegant Chateau Palmer (where a set lunch is often served) as well as the famed Chateau Margaux, and neighboring Chateau Prieure Lichine (owned and operated by the son of the late wine connoisseur Alexis Lichine). If there is time, the valley of the Garonne features Entre-deux-Mers (which means "between two rivers") and Sauternes. Our guide, Gilles Le Paire, took us up to the exquisite medieval village of St. Emilion; we tasted the wines of Chateau Ausone and Chateau Cheval Blanc, and bought some sparkling Bordeaux (yes, there is such a thing) in the ancient cloister of Cordeliers. Only the French would sell wine in a cloister!

If tasting the previous harvest is not your thing, there is plenty to do in Bordeaux itself. From the ship's berth just across from the Place de la Bourse (stock exchange), it is just a hop into the old section of town. Here, the narrow back streets are lined with wonderful old buildings and open onto delightful squares filled with cafes and tables in the sunshine. The city has some fine museums, including the Musee des Beaux Arts and the Musee D'Aquitaine, as well as an impressive Grand Theatre, considered one of the most beautiful in France. It is said that the double stairway inside was copied by the architect Garnier when he designed the Paris Opera House. There are some very pleasant restaurants lining the street beside the theater. I can't remember the name of the one we chose for that evening, but it had pink tablecloths and excellent local seafood. (Note: If you are interested in a wine cruise to Bordeaux, be certain the ship calls in September as *tout le monde* goes on holiday during the month of August and the chateaux are closed to visitors.)

From Marseille to Menton, the **French Riviera** unfolds a spectacular coastline onto a blue-green sea. The Cote d'Azur, as an obscure nineteenth-century poet named it, has almost eternal sunshine, sparkling waters, and flowered hills. It's not surprising that painters, poets, and other artists continue to find their muse here.

Queen of the Cote d'Azur is **Nice,** a year-round vacation spot and the cultural center of the Riviera. The city was founded in 350 B.C. by Greeks from Marseille, who called it Nike (victory), and has always been a popular watering hole for royalty, especially when they were out of favor at home. Napoleon visited in 1794 (when he lived at 6 Rue Bonaparte, three blocks behind the port) and in 1796 (when, anguished by parting with Josephine, he wrote her a famous letter from here). The British discovered Nice in the eighteenth century, as an alternative to their own dreadful winter weather. In 1820, the British colony paid for the magnificent boardwalk spanning the length of the Baie des Anges and appropriately named Promenade des Anglais. For over 160 years this promenade has been the meeting place for summer and winter visitors, with its one side facing the sea and the other lined with impressive facades of elegant hotels and mansions, public buildings, and casinos. Athough the beach in this area is not sand but rather large pebbles, this deters no one—it's body to bronze body from May to September! East of the Quai des Etats Unis is the Castle, and behind the port is the Old Town, where narrow, winding streets are lined with medieval houses, wonderful food shops, a few interesting museums, and the famous casinos. Less swinging and more sophisticated is the Cimiez district, up in the hills, which boasts Roman ruins, the former residence of Queen Victoria and her retinue, and the Matisse and Chagall museums. (Both Henri Matisse and Raoul Dufy are buried there.)

If your time in Nice can be extended (I am not suggesting you jump ship, but some cruises do embark and disembark here), you can take exciting excursions in all directions. From Nice to Menton, you have a choice of three different routes, or *corniches,* as the French say. The Corniche Inferieure (lower road) takes you through Villefranche (which also gets its share of cruise calls), Cap Ferrat, Beaulieu, Monaco, and Cape Martin. The Moyenne Corniche (middle road) offers good coastal views and access to the medieval mountain town of Eze. But the high road will thrill you most. The Grand Corniche, built by Napoleon along the remains of the ancient Aurelian Way, is definitely not for the tender-hearted! It's a continual grade that's straight up and then down, but a chance encounter halfway through is worth wearing the lining of the car's brakes. This is the small village of **La Turbie** (population: 1800), which overlooks Monte Carlo 1400 feet below and offers splendid panoramas of the coastline. In the center of La Turbie sits the famed Alpine Trophy, commissioned by the Roman Senate in 6 B.C. to commemorate Augustus's victory over forty-four previously unconquered tribes (uniting Italy with Gaul and Germania); erected with the aid of slaves and elephants on the spot where the principal roads crossing the Alps met, it's an astounding sight to come upon way up here. Even the poet Dante was so impressed he dedicated some verse to La Turbie. You can read it on the plaque of a nearby house.

All three routes terminate in **Menton,** the easternmost town of the Cote d'Azur. Smack at the Italian border, this resort has the warmest climate of all, influences from both countries, and was another favorite of the British. Artist Jean Cocteau decorated the Salles des Mariages in the Town Hall and left enough memorabilia behind for a museum in his honor, in a seventeenth-century fort near the harbor.

Modern French artists so loved the Riviera that they left memorials. Marc Chagall and his wife donated some 450 works of art to the country he embraced when he left his native Russia, and the French government built a museum in Nice, not far from the Matisse Museum.

Between Nice and Antibes, in the little town of Cagnes-sur-Mer, is Les Collettes, where Pierre Auguste Renoir lived from 1908 to 1919, now a museum. Four miles from Antibes is Diot, where Fernand Leger lived. After he died in 1955, his widow dedicated a museum with the largest collection of his artworks ever assembled. In Antibes itself is the Picasso Museum, another great collection personally donated by the artist (actually, it's on a permanent loan). I personally treasure the Matisse Chapel in Vence. In 1947 the seventy-seven-year old artist created this small chapel for Dominican nuns and then called it his "masterpiece . . . the culmination of a whole life dedicated to the search for truth."

Just outside the medieval town of St. Paul de Vence is the Maeght Foundation, a gallery occupying a magnificent site overlooking the Mediterranean to the south and the snowcapped Alps to the north. In a series of open and enclosed courts, surrounded by pine trees, rosemary, and lavender, are works by Braque, Chagall, Miro, Giacometti, Calder, Chillida, Ubac, and many, many more. Within the town is La Colombe d'Or (the Golden Dove), one of the region's most celebrated restaurants. Being lucky is sitting on the terrace and watching the doves turn golden in the sun!

If your cruise ship calls at **Cannes,** you may wish to remain on the western edge of the Cote d'Azur where the bikinis are said to be the briefest. Cannes has been fashionable since the mid-nineteenth century, and since then the Promenade de la Croisette has been sauntered along by everyone who's anyone. The harbor is packed with yachts during the season, and in the elegant shops and casino are tanned beauties of all sexes. Things are even livelier at bad-girl **St. Tropez,** the carnival town that Brigitte Bardot made famous a few decades ago. You will notice varying types of chic-ness along the Riviera, and St. Tropez is one extreme.

Traveling westward toward the Spanish border, your cruise ship may depart from **Toulon,** which has a beautiful, natural harbor and is the home of the French naval forces. During Roman times the port was famous for the purple dye it produced. It was also the site of Napoleon's first important victory—against the British—in 1793. During World War II this harbor was under German occupation. The National Memorial to the Provencal Landing is up in the peaceful hills, on the Corniche road to Mount Faron. The summit of this mountain has superb views. Stop also at the square featuring the craft workshops and studios—potter, weaver, ceramist, wrought-iron smith.

Marseille is the most famous name in this part of France, for it is the country's largest port and oldest city (founded in 600 B.C. by Greeks from Asia Minor). This city is credited with France's national anthem, although the song was actually written in Strasbourg as the war song of the Army of the Rhine. During the French Revolution, however, Marseille's 500 volunteers heard the song and sang it along the way to

Paris. By the time they arrived in Paris the tune was well known and identified with them, and so it was renamed the *Marseillaise* and adopted as the nation's anthem. In Marseille museums might easily be bypassed, but people-watching is a must—find a sidewalk cafe, have a coffee or a glass of local wine, and enjoy the variety of people that parade in this busy harbor.

Known as the Island of Beauty, **Corsica** has a rich and varied landscape that features beaches of honey-colored sand, secret coves, rocky crags, and rolling hills of pine, chestnut, oak, olive, and cork trees. Between the sea and the forests are scented herbs and bushes that perfume the air. "I'd know it if only from its fragrance," said Napoleon of the island on which he was born.

The main port of call for cruise ships to Corsica is **Ajaccio,** with a splendid harbor and a French-Italianate atmosphere. This is where old women walk slowly, slightly bent over and always dressed in black, cats dart about the narrow streets, and children play among donkey carts. You can visit the birthplace of Napoleon in town as well as the Napoleon room in the Hotel de Ville, or city hall, where you will find that nothing much has changed since the eighteenth century. Visit the Fesch Museum of Italian Primitives, and you'll understand a little more of this island that France has owned for just over two hundred years.

GIBRALTAR

This 2.28-square-mile British Crown Colony, sitting strategically on a peninsula at the mouth of the Mediterranean, was ceded to Great Britain by Spain in the Treaty of Utrecht of 1713. Spain has been attempting to recover it ever since. Relations between the two countries were so tense in the 1960s and 1970s that Spain closed its border with Gibraltar. Today the border has reopened as talks on control continue and a few thousand Spaniards enter "the Rock" daily to shop for duty-free British woolens and other luxury items. There are no natural resources here, other than a 1400 foot-high rock, a natural fortress that holds some of Britain's most sophisticated defense equipment. The commander of the fortress is also the Governor of Gibraltar and appointed by the Crown. About 30,000 people live in Gib or The Rock, mainly of Genoese, Portuguese, and Maltese descent. The two official languages are Spanish and English. With little to see or do, it's a perfect cruise stop for just a few hours. You can visit St. Michael's Cave, with its huge stalagmite and stalactite formations and a natural amphitheater that was the setting for a beauty pageant the day I visited. You can also go up the Rock by cable car for a spectacular view of the Spanish mainland and the African coastline. Don't forget a brief stop to see the wild Barbary apes—but hang on to the handbag. These apes are famous for being impolite!

GREECE

The Piraeus is the proper name for Greece's first port, and one of the largest in the entire Mediterranean. Gateway to Homer's "wine-dark sea"—the Aegean—as well as to all of Greece and the monuments of the Golden Age of Western Civilization, it dates from the third millennium B.C. and reached its peak in the fifth century B.C. In 493 B.C., Themistocles started the Long Walls that joined the port with Athens, seven miles away. Only sections remain, the rest having been destroyed by the Spartans at the end of the Peloponnesian War in 404 B.C.

Athens—thirty minutes away by taxi, tour bus, or electric train—is home to more than one-third of Greece's 9 million people, and it's difficult to do it justice in just one day. If you have extra time to spend abroad, spend it here. Syntagma, or Constitution Square, with the Parliament Building and Tomb of the Unknown Soldier, open-air cafes that seat 3000 people for hours on end, banks and travel offices, is the center of city life. The Plaka area teems in daylight with shoppers, and at night revelers at the tavernas enjoy tantalizing food, a fine variety of reasonably priced wines, and entertainment. (Some tavernas have rooftop gardens where you can dine under the spell of the Acropolis.) The Acropolis dominates Athens from "rosy-fingered dawn" to sunset, and if your visit coincides with a full moon you are lucky indeed. Air pollution, however, is speeding the city's disintegration more than all the centuries of war, and you are no longer allowed to wander through the Parthenon or to view the caryatids in their rightful place on the portico of the Erechtheum. (They, poor dears, are now captive in the Acropolis Museum.) Just below the Acropolis is the Agora, or ancient marketplace, where excavations for the past half-century have been under the direction of the University of Cincinnati and the American School of Classical Studies in Athens. This is a wonderful place to roam, and the Theseum, a temple dedicated to Theseus, perches on a grassy knoll overlooking it all.

When you have visited Hadrian's Arch and the Temple of Jupiter, the National Archaeological Museum, and the smaller Benaki and Byzantine museums, taken the tram up Mt. Lycabettus, and wandered the many back streets, it's time to see the rest of Greece. The local CHAT tours (4 Stadiou Street) have comfortable day trips to Sounion (where the Temple of Poseidon overlooks the sea and the cape), to Delphi on

Mt. Parnassus, and to the classical sites of Corinth, Mycenae and Argos, Nauplia and Epidaurus. Local buses are plentiful and a more adventurous way to get about. A trip to the Plains of Marathon, for example, is about one hour from Athens each way (unless, of course, you plan to run back). Rental cars are available, but gasoline is *very* expensive and you must know the rules of the road. If you park in an illegal zone, for example, the police teach a lesson by removing your license plates, making driving back impossible (and costly).

If the lure of the sea remains strong, excellent day trips from Palaion Phalero (between Athens and the airport) go to three nearby islands on a choice of cruise ships. (The cost for the day is about $40 including a lunch tray at sea, and the companies will pick you up and deliver you back to your hotel.) First call is usually at the island of **Aegina,** where a donkey ride through vineyards and pistachio fields will take you up to the Doric-style Temple of Aphaea or, if you prefer, you can have a swim in the bay of Aghia Marina. The next call is **Hydra,** an artists' colony with quaint, brightly colored houses along the waterfront. It's a wonderful place to stroll, shop, or sip ouzo. In the afternoon your ship visits the charming, unspoiled island of Poros, an important religious center in antiquity and home of the marble that was used, among other things, to build the Temple of Solomon. **Poros**—a weekend retreat of many Athenians who catch the hydrofoil on Friday evenings from Piraeus—has a beautiful harbor, windmills, fruit orchards, and olive groves. And then it's a two-hour sail back to Palaion Phaleron in the late afternoon, while you have a cool drink in the lounge and learn Greek dancing from the crew.

If you dock at **Itea** on the Gulf of Corinth and take the half-hour bus ride through Parnassus Country to **Delphi,** your route is through a sea of olives—probably the finest groves in all of Greece. First stop on your tour should be the Delphi Museum, with over ten thousand items found in the excavations begun by French archaeologists in 1892. Most impressive of the artworks is the bronze charioteer, dating from 478 B.C., a barefoot, life-size figure. Other works include stone friezes, toga-clad statesmen, a sixth-century B.C. sphinx presented by the island of Naxos to the oracle, and pottery fragments dating from the Mycenean period (1600 to 1100 B.C.).

Renowned throughout the ancient world, the Oracle at Delphi was often consulted for political reasons and thus thought to have changed the course of history many times. The woman who spoke was called a Pythia, and she had to fast three days and then bathe in the nearby Castalian Spring before she spoke. The upper precinct at Delphi includes the remains of the sanctuary, the Sacred Way leading to the Temple of Apollo, a fourth century B.C. theater, and a stadium where seven thousand spectators would watch the Pythian games every four years (it's a tough climb up to this one, but worth it.) The lower ruins feature a large gymnasium, the Temple of Athena, a lovely *tholos,* or round temple, whose purpose is unknown. The mystery makes it the most interesting structure of the lot.

During the Panhellenic games held in **Olympia** every four years, a "truce of God" was proclaimed. Rivalries were abolished so all of Greece could come to Olympia in safety for the spirit of the competitions and social functions that followed. The greatest honor and achievement was to be an Olympic victor and to wear a crown of wild olives. The winner would be feted, paraded, and even immortalized in poetry and sculpture. The status of winners was great; even important generals would defer to a winner. The first Olympic games were probably held in 776 B.C. and were continued every fourth year until 394 A.D., when they were abolished by the Roman Emperor Theodosius II on the grounds they were a pagan ritual. The games were held in midsummer under a full moon, and male athletes competed in the nude. Women were barred from the premises (and the events), but male spectators were encouraged to come from all over Greece and, indeed, the ancient world. The games were held on a site adjoining the Sanctuary of Zeus in Olympia, in the northwest area of the Peloponnese. This is where the Olympic torch is still lit today (with a magnifying glass and the rays of the sun) and then carried by runners to the location of the games, a tradition that began in 1936. As you walk among the ruins today, you pass through the fifth-century Temple of Zeus, the gymnasium, what is thought to be the oldest hotel in the world (to house spectators), the workshop of the sculptor Phidias (whose gold and ivory statue of Zeus here was one of the Seven Wonders of the ancient world), the house of Roman Emperor Nero (who introduced contests like singing into the games), and the fabulous stadium. (Perhaps one day the Olympic games will again be held here, where they belong.) The Olympia Museum displays artifacts found on the site (first excavated by French archaeologists in 1829 and continued by Hitler during World War II) and a scale model of the entire area. The Olympic Games Museum has a collection of memorabilia dating from 1896, when the games were revived in Athens.

Six of the islands in the Ionian chain—Corfu, Paxos, Lefkas, Ithaki, Kefallinia, and Zakinthos—lie off the western coast of Greece. The seventh is near the southeastern Peloponnese—this is Kithira where, according to Greek mythology, Aphrodite made her first appearance.

Of the Ionian group **Corfu** is an international tourist spot and popular cruise stop. It has an interesting history and provides a much-needed respite on sailings between Venice and Piraeus. All other Greek islands envy Corfu for its year-round greenness due to cypress groves and millions of olive trees. Of all the islands, Corfu is also the most un-Greek. Italian was spoken here for more than five hundred years, and the island was under the protection of the Venetian Empire from the fourteenth until the eighteenth century. Venetian occupation was followed by Russian, French, and British, the latter leaving a definite mark. The entire chain was ceded to Greece in 1864, and Corfu soon became a summer residence of the Greek royal family. Sailing into the port of Corfu you see the charming town nestled between two Venetian forts. The newer fortress (mid-sixteenth century) overlooks the port, while the older fort has a view of the Esplanade, or main square. The old Venetian-style town is fun to explore and good for shopping. Once in a while you'll happen upon a British legacy like the Royal Palace, the cricket field, and many of the statues in the Esplanade. Be sure to pay a visit to Saint Spiridon, the church dedicated to the patron saint, who is believed to have saved the island from plague in the seventeenth century and an invasion by the Turks in the eighteenth century. After you have wandered about the town, you may want to head for one of the beautiful beaches to sun on Corfu's famous golden sands. If your ship stays long enough, don't miss the Sound and Light performance (in English) in the Venetian Palace four nights a week.

Two out-of-town shore excursions of Corfu are known for fine views (and not much else). The first stop is Kanoni, a landscaped area named after the French canon that was once placed here. From this precipice you can photograph the so-called islet monasteries—the white convent of Vlachernae and the chapel on Mouse Island. When your eyes have absorbed the beauty of this setting, your tour will go on to the Achilleion, the former palace of Empress Elizabeth of Austria, which is now a casino/hotel near the village of Gastouri. The 200-year-old structure is rather hideous, due to the questionable taste of the empress as well as of Kaiser Wilhelm II (who owned it subsequently), but the proprietors and their guests certainly had lovely views from the terrace.

Shopping in Corfu town is always a pleasure, but remember that shopkeepers close from about lunchtime to 4 or 5 p.m. There is a very good branch of Lalaounis here, one of the famous Greek jewelers, as well as several other shops selling gold and silver at (almost) giveaway prices. Corfu also claims to make the best and the lightest olive oil in the world—and I paid about $8 recently for a two and a half gallon can. Getting it home was worth the agony!

Focus of the Cycladic Islands is the deserted island of **Delos,** whose only inhabitants these days are some caretakers of its ruins and a few archaeologists. According to Greek legend, Delos arose from the sea just in time for Leto, Zeus's paramour, to give birth to Artemis and her twin brother, the sun god Apollo. This has always been a sacred island, and when the cult of Apollo was prominently practiced it became wealthy as offerings to the Temple of Apollo filled its coffers. It was the banking center for the Eastern Mediterranean, with money loaned out to other islands at an outrageous rate, and its inhabitants also did a brisk business in the slave trade. Then, in 88 B.C., Delos was caught in a dispute between Athens and Rome. To make his point for the Athenian side Mithridates, King of Pontus, completely devastated the island, carrying off all the valuables. Delos never recovered, and its commercial role was usurped by Rhodes.

Walking tours of ancient monuments in Delos take about two hours and give you ample evidence of the island's glorious past. The most impressive memorial is the Terrace of the Lions, where five archaic beasts (seventh century B.C.) still hold vigil, crouching on their hind legs. You will also see the remains of the Temple of Apollo, the Sacred Lake (now dry), and ruins of elegant villas with their delicate mosaic floors in the Roman quarter. Especially beautiful houses are the Dolphin, the Trident, and the Masks. If you have time, climb the steps up Mount Kynthos for a splendid view of the other Cyclades—Syros, Naxos, Paros, Tenos, and Mykonos.

If I had a genie I would wish to be transported from time to time to the relaxing nearby island of **Mykonos.** Mykonos has some much-photographed windmills, a church (they say) for every day of the year, and a whitewashed maze of narrow and charming back streets that were designed to confuse raiding pirates. Refresh your soul by sitting in a sidewalk cafe by the seawalls and letting the sparkling sun take over. Because of the pleasant atmosphere and cordial natives, Mykonos has drawn artisans from all over the world who paint, make sandals, weave, sculpt, design jewelry, knit, crochet, and who can even make you a dress in two hours. One wonders why the sign on the pier—"Help Keep Our Island Clean"—is necessary. I like best the sign in front of the statue in the town square, "Please do not park backpacks here." While days may be spent on the beach, evenings are always spent in town, watching people parade and then finding a superb little taverna for a leisurely meal (my favorite is Antonini's on the square).

Santorini, sometimes called **Thira,** is the southernmost island in the Cyclades, and its eerie place in history is due to theories it may be the lost island of Atlantis. Recent excavations at Akrotiri reveal that a cosmic event in 1520 B.C. destroyed a flourishing civilization. As your cruise ship sails into the Bay of Santorini, note that this island, known as Strongyle or "the round one" in ancient times, is in five sections, of which Thira is the largest. Soaring 900 feet above the sea and plunging 1200 feet into the submerged core of its volcanic crater—which seems fathomless—the island has a feeling of bareness, with rugged black lava cliffs topped by whitewashed houses and chapels that have a frenzied, surreal look about them.

From your cruise ship to shore is undoubtedly by tender; from the shore up to the tiny, terraced town of Thira, you can either walk the winding and slippery eight hundred steps or pay a ripoff fee to ride a donkey. (While the ride is not one of my favorite travel memories, it is an experience you might want to try once! You may even buy a photograph of yourself to prove that you did it.) Once upstairs in the little town, you can shop around, have a coffee, or explore part of the island. If you have at least two hours before the tender leaves again, hire a taxi to visit the excavated site of Akrotiri, which is believed to have been contemporary with the Minoan civilization and then destroyed by the same holocaust of volcanic eruptions and tidal waves in 1300 B.C. If the site is closed, as it tends to be now on Sundays, you can take a twenty-minute taxi ride to the little town of IA at the other end of the island, where it's fun to walk among the whitewashed houses built into the cliffs and look out at the sea below. (Your cruise ship will look very, very far away from up here.) Our taxi driver on this excursion stopped along the way to show us a charming little chapel dedicated to St. George. If you happen to miss Akrotiri, findings from the excavations are in a special series of exhibit rooms on the second floor of the National Archaeological Museum in Athens and include wall paintings, pottery, and a small person's bed.

The most important city in Macedonia was named after the stepsister of Alexander the Great, Thessaloniki. Founded in 315 B.C. by one of Alexander's generals, **Thessaloniki** (also called **Salonika**) has had a stormy history, primarily due to its situation at the crossroads of the main routes between East and West, Asia and Europe. As a proud and cultured city, it is layered with the legacy of the Romans, Saracens, Normans, Venetians, Turks, Germans, Balkans, and more Turks, peoples who passed through and often conquered. Despite the frequent destructive fires and wars the city endured, you'll find early Greek or Macedonian treasures, Roman monuments, Venetian ramparts, Byzantine churches, and occasional vestiges of the Moslem culture imposed by the Ottoman Empire (although when the Greeks recaptured the city in 1912, they destroyed all the mosques and minarets within reach). Ironically, Thessaloniki, which boasts the tomb of Philip II of Macedon, father of Alexander the Great, is also the birthplace of Kemal Ataturk, who became the father of modern Turkey. A landmark of the city is the fifteenth-century White Tower, constructed by the Venetians at the boundary of the no-longer-standing city walls. Nearby is the Archaeological Museum, with findings from Hellenistic tombs and a rich collection of gold from Macedonia and neighboring Thrace. A road from the White Tower leads to the university named after the philosopher Aristotle, who came from Macedonia.

Either before or after your cruise from Thessaloniki, take a tour around the old town to see the prominent Rotunda, an ancient Roman structure intended as a mausoleum but turned into a Christian church in the fifth century (and dedicated to St. George by Theodosius the Great, who commissioned some fine mosaics). In the sixteenth century the Turks made it into a mosque and added a minaret (which is still there). A few minutes walk from the Rotunda is the house where Kemal Ataturk was born in 1881, preserved by the Turkish government and open to the public.

The Arch of Galerius is another Roman monument, built by the Emperor Galerius in 303 A.D. to commemorate his victory over the Persians. It's surrounded by wonderful old houses and tiny Byzantine churches, and straight up behind are the ancient city walls, with a fourth-century atmosphere and a fine view of the harbor. Cruise passengers are also offered an excursion to Pella—the capital of Macedonia from the fifth century B.C. to 168 B.C. and the birthplace of Alexander in 356 B.C.—with fascinating ruins here as well as beautifully preserved pebble mosaics, streets, and sewer systems.

A one-week cruise itinerary from Thessaloniki, in cooperation with the Greek government (which likes to see the tourist dollar spread around), calls at the islands of Skopelos, Skiathos, Lesbos, Lemnos, and Thasos as well as the port of Kavalla. No longer on most cruise schedules is the all-male enclave of Mount Athos, where women have not been allowed for over nine hundred years (cruise ships with women aboard may not even sail within 500 yards of the main port). Mount Athos, a holy mountain harboring ancient monasteries of the Eastern church, once welcomed male visitors for a meal and overnight. Today, however, men must apply at the Ministry of Foreign Affairs and prove they have serious religious or scientific interests which warrant a visit to the community.

Kavalla, at the Thracian border in eastern Macedonia, is the port for shore excursions to Philippi, another ancient city at the crossroads of history. On the plains of Philippi important battles took place and legendary figures met their fates. St. Paul preached here and sowed the seeds of Christianity before he was detained in prison and finally forced to flee. Brutus is said to have seen Caesar's ghost on the Philippian plains, just before he and Cassius were defeated by Octavian and Mark Antony in the famous 42 B.C. battle. Ruins here include a large agora, or marketplace, a Roman forum, some baths, the prison in which St. Paul languished for a spell, and some early churches.

Skiathos and Skopelos are members of the Sporades, or scattered islands. Beautiful **Skiathos** is known for wild strawberry bushes and olive trees as well as for lovely bays and beaches that invite lounging in the sun. Shore excursions here are relaxing—a short tour of the village and then a quick transfer to one of the beaches. Less than two hours by sea is **Skopelos** ("rock"), green as well as rocky, where charming, whitewashed houses have colorful shutters and doors. The island is noted for its plentiful fruit, especially the plums that you can taste fresh or in various stages of being cured for export.

Lesbos, the third largest island in the Aegean (after Crete and Rhodes), is close to Asia Minor and convenient for excursions by small boat to Dikili, the Turkish port near the archaeological site of Pergamum. Lesbos has played an important role in Greek literature since the eighth-century-B.C. school of poetry was founded here. Native sons and daughters have included Aesop, the great storyteller, and Sappho, who wrote erotic lyrics to other women and was said to have practiced what she preached. Her poems were allegedly burned by the church in the eleventh century. Nonetheless, she left a legacy to the world in the word "lesbian." Legendary figures associated with this island include the lovers Daphnis and Chloe.

Lesbos has a large population (about 150,000), many olive trees (approximately 11 million), and multitudes of sheep and goats. From the capital city of Mytilini you have wonderful views of Asia Minor plus relics of the long Turkish occupation. The countryside is especially beautiful, and shore tours visit the fishing village of Petra up the coast, the pottery town of Agiasos, and the quaint harbor of Molivos (swimming is available nearby). Because Lesbos is so close to Turkey, you will see many Greek soldiers on guard around the island, but don't be put off—it's a way of life that is unfortunately thousands of years old.

The last two islands visited on this special itinerary from Thessaloniki are Lemnos (or Limnos) and Thasos in the Thracian Sea. **Lemnos** is the larger and has the better beaches (your shore excursion will probably take you to Santa Barbara). Rich in legend, this island was home of Hephaestos, blacksmith to the gods. Greek mythology says the Argonauts stayed two years on Lemnos (fathering a generation of children) during their search for the Golden Fleece. A Greek warrior, Philoctetes, was marooned here during the Trojan War. The capital of Lemnos is Mirina (Kastron), a small town dominated by its Genoese castle built in the Middle Ages. The town has a cool, dry climate as well as an inspiring view of Mount Athos—especially at sunset. **Thasos,** in contrast, is hot and humid. Once a prosperous island-state, it was known in the ancient world for gold, marble, and wine exports. The main town of Limin (also called Thasos) is built around the ruins of an agora, a theater, and city walls. The local museum is interesting, but the best finds, alas, were reportedly carted off to the Louvre.

As a member of the baker's dozen Dodecanese islands in the Eastern Aegean, **Kos** lies close to Asia Minor and is best known as the birthplace of Hippocrates, the father of medicine. The main port, founded in the fourth century B.C., has relics of former glories of the Hellenistic, Roman, and Byzantine periods. A twelfth-century Venetian castle lies in ruins to one side of the harbor, its walls lined with the shields of the Knights of St. John, who stopped here in the fourteenth century on their way home from the Crusades. (Of all the sites on Kos, the castle is the least interesting—especially if your cruise is calling at Rhodes.) Just a few minutes' walk from the harbor you will find the ancient Greek agora as well as the temples of Apollo and Venus. For a splendid view from the top, climb up the tier of seats in the well-preserved theater. The museum on Liberty Square is also worth a visit. It has a 400 B.C. statue of Hippocrates, which was found under the theater, as well as a splendid Roman mosaic floor.

Two miles out of town on a beautiful hillside with pine forests, natural springs, and a view of the sea and Asia Minor, the Greeks built the Aesclepion of Hippocrates. One's imagination can run wild up here. Even historians admit they do not know what went on here in ancient times. You will find the Temple of Asclepios, the god of medicine and healing, several curative rooms, plus a swimming pool and a stadium for physical therapy. Some believe that the Greeks performed surgery here, but the Romans built their baths on top of the "operating" rooms. In town, natives will show you a plane tree that Hippocrates is said to have planted and lectured under but botanists today doubt this.

Northernmost island of the Dodecanese, **Patmos** is considered to be the loveliest of all, with beautiful bays and capes and spectacular views at every turn. Although barren like most of Greece (especially in summer), Patmos has on its southern side that sparkling-white architecture found also in the Cyclades islands. Patmos is a place of pilgrimage, for here St. John the Divine received the revelations and wrote the book of Apocalypse (which he actually dictated to a disciple), in a cave that is now enshrined by the Church of the Apocalypse. Nearby, the pretty village of Hora has an eleventh-century monastery founded by St. Christodoulos, a former hermit, as a School of Virtue and Holy Purpose. (For those whose purpose was considered unholy, burning oil was ready for pouring atop the gate.) A tour of this monastery is a must, although the lovely pebble beaches on the island also beckon. In the monastery compound is a treasury of costly icons and liturgical costumes and a library lined with glass cases containing over nine hundred handwritten books as well as some ninth-century illuminated manuscripts. You can also tour where the two dozen monks live, eat, and study. On the return to the port of Skala, stop in at the seventeenth-century house (if you can find it), a rich trove of folk art, furniture, and greenery.

Just over a mile from the shores of Turkey, **Samos** is another "Greece in Asia" island, known for its wine, its Temple of Hera (one of the wonders of the ancient world), and engineering marvels that still exist. Samos is characterized by mountainous terrain on which olives, dates, palms, poplars, and vineyards flourish. In the sixth century B.C. Samos was Queen of the Seas, due to its tyrant leader Polycrates, who used slaves from Lesbos to build the Temple of Hera, a harbor mole, and the mile-long tunnel that brought fresh water through the hills. Parts of the harbor mole and the tunnel are still around, but all that remains of the temple is a single, standing column a few miles west of Pythagorion (birthplace of the man who discovered that proportion forms the structural principle of the universe). Other sights on this lovely isle are two monasteries, the seaside village of Kokari, and many little mountain towns in sweet-smelling pine forests. If you are in the mood to taste a little of the local industry, visit the winery in Samos for a sampling of the new, young nectar of the gods. Some visitors also use Samos as the jumping-off point for a tour of the classical site of Ephesus (near Kusadasi in Turkey), while others head for the magnificent, uncrowded beaches.

When I asked Captain Michael Benas, now retired master of Sun Line's flagship, the *Stella Solaris,* which island in the Aegean was his favorite, he beamed and gave me a predictable answer, ''Why, Rhodes, of course!'' As we were sailing toward Rhodes at that very moment, I couldn't have been more delighted, for this island has long captured my fancy as one of the most enjoyable places in the entire world. **Rhodes** is the largest of the Dodecanese. Greek mythology tells us that the island rose from the sea and that Apollo took it as his domain, although he had to uproot some lesser gods who had already established squatters' rights. The island flourished as early as the eleventh century B.C. and reached its commercial and cultural prime in the fifth century B.C. Two centuries later, the Colossus of Rhodes was known as one of the Seven Wonders of the Ancient World.

This 100-foot bronze statue representing the sun god straddled the harbor of the ancient port of Rhodes. It was erected in 290 B.C. by a local sculptor to commemorate the steadfastness of the Rhodians and as a warning against invasion. It seems that after an Alexandrian military man withdrew his troops in frustration when his one-year siege failed to intimidate the Rhodians, they simply melted down his machinery and made their colossus. Unfortunately the Colossus toppled over in an earthquake about fifty years later, and its site is now marked by two pillars topped with bronze deer—the symbol of present-day Rhodes.

Rhodes, about six hundred square miles in area, has three separate layers of history to explore—the ancient, the medieval, and the modern. The most splendid of the three ancient cities of Rhodes is **Lindos,** about a forty-five-minute drive from port to the western end of the island. Lindians worshiped the goddess Athena, who is said to have rained gold down upon their city. Her fourth-century-B.C. temple on the acropolis of Lindos is one of the oldest sites in all of Greece. The acropolis, a steep climb up from the small town below, has wonderful views of the Bay of St. John and the harbor where St. Paul is reported to have landed in 51 A.D.

Your cruise ship will dock within sight of the old town of Rhodes, which lies within the reconstructed medieval walls built by the Knights of St. John in the thirteenth century. (Some of the larger passenger vessels must anchor out and tender passengers in, however.) In the northern section of the old town are the Palace of the Grand Master and the former inns of the crusaders that still line the Street of Knights. A fifteenth-century Hospital of the Knights houses the Rhodes Archaeological Museum, which has fine exhibits, including the lovely Aphrodite Thalassia found in the waters nearby and dating from the first century B.C. The medieval ramparts and buildings were all reconstructed during the Italian occupation, which lasted from 1912 to 1943 (all the good roads were built then too), and Rhodian guides will tell you that Mussolini had his eye on the 300-room palace as a summer residence (it's an impressive place, but I wouldn't want to live there). But Il Duce never got to fulfill this dream. An excellent Sound and Light show is aimed at the palace during the summer, and many ships stay in port for it. The English version begins about 9 p.m. And, if you prefer more sightseeing to shopping (the main area is Sokrates Street, the former Turkish bazaar), take a taxi to the mile-long Valley of the Butterflies—about twelve miles from the port of Rhodes along the western coastal road—to commune with millions of red and black butterflies that flutter through the trees.

Rhodes has thousands of foreign visitors (it's dubbed Scandinavian Haven) who fly in, come by overnight car ferries from Piraeus, or sail into the harbor on private yachts and sailboats from as far away as Australia. I love to walk along the breakwater, look at the boats, listen to the many languages spoken, and then sit in a waterfront cafe to watch the spectacle. This beats even the butterflies!

Crete is Greece's most southern island in the Aegean Sea and its largest (second in size only to Cyprus in the entire Mediterranean area). It is the legendary birthplace of Zeus, whose mother (Rhea) hid him in a cave lest his father (Cronos) swallow the baby whole as he had all preceding brothers and sisters. (Cronos did not want any competition.) Crete is also the birthplace of Domenico Theotokopoulos (El Greco) in 1545 and Nikos Kazantzakis in 1883 (whose popular novel *Zorba the Greek* is set here).

Heraklion (or Iraklion) is the most popular cruise port on the island, because it's closest to the Palace of Knossos and the fine Archaeological Museum. Although Heraklion has about 70,000 inhabitants, only a few Venetian relics (a castle, a lion, a fountain, and a loggia) are of interest here. But it is the gateway to a view of the magnificent Minoan civilization, which flourished here from 2000 to 1450 B.C., and the wonderful tales of King Minos, the bull, Daedalus, the Minotaur, Theseus, and Ariadne. No visit to the island is complete without a tour of Knossos. Excavations were undertaken by Sir Arthur Evans in 1900 to uncover and reconstruct the palace, which was the center of a large town that Evans felt had a population of around 100,000 at its peak. The palace, which had 1200 to 1400 rooms, is built on a plan so complex that archaeologists believe it is the origin of stories about the Minoan labyrinth. The complex was not even fortified, which meant that the king (both a divinity and a monarch) was as confident as he was powerful. Evans's restoration features large red wooden columns made broader at the top than at the base, wall reproductions, the throne room, the queen's bathroom (she supposedly took milk baths), and the sophisticated sanitary system. You can see charred remains from the fatal fire of 1450 B.C. that makes it seem people lived here only yesterday. You can also walk down the oldest street in the world, once lined with homes of aristocrats, and peek into the huge garbage receptacle where broken pottery was thrown.

At the Archaeological Museum in Heraklion, guides shout at the top of their lungs in every language possible. By all means avoid the frustrating tour here. Get away from your fellow passengers as quickly as possible, head upstairs for the frescoes, and then visit the 1:50 scale model of the Palace of Knossos and the cases downstairs. The museum is unique, in that it contains *all* the findings at Knossos and other sites in Crete. Not one object was carried off to European museums as happened so often at these classical sites.

If there is sufficient time before your ship sails, wander about the town a bit. The fruit market is spectacular, and you'll find interesting shops for souvenirs as well as tempting handwoven rugs in colorful Cretan designs.

ISRAEL

Whether your tour of the Holy Land begins in the well-equipped harbor of **Ashdod,** one of Israel's planned cities and perched on sand dunes, or in the three-tiered port of **Haifa,** populated since biblical times, you will find yourself on a journey like none other you have experienced before. Your cruise vessel may not be in port long enough for you to visit everything you would like, and you may have to choose between Jerusalem and Bethlehem, or the Nazareth/Tiberias/Sea of Galilee route.

If you are lucky enough to sail into Haifa, from the deep-blue sea to the top of "God's vineyards," Mount Carmel, you will enjoy panoramic views at every level: from the harbor with its broad bay, the Hadar or midsection business area; and the Carmel residential level of homes and parks and fine hotels. From Haifa, the heart of the Holy Land—Nazareth, Tiberias, and the Sea of Galilee—is easily accessible. Before you depart on your full-day tour give courtesy to Haifa itself, especially Elijah's Cave, where the prophet is said to have hidden from the wrath of King Ahab and his wife Jezebel, and where the Holy Family was sheltered on the return from Egypt.

The drive to Nazareth takes about an hour through Israel's largest and most fertile valley, an impressive array of fruit trees, vineyards, and green fields that were carefully nurtured from swampland. From the valley, your bus will maneuver hairpin turns through the King George V Forest and into Nazareth. Here is the Basilica of the Annunciation (built over the site of earlier structures), where the angel Gabriel is said to have announced to Mary that she would bear the Son of God. Nearby is a church where Joseph's workshop is thought to have been, and the synagogue Jesus attended. Two other historic sites are: Mary's Well, where you will see women carrying jugs of water on their heads just as they did in Jesus's time; and a Franciscan church, where Jesus is believed to have dined with his disciples after the Resurrection.

The road leads directly from Nazareth to the Sea of Galilee, a tranquil freshwater lake thirteen miles long and some seven hundred feet below sea level. En route you will pass by Cana, where Jesus is said to have turned water into wine, and you will glimpse Mount Tabor, site of Jesus's transfiguration. The ancient town of Tiberias, built by Herod in honor of the Roman Emperor Tiberias, was a major center of Jewish life in the Holy Land (the learned men of Tiberias introduced grammar and punctuation into the Hebrew language). This resort is still noted for curative hot springs famed for more than 3000 years. From Tiberias, you go on to the Church of the Multiplication of Loaves and Fishes and to the town of Capernaum, the center of Jesus's activities in the Galilee. On the return to Tiberias you will see the Mount of the Beatitudes, where the Sermon on the Mount was delivered and where Jesus is said to have chosen his twelve apostles.

Jerusalem, continually inhabited for more than four thousand years, is not only a great historical center but the cornerstone of the world's three great religions. Jews, Christians, and Moslems pay homage to their respective shrines. Jerusalem's inhabitants are thought to be members of the greatest melting pot mankind has ever known. The Old City, or walled section, of East Jerusalem is a living testament to that. Here you can visit the Wailing Wall (remnant of a wall that once supported the Temple on the Mount). Nearby is the gleaming Dome of the Rock, or Mosque of Omar, a Moslem sanctuary built over the spot where Abraham was prepared to sacrifice the life of his son and where Moslems believe that Mohammed ascended to heaven. On the Via Dolorosa, the route to Calvary passes fourteen Stations of the Cross marked for prayer. Pay a visit to the Church of the Holy Sepulchre, believed to be the site of the crucifixion. Also in the Old City are the Church of St. Anne, the Pool of Bethesda, and the Arch of Ecce Homo. From the Mount of Olives, you will catch your breath at the spectacular view of old and new Jerusalem before visiting the Church of all Nations, the Tomb of the Prophets, and the Garden of Gethsemane. From Mount Scopus, the panorama includes the Judean desert and the distant Dead

Sea. As your drive takes you through West Jerusalem, you will see the memorial to the six million Jews of the holocaust, Hadassah Hospital (largest medical center in the Middle East), and the Kennedy Memorial and Peace Forest where you can plant a tree for a small fee.

Bethlehem is seven miles south of Jerusalem from the Damascus Gate (it is traditional for pilgrims to walk it on Christmas). En route you will pass the Tomb of Rachel, wife of Jacob and mother of Joseph, and revered by Moslems, Jews, and Christians. At Bethlehem the Church of the Nativity on Manger Square is the principal shrine. The church is the oldest in the country, and the manger is believed to be in the crypt underneath the altar. Another historic site is the Milk Grotto, where Mary's milk is said to have turned the stones chalky white. And by all means, pay a visit to the bazaar where local merchants make a good living selling artifacts to the pilgrims.

ITALY

Italy's largest seaport, **Genoa,** is a spacious and attractive city that has some fifteen miles of quays receiving ships from all the seas of the world. A popular embarkation point for cruise ships sailing under the Italian flag, Genoa is an exciting port for the start of any adventure. The city is built up the side of a mountain and boasts many, many fine Renaissance palaces of the sixteenth and seventeenth centuries that overlook the bay (drive along Via Garibaldi and Via Balbi in the Porto Vecchio section). Genoa is midway on the Italian Riviera, which encircles the Ligurian Sea. The western end, or Riviera di Ponente, runs 101 miles to Ventimiglia and features such resorts as San Remo, capital of the flower section of this area and known also for its race course and casino. The eastern end, or Riviera di Levante, runs only seventy miles to La Spezia, a trading port and excursion center.

The rugged, rocky Portofino Peninsula is becoming a popular cruise call. **Portofino** is a small fishing village loved by artists. Except for the summer crowds and traffic, it's a rather sleepy, picturesque scene. My favorite walk is out to the lighthouse at sunset, to gaze out on the Gulf of Rapallo and along the coast to La Spezia harbor.

South of La Spezia is **Livorno** (Leghorn), an ancient trading port that one of the Medici princes linked by canal to Pisa in the sixteenth century. Pisa was a large commercial port in the eleventh century, rivaling Genoa and Venice, but her power declined after the fourteenth century, about the time the Leaning Tower was completed (it was built between 1174 and 1350). Since it began to lean, the tower has become Pisa's most renowned monument, and even native son Galileo used it in the seventeenth century to work out his theory of gravity. The tower leans almost fourteen feet now, due to a fault in the design of the foundation as well as to the poor subsoil on which it was built. It serves as the campanile, or bell tower, to the adjacent twelfth-century Romanesque cathedral and fourteenth-century baptistry.

Some cruise lines use Livorno for the port of entry to Pisa at the mouth of the Arno River, as well as for excursions to **Florence,** where the purest Italian is spoken (Dante was a native son) and some of mankind's most magnificent masterpieces were made. The artistic capital of Italy from the fourteenth to seventeenth centuries, Florence has always been pleasing to the eye to great patrons—the Pitti, Strozzi, Pazzi, and Medicis, whose names still linger on palaces, public buildings, and in dedications. Florence remains an art center and its modern craftsmen do beautiful work in leather, silver, wood, gold, and fashions. The term "Florentine" reflects a special style, just as it was during the Renaissance when talents included Botticelli, Leonardo da Vinci, Raphael, Michelangelo Buonarroti, Brunelleschi, Donatello, and Cellini. A visit to Florence is a delightful minicourse in the history of art—no musty classrooms, just beautiful buildings still in use, and paintings and statues everywhere. It's difficult to know where to begin, but the most practical place would be the Ponte Vecchio, that old bridge where the city began and which is now lined with shops.

If you have just one day to spend in Florence on a shore excursion, you will only get a taste of the beauty here. You won't want to miss the bronze doors of the Baptistry, or the Piazza della Signoria, the former center of political life and now the perfect spot to watch the action from a cafe or on the steps of the Loggia del Lanzi. The Pitti and Uffizi are two of the world's finest museums; but my favorite in Florence is the Bargello because it's small, is in a charming former palace, and has a lovely courtyard. It also has some interesting pieces by Michelangelo, Donatello, and Della Robbia. Save some time to walk around, have a *gelati* (ice cream) from a sidewalk vendor, and read the plaques on old buildings. The last time I was in Florence, I discovered Casa Guidi, at 8 Piazza San Felice, the former home of Elizabeth Barrett and Robert Browning.

On television I saw an old movie with the Bay of Naples in the background and an ocean liner anchored in the harbor; the hero had to choose between his wife on board the ship and a woman whose villa overlooked the bay. Well, the hero chose the woman with the villa, because of the magical quality of the bay. **Naples** is the prime port for passenger traffic in Italy. It is also the birthplace of spaghetti and pizza (the real thing, not what we find in America) and the capital of *bel canto.* A fascinating, frustrating, and continually surprising city, it is a world apart from the rest of the country. Neopolitans are known for being independent, crafty, tenacious, and wary of strangers. Families here are the brotherhood of man—once a member . . . never out of mind.

Naples began as the Greek colony Neapolis, and although conquered in the fourth century B.C. by the Romans, never gave up Greek language or customs until the end of the Roman Empire. Since then, seven "royal" families have reigned over but never really ruled Naples. From ancient times the city has been a popular winter retreat, and the bay has a deserved reputation for providing interesting environs, including mountains, lovely capes, and islands. Today, Naples is the jetty for cruises to Capri, Ischia, and Sorrento.

Naples is also the principal port for excursions to **Pompeii,** that ancient town smothered in molten ash in the year A.D. 79 from the eruptions of Mt. Vesuvius. The population of Pompeii—about 25,000 at the time, many of them wealthy aristocrats from Rome—had little warning. The entire area was quickly covered in hot lava and cinders, and was rediscovered in the seventeenth century. Excavations have been going since 1748, and today two-thirds of the city can be toured. It's an unforgettable feeling to wander among the uncovered ruins, to walk the stone streets still marked from chariot wheels, enter what were once luxurious villas full of exquisite frescoes and mosaics, and visit the Stabian Baths where both men and women exercised. It's as though the people of Pompeii have never left—their spirits still linger.

On the return to your ship you may want to visit Naples's old quarter (Quartiere Vecchio), the new castle (Castel Nuovo) built in 1282, and the National Museum located in a sixteenth-century palace full of treasures uncovered at Pompeii as well as at Herculaneum. **Herculaneum** was a nearby town buried in the same eruptions of Mt. Vesuvius but not excavated until the beginning of the nineteenth century. Historians have discovered that this town was for workers and the poorer folk, since instead of luxury villas they have uncovered what appear to be blocks of tenements.

If time allows, an excursion to the isle of **Capri,** a long-time haven for the international set, might be on your agenda. This island of dreams is four miles long and two miles wide, yet has some lovely wild and lonely spots, Blue Grotto sea cave, and 951-foot Monte Solaro (a chair hoist takes you up for a spectacular view). Or take a funny old convertible taxi up the Corniche Road to Anacapri, past the lovely villas owned by movie stars to the Piazza della Vittoria where you can sit in the sun, try the local wine, and drink in the atmosphere.

Since the reign of Emperor Trajan (A.D. 53–117), Civitavecchia ("old city") has been the port for **Rome,** capital of Italy and cradle of Christianity. Called the Eternal City, Rome is thought by historians, poets, and artists to have no equal in all the world. A brief, one-day cruise call can never do justice to Rome, but it can give you a feeling for the many great monuments that have existed here for centuries. Unlike many other historic cities, Rome is alive, vibrant, and full of action, which makes its many ruins more appealing, its piazzas more exciting, and its many churches more interesting. Legend says the city was founded by twins Romulus and Remus, the offspring of Mars and Venus, who were abandoned in the Tiber River and brought up by a she-wolf. Ancient Rome was first a republic, then capital of an empire whose influence reached to England and Asia, and later divided into the Western Empire (Rome) and the Eastern Empire (Constantinople). Under the reign of Constantine (324–337), Christianity became the state religion and the era of the pagans versus the Christians began. And when there were no more emperors in the political forum, the popes wielded power and often assumed absolute authority.

Any tour of this metropolis actually encompasses three separate cities—ancient Rome, Christian Rome, and the Rome of the people. This last is the Rome you can't miss even on a quick visit—tourists sitting on the steps of Piazza di Spagna, policemen in white gloves, cars and buses going in circles, and the new next to the old and the ancient.

Ancient Rome consists of the Forum, the Palatine Hill, the Coliseum (where gladiator contests took place and early Christians were confronted with lions), the Arch of Constantine, the Imperial Forums, and the Baths. Also visit the Pantheon, the most perfectly preserved ancient building in the world, and the beginning of the Appian Way (Via Appia Antica), which was built in 312 B.C. and runs all the way down to the port of Brindisi.

Christian Rome centers on Vatican City, which (with 109 acres) is the smallest independent state in the world. By tradition, its Swiss guards wear uniforms designed by Michelangelo and all come from the same town of Valais, in Switzerland. Walking through Piazza San Pietro is an overwhelming experience. This square is an extension of the basilica itself, site of papal funerals and the enthronement of new popes. The Emperor Constantine built the first St. Peter's on this site in the fourth century; the present basilica dates from the sixteenth century and is the combined work of Bramante, Sangallo, Raphael, and Michelangelo—who designed the dome. After St. Peter's, you may wonder if it's worth visiting other churches in Rome. Yes, but only at a very, very, leisurely pace. Dominating the Tiber River, and a personal joy, is Castel Sant'Angelo, built by the Emperor Hadrian in A.D. 135 as a mausoleum and turned into a fortress in the Middle Ages. It's connected to the Vatican by a tunnel—handy for several popes during difficult times. The interior is a museum of ancient weapons and some works of art. You can also see the prison cells and apartments of the popes (some combination!). From the top, the view of Rome is wonderful. I also like the seven hills of Rome, the white-marble Victor Emmanuel monument, Mussolini's balcony, and the Via Condotti where Gucci, Ginori,

Valentino, and Bulgari display their wares. But the fountains of Rome will beckon, and if you do not stop to throw two coins over your shoulder into the Trevi Fountain (one to ensure your return to Rome; the other to fulfill a wish), then you have not really been to the Eternal City.

Ever-changing **Venice,** one of the most romantic cities in the world, was used by Shakespeare as the setting for *Othello* and *The Merchant of Venice;* Thomas Mann wrote *Death in Venice;* and in Ernest Hemingway's *Across the River and Through the Trees* the last line is, "Take me to the Gritti [hotel]!" Of Venice's many painters, my favorite is the eighteenth-century Venetian who so frequently recorded the play of light on canals that he was called Canaletto. In this romantic city you'll fall under the spell of gondolas, narrow canals, bridges, the sun setting on St. Mark's Square, funny houses in back alleys with their balconies and flower pots, palaces of the rich and noble, and the sound of water lapping as you walk along the quiet streets. Once under this spell, you're under forever.

The best way to approach Venice is by water, for the city is wed to the Adriatic Sea. Alas, the waters rise more each year and the city sinks. Although pessimists predicted the city would not be standing by the end of this century, the Italian government finally began a preservation project to give Venice a long and happy life.

Founded in the ninth century, Venice was made a republic with a Doge (leader), and soon enjoyed such great prosperity via the Crusades (which were much more an economic than a religious endeavor) that an empire evolved. The Venetian Empire, whose influence reached as far as Asia Minor, was at its height in the first half of the fifteenth century and began to decline after midcentury, just as the arts began to flourish. The sixteenth century gave us the painter Titian as well as a special style of architecture that became synonymous with grand palaces and civic buildings.

The best way to see Venice is on foot, following no specific route (but with a good map in hand). I like to begin and finish each day in St. Mark's Square, home of thousands of pigeons, unending aperitifs, old-worn charm, and elegant shops. The square changes personality by the hour. On the square is St. Mark's Basilica, a jumble of styles put together through the centuries, which has played host to innumerable historic events and figures. The interior decoration is dazzling, but pay special attention to the bronze horses over the doorway, brought back from Constantinople in 1204 by one of the Doges. Unfortunately, what you see today are copies of the original works because the priceless bronzes were deteriorating from air pollution. Take a ride up the bell tower (this is a real campanile) for an overview of all Venice, and then tour the Doge's Palace, for a taste of how the city's famous leaders lived and treated their enemies to the famous Bridge of Sighs.

Venice consists of 117 islands, 150 canals, and some 400 bridges! A ride on the Grand Canal is mandatory—either by gondola in the moonlight or water taxi during the day—for the two-mile stretch of the largest concentration of twelfth- to eighteenth-century palaces in the world. Stop, if you can, at the Rialto Bridge (with the famous hump) and visit the shops and galleries overlooking the canal. This is the business section of Venice and a good place to browse.

Across the canal from St. Mark's Square is the Island of San Giorgio, a few minutes away by water taxi. Here, in a peaceful and serene atmosphere, the church of San Giorgio Maggiore is in stark contrast to the Basilica across the way. Sit for a spell on the quay, waiting for the *vaporetto* to return, to view the hustle and bustle going on across the water! For a lighter diversion the Lido is a fashionable resort about a half-hour's ride by water from St. Mark's Square. It's known for its lovely beach, beautiful people, and casino. Another popular excursion is the island of Murano, a glass works since 1292. You can visit the main canal-street, lined with Renaissance houses, and the glass works and museum, but shop prices are high here.

Italy's islands—Elba, the Lipari, Sardinia, and Sicily—are especially popular as cruise calls, for they offer a varied landscape and history. **Elba,** the largest in the Tuscan archipelago, is often called the Island of Sea Horses, but it is best known as the home of exiled Napoleon Bonaparte from 1814 to 1815. Here Napoleon reigned for less than a year following his abdication in Paris, and brooded over the view of his native Corsica. Cruise ships dock at Portoferraio, the sleepy capital of the island, guarded by two ancient forts. A walk along the waterfront and up the steps into the old section of town will take you to the Villa dei Mullini, where Napoleon often stayed and where he left mementos. A short ride from town is the Villa Napoleone at San Martino. Set in the beautiful hills, with terraced gardens overlooking the bay, this was the former emperor's summer residence, a miniversion of Versailles (but hardly so well kept—in fact, it's a *very* poor relative). Though the setting is lovely, I get a feeling of sadness.

The Lipari are an archipelago of seven small volcanic islands known for stark beauty and brilliant sunshine. Also known as the Aeolian Islands, because the ancients believed that Aeolus, the God of the Wind, lived here, the islands are Lipari, Vulcano, Alicudi, Salina, Filicudi, Panarea, and Stromboli. **Stromboli,** featured on the cruise circuit, has a smoking crater, vineyard-covered hills, and Moorish-style houses. The crater has minor eruptions of lava, and the spectacle of fiery stones falling into the sea is especially dramatic when seen from your ship at night.

Sardinia is a large island in the Tyrrhenian Sea, second in size only to Sicily, its southeastern neighbor. The island is said to have been colonized by the Cretans, which puts its first civilization around 2000

B.C., but a number of different peoples occupied it in rapid succession before the Spanish took over in the early eighteenth century. As a result, Sardinians have a keen sense of hospitality (they have no choice, one might say), honor, and are tough men and women of agriculture. **Cagliari,** Sardinia's capital, once a flourishing Carthaginian city, is now a busy seaport. It boasts a fine Roman amphitheater and a national museum of antiquities. St. Saturninus' Basilica dates from the fifth century and is thought to be one of the oldest Christian churches in the Mediterranean area. Cagliari's bustle is quite a contrast to the peaceful and rugged countryside, where native women wear long, pleated skirts and lace mantillas (left over from the Spanish days, no doubt) and shy away from the approach of strangers. Menfolk wear funny horned hats and are never far away from their dwarflike donkeys.

Sardinia was put on the map of the international set a few years ago when the Aga Khan organized the development of the Costa Smeralda area on the northeast coastline. Here, where the scenery is spectacular and the sea an emerald green, he poured millions of dollars into luxury hotels, seasonal apartments, and yacht basins for his friends and their friends. He used good taste—the buildings blend beautifully with the terrain and local Sardinian architecture. Those who do not come off yachts can fly into nearby Olbia for a visit to the eighty sun-filled beaches, or they can disembark for the day from cruise ships that dock during the season in the port of Olbia.

Sicily, the largest and most mysterious of the Mediterranean islands, home to some five million people noted for dark complexions— despite a few vestiges of the old Norman days in the occasional blond, blue-eyed baby. Sicilians are also reputed to have sinister characters, a sweeping and unfair appraisal drawn from movies about organized crime in the United States. The truth is, most Sicilians simply cultivate their vines, almond trees, fruits, and vegetables and have little to do with the outside world. Sicily is called the archaeological museum of Europe for its Greek temples and theaters, Roman bridges and aqueducts, Saracen mosques, Norman churches and castles. It houses so many interesting relics of European power struggles during the past 2000 years that it has many ports in which cruise ships call: **Agrigento,** with its Greco-Roman quarter and Valley of the Temples; **Catania,** which has been destroyed several times by eruptions from Mt. Etna; **Messina; Palermo,** the capital and chief seaport and the crossroads of civilizations for centuries; **Syracuse,** once the rival of Athens, with its beautiful bay and fine ruins of a former Greek city; and **Taormina,** a beautiful resort overlooking the sea and facing Mt. Etna.

Mt. Etna dominates Sicily in one way or another. It is the largest active volcano in Europe. In ancient times 135 eruptions were recorded, but the worst was in 1669, when the lava almost totally destroyed Catania. Already in this century Etna has erupted eleven times; another could occur at any moment. Nonetheless, visitors adore the ascent of the volcano to the huge black cone with fruit trees flourishing on its slopes. From Catania to the summit is about twenty miles, plus twenty minutes by cable car, and just under one hour on foot (high heels should not be worn on this climb). If you like to see the earth smoke and sputter, you will enjoy this excursion, provided you are dressed warmly enough. Otherwise, you may prefer a peaceful terrace in town and a glass of local wine. Later, stroll in the Bellini Gardens for a fine panorama of the city—and Mt. Etna.

MALTA

Your cruise ship will sail into **Valletta,** the capital that dominates the grand harbor of the Maltese Islands—Malta, Gozo, and Comino. These islands have had their share of shipwrecks—Ulysses supposedly spent some time in the arms of Calypso on the island of Gozo; and Apostle Paul is said to have drifted to shore in about 60 A.D. and lived three months in a cave between Rabat and Mdina while converting the island of Malta to Christianity. These islands, strategically located in the middle of the Mediterranean, have been the center of a struggle between maritime powers for centuries.

The Maltese Islands are thought to have been affiliated with Sicily as well as North Africa. The first known inhabitants were Sicilian Neolithic farmers of about 4000 B.C. The Phoenicians arrived later (700 B.C.) and used the fine harbors for their trading activities. They left the basis of a language that is still in use today. But Malta's most interesting period dates from 1530 to 1798 when the Knights of St. John made their home here and built fortifications, palaces, inns, and churches. Shortly after the knights arrived, in 1565, an attack by the Turks was repulsed and brought great fame to Malta. (This military prowess was repeated from 1940 to 1943 when Malta resisted the Axis powers.)

Valletta, founded in the mid-sixteenth century, reflects the islands' rich heritage. For a tour of beautiful places in the capital, begin at St. John's CoCathedral and move on to the Palace of the Grand Masters and Armory. A fine national museum of archaeology is housed in the Auberge de Provence, one of the inns of the Knights of St. John of Jerusalem (who founded Malta). Later than these midsixteenth-century structures but considered one of the oldest theaters in Europe, is the Manoel Theatre built in 1731 by one of the Grand Masters, Manoel de Vilhena. Outside of Valletta you can tour some unique sites, including the megalithic monuments of 2500 B.C., the Ghar Dalam Cave with fossils of animals that roamed some 170,000 years ago, a Blue Grotto that rivals the one in Capri, and the cave in which St. Paul is believed to have lived during his three-month stay in A.D. 60. (An account of his shipwreck can be found in Acts XXVII and XXVIII.)

The Maltese Islands also mean beautiful bays, beaches, and brightly colored boats called *dghajjes,* which you can take for touring the grottos and caves as well as for visiting the islands of Gozo and Comino. And when you're in the mood for shopping, the local crafts feature hand-made tiles, plates, and glassware and that wonderful Maltese cross!

MOROCCO

The Kingdom of Morocco, at the westernmost point of North Africa, is the land of the Casbah, couscous, caftans, and Casablanca. Once part of the Carthaginian empire and later a part of the province of Mauritania under the Romans, Morocco was conquered by the Arabs, the Portuguese, the Spanish, and finally the French. It first became an independent Arab kingdom in 788 but broke up by the tenth century. Independence from France was finally gained in 1956. Couscous (made of semolina, meat, and vegetables) is the national dish and caftans are the native dress. The famous Casbah, though, is in Tangier, which is a less frequent cruise call than Casablanca is. You can prepare yourself by catching the movie classic *Casablanca,* with Humphrey Bogart and Ingrid Bergman. Actually, the bustling city you sail into has no relation to the Casablanca of the 1940s; it is a thoroughly modern, twentieth-century city—the gateway to North Africa.

Casablanca has one of the largest harbors in Africa, and three gateways connect the old medina with the port. It's called "Casa" by those who live here and the "Great White City" by visitors. More new than old, Casablanca is also more Moroccan than French. It has both an old and new medina (the latter built by the French in 1921), a royal palace where the king stays when in town, United Nations Square, and Arab League Park. The most beautiful part of the city is the seaside residential area with lovely homes and romantic views. You may have heard of one quarter, Anfa, because Churchill, Roosevelt, and De Gaulle met here during World War II for the Casablanca Conference.

Just fifty-seven miles northeast along the Atlantic coastline is **Rabat,** capital of Morocco and home of King Hassan II. The drive is worthwhile. Only Moslems are allowed to enter religious monuments in Morocco, but you can visit the Quadias Casbah and Museum of Oudaia for a stroll through the gardens and the overwhelming displays of native arts and crafts. You may also climb the Tower of Hassan for a view of the city of Sale across the Bou Regreg. Take a walk through the medina, whose walls date from the twelfth and seventeenth centuries. Here you can peek at souk after souk, visit the old wool market, and pass by the mellah or Jewish quarter. And if an item grabs your fancy, bargain. The experts become serious only after your third offer.

The *piece de resistance* in Morocco is the all-day tour to **Marrakesh.** This imperial, red-ochre city founded by the Almoravids in the eleventh century is the jewel of the Islamic world. Marrakesh, 150 hot miles from Casablanca, is an oasis at the edge of the scorching Sahara Desert. The temperatures during the summer months average over 100 degrees (F), which is why the city was once a winter playground for the rich and famous. (Winston Churchill used to stay at the famed La Mamounia Hotel, whose gardens came straight from the Arabian Nights.) The landscape of Marrakesh is dominated by the pink sandstone Koutoubia, or Mosque of the Scribes, which has a minaret 222 feet high. This great monument of Moorish architecture and decoration was built in the twelfth century. Below the mosque is the Djemma El Fna, the country's largest marketplace and greatest free entertainment center, where you can buy anything in the world from just about everyone. This is the most famous square in all North Africa; and if you survive it, you're on your way to becoming a native. Some say that the profusion of water-sellers, story-tellers, acrobats, soothsayers, dancers, and snake-charmers create an incredible biblical atmosphere (in the epitome of a Moorish town). Other sights to tantalize the senses include the *medina* and *mellah,* the sixteenth-century monument of Medersa Ibn Yussef, the royal tombs, Bahia palace and gardens (provided no guests-of-state are in residence), Dar Si Said (arts and handcrafts museum), and the many imperial gardens. Marrakesh is famous for its beautifully planned gardens replete with olive groves, especially the Aguedal and Menara as well as the Mamounia (attached to the deluxe hotel of the same name). These gardens are all the more impressive and inviting when you remember that the mysterious desert is but a step away.

THE SUEZ CANAL AND THE RED SEA

The opening of the Suez Canal in 1869 was honored by the presence of royalty, including such personages as the Empress Eugenie of Austria, for whom a palace was built at the foot of the Great Pyramids (now the Mena House Oberoi Hotel where you may have lunch). Italian composer Giuseppe Verdi wrote his spectacular opera *Aida* (with live elephants on stage) just for this occasion, and the royal guests reportedly received it with a tumultuous welcome at the newly constructed

Cairo Opera House. What an inaugural for the 100.76-mile canal that joins the Mediterranean with the Red Sea!

It took a full decade to build the Suez Canal, and years of study and indecision passed before a shovel even touched the earth. The Suez is probably not the first canal on this site—scholars believe that a passageway of some sort existed between the two seas as early as the sixth century B.C. but was closed through neglect. From 1869 to 1980 the Suez closed only twice—the last time from the 1967 war to June 5, 1975, when it was reopened by Egyptian president Anwar Sadat. The western gateway to the canal is **Port Said,** a town that boomed during the late nineteenth century and is now known as a free port. You'll find little to do or see here, and most cruise ships call only as a courtesy and to offer full-day tours to Cairo, which comes into view at the end of a three-hour bus ride through the desert. (You can amuse yourself during the ride by counting the numerous checkpoints—rusted tanks left over from the recent battles—and the villages full of tents topped by television antennae.) From Port Said the transit through the canal to Suez takes about eighteen hours and passes by many little canal towns of which the prettiest is Ismailia. The city of **Suez,** the southernmost port of the canal, is a wonderful spot to view what you have just passed through (or if you are sailing in the opposite direction, what you are about to experience). Suez also sparks little interest for me, but it is another good embarkation point for visits to Cairo, since it's a reasonable two-hour drive from here.

Having transited the Suez Canal, your cruise vessel continues down the Gulf of Suez, between the Sinai Peninsula and Egypt's eastern desert. The first noticeable settlement of any size on this rocky, undeveloped Red Sea coastline is Hurghada, approximately 250 land miles south of Suez. From Hurghada you can see Mt. Sinai (Gebel Moussa) on a clear day. Just below the city lies the port of **Safaga,** from where all-day tours to Thebes, Karnak, and Luxor on the Nile River are arranged. The tours, although lengthy (twelve to fourteen hours), are wonderful, for you will visit the Valley of the Kings (tombs of Tutankhamen and Ramses VI) as well as the Temple of Queen Hatshepsut, eat an enjoyable lunch, and then ride by horsedrawn carriage to the Temple of Karnak. Following a visit to the Temple of Luxor, you may have time for a sunset sail on the Nile in a felucca before returning to your ship in Safaga for a late supper on board (according to the fine itinerary planned by Raymond & Whitcomb of New York). If your ship schedules another day in Safaga, try to fly down to the temple complex of Abu Simbel, about 160 miles south of Aswan (at a cost of about $150 per person). Here you can explore the Great Temple of Ramses II and the smaller temple dedicated to his consort and queen, Nefertari. These two monuments were rescued from the floodwaters of the Aswan Dam in 1969, in a scheme that involved moving the temples, piece by piece, to a new site that was seven hundred feet away but two hundred feet higher. The project took four and a half years and cost millions of dollars, and one engineer reportedly said that Abu Simbel qualifies as a wonder of both the ancient and modern world.

From Safaga your cruise vessel sails northeast to **Aqaba** in Jordan, a port town at the tip of the gulf that separates the Sinai and Arabian peninsulas. Aqaba is a biblical town, said to date from as early as the tenth century B.C. Known for its trading because of its location on the gulf, at one time it was a part of Egypt. Little of this past history remains, and the area now emphasizes splendid scuba diving on its beautiful coral reefs—equal to any throughout the world. As a result, Aqaba is becoming a fashionable Middle East resort. Even King Hussein finds the thirty-minute flight from Amman (capital of Jordan) short enough to make him a frequent visitor to his villa on the beach.

Two unforgettable shore excursions, to Wadi Rumm and Petra, leave from Aqaba. **Wadi Rumm** is a great desert valley, about an hour's drive from the port, through which the famous T. E. Lawrence passed in his pursuit of the Turks during World War I. The route that Lawrence and his Desert Legion followed is fascinating, and your journey, either by car or camel train, will eventually end at the fort of the Wadi Rumm Desert Patrol, which is also the home of several Bedouin tribes. Huge, red, stone cliff scenery; an almost perfect cloudless sky; and colorful Bedouin costumes combine to create an impression that boggles the mind. You may even be invited to a traditional Bedouin feast, although I understand that sheep's eyes are no longer served to foreign guests!

The rose-colored city of **Petra,** also known by the biblical name of Sela, lies in the desert near the Dead Sea and can be entered only through a narrow passageway that is just comfortable for humans and horses. Petra means *rock,* as does sela, and this narrow passage (or siq) is lined with towering cliffs of rosy-hued stone. Petra, one of the world's most unusual ancient sites, could date from as early as 2000 B.C. Through the centuries it was home to several different nomadic tribes, but the city reached its height under the Romans, who carved magnificent monuments out of the distinctive rock (the Treasury is the most perfectly preserved example). Later it became part of the Byzantine Empire, fell to the Arabs, and then was forgotten for centuries until it was rediscovered by a Swiss explorer in the early nineteenth century. What he found and what you see is a dazzling array of classical monuments, historic sites such as the Tomb of Aaron (the brother of Moses), and splendid views of the surrounding ancient lands. Petra's beautiful tombs and temples, and cliffs that change character with the rays of the sun, almost require you to set out with plenty of film and good hiking shoes.

~~~~~~

TUNISIA

Tunisia's leading seaport is **La Goulette** (Halq al-Wadi), famous for its sixteenth-century fort (built by Charles V of Spain to safeguard his many conquests in the Mediterranean) and its fish restaurants, which draw people from the nearby capital city of Tunis to the sidewalk tables. La Goulette is but a short distance from the capital the Romans once called Africa Vetus, and from the ruins of the ancient Mediterranean power of Carthage.

Approximately one million people live in greater **Tunis,** a typical North African metropolis that blends the old with the new, and the Oriental with the Occidental in a dizzying fashion. For here was a culture in which the conquering sword of Islam smote the early Christianity of Byzantium and brought about a vigorous flowering of new art forms. In the eleventh century, Tunisia entered another aesthetic era as influences shifted from the eastern Mediterranean to the Moslem West of Andalusia (southern Spain). The art of this period, delicate and refined, appears in illuminated manuscripts, copperwork, carved wood, and stucco lacework. In the sixteenth century Tunisia became part of the Ottoman Empire, and Turkish art introduced a new dimension that became increasingly baroque. In 1881 the country became a French protectorate. It received its independence in 1956 and today is a nation poised (as they say) on the brink of change.

Nonetheless, as you drive through Tunis you will see a city whose layers of history are evident on every street corner. The medina, or inner city of shops and old houses, is considered one of the most beautiful in the Islamic world. There is the great mosque Djamaa Ez-Zitouna, whose 184 columns were pilfered from the Roman temples of Carthage. The National Library of Tunis, which the Turks used as a barracks, has a remarkable collection of illuminated Koran manuscripts, and the beautiful Palace of Dar Ben Abdullah is one of the Tunisian great houses. Outside the Medina, boulevards and buildings with whitewashed fronts and light-blue shutters to filter the bright Mediterranean sun give the air of a French provincial town. (French is still the second language here, after Arabic.)

Just a short drive from this richness are the Carthaginian ruins of Punic and Roman Tunisia. The Phoenicians founded **Carthage** in 814 B.C., and the city became a Mediterranean power by the sixth century B.C., influencing civilizations as far as southern Spain and the Balearic Islands. As the ancient Romans grew stronger and conquered lower Italy, they disliked the Carthaginians more and more and referred to them as Punics, which applied not only to the language they spoke (a dialect of Phoenician) but also to the fact that they were considered treacherous and perfidious. A series of wars broke out, known as the Punic Wars; during the second Punic War (218 to 201 B.C.), a Carthaginian general named Hannibal crossed the Alps with the aid of elephants and invaded Italy, much to the disgrace of the Roman armies. Carthage was then totally destroyed, condemned to death by the Roman Senate in 146 B.C. The city, resurrected by Emperor Augustus, became a Roman province. The baths, built in the second century A.D. under Antoninus Pius, were among the largest in the empire. Built on the seashore near the site where the first Phoenician ships anchored, this magnificent structure measured seven hundred feet in length. Its sumptuous decorations were second to none. Other relics of these two Carthages that were nine centuries apart are: the Necropolis; the city gate; a theater; the Tophet (where Carthaginians first offered human sacrifices, then substituted animals); and some interesting, beautifully decorated private houses.

Some shore tours also stop at **Sidi bou Said,** a Moorish village along the coast from Carthage, and a photographer's paradise with its whitewashed houses untouched by the modern world. Here you can wander the steeply winding streets, past tiny shops, cafes, and benches crowded with village elders having a smoke. Where else, you may wonder, is the sky so blue, the cypress so green, and the bougainvillea so scarlet? Look across the Bay of Tunis to Bou Cornine, the twin-peaked mountain, and you will understand why this charming oasis is so popular with artists and lovers alike.

TURKEY

The little fishing village of **Dikili** on the edge of Asia Minor is a relatively new call for ships cruising the Aegean. A thrilling stop, Dikili is just a thirty-five-minute bus ride away from the classical ruins of **Pergamum,** the ancient city that flourished for some four centuries (from the second century B.C. to the second century A.D.). During the height of her power, Pergamum was a city of some 160,000 inhabitants and governed most of western and central Asia Minor. Bergama (the modern name) lies on a plain with the ancient Acropolis to the north and the Asklepeion to the southwest.

The Acropolis was the site of various kings' palaces, temples, a theater, and the second largest library in the ancient world (after Alexandria). The library is said to have contained approximately 200,000 papyrus scrolls; when the Egyptians stopped exporting papyrus (they were becoming slightly jealous of the competition), the people of Pergamum simply invented parchment and continued writing books. The

Egyptians, however, had the last word, for Mark Anthony carried away most of the library's contents in 41 B.C. as a present for his beloved Cleopatra. The beautifully restored theater, on the side of the Acropolis, features a white marble stage that hosts the annual Pergamum festival. Next to the theater sits a small temple dedicated to Dionysus, the god of wine. Archaeologists believe that this temple was placed on the first dead-end street in the world, for a covered walk led from here all the way down the hill to the Asklepeion, about a mile distant. The Asklepeion, a complex dedicated to the god of medicine and reputed to be the second largest hospital in the ancient world (after Epidaunus), specialized in psychotherapy. It was so popular that the coffers of Pergamum swelled from the many patients who came for treatments. The "cure" featured lolling in mud baths, getting lots of sleep, watching comedies (never tragedies) in the 3500-seat open theater, and running naked through the halls. Perhaps because of this last exercise, the treatment center had a central heating system.

A short twenty-five-minute drive from the small port town of **Kusadasi** brings you to the archaeological site of one of the most extraordinary cities of the ancient world, **Ephesus.** In just a few hours' tour it is impossible to absorb this great and vast metropolis whose life spanned two thousand years, especially when one realizes that less than 20% of the city has been uncovered—and excavations have been going on for more than a century! Late Mycenean pottery from 1300 B.C. has been found in the area, but historians say the city was first settled around 2000 B.C. on a sheltered harbor around a sanctuary dedicated to the goddess Cybele (later held equal to Artemis). As the harbor silted in, the city was twice relocated—in 1000 B.C. (Ephesus II) and in 334 B.C. (Ephesus III). Today the sea has receded all the way back to Kusadasi and left a valley fertile for the growing of tobacco, fruit, and olives.

The Temple of Artemis at Ephesus was one of the Seven Wonders of the Ancient World; at least one historian, Pausanias, considered it "the most beautiful work created by humankind." Artemis symbolized nature, virginity, and fertility and protected naval voyagers and wild creatures. The temple was destroyed several times but always rebuilt. Now, however, practically nothing remains so we can only speculate on its former beauty. The classical tour of Ephesus covers the remains of the third city, or Hellenistic period, as well as some monuments left from the following Roman era. (I had been told by the cruise director of the *Stella Solaris* that Ephesus would be the highlight of my Aegean cruise, and this was true.) The marble-paved streets lined with statues of important personages of 2000 years ago inspired me. Curetes Street, with its many shops and porticos, leads to the Library of Celsus and the junction with what is now known as Marble Road. On the right-hand side of this corner is every tour guide's favorite structure—the brothel! Scholars say it was constructed between A.D. 98 and 117 and featured baths, a public lavatory, and a series of small rooms on the second story. Mosaics depicting the four seasons and the usual pastimes of life inside a brothel have been found. Across the street from this building is an advertisement in the sidewalk—the head of a woman, a heart, and a foot pointing toward the brothel.

Arcadian Avenue leads from the huge amphitheater of Ephesus to what must have been the edge of the harbor in ancient times. The theater was renowned for its seating capacity of 24,000 and for its perfect acoustics. Now restored, it probably looks much like it did when St. Paul came to Ephesus in A.D. 54 to preach. If you have time and energy left after your tour of Ephesus, you can hire a taxi outside the gate at the end of Harbor Street and continue on to the Archaeological Museum, or drive up to the House of the Virgin Mary on Mount Solmisos (where it is believed she spent her final days) before you return to Kusadasi for some light shopping and the comfort of your cruise vessel. (By the way, tax-free liquor is sold on the pier here during the late afternoon.)

The approach to **Istanbul,** the city that spans two continents, begins about thirteen hours prior to reaching the port. Your ship must enter the Dardanelles, the narrow strait that separates Europe from Asia and the Aegean from the Sea of Marmara. This is the gateway to a strategic area that has been both the bridge and battleground between the exotic East and the Western world for more than two thousand years. Istanbul has been known by many names in its many-layered history. Founded about the fifth century B.C., it was first called Byzantium after the mythical figure, Byzas. As a crossroad between the East and the West, the city fell to the Persians and then to the Greeks. In the first century A.D., the Romans added Byzantium to their empire, and it remained in their interest for the next several centuries.

In A.D. 330, the Emperor Constantine I renamed the city after himself and pronounced it the capital of the East Roman Empire. Although these later Romans built some fine monuments in Constantinople, few of the structures remain, because the city was on the Crusade route and thus went through several severe sackings. In the thirteenth century, Constantinople again fell to the Greeks and then finally landed with the Turks in 1453. The Turks built mosques for the devout, palaces and other places of intrigue for the sultans, and beautiful fountains for everyone. They also changed the name to Istanbul, meaning city of Islams, and made it capital of the Ottoman Empire. When the empire fell, Kemal Mustafa (also known as Ataturk) formed the modern Turkish Republic and moved the capital to the more central location of Ankara in 1922.

Istanbul today is home to about two million people and more than four hundred mosques, whose domes and minarets make striking silhouettes on the busy skyline. It is truly a city of two continents, separated only by the eighteen-and-a-half-mile long Bosporus, the narrow strait that joins the Sea of Marmara with the Black Sea. Your cruise ship will dock in front of the old Customs House, or Yolgu Salonu, and you can see the newer section of the European side rising up before you. Across the Golden Horn, that inlet to the north, are the older quarters—Galata and Beyoglu. If you do an about face you'll be looking at the Asian side of Istanbul, which can be reached by numerous ferries as well as the only suspension bridge linking Europe with Asia. It's thrilling to sail into Istanbul (the only way I would ever want to approach this city), because you and your ship are immediately in the center of all the activity, the vibrancy, and the color that makes this area so fascinating. Churning, dirty, and busy Istanbul catches you in this crazy collage of colors, sounds, and smells as soon as you disembark from your cruise vessel.

One of your first stops should be the Blue Mosque, built by the Sultan Ahmed between 1609 and 1616, and covered on the inside with over 21,000 blue porcelain tiles that give it its popular name. One Turkish author writes that the exterior of the mosque, with its six slender minarets, "caresses the eyes like a beautiful flower." The interior is equally impressive because of the brilliant blue tiles overhead and the multipatterned Turkish rugs covering the stone floor. (You must remove your shoes when you visit a mosque, so carry a pair of heavy socks to counteract the dampness and chilliness of the stone floors.) Nearby sits another magnificent monument, Haghia Sophia, built by the Emperor Justinian between 532 and 537 with the aid of at least 10,000 slaves. The cost is said to have been some $7.5 million at the time, an amount that exhausted Justinian's treasury and forced him to impose new taxes. The ornamentation throughout was renowned, but little remains from the Fourth Crusaders' final looting in 1204. In 1453, Sultan Ahmed converted this ancient sanctuary into a mosque and covered many of the beautiful mosaics with Arabic script and sayings from the Koran. Then Ataturk made Santa Sophia a museum in 1935, so that all could enjoy the beauty of the building. He encouraged the restoration of the mosaics. On a recent visit, I was told that plans have been made to uncover the mosaics in the central dome, which are believed to be especially fine, but the procedure will be complicated because the Arabic script covering cannot be destroyed in the process.

Any tour of Istanbul must also include the Mosque of Suleiman the Magnificent, possibly the most beautiful Islamic structure in the city. It was constructed between 1550 and 1557, by the order of the Sultan whose forty-six-year reign of the Ottoman Empire was considered the Golden Age of literature, science, arts, technology, geography, and military tactics. The interior of this mosque is light and airy, despite the tremendous size of the structure. The echo heard in certain parts is one of its most distinctive features. If you have time to go about on your own, take a taxi to a small, jewel-like mosque (now museum) known as the Khora (Kariye in Turkish). Built around the seventh century, it houses priceless treasures in Giotto-style mosaics of the twelfth to thirteenth centuries.

Topkapi Palace, former home to the sultans and their 6000 or so retainers, is one of the most famous museums in the world. You may have even seen it in the movies. The palace contains the largest Chinese porcelain collection in the world, gathered by the sultans who believed that poisoned food served on this porcelain would change color and warn them. The palace has four rooms of ornaments made by the palace jewelers, some of which hold precious stones the size of your fist. Upstairs in another wing are the harem rooms, but they are only open at certain times, and not to large groups, so it's best to consult your guide if you wish to stay later to visit them. A separate room, open more often, gives an indication of the private lives of the sultans; and just outside, you can catch a glimpse of your ship in the distance. Before you leave Topkapi, follow the sign to the restaurant, stop at the first level, and take in a lovely view of Istanbul.

No visit to this city is complete without a tour to the largest oriental bazaar, or souk, in the world. Thousands of little shops comprise this covered bazaar, and untold numbers of peddlers try to entice you to patronize their stores (suede is a good buy). Most of the hawkers are downright annoying, but a few can be amusing, such as the man who promised he could find me a very nice flying carpet! Frankly, I prefer the smaller Spice (or Egyptian) Bazaar, which is quieter and redolent of the wonderful smells of local teas, pastries, and oriental spices. (If you're overcome by the aromas, you can take refuge in a very good restaurant here called Pandelis.) Another favored excursion in Istanbul requires you to hire a taxi and drive through the newer section of the European side—past the deluxe hotels and over the Bosporus Bridge to the Asian side. Two continents in one day is no small feat.

YUGOSLAVIA

The Dalmatian coastline is gaining in popularity for seven-day cruises from Venice, and well it should. For here, among the 1000 sun-kissed islands and the turquoise waters of the Adriatic Sea, are unforgettable panoramas and charming little ports of call. You can sun and swim or walk among Roman ruins, walled medieval towns, or Venetian fortresses. These cruises offer romance and adventure in the most delightful way, whether you are aboard the 150-passenger sailcruiser *WindStar* or the 280-passenger *Ocean Islander*. It depends entirely upon your own mood.

Among the island ports visited are **Hvar,** with its thirteenth-century walls encircling the picturesque harbor and its many fine medieval palaces. The island also boasts a Renaissance-style cathedral, and a Franciscan monastery with art treasures attributed to Titian, Bassano, and Rosselli. Everyone knows that **Korcula** was the birthplace of Marco Polo, who sailed from Venice in 1271 for China (to return with tales of riches in 1292), and several island inhabitants claim to be descended from the famed explorer. The port of Korcula has many fine historic monuments, including a Doge's palace, a cathedral with some paintings by Tintoretto, as well as medieval towers and homes of former aristocracy.

Opatija is considered among the most sophisticated resorts along the Dalmatian coastline and reminds some of the French Riviera. Located around a brilliant blue bay, it has cafes full of beautiful people, promenades by the sea, and some ritzy casinos. Opatija was a favorite of European royalty at the turn of the century, and you have some evening hours here to savour the nightlife and think of all those nobles who walked ahead. **Pula** is located at the tip of the Istrian peninsula and dates from Roman times, when it was an important port. Although a major commercial center today, Pula can still boast a 23,000-seat amphitheatre as well as other Gaulic leftovers. Cruise passengers can also opt for a side-trip to the twenty-one-mile long Postojna Caves, considered an underground spectacular.

Split is the cultural capital of the Dalmatian coastline. This city was built around the remains of the massive Palace of Diocletian, a native son who became one of Rome's most illustrious emperors. A walking tour here unfolds around lively cafes and homes outside the palace walls, a cathedral, mausoleum, and ancient Temple of Jupiter. **Zadar,** also on the mainland, was the ancient capital of Dalmatia and bears the symbols of many conquerors. The shore excursion will include a Roman forum, Trajan's Arch of Triumph, the ninth-century St. Donat's Church, and a thirteenth-century cathedral. A wonderful cherry brandy is made in Zadar, and no self-respecting visitor leaves without at least one bottle!

Called the Pearl of the Adriatic, **Dubrovnik** is an almost perfectly preserved medieval town, a treasury of cultural and historic monuments documenting a thousand-year history. This is historic Ragusa, which grew up in the seventh century and became a city-republic in the fourteenth century, second only to Venice in strength. With a fleet of ships some three hundred strong, it was the most important trading center in the Balkans, linking the Danube River to the Mediterranean. The republic, governed by dukes, produced many important men of science and

literature and lasted until 1806 when Napoleon entered the picture. Today the old walls and towers of Dubrovnik still rise dramatically from
the Dalmatian coastline. The city is the unofficial capital and tourist
center of Yugoslavia, a country comprising the people and customs of
Bosnia and Herzegovina, Montenegro, Croatia, Macedonia, Slovenia,
and Serbia, as well as the autonomous provinces of Kosovo-Metohija
and Vojvodina.

Cruise ships dock in the nearby suburb of Gruz, and your tour of
the medieval city (where all traffic is banned) will undoubtedly begin at
the western end through Pile Gate. From here the main street, or *placa*,
runs to Ploce Gate at the eastern end and is lined with the most marvelous old buildings and archways. A rewarding walk runs from the circular fountain to St. Blaise's Church, dedicated to the patron saint and
protector of the Republic who gave warning against and thwarted a
Venetian invasion. In front of the church stands a fifteenth-century pillar, formerly the site for official announcements and now a gathering
place for visitors from all over the world. Opposite Orlando's Pillar is
the lovely, sixteenth-century Sponza Palace that was both the customs-
house and mint for the Republic. Behind St. Blaise's Church, Gundulic
Square memorializes a sixteenth-century poet. It is filled with Slavs in
their colorful, native costumes selling produce in the morning and handcrafts later in the day. Dubrovnik's renowned Summer Festival takes
place here in front of the cathedral, and fifteenth-century Rector's Palace, which displays fine furniture, paintings, sculpture, and silver.

To be a true visitor, you must walk around the city walls (wear
sensible shoes) and get a realistic view of what life was and still is like
in this medieval town. You will pass such beautiful fourteenth- to sixteenth-century structures as the Dominican and Franciscan monasteries
and cloisters (the former is at Ploce Gate, the latter is at Pile). You will
also come upon the ruins of an old castle, built thirteen centuries ago;
the simple houses of the townfolk; the Fortress of St. John; and wonderful views of the harbor. The walls end on the harbor, a perfect place
to rest, sip a cool drink, and blend into the scenery.

South of Dubrovnik on the Adriatic coast, the Bay of **Boka Kotor-
ska** (Gulf of Kotor) welcomes cruise vessels that call in the only classic
fjord in southern Europe. The town of Kotor lies at the foot of Mt.
Lovcen in the province of Montenegro. The walled city has stood since
medieval times. In its bay are tiny islands such as the one on which an
orthodox church stands—the stalwart row to services.

THE PACIFIC

HAWAII

The glorious islands that make up our fiftieth state were formed from volcanic eruptions on the sea floor thousands of years ago. Inhabiting this landscape of red-hot volcanos, verdant mountains, paradisiacal valleys with daily rain showers, plus some of the most spectacular, unspoiled beaches in the world, is a potpourri of the earth's people: Polynesians, Orientals, Americans, Europeans, Africans, and the most exquisite combinations of all the above. What a pleasure to visit these islands—this land of "aloha" where everyone is gracious and friendly, the weather so sublime, and the sights so refreshing.

Most visitors to Hawaii arrive, alas, by air and thus miss the fun. Nothing is quite so thrilling as sailing to or from Aloha Tower in Honolulu, past Waikiki Beach and Diamond Head (an extinct volcano that was the legendary home of Pele, the fire goddess), to be greeted by the Royal Hawaiian band, complete with floral leis (if you throw your lei into the sea and it returns to shore, islanders say, you will return to this land). At this writing, American Hawaii Cruises offers regular weekly sailings from the famous Aloha Tower to four ports of call on three other islands. These popular and beautiful cruises are aboard the *Independence* and *Constitution,* formerly of American Export Lines, and well suited to sailing among these scenic islands.

Oahu: If you arrive at Honolulu International Airport dead beat, you will not be alone. It's a long flight from the mainland, as Hawaiians call the continental U.S., and a five-hour time change if you began your journey on the east coast. Have a good rest at your hotel along Waikiki (American Hawaii Cruises utilizes the Hawaiian Regent and it's an excellent choice), then a swim in the seductive Pacific Ocean and the world will look good again! As state capital, **Honolulu** is a thriving metropolis with more to its credit than that two-and-a-half-mile coastline called Waikiki, which lies in the shadow of Diamond Head. If you are planning to spend some time on Oahu, at either end of the cruise, rent a car or take TheBus for some spectacular touring. The Bishop Museum, Liliuokalani Gardens, Queen Emma Summer Palace, the National Memorial Cemetery of the Pacific (where 21,000 servicemen from two world wars, Korea, and Vietnam lie buried), the Royal Mausoleum (with the bodies of five Hawaiian kings and one Queen), and the East-West Center at the University of Hawaii. This center is a federally-funded institute to promote mutual understanding among the peoples of Asia, the Pacific, and the United States.

If you have only a few hours in the Honolulu area, the most important and sobering monument is the **Arizona Memorial** in Pearl Harbor. This monument was built over the sunken battleship where so many Americans lost their lives on December 7, 1941. If you take the two-and-a-half hour cruise aboard the *Pearl Kai,* you will also see the famous Battleship Row and memorial of the USS *Utah.* There is also a three-hour cruise aboard the *Adventure.* Both cost under $10 per adult. At the submarine base, there is a museum of some interest (Wednesday through Sunday) but you need a pass and instructions from the guard at Nimitz Gate (located off the highway of the same name). And, if tall ships are your thing, save some time for the *Falls of Clyde,* berthed at Pier 7 adjacent to Aloha Tower. The world's only full-rigged, four-masted ship is open to the public. For about $3, you may tour the *Clyde,* view the double-hulled Polynesian canoe *Hokule'a,* and see the maritime museum in Aloha Tower.

Hawaii: The big island of Hawaii celebrated its silver jubilee of statehood with the eruption of two of its five volcanos, **Mauna Loa** and **Kilauea,** among the world's most active. The **Kilauea Caldera** is the legendary home of the Hawaiian goddess of fire, Pele, and famous for the many rituals that have taken place here for centuries. From **Hilo,** the Big Island's major seaport and only city, visitors can travel along Chain of Craters Road up through the volcano country to the National Park Visitor Center. You can walk on lava along the way, and then dine at Volcano House, a hotel perched on the edge of Kilauea Crater.

The Big Island also claims some 22,000 different varieties of orchids, the 224,000-acre Parker Ranch (largest ranch under single ownership in the United States), which produces between 10 and 11 million head of beef annually, and an abundance of macadamia nuts. Halfway between Hilo and Kona is the town of **Honokaa,** known as the Macadamia Nut Capital of the World. There are factories and outlets all over the islands, but don't expect any bargains for this rare delicacy acclaimed as the ''perfect nut'' or in the more than 200 gift items related to it!

On the other side of the Big Island is the town of Kailua-Kona, known as **Kona,** famous for the wonderful coffee grown in the area.

Along the beautiful Kona coastline is Kealakekua Bay, a sacred place known as "pathway of the god," where Captain Cook arrived on January 17, 1779. Cook, the most famous navigator-explorer of his time, had "discovered" what he named the **Sandwich Islands** in 1778 at Waimea, Kauai. However, his return to these islands and this particular harbor was not fortuitous, and the dear fellow was murdered and dismembered by the natives less than a month after his arrival. He was just fifty years old. A 27-foot white pillar monument on the far shoreline of Kealakekua Bay was erected in his memory in 1874, and can be seen on both bus and cruise tours.

The most interesting part of the Kona coastline is the oasislike village of **Pu'uhonua O Honaunau** or City of Refuge. It is now a National Historical Park; but during ancient times, Hawaiians pardoned sinners of *kapu* (strict social laws) and other crimes who were able to reach sanctuary here. It was not easy to arrive here, because this area was owned by royalty and it was against kapu for any commoner to set foot upon royal ground. Nonetheless, enough swam ashore to make the place famous. The park provides a very nice map for your own walking tours as well as a short lecture by one of the guides. What is left of the sanctuary is worth visiting.

On the other hand, the village of Kona is tacky, tacky, with overpriced and overtouristed shops. Even Kona coffee seems to be less expensive on the mainland, and the selection of island wear (aloha shirts and muumuus) is better on Maui or Oahu. There is good snorkeling here, however, and a lovely private beach for the use of passengers. Those with real adventure in their souls will enjoy the deep-sea fishing aboard charter boats with a professional crew.

Maui: Many visitors agree with Mauians, who say "Maui No Kai Oi" or "Maui is the best ever!" Maui is the second largest island in the group, and **Kahului** is its principal seaport—although Lahaina (twenty-three miles away) is its historic heart and the first capital of the islands. This was the center of the whaling industry (1840–1865) and humpback whales from the Arctic still come to these Hawaiian breeding grounds during the winter months. But Maui is best loved for its magnificent scenery, especially the stunning white-sand beaches on the western shore, the lush Iao Valley that cuts through the island, and Haleakala National Park. It is said that Haleakala's enormous crater, with a circumference of twenty-one miles, could swallow all of Manhattan. It is called the House of the Sun, because Polynesian legend says that the demigod Maui captured the sun and held it captive to give his people more daylight hours.

Maui is definitely everyone's favorite island, if you only visit beautiful **Kaanapali Beach** with its fabulous resorts, great surf and snorkeling trails (be sure to take a little bread along for the fish). During the 7 a.m. to 6 p.m. call at Maui, passengers could even play golf or tennis at the Sheraton Hotel on Kaanapali Beach. In addition to being an old whaling town, **Lahaina** is great for shopping and there are many charming boutiques to peruse. As the "pineapple island," it is best to order a box of the succulent fruit for delivery to your flight in Honolulu. The prices at Take Home Maui are less than anywhere around, and the fruit was dutifully awaiting our check-in at the Honolulu airport. (Cash only, in case you are interested.)

Other shore excursions on Maui include the west coast and Launiupoko Canyon, Olowalu Valley and tallest cliffs in Hawaii tour by helicopter. Another expensive but unforgettable helicopter tour is of west Maui and the north shore of Molokai. This one features sea cliffs, cascading waterfalls, hidden valleys, and a rest stop on one of Molokai's inaccessible beaches.

Kauai: Just ninety-five miles northwest of Honolulu, Kauai is known as the Garden Island because an abundant rainfall makes for a wide variety of native flora as well as for large taro, pineapple, and sugar plantations. Kauai claims to have the wettest spot on earth—the 5170-foot Mount Waialeale, with 486 inches of rainfall annually. It also has the only navigable rivers in Hawaii. The Wailua River, where the first Polynesians landed in the archipelago some one thousand years ago, has a motor-launch cruise impressive for lush vegetation and unique tropical varietals. Nearby is the beautiful cave called Fern Grotto, its entrance framed by huge fishtail ferns. And a short distance by road is Wailua Falls where, if you survive the steep trail, you can swim in the natural pool surrounded by hala trees.

Lihue is Kauai's commercial center, but large vessels must dock south of it in the deepwater port of **Nawiliwili,** beside freighters loading sugar. More historic is **Waimea** where Captain Cook landed in 1778. No doubt, Cook explored the island's biggest tourist attraction, Waimea Canyon, a miniature version of the Grand Canyon—best seen from Puu Ka Pele mountain and the lookout at Kaana Ridge.

There are many popular shore excursions here, including the beach where *South Pacific* and other movies have been filmed. There is also a typical Hawaiian luau one evening that offers a flavor of the feast that some Hawaiians used to enjoy. The food is excellent and everyone loves the hula show afterward! Another popular excursion on Kauai is the one-hour flight by helicopter over the 5000-foot rim of the Waialeale Crater into the wettest spot on earth, down Waimea Canyon and along the Na Pali coastline with 3000-foot mountain walls. Hanalei Bay with its adjoining beaches is considered one of the most beautiful sights in the world, especially by air. All this for about $100, and those who took the ride said it was worth every penny! But only the brave should apply, as the ride is rather bumpy at times.

AUSTRALIA AND NEW ZEALAND

Australia: If I had to pick a good point to begin a South Pacific quest, it would have to be **Sydney,** capital of New South Wales and the oldest, largest (3 million people), and liveliest city in Australia. This bustling metropolis is home to more than 20% of the country's population, and its beautiful harbor is both a welcome and familiar sight to every sailor. Imagine yourself coming into this port aboard a luxury cruise vessel, past the sparkling new high-rises and the famous Opera House complex whose design is so evocative of billowing sails.

Sydney is often called the Cradle of the Country; it is the oldest civilized settlement in the southwestern Pacific (although one might question the criteria for being civilized). Nonetheless, history says that Captain Cook visited this harbor in 1770 and called it Port Jackson after a secretary of the British Admiralty. Actually Cook was only at the head of the harbor; and Captain Philip founded Sydney Cove on January 26, 1788, the anniversary of which is now celebrated as Australia Day. The best way to see Sydney is to emulate these founders; take a launch around the harbor to appreciate Harbor Bridge, the Opera House, and the skyline of the business district. Sydney has a small town mentality and a rather happy-go-lucky atmosphere—people seem to work only when they must, and the magnificent beaches north and south of the city are the most popular places to relax (the sun shines approximately 342 days of the year).

For a view of the city from fifty stories up, try the revolving restaurant at the top of the Australia Tower (actually on the forty-ninth floor), which takes two hours for a full 360-degree, effortless turn. Wander by Sydney's oldest building (the 1815 Cadman's Cottage near the passenger terminal), and the Argyle Arts Center where local craftsmen sell their wares. The latter is a large convict-built brick building that dates from the 1820s when convicts were once housed in the cellars. A stroll around Circular Quay brings you to the Opera House. Tours are conducted daily (except Saturday), and you can sit on the open-air terrace and watch ships sail by in the harbor. Other sites of interest include the Australian Museum (for a fine collection of aboriginal and South Sea art and the zoo). You are now in the land of kangaroos and koalas, and Taronga Zoo is one of the best in the world. For an even closer look, take a bus to Koala Park in Pennant Hills where you can cavort with koalas, kangaroos, and emus.

Sailing northward along the eastern coastline of Australia, your ship will enter the region of the **Great Barrier Reef,** a stretch of coral some 1242 miles long extending from Gladstone to Cape York. The reef teems with marine and bird life; they are among the world's most beautiful natural attractions. In this area totaling more than 80,000 square miles with over 600 islands live several hundred kinds of coral, at least 900 different species of fish, and birds that migrate from as far away as Japan and Siberia. Other birds that are nearing extinction elsewhere survive well here. Cruising the Great Barrier Reef is intriguing, and some of the larger islands have resort facilities, many of which are great for watersports. Your cruise vessel may also call at **Cairns,** one of the most northerly cities in Queensland, a tropical resort that serves as the base for excursions into the outer reef areas.

New Zealand: A certain amount of rivalry exists between Australia and her neighbor, New Zealand, and not all of it is simply on the surface. For example, New Zealanders are quick to point out that their country was not settled by convicts. Australians counter that they are not fifty years behind the times. Striking differences do exist between these two lands and cultures, which makes it a must to visit both. New Zealand is small compared to the vast continent next door. It consists of North, South, and Stewart islands which, all told, about equal the size of the state of Colorado. Called the land of the Long White Cloud by Polynesians some six centuries ago, New Zealand lies halfway between the Equator and the South Pole and has some of the most spectacular scenery in the world. Sheep outnumber people by eighty to one at last count, and there are about five and one-quarter million acres of national parks. The largest and most famous is South Island's Fjordland National Park that comprises some 3 million acres of bays and fjords, of which Milford Sound is the most popular for local cruises.

New Zealanders refer to themselves as Kiwis (turkeylike birds) and say that they live upon God's Own Country, which was discovered by a Dutchman in 1642 (who named it Nieuw Zeeland). The islands were pretty much ignored until Captain Cook arrived aboard the *Endeavour* in 1769. The first English settled in 1840 near Wellington. These new Westerners had to contend with a large native population who clung to their own considerable culture. These aborigines, the Maori, still number 8% of the population and contribute a great deal to life in this land.

Windy **Wellington,** a port city that will remind you of San Francisco, is the capital of New Zealand and named in honor of the Duke of Wellington's victory over the French in the Battle of Waterloo. The city is built upon a series of steep hills at the southwest tip of North Island. To best understand the layout, climb to the summit of Mount Victoria (558 feet) where you can see the entire harbor and, sometimes, the tip of South Island just twenty miles across Cook Strait. A bust of Wellington rests on this summit, as well as a memorial to the American explorer, Rear Admiral Richard Byrd, who used New Zealand as a base for his Antarctic expeditions. Wellington is a pleasant, clean, and very British capital of about 350,000 with some pleasant but not overly exciting sights to see. It is a government town, and one of the largest wooden buildings left in the world houses the government headquarters.

Auckland, often thought of as the largest Polynesian city in the world, is a much more exciting metropolis of about 800,000 people. Situated at the separation of two seas, the Pacific and Tasman, and two harbors, the Waitemata and Manukau, the city has been built on top of seven extinct volcanos—in addition, the volcano called Rangitoto Island sits in Waitemata Harbor. A former Maori fortified village, Mount Eden is a 643-foot cone of an extinct volcano from which you can see the Pacific on one side and the Tasman Sea on the other. One Tree Hill, another former Maori site, has one tree and a memorial to the Father of Auckland. The city offers a 300-acre park (where sheep graze close to the streets), a zoo where you can see the indigenous kiwi, a museum of transport and technology, and some lovely harbor cruises. Or you can take an excursion some 126 miles from the city to the Waitomo Caves to visit the Glowworm Grotto, eerie underground caverns illuminated by their many glowworms.

Far more interesting from a cultural point of view is **Rororua,** one of the country's prime attractions. Known as Sulphur City, this area about 150 miles south of Auckland is one of the traditional homes of the Maori people. From here, take an excursion to the thermal baths of Whaka, the Maori Arts and Crafts Institute, and the Ohinemutu Maori Village with its church and meeting house rich in local carvings. You can also attend a Maori concert and a typical Maori feast, which is cooked in the ground.

Sailing northward from Auckland, some cruise vessels call in the **Bay of Islands** for a brief visit to Russell and Waitangi. The latter is known as the birthplace of New Zealand history, for it was here that the Treaty of Waitangi was signed whereby, in 1840, the Maoris accepted the sovereignty of the British Crown in return for ownership of their traditional lands. Russell, across the bay from Waitangi, was the short-lived capital of this new colony; it still retains its Old World charm.

THE SOUTH PACIFIC

Following in the wake of Magellan were adventurers of the western world who discovered the paradisiacal islands in the South Seas that today are the last bit of exotica extant—Captain Cook, Captain Bligh and the crew of the *Bounty,* Robert Louis Stevenson, Henri Gauguin, and

Somerset Maugham. Many who came to the far-flung Polynesian kingdom stayed. For where else is the sky so blessed with sun and blue, are the beaches so shining and sensuous, the waters so clear, and the flowers so brilliant? Among all this perfection live people who are friendly and relatively untouched by the world outside.

Fiji: Fiji is an archipelago of more than three hundred islands, which are the most populous and economically advanced of the South Sea group. A tropical paradise 1100 miles south of the equator, Fiji is the center of communication for the area. An independent sovereign state, it holds a population of over half a million. Its capital is **Suva,** and its prime minister is an Oxford-educated hereditary tribal chief. Suva is a thriving commercial port with duty-free shops, Government House, a museum containing local artifacts dating from 2000 years ago, and the University of the South Pacific. Everything goes here, and the mode of dress ranges from the sulu of the local population to the sari of the large Indian community to the many varieties of European dress. One short excursion from Suva takes you to Orchid Island, where the flowers grow wild beside vanilla, coffee, and tea. You can also see mongooses, iguanas, and monkeys.

Fiji is also known for its *kava* and fire-walking. The former is a beverage made from the root of a pepper plant; the latter is practiced by both the native-born Fijians and the Indians who were imported by the British for labor and who now make up more than half the population. The fire-walkers are followers of Maha Devi. Visitors may be invited to the ritual now and then, for a small fee, of course!

The Samoas: The Samoas (American and Western) are considered the Heartland of Polynesia, and the same language and customs prevail on both sets of islands. Western Samoa is an independent Polynesian nation whose capital is **Apia.** American Samoa is an unincorporated territory whose native inhabitants are U.S. nationals but not citizens. Its capital is **Pago Pago** (pronounced Pango), made famous by author Somerset Maugham in a short story called "Rain." Anthropologist Margaret Mead also spent some time in American Samoa, which resulted in her book *Coming of Age in Samoa;* and Robert Louis Stevenson lived the last four years of his life in a large villa overlooking the port of Apia. While American Samoa is well subsidized by the U.S. and therefore rather rich, Western Samoa is poor. But the people on both groups of islands are simple and friendly, still ruled by the chieftain system and witchcraft. In fact, traditionalism caused both governments to issue a behavior code for tourists, which discourages revealing dress, requests no disturbances at prayer time, and advises how to eat and sit Samoan style (cruise passengers will probably not be bothered with the latter). Other than a few admonitions, Samoans just want you to enjoy the surrounding grace and beauty (and stay away from fiery kava and the local transvestites).

Tonga: Last of the Polynesian kingdoms and the only set of islands in the South Seas that has never been colonized, Tonga was a British protectorate and is now an independent nation within the Commonwealth. This group of 150 coral and volcanic islands, with a population of under 100,000, is one of the world's smallest nations. The name of its capital, **Nuku'alofa** (Land of Love), was chosen because Captain Cook supposedly referred to this archipelago as the Friendly Islands. Unfortunately, Tonga is very poor and rather feudal, and its present monarch (King Taufa Ahau Tupou IV) has had to rely on outside sources for funds (the USSR, Libya, and Japan); but he and his nobles hope that tourism will fill the coffers. Interesting sights around Nuku'alofa include the Royal Palace (which can be viewed over low walls but not visited), the Royal Tombs, and Ha'amonga Trilithon. The Trilithon is a stone calendar, erected about A.D. 1200 that predicts the summer and winter solstices. Not far from the capital in a village called Kolovai, flying foxes hang upside-down all day. They look like fruit and are considered sacred—only members of the royal family may touch them. For more natural phenomena, go see the blowholes where water shoots up sixty feet at high tide and visit the caves dripping with stalactites and stalagmites near the village of Haveluliku.

French Polynesia: French Polynesia consists of some 130 islands, of which **Tahiti** is the most familiar. The island was first sighted by Westerners in 1767 by the captain and crew of the English vessel *Dolphin*. A year later, French explorer de Bougainville claimed it for his country and left his name on the brilliant wild-flowers found everywhere here—the bougainvillea. Captain Cook arrived the next year aboard the *Endeavour* to set up a scientific observation post at Point Venus. Cook is also credited with giving Tahiti its name (from what he understood the natives call it), before he sailed away to discover the Society Islands, Australia, and New Zealand. He returned to Tahiti three more times; a monument to his memory stands at Point Venus. Another well-known captain to visit Tahiti, the infamous Bligh, was master of the HMS *Bounty*. In October 1788, the captain and his crew began a five-month stay on the island. Just after the vessel sailed again, the mutiny occurred, and Bligh was left in a boat along with eighteen of his men and some provisions. The group survived and landed in Indonesia. (The true story is even better than the movie!)

    Papeete, Tahiti, a bustling and noisy capital and port town, must rebuff complaints that it has lost its paradisical charm as high-rises replace interesting old buildings and powerboats replace outrigger canoes in the lagoon. But do not despair, just get out of town! Pay a visit to Point Venus, tracing the steps of the explorers and their men. Stop by the Museum of Discovery, with wax figures of captains Wallis and Cook and Frenchman de Bougainville as well as Tahitian chieftains and dancers. Some artifacts and engravings at the museum tell of the white man's arrival. **Papeari,** thirty miles southwest of Papeete, offers another museum of interest, the Gauguin Museum, which contains three original paintings as well as some drawings and doodlings made by the artist during his years on the island (it is said that he left some of his talent in one or two of the local population). And one thing is certain—you will eat very well (but not cheaply) on Tahiti.

If you are lucky enough to be aboard *Wind-Song* while sailing among these beautiful islands, your cruise will take you to Huahine, Tahaa and Raiatea, Bora Bora, and Moorea, but not necessarily in the order above.

Moorea, called the older sister of Tahiti, is actually twice the age of the better-known island and is separated by eight mountain ridges. The ship anchors in Pao Pao, or Cook's Bay, and even the well-known sea captain was said to have been overwhelmed by the island's natural beauties, which include Mou'a'-roa—the needle-shaped mountain known today as Bali Ha'i. Moorea is famous for its agricultural experimental park (full of vanilla, pineapple, and coconut plantations as well as farm animals, wheat, and corn) seen via air-conditioned Land Rovers, and Le Belvedere for spectacular views of both Cook's and Opunohu bays. Those preferring to be alone together on the island will find some lovely resorts and beaches (including one called Bali H'ai) as well as plentiful snack shops.

Bora Bora is the best known of the Society Island chain and the epitome of a South Pacific paradise. Our friend Captain Cook claimed the six-mile long island for England in 1777, but a more friendly invasion occurred during World War II, when some 5000 Americans were stationed here and rebuilt both port and land facilities. It is fun to rent a car in Bora Bora for a few hours and drive the 17-mile road around the lagoon, past many colorful villages and fabulous resorts—including Hotel Bora Bora, one of the most expensive in the South Pacific. Bora Bora is surrounded by charming ''motu'' or small islands where beach barbecues are often held. Another popular spot is Bloody Mary's Seafood Restaurant, a short drive from the pier by Le Truck bus. For those who enjoy seafood still squiggling, an outrigger canoe excursion features feeding the sharks (!) that congregate near a reef surrounding the island. Swimsuit, mask, and snorkel are necessary for this exercise.

Tahaa and **Raiatea** are also sister islands, now separated by a 2–3-mile-wide strait, though both geological and mythological evidence says they were once connected. Shaped like the flower of an hibiscus, Tahaa is reachable only by sea and surrounded by dozens of motu. Vanilla is grown here, and its distinctive fragrance fills the air.

Raiatea is considered the center of ancient Maori culture, from whence derived Tahitians, Tongans, and Samoans, as well as the original Maori who paddled all the way to New Zealand. When Captain Cook anchored *Endeavor* in Opoa Bay in July, 1769, he claimed Raiatea and all islands in sight for England, naming them the Society Islands (including Huahine, Tahaa, Bora Bora, and Maupiti). Known today as the leeward Society Islands, they were annexed to France in 1888.

As the largest of this group, Raiatea is also the most interesting and industrious, and its main town—Uturoa—is the administrative center for the islands. Raiatea boasts the group's only navigable fresh waterway—the Faaroa River—which is thought to be the ancient launching pad for those Maoris later found in New Zealand and Hawaii. Raiatea is full of legends and was once considered sacred in Polynesian history. Indeed, many Polynesians still feel that their soul will return to this spiritual homeland, known as Havai'i. An excursion up the Faaroa River is a lovely way to spend a morning, especially if your guide is the informative Tom, assistant manager at the nearby Bali H'ai Hotel. The energetic may enjoy a 3-hour walking tour to Mount Tapioi Point lookout, but there is no backup transportation available.

Huahine-Nui and **Huahine-Iti** (big and little) are another set of islands thought to have been united once as they still share a common barrier reef. Quiet and calm, the islands boast coffee, vanilla, and mango plantations, a main village called Fare, and an open-air museum of restored religious sites known as "marae." However, a Heritage Tour here is not worth the time and money. Most visitors can make use of the local beaches and nautical activities.

Shopping in Tahiti and the Society Islands is mind-bogglingly expensive. Even postcards cost around $1.25, and that doesn't include the airmail stamp! The black South Sea pearls are beautiful and an excellent investment, but my jeweler can get them cheaper in New York. Food and drink on the islands is very costly (a Coke is about $5) and most of the souvenirs are imported. In short, save your money; indulge in the beauty of the water, the sky, the beaches, and the lush mountainsides, especially if your ship is cruising at sunset.

SOUTH AMERICA

South America! That magnificent land mass that bulges east to west below the Equator, and then slims down to a graceful point at Tierra del Fuego, is often misunderstood and rarely visited by its friendly northern neighbors who also call themselves Americans. Hardly a continent to ignore, it covers some 12% of the earth's surface, has a population of well over the 200 million mark, and is growing rapidly. Its 6,866,000 square miles of land are bordered by the Caribbean as well as the Atlantic and Pacific oceans. South America claims the world's largest river, the Amazon (3915 miles); the world's three highest volcanos, Guallatiri (19,882 feet) and Lascar (19,652 feet) in Chile, and Cotopaxi (19,347 feet) in Ecuador; and the world's driest spot in Chile's Atacama Desert where the rainfall is barely discernible.

Culturally, this continent was influenced from the twelfth to sixteenth centuries by the fabulous Inca Empire that embraced some 25 million people and covered a territory that now includes Bolivia, Peru, Ecuador, northern Chile, and part of Argentina. Christianity was imposed upon the native population in the sixteenth century when the Spanish *conquistadors* and the Portuguese navigators began to colonize their discoveries, building churches and palaces lined with the newly found gold. The largest Spanish- and Portuguese-speaking population resides within the borders of South America; and races blend here unlike on any other continent. Called the ultimate in contrasts, South America boasts too much activity in all directions for any superlative to take hold. Here you can visit Machu Picchu (the mysterious legacy left by the Incas) and Brasilia (the ultramodern capital that symbolizes today's South America) in the same breath—and believe in both!

A decade ago, Grace Line offered weekly passenger service completely around the continent of South America. The good old days! Cruises to South America are now on an irregular basis and primarily during the winter season. Sun Line innovated excellent itineraries through the Caribbean and up both the Orinico and Amazon rivers on two different vessels. Ocean Cruise Line has followed suit up the Orinoco. Cunard/NAC has some Amazon river sailings as an annual cruise feature. Royal Viking Line, Royal Cruise Line, Sun Line, Epirotiki, Seabourn, Renaissance, and Society Expeditions all have South America on their winter schedules.

ARGENTINA

Buenos Aires, capital and port of Argentina, is considered the Paris of Latin America for its broad boulevards, sophisticated shops, art galleries, theaters, nightclubs, opera, and fine public buildings. It is also the city of Evita, where inflation can run extraordinarily high and where foreign business executives often hire 24-hour bodyguards as a deterrent to local terrorist groups. Despite the political and economic undercurrents, Buenos Aires still prides itself on its more than 150 beautiful parks and the best beef in the world. So, enjoy the romance and excitement of this city from the convenience of your cruise ship. Your city tour should include a visit to the Grecian-style Colon Opera House; Palermo Park on Avenida Libertador General San Martin (named after the national hero); the Plaza de Mayo and the pink Government House (known as Casa Rosada); the cathedral, which is one of the country's oldest buildings and where General Jose de San Martin is buried; and the Museum of Fine Arts. For a more charming and colorful view of life in Buenos Aires, you can visit La Boca, where local artist Benito Quinquela Martin helped change the scenery from slums to a picturesque fishing port. Don't miss the area museum stocked with his waterfront paintings. Some delightful restaurants are here too, where gourmet food is served with pride.

For a different look at this land of the *gauchos,* you can travel out of the city to a nearby *estancia* (ranch) for some congenial Argentinian hospitality that may include a sumptuous barbecue that would put even Texas to shame! Or you can take a two-hour cruise aboard a 160-passenger catamaran that allows a view of the Parana delta area and a peek at the Lujan, Sariento, Capitan, San Antonio, and Urion rivers.

Argentina stretches south some 2150 miles to Cape Horn at the lower tip of the continent. The bottom portion, called Patagonia (or Land of the People with Long Feet), boasts such fascinating place names as Tierra del Fuego and Ushuaia (the most southern town in the world). North of Cape Horn is the Strait of Magellan (see below).

BRAZIL

If I had to choose just one South American city to see, it would have to be **Rio de Janeiro.** Some say that this city has the most beautiful natural setting in the world. Truly, it competes with Hong Kong and San Francisco, and Rio is definitely a "fun capital," a city where the action rarely ceases from dawn to the following dawn. Brazilians love excitement, music, and the sun—and Rio has plenty of all three. Approximately sixteen beaches are within this beautiful fifteen-mile long bay—the most popular (and chic) is Copacabana, followed closely by Ipanema. If you want to "beach it" like a pro, go early in the day (8 a.m. to about noon) and wear as skimpy a suit as possible (remember, the "string" was invented here!). Leave everything you do not want to lose on the ship. Thievery is a real problem here, and some young natives are adept at stealing everything, whether one is wearing it or carrying it.

First among the city's attractions is the cable car ride to the top of Sugar Loaf; then in the late afternoon, take a taxi or the cogwheel train up to the Corcovado Christ for a sunset view. The famed statue that symbolizes Rio in many photographs was designed by a French artist. Standing 120 feet high and weighing about 700 tons, the statue was inaugurated in 1931 and paid for by contributions from the citizenry of Rio. Impressive from any angle, the statue gives way to an especially thrilling panorama of this seaside city as the sun sets and dusk signals the illumination of lights below.

Rio is a city of great wealth and great poverty (if you look at the *favela* hillside shacks). You may notice considerable French overtones. Its largest park was laid out by a French architect, and the Municipal Theater is an exact copy of the Paris Opera House. The many elegant and expensive shops feature the latest fashion ideas from Paris, either originals or quickly turned-out copies. Many women of Rio spend a lot of time shopping and dressing and adorning themselves. Rio is also the hometown of Hans Stern, the world-renowned jeweler who combines much gold with Brazil's fabulous array of semiprecious stones. On your walking tours, you may come upon some magnificent baroque churches with gold-covered interiors, the worthwhile Museum of Fine Arts, and many exciting restaurants featuring freshly caught seafood and the local specialty *feijoada* (traditionally served at Saturday lunch so you can rest after eating such a large meal). If your time allows for sightseeing outside of Rio, drive to Tijuca Forest, once a private estate; and to Petropolis where, in 1845, the Emperor Dom Pedro II built a summer palace that is now the Imperial Museum. Displaying items used by the Imperial family during this period, the museum is open daily (except Monday). The Emperor and his wife, Dona Teresa Christina, are buried in the cathedral nearby.

Just as I think Rio is an exciting tourist city, **Sao Paulo** is not. This metropolis of 10 million is the industrial center of Brazil—sprawling, congested, and stacked with new skyscrapers. The "Paulistas" love it, but a friend who lives there laments: "When visitors come, there's no place to take them, little of interest to see!" Well, there *are* lots of new buildings, including the largest snake farm in Latin America as well as Edificio Italia, the highest structure in South America. Sao Paulo also boasts one of the world's largest parks, Ibirapuera Park, and three art museums. The city's port, Santos, claims the biggest dock area on the continent in addition to its lovely tropical climate and beautiful beaches. Given the choice, I would venture no farther than the beaches.

THE AMAZON

The mighty **Amazon River** descends some 3000 miles from its source high in Peru down to the Atlantic Ocean. Early Spaniards explored the river around 1592, according to legend, and were so taken with its vastness that they called it *Rio Mar* or the River Sea. Legend also says that they came upon a race of women warriors they named the *Amazones*—from Greek mythology—and soon the whole region was called Amazon. In South America, distances are often larger than can reasonably be conceived, and the Amazon region covers some 3 million square miles—including 3900 miles of waterway from Atlantic to Pacific oceans and more than 10,000 tributaries along the way. Its width varies from a meager one-inch at the source (so they say) to more than 200 miles at the mouth at Belem. Large commercial vessels may navigate all the way to Iquitos, approximately 2700 miles upriver.

Although little of the Amazon region has been thoroughly explored, it totals some 25% of the world's fresh water and some of its most colorful jungle. Botanists say that there are about 18,000 different plant species in the Amazon Basin, and ichthyographers claim some 1600 species of fish. Plus the fact that the region is exceedingly rich in gold, diamonds, lumber, rubber, oil, and jute and has a population of less than 2 million people. Quite frankly, however, the only sensible way to explore the Amazon basin is by boat—particularly a comfortable cruise vessel that has air conditioning, hot water, a bar, a laundry service, and all those other wonderful things we can not possibly live without!

The port city of **Belem** is gateway to the mighty Amazon River, and located about ninety miles from the Atlantic Ocean. Although set in the midst of tropical foliage, it is a city of white buildings and wide boulevards. Tourist attractions include the Praca da Republica, the Goeldi Museum and Zoo, the Jungle Park public garden, and the Agricultural Institute. The port of Belem can be explored by motor launch, and the suggested best time for photographers is between 5 and 10 a.m. The really adventurous may also want to fly out to the Island of Marajo, a larger land mass than the country of Denmark, noted for its cattle production and lumber industry.

Santarem is located approximately 500 miles upriver, just halfway between Belem and Manaus. It is a city of about 150,000 inhabitants, which was settled by American Confederates from South Carolina and Tennessee in 1865. Indeed, the Confederate flag still hangs from some of the local wateringholes and some of the most common surnames in town are Higgins, O'Malley, and McDonald. Santarem is something of a boomtown these days because gold has been discovered, and the local citizenry are busy supplying prospectors. It is also a loading point for crude rubber out of the jungle. Away from the docks, you can see another world of primitive transportation and habitation.

If Santarem happens to be closed down because of a holiday (we visited on January 1st), bypass the city and head straight for the Tropicale Hotel, where there is a wonderful pool, lovely sunset views, a small zoo for the children, and nice cold drinks. Sun Line's evening excursion to a barbecue on the terrace is wonderful—the food and presentation are excellent.

The magnificent city of **Manaus** lies at the 1000-plus-mile mark of the Amazon and the confluence of the Rio Negro rivers, surrounded by dense jungle. The city became rich from the rubber boom of the late 1800s and nothing was too advanced for its inhabitants. It was the first city in South America to have streetcars and, it is said, many folk sent their laundry all the way to London! Its famous Opera House was completed in 1910, just as the rubber boom burst—but never mind, Jenny Lind once sang here. Never used for traditional opera, it is the town's number one tourist attraction and worthy of a visit. Following two years of scaffolding and $8 million, the Teatro Amazonas reopened in March 1990 with a Brazilian-composed opera, and the following weekend Placido Domingo (among others) flew into town to sing *Carmen*. Manaus entrepreneurs hope that this La Scala copy will once again attract well-known names, whom they plan to fly in from Miami, as the newly refurbished structure is gleaming and its red-velvet chairs are free from the termites that used to live under the covers!

Other sights to behold at this anomaly in the jungle are the Custom House and Lighthouse, which arrived dismantled from London, the Salesian Mission Museum, Taruma Falls, several churches, a rubber plantation or two, and the City Market Building. You can also take a boat trip on the Rio Negro into dense jungle, tropical birds, and wild monkeys. Since Manaus is a free port, its shops are stocked with goods from all over the world that have made the upriver journey, but most of the shops are selling electronic equipment—in fact, several blocks look like Little Tokyo. Beware also of the kids on the street selling fake perfume. The House of the Hummingbird is an interesting shop selling handicrafts, and the new Tropicale Hotel (far out near the airport) is fun for lunch and a swim. A branch of H. Stern is in the shopping arcade. Be sure you get taxis with meters and it won't take a fortune to go out and back.

CHILE AND EASTER ISLAND

Chile has to be the longest, narrowest country on earth, for it measures 2625 miles from north to south and only 312 miles at its widest point. Ships sailing through the Strait of Magellan often stop at its southernmost city, Punta Arenas. More interesting, though, is the seaport of **Puerto Montt,** gateway to Chile's lake district. Beautiful Lake Llanquihue is surrounded by magnificent volcanos, including the eternally snowcapped Osorno. Puerto Montt has a zone of glacial channels that offer fantastic views wherever you look, and is noted for fine seafood.

Valparaiso, Chile's main port, is colorful and enchanting. Founded in 1536, the old town and commercial section is built on reclaimed land along a low terrace, while the residential area clings to the slopes of the many hills surrounding the port. In between the two are narrow, twisting streets that delight tourists and photographers. Culturally, "Valpo" (as the locals say) has produced poets and writers, and its historical spots are many. For the best view in town, try the Miradero O'Higgins (named after the first ruler of the republic) located in the Alto del Puerto. Have a look also at the naval school, the Beaux Arts Museum, and the universities located here.

Just ten minutes along the coast from Valpo is the resort town of Vina del Mar, with beautiful beaches, lovely gardens and flowers, friendly atmosphere, and a large casino—one of the main attractions. But **Santiago,** on a 1706-foot plateau with the snowcapped Andes as an impressive backdrop, is the capital and center of Chilean life. Nature has endowed this setting with much favor; the city is built around beautiful hills. The most familiar is Santa Lucia, which has two fortresses, a lovely park, and superb view. Santiago also abounds with man-made beauty, exemplified by its many churches (the cathedral dates from 1558) and more than a dozen museums. If you disembark in Valparaiso, look into the many excursions possible in Santiago Province.

One excursion, albeit far out and remote, takes visitors to the mysterious **Easter Island,** the most eastern member of Polynesia, 2300 miles west of the Chilean coastline. Easter Island is considered an open-air museum, not to mention an archaeological question mark overflowing with evidence that a sophisticated and complex culture once flourished on this remote piece of land in the Pacific Ocean. Easter Island draws many eager cruise passengers to its isolated seven-by-fourteen-mile shores to see the intriguing masonry-lined caves, the gigantic statues, the engineering and astronomical accomplishments, and the petroglyphs, as well as the attractive beaches and the hospitable Polynesian people (who call their island Rapa Nui). If you can't make the journey out this time, console yourself with the excellent introduction to these artifacts in Santiago's National Museum.

COLOMBIA

Cartagena is a popular call on cruises to the lower Caribbean, for it offers a taste of South America—a mere whiff of what lies below the equator. Colombia's 1200-mile coastline borders the Caribbean, and Cartagena de Indias (the proper name) is the most important gateway. Founded in 1533, the city never allows visitors to forget its early history, and ancient fortifications still protect the harbor—reminders of seventeenth- and eighteenth-century attacks by the French and British. The old city is appealing, with Iberian architecture, narrow streets made crooked to deceive pirates, and baroque monuments to Christianity. Don't miss the spectacular view from La Popa, a restored seventeenth-century monastery, and the colorful local market surrounded on three sides by the bay. If you prefer a more relaxed day, taxi to the splendid Hilton Hotel for a fresh tuna, a swim, and some lovely local shops.

Sailing in and out of Cartagena is also quite spectacular, so find yourself a good vantage point on deck with camera ready. Although this beautiful and historic port has much to offer and is known for emeralds and other semi-precious stones, do not wander off on your own. Stick to the organized tour, which will offer every opportunity (including shopping). Cartagena is a drug haven and the U.S. government is cracking down on the cartels in town. Avoid doing business on the street and never, never accept a package for someone else.

ECUADOR

If your cruise vessel happens to call at **Guayaquil,** Ecuador's main port and largest city, my advice is to get out as quickly as possible. This metropolis of a million-plus people is a hot, dirty, sprawling flat area sprung from the Guayas River, about thirty-five miles from the Gulf of Guayaquil. That this city grew too big too fast is evident—don't try to mail anything from its *one* post office. It also has only one cemetery, which may be its most interesting feature. As one of my Quito friends said—typifying the rivalry between Ecuador's two major cities—"People are so brave to live in Guayaquil that they are given nice burials."

The best way to leave Guayaquil and see something of the country-side is by the *autoferro* to Quito, a twelve-hour journey of just under 300 miles. The autoferro is a single bus on rails, with a driver *(motorista)*, a conductor *(ayudante)*, reserved seats, a toilet in the back, and no food. It means planning ahead, spending the night in Guayaquil (where hotel rates are exorbitant), packing a lunch, and getting to Duran railroad station by 6 a.m. The train leaves approximately on time (at least by South American custom), and all seats not reserved by tourists are quickly occupied by locals traveling from one small village to another. In many of these villages, the autoferro is the only reliable source of communication, so the *motorista* and his *ayudante* deliver packages, messages, produce, and livestock along the route and pick up letters for the post office in Quito. Often, they will grab pieces of paper and envelopes from outstretched hands without even stopping. It's a unique performance, so try to get seats up front and watch.

If you're still sleepy the first few hours out of Guayaquil, don't worry, for the scenery is flat, tropical, and rather uninteresting. The spectacular views begin around 10 a.m. when the autoferro climbs one thousand feet up the Nariz del Diablo (Devil's Nose), a series of switchbacks and zigzags along a sheer gorge. From here it's a climb of 10,000 feet into the Andean highlands with breathtaking views of the snow-capped Mt. Chimborazo in the distance. If you're exceptionally brave, you are welcome to ride atop the autoferro, along with the chickens and the onions! The first and only rest stop comes around noon at Riobamba, capital of Chimborazo Province, a town known for its healthful, rarefied air at 9000 feet.

From Riobamba the line climbs to Urbina Pass, the highest point at 11,841 feet, and then skirts the base of Mt. Chimborazo to Ambato, an important Indian market town. From Ambato to Latacunga the line skirts Mt. Cotopaxi, which is not only the highest volcano in the world (19,200 feet) but also one of the most perfect cones. Then you coast into Quito, arriving between 5 and 6 p.m. It's a long but fascinating day, and there's no better way to see the country in between.

Quito, capital of Ecuador, is a charming city spread out on an Andean plain some 9375 feet above sea level. Because of this height, sightseeing should be taken slowly, otherwise you may feel tired and weak. Quito lies on the Equator (the marker is about a twenty-minute ride from town), yet has a splendid climate of sunny days in the seventies and brisk, cool nights. The colonial section of Quito, founded in 1534 by Sebastian de Benalcazar, was declared a site of world cultural heritage by UNESCO in 1979 and is now being carefully restored. Among the many fine projects in progress is the courtyard and cloister of the Monastery of St. Augustine, dating from 1573. The inner city is marked by churches and palaces whose interiors shine with gold culled by the Spaniards from their newly conquered land.

Among the gold leaf that impresses is in La Compania, one of Quito's most spectacular churches; visit also La Catedral, which has noteworthy artwork and the tomb of Antonio de Sucre, the liberator of Ecuador. Near the Plaza de Independencia are structures of great splendor—the Placio Nacional, the Palace of the Archbishop, and Arco de Santo Domingo—a classic arch dating from colonial Quito. A wonderful view of the city, including the historic district, can be enjoyed from Panecillo Hill, where it is said that Incans worshipped the sun.

While local Indians sell their wares on every street corner, there is a famous Saturday market at Otavalo that has handcrafts for everyone—no doubt sold by the cousins of the Quito merchants! Quito is a lovely city and there are many interesting things to do—as long as you are aware of the altitude and acclimate yourself accordingly.

GALAPAGOS ISLANDS

If you have never swum with a sea lion nor scratched the neck of a giant tortoise, one might say that you have not yet lived. Certainly, you have not yet visited the Galapagos Islands where these antics are commonplace and part of a thrilling cruise experience. The Galapagos form an archipelago of six minor and thirteen major islands covering some 3000 square miles across the equator in the Pacific Ocean. Discovered by Spaniard Fray Tomas de Berlaya in 1535, they were claimed 300 years later by Ecuador, whose coastline is approximately 600 miles due east. Shortly thereafter, Charles Darwin, the twenty-six-year-old British naturalist, visited while aboard the HMS *Beagle;* the rest is history. Here Darwin observed the relationships of land-, sea-, and air-life; these observations guided him as he wrote his controversial theories concerning the origin of species. Scientists and naturalists still use the Galapagos archipelago to study behavioral patterns of animals and plants. The Darwin Research Station on Santa Cruz (or Indefatigable) Island is especially well known.

Some visitors refer to these islands as the world's zaniest zoo, for here a multitude of animals coexist in their natural habitat: sea lions, fur seals, land iguanas, sea iguanas, lava lizards, Galapagos tortoises, penguins, cormorants, frigate birds, blue-footed boobies, lightfoot crabs, and at least thirteen different varieties of Darwin's finches as well as many other birds. The wildlife is safe, since the Galapagos were declared a national park in 1959 and tourism is tightly controlled. Cruises of three-, four-, and seven-day spans are available on government-approved Ecuadorian vessels only, and passengers are accompanied on each island by guides trained at the Darwin Research Station. Ecuador's National Park Service, which manages the islands, requests that visitors leave nothing more than footprints and take nothing but photographs. Other more stringent rules advise visitors what cautions should be employed when observing the flora and fauna on the islands, and that introducing certain foreign objects can destroy the delicate ecological balance.

Within this archipelago approximately fifty different inlets and areas are accessible, but the guides generally stick to the carefully marked paths on the less treacherous volcanic rock. Most landing parties use small boats, or *pangas,* that resemble lifeboats. Disembarking onto the islands for your twice daily (morning and afternoon) hike is often tricky and not recommended for the timid. Often to get ashore you must either jump feet first into the water (with pant legs rolled up and shoes in hand overhead) or jump onto slippery rocks. When a dock (or semblance thereof) is available, it seems an unaccustomed luxury. As your cruise within the Galapagos progresses, you will pick up a new language in addition to all the names of plant and animal life—"wet landings" and "dry landings." The islands generally visited are Santa Cruz (for the Research Station and giant tortoises), Santiago or James (for flamingos and fur seals), South Plaza (for land iguanas, sea lions, and swallow-tailed gulls), Hood or Espanola (for blue-footed and masked boobies, albatross from April to December, marine iguanas, and lava lizards), Floreana or Santa Maria (for flamingo), Tower or Genovesa (for frigate birds, red-footed and masked boobies, fur seals, petrels, and lava gulls), Isabela or Albermarle (for flamingos, Galapagos tortoises, flightless cormorants), or Fernandina or Narborough (for flightless cormorants, penguins, and marine iguanas), and Seymour (for frigate birds and blue-footed boobies).

Hood or Espanola (most of the islands have both an English and Spanish name) seems to be just about everyone's favorite. Here the hike lasts from three to four hours. You may become very fond of the blue-footed boobies, beautiful birds with blue feet and a rather dumb gaze that makes them appear like a dumbbell, or booby. They are charming, when caring for their young or squawking that you mustn't get too close to the nest. In the proper seasons, you can also watch an albatross mating dance, rather like a fencing match with beaks, or even observe the new mothers feeding their young with an oil secreted from their body. And Hood has the Blowhole, where the surf pounds upon the lava-lined shore and then blows straight up through a huge natural hole in the porous rock—a big hit with children, who adore the Galapagos. As one brother/sister pair said to me one summer, "This is much better than Disneyland!" The Galapagos Islands are definitely for the young in mind and body. In addition to the strenuous shore excursions with wet landings and extensive hiking in the hot equatorial sun, entertainment is limited to evolution, ecology, and the forces of nature. The islands did not strike me as being particularly beautiful. One might even say that they are ugly—volcanic, spare, and arid. Although it's possible to swim almost every day, I only saw one beautiful beach—Espumilla—where I had a lovely sunbath and an exquisite swim. When friends snorkeling off the end of the beach sighted some baby sharks, I swam closer to the shore; but there was no danger. As the equatorial sun is direct and strong, burning is a hazard, so beachtime should be used sparingly if you are susceptible. I also recommend that you wear a large-brimmed hat at all times to prevent sunstroke.

There are many small ships now allowed in the Galapagos, including those chartered by Special Expeditions (New York) and those operated by Society Expeditions (Seattle). Among the regulars with Ecuadorean flag is the *Santa Cruz,* a ninety-passenger vessel built in Spain in 1979 just for these islands. The *Santa Cruz* has a charming captain named Carlos, an excellent crew, and good facilities. Her guides conduct tours in four languages (English, French, German, Spanish), give fine briefings before each shore excursion, and are ready to answer questions. For most tours the passengers are divided into four groups (Albatross, Booby, Cormorant, Dolphin) to alternate embarkation of pangas for shore. The cruises are highly structured, so passengers see the most in the shortest time. Wake-up call is 6:15 a.m., breakfast at 6:45, and departures to the islands begin at 7:30. Return to the ship about 11:30 a.m.; lunch starts at 12:30 p.m. while the ship sails to another location; afternoon excursions are scheduled between 3 and 6; and dinner follows at 7, succeeded by a briefing of the next day's activities. Bed down early!

To get the most out of your Galapagos experience, spend a full week cruising the islands and fly to and from your vessel from either Guayaquil or Quito. These charter flights aboard Ecuadorean Navy planes are very safe. The best time of year to travel here is probably June through September, when the weather is coolest, although the seas can be a bit rocky. Since the *Santa Cruz* sails between 2 a.m. and 8 a.m. most mornings, the tossings can be a detriment to sleep. Metropolitan Touring's twelve-passenger *Isabella* is also popular, although rather less elegant. Its size, however, does allow calls at some smaller islands.

PERU

Peru's main port, **Callao,** lies a convenient eight miles from **Lima,** capital of this nation that was once home to the spectacular Inca civilization and the subsequent center of Spanish power in the New World. Lima was laid out along the left bank of the Rimac River in 1535 by Francisco Pizzaro, who named it Ciudad de los Reyes (City of Kings). Pizzaro, slain six years later by his own men, is famed as the conqueror of the Inca Empire as well as the founder of the Spanish Empire in South America. The city is centered around the Plaza de Armas, just as Pizzaro planned, but many of the fine colonial structures were destroyed by an earthquake in 1746 and have been replaced by modern buildings. Still, some survivors of the quake remain, and the churches lined with gold and intricate artwork are relics of a sumptuous seventeenth century. Lima claims the oldest university in the Americas, San Marcos, founded in 1551. Five thousand years of Peruvian culture lies within the Museum of Art, located in the 1868 Exposition Palace. The Museum of Anthropology and Archaeology displays more than 80,000 objects discovered throughout the country, in addition to a constantly changing exhibition of exciting new finds. Historical monuments mingle comfortably with modern life, for Lima lives very much in the present and its commercial activity is indicative of a prosperous future. Limenos relish a beautiful city in which to enjoy life. If you are offered a sip of Pisco Sour, a local cocktail, expect a kick.

For those interested in pre-Inca ruins, the nearest site is twenty miles south of Lima in the Lurin Valley. Known as **Pachacamac,** the four-square-mile area is believed to have been a sacred city from A.D. 600 to about 900. The Temple to the Creator God here has 400-foot terraces, frescoed walls, and doors inlaid with semiprecious stones. Irrigation and reservoir remains are also evident. Peru's leading tourist attraction and *piece de resistance,* however, are **Cuzco,** ancient capital of the Incas, and the mysterious fortress of **Machu Picchu** just seventy-seven miles away. Both take some doing to explore (Cuzco is 11,400 feet up in the Andes and Machu Picchu is another 1000 feet higher), so plan ahead for full enjoyment of one of the most exciting excursions of your travels.

STRAIT OF MAGELLAN

This passage between the Atlantic and Pacific oceans that many have called the greatest natural wonder on earth is just north of Cape Horn. The spectacular 340-mile Strait slices off a small portion of Argentina and Chile, and its navigation is the highlight of any South American cruise itinerary.

The Strait was discovered in 1520 by the global circumnavigator Ferdinand Magellan as he explored the Rio de la Plata and Patagonia regions of Argentina. Passage through the Strait takes most ships about thirty-six hours, but this depends upon the seas, which can be rough. Although much of the sailing takes place at night under the Southern Cross, you will want to be out on deck as much as possible; the majestic views equal or surpass Norway's fjordland and Alaska's Inside Passage. Often during the passage, Chile's Institute of Patagonia enlists passengers to spot whales and record data for a whale population study. A major portion of the world's whale population has been migrating to the peaceful environment of Patagonia and Tierra del Fuego. Passengers participating in the whale-spotting program are given full-color whale charts with illustrations and descriptions of the different species of whales, plus special forms providing space for information on type of whale spotted, time of day, latitude and longitude. When you've navigated from the Atlantic Ocean to the Pacific (or vice versa, as some ships sail), it's time to celebrate. After all, one does not do this sort of thing every day.

VENEZUELA

La Guaira is the bustling gateway to Venezuela's capital **Caracas,** which spreads along a valley some twelve miles from the sea via a winding mountain road. The city, founded in 1567 and christened Santiago de Leon de Caracas (after its patron saint), has lost most of its colonial character and is a major financial and commercial center with a nouveau riche atmosphere. An acquaintance who resides in Caracas said, "The already aggressive population has become even more so, because of all this new oil wealth." Nonetheless, the city is a major attraction in South America, especially noted as the birthplace of the continent's liberator and hero, Simon Bolivar. His family home, now called Casa Natal, is a national monument. Next door is the Bolivarian Museum, which details the Conquest, Colonial, and Independence eras of South America. Also on the heroic tour is Cuadra Bolivar, another restored home of the Bolivar family (Simon was born of noble and wealthy parents in 1783) that has a tamarind tree in the garden that is said to have been taken from the Santa Maria hacienda near Cartagena, where Bolivar died an impoverished and forgotten man in 1830.

Visit the Colonial Art Museum, a beautifully restored mansion filled with art and objects from the Spanish-influenced colonial era; the Plaza Bolivar and cathedral (the latter dates from 1595); Quinta Caracas, where local artists can be found at their easels on the colonial-style patio; and the 400-acre University City, a former sugar plantation. Designed by local architect Villanueva in free-flowing concrete, University City gives me a jolting, futuristic feeling. Adjacent to the university, where 50,000 students fill the campus each day, is the 175-acre Botanical Gardens— where you can refresh your spirit among elegant and abundant orchids and other tropical plants.

THE ORINOCO RIVER

Listed as the eighth largest river in the world, the mighty Orinoco extends some 1700 miles from its headwaters in the Parima Sierra (near the Brazilian border) to the Atlantic Ocean, where its enormous delta spreads some hundreds of square miles over tropical jungle. It is one of South America's major river systems and, with all its tributaries, provides over 10,000 miles of navigable waterway. The Orinoco is a mysterious river whose real source was only discovered in 1951 by an official expedition of the Venezuelan government. However, its vastness was not missed by Christopher Columbus, who is said to have remarked, "Never have I read nor heard of so much sweet water within a salt ocean." And his son Ferdinand wrote of the impact of the mid-rainy season outflow of the Orinoco on the Equatorial current flowing westward across the Atlantic from Africa, "The noise of the waves made it seem as though the very waters were fighting . . ." (The above was printed in *Ocean Islander*'s program, December 23, 1986, as the vessel entered the Delta Amacuro at noon that day.)

Ciudad Guayana was created in 1961 as a major port, but was actually founded in 1595 by Don Antonio de Berrio. Now a prime industrial center of Venezuela, the area boasts the famous Cerro Bolivar open cast-iron mine as well as one of the world's largest hydroelectric plants. **Ciudad Bolivar** is capital of the state of Bolivar and gateway to the Guayana Highlands, which lie just below the Andes. Ciudad Bolivar was originally named Angostura, and was the first home of the famous bitters.

Angel Falls is a great adventure for cruise passengers who fly over the giant cataract that is fifteen times higher than Niagara Falls and has a cascade of water of more than 3000 feet. The falls were first sighted by a Jimmy Angel, who crash-landed his plane on the rugged top of Devil Mountain in 1935, and they bear his name. A special Avensa-chartered Boeing 727 leaves Ciudad Guyana airport around 8 a.m. for the 35-minute flight. If the weather is good, the pilot can fly as low as possible over the falls and try to give both sides of the plane a peek. However, the windows are very small and most of them filthy, so don't expect breathtaking views. Following the falls, the plane drops in on Camp Canaima for a few hours. Here, passengers are offered a rum punch, a canoe ride, a swim in the lagoon and a walk around the grounds—there are a few souvenir shops in the area. The enthusiastic may also take a smaller plane ride over the falls or a jeep ride into the savannah—for an extra fee, of course!

WESTERN EUROPE

BRITISH ISLES AND IRELAND

Every harbor in this varied island world called the United Kingdom is loaded with history, pride, and tradition. Each has an individuality molded by adaptation to landscapes ranging from the isolation of the Shetland Islands to the subtropical Channel Islands to the highlands of Scotland, and the gentle lands of Ireland. Language has often kept these peoples together, while religion, politics, and plain stubbornness have set them apart. All share a fierce love for a rich past, however, and will proudly point out relics of the Stone Age, leftovers from Julius Caesar and four centuries of Roman rule, Saxon influences, and evidence that Saint Patrick really was here. Don't forget to appreciate the Norman towers, the country gardens, heather on the hillsides, and a misty climate that is thought to be good for your skin (since it is obviously not good for anything else). A cruise from the Atlantic Ocean to the Irish and North seas is one of the most worthwhile itineraries available.

The traditional gateway to England for seafarers, at least in modern times, is **Southampton.** Now the country's number one passenger port, Southampton dates from Saxon times. Both a local dwelling and a nearby abbey/monastery date from the twelfth century. One site not to overlook is the memorial tower to the Pilgrim fathers who set out for the New World on August 15, 1620, in a vessel called the *Mayflower*. Southampton is in Hampshire, whose most interesting city is Winchester—a historic center linked to the legends of King Arthur, with a cathedral dating from 1079.

The controversial **Channel Islands** are closer in culture and climate to France than to England. The two largest are Guernsey and Jersey, of which Guernsey is the more popular as a holiday (and tax) haven.

The main harbor is St. Peter Port, a small town with not much more than its gentle hills and Victor Hugo's house. The French writer, exiled here from 1855 until 1870, lived in a small house overlooking the harbor, and his mistress lived nearby. He is said to have written some of his masterpieces here, including *Les Miserables*. If you cannot find the house (the way is tricky), you can at least communicate with a fine statue of him in Candide Gardens, which also have a lovely view of the harbor.

The white cliffs of **Dover** have been famous ever since Caesar is said to have sailed past them. Some interesting Roman remains here, discovered in the 1970s, include a fort, bath building, and painted house. The port also has one of England's oldest and best-known castles, built by Henry II in the twelfth century and used again during World War II. In Queen Victoria's time Dover was a seaside resort, but today it is better known as the closest car-ferry port to France.

Hull is the port for one of England's most delightful towns, historic **York,** which is still encircled by thirteenth- and fourteenth-century walls. York was also known as a Roman town and, in fact, became a bishopric during the reign of Emperor Constantine (around A.D. 315). Today York is most famous for its minster, a cathedral surpassed only by rival Canterbury. Called the Church of St. Peter, the cathedral was built on the site of a Roman fortress and is the largest medieval cathedral in England. Also of interest are the York Castle Museum, a collection of everyday objects displayed in a former prison; the Treasurer's House, dating from the eleventh century and built over some Roman ruins; and the Shambles, the best-preserved medieval street in the country.

The port of **Leith** is the gateway to **Edinburgh,** the cultural capital of Scotland. Edinburgh Castle dominates the city; its origins as a fortress are thought to have begun as early as the Bronze Age. The castle building dates from somewhere in the twelfth century. Edinburgh comprises the medieval "old" section and the Georgian "new" districts. After paying a visit to the castle, walk along the Royal Mile to the Palace of Holyrood at the opposite end. Along the way you will see St. Giles Cathedral, John Knox's House (the fifteenth-century dwelling of the founder of the Scottish Presbyterian Church), and plenty of seventeenth-century timbered buildings with attractive overhangs. At the end is Holyrood Palace and Abbey, begun in the twelfth century, where Mary Queen of Scots lived between 1561 and 1567. (You can visit if the present Queen is not in residence.) Most interesting in the "new" towns is 7 Charlotte Square, a restored structure known simply as the Georgian House and headquarters of the National Trust of Scotland. This dwelling, an excellent example of eighteenth-century architecture, contains period furniture and decorative items. Also of great beauty is Hopetown House, the residence of the Marquess of Linlithgow. This huge country home (a minipalace) is on the Firth of Forth, a pleasant drive away from Edinburgh. Don't leave the city without paying your respects to the monument of Sir Walter Scott, the favorite native son, which is in the East Princes Street gardens. (Some of Scott's characters are part of the statue's design.) You may also find a theatrical performance or an evening of colorful and energetic Scottish dancers while your ship is in port.

Just off the tip of Scotland lie the **Orkney Islands,** sixty-seven small islands that the Romans described in writings from the first century A.D., although megalith monuments date from about 4000 B.C. The islands were settled by Norsemen, who built some exciting monuments that have been restored—St. Magnus Cathedral, Earls Palace, and Bishop's Palace in Kirkwall (which means Church Bay). Kirkwall, capital of the Orkneys, is the focal point of their culture. The cathedral has enjoyed more than 800 years of worship, and an annual music festival is held every June here (alas, too early for most cruise calls). You may also visit the Neolithic chambered tomb called Maeshowe (built sometime before 2700 B.C.) and the Neolithic settlement of Skara Brae on the western coast. This complex of seven stone houses connected by covered alleys was inhabited probably between 3100 and 2450 B.C.

Some cruises sail up to the Shetland Islands, but these are a bit distant for most casual tourists. Closer to the mainland of Scotland and a bit warmer are the **Hebrides,** which consist of Inner and Outer groupings. Largest of the Outer Hebrides is the island of Lewis and Harris, whose only town and port is called Stornoway. Apart from its Neolithic and Norse history, the island's biggest claim to fame is Harris Tweed, which has become Stornoway's best industry. It's not real Harris Tweed unless it's woven on this island. The lovely Island of Skye is a popular port of call in the Inner Hebrides. The scenery is magnificent and so is Dunvegan Castle, seat of the MacLeod clan since 1200. Open to the public, Dunvegan is said to be the oldest inhabited castle in all the British Isles.

Sailing southward between Britain and Ireland, some cruise vessels disembark passengers just below Conway Castle on the Welsh town of **Conway,** then reboard them in **Holyhead** on the island of Holyhead. This all-day tour of northwest Wales features a castle built by Edward I in 1284 and the surrounding town he laid out. The town is considered one of the most perfectly walled examples in Europe. Four miles south of Conway are Bodnant Gardens, seventy acres of plants and trees most suited to the wet climate of Wales. They overlook the lovely mountains of Snowdonia, through which you will drive on your way to Carnarvon Castle. Built by Edward I and finished in 1322, this well-preserved castle dominates the town's skyline. From the castle your tour will proceed across the Menai Strait and the island of Anglesey, to the port of Holyhead.

Eire, or the Republic of Ireland, is a delightful country to call upon, especially by the sea. Many charming port towns offer easy access to the heart of the land. **Waterford,** originally settled by the Danes but granted its first charter by King John in 1205, is famous for beautiful hand-blown crystal. At nearby **Cashel,** the Rock of Cashel is said to have been visited by Saint Patrick in A.D. 450. The thirteenth-century Cathedral of Saint Patrick shares the rock with the Round Tower and Cormac's Chapel. In the southwest section of the country, **Bantry Bay** lies at the head of Glengarriff and the gateway to the great lake district of Killarney. If you do not visit **Killarney,** you have not seen Ireland! The three lakes, surrounded by lovely scenery and some interesting historical sites, are worth the drive from Bantry Bay. Also within the lake district is an 11,000-acre national park presented to the Irish people in 1932 by its American owners, who also restored the property's famous mansion. Known as Muckross House, it was built in the midnineteenth century and received many important figures of the day. The house is now a fascinating museum that details local Irish life of the last century. For another view of Ireland some cruise vessels call in **Galway Bay,** gateway to the strongest of Gaelic traditions. People here are among the most individualistic, and the living can be rugged. The sea breaks against the rocks with such force that the spray is constant. In the bay are the Aran Islands, populated first in prehistoric times and much later by Christian hermits. County Galway boasts a fine monastery, the Ross Errily Franciscan Friary, founded in the mid-fourteenth century, although most of its buildings date from the late-fifteenth century. Your tour may also take in **Connemara,** known for its beautiful scenery and fine ponies of the same name.

THE NORTH CAPE

From Stavanger to Spitsbergen, along Norway's western boundary, the cruise passenger is treated to an unending spectacle of some of the world's most exciting scenery. This is the land of fjords, and nothing equals it. Mighty fingers of snow and ice reach out as you sail by, while white-capped mountaintops glisten in the brilliant sun. The views are the same whether you choose to cruise along in a luxury vessel or in a cozy mail boat laden with locals. Chances are you won't be tempted much by sleep, for this is also the Land of the Midnight Sun. From mid-May to the end of July, as you sail farther and farther north, the sun stays longer and longer within sight, until you can't get away from it at all. When you reach the island of Mageroy, the most northerly point of Europe, the entire disc of the sun is visible twenty-four hours a day.

If your journey northward to the Cape begins in **Stavanger,** you will find a romantic seaport full of historic wooden buildings and a modern boomtown full of North Sea oil-riggers. The cathedral here was dedicated in 1125, and the marketplace has been the center of life since the ninth century. The oldest wooden house, built in 1704 and known as the Consul Fred Hansen House, is now a shop (so you can visit it). Stavanger is a good starting point for explorations to the southern arms of the fjords, Lyse and Ryfylke, as well as the peaceful and unspoiled fishing port of Haugesund.

A few hours north by sea is **Bergen,** the country's second largest city after Oslo, founded in 1070 by the Viking, King Olav Kyrre. During the Middle Ages, Bergen became Scandinavia's primary port for trading. Many buildings from this period still exist, despite the ravages of nature and man. Don't miss the medieval fortress of Bergenhus, built in 1262, the coronation site of King Haakon. Bergen, a cosmopolitan city proud of its university and music, was the early capital of Norway. Just outside the city is the former summer home of composer Edvard Grieg where he composed many of his famous works. Amid all this culture and history you can find easy excursions to some of the most beautiful natural attractions in all of Norway—Sorfjord, Samnangerfjord, Tokagjel Gorge, and Steindalsfjoss Waterfall. Hardangerfjord and surrounding countryside is a visitor's haven from spring to fall, for the area is rich in flowers, especially orchids. You may also see Granvinfjord, with its crystal-clear lake; the Hamlagro mountain plateau; and the fertile Bergsdalen Valley. This is the classic "discovery route" and a splendid introduction to the natural resources that makes this country so special.

Eidfjord is the eastern extremity of the larger Hardangerfjord, and the village at the head of this fjord arm has served as a junction of eastern and western Norway for centuries. A shore excursion from the village takes cruise passengers along the banks of the river Eie (known for its abundance of trout and salmon) and into the majestic Mabodal Canyon. The bus ascends through the massive rocks and crags decorated with pines and wild flowers to the observation platform at the top, where you overlook the mighty Voringfoss Waterfall, one of the highest and most impressive in northern Europe—plunging six hundred feet to the floor of the canyon below.

The village of **Flam** lies by the end of Aurlandsfjord, which is at the tip of Sognefjord. Flam is famous for its twelve-mile electric railway that climbs 2845 feet to Myrdal through some dramatic panoramas. The train follows a serpentine path in and out of tunnels, but halts now and again so you can photograph some of the more spectacular waterfalls. From Myrdal station your journey will take you on to **Voss,** on the shores of Lake Vangsvatn. This village, known for its wealth of folklore, has a thirteenth-century Gothic church with a timbered tower, and a wonderful folk museum that traces the early farm life of the area. From Voss it's an easy drive along lovely Oppheimsvann Lake to Stalheim, where you can see Stalheimskleiv gorge and waterfalls. From here, travel down to the village of **Gudvangen** and return to your ship.

Geirangerfjord is one of Norway's most celebrated fjords; and what a sight it is to cruise by, passing the cascading Seven Sisters Falls. Nestled at the head of this waterway is the charming hamlet of the same name, **Geiranger,** one of the most popular resorts in the country. From here you may drive 5000 feet up to Mount Dalsnibba for a panoramic view of glaciers, waterfalls, lakes, and more mountains. You may even see your ship below like a tiny toy at anchor. If you begin your overland trip from **Hellesylt,** you will enjoy the same beautiful panorama of snowcapped peaks, glaciers, and the Geirangerfjord.

Molde's sheltered location and gentle climate warmed by the Gulf Stream make it the center of the country's rose industry, which gives it the nickname of City of Roses. Many of the buildings in Molde are recent because bombs and fire destroyed two-thirds of the town in 1940. Molde Church is the largest postwar church to be built in Norway. Its modern style is a great attraction in this tourist center, and over the baptismal font is a charred reminder of the bombed ruins. On the outskirts of town is the Romsdal Museum, an open-air complex of over two dozen wooden houses dating from the Viking period to the fifteenth century. During the cruise season, local children in regional costumes perform Norwegian folk dances and provide a colorful scene for photographers. Following the performance, take time out for the fabulous view of the eighty-seven peaks of the "Romsdal Alps" and the island-studded fjord below. Both can be seen from the deck of the Vardestua Restaurant some 1300 feet high.

From Molde you can travel overland to **Andalsnes.** Take a ferry across Romsdalsfjord to Vestnes, and then go by bus along Storfjord and Norddalfjord to the town of Valldal, noted for its mountain scenery and its abundant strawberries. From here the drive will take you along one of Norway's serpentine roads among the King, Queen, and Bishop mountains and by the 500-foot Stigfoss Waterfall, then down through the valley to the small village of Andalsnes on the banks of the Rauma River. (Or if you've had enough of fjords and high drives at this point, and it's the first week in August, check in Molde for the International Jazz Festival, fast becoming Europe's best.)

Trondheim is Norway's third largest city (after Oslo and Bergen) and one of its most interesting. It lies on the south bay of the Trondheimfjord, some 425 miles north of Bergen, and was founded by the Viking king Olav Tryggvasson in the tenth century. Trondheim was both the medieval capital of the country until the thirteenth century and the most important religious center in all of Scandinavia. Nidaros Cathedral, dating from the eleventh century, drew many a medieval pilgrim who came to worship at the shrine of the canonized King Olav. Ten Norwegian kings are buried here, and this was also the coronation site of King Haakon VII in 1906. Other attractions in Trondheim are the folk museum complex, with old timbered houses and a gold-colored stave church, and the Museum of Musical History at Rinvge Manor. The mansion, birthplace of a Norwegian sea hero, is often considered the highlight of the Trondheim tour, for it contains a collection of approximately 2000 musical instruments from all over the world. During the summer season daily tours in English are offered in the morning. Your guide will play a selection of the instruments, demonstrating their position in musical history.

If you're looking for the Midnight Sun, you'll find it in **Narvik,** a town situated 250 miles north of the Arctic Circle on the Ofotfjord. This industrial town that dates from 1903 has continuous sunshine from late May to mid-July, although August is known for having its share of mysterious lighting. Tours from Narvik may include a train trip to Riksgrensen in Lapland or to Gratangen for the thrilling panorama of fjords and mountains. **Tromso** is another town about 250 miles north of the Arctic Circle. Tromso, a boomtown, is very expensive now because of the North Sea oil projects. Skip it if you like, unless you're interested in visiting the world's northernmost university, which dates from 1972.

Hammerfest, the most northerly major town in the world, was founded in 1787 and then totally destroyed during World War II. Now very much rebuilt, it is a lively, ice-free port where fish and furs are loaded onto ships. Since it is also a shopping center for Lapps, you may see reindeer in town, so keep your cameras in focus. Here, too, the sun does not set from mid-May to the end of July; to offset this feat, it doesn't rise from late November to late January. The world's northernmost village and gateway to the North Cape is **Honningsvag,** on the southern side of Mageroy Island. Also situated on this island is **Skarsvag,** considered the most northerly point in Europe. Skarsvag offers a wonderful view of the Arctic Ocean from its 1000-foot elevation.

NORTHERN CAPITALS

Hamburg is one of those cities that belongs to the "Venice of the . . ." society. In this instance it is called the Venice of the North because of its many canals and its traditional coexistence with the sea. With nearly 2 million inhabitants, Hamburg is Germany's largest port, welcoming ships and sailors from every flag imaginable. It is the perfect starting point for the itinerary known as the Northern Capitals. A harbor cruise is a sensible way to begin a tour of this city, followed by a drive through the St. Pauli district to City Hall, the twelfth-century St. Petri church and the Altmannbrucke commercial center. Continue around the shores of Aussenalster, a lovely sheet of water in the center of the city, to millionaires' row and then to Poseldorf for some shopping and browsing.

The capital of tiny Denmark, **Copenhagen,** is as friendly and lively a city as one can find in the Baltic area. Here beautiful palaces and parks, great museums and shops share top billing with the world's greatest amusement park, Tivoli. Copenhagen, a charming port touched by the magical spirit of Hans Christian Andersen, is home to the Little Mermaid who sits in the harbor, a patient subject for your photographs. But where should you go first? There is so much to see—the dazzling display of the Danish crown jewels at Rosenborg Castle; Amalienborg Palace, where Queen Margrethe II lives; Gefion Fountain, named in honor of the Danish goddess who, in a single night, ploughed the island of Sealand out of Sweden, and the many fine art museums. But the best views come from the countryside of North Sealand and tours of the castles—Frederiksborg, built by King Christian IV in 1620 and now the National Historic Museum; Fredensborg Palace built in 1723 and still a summer residence of the royal family; and Kronborg in Elsinore. Renowned as the dramatic setting for Shakespeare's *Hamlet,* Kronborg was built by Frederick II between 1574 and 1585. Or, if you prefer a more rural atmosphere, visit the open-air museum of Frilandsmuseet, covering some forty acres. Here the Danish farmlife of yesteryear flourishes, with windmills, country houses, and period pieces and utensils. A drive back to Copenhagen will take you through even more countryside to Frederiksdal, one of the most beautiful areas in all Denmark. After dark, Tivoli offers diversions for all ages—a pantomime theater, a concert hall, ballet, clowns, acrobats, and aerialists—in a fantasy world of merry-go-rounds, swans and boats on the tiny lake, games of chance, a Ferris wheel, and plenty of places to dine. If this isn't enough, visit a brewery. It's free and you can drink all you want at either the Carlsberg or Tuborg breweries, where guided tours are available two or three times each weekday.

Oslo, at the mouth of the island-studded sixty-mile-long Oslofjord, is Norway's capital and largest city. It is, however, neither its most interesting nor cosmopolitan city (those honors go to Bergen). Oslo, founded by a Viking king in the eleventh century, was made capital of the country around 1300 by King Haakon V. In square miles, Oslo is one of the largest cities in the world but has a population of less than half a million, who live amid great natural beauty. In fact, many of the city's great attractions are out-of-doors, including the seventy-five-acre

Frogner Park where the city financed 175 sculptures by Norway's A. Gustav Vigeland—a monumental project that took some thirty years to finish. The thirty-five-acre grounds of the Norwegian Folk Museum on Bygdoy Peninsula exhibit other fine examples of local craft. The museum comprises 170 old buildings transported from all over the country, representing all facets of Norwegian life; it even includes the reassembled study of playwright Henrik Ibsen just as it was left at his death in 1906.

Also on the Bygdoy Peninsula are three of the famous Viking longboats, eighth- and ninth-century relics excavated at Gokstad and Oseberg, and the balsa-wood raft, *Kon Tiki,* that in 1947 Norwegian scientist Thor Heyerdahl and five colleagues sailed from Peru to Polynesia. The raft is housed in its own museum along with exhibits pertaining to Heyerdahl's projects, including his visit to Easter Island. You can also drive out to see Holmenkollen ski jump, one of the best known in the world and the highlight of the annual winter ski festival. A ski museum at the base of the jump houses many interesting exhibits. Your drive should also take you past City Hall (noted for both its modernity and ugliness) and Akershus Castle, built in 1300 and used as a fortress and royal residence for several centuries. Last but not least, save a little time for the Edvard Munch Museum, with its vast collection of works by Scandinavia's leading painter, who is most known for his melancholy and morbid depictions.

Stockholm, capital of Sweden, is a city built on fourteen islands. The water in every direction provides a good excuse to tour this beautiful archipelago by launch. After traveling the canals and waterways, under bridges of every shape and size and past all the important and historic buildings, you may wish to visit some of the more imposing structures—such as the eighteenth-century baroque-style Royal Palace or the thirteenth-century Riddarholm Church, the second oldest in Stockholm. The royal flagship *Wasa* is a Scandinavian vessel of renown that also has its own museum. The *Wasa* was raised from Stockholm harbor just twenty years ago, after she lay at the bottom for three centuries after the ignominious sinking on her maiden voyage in 1628. This capital also has a seventy-five-acre open-air museum, known as Skansen, where 150 eighteenth- and nineteenth-century dwellings have been reassembled. The museum offers continual exhibits of the country's crafts through many historical stages. For more modern artworks, visit the sculpture garden-by-the-sea of Carl Milles, Sweden's foremost sculptor and friend of Rodin (who is also represented here). The garden, on the residential island of Lidingo, provides a lovely setting as giant ships pass by on their way out to the Baltic.

On another island, in Lake Malaren, sits the eighteenth-century palace and theater known as Drottningholm. The palace is still visited by the royal family, and the theater still uses the original stage machinery and scenery. The delightful performances here complement the entire compound, one of the most charming attractions in all of Scandinavia. Before you return to your cruise vessel, make a walking tour of Gamla Sta'n or Old Town, which has wonderful antique shops, narrow cobblestone streets, and a historic marketplace.

Although the island of **Gotland** is not a capital, it is a popular call on Baltic cruises, for the walled city of **Visby** is considered one of the medieval jewels of Europe. The short-lived seat of the Hanseatic merchants from the late twelfth to early thirteenth century, the commercial Queen of the Baltic was sacked in 1316 by the Danes, and the island drifted into obscurity—not emerging as a tourist center until recent times, when its medieval ruins became known as the best in northern Europe. A tour will take you to the old Hanseatic harbor, past the town's oldest building (Kruttornet), and by two of the more famous towers in the old walls—Maiden's Tower, where a peasant girl was buried alive for helping a Danish nobleman, and Powder Tower, the most ancient fortification in Visby. Then you will drive by Gallow Hill, a medieval hanging station used until the mid-nineteenth century, and explore the ruins of the thirteenth-century monastery of St. Nicholas, where operas are staged for the Visby summer festival. Finally, a fine historical museum and the Botanical Gardens give Visby its title, the City of Ruins and Roses.

Helsinki, the white city of the North, is one of Europe's most underrated capitals. Although founded in 1550 by King Gustavus Vasa of Sweden, most of the city belongs to the twentieth century and is a tribute to modern Finnish design. Helsinki, built on a peninsula, is skirted by islands that dot the harbor. The marketplace at the water's edge, the most active and colorful square in town (especially in the early morning), is a good place to begin your tour. From here, you can take a ferry to Suomenlinna Fortress, known as the Gibraltar of the North, which has guarded the entrance to the harbor for two centuries. Another island to visit, Seurasaari, has its own open-air museum, which offers a view of Old Finland with seventeenth- and eighteenth-century structures, including an original sauna. In the summer, folk dancing delights many museum visitors.

Pride of the Finns, though, is **Tapiola,** a self-contained city-within-a-city, a look at the world of tomorrow. Perfectly planned, this striking area six miles west of the capital has parks, fountains, well-designed homes and apartment buildings, playgrounds, shopping centers, schools, and churches. If you're hungry, you can eat at a self-service restaurant that sits atop a large office building. Another area worth visiting is **Hvittrask,** a center for Finnish art and handcraft. Built in 1902 by three of Finland's noted architects—Saarinen, Lindgren, and Gesellius—for their residences and studios, the site features buildings made of natural stone and logs, which blend into the surrounding forest, lake, and majestic cliffs. Saarinen's house is open to the public, and the grounds outside contain many sculptures by all three artists. For a look at other artisans, pay a visit to the Finnish Design Center, which has a permanent exhibition and shop, and the Arabia ceramic house, which exports both utility pieces and artworks. A first-rate restaurant, sauna, beach, and natural park enhance the experience.

Many cruise vessels also call at the western seaport of **Turku,** just 102 miles from Helsinki. Turku is Finland's oldest city and considered the cradle of Finnish civilization, because it was an ecclesiastical center in the thirteenth century and the capital until the early nineteenth century. Among the sights here are Turku Cathedral, dating from the thirteenth century and one of the most important medieval monuments in the country; the equally old castle at the mouth of the Aura River, now the Turku Museum; and the open-air handcraft museum, perfectly preserved from the eighteenth century, in the only part of the city that survived the great fire of 1827. The houses of this compound—original, not reassembled, dwellings—are now the homes of craftsmen.

Leningrad, the second largest city in the Soviet Union, was the capital of the Russian empire until 1918. It was founded in 1703 by Peter the Great, who named St. Petersburg after himself. In 1914 it became Petrograd. Ten years later, the name changed again to honor Lenin after his death. By any name, this city is also called the Venice of the North for its many canals that connect some 100 islands. The city boasts over 1000 architectural and historical monuments and houses great cultural riches in more than fifty museums and 2000 libraries. Leningrad was the city of the Czars, great art collectors who also admired fine buildings and churches. The finest of all the buildings, the baroque Winter Palace now known as the Hermitage Museum, has more than 1000 rooms and reception halls, almost 2000 windows, and over 100 staircases. Many of the rooms have been decorated in semiprecious stones—malachite, jasper, and agate. A tone of malachite was used for just the columns in what is known as Malachite Hall. Amid all this splendor are more than 8000 paintings, a collection of artistic treasures almost unparalleled anywhere in the world. If you pay attention to nothing else in Leningrad, a visit to the Hermitage will make your trip worthwhile. Here are two dozen Rembrandts, a whole room of Rubens, numerous works representing five centuries of French painters, and masterpieces from the ancient world. Even the Impressionists are well represented (if you can make it to the top floor), with early works by Gauguin and Van Gogh that few people have ever seen. Truly one of the world's greatest museums.

Driving through Leningrad will acquaint you with the Admiralty built by Peter the Great, St. Isaac's Cathedral and Square, the Blue Bridge (which was once a serf market), St. Nicholas' Cathedral, and the Kirov State Theater. But a more popular excursion takes you fourteen miles south to the town of Pushkin (named in honor of the poet), where Catherine the Great built a palace and fine parks. Go four miles more and arrive at Pavlovsk, the site of another eighteenth-century palace and English-style park. Visits are allowed into the park only, which has interesting sculptures, artificial ponds, and wet jokes (if you happen to step under the wrong arbor, you will be drenched).

PORTUGAL

Portugal's capital on the Tagus River, **Lisbon,** is a low-key city that may seem drab in comparison to other European capitals, but visitors soon appreciate its special character. Legend says that Ulysses founded the town, but the credit to the Phoenicians in 1200 B.C. is more believable. Historically, Lisbon has gained many honors, for the great discoverers Vasco da Gama (the Indies) and Pedro Alvares Cabral (Brazil) set out from here in the late fifteenth century when Portugal reigned as a major maritime power.

Medieval Lisbon, the city's most fascinating section, begins with St. George's Castle overlooking the sea, then winds down into the Santa Cruz quarter of narrow streets and old houses. Between the Tagus and the castle is the Alfama, or former Moorish section, with stair-streets, tiny squares, and blind alleys lined with sixteenth- to eighteenth-century houses. Walking is the best way—indeed, the only way—to get around. From the castle, you can walk all the way down to the Praca do Comercio (Commerce Square) on the water. Here, where the Stock Exchange has replaced the former Royal Palace, the Portuguese king would walk down to greet every returning ship to collect incoming gold and riches.

Manueline Lisbon is up the Tagus in a suburb called **Belem.** A sixteenth-century monastery lies along the harbor here, its cloister a masterpiece of rich sculptured stone. On the riverside is a Monument to the Discoveries, erected in 1960 to honor the 500th anniversary of Prince Henry the Navigator. Nearby are the museums of popular art, ancient art, and the Coach Museum. The latter is installed in the former riding school of Belem Palace and holds some of the most ornate royal coaches from the sixteenth to nineteenth centuries. Most of them appear well-used, while others served merely as small gifts of appreciation between monarchs. All look extremely uncomfortable! Another museum worthy of a visit, the Gulbenkian, shows the extensive collection of an Armenian who willed his entire cache of artworks to his adopted country, Portugal, at his death in 1955.

Europe's longest suspension bridge spans the Tagus River. Originally called the Salazar Bridge after Portugal's hardy dictator, its name was changed after the 1974 revolution to the April 25th Bridge. Across the bridge are some interesting towns, especially those on the Atlantic coast—the quaint fishing village of Sesimbra; Setubal, with its sardine boats and twelfth-century castle; and Arrabida, where the scenery from mountain to sea is spectacular. Estoril, that fashionable gambling resort where deposed monarchs live out their twilight days in splendor, is only about fifteen miles south of Lisbon, and a few minutes more is charming Cascais, where former royalty also resides. But the most beautiful destination for a day trip from the capital is Sintra, nestled high in the Sierra de Sintra range; Lord Byron once called it a "glorious Eden."

At the end of the day in Lisbon, you must do what the Portuguese do— have a glass of red wine and listen to a little fado, haunting songs of fate sung to the accompaniment of romantic guitars. Early tradition held that only women sang these sad songs, but recently males have also sung them.

The 35-mile long island of **Madeira,** 560 miles southwest of Lisbon and on the same latitude as Casablanca, is often called the Pearl of the Atlantic because of its mild climate year-round, its lush subtropical vegetation, and its vast panoramas of volcanic landscapes. The Portuguese refer to Madeira proudly as the "floating garden" because the floral splendor includes bougainvillea, jacaranda trees, hibiscus, frangipani, poinsettia, Bird of Paradise, and all varieties of orchids. Madeira arose from the sea floor as the result of a volcanic eruption in the Tertiary Period. Thus, its rocky shoreline abuts right into high cliffs, and the only beaches are on the small, nearby island of Porto Santo. Inland, Madeira's mountains are so steep that farmers must not only dig out narrow terraces on which to plant, but also build *palheiros*—small thatched sheds—in which to keep their cows (lest the cows miss their step and fall over the cliff).

Funchal, capital and chief port of Madeira, was named for the sweet smell of fennel. When Portuguese explorer Joao Gonclaves Zarco "discovered" the island in 1419, called it Madeira (wooded isle), and claimed it in the name of Prince Henry the Navigator, he also named Funchal. The English relate a more romantic tale: they say the island was first found by the English adventurer Robert Machim, who was shipwrecked here (with his mistress) in 1346. Perhaps because of this story, but more likely because of the comfortably mild climate, the English love Madeira.

Cruise ships dock in Funchal, which lies at the end of a beautiful bay. Most of the city's 98,000-plus inhabitants live in charming white houses perched on terraces in the surrounding hills. At night the twinkling city lights give off a fantasy-land feeling. And if you're an early riser, just a few steps from the cruise ship pier you can find the small flower market where local women in traditional costumes are as colorful as their merchandise. If you wish to "have some Madeira, m'dear," this is the right place. The Madeira Wine Association on Avenida Arriaga has a tasting lodge (as do all the local firms) where you can sample as much as you like, from the sweetest Malmsey (Duke of Clarence is the most popular brand) to the driest Sercial. Whatever you wish to purchase will probably be packed in a locally made wicker basket. Wicker and exquisite embroidery are two of the island's best known cottage industries; both products are worth the entire visit.

Your sightseeing excursions should include a visit to Quinta das Cruzes, a villa (built by Zarco) that is now a museum surrounded by a beautiful orchid garden; Camara de Lobos, the fishing village Sir Winston Churchill painted on his visits to the island; further along the coast, Cabo Girao, the world's second highest sea cliff (at 1900 feet), with a proper railing so you can look without falling off. And if you like a thrill now and then, take a toboggan ride down to Funchal from Monte, four miles away. Two straw-hatted professionals who wear rubber-tire shoes will guide your toboggan, a wicker basket on wooden runners, as you slip and slide down the smooth pebble path. Each toboggan holds two people, so you can cling together during the fast turns.

The area around Funchal has many good restaurants and smart hotels. My favorite is the famous old Reid's Hotel (again, where Churchill loved to stay) where the terrace view of the harbor is lovely. Reid's also has a wonderful garden, and if you're confused about the name of a particular plant or flower, the manager might just get out his book and look it up for you. Closer to town is the ultramodern Casino Park Hotel, designed by the renowned Brazilian architect Oscar Niemeyer, in a complex that includes the Casino of Madeira (so if you like roulette, blackjack, French bank, and slot machines, drop in between 4 p.m. and 3 a.m.). If you hunger for real country food, take a taxi up into the hills where the restaurant A Seta serves hot, crusty bread, *espetada* (beef on a spit); pitchers of local wine; and Madeira honey cake for a bargain price.

SPAIN

As your cruise ship sails into the harbor of **Barcelona,** your senses will tell you that full enjoyment lies ahead. For Spain's second largest city and principal port has character, beauty, and charm. The people who live here call themselves Catalans and speak their own language, which they insist is not a combination of French and Castilian Spanish. But they, and the city in which they live, are certainly influenced by the proximity to neighboring France as well as to the varied cultures that have come through this port since the third century B.C.

Barcelona has wide boulevards lined with sidewalk cafes and elegant shops; flowers everywhere and palm trees (which tell you about the climate); a gothic quarter with narrow streets and thirteenth- to fifteenth-century buildings (visit the Palacio Real where Columbus paid a visit following his return from the New World); Montjuich Park and Tibidabo Mountain; the Ramblas section; and the historic port section with a statue of Columbus, a replica of the *Santa Maria,* and an interesting Maritime Museum. While touring the city, every visitor must stop to pay respects to two favorite sons: Pablo Picasso and Antonio Gaudi, the latter a surrealist architect who died in 1926 (run over by a tram). Gaudi left behind some crazy concoctions, the most famous of which is the church of the Sagrada Familia (Holy Family), begun in 1884 and still unfinished because he left no plans (and so far, no one has been able to interpret his motives). Other examples of "gaudy" works are Guell Lodge and Park and some luxury flats on the Paseo de Gracia. By contrast, the Picasso Museum will seem like an old friend. Located in the fourteenth-century Aguilar Palace at 15 Calle Montcada (the street is lined with medieval Catalan architecture, so be sure to walk the entire length), the museum contains some 2500 works donated by Picasso. The artist lived here as a young man, in Bohemian style down near the port. Some of his wonderful early sketches of Barcelona show us what the city was like around the turn of the century.

Malaga is the undisputed capital of the Costa del Sol, Spain's sun coast and a year-round tourist spot. It is also the most important town on the Mediterranean side of Andalusia. The Moors, who occupied this part of Spain for eight centuries, gave it the name Andalusia, and the Arab influences are still very much felt in Malagan houses, folklore, and colorful native costumes. Some say the best flamenco, the soul of Andalusia, can be seen here—a good complement to gazpacho, the region's gastronomic specialty. Malaga, prosperous and lively, is protected by mountains in the north and the sea to the south. Not far from the harbor and the lovely, park-lined Paseo de Cintura del Puerto are two fortresses that made Malaga one of the major strongholds of Andalusia. The higher one, Gibralfaro, commands a spectacular view from its fourteenth-century ramparts. The lower, Alcazaba, was built over a Roman amphitheater and has lovely Moorish gardens, art, and atmosphere. Walk back to the seafront via the sixteenth-century cathedral and the fascinating shops along Larios Street. Stop at a local cafe for a glass of wine, some crusty bread, and a bowl of iced gazpacho.

Only one small town in Sicily gets as much sunshine as Malaga, I've heard, so when you're ready for the beach, take a tour to **Torremolinos** where the white, sandy beach is five miles long. It's no longer a quaint little village supported by the sugar cane industry. Now it's row upon row of modern, high-rise hotels and apartment houses. When you've had enough of this impersonal air, you can always return to the

Old World atmosphere of Malaga, the Arab-Spanish-gypsy town that gave birth to Pablo Picasso at 15 Plaza de la Mercĕd.

The port of **Vigo,** on Spain's Atlantic coast just north of the Portuguese border, has been an important natural harbor since Roman times. Primarily, it is the point of entry for **Santiago de Compostela,** Spain's holiest of cities. Since the Middle Ages, pilgrims from all over the world have made their way to Santiago where, it is believed, the remains of the Apostle St. James the Greater were buried. The relics were discovered early in the ninth century, and by the eleventh century a pilgrimage to St. James' shrine in Santiago de Compostela ranked equally with a visit to Jerusalem or Rome. The Apostle became Patron Saint of Spain during the Reconquest. For the half to two million pilgrims a year, a Pilgrim Guide existed, written in the late twelfth century by Cluny monks. It described the best routes to take and what sights to enjoy along the way (this may have been the first guidebook ever written).

Santiago de Compostela has changed little since medieval times. One can still wander the winding, stone streets that lead to the plaza and cathedral, just as devoted Christians have done for centuries. The present cathedral, believed to be on the very site where the Apostle's tomb was found, dates from the eleventh through thirteenth centuries. Its huge edifice is always welcoming the faithful and curious who come to pay their respects to the thirteenth-century statue of St. James and to his relics. If you happen to visit the cathedral on a holy day, as I did a few years ago, you may be able to observe the ceremony of the incense, when a huge, smoking pot is thrown from side to side in front of the altar. I was lucky; in the crowd that day was Spain's handsome King Juan Carlos who had come to pay his respects, and he personally greeted everyone within sight, including a friend and me! In 1982 Santiago de Compostela celebrated a Holy Year Jubilee, a year-long fete that occurs only when July 25, the Day of St. James the Apostle, falls on a Sunday. The jubilee officially begins on December 31 of the previous year, and the Holy Doors on the east face of the cathedral are opened at this time. Like the Holy Doors at St. Peter's Basilica, these doors are allowed to be opened only during a jubilee year.

A tour to Santiago is not complete without a visit to the Hotel de Los Reyes Catolicos on the cathedral square. This remarkable *parador* (government-run inn) was founded by Ferdinand of Aragon and Isabella of Castile in the late fifteenth century as a pilgrim inn and hospital. Most of the original carved columns and grillwork are still intact; enjoy them as you walk through the four beautiful patios, large dining room, and lovely, antique-filled guestrooms. On the same Plaza de Espana (the cathedral square) are the twelfth-century Bishop's Palace, the eighteenth-century Raxoy Palace (now the Town Hall), and the seventeenth-century San Jeronimo College. Take your camera. All are worth several thousand words!

Balearic Islands: One of Spain's forty-nine provinces is the Balearic archipelago, which consists of Mallorca, Minorca, Ibiza, and the small Formentera. Capital of the group and most popular tourist center is **Palma de Mallorca,** a port city spread around the back of a beautiful, wide bay. Palma has a mild climate year-round, lovely old mansions of the fifteenth and sixteenth centuries, and an interesting harbor. It claims to receive more visitors (by air and sea) than any other place in Spain. The island has been a part of Spain for most of its discovered life (with the exception of three hundred years during Moorish occupation) and boasts its own school of painting (from the fourteenth to fifteenth centuries) and at least one well-known native son, Junipero Sera (1713–1784). Born in Petra (a town near the center of the island), Sera became a Franciscan, went to the New World to work with Indians in Mexico and California, and founded several missions and the cities of San Diego, Monterey, and San Francisco. Not bad work for a local boy.

Along the waterfront you can see the cathedral, which took from the thirteenth century to the year 1601 to complete; the Bishops' Palace; Almudaina, former residence of the Moorish kings; and Lonja, a fifteenth-century commercial exchange. But save some energy for a stroll through the Old Quarter with its many beautiful old mansions, public buildings, and Moorish Baths left behind from the days of Palma's caliphate. A long climb westward (about two miles) brings you to the site of the fourteenth-century Bellver Castle, summer residence of Mallorcan kings and later a prison. If you still have the energy to climb the winding steps of the tower, you will enjoy a panoramic view of Palma Bay. And if you are in the mood for shopping, you will find good quality leatherwork here. For a view of the countryside take a tour to Valledemosa, an old Mallorcan village and Carthusian monastery that harbored two famous visitors during the winter of 1838—composer Frederick Chopin and French author George Sand.

The second largest of the Balearic Islands is the cavernous **Minorca** where the remains of a Bronze Age people have been found in the form of *talayots*. These great stones, used to cover funeral chambers, perhaps also formed the bases of primitive houses. The thirty-mile island is dotted with them. Other interesting finds include Stone Age monuments called *navetas,* or upturned boats, that may have been tombs. Check the Archaeological Museum at Conquista Square in Mahon, the capital, for more complete information on and examples of the findings. Minorca is quite a different island from Mallorca, and suffers from its second-best rating. Tourism is less developed here, and the atmosphere is more peaceful and subdued. A certain eighteenth-century British influence flourishes, attributable to a British occupation of the island. Admiral (Lord) Nelson is said to have visited briefly and even put the finishing touches on a book here during the fall of 1799. And the fishing is reputed to be superb around Minorca. The locals even claim to have invented mayonnaise to serve with their catch of the day.

Tourism is growing on **Ibiza,** the third largest of the Balearic Islands, often called the White Island because of its many whitewashed, limestone buildings with terraced roofs designed to catch rainwater. This mountainous island, with a population of only 35,000 on its twenty-five miles, has been important to Mediterranean trade routes since the tenth century B.C. when the Phoenicians stopped here en route from Spain to Africa. They left behind a splendid graveyard, a necropolis, overlooking the main harbor, with some 2000 tombs. La Ciudad—the city—is the primary port town, with about 20,000 inhabitants, busy streets lined with shops, and open-air cafes along the waterfront. In the fishermen's quarter the cubic, whitewashed houses are built one atop the other, leaving space for nothing in between. The pine forests, which fringe the island, explain why the Greeks called this place Pitiousa, or Pine Island. But there are other trees: almonds, olives, figs, and palms. Just three and one-half nautical miles south of Ibiza lies the Wheat Island, the eight-mile long Formentera. Fourth in size of the Balearics, Formentera has little to attract tourists, but your cruise vessel will probably sail by closely enough so you can see the small harbor of Cala Sabina.

Canary Islands: Another island-province of Spain, the Canaries lie just 72 miles northwest of Africa and 650 miles south of Europe. The islands comprise Furteventura, Grand Canary, Lanzarote, and Tenerife. Cruises often call at the popular ports of Las Palmas and Santa Cruz de Tenerife. **Las Palmas,** capital and main seaport of Grand Canary, is a scallop-shaped island with steep cliffs on the north and south coasts. Founded in a palm grove in 1478, Las Palmas was visited by Christopher Columbus at the commencement of each of his discovery voyages to the New World. Where he actually stayed in 1502 became the palace of the island's first governors and is now a museum of fine arts with a collection of fifteenth-century maps, charts, and navigational equipment used at the time of these voyages.

Like the whole chain, volcanic **Grand Canary** offers some spectacular views from the mountainous areas of black sand beaches over lush fruit trees and tropical flowers. Wonderful excursions begin at Las Palmas, the most interesting of which is to Cruz de Tejeda where, at 4750 feet, you can see a petrified forest. Actually, it's the village of Tejada that stands in a huge volcanic basin. If you climb even higher, to 6496 feet, you can see the island's meterological station as well as a panoramic view of the countryside, the coastline, and the sea.

Tenerife, largest of the Canary Islands, possesses the highest summit on Spanish territory, the snowcapped volcanic peak named Mount Teide, on the Las Canadas plateau. For one of the most breathtaking views in the world, visit the cone. You can do so from Santa Cruz, the island's capital and main port. The drive from Santa Cruz passes through La Laguna, the oldest town on Tenerife (founded in 1496) and its first capital. Travel on to the floral paradise of Orotava where the ascent begins. The road up to Teide is twenty-four miles long, past the Agua-mansa woods, by the Dornajito and Monteverde springs, and then to the Altavista Resthouse where the funicular will whisk you up to the cone. From here, it's a forty-five-minute climb to the edge, where at 11,664 feet, you'll get one of the thrills of your lifetime. If you prefer to stay in town, Santa Cruz, a free port since 1852, has some charming old houses with wooden balconies that are typical of the island.

GOING ASHORE

A friendly male voice left a message on my telephone answering machine the other day, requesting that I consider giving stars to shore excursions. It's a wonderful idea and I do appreciate his concern for making this book better; however, it is quite impossible. We all understand that there are good shore excursions and there are the antithesis—*dreadful*! What's more, there are good and dreadful ones on the same route in the same week. And, unless a cruise vessel staff member is on each bus of each tour, there is no immediate control concerning guide courtesy, value information, relation of shopping stops versus seeing the sites, etc.

In my opinion, most shore excursions begin too early—after all, we are supposed to be on vacation! However, moving large shiploads of people is a tedious task and time in port is restricted. To visit the ancient city of Pergamum, during a Greek Island cruise several years ago, we embarked the tenders around 7 a.m., but still savor memories of every moment we spent ashore in Dikili, Turkey.

Thank goodness, the Greek Islands/Turkey are back in favor, because the shore excursions in this area of the cruise world are some of the best—even if you abhor ancient ruins. There is plenty to do on every island, from shopping for local handicrafts to just sitting in the sunshine (with a glass of ouzo at your elbow) watching the scenery go by. The Greek Islands are a favorite with Scandinavians seeking the sun after their long winter, and the sight of those lithe, tanned Vikings (of both sexes) is something to behold!

Some people never go ashore. They just love ships, sailing, and the whole concept of a cruise; they feel no need ever to set foot in port. However, most of us eagerly await each port of call and, in fact, we often choose our cruise holidays as much by the itinerary offered as by the passenger vessel. Ship lines are cognizant of passenger preferences and pay particular attention to what ports receive the highest praise and offer the most rewarding cruise call experience. Ship lines also consider integration of on-board and onshore activities, convenience and comfort for passengers, availability of sightseeing attractions and shopping opportunities, and rigid navigation safety standards. It is safe to assume that what happens ashore affects your entire cruise experience. The physical facilities for every potential port of call must meet stringent standards and offer adequate vessel accommodations. Most ship lines prefer ports with dockside berthing, since it is more convenient for passengers to walk ashore. Most lines also seek ports that have sufficient emergency facilities (doctors, dentists, hospitals, ambulances), just in case. Many ports offer everything, while others may excel in history and archaeology or be just the place for sunbathing.

I pay particular attention to destination, hours spent in each port, arrival time and day of the week (are the shops open, is it a holiday, is there a strike of some sort?). These questions are very important, because I try to plan as much exploration time as possible, while also calculating how much time to allow for shopping and indulging in local specialties. Thus, it can be most disappointing if the program changes without your knowledge. Often the changes are to passengers' benefit; however, your travel agent should be advised of any last-minute alterations to the schedule and she or he should inform you. Ship lines are responsible and can always verify their notification of travel agents, so check carefully into such matters before any complaints are registered.

INFORMATION ON PORTS OF CALL   Long before each port of call looms over the horizon, a member of the cruise staff will give an on-board briefing detailing the latest information on arrival and departure times (they tend to vary according to sailing conditions and any unforeseen circumstances), the vessel's mooring plans, dress suggestions considering local custom and weather, currency rates, shore excursions (if you have not already bought the full package), and free time. If you plan to do any exploring alone or in a private group, you will also wish to know taxi and other transportation rates, where to eat and shop, and how long it takes to get from place to place. The briefings may even include a short film or slide show to acquaint you with the location of famous sights. However, most of these port talks provide only adequate information, and you may want to supplement them. A map is always helpful, whether you join the organized tour or not. Most ships sell maps in the purser's office (but the supply is limited so get there early). The best maps have famous sites sketched on, so that even if the taxi driver cannot read English, he can at least recognize the monument (this was a godsend in China). Some cruise lines—Royal, Pearl and Cunard—give their passengers complimentary copies of a mini-Berlitz guide relating to the itinerary. Frankly, these booklets are not worth the paper they are printed on—even a crude map drawn by someone on board who knows the area well is better. The best advice is to bring along your own favorite guidebook.

Guidebooks furnish both background material and practical information concerning your ports of call. Historical novels are a good source for atmosphere, and since port cities were often the first settled or colonized, plenty has been written about most of them. Friends and colleagues may offer tips, and perhaps your travel agency has its own cache of materials. If you are booked on a serious cruise (Swans Hellenic, Special Expeditions, or Society Expeditions), you may receive a reading list to prepare yourself for the sights and sounds ahead. And if you're really lucky, you may discover some picture books and such in the ship's library. Advance preparation—your local library, museum publications and videos from a favorite shop—is the best way to enjoy your cruise. In addition, I try to have some local currency ready so I can purchase a book or two in port. Although many are not bound very well and tend to fall apart with use, the local books, usually written by native scholars, are a good primary source.

BUYING SHORE EXCURSIONS   You may prefer to purchase every shore excursion available and leave the driving and the thinking to someone else. Buying the complete package of port tours when you book is the very best way to purchase these tours, because the price quoted should include all the extras, and you're done with it. Procuring shore excursions piecemeal can be bad psychologically; you begin to think too much about price and lose your enthusiasm. Of course, if you have booked a cruise operated by the specialty companies mentioned before or on many of the lovely barges in Europe, the shore tours are all-inclusive (and how excellent they are).

The average shore excursion, developed between the ship line and a local tour operator in each port of call, is generally well organized and well managed. You don't have to worry about safety or buses running out of fuel, because the ship line plans carefully. What the company cannot control is the turnover in tour guides, some of whom are in it only for the money. Beware of guides who put green dots on your collar or flowers in your buttonhole for identification. Guides may use these symbols to tip off shops that you are a "wealthy" tourist. (It's an old trick and still used worldwide.) If you feel your guide has not fulfilled her/his duties gracefully or has attempted to obtain extra charges from the bus group, complain at once to the purser's office. You deserve a rewarding and hassle-free experience in return for the price paid.

Shore excursions are expensive for many reasons. Often, the ship line must deal with countries where the cost of fuel and vehicles is almost prohibitive. Add this to the greed that tourism breeds, and you have inflated prices. I understand that tour guides in the Caracas area want $500 a day, which explains why a short morning tour of Caracas from La Guaira costs far more than it is worth. Then, remember that you buy the tour from the ship line, which buys from the tour organizer, which buys from someone else. Each party marks the price up a little bit. Actually, ship lines claim that they only add a little to the price to cover the expenses (and commission to the travel agent). However, ship lines would not have tour-desk personnel if they did not make their salaries.

Despite the cost, the morning spent at Ephesus will remain one of the great travel memories in my husband's and my album. There are many others: a late evening gondola ride through the back canals of Venice; the magnificent mosaics in Ravenna—best viewed with a proper guide and torch; a long day's journey into San Jose, capital of Costa Rica, and return right to the gangway of the ship via a 100-year-old train; a barbecue at the Tropicale Hotel in Santarem under the stars; a tour of the great houses in Newport, Rhode Island; wine tasting in the chais of Bordeaux; a drive through the sugar plantations in Barbados; China!

Many other areas in the cruise world demand—price be damned— the shore excursions. These include the USSR and China (where it's obligatory for the most part), North Africa, the Red Sea (especially to Petra), some South American and North Cape calls, and Alaska. One of the most popular but very expensive excursions on Alaskan cruises is a seaplane tour which, if it includes lunch at the charming Taku Lodge, could be well over $100 per person. A forty-five-minute heli- copter tour of Sitka Sound, St. Lazari Island National Bird Reserve, Mt. Edgecumbe, and a quick landing nearby to see goats, seals, whales, and bears costs almost as much. But, all who take this short ride say it is the highlight of the entire Inside Passage sailing.

ON-YOUR-OWN SHORE EXCURSIONS   If you are counting pen- nies, you can save by touring many ports on your own, especially if they have few tourist sites and are more renowned for their beauty and fine beaches than their costlier attractions; try the Mexican Riviera or many of the Caribbean Islands (especially Puerto Rico and St. Thomas) for this. Toss aside frantic sightseeing tours of these ports and indulge in a leisurely catamaran cruise in the harbor or a stroll through the narrow back streets to reward yourself. Tours around the Hawaiian is- lands are excellent as there is much beauty and drama to see here. How- ever, if you are as allergic to buses as I am, you may prefer to rent a car and swim off less congested beaches. American Hawaii Cruises packs tasty picnic lunches and the rental car agencies (Budget, Avis, Hertz, etc.) all have good road maps. Any driver's license of the fifty states is valid, of course. Know what is available before you go; some of these agencies will offer a bargain weekly rate, and have a car waiting at each port call in the islands.

In some port cities, knowledge of the area and a friend to help share taxi expenses make for a thrifty and enjoyable exploration, espe- cially in the northern capitals of Europe, Athens, and Hong Kong. Some excursions—sailing the Orinoco River or transiting the Panama Canal, for example—are exciting enough in themselves, and you never need to

240 · · GOING ASHORE

go ashore. However, I would not miss the temple tour in Bangkok, the Japanese garden tour in Kyoto, or any tour of that "Morning of the World" island, Bali. And, if you spend the time and energy to sail up or down the Nile, you must take every tour of the temples and monuments—no matter what the temperature or the hour!

Many of the local cruise and beach tours around the Caribbean sound splendid, and some ship lines even arrange their own. Norwegian Cruises has offered a very successful beach party on Grand Cayman and now adds turtleburgers to the luncheon spread. Its other vessels have dropped anchor off one of the uninhabited Berry Islands, and the *Norway* uses Little San Salvador to treat its passengers to sun, sail, waterski, and snorkel between rounds of beer and soda, hamburger and hotdogs. Royal Caribbean Cruise Lines has spent millions of dollars so passengers can enjoy the day at Labadee, its private resort on the corner of Haiti. Snorkeling is a popular pastime at many calls in the Caribbean and should be included in your shore excursion budget, for it's pretty hard to beat the beauty and excitement of this underwater world. Activities like these also present a wonderful way to meet other people on the ship with shared interests. You may even make lasting friendships. Often, passengers will become friendly during an organized tour in one port and decide to share expenses and explore together during the next call.

On the new, smaller vessels (*Seabourn Pride* and *Spirit, Sea Goddesses, Windstar* fleet), you don't need to bother with local beaches because unique stern platforms allow watersport amenities then and there. The platforms are lowered when the ship is at anchor, for swimming, water skiing, jetskiing, windsurfing, sunfish sailing, snorkeling, or just hitching a Zodiac ride. These platforms are a wonderful invention and a great way to spend a few hours—especially if the majority of passengers have disappeared on a shore excursion!

If you do decide to explore alone, pay particular attention to checking off and on the ship and allowing plenty of time for coming back aboard. (Many cruise staff personnel insist they will not wait for returning passengers.) If the port is small and lacks the proper facilities, your vessel may have to anchor out. This means "tendering in," which cuts your time in port considerably; remember it is your responsibility to know the times of the last tender. Frequently, the boats leave the ship every fifteen minutes or so for the first hour and then make returns every hour on the half hour. Ship lines often leave a crew member on the pier to check your boarding tag numbers, especially if you opt for the last launch back, to prevent anyone's being left behind. But you never know. The port calls and shore periods have been carefully planned by the ship line for passengers' fullest enjoyment. But don't miss the boat; the next port may be even more exciting!

CHANGES IN ITINERARY   If weather or some other unforeseen circumstance prevents your cruise ship from completing the full itinerary in the time allotted, you can do nothing but accept the situation gracefully. Hurricanes in the Caribbean and monsoons in the South China Sea are "acts of God," so we can't hold the ship line responsible. If this happens to you, be grateful for the competency of the captain and thank him when it's all over. On the other hand, if the boilers break down and the entire cruise is ruined, you will definitely receive some recompense—which may be a considerable refund, a discount on a future cruise, or both. Since happy passengers take future cruises—and even tell their friends—no ship line will let you down the gangway discontented!

SHOPPING

Browsing through the local markets and shops is definitely an important pastime on travels. Just consider how the art of shopping introduces us to the local people, products and specialties of the land. I never fail to come away with something unusual and enjoyable by spending a little time looking at what is available both aboard ship and in ports of call. In addition to the usual souvenirs—or remembrances—of where I was through T-shirts, hats and accessories, perfumes and other paraphernalia, there are fragrant spices for a song as well as flavorful liqueurs in interesting bottles and charming works of art that make memories linger long after the cruise is over.

SHIPBOARD SHOPPING   A great deal has changed in the past few years in shipboard shops, so I never fail to check them out in my annual inspection tours. Although many are run by outside franchises and have a certain amount of junk merchandise that shouldn't be allowed valuable space, most of the shops these days have excellent buys in jewelry, handbags, scarves, perfumes and cruisewear.

Shipboard shopping has become a multi-billion dollar business, and warehouses in south Florida are brimming with goods from all over the world to be loaded onto cruise ships sailing the Caribbean. According to shop managers, Gucci handbags are the number-one seller afloat—followed by perfumes and fancy watches. But don't be surprised to see fox and mink joining the ranks of Hummel and Majorcan pearls!

When the "new" *Queen Elizabeth 2* returned to service in May 1987, she boasted a $7 million shopping arcade filled with Gucci, Dior, Louis Feraud, Aquascutum, Pringle, etc., and with prices to match. The Garrard jewelry shop featured a $250,000 graduated diamond necklace—in case one of you wins big at the tables. In the Dunhill shop, men's blazers are a mere $500-plus (compared to $750 on land). One shop rents and tailors tuxedos for men, while another sells such English delicacies as smoked salmon and Stilton cheese as well as jams and a variety of tea. It is a lovely arcade and a wonderful place to browse—especially on a transatlantic voyage when the foghorns can be heard in the distance.

The *Norway* has a two-level emporium—Le Drugstore on one deck (sundries, paperbacks, cigarettes and liquor) with Upstairs at the Down-stairs above, where unusual gift items, china, crystal, and porcelain as well as a selection of fine watches are displayed. The Golden Touch has fine jewelry; Dimensions has chic cruisewear for women, and the Islander caters to the male ego. Faces and Fragrances sells cosmetics and perfumes, and Norway Nights is a new boutique featuring evening wear and furs for both sexes. At the end of the promenade is a conve-niently located ice cream parlor (adjacent to the children's computer room), where you can satisfy your soul with one of Sven's favorite flavors.

Onboard the largest cruise ship in the world, the 74,000-ton *Sov-ereign of the Sea,* a total of eight different boutiques line the shopping area known as Shops of Centrum. The arcade's designer calls it Lon-don's Bond Street/Miami's Bal Harbour/Los Angeles' Rodeo Drive col-lectively. Among the fancy storefronts are Gucci, of course, a fabulous perfumerie, a Scandinavian shop featuring Orrefors crystal, local crafts, and Blue Fox fur jackets. A jewelry shop, a boutique full of elegant evening clothes, and an all-purpose sundry/reading material/liquor/cig-arette, etc., complete the Centrum Mall.

The sailing area of ships is a clue to what the shops may feature. For example, onboard *Ocean Islander* during an Orinoco River cruise, we found Venetian leather goods and glass beaded necklaces as well as an enticing Italian line of handknits—all a result of the vessel's Venice port calls the previous summer! Royal Cruise Line, which travels around the Greek Islands from spring through fall, stocks lovely Greek gold in its shops—including pieces from the famed jeweler, LaLaounis—I saw a lovely necklace for about $7500! On board *Wind-Song* in French Polynesia, one shop featured the distinctive black pearls of the South Seas—beautiful but costly! Nonetheless, we all had a good look—and a drool. While some passengers did buy earrings and such, it is always a bit dicey to spend so much money unless one is an expert on the quality and color of semi-precious or precious stones. It would be so disheartening to have such a purchase "devalued" back home. If you plan to do any serious shopping aboard or abroad, discuss it first with your local jeweler (or banker).

Holland America's vessels have terrific shopping areas, with cases full of Waterford, Royal Worcester and Royal Copenhagen, as well as the usual handbags and scarves, watches and jewelry. The *Nieuw Am-sterdam*'s shopping arcade is named Perel Straet after the Dutch Col-ony's center of import-export activity, so plan to buy your Dutch chocolates here. This same area is known as Canael Street on the *Noor-dam,* and the shops reflect the ship's east/west theme of exploration and discovery.

Muumuus and aloha shirts are the most popular items in the *Inde-pendence* and *Constitution* shops, and they disappear rapidly from the racks when Hawaiian night occurs on each ship! Even though each line attempts to "theme" its shops with items relating to itinerary and clientele, the world is small and products will pop up from just about anywhere! As on land, consider the price carefully and if you still love it—buy it as a wonderful memento of your cruise.

SHOPPING AT PORTS OF CALL   Enticements lie around the corner of every street and lane in your current port of call! Tax-free temptations are just too irresistible, no matter how hard I try. On several visits to **Bermuda** I have managed to collect an entire set of Herend hand-painted china from Hungary at 40% below New York prices. Other good and frequent purchases from Trimingham's and Smith's and Cooper's include shetland pullovers in beautiful colors, Liberty of London prints, and Bermuda bags with cedar handles. After I check Blucks' once again to convince myself a new piece of Herend has not snuck into the shop, I never fail to feed another addiction. I pay a call on the island's artist laureate, Alfred Birdsey, to add a few more watercolors to my collection. No one has brought the spirit of Bermuda to paper so well as Birdsey. (I have called him an eccentric elsewhere and I shall continue to do so, because he loves it!) If your cruise vessel is **Bahamas**-bound or if you just pop over for the weekend out of Miami, you will want to save a few pennies to spend at the Straw Market in Rawson Square for bags and hats and such. This is about the only fun shopping left in the Bahamian capital, as Bay Street is no longer very interesting (unless you have a hankering for American-fast-food-chain chicken or hamburger).

In the **Caribbean** most cruise vessels aim their bows straight for St. Thomas, USVI, and do not even bother to pass go, for the charming town of Charlotte Amalie might just well be the bargain center of the entire Western Hemisphere. Most travelers consider it such, and even U.S. customs waxes so enthusiastic that returning citizens are allowed double duty-free purchases from here ($800 per person). As a bonus you may even bring back a gallon of liquor acquired here (versus the quart from elsewhere). Liquor is such a popular item for purchase in St. Thomas that the larger (and more aggressive) stores will come aboard, take your orders, and deliver the five-pack in bond before you have the chance to say "boo." Of course, if you prefer to walk the streets and alleyways of Charlotte Amalie, you will find many other ways to break the bank. For example, Hummel figurines, Irish Beleek, Limoges, perfumes, cameras and lenses, tape machines and other grown-up toys, watches galore, and jewels will knock your eyes out. The town even has a Hans Stern outlet as well as Little Switzerland, Gucci, St. Michael (the Marks and Spencer people), a store just for tablecloths, and T-Shirt World. If you buy something that is made or bottled here, a 100-year-old work of art, or a contemporary painting, you may bring it home duty-free. Now you understand why cruise passengers go bananas when the captains say "St. Thomas."

Throughout the Caribbean you can buy some lovely handcrafts as well as tax-free European imports. Haiti is known for its primitive paintings, voodoo drums, and Iron Market. San Juan has *Santos* (small religious wooden figures that are handcarved and very traditional), a Bacardi Rum factory, and a Hathaway shirt outlet in the center of the shopping district. In fact, San Juan has excellent outlet stores, including a Bass Shoe shop and two-story Ralph Lauren boutique where bargains abound for both sexes. I don't recommend Barrachina, which has promised free pina coladas (a thimbleful) and two-dollar rides to the airport. When I went, the place was dirty and overpriced (and extremely rude when I refused to buy). You can find delft jugs and orange liqueur in Curacao, lovely filigree jewelry and Dunhill pipes in Trinidad, perfumes and French crystal in Martinique, and straw items wherever your cruise calls. Silver jewelry in **Mexico** is not the bargain it once was—but prices are better than they have been for a few years. Take lots of cash if you plan some purchases—discounts abound with greenbacks. Mexico is also the home of Aca Joe for casual wear, and there are some good Polo outlet shops—with pullovers, slacks, etc., for quite a savings. **Alaska** has fur boots, ivory curios, gold nuggets, totem-pole souvenirs, and packaged fish products. It also boasts some fine local artists, so check out the galleries wherever you go. A recent call in **Costa Rica** brought a gold mine in coffee—at $1 a pound!—as well as hand-carved salad bowls, trays, and some lovely handcrafts at the museum in San Jose. If I had a place to park one of the colorful hand-painted ox carts, that too would have been a memorable purchase.

If your cruise includes ports in **South America,** you will have even more fun shopping. Favorite items in the popular port of Cartagena include tooled leather goods (a traditional Colombian art form), macrame purses, and jewelry of gold and emeralds. Hans Stern, who lives in Rio de Janeiro, is a jeweler known throughout the world for his good and sometimes gaudy designs featuring gold and Brazilian semiprecious stones. His stores will literally follow you around South America, and he has also opened in New York, Paris, Lisbon, Madeira, Frankfurt, Tel Aviv, and Jerusalem. The stores are reputable, as far as I can gather, and the tag prices prevail (no bargaining). In Caracas you can buy jewelry made from cacique coins, the familiar Hand of Fatima, *chinchorros* (hammocks), handbags, and sandals. Rio combines Acapulco and Monte Carlo, with its high-style and very expensive shops touting gold and stones, the latest fashions from the Continent, and the briefest of bikinis.

If your vessel calls at Montevideo, you may want to pick up a few amethysts (they are considered the best in the world here), a suede or antelope jacket, and nutria or seal coats. Or perhaps a nice gaucho hat with boots to match. Chilean specialties include colorful, hand-woven ponchos, vicuna rugs, and artisan copper work. Chilean contemporary art is extremely interesting, and the rock shops feature locally mined lapis lazuli, jade, amethyst, agate, and onyx. Although Lima overflows with silver and gold, you should also look for the many Indian items available, such as baskets, gourds, textiles, and rugs of alpaca and llama fur. When you get to Ecuador, you have landed where the very finest Panama hats are made. Ecuador has some lovely early Indian artifacts, and some fine contemporary painters gain their inspiration from the pottery. The country has presented an artistic medal of honor to Olga Fisch, who turns out one-of-a-kind carpets and wall-hangings with early Indian motifs. They are worth every penny.

Sailing slowly along the **Amazon** will do wonders for your cruise diary and photo album, but don't expect to complete your Christmas list will all the exotica for sale. Other than some attractive round baskets (that fall apart on the way home) and some bowls made from gourds, there is not much available in the native inventory. Manaus, the former boom town 1000 miles up the Amazon, is a so-called free port but the shops are full of electronic goods and little kids sell fake perfumes on every street corner. There is one local handcraft shop, House of the Hummingbird, where everyone stops and rainmakers (a grass tube filled with sand) can be bought for about a dollar.

If your ship sails to the heart of the **Pacific islands,** pick up some macadamia nuts in Honolulu, some sarongs in Tahiti, finely woven placemats in Samoa, and a few baskets in Suva. Although koala bears are not for sale in Sydney, Maori carvings are the thing to buy in New Zealand (along with anything wooly, of course).

If you're bound for the **Far East,** head straight for Hong Kong; it has everything anyone has ever wanted, and for the best price! While not the idyllic shoppers' paradise it once was, Hong Kong is still the number one shoppers' call on world cruises. Singapore tries to match Hong Kong as a free port but has never succeeded (there is less choice in products and the prices are slightly higher, probably because the shelves are cleaner). It's simple to spend money in Hong Kong, as it's rather difficult to find anything else to do. Your ship docks right at Ocean Terminal, itself a huge shopping complex and only a short walk from the Nathan Road area where buying and selling is practically a religion. Here you can still have a silk dress made in forty-eight hours (but don't expect it to fit like standard-size clothes), find a setting for your new stones, buy photographic and stereo equipment, and even pick up a Camcord at prices lower than anywhere else in the world (if you pay cash). If you insist upon using a credit card, the shop may charge you an additional percentage to cover the carrying charges. However, it is pretty hard to beat Hong Kong's prices if you shop carefully and follow the advice of the free *Stop and Shop Bargain Guide* (issued by the Hong Kong Tourist Association), which outlines licensed dealers for every type of equipment and product sold and gives suggested retail prices (which I have always found to be quite accurate). It is especially important to follow this guide for photographic equipment purchases. I am still staggered that my husband recently got more trade-in allowance for a lens than I originally paid in Hong Kong eight years ago. Such is Hong Kong.

A word to the world traveler. Avoid the fancy European designer shops—only the Japanese frequent them these days—as they are rather expensive and often more than what you would pay at home (especially if your own shops have good sales). Stick to what Hong Kong is famous for—Chinese-made goods and wearing apparel. The tourist association has a good list of factory outlets (with maps and taxi instructions) that are great! Here you can buy lovely silk pants suits, shirts, lounging outfits and plenty of designer dresses. The labels are often missing—but who cares?

If you plan to skip the People's Republic of China, you can make do with one of the many terrific Chinese department stores, completely owned and operated by the PRC and often offering better prices than in Guangzhou (Canton) or Beijing (Peking). These department stores market lovely silks and embroideries, carpets, jade, Ming dynasty-style vases, and gold (the gold is only 9-karat, I believe). The best department store, China Arts and Crafts, has a Kowloon branch catty-corner to the Star Ferry Building (the one with the clocks), on the left-hand side as you walk from Ocean Terminal to Nathan Road. Hong Kong has also become quite a diamond center, but check first with the Hong Kong Tourist Association for their list of reputable dealers. And never pay attention to people on the street who offer you gold watches and such. They think they can always spot a victim, so prove them wrong!

If your Far East cruise does include China, spend some time shopping in this fascinating country. The Chinese now accept travelers' checks as well as some credit cards in the government-run Friendship Stores. You may browse in other stores, of course, such as the famous Number One Department Store in Shanghai, which has a money exchange on the top floor and is quite accustomed to foreign guests. If you enter the smaller shops, be certain to have plenty of *Renminbi* with you. The most popular items are Mao jackets and hats that now come in extra large sizes to fit the Western figure. Silk pajamas and lounge suits abound, but often the prices are better in Hong Kong, where there is more competition. If you get into a government-controlled antique shop, you will be staggered by the prices; take care in what you buy. Nothing really old is allowed out of China these days, so you may be the owner of an authentic reproduction (despite the dynasty chart the sweet little girl explains to you in great detail). Good buys in China are jade (if you have lots of money with you), embroidered silks and linens, souvenirs like sandalwood fans or hand-painted silk fans, and handkerchiefs. The silk fans are my favorite item, however, for they make wonderful spur-of-the-moment gifts and only cost about the equivalent of thirty cents. If you're lucky enough to visit a silk fan factory, buy them there and save a penny.

Shopping in Japan, a subtle and sensitive art form, includes the play of nimble fingers over an abacus to finish every deal. Although prices remain out of sight, the Japanese make some of the most beautiful things in the world. This is the land of pearls, woodblock prints, happy coats and kimonos, exquisite lacquerware, and imaginative folk crafts. *Mingei* (folk art), found primarily in paper, wood, and pottery, make the local shops seem like art galleries, they are so bursting with charming designs. The tape recorders and computer products are better bought in Hong Kong, where fierce competition keeps the prices low. For the real experience of shopping Japanese-style, stick to the arts and crafts of Japan.

Elsewhere on your Far Eastern cruise, you will find brilliant silks in Thailand, as well as shops full of rings set with semiprecious stones. Singapore is a clean version of Hong Kong, and Penang has little but Malaysian batiks. Indonesia offers beautiful, rich brown and blue batiks (and the antique irons used to make them are wonderful bookends). Buy dolls of old coins in Sumatra, *wayang* puppets in Bandung (wonderful souvenirs), and art (paintings, carvings, sculpture) in Bali. In the Philippines you will find the wonderful *pina* fiber (made from pineapples) that the *barong tagalog* shirt and ladies' pantsuits and dresses use (but no matter how interesting they look, beware; they can be very hot!). Taiwan is a shopper's paradise for brass, baskets, and tailoring at low prices. Semiprecious stones sparkle in Sri Lanka, which has sapphires, chameleonlike alexandrites, cat's eyes, rubies, and aquamarines. And if your vessel calls at Bombay, seek out some lovely saris and exquisite Moghul miniatures (that are mostly fakes, but never mind if you don't pay too much).

Cruising **Europe**'s waters brings you into contact with many familiar items, but before long you realize that many of your favorite things are actually cheaper at home. Most European countries have Value Added Tax (VAT), which raises the price of luxury items by as much as 33.33%. Unfortunately, this tax is unavoidable if you buy less than $100 at a time and carry the item back on board. The Scandinavian countries have among the highest goods taxes in Europe (Iceland—23.5%, Sweden—22.3%, Denmark—22%, Norway—20%) but have instituted a cash return of the tax paid before you sail away (be sure to check with the local customs at the pier). It is almost impossible to get the VAT returned from shops in France and England without some reminder, especially if a considerable amount is involved. Spain and Portugal are still wonderful countries in which to shop, and Lisbon is a popular shopping port call. But if you have the luck of stopping by Madeira, you are very fortunate. Here amid a floating garden, are wonderful wicker products, exquisite hand-fingered embroideries, and plenty of the local wine.

Specialties along the shores of the **Mediterranean** include whatever you can find in the famous souks of Morocco, wonderful white filigree birdcages from Tunisia, scarabs from Egypt as well as busts of Nefertiti and *jellabas* and *caftans.* Actually, the most popular Egyptian souvenir is the *cartouche,* an insignia bearing a pharaoh's name in hieroglyphics; you can buy it as a necklace, in gold or silver. If you would rather have a Muslim charm, the Hand of Fatima is here, too. Since most cruise vessels that call in Egypt now also continue on to Israel, prepare yourself for the woven and hand-stitched crafts available, as well as the olive wood items, the copper and brass work, pottery and basket ware.

On a Greek island and Turkey cruise, you will be tempted by rugs, rugs, and more rugs. All are fascinating and if you buy one, carry it home. The covered bazaar in Istanbul is a wonderful place to get lost and you will be approached time and time again by people pushing rugs. (I even had an offer of a flying carpet.) Turkey also has wonderful brass and copper items, spices, leather coats and jackets, and meerschaum pipes. Everything in Greece is a temptation, and I have a very hard time resisting, especially among the various island ports. Crete offers impressive red rugs (they're best as wall hangings), and Mykonos displays the most splendid-looking handmade sweaters in the world, and Rhodes (glorious Rhodes) has just about everything. I buy all my gold jewelry in Rhodes, among the shops just off the Palace of the Knights, and I always dream about the pieces left behind! Souvenir items in Greece include fine reproductions of pottery found in the ancient tombs— hand-painted and very reasonably priced.

With the **Black Sea** ports back in favor and the European capitals of the **Baltic** a popular summer destination, passengers will have opportunities again to buy lovely painted wooden boxes, bowls, and dolls in Russia as well as fur hats and ethnic costumes for children. Unless you are familiar with the workings of the USSR, shop only in recommended stores and never, never make a currency exchange with anyone on the street—no matter how good his story seems to be.

U.S. CUSTOMS   ''Sailing Through Customs'' is Norwegian Cruise Lines' catchphrase for declaring all your new purchases. According to the U.S. Customs laws, each returning resident may bring back up to $400 worth of acquired merchandise (including gifts), duty free, every thirty days. The only exception is from the U.S. Virgin Islands, American Samoa, or Guam, where the allowance is $800 (if you return directly and at least half of your bundle was purchased there). Original works of art and antiques (at least 100 years old) are exempt from duty, as are any items made on these U.S. territories (perfume, clothing, jewelry, and handbags). If you travel as a family, the duty-free allowance lets you pool your purchases, which means that a family of four has a combined allowance of $1600. If your acquisitions exceed this (and the customs officials are very lenient), a flat rate of 10% is assessed on the first $1000 over the limit. After that the rate of duty reverts to the old laws and varies widely. If all your purchases were made in U.S. territories, the flat rate is only 5% for the first $1000 worth of goods over the allowance.

If you plan to return with tobacco and liquor, first check your state laws, for federal and state regulations differ widely. For example, California residents should be aware that importing more than one bottle of wine is illegal. Basically, your duty-free limit is one carton (200) of cigarettes per person or 100 cigars. Each U.S. resident (age twenty-one and over) is also allowed one quart of liquor duty free. Cruise passengers returning from the U.S. Virgin Islands may import one gallon (five fifths), provided at least four fifths were bought in St. Thomas. It is also forbidden to bring any live plant, piece of fruit or vegetable, plant cutting or seeds, or unprocessed plant product into this country. Other items banned include Haitian goat skins, certain ivory items, alligator products, and any articles made from the skins of endangered species. Trademarked products may be imported now for personal use only; the limit is one item.

If you plan to send gifts from abroad, restrict yourself to one per address and no more than $25 worth, duty free ($40 if sent from St. Thomas) to stay within the limit. When you send presents through the mail, be careful which countries you choose; know the regulations and be certain to insure the packages properly. Write in large letters on the outside of the wrapping, "Gift enclosed, value under $25" ($40 if from St. Thomas).

The Generalized System of Preferences, instituted in 1976 to help developing countries improve their financial or economic condition through export trade, provides for duty-free importation of certain products from certain nations. Many of these are tourist items. The list, which is renewed each year, includes 107 nations, 32 dependent territories, and approximately 2700 items—Turkish rugs, loose semiprecious stones, rattan (other than furniture), shell products (except from the Philippines), toys (except from Hong Kong and Taiwan), and wigs (except from South Korea) to name a few. If your cruise encompasses a great many calls in developing nations and territories, you may wish to check which potential purchases might be duty free. Under the Trade Act, however, certain items—like most footwear, textiles, watches, some electronic products, and some glass and steel products—are specifically excluded from any GSP benefits. The U.S. actually prohibits importation of many articles, such as many types of ivory, skins from endangered species, plants and animals, and foodstuffs that could carry contamination. If you feel a buying spree approaching, contact your nearest U.S. Customs office for updated information. Or write to: Department of the Treasury, U.S. Customs Service, Washington, DC 20229 for *GSP & the Traveler* and *Customs Hints—Know Before You Go.* If you contemplate purchases of ivory, skins, fur, etc., contact the U.S. Fish and Wildlife Service, Department of the Interior.

Because cruise traffic has grown so rapidly in recent years, returning to U.S. ports is no longer the simple procedure it once was. Chances are your luggage will be placed on the pier according to the first letter of your surname. Alas, confusion is rampant as you collect all your baggage and lug it over to the nearest Customs official for clearance. I have great respect for Customs officials and make a point of making their day as pleasant as possible. With the very generous duty-free allowances that we Americans receive, there is no reason not to make the clearance process hassle-free.

The only time Customs officials will spend more than the time to say "Welcome home" is when you traveled in hot drug- and diamond-smuggling spots. Since most cruise vessels no longer frequent such areas (as Cartagena), there is little to worry about. I have been scrutinized beyond the call of duty twice—once returning from Amsterdam and the other from Ecuador—but both arrivals were at JFK Airport in New York City.

If you are on an overseas air-sea program, you will return to the U.S. through a major gateway like New York City. The rule worldwide is the first point of earth you touch in any country is where you must clear both Customs and Immigration. Fact of life. Just have your forms filled properly, get in the correct queue, and smile. You'll enjoy it!

INLAND WATERWAYS

ABERCROMBIE & KENT INTERNATIONAL, INC.

1420 Kensington Road
Oak Brook, IL 60521
tel: (312) 954–2944
   (708) 954–2944
   (800) 323–7308

Abercrombie & Kent has been a premiere tour operator for three decades. First love and area of expertise is the Africa of safaris, but A & K has extended its tours to feature such inland waterways as the Nile River, barge trips in France, England, and Holland/Belgium, and China's Yangtze River. Other cruises offered are along the Turkish coastline, in the Galapagos Islands, and among the Indonesian archipelago. The company is owned by Geoffrey and Jorie Butler Kent, two intrepid travelers whose picture cannot be missed in every brochure. Geoffrey confesses that he added the Abercrombie only to ensure an early listing (the *A*s) in any travel agent compendium!

A & K utilizes the 46-passenger M.S. *Sun Boat* for its Nile cruise programs. This privately owned vessel (most Nile boats are owned by the Egyptian government, which has its own rating system) has 23 air-conditioned outside cabins on three decks, plenty of public space, and a small, refreshing swimming pool. There is one crew member for every two passengers and a qualified Egyptologist-escort offers daily briefings on the historic sites. The Nile Explorer and Nile Discoverer programs feature a 5-day (4-night) *Sun Boat* cruise between Luxor and Aswan, while the Pharaohs and Pyramids includes two extra days in Aswan for a one-week Nile cruise. A & K prices are high, but so is the quality of service and experience.

More recent to A & K's extensive offerings is barge cruising on the delightful rivers and canals of France, England, and Holland/Belgium. It is simply ''the best way to travel,'' according to Gerard Morgan-Grenville, author of several books on the subject and owner of two very special charter barges, *Virginia Anne* and *Fleur De Lys*—both marketed by A & K.

The 7-passenger *Fleur de Lys,* considered the flagship of the A & K fleet, is the most elegant and spacious vessel on any inland waterway. Her accommodations boast a suite with king-size bed and bathroom with full tub and twin sinks. There is a baby grand piano in the antique-filled main salon and a heated swimming pool on the aft deck. (As yet, no other charter barge features such impressive amenities—although *The Princess,* industrialist Ludwig's 10-passenger charter vessel, is not far behind.) Three-, six-, or nine-day charters are available throughout the season in Alsace, between **Nancy** and **Strasbourg** in northeastern France. Prices are stiff but include gourmet meals, wines and bar drinks, all excursions, and the loving care of the crew. Passengers are transported to and from *Fleur de Lys* from train, plane, or hotel in the area. The *Fleur de Lys* is an experience "extraordinaire," and one that my husband and I still savor.

The 6-passenger *Virginia Anne* is a charter barge with a different character—a period vessel originally built of iron in 1911. One of the pioneers of this popular way to travel, she is the subject of *Barging into France* by her owner/author Gerard Morgan-Grenville. *Virginia Anne* spends the season (April through October) in the Nivernais region of Burgundy on 3-, 6-, and 9-night cruises between **Auxerre** and **Dirol.**

Also well known as a charter vessel is the 4–8-passenger *Mark Twain,* which cruises on three routes in Bordeaux and Midi. The *Mark Twain* has four twin cabins, plus a spacious wood-paneled salon and sundeck with traditional ambience from a Dutch 19th-century origin. The Bordeaux cruises are between Moissac and Castets. In the Midi, *Mark Twain* covers the area between **Toulouse** and **Carcassonne** or **Carcassonne** to **Agde.** The fourth charter barge in the A & K fleet is *Alouette,* converted in 1986 to a canal boat for 6 passengers. *Alouette* offers cruises from April to November throughout Burgundy and the Loire valley.

Hotel barges generally carry more passengers (in smaller cabins) and are individually booked. They include the 22-passenger *L'Abercrombie* on 3-to 9-night cruises in lower Burgundy, the 20-passenger *Litote* (Understatement) on 6-night cruises in central Burgundy, and the 22-passenger *Lafayette* in **Sancerre** and the Upper Loire Valley for 3 or 6 nights. Hotel barges are less pricey and great fun—my husband and I took *Litote* about ten years ago and have fond memories. We still correspond with some fellow passengers. Travelers are met in Paris, usually at the Hotel Lutetia-Concorde on the Left Bank, for transportation to the barge. During the cruise, ballooning may be available for an extra charge of about $200 per person. Drifting slowly over the vineyards of France is a sensation worth the money!

The 12-passenger *Actief* is A & K's offering on English waterways. Converted from a Dutch clipper in 1977, the *Actief* cruises the River Thames between **Windsor** and **Shillingford Bridge** (a few miles from Oxford). The 3- or 6-night cruises along the so-called Queen's Waterway feature the playing fields of Eton, the spires of Oxford University, and some charming little villages. The *Actief* is a comfortable vessel with a total English atmosphere. In the low countries, the 17-passenger *Rembrandt* offers a choice of cruises round-trip from **Amsterdam** or **Amsterdam/Bruges.** The Dutch-owned and -managed *Rembrandt* has six twin staterooms, the Van Gogh and Rembrandt suites, and one single cabin. The Holland cruises visit Kaag, The Hague, the famous cheese town of Alkmaar, and Marken. (When we were aboard a few years ago, a rijstaeffel farewell dinner was a nice complement to the hearty Dutch food served daily!) The Amsterdam to Bruges itinerary features Haarlem, Delft, the other famous cheese town of Gouda, Hansweert, Ghent, and Bruges.

Abercrombie and Kent reinstated its China tours in 1990, including Yangtze River cruises aboard the 68-passenger *Bashan*—the vessel formerly utilized by Lindblad Travel (now bankrupt). The well-appointed *Bashan* boasts 26 cabins and 8 suites, all with private facilities and large picture windows, a swimming pool, single-seating dining room, library, glass-enclosed observation area, and many other modern amenities. The 5-night sailings can be booked on a cruise-only basis and all feature the famed Yangzi Gorge between Chonqqing and Yichang. *Bashan* is now under exclusive contract to A & K; cruise director Bill Hursh, who has guided the vessel since the maiden voyage and is also a special consultant to the Yangzi River Shipping Company, is happily on board.

In addition to Galapagos Island cruises aboard the 34-passenger *Isabella II* (which other tour operators also utilize), A & K offers travelers 4- or 7-day sailings along the Turkish coastline in the Gulf of Fethiye aboard the 30-passenger M.Y. *Halas*. A former Bosphorus Sea ferry recently converted to a private yacht, *Halas* boasts three French double, eight standard twin, two large twin, and two sumptuous suites (Lycian and Bridal) as well as a crew of 26 to cater Turkish/Continental cuisine, local wines, and two well-stocked bars, and all watersports equipment. The *Halas* also boasts such modern amenities as cellular telephones and Fax machines!

Last but not least of A & K's diverse cruise offerings is the 36-passenger *Island Explorer,* a twin-hulled catamaran sailing among Indonesia's exotic Spice Islands. The one-week programs can be combined for longer cruises and have such enticing names as Sandalwood and Dragons, Dance of Welcome, Volcanos, and Wildlife (see cruise ship listings for more information on *Island Explorer*).

BARGE ABOUT FRANCE

B & D de Vogue International
P.O. Box 1998
Visalia, CA 93279
tel: (209) 733–7119
   (800) 444–1188

Barge About France represents six privately owned hotel barges on the waterways of France. President of the company is Patricia de Vogue, Comtesse Walewska, who offers passengers private visits to the chateaux of her relatives and friends. She mentions particularly her sister, Duchesse Pozzo di Borgo, who could open her Chateau de Dangu near Monet's former home in Giverny, and a cousin, Comtesse de Vogue, with Chateau de Commarin in one of the loveliest parts of Burgundy. Even as a paying guest, it sounds interesting! There are a total of 70 chateaux in France available through this company.

The fleet of hotel barges offered by B & D de Vogue tours has also grown—to six—all with a Moet & Chandon champagne welcome on 3- or 6-night cruises. The newly converted hotel/charter barge *Lady A* can be found on the famous Canal de Bourgogne between **Dijon** and **Pouilly-en-Auxois.** Captain/owner David Bourne and wife Lisa will share their passion for the countryside and personally escort wine tastings as well as host a typical Burgundian feast ashore one evening! *Lady A* accommodates just 6 passengers in three twin cabins and a crew of three.

Reine Pedauque also cruises Burgundy on 3- or 6-night programs that begin and end in **Dijon.** The charter barge carries 10 to 12 passengers and a crew of five on gourmet cruises through the heart of "Grand Crus" country, which the *Reine Pedauque* captain knows well, and offers a view of some private vineyards. The 8-passenger *Anjodi* is a hotel/charter barge on the 300-year-old Canal du Midi, and passengers are escorted from and to **Montpellier** for the 3- and 6-night cruises. The *Anjodi* has four twin cabins (air-conditioned) and a crew of four. Also on the Canal du Midi, enjoying the quiet splendor of the region known as Languedoc, is the 12-passenger *Athos*, with welcoming by the captain in either **Toulouse** or **Montpellier** for 3- or 6-night cruises. The *Athos* has five twin and one double cabin (air-conditioned) and a crew of five.

The beautiful Canal de la Marne au Rhin in Alsace-Lorraine is where the *Stella* cruises, carrying 8 passengers in four twin cabins. This is a lovely area, and the *Stella* program features excursions through lakes and forests of the Parc de Lorraine and Forest of Fenetrange, with a special visit to view the 18th-century architecture of Nancy. The *Royal Cognac* cruises the Charente River, which French King Francois I called "the most beautiful stream" in his kingdom. A tasting at the Hennessey distillery, home of the most prestigious cognac in the world, and some private eau-de-vie makers is one of the cruise highlights. The *Royal Cognac* carries 8 passengers and a crew of four on 3- and 6-night cruises. Pick-up and drop-off of passengers is **Angouleme.** Moorings include Port d'Envaux, La Beyne, Chez Lardard, Cognac, and Carde Moulin for the barge.

One-hour balloon flights are available on most itineraries for $250 per person per hour. Transfers from your hotel in Paris by private car to the railway station and round-trip high-speed express train (TGV) tickets are available for approximately U.S. $250–$300 per person.

CRUISE COMPANY

33 Lewis Street
Greenwich, CT 06830
tel: (203) 622–0203
   (800) 825–0826

Cruise Company has been offering barging holidays since 1976 through veteran John Liley, whose book *France—the Quiet Way* is definitive on the subject. The 14-passenger, 6-crew *Luciole* was completed under Liley's direction, and cruises the waterways of western Burgundy—the canals de Bourgogne and Nivernais between Dijon, Auxerre, and Nevers. Passengers visit the famous vineyards and historic sites of the region on daily excursions. Personally escorted service between **Paris** and **Dijon** via high-speed (TGV) train is available for approximately $150 per person.

Cruise Company also represents the *Shannon Princess,* a former Dutch barge accommodating 12 passengers in four twins, one double, and two single cabins. The *Shannon Princess* is the largest vessel to navigate the lovely Shannon River and surrounding lakes. Guests are met at Shannon Airport on Sundays and escorted to the hotel barge for the 6-night sojourn that culminates in a traditional Irish medieval banquet! The itinerary also features visits to Limerick, Killaloe, Nenagh, Dromineer, Portumna, and many, many singing pubs along the way!

And, if you have wondered what ever became of the *Sea Cloud,* the famous yacht built by E. F. Hutton for his bride, Marjorie Meriweather Post, Cruise Company has the particulars and you can book here! *Sea Cloud* sails the Caribbean from Antigua during the winter months and in the Mediterranean during the summer season.

ESPLANADE TOURS

581 Boylston Street
Boston, MA 02116
tel: (617) 266–7465
  (800) 628–4893

Esplanade Tours has exclusive representation for the six-passenger *Berendina*, owned and operated by Captain Roy Smith and Jill. The 70-foot charter barge accommodates 4 to 6 passengers and is comfortable—the aft cabin even has a bathtub! The *Berendina* cruises the Canal du Midi from early April to late October. Much emphasis is placed on food and wines, and private vineyards are visited during the week. Roy and Jill have spent 20 years in France and everything is included in the cruise price, including drinks. Captain Smith has a small house near Narbonne on the Canal du Midi, and invites his guests to enjoy a meal overlooking the waterway—with the Pyrenees in the distance.

In the Midi, the *Berendina* cruises between **Carcassone** and **Beziers** on a weekly Wednesday to Tuesday program. Beziers is considered the wine capital of the Languedoc region and Carcassonne is a medieval walled city in Mediterranean France. Excursions by mini-bus feature the pink city of Toulouse, the market town of Mirepoix, and Bassin de St. Ferreol—where picnics are popular.

Jacqueline Keith, president of Esplanade Tours, also represents sister hotel/charter barges *La Tulipe* and *Vios*. Both are owned and operated by young English couples who share their love of Burgundy with just 4 passengers each in twin bedded (no bunks) cabins. The *Vios* hosts are Captain Jon Brine and chef Trini Brine, who invite you to their "house party" barge. Cruising in tandem with *Vios* is *La Tulipe,* with Captain Richard van Wissen and chef Viola van Wissen. Together the two barges cover Burgundy from early April through October, following the Canal de Bourgogne, River Saone, Canal du Centre to Canal Lateral a la Loire, Canal de Briare, River Yonne, and Canal du Nivernas. The two barges sound delightful, with very personal and caring service, and seem ideal for family or friends traveling together.

Jackie Keith represents the deluxe, 8-passenger *Panache* in Alsace and Franche-Comte, where the local specialties are crystal, antiques, pottery, wines, and foie gras. The Wednesday to Tuesday programs feature **Strasbourg** to **LaGarde** and **Dole** to **Montbeliard,** with a Michelin-starred restaurant included during the program. The vessel is available for full charter only, and rates include all gourmet meals, wines, and bar drinks, as well as sightseeing and excursions.

Jackie is also the sole representative of Swan Hellenic Cruises, which is famous for its Nile sailings with Egyptologists aboard the 68-passenger *Nile Star* between Cairo and Aswan. The vessel has both single- and twin-bed cabins, an attractive lounge/bar, and one-seating dining room. On the upper deck is a small reference library and sunning area. The programs are **London/London,** with excellent guides who render lectures, maps and reading lists.

These are definitely among the very best cruises up and down the Nile offered, and there are several different itineraries and lengths available from 9-day Luxor/Aswan cruises (with optional land extensions to St. Catherine's Monastery and Mount Sinai or to Israel) to 17-day Cairo/Aswan or 17 days on the Upper Nile (Aswan/Abydos/Aswan). Jackie can quote complete rates from the U.S. and arrange all air transportation.

A more recent addition for Swan Hellenic are 500-mile Rhine/Moselle cruises aboard the 90-passenger *Poseidon,* a spacious vessel flying the Dutch flag. Air-conditioned cabins have large picture windows and private facilities. There is a comfortable lounge/bar, single seating dining room, and large Sun Deck. The all-inclusive 10-day cruises are **London**/Cologne/Basle/**London.** What a wonderful way to see "the heart of Europe," especially in the spring and early fall. All sailings are accompanied by a guest lecturer and cruise manager, and are exclusive to Swan Hellenic.

EXPRINTER

500 Fifth Avenue
New York, NY 10110
tel: (212) 719–1200
   (800) 221–1666

Fred Mayer represents the *Danube Princess* on one-week cruises from Passau to Durnstein, Bratislava, Budapest, Esztergom, Vienna, and Melk. Passengers are escorted between Passau and Munich Airport for flights to and from the U.S. The participating carrier is Pan Am.

The 364-foot *Danube Princess* was built in Germany and launched in March 1983. Two years of planning and design result in four comfortable passenger decks, full air conditioning, a one-seating dining room, and open-air swimming pool. There are 101 cabins to accommodate 215 passengers (with a crew of 62). There is a large wood-paneled main lounge with picture windows, bar, small library, hairdresser, Information bureau, and small onboard shop for newspapers, film, cigarettes, etc. Cabins are spacious for a riverboat and have telephone, TV and radio, telephone, and private facilities.

Meals aboard the *Danube Princess* reflect the European crew, the passing countryside, and the passenger complement. There are American or English breakfasts, German/Austrian/Hungarian/Italian specialties at lunch or dinner, and local wines. Bouillon at 11 a.m. and a midnight buffet are also available. Jacket and tie is expected for dinner and there is evening entertainment and dancing in the lounge. The small onboard orchestra also plays during the day—since the River Danube has been a muse to many composers and musicians in the environs.

Passengers are met at the *Danube Princess* counter at **Munich** Airport and treated to a bus tour of the Bavarian capital before lunch in the countryside at Altotting. A brief visit here includes an organ recital in the cathedral before boarding the riverboat in Passau where the Danube, Inn, and Ilz rivers meet. The vessel sails at 7:30 p.m. that evening (Saturday) and spends all the next day cruising the river. Sunday evening is spent in Durstein, Austria, heart of the Wachau region. All day Monday is spent in Bratislava, Czechoslovakia, the capital of the federative Slovak Socialist Republic and 16th-century capital of Hungary. Tuesday is Budapest, Hungary—the Queen of the Danube, with the ancient city of Buda on one side of the river and the younger Pest on the other.

The ship docks in Esztergrom, cradle of Hungarian Christianity, on Wednesday afternoon for a tour of this town founded 1000 years ago by St. Stephan. All day Thursday is spent in Vienna, the Austrian capital of music, *sachertorte,* and the Spanish Riding School. Vienna is one of the great cities of the world, full of palaces, parks, theaters, and museums. The city also boasts about a thousand cafes, since coffee was introduced here by the Turks and taken very seriously. Last call is at Melk, seat of the first Austrian monarchy in 976 until Leopold III moved his court to Vienna at the end of the 11th century. On the return to Passau early Saturday morning, passengers continue along the Danube by bus via Straubing for lunch in Regensburg before the afternoon flight from Munich Airport. What a wonderful week!

The *Danube Princess* has been so successful during her five seasons on one of the world's most famous rivers that two longer sailings of 12 days and 8 countries are now available in late June and July. The vessel cruises between **Passau** and **Constanta** (Romania), and passengers fly one way. Success also breeds more ships, and the 150-passenger *Passau Princess* begins round-trip sailings from Hamburg in March 1991. A sistership to the *Danube Princess,* the slightly smaller vessel cruises the Elbe River calling in Schnackenburg (side trips to Berlin available), Tangermunde, Wittenberg, Bad Schandau (side trips to Prague available), Konigstein, Dresden, Meissen, and Magdeburg. **Passau Princess** features 75 outside cabins, heated swimming pool, library, boutique, and beauty salon, and single seating dining room.

Exprinter is also general sales agents for the *Berlin* (see cruise ship listings). All three vessels are owned and operated by Peter Deilmann Shipping and are marketed in the United States through EuropaAmerica Cruises, a division of Exprinter, located at the same address.

FIRST DANUBE STEAMSHIP COMPANY

c/o Austrian National Tourist Office
500 Fifth Avenue
New York, NY 10110
tel: (212) 994–6990

The 239-passenger *Mozart* is one of the more stylish vessels sailing the famous Danube River—in fact, the First Danube Steamship Company considers it a "five star" ship. There are 113 large cabins on board, of which 16 can be converted to suites. Each cabin is 207 square feet and features a TV, telephone, hairdryer, and double/twin beds, as well as large picture window. All cabins are on the lower Dorabella Deck, or Taminio Deck, where there is a reception area, beauty salon, and fitness center with indoor swimming pool/sauna/massage/gym/solarium. Up on Don Giovanni Deck is the main lounge with stage, game room, library, a Viennese coffee house called Amadeus, and the Magic Flute single-seating restaurant. There is also a duty-free shop on board. Top deck is the open-air Papageno Deck.

From the end of April through mid-September, *Mozart* offers 3- and 4-day segments between Vienna and Passau. Shore excursions for cruise-only passengers are not included in the fare. However, these mini sailings are combined by many tour operators into one-week or more programs of the area. Check with the Austrian National Tourist Office for a list of the operators and what they offer.

On the Canal du Bourgogne . . . a lockkeeper and barge captain catch up on local gossip!

La Litote ("the understatement") is a very special hotel barge now marketed by Abercrombie & Kent.

Noordam and *Sovereign of the Seas* prepare to depart Charlotte Amalie, St. Thomas, USVI.

The popular *CostaRiviera* returns to her Port Everglades berth on Saturday mornings.

The newly stretched *Westerdam* en route to the Caribbean.

The back end of *Star Princess* . . . a bit boxy,
but she handles "like an angel."

Royal Viking Star salutes the Statue of Liberty twice weekly during the summer season.

Celebrity Cruises' *Horizon* is escorted by a Moran tug on her arrival in New York harbor.

Nordic Prince boasts one of Royal Caribbean Cruise Line's first distinctive Crown lounges cantilevered from the smokestack.

Carnival Cruise Lines' famous logo is a familiar sight in Nassau.

The California Golden Door's eastern philosophy translates well to its spas at sea aboard the *QE2*, Cunard/NAC, and Sea Goddess ships.

FLOATING THROUGH EUROPE

271 Madison Avenue
New York, NY 10016
tel: (212) 685–5600
     (800) 221–3140

Floating Through Europe has found a successful formula during its 15 years of operation, offering 6-night cruises for 8 to 20 passengers on hotel barges throughout Holland, Belgium, France, and England. The company has been innovative in its tulip cruises, art cruises, wine and gourmet cruises in France, and Shakespeare cruises in England. For the 90s, Floating Through Europe has extended its operation from April 1 to early November.

Floating Through Europe caters to people who know better and like it. Not everyone is suited to the spirit and intimacy of barge travel—but those who are, certainly enjoy cheerful cabins (albeit tiny) and memorable meals. They are also pleased with well-planned excursions in the barge's own mini-bus, which miraculously appears at every mooring. The FTE six-member barge fleet offers comfortable accommodations, good private facilities, charming public areas, and pleasant crew. FTE does not stint, especially when satisfying passengers' palates! Young Cordon Bleu graduates do the planning, shopping, and cooking; and the meals are mainly *nouvelle cuisine* (no matter which country one happens to be cruising through)! Fresh produce is purchased almost daily from the local markets, and you can count on plenty of wonderful and interesting cheeses, pates, breads, and salads, not to mention the local bottled grape that is carefully chosen to complement the menus.

In the Burgundy wine country, the 22-passenger *Janine* offers a round-trip program from **Dijon** on the River Saone, Canal du Centre, and the Canal de Bourgogne. The *Janine* has been in Burgundy since 1979 and was the first nonperson to be honored by the French Wine Society when she was made a member of the Confrerie St. Vincent et Disciples de la Chanteflute de Mercurey. She is noted for having aboard Jean Michel Lafond, a professor of gastronomy at Dijon University and popular raconteur of the area.

Guests are met in Dijon at the Hotel de la Cloche and bussed to the *Janine* in **Montceau-les-Mines** for a champagne welcome and dinner. The barge cruises to St. Julien, Fragnes, Chalon, Seurre, and St. Jean de Losne, with many calls (by mini-van) at famous vineyards for tastings and visits to the historic sites along the way. Highlights include a visit to Clos de Vougeot, where the Confrerie des Chevaliers du Tastevin meet and the Gregorian chants of the monks at the abbey of Citeaux. Hot-air balloon flights by Air Escargot (!) can be arranged on board for an additional fee (about $200 per person).

The 14-passenger *Linguenda* cruises Champagne country between **Paris** and **Reims** along the River Seine, the River Marne, Canal Lateral a l'Aisne, and the River Aisne, calling at Meaux, Chateau Thierry, Damery, Tours-sur-Marne, Sillery, and Reims. Passengers tour Hautvillers (where monk Dom Perignon "invented champagne"), the Cathedral of Notre Dame in Reims, and other monuments of this historic region known for Joan of Arc, Napoleon III, and two costly world wars. Champagne tastings are organized in the private caves of Moet and Chandon and Dom Ruinart—the oldest champagne house in existence. Dom Ruinart was a disciple of Dom Perignon, and the limestone caves in Reims are a "national treasure." A hot-air balloon flight by Air Champagne can be arranged on board for an extra per-person fee.

In the south of France the 8-passenger *Bonjour* cruises between **Carcassonne** and **Port Beziers**. Passengers are met in **Montpellier** and escorted to their hotel barges moored on the Canal du Midi just above Carcassonne. Historic and beautiful places en route are Marseillette, Homps, Paraza, and Capestang. The Sunday to Saturday programs begin with a complimentary stay at the Hotel Sofitel in Montpellier and end with a farewell at **Montpellier**'s railway station.

In Alsace Lorraine, the 8-passenger *Lys* cruises between **Strasbourg** and **Nancy** on a Sunday to Saturday schedule along the Canal de la Marne Rhin. Stops along the way include Waltenheim, Saverne, Lutzelbourg, Niderville, and Einville. There are lovely drives through this beautiful scenery as well as wine-tastings of the refreshing white of the Alsace region. There are plenty of tow paths for walking, cycling, or jogging, and plenty to see—satisfying everyone's taste.

Returning for another season on the River Avon are the *Beverly* and *Jean,* a pair of traditional English "wide boats" decorated with roses and castle insignia, which travel in tandem on Shakespeare-country cruises. This delightful pair is especially charming in the world of river barges, for one vessel is fitted with six cabins for 12 passengers and the other is for dining, the galley, and the crew's quarters. The *Beverly* is the service boat and the *Jean* is for changing and sleeping. The two have been cruising this river together since 1978 and are well known on this pastoral waterway. The food is delicious and served on Royal Worcester china made in the area, as passengers float peacefully between **Stratford-upon-Avon** and **Tewkesbury.** The week includes healthy walks on the banks of the Avon, helping with the self-service locks of the river, and side excursions to snug little villages, stately manor houses, the Royal Worcester Porcelain Works, the Norman abbey at Tewkesbury, and an evening at the Royal Shakespeare theater. This is a wonderful part of England, and passengers soon understand why the world's number one playwright made his home here.

Passengers on all River Avon cruises are escorted to and from central London with meeting point at Cadogan Hotel.

Delightful Holland is offered aboard the 18-passenger *Juliana,* which sails round trip from **Amsterdam** every Sunday from June through October. The Dutch-built vessel cruises the River Amstel, Becht, Lek, and in the 19th-century North Sea Canal to Haarlem. Other stops include Leidschendam, Gouda, Schonhoven, and Ouderkerk. Passengers are met at the Schiphol Hilton and escorted back to the airport.

During tulip time, the 24-passenger *Juliana* and the 14-passenger *Linguenda* join the *Lys* on three- and six-night floral cruises from early April through May. This is a wonderful way to see the flowers and this beautiful country of canals and dikes in the spring.

Floating Through Europe offers all-inclusive cruises, even with bar drinks, and takes excellent care of its passengers. Many of the vessels can be chartered—for the whole family—and the chefs promise American-style food for the young people. Special cruises in delightful Belgium are also offered from time to time during the season, usually by popular demand.

Life is forever exciting at Floating Through Europe!

FRENCH COUNTRY WATERWAYS, LTD.

P.O. Box 2195
Duxbury, MA 02331
tel: (617) 934–2454
    (800) 222–1236

French Country Waterways, Ltd., has blossomed recently through the marketing and management of the *Nenuphar, Horizon II,* and *Liberte* (former Horizon Cruises vessels) as well as the *Esprit,* which is owned and operated by FCW owners Jim and Pat Tyng. The lovely *Esprit* was completed in 1986 under the supervision of Charlie Pope, a veteran hotel barge captain formerly with Horizon and Continental Waterways, who commands the 18-passenger vessel. *Esprit* cruises from April to October between **Nancy/Strasbourg,** Strasbourg/Montreux-Chateau, Montreaux-Chateau/Dole and **Vandenesse/Auxonne.** Under such fine tutelage, passengers aboard *Esprit* can enjoy a very special experience and plenty of information on the cruising areas.

Horizon II is the flagship of Horizon Cruises, a company owned by Chicago attorney Rex Carr. For the past few years, the vessels were marketed by Hemphill-Harris, a California-based tour operator and another disaster of 1989. The three-barge fleet is now in the good hands of the Tyngs who will market and manage the vessels with loving care. *Horizon II* accommodates a dozen passengers and a crew of six on Canal de Bourgogne cruises through the popular Cote d'Or (golden coast) Burgundy wine region between **Pouilly-en-Auxois** and **Dijon.** *Horizon II* is decorated with oriental carpets and antiques and features one suite, one double, and four twin cabins—all air-conditioned.

The *Nenuphar* (water lily) also accommodates 12 guests and a crew of six in air-conditioned comfort with all luxurious suites furnished in French antiques. *Nenuphar* cruises the northern section of Canal de Bourgogne between **Montbard** and **Tonnerre,** with escorted visits to the 18th-century Forges de Buffon, the 12th-century Abbaye de Fontenay, and the 16th-century d'Ancy-le-Franc, as well as the vineyards of Chablis.

The 10-passenger *Liberte* explores the romantic Canal du Nivernais between Auxerre and Villiers. This area produces France's famous chablis wines and ballooning over the vineyards is an option (approximately $225 per person) on *Liberte* and other French Country Waterways cruises. The three Horizon Cruises vessels all depart on Sundays (the *Esprit* on Saturdays) from April through October. Passengers are escorted to and from Paris to their luxury hotel barge.

FRENCH CRUISE LINES

701 Lee Street
Des Plaines, IL 60016
tel: (708) 824–4577
    (800) 222–8664

French Cruise Lines is a new company operating two 100-passenger vessels, the *Arlene* and the *Normandie,* on weekly cruises from late March/early April through October. Both vessels feature French crew, ambience, and cuisine, and have been constructed to navigate the Seine through Normandy and the Rhone and Saone through Provence. They are the first vessels of their size and type on these rivers as most others are former working barges converted to accommodating 4–24 passengers and offering luxury floating hotel service for 6 nights.

French Cruise Lines is an affiliate of AHI International, an American tour operator based in Chicago that has offered unusual charter cruises to special interest and alumni groups for almost three decades, and Aqua Viva—a French shipping company that constructed and owns the ships. The twin vessels have just two passenger decks on which are located air-conditioned cabins with large windows, color TV, multichannel music system, hairdryer, climate controls, telephone, and tiled bathroom. A single seating dining room, lounge, and spacious sun deck complete the picture.

The *Arlene* sails the Rhone and Saone rivers between **Avignon** and **Macon,** calling at Arles, Viviers, Tournon, Vienne, and Lyon. Optional excursions are available to Berze, Cluny, Ardeche, Grignan Castle, and the Camargue's Les Saintes Maries de la Mer. These one-week Provence-Burgundy cruises operate continuously from the end of March through October in alternate directions. The *Normandie* can be found on the River Seine between **Honfleur** and **Paris.** The 6-night cruises visit Rouen, Villequier, Caudebec, and Les Andelys, with optional full-day excursions to Bayeaux, Caen, and the famous Omaha Beach along the Norman coastline. The highlight of the cruise is sailing into the ''City of Lights'' on the Seine, the evening before disembarkation.

HILTON INTERNATIONAL

P.O. Box 257
Cairo, Egypt
or
tel: (800) 445–8667

The Nile Hilton in Cairo operates two of the most popular boats that cruise the Nile River—the 270-foot, 90-passenger twin vessels, the *Isis* and *Osiris,* which sail between Luxor and Aswan on four-night/five-day excursions year-round. These vessels are alike, simple but very comfortable, and are considered as floating hotels of Hilton International standards. A number of top-quality tour operators who specialize in Egypt, use the twins. The vessels were overhauled recently and are very popular for short Nile cruises.

The *Isis* and *Osiris* have four passenger decks and are fully air conditioned. The cabins, small and simple, can sleep from one to three persons in all outside accommodations with private facilities. On the top, or Bridge Deck, are a good swimming pool, open sitting area with awning, and enclosed lounge. The first deck has a pleasant dining room with bar, a lounge, and a small boutique. The front office and beauty salon are located on the main deck, along with passenger cabins, and the lower deck is all accommodations. Although Egypt bills itself as a year-round destination, the best time for cruising along the Nile falls between September and the end of May, when the days are sunny and warm and the nights cool. From December through February the weather is also pleasant, although the evenings can be chilly. June through August should be avoided if you cannot take heat and bone-dry air (the vessels are well air conditioned, but the monuments are not). At all times of the year, though, the sightseeing excursions occur only during early morning and late afternoon hours, because the Egyptians fully agree that "only mad dogs and Englishmen" are crazy enough to sit in the midday sun.

The ships alternate sailing every five days from **Luxor** to **Aswan** and vice versa. The Luxor/Aswan itinerary includes the great temples of Luxor, Karnak, and Abydos. You will visit the Temple of Hatour, Thebes' Necropolis, Valley of the Kings, and Tomb of Tutankhamon. The Temple of Queen Hatshepsut at Deir al Bahri, the romantic Valley of the Nobles, the Valley of the Queens, the Temple of Medinet Habu, and the famed Colossi of Memnon will awe you. Then, an early morning departure for Esna takes you to the Temple of Esna and on to the Temple of Horus (237 B.C.), the most complete example of the remaining Egyptian temples. During your last day you will see the Ptolemic Temple of Kom Ombo, with its beautiful murals, fascinating reliefs, and fine view of the river. A morning sailing to Aswan includes a visit to the Botanical Island and Mausoleum of Agha Khan by *feluccas* (small native sailing craft).

K.D. GERMAN RHINE LINE

Rhine Cruise Agency
170 Hamilton Avenue
Suite 317
White Plains, NY 10601
tel: (914) 948–3600
or
Suite 619
323 Geary Street
San Francisco, CA 94102
tel: (415) 392–8817

KD German Rhine Line is well on to its 165th anniversary in operating passenger services on the river that flows through the very heart of Europe. The Rhine has often determined the course of European history. It flows from the romantic Alps of Switzerland and France to the rugged North Sea—820 miles of important trade routes, historic towns and cities, and cultural monuments that give a fine taste of the civilizations that developed here for several centuries. The river touches upon the banks of four European countries—Switzerland, France, Germany, and Holland—and the variety of scenery you pass through and impressions you receive will seem endless. It's exhilarating to cruise along this stalwart waterway trying to absorb almost 2000 years of art and history.

This is the ''rich and romantic'' Rhine, where the famed Lorelei reclined some 433 feet above, combing her locks and singing a siren song that lured fishermen to the rocky shores. Here Caesar's legions bridged the floodwaters and General Eisenhower battled the army of Hitler. Industrial areas spew saffron smoke into the air, a stark contrast to the castles dating from the 12th century when you could almost see the dragons who inhabited the cliffs. Wooded hills, vineyards, and the spire of a distant church all tease the senses.

KD German Rhine Line operates some 28 different passenger vessels, including eight comfortable cruise liners: the *Deutschland, Britannia, France, Nederland, Austria, Italia, Helvetia,* and *Europa.* The ships average about 330 feet long and 40 feet wide, and sail about 10 miles per hour upstream, 16 miles per hour downstream. Each vessel carries about 200 passengers in clean and simple all-outside cabins, which have one sofa-bed, one folding bed, a large window, and private facilities. The public areas feature a spacious observation lounge with double-length windows for uninterrupted views of the river and a cozy bar, reading room, dining room, and shopping arcade.

All the ships have large sun decks and, except for the *Italia* and *Austria,* all have a heated outdoor swimming pool. The cuisine on board favors Continental specialties, with plentiful Rhine and Moselle wines at moderate prices. On four of the vessels—the *Europa, Austria, Helvetia,* and *Italia*—simple dining offers buffet breakfasts and three-course luncheons and dinners. This, instead of served breakfasts and five-course meals the rest of the day, results in lower prices (by about thirty percent) as compared to ships with First and more elegant service.

These eight vessels sail from the source of the Rhine to its mouth between April and the end of October, with some special cruises offered in December. It takes one week to ''do'' the river, but most of the sailings range from two to five days in either direction. Major places of interest along the way include Basel, Strasbourg, Braubach, Speyer, Koblenz, Bonn, Cologne, Rudesheim, and Nijmegen. The ships anchor each evening along the riverbank, so passengers can take a stroll after dinner or go into the nearest village for a beer, and get underway again in the wee hours of the morning.

A few years ago, my husband and I spent a delightful three days on board the first-class *Deutschland* from Dusseldorf to Cologne, Boppard, and Mainz during a special Karneval Cruise, and it was great fun. Although the weather outside was cold and rainy, inside the ship was warm and inviting and everyone was in good form, roaming the wet/cold streets of Cologne, watching the Rose Monday parade in Mainz, or attending a local Karneval Ball in costume (well, as much costume as I could persuade my husband to wear!). We were both impressed by how friendly the people along the Rhine River really are, and how comfortable the *Deutschland* was. Although cabins are small (and bathrooms even smaller), the main salon and dining room are spacious. Wine and beer is served with lunch and dinner and you may dine heavy or light. As the ships dock right in the middle of town or city, there is never a problem walking around on your own. Cruising any waterway is a delightful way to spend a few days; we found the Rhine River and *Deutschland* exceeded our expectations.

KD German Rhine Line has so many different programs each season that it is somewhat difficult to keep abreast. More than 350 different cruises are scheduled during the season. First-class cruises on *Britannia* and *Deutschland* follow the Rhine through Switzerland, France, Germany, and Holland. Three-country first-class cruises operate between **Strasbourg** and **Amsterdam.** Four-country Europa-class cruises operate between **Basle** and **Nijmegen.** Two- and three-day Rhineland Explorer cruises operate between Frankfurt on the Main and Cologne. The *Europa* offers a total of 75 short cruises along the Moselle River between **Koblenz** and **Trier,** where dry white Rieslings are world famous.

Theme cruises each season feature Floating Wine Seminars, Waterways of Holland cruises that circle the country from Rotterdam to Nijmegen, and Christmas/New Year cruises.

There are also some new programs in conjunction with First Danube Steamship Company's elegant *Mozart.* And, in summer and early fall, over a dozen Rhine in Flames cruises are scheduled, which feature spectacular fireworks at four places along the river: the wine village of **Rudesheim; Koblenz,** where the Rhine and Moselle rivers meet; **Oberwesel,** a town dominated by Schonburg Castle; and **Goarshusen,** beneath the Lorelei rock.

In early 1990, officials from KD German Rhine Line of Cologne and VEB White Fleet of Dresden met to discuss a joint venture for cruises on the Elbe River. The 4- to 5-day cruises would operate between Hamburg, West Germany's largest city and port, and the East German cultural capital of Dresden, beginning in 1991.

SHERATON NILE CRUISES

Sheraton Hotels
P.O. Box 125
Orman, Giza
Egypt
or any Sheraton reservations center

Sheraton Hotels in Egypt operates four identical hotel barges year-round on the Nile River between Luxor and Aswan. These 89-cabin vessels built in Scandinavia, named the *Tut, Aton, Anni,* and *Htop,* have a total of about 25 sailings each month of either four or seven nights. The 235-foot barges carry 178 passengers in two-berth cabins (some have an additional berth for a third person). All accommodations have private facilities, air conditioning, and lots of wardrobe space. In addition, each barge has a large restaurant and lounge/bar that converts to a disco in the evening. Live entertainment, a swimming pool, and a sun deck that is popular at cocktail time provide pleasant distractions. Two meal seatings offer lunch at noon or 1:15 p.m. and dinner at 7 p.m. or 8:15 p.m. All meals, plus afternoon tea, shore excursions, and entertainment are included in the cruise fare.

The four-night cruises visit the temples at Luxor and Karnak, the Valley of the Kings, Esna, Edfu, Kom Ombo, and Aswan. The seven-night itinerary features Luxor and Karnak, Thebes, Nag 'Hammadi, Abydos, Dendera, Esna, Edfu, Kom Ombo, and Aswan/Elephantine/Kitchener/Aga Khan Mausoleum as well as the High Dam/Old Dam, granite quarries, and Philae Temple. The order of sites reverses when the barges sail from **Aswan** to **Luxor.** These are spacious vessels—perfect for travelers who enjoy having a little legroom.

ADMIRAL CRUISES INC.

1220 Biscayne Boulevard
P.O. Box 010882
Miami, FL 33101
tel: (305) 374–1611
    (800) 327–2056

In the fall of 1986 Eastern, Western, and Sundance Cruises combined to form one company called Admiral Cruises—to operate the *Emerald Seas* from Miami, the *Azure Seas* from Los Angeles, and the *Stardancer* to Alaska and Mexico from the west coast. The combined fleet had a capacity for more than 2700 passengers in a variety of 3-, 4-, and 7-day cruises.

Through a number of maneuverings with parent company Royal Admiral and sister ship line Royal Caribbean Cruise Line, Admiral Cruises has been reduced to the vessels previously operated by Western and Eastern Cruise Line—the *Emerald Seas* from south Florida and the *Azure Seas* from southern California. The former *Stardancer* has been refurbished, renamed *Viking Serenade,* and now sails under the RCCL flag to Alaska during the summer season and the Mexican Riviera in winter (her usual itineraries). There was talk of the sale of one or both Admiral vessels—since they are a bit on the older side—but negotiations seem to have failed at this writing. So, here we are—onward Admiral Cruises and all who sail with her—the price is fantastic and the vessels are well maintained and earn high marks from travel agents and past passengers.

The twin-funnel, 980-passenger *Emerald Seas* is one of the oldest ships at sea, but still steaming along as strong as ever. She was last refurbished in September 1988 and looks great.· Cabins are spacious, befitting a former ocean liner. She was the first to operate 3- and 4-night cruises to the Bahamas from Miami (since May 20, 1990, *Emerald Seas* was reberthed to Port Everglades for Bahama cruises), and a highlight is the full day at Little Stirrup Cay, the ship line's private island in the Bahama chain, which boasts four beaches, coral reefs, two lakes, calypso band, barbecue lunch, and even a straw market. In addition to normal cruise food, Admiral now offers a choice of vegetarian dishes, menus suggested by the American Heart Association, and kosher dishes supervised by the Union of Orthodox Jewish Congregations of America at lunch and dinner.

The 400-plus passenger *Azure Seas* sails Monday and Friday from San Pedro, the port for Los Angeles, to Catalina Island, San Diego (on the four-day cruises) and Ensenada, Mexico. The *Azure Seas* was the first to choose Catalina Island as a port call, and it has been most successful—also copied.

AMERICAN CANADIAN CARIBBEAN LINE

461 Water Street
P.O. Box 368
Warren, RI 02885
tel: (401) 247–0955
    (800) 556–7450

American Canadian Caribbean Line (ACCL) has been operating cruises along the New England coastline and the inland waterways of Canada as well as throughout the Caribbean for just over a quarter century, and its small vessels have sailed many more than a million miles.

It all began when Luther Blount (now in his 70s), inveterate mariner, explorer, ship designer and builder, and native Yankee took groups of friends on informal mini-cruises along the historic Erie Canal. These social expeditions became a business, aboard small ships designed and built at Blount Marine—located on the Warren River in Rhode Island. ACCL's two cruise ships depart from the Blount dock on their summer itineraries, along with a popular dinner boat—*Bay Queen*—which cruises Narragansett Bay to fashionable Newport, Rhode Island, and returns.

The two ACCL ships in operation attract middle-aged folk who have experienced the dress-up, larger vessels and are seeking a more informal and intimate atmosphere. Repeat business is over 60% and ACCL adds one new itinerary each winter season so "repeaters" need not repeat a cruise! At a time when other small ship companies have gone out of business, ACCL enjoys great success due to its special itineraries and the TLC with which passengers are treated. The entire ambience is of a "family," as this is a family-run business.

To begin the decade of the 90s and celebrate that silver anniversary with style, Blount has added a Belize/Guatemala cruise (after sailing the Yucatan coastline as well as the Gulf of Honduras and up the Rio Dulce into Lago Izabal). Long a student of Christopher Columbus and his travels to the New World, Blount is also offering two itineraries that closely follow the same routing—in anticipation of the great interest to be generated by the 500th anniversary (1992) of the explorer's arrival. And from all reports, these cruises are already popular with ACCL passengers and selling fast!

The *New Shoreham II* sails out of Warren, Rhode Island, during the summer season from June through October on 12-day cruises to the Saguenay River (with connecting buses for the return trip). On these voyages the vessel cruises the Hudson River, the Erie Canal, Lake Ontario, and the St. Lawrence and Saguenay rivers. Fall foliage cruises take place in October, and in November the *New Shoreham II* sails from Warren to West Palm Beach, Florida, on a leisurely 15-day repositioning cruise.

In December 1983 Luther Blount inaugurated his latest design in mini-cruise ships—the 80-passenger *Caribbean Prince*. The 160-foot vessel has a spacious, ultramodern interior with a yachtlike ambience. Air-conditioned cabins have large picture windows, private facilities, teakwood trim, and a choice of sleeping arrangements (twin or double). There are six nonporthole cabins below for the economy-minded. The *Caribbean Prince* also boasts the Blount specialty—a ramp that goes down from the bow and allows passengers to walk right off the ship onto the beach. Blount calls it his Bow Ramp design, a feature that enables the vessel to stop at off-beat places that other ships may not be able to reach.

During the winter season, the *Caribbean Prince* offers a unique 12-day itinerary from Cancun to the large barrier reef off Belize where the snorkeling is supposed to be superb. Passengers fly to and from Cancun to pick up the boat. Swimming, snorkeling, bonefishing, sailing (the ship carries small boats), and collecting shells are the order of the day, but tours to the local ancient sites are also available. Life is very casual on board. The cabins are rather small, so luggage should be kept to a minimum. Days are spent playing in the water or walking on the beach, and in the evening you are left to your own entertainment devices. The dining room seats all passengers at one time, and meal service is family style, with menus geared to American taste buds (and now very much on the "light" side if you so desire). There is no need to dress up; a nice sports shirt for men and a long cotton skirt for women are appropriate. The brochure advises to BYOB (bring your own bottle), although sodas are supplied. No money on board is necessary other than any gratuities you wish to present at the end of your wonderful cruise.

From mid-December through April, the *New Shoreham II* offers unusual Virgin Islands cruises of 12 days as well as some Caicos-San Salvador-Nassau itineraries. Both vessels are involved in the "footsteps of Christopher Columbus" cruises that have several different routes and should become more popular as 1992 approaches. She returns to Rhode Island from West Palm Beach in May for a series of Saguenay cruises from Warren, Rhode Island. Two Fall Foliage cruises to Montreal and Quebec are offered in late September and October.

American Canadian Line is (without doubt) a family-run company; Luther Blount's daughter, Nancy Palumbo, is Director of Operations. The ship line's philosophy is cruising areas that are "uncommon, unhurried and unspoiled." While the ships are small and cabin space cramped, passengers find a big welcome and most friendly atmosphere on board. Rates are also among the lowest in the cruise industry—an incentive for repeaters.

The venerable Luther Blount has also designed and built in his shipyard the restaurant day-cruisers *Spirit of New York, Boston* and *Chicago,* as well as *The Spirit* of Norfolk, VA. The boats are very comfortable and are a wonderful way to spend a few hours seeing a skyline by water. His latest invention, we are told, is a head (toilet) that flushes silently on one pint of water!

AMERICAN HAWAII CRUISES

550 Kearny Street
San Francisco, CA 94108
tel: (415) 392–9400
    (800) 765–7000

American Hawaii Cruises has just celebrated a full decade of sailing among the God-given islands of our 50th state. The company has survived and offers excellent value where others have failed—namely, Aloha Pacific *(Monterey)* and Exploration (with its executive catamaran that never caught on). While the ship line experienced some rough weather in its start-up days, and has changed ownership in the past few years, it offers a consistent itinerary—and a most beautiful one—so that passengers know what to expect and where they are going.

It all began when the late C. Y. Tung, a Hong Kong shipping magnate, bought the famous *Independence,* a 30,000-ton vessel built at the Bethelehem Quincy shipyard in Massachusetts and formerly a member of American Export Lines' fleet. The Tung Group refurbished the vessel in Taiwan, and Congress approved her return to U.S. registry and cruising the warm waters of Hawaii. It was a wonderful idea and, although the Tung Group is no longer involved and Chinese/American businessman Peter Huang is, the idea has proven successful.

The 30,000-ton *Constitution,* a true sister ship of the *Independence* and also built at Bethelehem Quincy Shipyards in Massachusetts in 1951 for American Export Line, was also returned to U.S.-flag status by executive order in the early months of 1982. At inauguration the late Princess Grace of Monaco smashed a bottle of champagne against the ship's bow in Kaohsiung, Taiwan, where the vessel was being refurbished for inter-Hawaiian-island cruises. The *Constitution* was always a favorite of the Princess. As Academy-award-winning movie star Grace Kelly, she sailed aboard the *Constitution* to her fairy-tale wedding and principality on the Cote d'Azur. She later boarded the vessel with her Monarch-of-Monaco husband, Prince Rainier, and then took an additional voyage alone.

The *Constitution* is the more glamorous of the two ladies, and a lovely writing room has been dedicated to the late princess as a fitting tribute. The Constitution Lounge is also a handsome public room, although Commodore Harry Wu prefers the smaller Friendship Bridge Room for his many cocktail parties. Commodore Wu is a wonderful person, and he runs an excellent ship. Shanghai-born, the captain came to the United States after the second world war and is now a proud citizen. Both his crew and passengers adore him, and he makes many fans for the ship line.

The recent $25-million-dollar refurbishment of both vessels features new interiors in public rooms and cabins designed by a Honolulu firm and prints by Hawaiian artist Pegge Hopper. In addition to routine maintenance while in drydock, the vessels received new bridge and lifeboat equipment as well as a careful U.S. Coast Guard inspection. Other improvements include Owner's Suites on both vessels, with another small cabin attached for children-nanny or valet! A new director of Passenger Services is on board both vessels as well as notable changes in entertainment, service levels, uniforms, and menus. There is a variety of selections in lighter fare, with the variety of fresh fish available in the waters below and the abundant tropical fruits, plus the popular ice cream socials and hamburgers/hot dogs on deck every afternoon (following a day at the beach or shore excursions). Although American wines are most familiar to passengers, American Hawaii Cruises has bottled and labeled its own French sparkling wine, Grandin Blanc de Noir from the Henri Grandin family vineyards of Nantes, France—made in the Methode Champenoise process. The ship line suggests this new product as shipboard gifts or souvenirs. As expected, the atmosphere on board is "casual American"—although not so casual as it was once. Appropriate dress, including footwear, is required in the dining room.

American Hawaii's itinerary is so enjoyable that members of the World Ocean and Cruise Liner Society voted it the Number One grade of any on the market a few years ago! The *Constitution* and *Independence* sail in tandem every Saturday at 9 p.m. from the Aloha Tower near Honolulu's famed Waikiki Beach and it is a glorious sight to see. Both vessels spend the first day at sea, cruising slowly among the beautiful islands. Both visit the same islands and ports, but in reverse order, and both spend an overnight on Kauai or Maui. Other port calls are Hilo and Kona on the "big island" of Hawaii and Nawiliwili on Kauai. The vessels then meet outside Honolulu harbor to return together to the Aloha Tower.

New a few years ago and very popular are the 3- and 4-day cruises aboard either vessel between Honolulu and Hilo, with the rest of the package on one of the islands for golf, tennis, or just beach time. There are several different itineraries available in this Cruise and Resort program, including honeymoon and anniversary packages, with air supplements from North America. All-inclusive prices are very reasonable (especially from the west coast), and popular with the younger/more active set who wish to try their "sea legs" before committing to a full week's sailing. Once on board, this group finds plenty of activities in respective fitness center/health spa and super-healthy menus—just like home!

During the summer months, both the *Constitution* and *Independence* are terrific for families and there are plenty of counselors and activities on board for all age groups. To encourage families traveling together, American Hawaii offers the "free kids" program for up to two children (16 and under) sharing a cabin with two full-fare adults. The ship line's youth directors guide special activities for the young passengers, such as beach and pool parties, Captain's Coke-tail party, treasure hunts, and video games.

American Hawaii Cruises is committed to supporting the humpback whales that migrate from Alaska each winter to breed in the warm Hawaiian waters. Ship-line chairman Peter Huang has made a personal commitment to the preservation of the humpbacks through benefits and donations. He also added a Whale Gallery to each vessel, featuring color photographs of the mammals as well as migratory details and current research data. Other photos of humpbacks hang throughout the corridors of the ships.

Special one-week cruises in April are designed to generate humpback whale awareness through lectures, slide presentations, and shore excursions on Maui with experts. Researchers, photographers, and marine biologists are on board. Check with American Hawaii Cruises for exact sailings, and don't miss this added bonus of cruising among the beautiful Hawaiian Islands!

BERGEN LINE

505 Fifth Avenue
New York, NY 10017
tel: (212) 986–2711
   (800) 3–BERGEN

The original Bergen Line steamship/mail cargo system dated from 1851 in Bergen, Norway, and it provided reliable and regular service between key Norwegian coastal cities and major ports such as Hamburg (Germany) and Hull (England). The Bergen Line that we know today does not operate any coastal routes; rather it markets the products of steamship companies in Scandinavia and other travel-related firms. In 1985, Bergen Line became a subsidiary of the Kosmos Group, a Norwegian travel and transportation conglomerate.

Bergen's most popular representations are Norwegian Coastal Voyages and Fjord Steamers, all of which begin in Bergen. The voyages cover 1250 miles of Norway's western coastline via a fleet of 11 mail cargo vessels calling at some 35 villages and towns along the route to Kirkenes, which is well above the Arctic Circle. The working steamers sail year-round and offer unpretentious but comfortable accommodations plus three hearty meals a day. Passengers are encouraged to disembark to stroll on their own or sign up for an organized shore excursion. In addition to crossing the Arctic Circle, steamer travelers can trek through Lapland, photograph enormous glaciers, and walk to within 10 feet of the Russian border.

The Fjord Steamers are also working vessels—full of local passengers and cargo—which begin their journey in Bergen harbor (one of the prettiest in the world) to make 2- or 3-day minicruises to four different fjords. Fine food and clean, simple cabins are a feature of this most affordable package, but reservations well in advance are a must, as these fjord minis are very popular in summer season. Three routes are available: Bergen/Gudvangen; Bergen/Flam; and Bergen/Sandane.

Bergen Line, Inc., represents Silja Line, Gota Canal, and Gotland Line as well as Jahre Line, Norway Line, and Fred Olsen Lines. Silja Line is an overnight car/ferry servicing Helsinki, Stockholm, Turku, and Mariehamn, with a Finnjet from Helsinki to Travemunde (West Germany) in less than 23 hours. The service is very popular with Scandinavian groups and conventions because of the duty-free shopping available on board (if you saw what they must pay on land for luxury items, you would understand!)

Gota Canal offers 2- to 5-day packages across Sweden between Stockholm and Gothenburg on a slow-moving canal boat, and it is lovely in perfect weather. Gotland Line offers both ferry and catamaran service from Stockholm to Visby, Vastervik, and Oskarshamn—for travelers who loves small towns!

Jahre Line sails the 19-plus hours between Oslo and Kiel. Norway Line services Bergen, Stavanger, and Newcastle (England); and Fred Olsen Lines makes the journey between Harwich, England, and Oslo, Norway, with a stop in the delightful Danish port of Hirtshals. Bergen Line, Inc., also offers complete packages which range from kyacking in Norway to unlimited mileage in a Mercedes Benz 190—not to forget hot air ballooning and mountain climbing!

In addition to its already extensive offerings, Bergen Line now markets Baltic Shipping cruises of 4 and 5 days from Stockholm to Leningrad aboard the Russian-crew *Ilich,* with longer programs that include Helsinki. There are also sailings along the Rhine and Moselle rivers aboard the *Victoria* and the Danube aboard the *Rousse.* Programs with the 120-passenger *Victoria* feature an 8-day cruise with two days on land in Cologne. The Danube River itinerary is 11 days, with 2 nights spent in Vienna. All-inclusive packages from North America are available for both river ships. And, if you favor the far north, a 10-day Smyril line package features Iceland's Westman Islands and the Danish Faroe Islands. This one boasts a most reasonable price and appears to be made for the adventurous!

B.S.L. Cruises, Inc.

1086 Teaneck Rd.
Teaneck, NJ 07666
(201) 837–0400
tel: (800) 237–5361

This cruise company has been born yet again (and I wrote these very words in the last revision of this guide). At the time, Bahama Cruise Line had recently been renamed Bermuda Star Line to reflect its seasonal schedule from New York to Bermuda. At this writing, the name of the company is B.S.L. Cruises, Inc., and the ships no longer sail to Bermuda on a regular basis. The company is now owned by Rederi Effjohn of Scandinavia, which also owns Commodore Cruise Line and has begun another ship line in Europe called (appropriately) Europe Cruise Line. Effjohn also operates 14 ferries in Europe, under the names of Sally Line and Silja Line, but was very keen to enter the cruise business—and so it has, with fervor. Do not be surprised if Effjohn combines B.S.L. and Commodore into one ship line, soon!

B.S.L. Cruises operates the 725-passenger *Bermuda Star* and 725-passenger *Queen of Bermuda* (but not *Veracruz,* which has reportedly been sold). The vessels were renamed a few years ago (the *Queen of Bermuda* is celebrating her sixth personality), but they no longer have destination meaning. Is yet another name change on the horizon for these sister ships, which have survived so many different identities but still remain comfortable and respected vessels in the industry?

The *Queen of Bermuda* spends the fall, winter, and spring in New Orleans, offering weekly sailings to Key West, Playa del Carmen (for Cancun), and Cozumel. During repositioning cruises to New York in spring and fall, *Queen of Bermuda* "visits" the Panama Canal from 7 a.m. to 4 p.m. one day. During the summer season, the vessel offers 10-day Caribbean cruises from New York calling at four islands with occasional "visits" to Bermuda.

Meanwhile, the *Bermuda Star* spends the fall, winter, and spring in San Diego offering weekly sailings to Puerto Vallarta, Mazatlan, and Cabo San Lucas. This sounds like a very relaxing cruise as it also features three full days at sea. Spring and fall repositioning cruises to New York transit the Panama Canal and can be embarked from 13 to 28 days—at bargain rates as well! During the summer season, *Bermuda Star* sails from New York to Montreal on a New England/Canada itinerary that combines the best of all worlds—scenic routes, famous waterways, and a fjord and wonderful cities. The one-week cruises begin in New York northbound and Montreal southbound.

CARNIVAL CRUISE LINES

5225 N.W. 87th Ave.
Miami, FL 33178-2193
tel: (305) 599–2600
 (800) 327–9501

Carnival Cruise Lines has grown in the past two decades from a "mom and pop" organization with two vintage vessels to a giant in the industry—*the* giant. Carnival carries more than 25% of all cruise passengers recorded, with occupancy levels exceeding 100% (based on two to a cabin) and impressive revenue levels. The ship line went "public" in 1987, offering some $400 million in shares, and is considered a multibillion-dollar company involved in cruises, gambling casinos, related resort properties, and an airline. The ship line currently operates a series of 3-, 4-, and 7-day cruises aboard eight large vessels (with another ship expected in spring 1991 and yet another in negotiation)—to the Bahamas and Caribbean from south Florida and to Mexico from the west coast.

Carnival launched the first of its soon-to-be super fleet with the flagship *Mardi Gras* in 1973. This 27,250-ton vessel carrying an easy 906 passengers, was the former *Empress of Canada*. A year later Carnival developed the "Fun Ship" theme, which soon became associated with sparkling white exteriors and a red, white, and blue smokestack that is recognized in every Caribbean port. In 1976 the ship line launched the *Carnivale,* the former *Empress of Britain,* sister ship of the *Mardi Gras.* Both vessels were converted from North Atlantic sailings to full-time Caribbean cruising, and through continual refurbishment, the old-world ambience and dark woods have been replaced to reflect Caribbean lifestyle and colors. These ships do well, catering to the night-owl set, who love to eat, drink, and be merry on into the wee hours. The *Carnivale* set occupancy records since her launching, carrying well over the 950-passenger complement forecast.

Then, the 38,175-ton *Festivale* joined the fleet in 1978. The former SA *Vaal* of Trans-Vaal Castle Line carries just over 1400 passengers and has done very well since her relaunching as a Caribbean cruise ship.

Carnival introduced in 1982 its much-touted ship of the "90s" to cruise clientele in the Caribbean. Called the *Tropicale,* the $100 million, Danish-built vessel has a capacity for 1200-plus passengers and quickly became *the* top fun ship of the then-four-vessel fleet. The vessel has been well-designed, with plenty of deck space for the swinging crowd, an enormous casino, and just enough spit-and-polish to be vaguely impressive. Cabins are comfortable and, with the exception of twelve veranda-suites on Verandah Deck, all are the same size with large windows, closed-circuit color television, and twin beds that can be joined for a king-size treat. Emphasis is on having a good time and dropping lots of money in the casino or at any of the several bars. However, a Carnival spokesperson once admitted that the line actually made more money at the bar than in the casinos. Hard to believe, but if you want a proper ''drink''—watch carefully as it is concocted.

The 46,000-ton *Holiday* entered Caribbean service mid-July 1985, carrying 1452 passengers and a normal crew size of 660. The vessel, constructed in Denmark, with public areas and cabins under the design supervision of Joe Farkas, represents a definite departure for Carnival in on board ambience. While the cabins are standardized and easily convertible from L-shaped twin configuration to together-beds, there are some interesting public areas. The two dining rooms offer a much more gracious meal experience than ever before found on a Carnival ship (even though the food presentation and quality needs an uplift), and such spaces as the Carnegie Library and Rick's Cafe American (piano bar) are pleasantly relaxing, indeed.

A year later, the 1500-passenger *Jubilee* entered service in the Caribbean and was followed in March 1987 by sister ship *Celebration.* Both vessels boast 48,000 tons and created a new concept in cruising for Carnival, which touted itself as the mega-vessel company. So, Carnival ordered three more—to be even bigger and more glitzy—and astounded the industry with their names . . . *Fantasy, Ecstasy, Sensation!* Alas, the shipyard in which this superliner trio was to be constructed underbid the contract and fell into grave financial difficulties that Carnival was forced to help rectify. The first of this ''new generation of cruise ships'' at 70,000 tons, *Fantasy* was a bit delayed but arrived in Miami in February 1990—complete with 12 miles of neon tubing installed in its walls and ceilings (that changes color, of course, throughout the day) and a 20-foot-tall kinetic sculpture—among other accoutrements. Sister ship *Ecstasy* is also a bit delayed, but expected arrival is June 1991.

Meanwhile, Carnival Cruise Line has not been resting upon the laurels of its success and its cash-rich basis. Anxious to be ''respectable'' in this crazy industry, Carnival purchased the travel and tourism activities of Holland America Line and all its subsidiaries—Westours, Westmark Hotels, and Windstar Sail Cruises—for approximately $625 million in January 1989. This is an upscale image for Carnival, which does not intend to tamper with an already fine product. More recently, Holland America and Carnival announced the order of three 50,000-ton cruise ships for Holland America to be placed in service between 1992 and 1994. The ships will be registered in the Bahamas and will be quite luxurious. When all is accomplished in the new cruise ship department by the end of 1994, Carnival Cruise Line will be operating a total of 20 vessels under three separate companies.

The *Festivale* sails from San Juan to St. Thomas, St. Maarten, Barbados, and Martinique. The *Tropicale* also sails from San Juan to the lower Caribbean—St. Thomas, Guadeloupe, Grenada, La Guaira, and Aruba. From Miami, the *Holiday* visits Playa del Carmen, Cozumel, Grand Cayman, and Ocho Rios, while the *Celebration* calls at San Juan, St. Thomas, and St. Maarten. From Los Angeles, the *Jubilee* sails every Sunday for Puerto Vallarta, Mazatlan, and Cabo San Lucas (weather permitting). Three- and four-day cruises to the Bahamas feature the *Mardi Gras* from Port Everglades, the *Carnivale* from Port Canaveral, and the *Fantasy* from Miami. Air-sea programs, pre- and post-stays are available for all programs.

CELEBRITY CRUISES
CHANDRIS FANTASY CRUISES

900 Third Avenue
New York, NY 10022
tel: (212) 750–0044
    (800) 621–3446

Like many other ship lines, Chandris Inc. has not stood still the past few years. This family-owned company has been busy. It concluded that, in addition to the Chandris Fantasy Cruise fleet in the Caribbean and Mediterranean, it needs a more upscale product to offer loyal passengers. Hence, Celebrity Cruises was announced mid-1989 with a personal commitment to the industry by John Chandris. It boasts a fleet of two vessels at this writing—the 30,000-ton *Meridian* (ex-*Galileo*) and the spanking-new 45,000-ton *Horizon*, finished in Papenburg, Germany, in May 1990. A third vessel, a 45,000-ton sister ship to *Horizon* to be called *Zenith* has been ordered from the same shipyard for delivery in 1991.

Celebrity Cruises is quite a departure for the Chandris Group, which was founded in 1915 with cargo business, but known the past decade or so for its Fantasy Cruise "value" sailings. The new subsidiary offers passengers a chance to "trade-up" cruises to more glamorous and glitzy digs and still feel part of the Chandris family. Celebrity began its inaugural season by sailing from New York to Bermuda on both vessels—the *Horizon* to St. George's and Hamilton, the *Meridian* to Somerset—on a weekly basis. Winter itineraries feature the *Meridian* from Port Everglades on a 7-day schedule to Antigua, St. Thomas, and Nassau, and the *Horizon* sailing every week from San Juan to the lower Caribbean ports of Martinique, Barbados, St. Lucia, Antigua, and St. Thomas.

The 1106-passenger *Meridian,* with an international crew of 480, was completely reconstructed in Germany from the former *Galileo.* The $45-million rebuilding created structural changes in the public areas as well as some cabins, with floor-to-ceiling windows and suites with skylights. The 1354-passenger *Horizon* is the first new building in the Chandris fleet—the $165-million vessel was designed by a consortium of well-known ship architects, including the famed husband-and-wife Katzourakis team whose fine work appears on so many other vessels.

Creating special recipes and menus and acting as consultant to Celebrity Cruises is Michel Roux who, along with his brother Albert, are Britain's most famous French chefs and restaurateurs. Food consultants are very popular now with many ship lines, and Roux has promised to watch carefully over the flock in the kitchen and to change the menu every few months. In addition to two restaurants in London, Roux has also created menus for British Airways Concorde.

The Chandris Fantasy Cruises division operates the *Britanis, Amerikanis, Victoria, The Azur,* and *Romanza* in Mexico, the Caribbean, and the Mediterranean. From April to November, the *Romanza* and the *Azur* sail the Mediterranean, Aegean, and Black Sea. More recently, the *Victoria* returned to Europe for the summer season to offer North Cape and Baltic Sea cruises. Meanwhile, the *Amerikanis* and *Britanis* maintain a year-round presence in the Caribbean. During the summer months, the *Britanis* sails from Miami on 2-night cruises to Nassau and 5 nights to Mexican ports. From early September through October, the vessel makes a long cruise around South America that has become very popular with both Europeans and North Americans. The *Britanis* is very well maintained, and the per diem "value" of such a long cruise is excellent. Good reports have been received!

The Chandris Group also operates the largest privately held hotel group in Greece with five luxury properties in Athens, Chios, Crete, and Corfu that appeal to the full range of today's travelers in the leisure and business categories. Cruise and Stay packages are available with the Chandris vessels. *(Romanza* and *The Azur)* in the sailing areas during the season.

As the garden of ship lines throughout the industry has grown and blossomed, so has Chandris, and we expect more from this very creative and energetic organization.

CLASSICAL CRUISES

132 East 70th Street
New York, NY 10021
tel: (212) 794–3200
   (800) 252–7745

Classical Cruises is a new addition to the cruise family, but not that much of a stranger since its one ship—the 140-passenger *Illiria*—is well known in refined circles. The *Illiria* has been marketed by Travel Dynamics of New York for several years to museum and gallery groups, alumni associations, garden clubs, and such for what one would call "classical" cruises. The above company was formed to offer these cruises to the general public, and they are quite a bit apart from the normal offering, for there is more time in port to enjoy the classical sites on in-depth sightseeing tours for which the ship's lecturers have thoroughly briefed passengers. The ship is a classic beauty inside and beautifully maintained. She was just refurbished and boasts an art collection that ranges from Etruscan objects to works by Calder and Dali. The *Illiria* is a comfortable yachtlike vessel with interesting fellow passengers.

During Classical Cruises' inaugural season (April through October 1990), the company offered five different air/land/sea programs to classical sites in Turkey, Yugoslavia, Egypt, and the Greek Islands that included a week's cruise aboard the *Illiria*. The most interesting programs featured In the Spirit of St. Paul and In the Steps of St. Paul (which began in Thessalonica, capital of northern Greece). During the 1991 season, the same cruise itinerary to Turkey and the Greek Islands will be offered, as well as one-week cruises in the Black Sea. All sailings begin and end in Istanbul. During the winter, *Illiria* is in Antarctica.

CLIPPER CRUISE LINE

7711 Bonhomme Avenue
St. Louis, MO 63105
tel: (314) 727–2929
    (800) 325–0010

It might occur to you that St. Louis is rather a funny place for a cruise line whose fleet is intended to sail along the eastern seaboard and intracoastal waterway, and then spend the winter season among the Virgin Islands. The reason: Clipper Cruise Line is owned by Barney Ebsworth, who also owns and operates the much-respected and highly successful tour company known as INTRAV, based in St. Louis. Clipper is not a wholly owned subsidiary of INTRAV, but a separate company whose sales team works closely with the tour operation.

Clipper was conceived to operate three ultrayachtlike vessels, on which 100–138 passengers can explore the historic towns that have grown up along America's waterways. The ship line is attracting sophisticated passengers who have done it all elsewhere but come aboard for a different view of America the Beautiful. These vessels are not for people who need a casino, disco, midnight buffet, or nightclub shows. One is encouraged to enjoy the best of American-style cuisine, do-it-yourself walking tours when the ship is in port, and quiet evenings with local entertainment and fellow passengers. During the day there are excellent port lectures and ever-changing scenery, since the ships are never far from shore.

In the past year, Clipper has expanded its cruise destinations to provide loyal passengers with ever more adventure and an opportunity to experience more of the travel spirit they encompass. The company is taking full advantage of the small size of its ships and their shallow draft to go into such places as Alaska's Inside Passage, the Northwest's Columbia River, and even California's Sacramento River. Other new destinations include the Orinoco River and the lovely country of Costa Rica. Wherever they sail, the Clipper fleet does it with style, and passengers rave about their time on board and their experiences.

The *Newport* and *Nantucket Clipper* are sister ships that carry a total of 102 passengers each in 51 small but adequate cabins, while the brand-new and very glamorous *Yorktown Clipper* accommodates 138 passengers and was constructed at Clipper's own First Coast Shipbuilding Company near Jacksonville, Florida. It began cruising the scenic waterways of the eastern seaboard in June 1988.

The *Newport Clipper* is on charter to a French company until March

1991 but will return to service for the summer season in eastern Canada, then reposition to the Caribbean for the winter months. *Nantucket Clipper* carries on the Eastern seaboard/New England tradition from spring through fall and then repositions to the Virgin Islands for the season, sailing weekly from St. Thomas. The *Yorktown Clipper* has become the real adventurer of the fleet, offering Panama/Costa Rica and Orinoco River cruises during the winter months and then cruising up the western coastline to Alaska for the summer season. Some Columbia and Sacramento river sailings are also on the schedule. Wherever they cruise, these three vessels offer the unusual in secluded coves, coming so close to shore sites that passengers can just about reach out and touch something.

CLUB MED

40 West 57th Street
New York, NY 10019
tel: (212) 977–2170
    (800) CLUB–MED

Club Mediterranee, the famous French resort company, has joined forces with three French banks—BPN, Credit Lyonnais, and Societe Generale—to construct a 425-passenger, $100-million sail cruiser with five masts and 2990 yards of sail. The vessel was ordered from Societe Nouvelle des Ateliers et Chantiers du Havre, the same shipyard that was responsible for the three 150-passenger Windstar sail cruisers. However, the Club Med ship has been designed with 8 decks, is 617 feet long, 66 feet at beam, and has a draft of 16 feet. She has a total of 197 cabins, of which four are ''central'' (inside) and two are suites. Contrary to Club Med tradition, all cabins boast telephone, refrigerator, TV/stereo/VCR and private facilities. In-cabin service is available but—contrary to cruise tradition—there is a charge!

Club Med I has two restaurants—one buffet style—and complimentary wine is served with lunch and dinner. There are 5 bars, 2 swimming pools, other necessities, a sports platform on the stern, and 60-plus GOs (gentle organizers). The vessel is spectacular from all reports (I have only seen a model) but these same reports do not recommend Americans sign on unless they 1) speak fluent French and love French people, and 2) love the Club Med experience. This is a floating Club Med that departs weekly from Guadeloupe during the winter season and from Villefranche in the summer months. There are seven different rates published; air fare is additional.

COMMODORE CRUISE LINE

1007 North America Way
Miami, FL 33132
tel: (305) 358–2622

This Florida-based cruise line, with offices right on Dodge Island in the heart of the active Port of Miami, operates the 17,000-ton *Caribe I,* the former *Olympia* of Greek Line, which accommodates 1100 passengers and departs Miami every Saturday afternoon for Puerto Plata, San Juan, St. John, and St. Thomas. Commodore was known for its loyalty to Haiti, but dropped a call at Cap Haitien a few years ago following State Department advice. *Caribe I* is a ''value'' product with many first-time cruise passengers from the midwest and southeast. During the winter, the ship line admits playing host to an older group of passengers while the summer crowd is younger and includes many families who enjoy the larger cabins aboard.

The food on the vessel has a fair—hardly gourmet—reputation, and the ship line makes a point of saying that it does *not* concession any of its food and beverage services, as so many ships in the Caribbean do. Lively entertainment on board befits the type of passengers, and the line specializes in Oktoberfest cruises, with lots of good German beer, pretzels, and all the trimmings during the month of October. Other theme cruises are available, and families are encouraged to bring their entire entourage during the summer months. Reasonable prices and the four-port itinerary attract many passengers.

Commodore Cruise Line, now owned by EffJohn International, a shipping group combination of the Johnson Line of Sweden and Effoa of Finland, which are two of the largest ferry operators in the Baltic, also owns B.S.L. (Bermuda Star Line), headquartered in New Jersey. Recently, EffJohn ordered two vessels worth $100 million each from a Spanish shipyard. The first, which Commodore expects to operate beginning spring 1992, will carry 800 passengers on one-week Caribbean cruises. The second vessel, due for delivery in 1993, will be operated by either Commodore or B.S.L.

Meanwhile, EffJohn acquired the former *Orient Express,* which it intends to operate year-round. Renamed *Eurosun,* the 670-passenger vessel sails around the Canary Islands and Morocco during the winter season and from Venice in summer under the aegis of Europe Cruise Line. The vessel is marketed through Commodore, but one would never know because several calls for background material and new brochures produced nothing. I could have told you more—but the ship line has to get its act together, first! Watch for a combined ship line of Commodore, B.S.L., and Europe Cruise, soonest!

COSTA CRUISES

World Trade Center
80 S.W. 8th Street
Miami, FL 33130-3097
tel: (305) 358–7325
(800) 332–8263

Costa used to boast that it was the largest cruise line in the world, and it was, without doubt, during the early years of the North American cruise industry. Costa is also one of the oldest privately owned maritime firms in Italy, established in 1924 with the purchase of the freighter *Ravenna,* although the Genoa-based family has been in the olive oil business since 1860. Over a century ago, Giacomo Costa and his brother began importing the oil from Sardinia, refining it, and exporting it throughout Europe. To do so, they needed vessels and a soon-booming cargo business led to passengers and cruises. By 1935, seven more freighters joined the Costa fleet. Following World War II, Costa was left with just the tiny ship *Lagano,* but bounded back quickly with some 12 vessels flying the house flag from 1946 to 1948. Passenger service between Genoa and South America began in early 1948, with the 850-passenger *Anna*—and air-conditioned too (so they claim)!

Three more passenger vessels were added to the fleet—the *Andrea C., Giovanna C.,* and *Franca C.* The 1200-passenger *Frederico C.* (now Star/Ship *Royale*) was constructed in the late 1950s, and the new flagship *Eugenio C.* began service between Italy and South America in 1966. The *Enrico C.* (formerly the *Province*) was also placed on this run.

In the late 1960s, Costa acquired the *Carla C.* (former *Flandre*), the *Fulvia* (former *Oslofjord*), and the *Flavia.* During the 1970s, Costa operated eight of its own vessels and chartered six others, with a fleet deployed in the Mediterranean, Caribbean and along the eastern coastline of South America. The company claims it pioneered Caribbean cruises from San Juan in 1968, and today home-ports the *CarlaCosta* year-round and the *Daphne* during the winter season in Puerto Rico.

Through attrition and other facts of life, the Costa fleet is now the very manageable size of six: the *EugenioCosta* and *EnricoCosta* in Europe and South America; the *Danae* in Europe and around the world;

and the *Daphne, CarlaCosta* and, *CostaRiviera* catering to the North American market.

A few years ago, Costa began to use a little sex in its advertising, and its "Cruising Italian Style" motto has certainly been successful. Indeed, Costa is the last true Italian ship line, with warm and caring Italian officers, an Italian kitchen with a fabulous reputation, and mainly Italian service crew, offering cruises covering most of the world. And the ships filled up—aided in part by the latest terrorist happening a few years ago *(Achille Lauro)*—because North Americans would rather "Cruise Italian Style" in their own backyard (the Caribbean and Alaska) than in the Mediterranean.

Costa has also upgraded its brochures—now adorned with lovely watercolors—and its vessels. The venerable *CarlaCosta* (all ship names are now jammed together) has had a wonderful facelift and returned to the ambience of her art deco period when it was known as the *Flandre* in the 1950s. The *Daphne* and *Danae* have been refurbished, and one-seating dining has returned to the Trevi Restaurant—at least on most cruises. The *EugenioCosta* has also been refurbished in the public areas and is marketed to North Americans during the Mediterranean summer season, although the venerable vessel is the lesser of the fleet.

The old-world, 770-passenger *CarlaCosta* sails year-round from San Juan on 1-week cruises to the lower Caribbean. She is joined during the winter season by the 424-passenger *Daphne,* which offers something called "resort cruising" on seven different Caribbean islands. From mid-May to mid-September, the *Daphne* sails from Vancouver on 1-week round-trip cruises through the Inside Passage. The vessel also makes a pleasant repositioning cruise through the Panama Canal in spring and autumn.

Sistership of the *Daphne* is the *Danae,* which summers in the Mediterranean and offers global or orient cruises during the winter months that suit her intimate 420-passenger capacity. Both vessels are quite different from the Costa family but seem to have fit nicely into the fleet during the past decade. The 700-passenger *EugenioCosta* (formerly known as the *Eugenio C.*) received a multimillion refit recently but is most suited to Italian- or Spanish-speaking passengers, who make up the majority on board.

The 1000-passenger *CostaRiviera* has been a popular vessel since her introduction in 1985 and now offers alternate East and West Caribbean itineraries from Port Everglades that can be enjoyed "back to back." Costa created a health/fitness program especially for the *CostaRiviera* that offers passengers exercise, body pampering, and diet. The Spa-Costa packages can be purchased for 1 to 7 days through a travel agent, regardless of your cabin category.

New to the Costa family during the summer of 1990 was the 770-passenger *CostaMarina,* a 25,000-ton former container ship rebuilt in

Genoa (where *CostaRiviera* was converted). The vessel looks very solid in the Costa tradition. Another vessel—a 50,000-ton new building—is being prepared at the Fincantieri Shipyard in Italy for delivery in 1991. Viva "Cruising Italian Style"!

CROWN CRUISE LINE

P.O. Box 3000
2790 North Federal Highway
Boca Raton, FL 33431
tel: (407) 394–7450
   (800) 447–2290

Crown Cruise Line, owned and operated by Norwegian-born Oddmund Grundstad, has been in existence for over five years, but no one took the company seriously until it moved to the Port of Palm Beach and began building tonnage. The first vessel, *Viking Princess* (ex-Ilmatar of Silja Line ferry service in the Baltic Sea) carries a maximum of 700 passengers and a Filipino crew of 110 on day cruises from the Port of Palm Beach to the Bahamas.

In early 1989, Crown added the 486-passenger *Crown del Mar,* another former ferry called *Las Palmas de Gran Canaria* by its Spanish owners, on 2-day cruises to the Bahamas and 5-day cruises to Key West and Mexico. Following a $35-million renovation in Valencia, Spain, the 10,000-ton vessel has 138 outside staterooms and 86 inside. Officers are Norwegian and service staff is Filipino/international. Another vessel, the $60-million *Crown Monarch,* is being constructed in Spain to carry 560 passengers in 16,000 tons on one-week cruises from the Port of Palm Beach. In fact, a $1.7-million cruise terminal for Palm Beach was constructed with Crown Cruise Line in mind; its three vessels will have exclusive use year-round.

Crown also operates two dive and live-aboard vessels—the 31-passenger *Crown Diver* and 33-passenger *Crown Islander,* which cruise the Bahamas on 3-, 4-, and 6-night excursions for underwater aficionados. A third vessel is projected for the 1990s, possibly for Belize.

CRYSTAL CRUISES

2121 Avenue of the Americas
Los Angeles, CA 90067
tel: (213) 785-9300

Crystal Cruises has entered this world as a west-coast cruise line boasting it plans "to provide the most elegant, most luxurious cruise experience anyone has ever known." It is rather wonderful to want to provide elegance and luxury, but the comments of Crystal Cruises' staff have been a bit overblown the past two years and, in fact, an insult to many within the industry who have already done well in providing passengers with superb surroundings and service. Its first vessel, the 960-passenger *Crystal Harmony,* began her inaugural season July 24 (1990) on four 12-day sailings from San Francisco to Alaska and Canada. Crystal Cruises is a subsidiary of NYK (Nippon Yusen Kaisha) Line, headquartered in Tokyo, the largest shipping company in Japan, which has announced a $1-billion total investment in the passenger ship industry. (For NYK Line this is a re-entry, since it operated passenger liners from Seattle and San Francisco to Japan between the world wars.) Crystal Cruises (for luxury) and Frontier Cruises (for adventure) are just two of the companies this wealthy ship line plans to build. Both are aimed at the western market—in fact, potential Japanese passengers are under a quota, and not more than 10% may be aboard any cruise!

The 49,400-ton *Crystal Harmony* was constructed by Mitsubishi Heavy Industries in Nagasaki, Japan, where the most advanced technology was married to Scandinavian design and American comfort. No doubt, the *Harmony's* announced sister ships (1992; 1993) will also be constructed here, although NYK Line is making a token effort to receive bids from European yards.

Following the Alaska/Canada season and a series of trans–Panama Canal cruises during the winter months, the $200-million *Crystal Harmony* will make her debut in the Mediterranean for the 1991 Europe season, which is expected to be very strong. China was originally on the 1991 schedule but was cancelled due to lack of passenger interest. Watch for other happenings from this new and most energetic ship line that utilizes crowned sea horses to symbolize its philosophy of "unequalled elegance." Let us hope that its most boastful pronouncements are all true!

CUNARD LINE

555 Fifth Avenue
New York, NY 10017
tel: (212) 880–7500
    (800) 221–4770

Cunard Line, which started life as the British and North American Royal Mail Steam-Packet Company just over 150 years ago, was the first to offer regular transatlantic passenger service and has remained the last. The visionary behind such an undertaking was a merchant from Halifax, Nova Scotia, named Samuel Cunard, who took an idea to London in 1839: scheduled mail service on the North Atlantic was possible. A few passengers could come along too, he added. Cunard cajoled a mail contract out of the British Admiralty, and a year later he launched the *Britannia,* which left Liverpool on July 4, 1840. The voyage to Boston took fourteen days and eight hours, and the *Britannia* received a tumultuous welcome. The Boston citizenry were so proud of this new service that they presented Cunard with an enormous sterling silver loving cup as a memento. Miraculously, the cup has survived 150 years of stormy seas and wars, and is on view just as you enter the Columbia Dining Room of the *QE2.*

The *Britannia* was a wooden paddlesteamer of 1150 tons with a 207-foot hull. She carried noteworthy passengers including novelist Charles Dickens, who sailed to Boston in 1842 and was shocked to discover his stateroom was nothing more than a closet, even though he had booked deluxe accommodations. He called it "utterly impractical, thoroughly hopeless, and a profoundly preposterous box." However, he and his two roommates finally agreed that the cabin could be quite spacious, especially if they all turned around in unison!

In 1847 Cunard added the port of New York to the transatlantic itinerary, and the Admiralty agreed to increase his mail subsidy. By the end of the decade the fleet had doubled and the North Atlantic was becoming "crowded," Cunard cried. After all, this not too minor body of water was already known as "Cunard's Pond." But in 1856 he launched the biggest ship ever—the *Persia*—twice the length of the *Britannia,* with paddles that were no less than forty feet in diameter, a capacity for three times more passengers than before, and a record speed of fourteen knots. Although Cunard Line never formally recognized the famous "Blue Riband," the award to the fastest ship on the Atlantic service presented from the 1880s to the end of the 1960s, the launching of the *Persia* began a racetrack atmosphere.

Hence, the history of passenger service on the North Atlantic closely parallels the development of Cunard Line (its denouement in the early 1970s and its renaissance in the 1980s). At the end of the 19th century Cunard was building ships in pairs, following specifications laid down by Lloyds and decorating them in the manner of the day—Victorian— with velvet drapes, stained-glass cupolas, and the wooden paneling. The 20th century brought the turbine engine and such sister ships as the *Carmania* and *Caronia, Mauretania* and *Lusitania*.

But the most famous of all Cunard's vessels are, undoubtedly, the *Queen Mary* and *Queen Elizabeth*. These two ships were planned with dollar signs in the eyes of company officials, so that every week of the year (with the exception of brief overhaul periods) one *Queen* would depart Southampton, the other New York, at a speed of about 28½ knots. The *Queen Mary* was launched in 1937 and, by the next year, was the fastest ship in Atlantic service. The *Queen Elizabeth* did not fare so auspiciously at first, but began life stealing across the North Atlantic under the cover of wartime gray. The vessel did not carry any paying passengers until after the war. During the war the two *Queens* had together transported over a million troops back and forth across the seas. Of this service Winston Churchill commented, ''The world owes them a debt that it will not be able to measure.''

In the postwar years when Europe was again reachable, life was heady for Cunard Line. The two *Queens* were the most prestigious ships on the transatlantic run, not for their cuisine especially but for their traditional British-style service and for afternoon tea and violins among the palms—and for all the elegant people (not to mention the misplaced royalty) who sailed aboard them! But within two decades, the dream faded. In September 1967 the *Queen Mary* tooted to her younger sister, the *Queen Elizabeth,* for the last time as they passed midway across the Atlantic. Less than one year later, the *Elizabeth* was retired and on her way to an ignominious end—to be ravaged by fire in Hong Kong harbor.

Cunard was not without a *Queen* for long. In the spring of 1969 Queen Elizabeth II used the same pair of gold scissors to cut the launching cord of the *QE2* that her mother and grandmother had used while christening the two ships named after them. It was a lovely beginning for the splendid new 67,107-ton vessel filled with the latest in transport technology. Her 1700 passengers have thirteen decks and fourteen public rooms through which to roam, as well as four swimming pools, two gymnasia, several saunae, and a complete hospital. One can get lost but not bored on the *QE2*. And the grand dame hangs in there, offering the only regular passenger service from New York to Southampton between April and December, interspersed with more lucrative short cruises. From

January to April she circumnavigates the world—sometimes in as little as eighty days, just because she's the only ship that can do so.

The *Queen*'s schedule was disrupted in 1982; the British government requisitioned her for war service in the Falkland Island crisis. The interior of the vessel was stripped down to carry troops, and helicopter pads were welded to the top decks. Over seven hundred members of her crew volunteered for service and received combat pay as well as a citation from Her Majesty's government. Fortunately, the vessel received no damage, just a heroine's welcome upon her return to Southampton in July. She was completely refurbished, more outdoor dance space was designed, and the ship was fitted with a floating Golden Door health spa for all passengers' use. The *QE2* returned to service on August 14, 1982, a wiser and more respected lady of the sea.

As the most publicized vessel afloat, the *Queen* doesn't do too badly! Her two dozen or so transatlantic crossings have a healthy passenger complement and why not? With such enticements as riding the Concorde for a song, putting up at the Ritz or the 18th-century Hotel Stafford in London, as well as discounts on Godfrey Davis cars and even the Simplon Orient Express, it's absolute madness to stay at home. Not to mention that once afloat, there are hourly fitness sessions a la Golden Door (even skeptics will agree that these classes can be very habit-forming); or, you can get a jump on your children and take some computer lessons; take a swim in the $2 million Lido area; hobnob with certain celebrities singing for their supper at twice-weekly lectures; enjoy first-run movies; break the bank in the casino; or just eat and drink. The Golden Door takes care of the calories. The *Queen* is the most sophisticated ship on the sea, and it is amazing how quickly the days pass between Southampton and New York harbor. In between regular crossings the vessel makes some short cruises here and there—an excellent way to find one's sea legs.

To ensure the *QE2* a place in history well into the 1990s, as the ultimate ocean liner, Cunard committed some $150-plus million to a major refit in Bremerhaven, Germany—primarily to install the largest diesel electric plant on any passenger vessel. Fortunately, some of the funds were allocated for public rooms and private accommodations and the result is nothing less than spectacular! Gone at last is the gloomy, British look that haunted the interior of *QE2* since her 1969 arrival. Also gone is a large but tacky shopping area atop the former Double Down Room. In its place is an enticing and very large shopping promenade full of fancy names and prices. There are some very fine buys here in French, British, and Italian clothing and accessories, some badly designed but nonetheless expensive jewelry, and the usual shipboard junk decorating a shop at the back.

Below this popular promenade is the two-level Grande Lounge entertainment area, with a horseshoe-shaped double stairway that becomes part of the stage. Seating has been tiered, with a bright and uplifting decor. Behind, the former dreary Double Down Bar has been reborn as the Yacht Club—with a transparent plastic piano top and deck-to-deck windows looking out on a new sports facility. In other areas, a handsome Boardroom has sprung from the former Computer Centre (now located down near the Purser's Office) and the four restaurants received good care. All accommodations have been spruced, and there is a new series of elegant penthouse suites with private verandas.

Despite the fact that *QE2* spent six months in Japan during the winter of 1989/90, she managed to make 18 transatlantic crossings during the '90 season and is returning to her former life with a 1991 world cruise. What the future holds for this flagship is uncertain, however, as rumors float along atop the waters. Be sure that Cunard has something up its sleeve, however.

Meanwhile, Cunard Line celebrated the 150th year of Samuel Cunard's vision in grand style—with a series of gala events in England as well as New York harbor. A dramatic Spithead Review, in company with Royal Navy vessels while the Royal Air Force saluted with a fly-over display, was the highlight. Former captains of the vessel came aboard during the event, and passengers on all anniversary sailings were presented a commemorative gift of Waterford crystal. In North America, the flagship called at Halifax, Nova Scotia (Cunard's birthplace), and Boston, MA (his first transatlantic port of call), during a four-day celebratory cruise.

Cunard also operates two warm-weather, short-cruising vessels, the *Cunard Countess* and the *Cunard Princess*. In the ship line's tradition, the two vessels were designed identically and built simultaneously. In August 1976 the *Countess* was christened in San Juan by Mrs. Neil Armstrong (wife of the first man to walk on the moon), who was chosen to symbolize the vessel's interior astrotheme. The *Princess* was christened in New York harbor by the late Princess Grace of Monaco in March 1977. Both 17,500-ton ships carry up to 800 passengers.

The *Cunard Countess* cruises year-round from San Juan, where she is in good company. She operates on alternating itineraries: Saturdays to the Caribbean Capitals or Grenada, Trinidad, Barbados, Martinique, and St. Thomas; followed by Saturdays to Seven Plus, featuring calls at Tortola, Guadeloupe, St. Lucia, St. Maarten, Antigua, and St. Thomas. The two can be combined for La Grande Caribbean—a 2-week cruise featuring 12 different ports. Prices are reasonable and cruises can be booked as a Sail 'n Stay program for an extra week at either Hotel La Toc and La Toc Suites on St. Lucia or Paradise Village and Beach Club on Barbados, both Cunard-owned resorts.

While the *Countess* has sailed from San Juan since her christening, the *Princess* has been all over the map—the Caribbean, Bermuda, trans–Panama Canal, Alaska—trying to find her place, poor thing. The latest itineraries in the Cunard sketchbook are sailing in European waters year-round. The vessel is well suited for the English market, which doesn't want to pay for too many frills and doesn't mind small (and noisy) cabins and even tinier bathrooms. The winter program is based in Malaga for Saturday departures to Casablanca, Madeira, Las Palmas, Tenerife (where 7-day passengers disembark/embark), Lanzarote, Agadir, Madeira, Tangier, and Gibraltar. These 14-day Canary Islands itineraries feature Sail and Stay packages in Malaga or London.

From April to November, *Cunard Princess* sails between Venice and Piraeus (port for Athens) on two-week itineraries that feature Black Sea, Ancient Mediterranean, Classic Mediterranean, and Mediterranean Odyssey, with Sail and Stay packages available in either Athens or Venice. Round-trip airfare is free in some instances (if you can decipher the confusing brochure). *Cunard Princess* returns to Malaga mid-November for the winter season.

Cunard Line acquired the top-rated *Sagafjord* and *Vistafjord* in late 1983 and both ships have fared very well, indeed, with the infusion of several million dollars on decor, new penthouse/veranda cabins, sea-view dining room on *Sagafjord,* the Golden Door Spa at Sea, a computer center *(Vistafjord),* and daily editions of the *International Herald Tribune* printed on board. The *Sagafjord* (which has a definite edge over her sistership because of the personalities involved) continues with her annual world cruise each year, and spends the summer on 10- and 11-day sailings in Alaskan waters between Vancouver and Anchorage. Following her successful season in Alaska, the *Sagafjord* sails for the South Pacific until mid-November and then transits the Panama Canal to the Caribbean for three cruises from Port Everglades, including a gala Christmas/New Year's sailing. In early January, she departs south Florida for her annual global voyage—one of the most popular offered.

Meanwhile, sister ship *Vistafjord* summers in northern Europe on 14-day cruises from Hamburg with a few eastern Mediterranean sailings as the season progresses. Following a southern transatlantic repositioning cruise, the *Vistafjord* sails from Port Everglades to Los Angeles to prepare for a 28-day Polynesian cruise from Los Angeles before returning to North America and the Caribbean for the rest of the winter 1991.

Sea Goddess I and *II,* Cunard's precious but problematic small vessels, originally constructed by the now-bankrupt Wartsila Shipyard in Finland for Sea Goddess Cruises, were designed for just 116 discerning passengers who didn't mind paying a premium for good service, excellent food, complimentary champagne (plus all drinks) and caviar, and cabins that are a bit of a squeeze (including a bathroom built for a midget). Both vessels spend the "season" in the Mediterranean, where they are ideally suited. During the winter months, *Sea Goddess I* plys the Caribbean from St. Thomas or Barbados and *Sea Goddess II* is in the Far East with a series of fascinating itineraries. Cunard has kept up the standard of Sea Goddess Cruises' original intent, without the fancy clientele. Leave grandmother's jewels at home—believe me, no one else on board has any! Life on *Sea Goddess I* and *II* still offer the penultimate cruise experience.

DELTA QUEEN STEAMBOAT COMPANY

30 Robin Street Wharf
New Orleans, LA 70130
tel: (504) 586–0631
    (800) 543–1949

The Delta Queen steamboats are as much fun to think and write about as they are to sail upon. As two of the only paddle-wheel overnight boats left in America, they are charged with the glorious mission of keeping alive a more than 150-year tradition as they cruise over 35,000 miles each along the Mississippi and Ohio rivers, at the speed of some eight miles per hour. Between these two paddle-wheelers, a dozen states are visited each year as well as hundreds of large and small river towns.

The company celebrated its centennial year in 1990—to much fanfare, as it is the oldest surviving cruise line in America and has operated some 29 steamboats on the Mississippi River and its tributaries. The company began in 1890 when a young river pilot, Gordon C. Greene, bought his first steamboat and ran it with his wife, who also had her masters license. Their son, Tom (born aboard an ice-bound steamboat), would later bring the *Delta Queen* to the Mississippi River from California.

The *Delta Queen,* last of the old-time steamboats, was constructed in 1926 with no expense spared in the teakwood handrails, stained-glass windows set with copper instead of lead, brass fittings and posts, and paneling of either oak or mahogany. These irreplaceable features cost $850,000 at the time. During World War II the U.S. Navy commissioned the *Delta Queen* to ferry wounded and healthy troops across San Francisco Bay. In 1946 she was sold to the president of Greene Line Steamers (the former name of the Delta Queen Steamboat Company) who had the paddle-wheeler towed home to New Orleans. (It was a long journey down the Pacific Coast, through the Panama Canal, and across the Gulf of Mexico, even if in a crate!) From there, the *Delta Queen* traveled to Pittsburgh for a thorough remodeling and refitting. She began her new life in the Mississippi River in June 1948.

For the next two decades this steamboat cruised slowly up and down the main arteries of the Midwest, offering her passengers the treat of experiencing American river life. Then the controversy began—a new Safety at Sea law required all vessels carrying over 50 passengers overnight to be constructed entirely of steel. Facing threats that the venerable old lady might be forced to retire, her loyal subjects rallied and not only obtained six subsequent exemptions from the law, but also enjoined the Department of the Interior to list the *Delta Queen* in the National Register of Historic Places. The current exemption was extended by President Reagan in August 1986.

The *Delta Queen* follows an itinerary of 3- to 12-night cruises that stop along the Mississippi and Ohio rivers from early March through November. The final sailings of the season are 4-night cruises round-trip from New Orleans in late November with an old-fashioned holiday atmosphere. A popular annual summer event for the sister *Queens* is the Great Steamboat Race during the 11-night Mississippi Explorer itinerary from New Orleans to St. Louis (in June). Steamboat racing was a colorful pastime on American rivers during the last century, and the Delta Queen Steamboat Company was able to revive the tradition a few years ago. The two *Queens* vie for the coveted Golden Anchor Award, which passes between them quite fairly from year to year. The annual Races are a colorful occasion, as both ships perform 11-day cruises from New Orleans to St. Louis via Baton Rouge, Natchez, Vicksburg, Memphis and Cairo. It's wonderful fun with races between the steamboats and contests between the complement of passengers. Streamers, shouting, clapping, New Orleans jazz, and nonstop libations add to the excitement.

While some aficionados prefer spring and others wouldn't miss the fall foliage, any time of the year on the river is special, for life is relaxing and the livin' is easy aboard these boats. I suggest comfortable sportswear for both men and women, and good walking shoes are helpful for visiting plantations, small towns, and such along the way. Jackets and ties, although not required for dinner, are in good taste for the formal evenings on board. There are two seatings for each meal, and shore tours are arranged at most stops. The cruise director will advise you of all activities in the daily *Steamboat Times,* so nothing will pass you by. Service on board both *Queens* is special. The average age of the crew is about thirty years old, and all are totally dedicated to their work on the river. During the summer you may find occasional students who have joined the staff hoping to get a flavor of life on the Mississippi, but all are perfectly professional and should be treated with the same courtesies (that means tips) as the crew aboard a large cruise ship.

The enthusiastic entertainment on board both steamboats is strictly river-oriented (that's what you came for), sweeping you up with singalongs, Dixieland jazz bands, barbershop quartets, and concerts of river songs. How long has it been since you've heard "Bill Bailey," "My

Old Kentucky Home,'' "Camptown Races,'' and everyone's favorite tune "Ole Man River''? As the entertainment fires up spontaneously at times, you may find yourself the recipient of a tableside serenade at dinner, which by the way, is strictly American fare. Expect the menu to offer such items as southern fried catfish from Arkansas (an old Mark Twain favorite, they say), creole dishes, peanut butter soup, and corn-bread in all disguises. And whether you've ordered them or not, you'll probably find grits with your scrambled eggs at breakfast. Wines tend to be domestic, and the Bloody Marys are famous for being hot and spicy.

Life on board the *Mississippi Queen* is slightly more formal be-cause of her size, her greater luxury, and her well air-conditioned public rooms (which means more dressing up). Personally I prefer the *Mississippi Queen,* because she has a small Jacuzzi and Nautilus gym as well as 14 spacious veranda suites up on Promenade Deck. The newest stern-wheeler, launched in 1976 (at a final cost of $27 million) and Old World in concept is a thoroughly splendid and modern machine. In appear-ance, the two boats are similar, although the *Mississippi Queen* is much larger by approximately 100 feet and almost 3000 tons. But both have the same layer-cake look and both seem to cruise along the rivers lead-ing with their tongue, or "stage" that sticks straight ahead. The *Mississippi Queen,* however, has benefited from the most advanced technol-ogy, for her huge 35-by-25-foot paddle wheel is turned by a four-cylinder "horizontal tandem compound condensing steam engine.'' Her automatic boilers (which use oil like everything else) and her steam turbine generators can provide enough electricity to power a small city. Inside, her moldings, mirrors, polished steel, and brass all evoke the past in 19th-century detail, but nothing is made of wood. Even her calliope, considered to be the world's largest and lustiest, is computer-ized so that both professionals and passengers can play onto a digital tape, push a button, and hear it all come back. And if you happen to be sitting on the top deck near the Jacuzzi, you really hear it!

Both vessels offer "Bodacious Steamboatin' '' with ongoing pro-grams—Music of the Rivers, River Heritage, and Crafts, Food and Folklore. Theme Vacations are also an annual event—The Great Steam-boat Race, Big Bands, Mardi Gras, Mark Twain Celebrations, Fall Fo-liage Vacations, Cajun Christmas/Shopping Spree, Taste of the Mississippi, and American Anthology Vacations. There are also annual Feature Cruises—Memorial Day/Civil War, Antiques, Mystery Cruises, Victorian Lifestyle, even Women in Politics.

Chattanooga, Tennessee, was added as a new port city a few years ago, and the *Delta Queen* does call there once. Delta Queen also is offering a new series of port city packages for passengers before or after their cruise. The 2- or 3-night packages are available in New Orleans, Memphis, St. Louis, and Minneapolis/St. Paul on the Mississippi River sailings; Cincinnati and Pittsburgh on the Ohio River; and Nashville on the Cumberland River. What a wonderful way to see the heartland of America!

DIAMOND CRUISE LTD.

c/o Radisson Hotel International Inc.
12755 State Highway Fifty-Five
Minneapolis, MN 55441
tel: (612) 540–5451

Diamond Cruise Ltd. was announced to the American public in May 1990 but actually formed in Helsinki, Finland, in November 1986 by Captain Offe Nyblin and his partner, Christian Aspegren. The two Finnish entrepreneurs seemed to know their minds and engaged the respected Rauma Yards in Rauma, Finland, to construct a $125-million vessel with a revolutionary design technology called SSC (Semi-Submersible Craft). At first glance, the vessel looks like a catamaran because it is lifted above the water on two large struts that are attached to two submerged hulls that provide buoyancy. The executive vice president of Rauma shipyard, Pekka Laxell, said this sensational design would offer maximum comfort and quality of cruise experience to passengers—even providing a larger and wider deck. We shall see when the vessel appears in 1992.

The 18,400-ton cruise ship will be 410 feet long and 105 feet at beam. She will carry a passenger complement of 354 and a crew of 170, and per diems are expected to be in the $600 range. The ship has been named *Radisson Diamond* because Radisson Hotels International will manage and market the new vessel, whose sister ships contemplated for the later 90s will be called *Radisson Ruby* (1994) and *Radisson Sapphire* (1993). Interiors of *Radisson Diamond* are being designed by Vincent Kwok Interiors of Minneapolis. Focal point of the lobby will be a five-story atrium with glass elevators as well as a grand staircase. The all-suite accommodations will feature terraces as well as state-of-the-art amenities and communications technology for the executive class that Radisson Hotels attracts. The dining room will be a world-class restaurant and the eight-deck lounge will have panoramic sea views. Recreational features include an outdoor swimming pool and Jacuzzi, ice pool, health and fitness center, jogging track, and floating marina at the rear of the vessel—a staging area for watersports.

The preliminary schedule for *Radisson Diamond* is a series of one-

and two-week cruises in the Caribbean during the winter season and following the sun worldwide in other months.

DOLPHIN CRUISE LINE

1007 North America Way
Miami, FL 33132
tel: (305) 358–2111
　　(800) 222–1003

　　Dolphin Cruise Line has come a long way since it was formed in 1984 to take over the marketing of 3- and 4-day cruises aboard the *Dolphin IV,* a 590-passenger vessel relinquished in the industry by the former Paquet Cruises. Since then, the company has done nothing but upgrade its product and become a much-respected entity. In 1989, Dolphin expanded into the one-week cruise market with the acquisition of the *Seabreeze* (former Starship *Royale* of Premier Cruise Line, ex-*Federico C.* of Costa Line), on which it spent $5.5 million in refurbishment.

　　Life is sailing along very well at Dolphin Cruise Line. The *Seabreeze* is departing at an average 100% capacity, and the baby *Dolphin* continues to appeal. In fact, ship-line executives are now looking for another vessel—to be placed in Europe—and then another and another vessel.

　　The company painted both ships white with a blue-on-blue stripe and put an adorable dolphin logo on the smokestacks. Let us hope that this good value cruise line continues to expand and offer cruises at very reasonable rates.

EPIROTIKI LINES

551 Fifth Avenue
Suite 1900
New York, NY 10176
tel: (212) 599–1750
    (800) 221–2470

This family-owned Greek shipping company is thriving under the fourth generation leadership of brothers George and Andreas Potamianos, great-grandsons of the adventurous youth from the island of Cephalonia who first hauled cargo and a few passengers up and down the Danube River in the 1850s. The company was named after Epirus, the hometown in northwestern Greece where Tassos Potamianos, grandson of the originator and a pioneer of cruising in the Aegean and Mediterranean, first launched his ships. It was Tassos who created the company symbol, a stylized gold Byzantine cross on a sky-blue background, which has now become a familiar sight in cruise ports around the world.

World headquarters of the ship line is the Epirotiki Building, a modern, steel and tinted-glass structure right on the harbor in Piraeus. From this building, which has already become a city landmark, the brothers command the largest Greek-flag cruise fleet in the world, a total of eight passenger vessels that sail most of the year, either on company-operated cruise programs or on charters. A good 80% of the ship line's business comes from the chartering of their vessels to tour operators in the U.S., the U.K., and Germany.

Epirotiki is considered the pioneer in Greek cruising. In 1930 and 1939 the company organized and operated the first cruises in the Aegean, for American archaeological groups. In 1946 Epirotiki operated the first passenger ship linking the Ionian Islands, and the next year introduced the largest vessel available for Greek coastal service. In 1954 the Greek National Tourist Organization joined with Epirotiki to undertake a new concept in European holidays—regularly scheduled cruises around the Aegean. This experiment was such as success that it spurred the growth of cruises throughout the world. The first passenger-plus-car ferry service between Brindisi (Italy) and Patras (Greece), launched in 1959 by Epirotiki, opened up another new type of European vacation car touring. In 1960 Epirotiki extended this service to link Europe with Asia (Turkey).

From 1965 to 1973 Epirotiki launched seven ships that were either newly built or recently refurbished specifically for the cruise market.

The first to usher in this new era of cruising was the 200-passenger *Argonaut,* a vessel originally built in 1929 as a private yacht. The *Argonaut,* still considered the flagship of the fleet, sails under the auspices of Raymond and Whitcomb of New York City, a tour operator that specializes in high-caliber programs for members of museums, college alumni associations, and special-interest groups. The yachtlike *Orpheus* has found a good home with Swan Hellenic Cruises, which offers excellent and very high-caliber programs to its clientele—80% of whom are British.

In 1966 the newly built *Jason* made its debut. The refurbished *Orpheus* and *Apollo* both arrived in 1970. The 9000-ton *Jupiter,* which debuted in 1971 in both the Aegean and Caribbean, became the largest of the ships thus far. Epirotiki launched the 4000-ton *Neptune* in 1972, and the next year cruise passengers saw the 16,000-ton *Atlas* (first built in 1951 as the *Ryndam*) in both the Aegean and Caribbean. In 1977 Epirotiki introduced the 2500-ton *Hermes* for seasonal one-day cruises to the Saronic Gulf islands, and some 300,000 tourists now take this ship annually. Two more vessels joined the fleet in 1978: the 12,000-ton *Oceanos,* which began life in 1952 as the *Jean Laborde* of French Line and the 12,000-ton *World Renaissance,* which was built in 1966 as the flagship of Paquet French Line (then named the *Renaissance*). Within the very week that Epirotiki purchased the latter vessel, she was leased on a long-term basis to Costa Line. The *World Renaissance* returned to the Epirotiki family in time for the 1984 Aegean season, and is considered the top vessel in the fleet.

Epirotiki runs a good, solid fleet that is not luxurious by any standards, but the ships are well-maintained and the service is reported to be pleasant. With so many cruise vessels to care for, Epirotiki manages its own workshop for repairs. The company also has had a long and fruitful relationship with American interior designer Maurice Bailey, who moved to Greece in 1962 to design the interior of the Athens Hilton and who now has more than 100 hotel interiors to his credit. A few years after he arrived in Greece, Bailey took on the interiors of the *Argonaut,* followed closely by the *Jason, Orpheus, Apollo, Jupiter, Neptune,* and *Atlas.* Bailey and his artists, namely Arminio Lozzi and Russell Holmes, have integrated the mythological tales and escapades of the legendary figures after whom each ship is named into the cabin murals, beautiful tapestries and sculptures in the public rooms, mosaics in the swimming pool, and even into the carpet designs. Delightful and appealing schemes appear throughout each ship. The *Neptune* has trident carpets and a large Poseidon tapestry in the Lounge of the Tritons as well as handmade brass lamps depicting Poseidon's Castle. The main lounge bar of the *Jason* displays a huge tapestry of Jason yoking the wild bulls in the sacred field of Ares. Walking up from the *Jason*'s reception hall, you see a sculpture of *Argo,* the ship that carried Jason and his Argonauts on their search for the Golden Fleece. And each cabin in the *Jason* has my favorite mural—a scene of the mysterious island of Santorini (Thira).

In May 1986 Epirotiki acquired the 632-passenger *Pegasus* (former *Sundancer* and *Sven Corona*), which spent the summer of '86 in Vancouver as a floating hotel during Expo 86. The ship line acquired its 11th vessel, the 340-*Odysseus* (ex-*Aquamarine*), in February 1988, and Epirotiki became operator of the largest privately owned cruise fleet in the world whose primary market is the Mediterranean and Aegean from spring through fall. (*Atlas, Jupiter,* and *Apollo* have since been sold and are no longer part of the Epirotiki fleet.) Disruptions in the area a few years ago affected Epirotiki's fleet more than any other. Business has returned strongly, however, as the ship line offers excellent value and variety of itineraries.

Epirotiki Lines is affiliated with a cultural association (perhaps its own?) called CruiseWorld Society that invites established (past) passengers to join and contribute their suggestions for special theme and musical cruises. During the third year of CruiseWorld Society (spring 1990), a special two-week Easter Cruise took place aboard *World Renaissance,* a one-week Music Festival occurred on *Odysseus,* and the *Pegasus* offered a special repositioning cruise from Malaga to Piraeus. In addition, *Odysseus* sailed between mid-May and mid-October on two-week Seven Seas cruises from Genoa to Venice (or vice versa) with enrichment lectures in five different languages!

Although Epirotiki Lines often replaces one vessel with another—mainly due to popular charters—it does utilize most of its fleet during the summer season on 3-, 4-, and 7-day cruises that are combinable. One-week cruises are called The Alexandrian, The Golden Fleece, and The Homeric, depending upon itinerary. Three-day cruises are either Aegean Hellenic or Aegean Minoan, while 4-day sailings are Aegean Byzantine or Aegean Classical. A 1-day excursion is available for those who just want to get their big toe wet.

During the winter season, Epirotiki is a presence in South America and the Caribbean, with departures from Rio, Manaus, Port Everglades, and Trinidad, generally on *World Renaissance, Pegasus,* or *Odysseus.* New for the 1991 winter season is a series of Red Sea cruises aboard the *Oceanos.* A dozen one-week offerings depart Port Said, visiting such exotic places as Aqaba, Luxor, Eilat, and Sharm El Sheikh (a center of Bedouin culture). There are also some longer sailings available. These cruises have never caught on—let's hope Epirotiki is successful!

Epirotiki Lines must be commended on its very fine brochure, which is well organized and a joy to read. If a brochure is meant to enlighten and entice, this one succeeds!

GALAPAGOS CRUISES

% Adventure Associates
13150 Coit Road, Suite 110
Dallas, Texas 75240
tel: (214) 907–0414
    (800) 527–2500

Galapagos Cruises, a division of Metropolitan Touring of Quito, Ecuador, was the pioneer in offering pleasure cruises to the Galapagos Islands. Ecuadorean Eduardo Proano, president of Metropolitan Touring, is deeply concerned with both promoting and preserving these enchanted islands. He brings in most (if not all) of the allotted twelve thousand tourists annually. Proano opened the area to tourism in 1968.

Flagship of Galapagos Cruises is the 1500-ton *Santa Cruz,* a 90-passenger, all first-class vessel built in Spain in 1979 especially for these cruises. The *Santa Cruz* offers a three-, four-, or seven-day program among the islands, but the best is a seven-day itinerary (a combination of the three- and four-day), with flights to and from the ship. In addition, the company operates the new *Isabela II,* a 40-passenger yacht (which Galapagos National Park regulations restricts to a capacity of just 34) on 7-night itineraries from Baltra to Plaza, Hood, Floreana, Barrington, Santa Cruz, Tower, Isabela, Fernandina, James, and Bartolome islands. The 166-foot yacht has 20 outside twin cabins, each with two lower berths and private facilities as well as a salon/bar, spacious dining room, and separate reading and games rooms. It carries a crew of 17, including two multilingual naturalist guides.

Metropolitan Touring also operates a series of smaller yachts accommodating from 6 to 14 passengers each—the *Merak, Encantada, Mistral, Nortada, Amigo I,* and *Beagle III*—and develops itineraries to suit your needs. Introduced in 1989 were inexpensive hotel and day cruise packages utilizing the 36-passenger motor yacht *Delphin II* and the Hotel Delfin, built around a tidal lagoon in Academy Bay on Santa Cruz Island. Travelers can choose as many days as they like of the package, but the itineraries are designed with guaranteed air space from Guayaquil on the 3-, 4-, or 7-night cruises. During the various Galapagos programs that highlight the most popular islands, guides trained by the Darwin Research Station come aboard each vessel. Metropolitan offers more than 60 different tours within mainland Ecuador, ranging from city sightseeing and visits to Indian markets to countrywide itineraries, mountain climbing, trekking, birdwatching, a look at the equator marker, etc.

Galapagos Cruises also operates a three-deck, 56-passenger flotel *Orellana* on Ecuador's Napo River for two- to four-night jungle cruises. The two- to four-berth cabins all have private facilities, and the flotel has a large sun deck, salon, and dining room. Shore excursions into the rain forests in motorized dugout canoes travel to such places as the Jivino River, Monkey Island, Primavera, Limoncocha, and Lake Taracoa—not for the timid, but worth it for the colorful scenery and thousand new sounds.

GALAPAGOS INC.

7800 Red Road, Suite 112
South Miami, FL 33143
tel: (305) 665–0841
    (800) 327–9854

This Florida-based company represents the *Galapagos Explorer*, a vessel carrying 90 passengers in air-conditioned comfort around the Galapagos Islands. Like the *Buccanero* before, the operators say this is the largest cruise ship operating in the islands. The ship boasts such amenities as a swimming pool, solarium, spacious dining room, two bar areas, and music for dancing. Five naturalist guides, who studied at the Charles Darwin Research station, are also aboard, and the 3- and 4-night cruises can be combined to a full week. Flights from Guayaquil carry passengers to San Cristobal to catch up with the *Explorer*. The Wednesday to Saturday or Saturday to Wednesday departures are year-round. Galapagos Inc. also offers yacht cruises of the islands aboard the first-class *Dorado*, tourist-class *Yolita* and *San Pedro*, economy-class *Darwin*, *Albatros*, *Poderoso*, *San Antonio*, and *Aida Maria*, as well as some charter boats upon request.

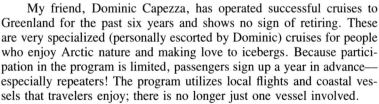

GREENLAND CRUISES

10 Park Avenue
New York, NY 10016
tel: (212) 683–1145
    (800) 648–2544

My friend, Dominic Capezza, has operated successful cruises to Greenland for the past six years and shows no sign of retiring. These are very specialized (personally escorted by Dominic) cruises for people who enjoy Arctic nature and making love to icebergs. Because participation in the program is limited, passengers sign up a year in advance—especially repeaters! The program utilizes local flights and coastal vessels that travelers enjoy; there is no longer just one vessel involved.

The tours depart in July and August to the land of the ever-shining sun, where primary destinations are Nuuk/Godthaab, Ilulisat/Jakob-shavn, the Ice Cap, Umanak, and Qilakitsoq. Highlights are flightseeing as well as hiking through small villages and meeting the townsfolk. The all-inclusive prices feature round-trip air travel from Ottawa, with ar-rangements possible for extended time in Greenland and Baffin Island.

HAPAG-LLOYD TRAVEL (AMERICA) INC.

c/o Hapag-Lloyd Tours
1640 Hempstead Turnpike
East Meadow, NY 11554
tel: (516) 794–1253
    (800) 334–2724

The much-respected Hapag Lloyd shipping line is the result of a 1970 merger between the famous Hamburg-America line (Hapag) and North German Lloyd (NDL). Lloyd dates from 1857 and began service between Germany and North America in 1858 with the steamer *Bremen;* Hapag was founded a decade earlier. The two companies were constant rivals in both service and speed as they carried passengers between the Old World and the New. By 1881, NDL's steamer *Elbe* had reduced crossing time between Southampton and New York to only eight days, 12 hours, and 50 minutes. A Hapag ship, the *Furst Bismarck,* set a record of six days, 11 hours and 44 minutes on the same route in 1889. NDL retaliated with a fleet of four-funnel-class vessels capable of mak-ing the North Atlantic crossing in less than six days. The battle for the Blue Riband had begun!

Even before the century turned, the two companies were expanding dramatically worldwide. In 1913 the ten-millionth passenger was re-corded aboard a Lloyd vessel, while Hapag was reportedly the largest shipping line in the world. These golden days, however, ended with the advent of World War I. When it was over, only a few vessels remained to both companies. But by 1930, NDL boasted two Blue Riband win-ners—the *Bremen* and the *Europa.* Again, such glorious times were fleeting, and World War II brought total destruction to both fleets.

Today, Hapag Lloyd's strength lies in freighters and container ships that carry their cargo all over the world. The company also operates one cruise vessel, the *Europa,* which replaced the former *Kungsholm I* in 1982. The 34,000-ton vessel, built in the Hapag-Lloyd yard in Bremer-haven, is very popular with the Germans—for whom she was con-structed! The vessel boasts eleven decks, ''an overall design ahead of its time,'' noiseless and spacious cabins, and a passenger capacity of between 600 and 1000 plus crew space for about 300. She cruises the world, following the sun and offering her passengers interesting itineraries and great comfort on board. However, this vessel does not really belong in a book written especially for North Americans because *Europa* is Germanic through and through. Food, service, entertainment, on-board ambience, and crew are all German; all passenger services are provided in the German language. Occasionally, if a large enough group on board warrants, an English-speaking host will translate and take care of you. This is not an "international" vessel on which many European nationalities are present and mingling; this is a German vessel, and passengers who do not speak the language are foreigners.

HOLLAND AMERICA LINE

300 Elliott Avenue West
Seattle, WA 98119
tel: (206) 281–3535

The beginning of Holland America Line fits into modern history. The future of Rotterdam as a port looked rather bleak in the early 1870s because ship owners seemed to prefer rival Amsterdam. Therefore, to try to develop some necessary trade between Holland and America, two young Dutchmen commissioned the SS *Rotterdam,* an iron vessel of 1700 tons that could carry eight passengers in first-class accommodations and 380 in steerage, as well as 1500 tons of cargo. Her maiden voyage took place in October 1872, and her subsequent voyages were so successful that the two young partners joined with a third to form the Netherlands-America Steam Navigation Company in April 1873. It became known simply as Holland America Line in 1896.

From the very beginning, Holland America's flagship has been named the *Rotterdam,* one in a fleet that features such names as *Nieuw Amsterdam, Potsdam, Ryndam, Noordam, Maasdam,* and *Statendam.* In addition to weekly service between Rotterdam and New York, the company began cruises to Copenhagan as early as June 1895 aboard the *Rotterdam* (the second). Another cruise offered during the first decade of the 20th century, aboard the *Statendam,* included a visit to the Holy Land. A few years later the company ordered a new 32,000-ton *Statendam,* which was destined to become a giant among passenger vessels, but alas, never carried a paying passenger. The ship launched just as World War I broke out, was fitted to transport troops, only to be sunk at sea—a U-boat victim.

Another new *Statendam,* ordered in the mid-1920s, sailed on her maiden voyage in April 1929, arriving in New York on the 300th anniversary of the landing of the Dutch ships that carried the founders of the settlement once known as New Amsterdam. The decade of the 1930s was a slump time for shipping, due to the world economic situation. By May 1940 Germany had invaded Holland and Dutch shipping ground to a standstill. At this time, however, Holland America transferred its headquarters to Curacao in the Dutch West Indies, where it remains.

In the postwar period Holland America launched the 15,000-ton *Ryndam* (most recently the *Atlas* of Epirotiki Line) and the *Maasdam* (now the *Stefan Batory* of Polish Ocean Line). The former *Statendam* (fourth of her name), launched in 1957, now sails as *Regent Star.* In 1958 Queen Juliana launched the fifth *Rotterdam;* her maiden voyage took place a year later. Both vessels easily converted to one-class cruising ships to accommodate the demand of the past few decades.

The 38,000-ton *Rotterdam* is now the grande dame of the Holland America Line fleet. Worldly and gracious, the *Rotterdam* has a fine following and (at thirtysomething!) has received a $15-million facelift to take her into the 90s. The vessel made 25 global voyages, the last one in 1986 when HAL management decided the long cruise market was "passing away." But times have changed again, and the *Rotterdam* began the 90s with a 47-day Around South America cruise as well as an Around Hawaii sailing. The ship was designed for long, leisurely ocean voyages and will, hopefully, be utilized for such in the future.

Two 32,000-ton sister ships, the 1200-passenger *Nieuw Amsterdam* (1983) and *Noordam* (1984) have proved successful for Holland America, as they are well suited to short Caribbean cruises during the winter months as well as the Alaska season in summer. Both vessels are beautifully designed and decorated—the *Nieuw Amsterdam* has the ambience of a 17th-century sailing ship and over $1 million in nautical artifacts, while the *Noordam* received an 18th-century interior and also $1 million in lovely antiques.

Fourth and largest of the fleet is the 52,000-ton *Westerdam* (former *Homeric*), which received a $65-million expansion and redesign in the Papenburg, West German, shipyard where she was originally constructed (1986). The insertion of a 130-foot section increased the ship's passenger complement to 1476 and her length to 798 feet. Another million dollars in 17th- and 18th-century art and antiques to reflect Dutch exploration were also added.

Holland America, whose motto is "Tradition of Excellence," is known for its Dutch officers and Indonesian crew trained at a special school in Jakarta (Filipinos have since been added). The line is also known for its No Tipping Required policy, the spirit of which seems to work well as the crew all appear to have happy faces. However, exceptional service is not expected to go unrewarded, so tipping aboard HAL ships is not a bad word; it's just not a continual word!

Holland America, through its Westours subsidiary, has been a major force in Alaska and the Yukon territory for two decades. It also operates Gray Line of Alaska, Westmark Hotels and Inns, several large excursion boats, and the McKinley Explorer glass-domed railway cars. Alaska, where Holland America places all four vessels for the summer season and offers over 50 Inside Passage cruises (plus another 16 on *Wind Spirit*), is considered one of the top travel destinations of the 1990s—the ship line saw an increase of 15% in cruise passengers as the decade unfolded.

In 1987 and 1988, Holland America acquired half and then full interest in Windstar Sail Cruises, whose small vessels are *Wind Star, Wind Song,* and *Wind Spirit.* In January 1989, Carnival Cruise Line completed acquisition of Holland America Line, which is treated as a wholly owned subsidiary. Before the end of that same year, the two companies announced an order for three new Holland America vessels to be constructed at Italy's Fincantieri shipyard. The 50,000-ton cruise ships, to be registered in the Bahamas, will accommodate 1250 passengers in more splendor than HAL has ever offered and be designed for world-wide itineraries. Delivery dates are 1992, 1993, and 1994.

INTERNATIONAL CRUISE CENTER

250 Old Country Road
Mineola, New York 11501
tel: (516) 747–8880
     (800) 221–3254

International Cruise Center, a company begun in 1982 by a former Yugoslavian cargo captain, is discovering a happy place in the world for it markets cruise tours primarily to Eastern European countries aboard vessels (primarily) registered in the USSR. These cruises are for travelers who prefer adventure to luxury and believe in "glasnost." Although ICC does send along an English-speaking guide/lecturer, it sometimes helps if potential passengers speak an Eastern European language—or Russian—which was definitely necessary to enjoy the USSR-flag vessels when they were allowed to sail from U.S. ports.

Among the cruise tours available from ICC are Danube River sailings aboard the *Volga* and the Black Sea aboard an ocean liner named *Ayvazovsky.* Other Baltic adventures are featured in mini-cruises aboard *Ilich, Konstantin Simonov,* or *Georg Ots* from Helsinki to Leningrad, Stockholm, or Tallinn (Estonia). If you wondered whatever happened to the *Astor,* the vessel is now called *Fedor Dostoevsky* and sails the world with the *Odessa*. Both vessels fly the USSR flag but are under West German management; ICC can book a cruise around Europe, to Indonesia, or up the Amazon River if you are interested.

Another vessel that surfaced in ICC literature is the former *Aquarius* of Hellenic Mediterranean Line (a company that folded during the terrorism travel problems). This 300-passenger charmer is now called *Adriana* and is a member of the Jadrolinija Shipping Company of Yugoslavia. She offers cruises from Dubrovnik of 9- and 12-days to the Greek Islands and Turkey at reasonable rates. Transportation to the Greek Islands and Turkey is also available through Minoan Lines car ferries, which seem to have a year-round schedule.

In addition to the Russian-flag vessels and cruise ferries in Scandinavia and the eastern Mediterranean, ICC also represents the *Hebridean Princess* and Hebridean Island Cruises around the northwest of Scotland. The 48-passenger vessel was converted recently from a Scottish ferry. British, Irish, and Scottish ferries are all on file with ICC, which will plan an entire land/cruise package around a ferry ride!

IVARAN LINES

One Exchange Plaza
New York, NY 10006
tel: (212) 809–1220

The Oslo-based Ivaran Lines is no stranger to the East Coast of the United States nor to South American ports. For almost 70 years, Ivaran has been sending its cargo vessels, also carrying a few passengers, on these routes. In March 1988, the company inaugurated a glamorous 19,500-ton passenger/container vessel constructed in Korea for 46-day sailings/cruises from New York (Brooklyn) to South America and return. The concept is a reincarnation of the famous Grace Line cargo liners that left the West Coast (Vancouver/Seattle/Portland) every two weeks like a clock and sailed around South America for up to two months. Alas, they were laid up in the late 70s by Delta Line of New Orleans (which purchased the company and then claimed they were too costly to operate).

Ivaran is offering an excellent service aboard its 88-passenger *Americana*—a pair of sister ships called *Brasilera* and *Argentina* are promised—for the ship is well designed and maintained and a good time is had by all aboard. Registry and officers are Norwegian, of course, and the hotel staff is a well-trained group of young Argentinians who complement nicely the "retired age" and very experienced cruise passengers. The interior spaces are Scandinavian decor, with light woods and an airy ambience. Cabins are cheerful and well designed for long voyages with such amenities as small refrigerator, private safe, TV/

VCR, desk/vanity, sitting area, and bidet in the bathroom. The single-seating dining room has spectacular seaviews and a cuisine that keeps one's interest still keen after six weeks!

Ivaran overbid its per diem the first year and had to adjust prices to market level. The average per diem going into the 1990s is over $200—fairly high for a slow boat, but this one is top of the line. While the ports may be interesting—Charleston, Savannah, Jacksonville, Miami, Rio de Janeiro, Buenos Aires, Montevideo, Rio Grande, Santos, Bahia, Fortaleza, Norfolk, Baltimore, and Philadelphia (or any combination of the above)—there are no organized shore excursions, so do your homework and make your own. And there is no after-dinner "show" either; that is also make-your-own.

NORWEGIAN CRUISE LINE

2 Alhambra Plaza
Coral Gables, FL 33134
tel: (305) 447–9660
    (800) 327–7030

It seems a long way from hauling coal around Scandinavia at the turn of the century to buying one of the most famous ships afloat and converting her into a fun-filled resort called the *Norway,* but that is just the history of the family Kloster. The *Norway* is just one of the many coups of the grandson of the original Kloster ship owner, who bought his first steamer of 830 tons in 1906. Knut Utstein Kloster.

You may still think of this company as Norwegian Caribbean Line— it still is NCL—but it has a new name, logo, and address that is here to stay! The new name, *Norwegian Cruise Line,* reflects the changing scope of the company from just offering cruises in the Caribbean to other areas—Bermuda, Alaska, the west coast, and possibly Europe. Other changes in ship-line policy include reflagging all vessels to Bahamian flag and changing Kloster Cruise Limited (the parent company) to headquarters in Bermuda. While all ships will continue to be operated primarily by Norwegian officers, the corporate changes were strategic to containing costs and restructuring debt. In order to raise financing for the new vessels, Kloster Cruise planned a $100 million stock offering in late 1987 that has been indefinitely postponed due to stormy weather on Wall Street since the so-called October 19 market crash. Alternatives are being studied by this pioneering company, which has a reputation for doing the unexpected and doing it with panache. Its first venture into the cruise business occurred in 1966 with the introduction of the

Sunward on three- and four-day cruises to the Bahamas from Miami. Since that time Caribbean cruises and this company have grown so rapidly that NCL has been a major force in the cruise industry for over two decades and has carried several million passengers during that time.

The original *Sunward* (now retired) was soon followed by the 16,000-ton *Starward* in 1968, which pioneered weekly cruises to Jamaica. In 1970 the company introduced the 16,250-ton *Skyward* on weekly cruises that featured a call at Cap Haitien, home of the renowned Citadel Laferriere. Two years later NCL launched the 16,607-*Southward* on 14-day cruises, but then changed her itinerary to a seven-day program in 1975. Then NCL bought the ailing Cunard *Adventurer,* completely refitted her, and changed her personality to fit three- and four-day Bahama cruises. She took to the seas again in 1976 as the *Sunward II* on sailings that featured Nassau as well as an Out Island, just for the fun of it! The ship line made a rather bold move when it decided to just plop people down on a beautiful beach for a day, disregarding vacationers' gambling and shopping instincts. It has been a noteworthy success. As one contented passenger said recently, "It was the most relaxing five hours I have ever spent. When I saw those sparkling sands, I knew what it was like to be a beach bum!" NCL's own Out Island in the Bahamas originally was called Great Stirrup Cay; it is now known as Pleasure Island.

Sometime during this history, Kloster bought real estate in Jamaica so passengers aboard the *Starward* could enjoy a cruise-and-stay holiday at Jamaica Hill near Port Antonio. Unfortunately, the 44-villa resort on an old estate with acres of lawn, tennis courts, and a swimming pool overlooking miles of beautiful beaches, has not been a success and is no longer part of the NCL package. But Knut Kloster's most bold cruise-oriented move was the purchase of the SS *France* and her conversion into a $130-million floating resort, the *Norway.* No one said it would work, but once again Kloster succeeded (despite some severe problems). A handsome vessel, with the most beautiful public rooms on the sea and a wonderful spirit from top to bottom, it charms even those who knew her as the *France* to say that her reincarnation was well planned and well done. The 1035-foot *Norway* is truly her own cruise destination and has proved to be one of the most relaxing one-week holidays available.

The "white fleet"—Skyward, Southward, and Starward—are good, solid ships that have been refurbished over the past few years to the tune of more than $60 million, with new designs by Jeffrey Howard Associates of Miami. Public rooms are renamed and redesignated to allow for upgraded standards of service, especially in the dining area. While the ships have no pretenses to elegance—which makes them credible—they do offer interesting itineraries and a casual ambience. All cabins have received attention in new rugs, bedspreads and curtains, and new fixtures of brass and glass. Passengers can depend upon these vessels and are rarely disappointed. If you are in the mood for just three or four days in the Bahamas, the *Sunward II* has a fine reputation for onboard service, food, and just plain fun. The *Norway* is still the ultimate floating resort—with nothing overblown, nothing overdone—with plenty of "name" entertainment on board, some of it very good indeed. NCL has added some ports of call to the *Norway* schedule so that she now visits St. John, St. Thomas, St. Maarten, and a beach party on Great Stirrup Cay, NCL's Pleasure Island.

Always an innovator in the cruise industry, NCL emphasizes good clean fun that is very popular with its passengers. One of the most memorable programs available is the Dive In, for which a staff of some 15 certified diving instructors offers lessons, equipment, and guidance on undersea tours around the Caribbean. Since its debut in 1978 aboard the *Sunward II,* the Dive In program has led approximately a million NCL passengers in colorful explorations below the water. All NCL vessels now offer the program, and you do not even have to swim to participate and enjoy! (A safety vest protects nonswimmers from danger.) Most of the Dive In programs occur on the ship line's Bahamian Out Island, but other ports of call are now also included.

In redeploying the fleet, NCL has moved the *Starward* to San Juan for year-round weekly cruises to Barbados, Martinique, St. Maarten, Antigua, and St. Thomas. She was joined recently by the *Skyward,* departing Saturdays for Barbados, St. Lucia, Guadeloupe, St. Thomas, and St. Maarten. In May 1988 the *Southward* began 3- and 4-night cruises from Los Angeles to San Diego, Ensenada, and Catalina Island. Three of NCL's vessels still call Hawaii "home"—*Sunward II, Norway,* and *Seaward.*

The $120-million, 42,000-ton *Seaward* made her debut in New York harbor in May 1988 and was christened by Norwegian running star Grete Waitz in ceremonies followed by a gala fund-raiser to benefit the U.S. Olympic team. The vessel accommodates approximately 1500 passengers and sails every Sunday to NCL's Pleasure Island, Ocho Rios, Grand Cayman, Playa del Carmen, and Cozumel.

The *Seaward,* although seemingly built in haste by the former Wartsila Shipyard in Finland, has proved to be very popular with NCL passengers and a successful addition to what company executives consider "mass-market" cruising.

Those same executives have not been idle in preparing for the new decade and have promised more new vessels for the ship line. Meanwhile, a $40-million enhancement to the *Norway* raises her tonnage to 75,000 and passenger complement to 2044 while also adding some of the most glamorous accommodations (in two new glass-enclosed decks) and facilities afloat—including a 6000-square-foot Roman Spa down on

Dolphin Deck—if you can find it! It makes good business sense to "enhance" the *Norway* by $40 million after ten years of service, they say, because her replacement value is approximately $500 million!

NCL likes to offer an appeal to just about everyone (the masses, one might say) and promotes its theme cruises on all six vessels. Country music, jazz, golf, tennis, football stars, even how to ski (!) are just some of the "theme" cruises available throughout the year. The company has also announced a multi-year commitment with Universal Studios of Florida and Hollywood (CA) for special cruise/land packages as well as a whole new world of entertainment at sea.

Kloster Cruise Limited is the umbrella under which Norwegian Cruise Line operates. In 1984, Kloster acquired the posh Royal Viking Line and took delivery of the elegant, 740-passenger *Royal Viking Sun* in 1988 (which became immediately one of the premiere cruise vessels afloat). Since, Kloster consolidated these two companies in Coral Gables, although it has not tampered with RVL's upscale image and product. In 1989, Kloster acquired the San Francisco–based Royal Cruise Line and its two very fine vessels—*Golden Odyssey* and *Crown Odyssey*—important additions to its luxury division. Kloster Cruises Limited has announced that all three companies will be operated as separate entities—at least for the present time.

OCEAN CRUISE LINES

1510 S.E. 17th Street
Fort Lauderdale, FL 33316
tel: (305) 764–3500
    (800) 556–8850 (East Coast)
    (800) 338–1700 (West Coast)

PEARL CRUISES

tel: (800) 426–3588 (East Coast)
    (800) 338–1700 (West Coast)

As this guide goes to press, Paquet French Cruises has announced the purchase of Ocean Cruise Lines and Pearl Cruises, which it promises to operate as separate entities, although in the same south Florida location. Paquet French Cruises, with its flagship *Mermoz*, has just returned to the North American cruise scene and a marketing agreement had been signed already between the companies for Paquet to represent Ocean and Pearl in France. Obviously, Paquet took a large leap and bought the entire operation from the Swiss-based 2000 Corporation, which formed Ocean Cruise Lines in 1983 and then acquired Pearl Cruises in 1987. The two cruise lines operate the *Ocean Princess* and *Ocean Pearl*. The 250-passenger *Ocean Islander* left the family in October 1990 following the Mediterranean season and will no longer be sailing for Ocean Cruise Lines. However, Paquet is looking for growth in its new enterprise, so watch for additional vessels to join the Paquet/Pearl/Ocean fleet!

The 12,200-ton *Ocean Princess* (ex-*Italia*) is registered in the Bahamas but has Greek officers and a Greek/Italian crew. It was extensively redone by Agni and Michael Katzourakis, Greek-born interior designers well known in cruise circles as they have to their credits the *Golden Odyssey, Royal Odyssey,* and S/S *Oceanic* (of Premier Cruise Line). They have managed to give all these vessels the appearance of being completely new.

The 460-passenger *Ocean Princess* cruises in northern Europe from spring through fall, offering one-week Fjord and Fairytale sailings from Copenhagen alternating with Scandinavia/Russia ports of call so passengers can embark for a full two weeks. A special two-week North Cape/Spitzbergen cruise departs Copenhagen mid-June. Transatlantic and Grand Europe Cruises are also available. During the winter season, *Ocean Princess* cruises in the Caribbean plus as many as nine varied itineraries to South American ports of call, including the Amazon, Rio, and Buenos Aires. Recently, Ocean teamed with travel pioneer Lars Eric Lindblad (whose own company went bankrupt in 1989) to offer adventure cruises aboard the *Ocean Princess* to Antarctica, the Falkland Islands, Patagonia, and other exotic global places. The cruises, called Lindblad Limited Editions, will sometimes feature Lindblad on board as lecturer/escort on both this adventure series and on the return of *Ocean Pearl* to China. Lindblad is an expert on China and assisted in opening the country to North Americans during the 1970s.

Ocean spent several million dollars refurbishing the *Ocean Pearl* (formerly known as *Pearl of Scandinavia*), which included expanding the berth count from 428 to 500. The vessel sails year-round in the Far East, offering several different two-week itineraries. They have such names as The Spice Islands, Bangkok/Bali & Beyond, Great Cities of Asia, and China Dynasty. After a year of pussyfooting, Pearl Cruises has returned to China, and the response from passengers has been fine— if not yet overwhelming. New on the *Ocean Pearl* itinerary are cruises between Bombay and Singapore, called Jewels of India, and between

Bombay and Mombasa, called Passage to Africa. So, the vessel is covering more than the Far East and extending its appeal to Ocean Club (past passenger) members.

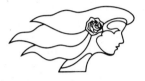

OCEANIC CRUISES

SMI Group—Suite 500
188 The Embarcadero
San Francisco, CA 94105
tel: (800) 545–5778

"Cruise Japanese Style aboard the *Oceanic Grace,*" says the attractive brochure. Oceanic Cruises is another of the booming Japanese companies to enter the industry with a luxury vessel. The company is owned by Showa Line, one of the six largest steamship companies in Japan involved with commercial shipping worldwide. According to Showa's corporate profile, the company operates containers, liners, tankers, and transport and bulk carrier services, involving 113 different owned or chartered vessels. To enter the cruise/leisure industry seems a logical extension of such success.

The 118-passenger *Oceanic Grace* was built in Japan and began service in April 1989. It was designed by the Studio Yacht group of Holland and closely resembles the *Sea Goddess I* and *II,* except the chairs are shorter, the beds are harder, and the bathtubs are only four feet long! While the vessel caters primarily (80 to 90% at this writing) to the Japanese market, we understand that Americans and Europeans are very welcome and the Japanese passengers on board are such that they are eager to interface with westerners.

For the 1991/92 season, *Oceanic Grace* offers one-week cruises from Nagasaki, Yokohama,Tokyo, Kobe, and Hakodate and Niigata. She is the only vessel sailing exclusively around the Japanese archipelago so extensively, and her 5000-ton size allows visits to both large and small ports. Sounds wonderful, and we wish her well!

P & O CRUISES

c/o Princess Cruises
10110 Santa Monica Blvd.
Los Angeles, CA 90067   or
tel: (213) 553–1770

Canberra House
47 Middlesex Street
London E17AL
England
tel: (01) 283–8080

The Peninsular and Oriental Steam Navigation Company, England's largest and most prestigious passenger and cargo line, began in the early 1800s and grew steadily in the 19th and 20th centuries through a series of astute acquisitions (and some romantic seafaring history). The company flag, a combination of the blue and white national colors of Portugal quartered with the red and yellow colors of Spain, symbolizes the highest of honors that both countries bestowed upon the ship line in the 1830s, commemorating valuable services rendered to Queen Maria of Portugal and Queen Isabella of Spain. Another interesting episode in the annals of P & O history dates to the opening of service between Egypt and India, which added a new word to the English language: *Posh* appeared stamped on certain steamship tickets to indicate that the passenger had bought the best (and coolest) cabin—which happened to be "Port Out (to India), Starboard Home." Since this cabin was in the most expensive category, the new word began to connote wealth and elitism.

According to company correspondence, P & O Line had such a fine reputation in the Victorian 19th century that even its shipwrecks were considered the best of any passenger fleet! In a letter dated 1863, from a Mrs. Dulcimer to her friend, Laura, the writer advises, "If you are ever shipwrecked, do contrive to get the catastrophe conducted by the Peninsular and Oriental Company. I believe other companies drown you sometimes, and drowning is a very prosaic arrangement fit only for seafaring people and second-class passengers. I have just been shipwrecked under the auspices of P & O, and I assure you that it is the pleasantest thing imaginable. It has its little hardships to be sure, but so has a picnic, and the wreck was one of the most agreeable picnics you can imagine." What a recommendation!

P & O Cruises, which celebrated its 150th anniversary as a passenger ship company in 1987, is part of a huge conglomerate of companies in Britain involved in cargo/container shipping as well as construction and real estate. In passenger services, P & O owns and operates Princess cruises of Los Angeles *(Royal Princess, Sea Princess, Island Princess, Pacific Princess, Fair Princess, Dawn Princess, Sky Princess, Crown Princess, Star Princess, Regal Princess)* as well as the Swan Group (Swan Hellenic Cruises aboard the *Orpheus,* Nile cruises aboard *Nile Star,* and new Rhine cruises in season) and Canberra cruises, which markets the last of the great ocean liners, *Canberra.*

The 44,807-ton *Canberra* was built in Northern Ireland in 1961, but has been refurbished twice in the past decade to bring her up to 1980s standards. She carries 1400 passengers (double occupancy) as well as a crew of 805 that represents the far reaches of the former British Empire—British officers with Indian (Goanese), Pakistani, and Chinese deck and engine. Many cabins still do not boast complete private facilities (wc and showers are down the hall a bit), but the Great White Whale, as she is so affectionately termed by her loyal passengers, is certainly the last of a breed. She is very popular with a wide range of English-speaking nationalities, and makes a world cruise every winter as well as round-trip sailings from Southampton to ports throughout the Mediterranean, Black, and Baltic seas—never repeating an itinerary if she can avoid doing so!

In spring 1991, the lovely *Sea Princess* (former *Kungsholm*) returns to the P & O family where she began her second life as *Sea Princess* in 1979. The 28,000-ton, 710-passenger, all first-class vessel with traditional ambience will offer round-trip sailings from Southampton during the season and follow the sun during the winter months. She returns to P & O by popular demand, not only for the vessel herself but for the additional berths she brings to the British market where cruises are *in!*

PAQUET FRENCH CRUISES

1510 S.E. 17th Street
Fort Lauderdale, FL 33316
tel: (305) 764–3500
　　(800) 999–0555

Paquet French Cruises has returned to the North American scene after an absence of several years. The French-based company, known as Compagnie Francaise de Crossieres in Paris, is owned by two large conglomerates—Chargeurs S.A. and Accor (one of the largest hospitality corporations worldwide and owners of both Novotel and Sofitel hotels). Paquet was originally founded by Nicolas Paquet in 1860 as a merchant shipping operation between Marseilles and Morocco and has survived several diverse lives since then!

Not only did Paquet announce its return to the North American market in early 1990 but it made a major splash in May of the same year by acquiring Ocean Cruise Lines and Pearl Cruises from the 2000 Corporation. In doing so, Paquet increased its fleet from a 530-passenger flagship, *Mermoz,* with the 460-passenger *Ocean Princess* and 500-passenger *Ocean Pearl.* There are plans for more expansion, which means more cruise ships and more destinations. Watch for happenings!

Meanwhile, the *Mermoz*—which flies the Bahamian flag but features French officers—sails in the Mediterranean during the summer as well as through the fjords of Norway. In the fall and early winter, she travels to ports around South Africa following the ancient spice route and then sails to the Caribbean for cruises out of San Juan, Guadeloupe, Fort Lauderdale, and Martinique. South America and the Galapagos Islands are also on the winter agenda.

PREMIER CRUISE LINES

400 Challenger Road
Port Canaveral, Cape Canaveral, FL 32920
tel: (407) 783–5061
    (800) 327–7113 (outside Florida)

Premier Cruise Lines has become the "official" cruise line of Walt Disney World, and offers an all-inclusive package to the world's number-one tourist destination with every sailing. The Greyhound-backed ship line is managed by two co-executives whose ambition—to offer 3- and 4-day cruises to the Bahamas from Port Canaveral that would appeal not only to families but to anyone young at heart—is sound and very successful. The company offers an excellent concept with good ships and service for exceptional prices. This is truly the best way for all generations to enjoy the same holiday, and family-size cabins accommodate as many as five people (providing that three are small ones).

Premier Cruise Lines made its debut in March 1984 with the 21,000-ton *Royale,* the former *Frederico C.,* which has been sold to Dolphin Cruise Line and become the *Sea Breeze.* The company brought the well-known 40,000-ton *Oceanic* into service in late April 1986, followed by the former *Atlantic* and the former *Sun Princess.* These are now known as Star-Ship *Oceanic,* Star-Ship *Atlantic,* and Star-Ship *Majestic.* All vessels are painted with Premier Cruise red on the hull, and the *Oceanic* has been nicely refurbished by the husband and wife team, Agni and Michael Katzourakis, who brightened interiors and added a number of kiddie and adult play areas—casino, teen center, video game room, fitness center, etc. Cabins were not paid much attention, although Premier did add some double beds for the younger crowd. Also for the grown-up contingent is "name" entertainment, decent food, some excellent bars, and good company among the passengers. After all, other people who bring their children along on vacations have to be okay!

Premier offers the ease of a 3- or 4-day cruise to the Bahamas aboard three very different vessels as well as a 4- or 3-day Disney World vacation package for one price, with one booking. What could be more convenient? And the cabin category you choose for the cruise is related directly to the hotel at Disney World. All you have to do is buy a round-trip airline ticket and off you go. The package also includes a 7-day rental car and a tour of the Kennedy Space Center. It sounds pretty good to me—tromp around Disney World/EPCOT Center for a few days and then rest. up on board ship the rest of the week on a cruise to the Bahamas.

Premier Cruise Lines has been awarded the Grand Prix Mondial du Voyage by the World Travel Award Committee for four consecutive years. Whatever it is, it sounds good, and I'm sure that Premier is quite deserving of the honor. From Port Canaveral, Star-Ship *Atlantic* and Star-Ship *Oceanic* sail every Monday and Friday year-round to Nassau and Salt Cay, an out island in the Bahamas. Star-Ship *Majestic* sails every Thursday and Sunday year-round to Abacos, Treasure Cay, Green Turtle Cay, Great Guana Cay, and Man-O-War Cay in the Bahama Islands.

PRINCESS CRUISES

10100 Santa Monica Boulevard
Los Angeles, CA 90067
tel: (213) 553–1770

Princess Cruises was founded by Seattle industrialist and entrepreneur Stanley B. McDonald in 1965, when he pioneered cruising to Mexico's west coast aboard the 6000-ton ferry vessel named *Princess Patricia*. Two years later he brought the *Princess Carla* into year-round service that combined the Mexico cruises during the winter with Alaska sailings all summer. McDonald sold his company to Boise Cascade in 1968 but bought it back again (for a song) in 1970. Four years later McDonald sold the company once and for all to P & O, who promised to retain the Princess name.

At the time (and to this day), the prestigious Peninsular & Oriental Steam Navigation Company (P & O) prided itself on having "invented" leisure cruises when William Makepeace Thackeray took a series of P & O vessels around the Mediterranean in 1844 and wrote "From Cornhill to Grand Cairo"—which enticed other writers (Kipling, Forster, Trollope) to follow in his wake. With the union of Princess Cruises and P & O in 1974, the popular *Island Princess* was purchased outright and so was sister ship *Pacific Princess*. P & O's new *Spirit of London* became *Sun Princess* so that by the end of 1975 Princess Cruises boasted a three-vessel fleet. In November 1984, Her Royal Highness the Princess of Wales christened the company's trendsetter in superships, the 45,000-ton *Royal Princess,* which carried her complement of 1200 passengers in all outside cabins—many with terraces. The Princess Cruises family expanded to five members in December 1986 with the addition of *Sea Princess* (former *Kungsholm*), formerly operated by P & O in Australia/Europe trade.

Not to rest on well-known laurels, Princess Cruises/P & O bought out the competition—Sitmar Cruises—in July 1988 and acquired three vessels in operation (*Fairwind, Fairsea, Fairsky*) as well as three under construction. The 925-passenger *Fairwind* and *Fairsea* were renamed *Fair Princess* and *Dawn Princess*. The 1200-passenger *Fairsky* is now *Sky Princess*. The 1470-passenger *Star Princess* was christened by the lovely Audrey Hepburn in Port Everglades in March 1989, and the 1590-passenger *Crown Princess* received her blessing from actress Sophia Loren in New York harbor in September 1990. Her sistership, *Regal Princess,* will be introduced in 1991.

Princess Cruises is a burgeoning company, as they say, and can boast a fleet of nine vessels carrying more than 350,000 passengers worldwide each year. Although *Sea Princess* is returning to P & O auspices for the British market on European cruises, the vessel will be replaced by the arrival of *Regal Princess*. During the summer season, Princess Cruises is quite a presence in Alaska, with some 93 departures on six different ships from May to September. The 7- and 10-day itineraries feature the Inside Passage and Gulf of Alaska from San Francisco, Vancouver, and Whittier. Princess vessels can also be found in Europe, the South Pacific and Orient, through the Panama Canal, to the Mexican Riviera, and in the Caribbean. The company is committed to the Caribbean and plans to become a dominant presence in the "premium market" beginning 1991, with *Regal Princess, Crown Princess, Star Princess,* and *Sky Princess*.

Princess is the cruise line that said yes to *Love Boat,* the long-running television program that brought the idea of taking a cruise to millions. *Pacific Princess* is the original "Love Boat," but the series has sailed and filmed aboard *Royal, Island, Pacific, Sky,* and *Sea Princess* ships. In syndication, the series has been translated into 29 different languages and viewed by millions in some 93 countries.Now that *Love Boat* is no longer in production, Princess has contracted the familiar face of Gavin MacLeod as its spokesperson—just in case you miss the show.

Princess Cruises celebrated its 25th anniversary in 1990 and there were some in the company who remembered the 6000-ton ferry *Princess Patricia* that gave the ship line its name!

REGENCY CRUISES

260 Madison Avenue
New York, NY 10016
tel: (212) 972–4774
    (800) 341–5566

Regency Cruises was founded in November 1984 and completed its initial public offering in June 1985 with some 6.5 million units sold for over $5.5 million. The new cruise company began operation in mid-November 1985 with service aboard the 722-passenger *Regent Sea* (former *Gripsholm, Navarino*) from Montego Bay every Sunday.

Chairman and Chief Executive Officer of Regency Cruises is the respected industry veteran William Schanz, one of the founders who was formerly associated with Paquet French Cruises. Schanz has built the company's executive team, its European on-board ambience, and watches the pursestrings tightly so that a profit has been enjoyed from the very beginning of operations.

From the beginning, Regency has been committed to the Caribbean—innovating one-week cruises from Montego Bay, Jamaica, that featured a partial transit of the Panama Canal. In July 1987 the 950-passenger *Regent Star* (former *Rhapsody* and *Statendam*) began 7-day cruises from Montego Bay as well, while the *Regent Sea* journeyed to Alaskan waters for the summer season. Both have offered good value for the vacation dollar and high occupancy levels.

With the acquisition of a third vessel in December 1988, the former *Royal Odyssey/Doric* and renamed *Regent Sun,* and a certain tension in the Panama political climate, Regency began to offer alternative Caribbean itineraries to its loyal passengers and try other ports of departure. Montego Bay is still home port for the *Regent Star* for the winter season, offering Regency's signature cruises of a partial transit of the Panama Canal. After a series of two-week trans–Panama Canal cruises between Los Angeles and the Caribbean, *Regent Sea* and *Regent Sun* spend the winter months in San Juan offering one-week Islands in the Sun and Gems of the Caribbean, respectively. The cruises depart on Sundays.

During the summer months Regency sends two of its vessels to Alaska—*Regent Sea* and *Regent Sun* for a total of 34 departures (Sunday or Friday) between Whittier (Anchorage) and Vancouver. At the end of the season, Regency offers its popular Jazz Festival at Sea aboard the *Regent Sea* between Vancouver and Los Angeles. New for Regency Cruises is placing the *Regent Star* on one-week sailings between New York and Montreal from late June to early October. Following the success of the 1990 summer program, one can expect that *Regent Star* will return to the lovely Northeast and Canada in successive years.

RENAISSANCE CRUISES

1800 Eller Drive—Suite 300
P. O. Box 350307
Fort Lauderdale, FL 33335-0307
tel: (305) 463–0982
    (800) 525–2450

Renaissance Cruises, another addition to the boutique (small ultra-luxury vessels) niche in this diverse industry, plans to have eight 100–114 passenger ships—all named *Renaissance*—sailing the oceans and seas of the globe by early 1992. The first *Renaissance* vessels have arrived, and their destinations feature the Far East, Mediterranean, European, and Scandinavian ports, Black Sea and Red Sea as well as ports and islands around Africa and South America, and in the Caribbean. Although the ships are beautifully designed, spacious for the passenger complement, and well appointed, their destinations are the primary theme of this company. In fact, the ship line boasts that the total itineraries of its vessels will encompasss some 180 ports (about one-third of them exclusive to Renaissance Cruises) in 50 countries on four continents. When the ice-class-rated *Renaissance VII* and *VIII* arrive in 1992, they will most likely add Antarctica to their itinerary—another continent.

Renaissance Cruises is owned and operated by prestigious Fearnley & Eger, a 120-plus-year-old Norwegian shipping concern based in Oslo. The parent company is no stranger to the cruise industry, having dabbled in it for almost three decades. The vessels were and are being built in La Spezia, Italy, where certain delays have taken place—a natural occurrence in any shipyard. Their design is sleek and simple, with all-outside suites of 200-plus square feet and stocked with modern amenities.

The destination-oriented *Renaissance I–VIII* will cruise primarily during the night to leave the daytime hours for port calls. On board are guest lecturers who profess to be experts in their particular fields; pre-cruise information packets as well as suggested reading enable passengers to prepare for the destinations. Both organized shore excursions and independent touring are available.

Back on board, passengers may relax at the outdoor pool and spa, sports platform, piano bar, blackjack table, or watch a video in their spacious suite. Buffet breakfast and lunch are served al fresco, weather permitting. Dinner is available in the elegant dining room where there is open seating and extended hours. The cuisine has an Italian accent, with an emphasis on the new and lighter preparation. Menus are rotated every 21 days, so passengers can take back-to-back one-week cruises and not have a dish repeated.

Itineraries such as those in the Mediterranean—Barcelona/Rome, Rome/Venice, Venice/Istanbul—can be combined in what the ship line calls a "modular concept" of three one-week cruises. All itineraries include round-trip airfare from departure gateways as well as up to three nights in a deluxe hotel at both beginning and end of the cruise. Or, travelers may prefer to make their own arrangements and thus receive the appropriate discount on the package rate.

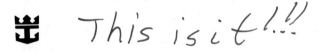

This is it!...

ROYAL CARIBBEAN CRUISE LINE (RCCL)

903 South America Way
Miami, FL 33132
tel: (305) 379–2601
    (800) 327–6700

In the highly competitive world of cruise companies based in Miami for sailings around the Caribbean, Royal Caribbean Cruise Line consistently earns top honors in quality of its ships, itineraries, and on-board amenities. The ship line was founded in 1969 as a partnership of three respected Norwegian companies, long experienced in offering solid products worldwide: I.M. Skaugen is involved with supertankers; Anders Wilhelmsen operates the Barber Line freighters among other shipping interests; Gotaas Larsen has tankers and freighters and is involved with Admiral Cruise Lines of Miami and Los Angeles. While Royal Caribbean's headquarters and fleet is registered in Oslo, its North American management team is in Miami and very aware of passenger preferences and fluctuations. The scene has changed a bit the past year or so at the formerly conservative RCCL in Miami, with the departure of some high executives as well as the arrival of the largest cruise ship in the world. By its own cognizance, the company has become involved in the "volume economy market," which will extend into the mass market in the very near future.

RCCL (as the company is affectionately called) has not been idle as the cruising decade of the 80s went by and the 1990s began. In January 1988, the French-built *Sovereign of the Seas*—largest cruise ship afloat (at this writing)—made her cruise debut from Miami to great acclaim. The vessel has proved so popular with loyal RCCL passengers that the company has ordered two more! The keel was laid for *Sovereign II* on July 31, 1989, for Spring 1991 delivery. *Sovereign III* will be delivered approximately one year later, and both vessels will sail the Caribbean on one-week cruises—the 3000-passenger (maximum) *Sovereign II* from San Juan. Not content with major success, RCCL added two more vessels to its fleet—the 976-passenger *Viking Serenade* in January 1990 and the 1610–2000-passenger *Nordic Empress* in June of the same year. *Viking Serenade* is the former *Stardancer* of Admiral Cruises, and it sails in Alaska during the summer season and to the Mexican Riviera in winter. *Nordic Empress* was originally ordered by Admiral Cruises as the *Future Seas*. She will now sail under the RCCL banner on 3- and 4-day cruises to the Bahamas, with a call at RCCL's own out island—recently renamed CocoCay. In addition to all the above, Royal Caribbean placed the *Sun Viking* on a European itinerary beginning summer 1990—an indication that the company is becoming more "global" (which it suggested a few years ago).

So, the RCCL fleet will eventually number nine, of which the original four were built in famed Wartsila Shipyard near Helsinki (now known as Wasa due to bankruptcy difficulties). The *Song of Norway* began service in November 1970 and for a decade made a consistent seven-day pattern, often filled with first-time RCCL passengers. Sister ships *Nordic Prince* and the *Sun Viking* arrived in 1971 and 1972 respectively, to be placed on two-week itineraries that departed Miami on alternate Saturdays. As originally designed and constructed, all three vessels were approximately 18,600 tons and carried some 700 passengers. Each ship is immediately recognizable in any Caribbean port by the distinctive, circular Viking Crown Lounge, which sits about ten stories above the sea and is cantilevered from the smokestack.

The very popular *Song of Norway* returned to her place of birth, Wartsila shipyard in Helsinki, to be enlarged in 1978. The *Song* became the first of several cruise ships to be "stretched," a sophisticated method of adding tonnage and capacity to its midsection. The *Song* (and later the *Nordic Prince*) both had 85-foot-long insertions, increasing the ships to 23,000 tons and capacity for just over 1000 passengers. Public rooms were increased in size and space and about 80 crew members added. In true RCCL fashion, cabins are small, but public rooms are spacious.

Royal Caribbean's *Song of America,* arrived on schedule in Miami on December 5, 1982, for her maiden season. The vessel was four years in the planning/construction, and her design is based on the Finnjet approach that places most of the cabins in the forward section to eliminate unnecessary noise problems. The ship's main lounge has a multilevel seating arrangement to improve passengers' visibility of entertainment, and the Madame Butterfly dining room has a U-shape configuration with two terraced galleries for dramatic ocean viewing while eating. But the cantilevered Viking Crown Lounge, hallmark of the ship line, provides the most dramatic departure of all. It completely encircles the funnel some 12 decks above the waterline and provides a 360-degree panorama for its 140-person capacity. It is also reachable by an inside elevator, a feature much appreciated by passengers.

The public rooms on all Royal Caribbean vessels are themed after hit Broadway musicals. The *Song of Norway* features The King and I, My Fair Lady, and South Pacific lounges; the *Nordic Prince* boasts Camelot, Carousel, and Showboat; HMS Pinafore, The Merry Widow, and Annie Get Your Gun can be found on the *Sun Viking;* and the *Song of America* inaugurates Can Can, Oklahoma, and Guys and Dolls. Deck space is superb on all RCCL vessels and outdoor pools are among the best afloat. In addition to the distinctive Viking Crown Lounge, the late-night spots have simultaneous slide presentations put together by the ship line's own photographer, who roams the world in search of good shots. Dining-room service is excellent and once again, each night of the week is themed with different table settings and menus. Waiters seem to be hired as much for their ability to take "orders" as for their agility in singing and entertaining guests.

Royal Caribbean's attention to quality is evident in its highly rated food and service, entertainment that rotates weekly among the fleet, and cabin cleanliness. Passengers report that breakfast arrives promptly every morning when requested, ice and fruit are replenished daily, covers are turned down with soft lights turned on, and a chocolate is on every pillow before bedtime. All Royal Caribbean vessels receive superlative reports each year by members of the World Ocean and Cruise Liner Society, in an annual review of cruises. The society itself lists the vessels as "superior quality" and passengers agree consistently. The *Song of America* has proven to be another RCCL success story, and there is a terrific spirit onboard among the cruise staff. And, in order to appeal to the lowered average age of clientele on all RCCL vessels, shipshape programs and family cruising are part of the experience.

Cabin size is my major gripe with RCCL, and how they expect two, let alone four, passengers to enjoy those boxes is beyond me. These are the ships on which I always say travel with someone friendly because you will lock knees when you sit down in the cabin! However, passengers don't seem to mind because RCCL keeps everyone too busy to think about the small space provided for their private lives. In addition, the ship line takes such good care of passengers and their travel agents from start to finish that only praises come forth.

RCCL's biggest splash, *Sovereign of the Seas*, finally happened, and it was quite overwhelming for all those who had the first peek/cruise. The 74,000-ton vessel has a total capacity of 2690 in 1141 cabins. Although enormous by any standards, the vessel is well designed and something to behold for most cruise passengers. People who have not cruised before should avoid *Sovereign of the Seas*, because they will expect all others to look like this—a floating Hyatt Regency Hotel! Despite the feeling that you are not really aboard a proper ship, the experience is interesting. *Sovereign* should do very well in the incentive market because she can handle a great many people in a group without disturbing the other passengers, and there are ample meeting and socializing areas available on board. *Sovereign* was quite a feat to accomplish, and RCCL has two more of the same being constructed in the same St. Nazaire (France) yard, which will increase the ship line's capacity by some 75%.

RCCL now offers cruises to ports in Alaska, Mexico, Europe, the Bahamas, and Bermuda as well as the Caribbean, ranging in length from 3 to 12 days and departing from Miami, Los Angeles, Vancouver, New York City, San Juan, Lisbon, and London. *Nordic Empress* sails Mondays and Fridays to the Bahamas; *Song of America* sails Sundays from Miami to the Western Caribbean; *Sovereign of the Seas* departs Saturdays from Miami to the Eastern Caribbean; *Nordic Prince* sails Sundays from New York to Bermuda during the summer season and on 8- and 10-day Caribbean cruises from Miami during the winter months; *Viking Serenade* departs from Los Angeles on one-week cruises to Mexico during the winter, and from Vancouver to Alaska during the summer season; *Sun Viking* cruises in the Mediterranean, the Baltic, and along the coast of northern Europe during the summer, and from San Juan to the Southern Caribbean during the winter; and *Song of Norway* departs San Juan year-round on her southern itinerary. And if you can't bear to leave your golf clubs behind, Royal Caribbean Cruise Line has been designated the official ship line of the PGA, and passengers are invited to play on over a dozen different courses in the Caribbean, the Bahamas, and Bermuda. So, bring along money and your handicap for the best of both worlds!

ROYAL CRUISE LINE

One Maritime Plaza
San Francisco, CA 94111
tel: (415) 956–7200
    (800) 227–5628

Royal Cruise Line, founded in Greece by chairman Pericles S. Panagopoulos in 1971, was acquired recently by Kloster Cruises Ltd.— a company that owns Norwegian Cruise Line and Royal Viking Line. Royal Cruise Line is another "upmarket" addition to Kloster as its vessels, itineraries, and personnel are considered to be top quality and operate in the Mediterranean, Scandinavia, South America, and Caribbean with great success. Kloster insists that it will not tamper with the fine products, and the North American branch of the company (at this writing) will remain in San Francisco.

For the first decade of its existence, Royal operated a single vessel—the 10,500-ton, 460-passenger *Golden Odyssey*. The vessel was built in Elsinore, Denmark, in 1974 under the direction of Tage Wandborg, one of the world's leading naval architects, and is still considered the premier cruise ship of Royal's small fleet. After a lengthy search for more tonnage, Royal purchased the former *Doric* (Home Lines) in late 1981 and spent some $20 million transforming her into the *Royal Odyssey*. The vessel was very popular with Royal's loyal clientele, but the ship line sold her to Regency Cruises, where she has been sailing as the *Regent Sun,* since December 1988. The transfer of *Royal Odyssey* to another line was to pave the way for the $160-million *Crown Odyssey,* a 40,000-ton vessel accommodating 990 passengers, which was built in Papenburg, Germany, and delivered to Royal Cruise Line in June 1988.

The new vessel, with interiors inspired by the art deco style of the 1920s and 1930s, spent her inaugural summer in Northern Europe on a Scandinavian Capitals and Russia itinerary. Itineraries for the *Crown Odyssey* in the early 1990s feature Europe and the Mediterranean, Scandinavia, transatlantic repositionings, South America, Mexico, Hawaii, the Panama Canal, and the Caribbean.

Meanwhile, a $10 million refurbishment program was completed aboard the 460-passenger *Golden Odyssey,* which sails in the Caribbean and trans–Panama Canal during the winter months, transatlantic and in the Mediterranean from spring to fall. Royal Cruise Line is bullish on the Mediterranean and Europe and offers more than 30 departures with eight different itineraries during the season—including a new Greek Island cruise and the chance to visit Bucharest (Romania) on Black Sea sailings.

Royal is also continuing its successful "host program" of inviting distinguished gentlemen aboard cruises to act as "unofficial" hosts, serving as dinner, dancing and card partners. They also escort groups of single ladies ashore, to cocktail receptions and other shipboard activities. They are on board strictly to "mingle" and not favor any one lady. Meanwhile, the ladies love the program!

Since unattached men are always a benefit to any gathering, Royal went one step further in 1986 and initiated a Commanders' Club in which single men receive a variety of benefits and discounts, including a single cabin supplement for a very reasonable per diem (in selected categories). No interview is necessary and it is understood that members of the Commanders' Club will join in all the activities and be nice to the ladies. Another new program is the Crown Card, Royal's own credit card in conjunction with the Imperial Bank. Passengers may charge their entire air-sea package on the Crown Card as well as shore excursions and shipboard purchases. It promises a lower rate than average and there is no annual fee or payment penalty. Passengers also receive automatic travel accident and baggage insurance when they use the Crown Card.

Both vessels have all-Greek crew and a solid reputation for helpful and attentive service. Dining-room meals are geared to California palates—quality and simple preparation of plentiful fresh fruits, salads, and beef dishes. Forget the haute cuisine and fancy menu nonsense, this company offers food that everyone can understand, whether it arrives labeled under Greek Night, Pastel Night, or whatever.

Royal Cruise Line is proud of its Eating Away From Home program, in conjunction with the American Heart Association. As so many of Royal's passengers have come from retirement homes in California, it is only fitting that the AHA take part in dietary recommendations to these travelers. A special booklet published jointly by the AHA and Royal Cruise Line describes everything you have ever wanted to know about keeping a healthy heart, along with a number of luncheon and dinner dishes recommended for their sensible nutrient content. Also popular on board is the invigorating "New Beginnings" lecture series, regarding health of the heart and soul!

The shore excursion programs provide another example of Royal Cruise Line's attention to detail. These are under the very expert and personable care of John Tirrell, who travels the world to ensure that Royal Cruise Line passengers receive memorable times ashore in every port. And I can guarantee that this is so—my husband and I enjoyed a romantic gondola tour of Venice one evening, and an art history tour of Ravenna the next day that was simply wonderful! Some cruises, such as the Great Capitals of Europe, include complimentary tours of nine ports of call, but the majority have reasonable prices and are purchasable (and chargeable) prior to sailing.

ROYAL VIKING LINE (RVL)

95 Merrick Way
Coral Gables, FL 33134
tel: (305) 447–9660
   (800) 422–8000

Royal Viking Line is at the tippy-top of world-class cruise companies, and its fleet of three identical white vessels (and a newer, larger version) with a crimson sea eagle emblem on the smokestacks are a familiar and respected sight in ports of call throughout the world. The ship line was formed in Oslo in 1970, with American expertise at the helm, and aimed at the quality market. When constructed, these three vessels were 22,000 tons and just 500 passengers. They were "stretched" a few years ago to raise the passenger complement to 725—which seemed outrageously large at the time, but is once again considered small (considering all these behemoths arriving with regularity!) The *Royal Viking Sea, Sky,* and *Star* were joined in December 1988 by the 740-passenger *Royal Viking Sun*—a larger and even more luxurious vessel.

Royal Viking Line was acquired a few years ago by Kloster Cruise Ltd., a parent company that also owns Norwegian Cruise Line and more recently acquired Royal Cruise Line. All three ship lines remain separate entities, although Royal Viking Line's staff has moved to Florida from San Francisco. Will Royal Cruise Line be far behind?

RVL's strength lies in the fact that its fleet of four top-class vessels covers the globe and every port worth visiting. The annual cruise atlas lists sailings for Around the World, trans–Panama Canal/Caribbean/Mexico, the South Pacific/Orient, Northern Europe, the Mediterranean and Greek Isles, Canada and New England, and Alaska.

Royal Viking Line continues to offer upscale cruises and travel experiences, but is trying to appeal to a younger clientele with its shorter sailing schedules that can be combined into much longer cruises for the more leisurely set. In catering to affluent and sohisticated travelers, Royal Viking Tours has been formed to offer a total vacation package to RVL passengers.

There are some nice features on board all Royal Viking ships. Gambling is in with the Casino Royale Casino (blackjack tables, roulette, and slots), but definitely low-key. The Sky Deck lounge is wonderful for parties and doubles as a supper club on sailings of three weeks or more. For formal seated dinners, the club holds only 60 passengers—but is a great concept that should be carried through on sailings of at least two weeks, if possible. The penthouse suites have their own butler (just one) who will arrange cocktail parties, luncheon and dinner parties, etc. (He must be the wealthiest man on board!) Reception has a concierge—who is just a member of the purser staff who wears a different hat. The sports deck has tennis, golf driving range, jogging course and parcourse.

One interesting innovation on all RLV vessels now is golf—for those diehards who would never *dream* of taking a cruise lest it keep them from the links. RVL has made arrangements on many of its itineraries for people to play at top courses around the world, mingle with the well-known names on board, and generally combine the best of both worlds. The company's international golf adviser is Gary Player, a well-known name and winner of over 125 PGA tournaments. Another well-known name who likes to sail aboard RVL is Omar Sharif, who brings a bevy of other experts for Goren World-of-Bridge cruises.

But hang onto your mallets and whites, folks, because *croquet* became the *in* game on the elegant 740-passenger *Royal Viking Sun*. The 36,000-ton vessel was designed and constructed at the famed Wartsila shipyards in Turku, Finland, where the original fleet was born. More than one-third larger than the existing RVL vessels, and boasting more space per passenger than most other luxury ships, *Royal Viking Sun* has such glamorous features as walk-in closets, a swim-up bar, and wood-panelled lounge with fireplace. In addition to an informal cafe for breakfast and lunch and formal seaview dining rooms, there is also a permanent a la carte restaurant at the top of the vessel for even more formal dining, under consultation of renowned French chef Paul Bocuse. Over one-third of all staterooms have private verandas and 96% of the 370 passenger accommodations are in an outside configuration. *Royal Viking Sun* is utilized for both long and short cruises, including the prestigious annual global voyage, which is quite spectacular according to all reports.

Royal Viking line recently was inducted into two prestigious culinary associations, Les Toques Blanches and Master Chefs Institute. It also has working relationships with the top hotel schools in the world—from Cornell to Lausanne—and has long been a member of La Confrerie de la Chaine des Rotisseurs, the world's oldest food and wine society. So all is well at Royal Viking Line as it enters an exciting new decade of cruises and passengers.

SALEN LINDBLAD CRUISING

133 East 55th Street
New York, NY 10022
tel: (212) 751–2300
    (800) 223–5688

Salen Lindblad Cruising (SLC) was formed in July 1982 to operate and market the *Lindblad Polaris, Lindblad Explorer,* and *Yao Hua*— none of which still exists by those names. In fact, Lindblad Travel is no longer in business, and SLC has had no connection with the company for the past several years. However, Salen Lindblad Cruising continued with great success to represent many other expedition-type vessels and never was lacking fascinating itineraries.

Salen Lindblad Cruising now operates the recently acquired *Caledonian Star* (former *North Star*), a charming small vessel accommodating just 140 passengers (one of my favorite) and utilized as an expedition ship by SLC to visit remote and exotic areas around the world. Her first series of voyages were across the Indian Ocean and through the Red Sea, and Expedition Leader Tom Ritchie was delighted to be back in business aboard an SLC-owned ship! Other expeditions aboard *Caledonian Star* will sail as far north as the Baltic Sea, around Europe and the Mediterranean to the Black Sea and a return to the Indian Ocean.

More good news from Salen Lindblad Cruising is the introduction of the 164-passenger *Frontier Spirit,* the first expedition-type vessel to be newly constructed since 1974. The vessel is a joint venture between NYK Line (which also owns Crystal Cruises), Mitsubishi Corporation, Mitsubishi Heavy Industries (the ship was built in its Kobe yard), Hapag-Lloyd, and Salen Lindblad Cruising. *Frontier Spirit* is an "environment-friendly" expedition vessel, which means her state-of-the-art equipment will not harm the fragile ecosystems in which the vessel sails and visits. The 6700-ton *Frontier Spirit,* with Super Ice Class rating and double-bottom hull, boasts a tempting schedule through 1992—beginning November 1990 from Palau to the Caroline Islands in Micronesia. Other cruising areas feature Tasmania, Australian and French Antarctica, the Ross Sea, New Zealand Islands, and Australia's Great Barrier Reef, on sailings that range from 8 to 27 days but average about two weeks during her first year of operation in 1991. There is also the Orient, the Americas, Alaska, and the Northwest Passage from West to East (an historic 31-day voyage).

With two such comfortable expedition vessels offering exciting itineraries, Salen Lindblad Cruising should enjoy continued success in the coming years.

SEABOURN CRUISE LINE

55 Francisco Street
San Francisco, CA 94133
tel: (415) 391-7444
    (800) 351-9595

Seabourn Cruise Line was founded in 1986 by Norwegian investors interested in the super luxury resort/cruise business. They brought the highly respected veteran of the top-quality cruise business, Warren Titus, out of retirement from Royal Viking Line to CEO the new company. Titus did an excellent job in launching *Seabourn Pride* (December 1988) and *Seabourn Spirit* (November 1989) and has now moved up to chairman of the company. The twin vessels, with all-suite accommodations and spacious public areas, have created a special place in the cruise industry and appeal to a discriminating clientele.

The $50-million (each), 10,000-ton *Pride* and *Spirit* carry a maximum of 212 passengers—but rarely more than 190—in beautfully appointed staterooms/suites that feature five-foot seaview picture windows with automated shades (if you can find the button!) Deck space is enormous, and a generous Spa/Fitness Center overlooks the sea—so does the beauty salon. Walk-in closets with a private safe and a marble bathroom with tub and two sinks are also well-considered amenities for such an exclusive vessel.

In case you haven't noticed, Seabourn Cruise Line has some of the most elegant advertisements in any industry, and its 1991 brochure certainly belongs on the coffee table. The burgundy-covered booklet has lovely (and authentic) photographs of the vessels and clear maps of their itineraries—Mediterranean, Northern Europe, transatlantic, Panama Canal, Mexican Riviera, Caribbean, South America, and New England/Canada. The per diems are hefty, but so is the experience of Seabourn Cruise Line.

SOCIETY EXPEDITIONS CRUISES

3131 Elliott Avenue
Suite 700
Seattle, WA 98121
tel: (206) 285–9400
  (800) 426–7794

Society Expeditions Cruises was formed in September 1979 to handle the cruises aboard the *World Discoverer* for members of the Society for the Preservation of Archaeological Monuments (incorporated in Washington state). Sole stockholder until August 1987 was a very serious fellow named T. C. Swartz, when Society was assumed by a German businessman named Heiko Klein, who is chairman of Discoverer Reederei—the company that owns both of Society's vessels. (One can only assume that Klein took over Society to be assured of regular rent checks.) Nonetheless, we feel that Society is now in excellent and businesslike hands with a new management team.

Society operates both *Society Explorer* (former *Lindblad Explorer*) and *World Discoverer,* which accommodate 100 and 140 passengers respectively. Cruising expeditions include: Alaska, Canadian fjords, Northwest Passage, St. Lawrence Seaway, Panama Canal and South America western coast, Antarctica, South Pacific/New Guinea, Indonesia/Malaysia, Amazon, West Africa, Europe, Norwegian fjords and Greenland, China and Japan!

Passengers can be assured that each cruise is carefully planned and a goodly number of naturalists, ethnologists, historians, and fellow explorers are on board. As with most cruises of this type, only the healthy need apply, since some of the shore excursions can be rigorous. Simply climbing in and out of the Zodiacs takes some agility—especially in the rain! Both vessels are extremely comfortable and passengers receive a great deal for the money spent (which is considerable), even including windbreakers and complete notebooks of the lectures involved. Both vessels have lecture/lounge areas, excellent libraries, fitness centers, good food, and fine wine lists.

In an attempt to streamline operations and allow passengers to make plans a year in advance, Society has published a brochure that specifies exactly where each ship will be at what time—from year to year. The brochures are very beautiful—well researched and written by an in-house team. These are cruises for passengers who want their adventure and their dry martini too! Nothing is too small a detail for Society—and this is one of the perfect companies for those people who wish to explore with naturalists, ethnologists, historians, and other learneds, yet know that all the "comforts of home" await at the end of each exciting but probably tiring expedition.

Unfortunately, Society Expeditions has become a little "too too" recently and bombards one with paper material (please savor the trees) that is quite unnecessary. One complete brochure and a few important news-breaking press releases are just fine—not dozens and dozens! Society has also taken upon itself to advise people on behavior in fragile ecologies—as if we were not already sensitive and caring.

In order to keep up with the competition coming from Salen Lindblad Cruising and Special Expeditions, Society Expeditions Cruises has ordered two new vessels from the Rauma Shipyard in Finland for delivery June 1991 and June 1992. The $68-million (each) vessels have a capacity of 160 passengers and 125 crew plus a "hands on" laboratory, complete with whale and marine mammal sounding equipment, microscopes, and fresh/saltwater aquaria. The vessels also boast glamorous staterooms, state-of-the-art waste disposal equipment, 14 zodiac landing craft, four launches, a glass-bottom boat, plentiful snorkeling gear, and full diving equipment for 20 persons. Itineraries feature Greenland, Canadian High Arctic, and Maritime Provinces, as well as the U.S. Northeast, Orinoco and Amazon rivers, and Antarctica.

SPECIAL EXPEDITIONS

720 Fifth Avenue
New York, NY 10019
tel: (212) 765–7740
  (800) 762–0003

Special Expeditions was formed several years ago by Sven-Olof Lindblad (son of Lars-Eric Lindblad) "dedicated to the spirit of discovery" and to use travel to focus on a greater depth of exposure in a few select areas of the world. The company caters to small groups with an interest in obtaining an intimate view of marine and shore life, especially at times of migrations. The company operates the 80-passenger *Polaris* (formerly known as *Lindblad Polaris*), a most comfortable but hardly fancy vessel equipped with a fleet of zodiacs as well as a specially designed "bottom boat" outfitted for both day and night viewing, which enables passengers to explore the rich and colorful world under water. *Polaris* has both Swedish/American command and boasts a most pleasant ambience, with lounge/bar, quiet library, good deck space, seaview restaurant, sauna, and a variety of cabins. Lindblad refers to his company as one of the pioneers in the expedition cruising field and defines his market as those with a "definite craving for travel experiences that enrich and stimulate the mind."

As expedition cruises account for 90% of the company's business, recently it acquired two smaller vessels built months apart in 1981 on Whitby Island (just outside of Seattle, Washington). Formerly members of Exploration Cruise Line's fleet, the two vessels have been cosmetically and technically refurbished and are now known as the 70-passenger *Sea Bird* and *Sea Lion*. Special Expeditions had chartered the vessels from Exploration from time to time, so they are familiar entities but now are considered a bit more comfortable. As the ships are small, they can navigate the Columbia & Snake rivers "In the Wake of Lewis & Clark," closely explore Alaska's Coastal Wilderness, and offer the Voyage to the Sea of Cortez. Operating *Sea Bird* and *Sea Lion* allows Special Expeditions to place the *Polaris* in Europe during the summer and around Central America in the winter season.

Just some of the many programs offered by Special Expeditions throughout the year include: Exploring Coastal Iberia, France and Britain; Impressions of an Arctic Summer; Exploring America's Maritime Heritage—a 2000-mile journey from Nova Scotia to Savannah, Georgia; A Thousand Miles up the Amazon and Orinoco in 16 days; Beyond the North Cape; and the popular 11-day voyages between San Diego and La Paz on the Sea of Cortez. During Baja and the Sea of Cortez cruises, approximately 122 different birds, 108 fish, 68 plants, and 14 marine mammals (including six species of whales) have been recorded in the ship's log. These are very special expeditions, indeed, for those who enjoy the company of naturalists, artists, photographers, and writers—all of whom accompany each cruise.

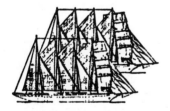

STAR CLIPPERS INC.

2833 Bird Avenue, 2nd Floor
Miami, FL 33133–4604
tel: (800) 442–0551

This brand-new cruise line plans to operate two four-masted sailing ships constructed in Belgium for service in the Mediterranean and Caribbean. The 180-passenger *Star Clipper* (late 1991) and *Star Flyer*

(1992) will be manned sailing ships (as opposed to the Windstar fleet, which has a computerized sailing system). The company was founded by Mikael Krafft, who previously owned a shipping company in Sweden and decided what the cruise world needed was a blend of the casual Windjammer ships and the more "chicly comfortable" Windstar fleet. Passengers will be invited to participate in the sailing experience while also enjoying the elegant wood-panelled library with fireplace, piano bar, Jacuzzis, and in-cabin toys like TV/VCR.

Star Clipper will be homeported in St. Maarten for one-week sailings alternating between the Virgin Islands (Virgin Gorda, St. Thomas, St. John, Tortola, Jost Ban Dyke, Anguilla, and Peter Island) and the Leeward Islands (St. Barts, St. Kitts, Montserrat, Antigua, Nevis, Statia, Saba, and Barbuda). The sailings can be combined for two full weeks, with rates at approximately $250 per day. *Star Flyer* will begin her career in the Mediterranean, most likely from Monaco, before repositioning in St. Maarten for the winter season.

SUN LINE CRUISES

One Rockefeller Plaza
New York, NY 10020
tel: (212) 397–6400
    (800) 445–6400

Sun Line Cruises is owned by Keusseoglou family interests. The company was founded in 1958 by the late Ch. A. Keusseoglou, who remained chief executive until his passing in May 1984. A former executive with Home Lines, Keusseoglou launched the *Stella Maris I* as Sun Line's first vessel for Aegean cruises from the port of Piraeus. In 1963 the *Stella Maris II* replaced her namesake, and the *Stella Oceanis* became a Sun Line ship in 1967. Flagship and pride of the fleet, the *Stella Solaris,* made her maiden voyage in 1973. Isabella Keusseoglou supervised the interior design of all three Sun Line vessels and still takes an active part in the day-to-day "housekeeping" from the family home in Monaco and a New York City pied a terre. President of the company is M. P. "Pilli" Keusseoglou, who lives in Athens; vice-president is younger brother, Alex "Aleco," who manages the marketing aspect from New York City. Mrs. K. is rightfully proud of her two sons.

Sun Line has always been considered one of the premier cruise lines in the Mediterranean/Aegean. From spring through fall, Sun Line offers 3-, 4-, 7-, 14-, and 21-day sailings from Piraeus, Venice, and Nice aboard *Stella Maris, Stella Oceanis,* and *Stella Solaris.* From May to October, the *Stella Oceanis* sails from Piraeus on 3- and 4-day Greek Island/Turkey cruises. The baby *Stella Maris* makes one-week Greek Island/Turkey cruises in April-May and September-October from Piraeus, then transfers to Nice/Venice for weekly departures in June, July, and August of her Around Italy program. The *Stella Solaris* sails every Monday, alternating between Greek Islands-Turkey and Greek Islands-Egypt-Israel-Turkey. The two cruises can be combined for a lovely 14-day experience that encompasses the best of this region.

The 18,000-ton *Stella Solaris* was built in 1973 and carries just 620 passengers—an intimate vessel by current standards. She has none of the razzmatazz of modern cruise ships, but her 330 Greek crew members epitomize warm and personal service. Many of them have been with the company for years and love to see returning passengers. The same is true of the smaller vessels—the 5500-ton *Stella Oceanis,* which carries only 300 passengers and the yachtlike *Stella Maris* with her 175 passenger complement. Indeed, it is quite usual and very flattering for staff members on any of these vessels to make an effort to remember not only your face but your name as many as five years hence! But, that is the Sun Line trademark and it is very special.

During the winter season, only the *Stella Solaris* repositions to the Western Hemisphere to offer innovative South American cruises that feature such exotic areas as Angel Falls, sailing the Amazon River, the Valdes Peninsula of Argentina, and a fly-over of Antarctica. Also on the itineraries are the exciting port cities of Buenos Aires, Montevideo, Valparaiso, and Rio de Janeiro. Two cruises pass through the Strait of Magellan, where the fly-over of Antarctica and Cape Horn is available as an optional shore excursion. Following this schedule, Sun Line's famous 21-day Primavera Cruise aboard *Stella Solaris* departs Port Everglades in April for Piraeus and another season in the Aegean.

The 4000-ton *Stella Maris II* is the baby of the fleet and everyone's favorite. Carrying not over 180 passengers and a crew of 100, the vessel sails from Piraeus on three- and four-day Greek Island/Turkey cruises beside the *Oceanis* during the spring and fall months. During the summer she offers one of the best itineraries in the Mediterranean, on weekly sailings between Nice and Venice. This popular cruise is sold out early, so hurry! The *Stella Maris* is one of my favorite cruise vessels. Everyone who has ever been aboard agrees that this ship has a special personality. The service is superb and there is a wonderful feeling of "getting to know you" among the passengers and crew. The Nice/Venice program can be combined with all sorts of wonderful experiences, like the Concorde to Paris and the Simplon Orient-Express to or from Venice. Not to be missed!

SWAN HELLENIC CRUISES

% Esplanade Tours
581 Boylston Street
Boston, MA 02116
tel: (617) 266–7465
    (800) 426–5492

The prestigious London travel firm of W. F. and R. K. Swan has been operating Mediterranean cruises since 1954 on a regular schedule and Nile cruises since 1960, in addition to the quality tours arranged to more than forty different countries since the 1930s. In 1980 R. K. Swan inaugurated Around Britain cruises. For the first time in 25 years he repeated an itinerary. This was an earth-shattering event, for Swan prided himself on never duplicating cruise itineraries. Although Swan sold out to P & O in 1983 and still remains as an active consultant, nothing has changed with the company or its programs. Expect the same high quality as ever.

Swan Hellenic Cruises, as they are called, are more than just cruises. The ship is mere transportation, but coupled with mini-courses in the archaeology, history, and culture of the area visited, the cruises attract travelers who wish to learn as much as possible from their experiences. Lecturers on board each cruise, drawn from the corridors of Cambridge, Oxford, and other notable colleges (even from Princeton and Yale) entertain and enlighten passengers on what they are about to see and do. Although this may sound a little too cerebral, it's really not because R. K. Swan remembered that his clients are "on holiday," after all. You can just as well sit in a deck chair with a beer, or you can listen to the lectures in the privacy of your cabin. But the high-caliber, optional lectures are well worth the effort to attend.

R. K., as he was known to his colleagues, believed in delivering as much value for the money as possible to his passengers. Included in the cruise fare are all port taxes, shore excursions, site fees, gratuities, and literature. And the literature is superb! Each cruise has its own special handbook with maps, a quick reference of selected dates and historical events, a short description of each place visited, and a glossary of technical terms. If you don't wish to carry the whole book, take a tear sheet, available for each separate excursion, with you. Most tours, planned as only half-day events, leave plenty of time for study and relaxation. Often an artist will be along to take care of a group of sketchers, because R. K. insisted that you cannot do both—sketch and listen to the guide!

All cruises are aboard Epirotiki's 300-passenger *Orpheus* because she does so well with passengers. The ship is comfortable and simple, but during eight months of the year is full of spirit and intellectual pursuits as she cruises around the Hellenistic World of the Aegean, Mediterranean, Black Sea, and Adriatic. The all-Greek crew is carefully picked because there is a no-tipping policy aboard—all gratuities are included in the reasonable cruise fare. In fact, just about everything is included in the cruise rate (shore excursions, entrance fees, all flights) exept personal bar and laundry. Life on board is relaxed and friendly and passengers need not worry about a thing—except having a wonderful experience, making many new friends, and learning a great deal about the ancient and modern world.

In early 1988, my friend Jacky Keith was reappointed U.S. general sales representative for Swan Hellenic Cruises and we welcome her back most warmly! She is most familiar with the programs and can arrange tender, loving care programs for all passengers from the U.S. to London to embark flights to the *Orpheus*. The brochure is enticing and a list of guest lecturers is announced for every sailing. The map of the Mediterranean ports of call is mind boggling and there is much, much more on the plate. New in 1990 and rather a departure from Swan's proven Mediterranean/Aegean itineraries was a cruise around northern Europe to the Scottish Islands, Norway, and Denmark. She also sailed into the Black Sea to visit southern Russia and introduced two shorter cruises of 8 days each in the Aegean. And, to attract some younger passengers on board, the company is offering 50% discounts on certain sailings when they travel with an older relative or friend. This is a wonderful marketing ploy and should result in many future Swan Hellenic fans.

Swan Hellenic also has Nile and Rhine river cruises (see related chapter) as well as Natural History and Art Treasure tours of the world. These are programs for the young in mind—at any age!

WINDSTAR SAIL CRUISES

300 Elliott Avenue West
Seattle, WA 98119
tel: (206) 286–3210
   (800) 258–SAIL

It seems like yesterday, but it was December 1984 when an invited group of friends and press gathered at the New York Yacht Club to hear plans of this new and unusual company to operate a series of 150-passenger sail-cruise vessels, originally designed by Kai Levander of Finland's famed Wartsila Shipyard near Helsinki. The four-masted, computerized sailing vessels would be constructed in France at the Societe Nouvelle Des Ateliers et Chantier du Havre for one-week sailings in the Caribbean, Mediterranean, and French Polynesia.

The principle figure and chairman of this young cruise line is a creative and dynamic 42-year-old Finn named Karl Andren, descendant of a proud Aland Islands seafaring family, who arrived in America as a young boy and was soon smitten with the hurly-burly vibrance of New York harbor. It did not take Karl long to combine an MBA with his love of the sea. He bought Circle Line and developed the sail-cruise concept. Along the way, he acquired a notable partner, Norwegian ship owner and fellow entrepreneur Jacob Stolt-Nielsen, and well-known cruise industry figure Jean Claude Potier as company president. Potier has been associated with French Line, Sun Line, and Paquet French Cruises.

Other Scandinavian shipping friends joined the group to offer advice and help develop the concept. Parisien designer Marc Held worked with Louise Andren on the interiors; Tom Heinan is credited with designing the spectacular clover-shaped bathroom, and his wife assisted in selecting the contents of each library. The result of everyone's endeavors—the Windstar Sailship—is an object of breathtaking beauty inside and out, complete with state-of-the-art technology and creature comforts to complement the unstructured ambience of *sailing.* To sit on deck watching the white sheets unfurl and feeling the vessel respond to wind conditions is akin to understanding the drama and sense of adventure that compelled such writers as Herman Melville and Joseph Conrad to share their seagoing experiences.

The first vessel, *Wind Star,* was christened by Louise Andren in the fall of 1985 at the French shipyard and made her sailing debut in the Caribbean, December 1986. The second vessel, *Wind Song.* arrived in New York harbor in the spring of 1987 and was christened by Nadia Stolt-Nielsen, wife of the vice chairman. *Wind Song* made her debut in French Polynesia that summer, on a year-round program every week from Papeete, Tahiti. The third vessel, *Wind Spirit,* was christened in Monaco's tiny harbor by Clara van der Vorm, wife of then Holland America Line chairman, in April 1988, and sailed the following day on her inaugural cruise of the French and Italian rivieras. Since all these festivities occurred, Holland America Line went from half-interest owner in Windstar Sail Cruises to full ownership, and then Carnival Cruise Line acquired Holland America Line—and Windstar in the bundle!

All three vessels are alike in design, concept, and spaciousness— although the main lounges of each have been gradually improved (one learns by experience). The cabins are cozy, cheerful, and roomy enough for two (honest), without losing the effect of being aboard a "sailing vessel.'' The bathrooms, however, receive more comment and praise than any other area on board! Cabin and bathroom amenities include: TV/VCR; refrigerator with mini-bar; state-of-the-art telephones; twin/queen beds; wall safe; gray terry-cloth robes with matching towels; a shower designed for two friendly people; hair dryer; Roger Gallet soaps and shampoo, as well as a small atomizer of Evian water (for the skin, not the stomach).

The atmosphere on board Windstar Sail Cruises is deliberately unstructured and aimed at sports-minded young or young at heart. These vessels are suited to newlyweds as well as those celebrating their silver anniversary; they are not suited to the single passsenger who cannot make his or her own entertainment. There are few activities of a group nature and meals are casually elegant; you dine when you wish (within certain hours) and sit where you please. There are no assigned tables and nighttime entertainment is minimal—a small band in the lounge for after-dinner dancing, a library, a casino, and lots of video tapes available at the purser's office.

The vessels anchor out of port as much as possible, so that passengers can enjoy the wonderful sports platform aft, which sits atop the sea for swimming, water skiing, wind surfing, etc. The platform is also convenient for embarking boats for water tours, as the one offered up-river in Raiatea. Another friendly design features a navigation platform aft for passengers as well as the open wheelhouse forward. Indeed, passengers are encouraged to absorb the entire *sailing* eperience, and I know one energetic passenger named Bob Gates who doesn't feel the vessel should leave harbor unless he is within the vicinity of the wheel-house!

These vessels are absolutely for people who enjoy a casual, elegant environment, a young and energetic crew, good food and drink, lovely vistas, and the feeling of *sailing*—for it is the sailing experience that makes Windstar different from any other cruise line.

Wind Star winters in the Caribbean and summers in the Mediterranean—what could be more glamorous? She sails on one-week cruises from Antigua from October to April, and offers a fun transatlantic crossing to Las Palmas and thence to Monte Carlo for the start of the summer season. One-week cruises from Rome, Venice, and Monte Carlo alternate from June through September before the vessel returns to the Caribbean. *Wind Song* continues her successful departures from Papeete through the Society Islands (Huahine, Raiatea, Bora Bora, and Moorea) year-round, and also offers two special 14-day sailings through the Marquesas in June and September. *Wind Spirit* sails weekly from St. Thomas and Barbados during the Caribbean season, then repositions to Alaska for a brand-new sail cruise experience between Prince Rupert and Juneau—another first for Windstar!

WORLD EXPLORER CRUISES

550 Montgomery Street
San Francisco, CA 94111
tel: (415) 391–9262
   (800) 854–3835

World Explorer Cruises is a name now synonymous with Alaska as its one and only vessel, the *Universe,* has been offering in-depth sailings along the coastline of our 49th state for well over a decade. Alaska has been called one of the top destinations of the 1990s, and this is an Alaskan cruise for passengers who value their money and their time—more is explored and accomplished on these two-week voyages than aboard any of the more luxurious, glitzy vessels. The ship line offers a total of nine ports of call on every cruise, as well as excellent lecturers and guides, 44 different optional shore excursions (the expensive flight-seeing tours seem to be the most popular), and vacation extensions in Vancouver or Seattle either before or after your cruise.

World Explorer Cruises operates the 550-passenger *Universe,* a modest vessel with Chinese officers and crew but American cruise staff and lecturers. Twice a year, in September and January, the *Universe* does perform as a seawise university on around-the-world voyages. These sailings can accommodate 500 students, who receive credit for the semester at sea, and return home very enthusiastic for the world they have experienced! World Explorer Cruises also offers extension credits to Alaska passengers in conjunction with California's Chapman College. Courses are taught on board, and there is no pre-registration requirement. There is, in addition, a 12,000-volume library on board for browsing or writing a serious paper!

From May through August, the *Universe* can be found in Alaskan waters, departing from Vancouver every two weeks. The vessel is quite unique in the world of cruising, and rave reviews occur after every sailing—from a wide range of passengers. So, leave your fancy clothes behind and discover Alaska!

THE SHIPS AND THEIR RATINGS

★★★★AMERICANA

Ivaran Lines; Norwegian registry and crew; built in Korea in 1988; 19,500 tons; 578 feet long; 85 feet at beam; 88 passengers; crew of 44; cruising speed of 20 knots; 5 decks.

This still new vessel combines carrying cargo with luxury space for passengers on the leisurely around South America run. The concept is certainly reminiscent of the once familiar Grace Line vessels that departed from the West Coast every two weeks on their South American journeys. The *Americana* departs from Brooklyn Passenger Ship Terminal down the eastern seaboard to South American ports—hopefully, with as many as 50 passengers on board—to ensure priority berthing and an ability to keep on schedule. Built at South Korea's Hyundai yard, the ship has space for over 1100 containers of 20 feet each, and the passenger space is prefabricated components from Scandinavia and Japan as well as other countries. The result is impressive, modern and bright, and passengers will not be disappointed with their environment.

Public rooms include a lounge/bar, swimming pool with lido area, one-seating dining room with large picture windows and adjustable tables, library, a few slot machines, health club, and hairdresser. The spacious cabins feature telephones, closed-circuit VCRs, safe and mini-bar. Some of the bathrooms boast bidets (as though anyone ever uses them). There are 22 double cabins, eight deluxe (four with private balconies), two suites, eight single outside and 12 single inside (convertible to double) accommodations. Entertainment is the do-it-yourself variety, and shore excursions along the east coast and South American ports will focus on the cultural—with a minimum of 12 hours spent at each call. Passengers are primarily of the retired and well traveled sort who seem to know more about the South American ports than others on board and are happy to share their knowledge.

344

Ports scheduled on the 46- to 48-day round-trip sailings from Brooklyn, New York, include: Baltimore, Norfolk, Charleston/Savannah, Jacksonville, Miami, Rio de Janeiro, Santos, Buenos Aires, Montevideo, Rio Grande do Sul, Paranagua/Itajai, Ilheus/Salvador, and Fortaleza. Prices are not inexpensive, but approximately $210 per diem per person for a deluxe double suite. It really depends upon whether you want a slow boat to South America or a faster one! Ivaran Lines is planning a pair of sister ships for the *Americana*—to be called *Brasilera* and *Argentina*. We await their arrival as time will bestow upon Ivaran an excellent reputation for its passenger division.

★★★AMERIKANIS

Chandris Fantasy Cruises; Panamanian registry; Greek officers and international crew; built in 1952 as Kenya Castle*; rebuilt in 1968 by Chandris and renamed* Amerikanis*; last refurbished 1987; 20,000 tons; 576 feet long; 74 feet at beam; 606 passengers; crew of 400; cruising speed of 16 knots; 8 passenger decks.*

If anyone mentions a Chandris vessel, the *Amerikanis* will receive the most affectionate responses and for good reason. Built as a one-class vessel for the round-Africa service, she was acquired by Chandris in 1968 and rebuilt as a cruise vessel—sailing for Chandris and then on charter to Costa Line for many years. Since the return of the *Amerikanis* to Chandris Fantasy Cruises, the vessel has been spruced up and was most recently refurbished in June 1987 (including complete interior carpeting).

Cabins aboard the *Amerikanis* are spacious and old-world with fine wooden details and plenty of closets. Bathrooms are very old-fashioned—a pleasure to turn around in! (No problems with dropping the soap here.) Of the total 306 cabins, 212 are outside and 67 boast double beds. The 54 minisuites are approximately 250 square feet and even the lowest-priced cabin is not smaller than 165 square feet. This ship represents the good old days, folks, although closed-circuit TV has been added to all cabins.

The large Galaxy Disco is located up on Sun Deck and, before hopping begins, is a splendid gathering place for private parties. Below on Athens Deck are the large Neptune Casino, shops and small rooms, the Mayfair Ballroom (main lounge) and Rendezvous Bar. The 360-degree Rendezvous Bar commanding this spacious room is very popular and a good place to become acquainted with fellow passengers—at cocktail time or after dinner and before things begin to awaken in the disco.

The Silver Carte and Silver Leaf restaurants are located below on Rome Deck and offer a nice, cozy feeling. There are two seatings for all meals; if traveling with friends, be sure to book the same dining room at the same time. Food and service have been improved by the new, tough management that puts up with no nonsense. (Any complaint from passengers is immediately rectified.) A gym/sauna is located on Lisbon deck, the cinema on Ottawa deck.

The *Amerikanis* was a much-beloved presence in Bermuda during the season but now sails year-round from San Juan, departing for the lower Caribbean every Monday at 11:45 p.m. The one-week cruises call at St. Thomas, Guadeloupe, Barbados, St. Lucia, Antigua, and St. Maarten during the winter/spring season, and St. Thomas, Martinique, Grenada, La Guaira, and Curacao during the summer/fall months. Special 6- and 8-day cruises are also available during the holiday season. Sea and San Juan pre- or post-cruise packages feature stays at the elegant El San Juan Hotel & Casino or the Condado Beach in San Juan, Puerto Rico.

★★★ARGONAUT

Epirotiki Lines; Greek flag and crew; originally built in 1929 and rebuilt in 1965; 4500 tons; 330 feet long; 47 feet at beam; 150 passengers; crew of 102; cruising speed of 14 knots; 4 passenger decks.

The *Argonaut* is on a long-term charter agreement to Raymond and Whitcomb, the travel firm that specializes in cruise programs for museums, private clubs, and college alumni associations, as well a other travel firms. Billed as the "exceptional" *Argonaut* and originally built as the world's largest private yacht (for an American, in 1929), the ship was rebuilt and refurbished in 1965 and launched as the flagship of Epirotiki Lines. This small vessel can carry 200 passengers, but Raymond and Whitcomb keep the capacity to 150 to ensure greater comfort.

Although it lacks a certain luxury, the *Argonaut* is a pleasant and charming vessel with a congenial personality and a crew that prides itself on offering excellent service. A graciousness and warm informality that is lost on larger vessels exists on the smaller *Argonaut*. The only large public room is the Golden Fleece Lounge, but smaller coffee and garden lounges often hold art lectures. The dining room is simple and large enough to accommodate all passengers at the same time, permitting free seating. The Greek/Continental cuisine is definitely modified to suit American taste—another plus. The vessel also has two cozy bar areas, a small pool, boutique, and beauty shop, but my favorite feature is the central winding stairway.

★★★+STAR/SHIP ATLANTIC

Premier Cruise Lines; Liberian registry and Greek officers; international crew; originally built in 1982 for Home Lines; acquired by Pre-

*mier and refurbished 1988; 36,500 tons; 671 feet long; 90 feet at beam;
1068 passengers; crew of 550; cruising speed of 24 knots; 7 passenger
decks.*

The *Atlantic* is a very sturdy ship, as she was built for Home Lines,
and has a high degree of spaciousness; Premier has not tampered with
the passenger configuration. While not so elegant in design as the
Oceanic—especially the exterior—the vessel is a very pleasant one and
suited to all ages. A jogging track has been installed on Sun Deck,
around the Magradome (sliding roof) of the Riviera pool and terrace on
Pool Deck below. This deck also boasts the Satellite Cafe for buffet
breakfasts and lunches as well as the Seasport Fitness and Health Center, two bars, an ice cream parlor, and the Calypso Pool aft.

Lounge Deck, below, features superior cabins with queen-sized beds
as well as Club Universe (for evening shows), Lucky Star Casino, shops
and photo gallery, Space Station teen center, and the Junkanoo Club/
Bar. Forward on the deck below is Pluto's Playhouse—children's recreation center and pool. The Galaxy dining room is a few decks down—
next to the infirmary.

Star/Ship *Atlantic* sails from Port Canaveral every Friday and Monday for Nassau and the Bahamian Out Island of Salt Cay. All cruises
include a visit to the Magic Kingdom Park, EPCOT Center, and the
new Disney-MGM Studios Theme Park, as well as tours of NASA's
famous Spaceport USA at Kennedy Space Center.

★★★THE AZUR

*Chandris Fantasy Cruises; Panamanian registry, Greek officers, and
international crew; originally built in 1971 and named the* Eagle; *rebuilt and renamed* Azur *in 1976; 15,000 tons; 466 feet long; 72 feet at
beam; 665 passengers; crew of 340; cruising speed of 18 knots; 7 passenger decks.*

The *Azur* is now very much a member of the Chandris Fantasy
fleet. She was acquired from Paquet in spring 1987 and placed in the
Mediterranean for the season. Every year, from June through October,
The Azur sails from Venice to the Greek Islands, Turkey, and the Black
Sea, or to the Greek Islands, Egypt, and Israel on 10- and 11-day cruises.
The ship is ideal for these itineraries, and Chandris offers excellent air-
sea programs.

Following a repositioning cruise to the Caribbean—which Chandris
sells privately to Europeans—*The Azur* sails from San Juan every Monday evening for St. Thomas, Bequia, Barbados, Martinique, and St.
Kitts.

Because *The Azur* is a former car ferry, a two-deck space aft has been retained for an on-board sports center where passengers can play volleyball, table tennis, squash (I believe this is the only squash facility afloat) and use the typical gym-style machines. As a complement to this fine sports center, Chandris has devised a group of outside facilities for passengers to enjoy. Here, they can play golf or tennis, snorkel, water-ski, windsurf, use a health spa, etc., at *The Azur*'s ports of call. They are: Beach Club of Suncrest in Barbados; Hotel La Bateliere in Martinique; Frigate Bay in St. Kitts; El San Juan Hotel & Casino in San Juan; and Cokki Beach in St. Thomas. These are optional shore excursions, for which prices vary according to island and program selected. Additional sporting shore excursions include deep-sea fishing in Barbados and parasailing or a ride in the Looking Glass Submarine in St. Thomas.

The Azur has very attractive public areas, including the seaview Riviera Restaurant, Casino, Tahiti Club, Azur Bar & Lounge, and two large pool areas. Buffets are served on Sun Deck, which is an active and popular place from morning until moonlight!

★★★AZURE SEAS

Admiral Cruises, Inc., Liberian registry and international crew; originally built in 1955 and formerly named the Southern Cross, *then* Calypso; *last refurbished 1989; 21,486 tons; 603 feet long; 78 feet at beam; 756 passengers; crew of 370; cruising speed of 20 knots; 9 passenger decks.*

The *Azure Seas* now sails under the Admiral Cruises banner, which is a sister ship line of Royal Caribbean Cruise Line. Royal Admiral is the umbrella under which both companies operate.

Western Steamship Lines, a subsidiary of Eastern Steamship Lines of Miami (the former cruise company), began operating 3- and 4-night cruises from Pier 93 in San Pedro (the port for Los Angeles) to Ensenada in Baja, California, in mid-November 1980. The cruises, billed as "Let's Go" and "party" sailings, offer a fully equipped casino and top nightclub entertainment on board. The *Azure Seas* now also calls at Catalina Island on both 3- and 4-night sailings.

The *Azure Seas* departs San Pedro every Friday at 7:45 p.m., calls at the enchanting island of Catalina on Saturday, and Ensenada on Sunday, before returning to port on Monday at 8 a.m. The 4-night midweek cruise departs San Pedro on Monday at 4:45 p.m., drops anchor off San Diego and Catalina Island, spends Thursday in Ensenada, and then returns to San Pedro on Friday at 8 a.m.

Azure Seas has a total of 370 cabins, all with private facilities. ₃as feature an enormous two-level casino (with slot machines) Deck; the Rendezvous Lounge-Showroom, the Mayfair, and

Cafe Miramar on Promenade Deck; and the Caravelle Restaurant on Caravelle Deck. In addition to these areas the ship has a disco (on Disco Deck), the double-tiered Rialto Theater and meeting rooms on Boat Deck, library, card room, swimming pool and heated whirlpool/spa, and huge sun deck. Two seatings apply for all meals in the Caravelle dining room, and passengers embarking on Fridays are invited to an extensive buffet dinner from 6 to 10 p.m.

The ship line has spent several million dollars in the past few years making *Azure Seas* competitive, and it is apparent in the cabin decor (there are 12 spiffy new suites with tubs and TVs), kitchen and food service, and the nightclubs. There has been a determined effort to offer passengers the entire cruise package, and it seems to be working. The food has received high marks, and the weekend sailings now appeal to the whole family. The casino is still very much on board, but it has become just another amenity. First and second passengers (in a cabin) fly free from selected gateways nationwide. Up to 7-day Supercruise Vacation packages are available in southern California and San Francisco at excellent rates.

★★★BERLIN

Peter Deilmann-Reederai; (EuropAmerica Cruises gsa) West German registry; European officers and Asian crew; built in 1980 in Kiel as Berlin; *also known as* Princess Mahsuri; *rebuilt 1986 as* Berlin; *9570 tons; 460 feet long; 58 feet at beam; 470 passengers; crew of 190; cruising speed of 17.5 knots; 5 passenger decks.*

The *Berlin* entered a German shipyard during the fall of 1986 for a little stretch. Added to the vessel were 58 feet and some 2000 tons. Her capacity increased from 300 to 470 passengers, accommodated in a total of 216 cabins. All are compact, with air conditioning and private facilities. I have not seen this vessel in several years, since she was cruising the Caribbean as the *Berlin*. She then went to the Far East, to offer exotic cruises—in conjunction with Pearl Cruises—but the affiliation was short-lived despite an elegant brochure.

As I recall, the public rooms of the *Berlin* flow nicely into each other. For example, the Lido Bar on Promenade Deck opens onto Sun Deck and the glass-sheltered outdoor swimming. New midships on Promenade Deck is a small Taverna for casual meals; the club/casino is forward. Another lounge with dance floor and stage is located on Main Deck, and the restaurant on A-Deck now has two seatings for all meals. A fitness center and sauna can be found down on B-Deck—next to the hospital!

The *Berlin* summers in Europe on a wide-ranging itinerary that stretches from Norwegian fjords to ports in the Black Sea and Eastern

Mediterranean. She sails from Genoa, Limassol, Aqaba, Instanbul, Venice, Kiel, Bremerhaven, Tromso, and Travemunde. During the winter season, the *Berlin* cruises the Caribbean between Santo Domingo and Barbados. This is a German flag ship and attracts a goodly number of German passengers. Although announcements are in both languages, unless you love Germans—watch out! *Berlin* is represented in the U.S. by EuropAmerica Cruises, a division of Exprinter that was formed to represent Peter Deilmann's *Danube Princess, Passau Princess,* and *Berlin.*

★★★BERMUDA STAR

Commodore Cruise Line; Panamanian registry; international crew; built in 1957 for Moore-McCormack Lines and originally named Argentina; *also known briefly as* Monarch Star *before returning to Holland America Cruises as* Veendam; *rechristened* Bermuda Star *in 1984; 23,500 tons; 617 feet long; 84 feet at beam; 725 passengers; crew of 300; cruising speed of 18 knots; 7 passenger decks.*

The former *Veendam* has been sailing as *Bermuda Star* for over half a decade now and is a happy vessel. Now owned by Rederi Effjohn of Finland, the group that bought Bermuda Star Line and changed its name to Commodore Cruise Line Cruises, the ship has been refurbished, but no changes in itinerary have been planned.

Other new features on the *Bermuda Star* have to do with dining. A Palm Cafe and Brass Grill have been installed in the former Lido buffet area. The Palm Cafe has table service only for continental breakfast early, then limited egg selections until 10:30 a.m. Through the rest of the day the cafe serves a number of exotic coffees (for $1 each) as well as complimentary pastries. Around the perimeter is the exclusive Brass Grill, a 75-person restaurant with two seatings for passengers in Categories 1–3 on a first-come basis. The grill has an intimate atmosphere, many tables for two by the window, deep burgundy-upholstered chairs, and excellent service. It was planned to offer a special dining experience—complete with string trio playing classic and popular background music.

The menu in the Brass Grill is the same as that in the main dining room as Commodore Cruise Line insists upon maintaining the one-class atmosphere. Both menus offer the usual high quality cruise food, but feature each night a different specialty relating to Delmonico's At Sea during the Bermuda cruises or Antoine's French Cajun cooking during the New Orleans departures. Some selections from the Delmonico's At Sea are: Filet Mignon; Prime Rib; T-Bone steak; Lobster Tail Wellington; Veal Chop Normandie or Broiled Lobster Tail. Special attention to food quality is part of the new *Bermuda Star* image, and early reports are excellent.

After-dinner entertainment in the Star Lounge features minimusicales such as *My Fair Lady* or *South Pacific,* complete with full show band. The lounge has a large "No Smoking" section but there is a nice, small library aft where Julio del Valle (former president of Bermuda Star Line) likes to have an after-dinner cigar. There is a small bar here that will be open during the evening hours. Other *divertissements* aboard are a large casino, the Safari disco (which may be repositioned out on deck in good weather), and the Observatory. Located one deck above the bridge, this charming hideaway is ideal for sunset cocktails or late-night piano-bar get-togethers.

Cabins aboard the *Bermuda Star* are spacious, to say the least. They are "old world" in the use of wood; they also need some refurbishment, which is forthcoming. Otherwise, the *Bermuda Star* is an excellent value and on the right course. Some 13 cabins in minimum-range have been added to Dolphin Deck (but watch for size).

During the summer season *Bermuda Star* sails between New York and Montreal on one-week cruises of New England, the St. Lawrence River, and French-speaking Canada. The vessel also departs from Penn's Landing in Philadelphia, in conjunction with Constitution Cruise Lines. Two-week cruises of this spectacular northeastern area can be combined at a discounted rate. Ports of call are Newport, Sydney, Nova Scotia, Gaspe, and Quebec, with cruising around Bonaventure Island, Perce, and the Saguenay fjords on the northern portion. Sailing south, *Bermuda Star* calls at Halifax, Martha's Vineyard, and Fall River, MA.

During the winter months *Bermuda Star* sails from San Diego to the Mexican Riviera, calling at Puerto Vallarta, Mazatlan, and Cabo San Lucas on one-week cruises that are popular and offer excellent value. Repositioning cruises through the Panama Canal between San Diego and New York are available from 13 to 28 days in the spring and fall. Free air is also available for all programs.

★★★BRITANIS

Chandris Fantasy Cruises; Panamanian registry; Greek officers and international crew; 26,000 tons; originally built in 1932 in Quincy, MA, and formerly named Monterey, Matsonia *and* Lurline*; refitted in 1971 and renamed* Britanis*; last refurbished in 1987; 26,000 tons; 638 feet long; 82 feet at beam; 926 passengers; crew of 530; cruising speed of 20 knots; 8 passenger decks.*

The *Britanis* has a great history in American passenger service. She was built by Bethlehem Steel Company in 1932 for the Matson Navigation Company and sailed that romantic route between San Francisco and Honolulu as the *Lurline* before the war, the *Matsonia* following. But life was never the same, and the ship became the *Monterey;*

however, the U.S. government decided (wisely) to no longer subsidize the salaries of U.S. crew aboard leisure passenger vessels, so the ship and company went out of service.

The vessel was purchased by Chandris Inc. in 1971 and converted from a trans-Pacific liner to one-class Caribbean cruising. She is no glamourpuss but a traditional vessel with old-world ambience, and is among the most worthy ships afloat. When it was suggested to young John Chandris that he replace the *Britanis* with another known vessel, he replied astutely "Why should I buy that ship whose boilers are always blowing up? The *Britanis* has six sound boilers and never a problem!" Well said.

The 926-passenger *Britanis* has a total of 463 cabins (of which 87 are rock-bottom value because they share facilities). Double cabins top at 225 square feet and large suites are about 405 square feet. Public rooms are located on Promenade Deck, with a large casino, several bars, the ballroom and shopping arcade. The outdoor swimming pool with bar area (becomes late-night disco) is located on Upper Deck; a gym and library/card room are forward on Main Deck. The Waikiki (they never changed the name, it seems) and Coral dining rooms are on Barbados Deck (with sauna way, way forward) and the theater is on Dorado Deck. The vessel is always well maintained and is in good form for such a grande dame. The food on board is good quality, especially for the price, and there are two excellent musical groups for dancing and serenading. This vessel offers terrific value for your dollar and an interesting itinerary, with an interesting passenger mix of Americans, Canadians, and Europeans.

From September 6 to October 26, 1990, the *Britanis* made her fourth annual circumnavigation of South America, and there is no reason to stop now! Passengers love the long, leisurely cruise aboard such a great lady, and the articles they write in Travltips are very touching, indeed. For the rest of the year, *Britanis* sails from Miami on 5-night cruises to Key West, Playa del Carmen, and Cozumel every Sunday, and 2-night Fantasy Champagne Weekend cruises every Friday to Nassau. Sounds like fun!

★★★★CALEDONIAN STAR

Salen Lindblad Cruising; Bahamian registry; Scandinavian officers and international crew; formerly known as North Star; *acquired by SLC November 1989; refitted and refurbished May 1990; 3095 tons; 295 feet long; 46 feet at beam; 130–140 passengers; crew of 70; cruising speed of 13.5 knots; 5 passenger decks.*

The *Caledonian Star* (former *North Star*) is a charming vessel, and I am so happy that she has found a new life with Salen Lindblad Cruising. On board everything is casual but comfortable, with small but all-outside adequate cabins (refurbished to feature TV/VCR and refrigerator), a main lounge/bar/lido bar and small swimming pool with plenty of deck space, a small library, theater, and enlarged dining room that now seats all passengers. There is also a small boutique (where I bought my husband a beautiful watch a few years ago) as well as the famous "Baby Star" tender and a fleet of Zodiac landing craft.

Caledonian Star is a sturdy ship (she was originally built in Bremerhaven in 1966 and employed as a German fish factory vessel) and well suited for expedition cruises. I had a wonderful week aboard (as *North Star*) from Gothenburg, Sweden, into the spectacular Norwegian fjord country, and felt very happy in my cabin on Upper Deck with its single bed and convertible sofa. The two windows were perfect for viewing the passing scenery over early morning coffee and yogurt, nicely delivered by the young Scandinavian stewardess.

Caledonian Star plans to explore the Gulf of Siam and Straits of Malacca, the Bay of Bengal, the Maldives and Seychelles, the Red Sea, eastern Mediterranean and the Black Sea, through the western Mediterranean to northern Europe and the Baltic. The expeditions range from two to three weeks, and plenty of naturalist/lecturers are on board.

★★★ + CANBERRA

Canberra Cruises; British registry and crew; built in 1961 in Great Britain; 45,000 tons; 819 feet long; 107 feet at beam; 1735 passengers; crew of 802; cruising speed of 26 knots; 10 passenger decks.

Former flagship of the proud P & O fleet and now marketed under Canberra Cruises, the *Canberra* is one of the last remaining passenger liners to carry on that old-world tradition. Launched in 1961 when shipboard travel was still the traditional way to cross oceans, her ambience remains that of a great liner. She has ten passenger decks and a wealth of open space. Just four times around her Promenade Deck is equal to one mile. There are three swimming pools, fifteen public rooms, nine bars, two restaurants, four shops, a children's playroom, launderettes, and several other amenities. Many cabins are inside and do not have private facilities.

According to P & O Line, the galleys on board cater to an average of 7500 meals each week, with approximately 4840 eggs cracked and 6500 rolls baked daily. The *Canberra News* publishes 1500 copies daily, and the ship photographers shoot some 4000 pictures per two-week cruise. The vessel was named after the capital of Australia, an Aboriginal word meaning "place by the water" or "meeting place." And passengers on board the *Canberra* can meet at any one of some forty different activities, not including special events like instruction in bridge or dancing offered by selected guest celebrities on special cruises.

Passengers in the more luxurious staterooms (1 to 102) dine in the Pacific Restaurant (where slightly more menu choices are available), while all others (cabins 201 to 333) dine in the Atlantic Restaurant. There are two seatings for all meals. The vessel draws people of all interests worldwide, and children are well entertained during the day with their own activities. In addition to the many large lounges, some more intimate areas are the very-English Cricketers Tavern and the Crystal Room (often used for private parties).

Following her great heroism in the Falkland Islands, the *Canberra* picked up a large and loyal following from both the troops she transported and past passengers.

Since she celebrated her quarter century of service in June 1986 and is still going strong, P & O decided to spend several million British pounds on giving the grand lady a much needed body lift. Additions and improvements included the installation of a gym, redecorated theater, new casino facilities, TV and video rooms, more premium cabins, family cabins, night nursery facilities (complete with nannies), computer games rooms, redecoration in cabins and public areas, and the opening up of more deck space for passenger use. The reasoning behind the investment was to bring the vessel in line with a younger and more active group of passengers, especially professional couples with children of any age. The vessel is filled primarily with British passengers, with the exception of the annual world cruise (January to April), which does call in North American ports (New Orleans, San Francisco, Los Angeles) and picks up passengers at these points.

During the rest of the year the *Canberra* follows the sun sailing from Southampton on a variety of itineraries and cruise lengths. She is a familiar sight in the Mediterranean as well as in such popular ports as Tenerife, Las Palmas, and Madeira. For a bit of the Britain that once was, a cruise aboard the *Canberra* is an excellent buy and experience!

★★★CARIBBEAN PRINCE

American Canadian Caribbean Line; American registry and crew; designed by Luther Blount and built in Warren, Rhode Island, in 1983; less than 100 tons; 160 feet long; 35 feet at beam; 80 passengers; crew of 15; cruising speed of 12 knots; 3 passenger decks.

The *Caribbean Prince* is the latest (but not last) of shipbuilder Luther Blount's creative designs. Blount specializes in small vessels with shallow drafts and a bow that folds down right onto the beach! Hence, the cruise line's philosophy and itineraries are rather like those of a private yacht. The *Caribbean Prince* has three passenger decks, with 32 spacious picture-window cabins on Sun and Main decks and six economy nonporthole cabins on Lower deck. All have private facilities, and the Sun/Main deck cabins have a choice of sleeping arrangements (double or twin configuration). The dining room and main lounge are located on Main Deck, and both spaces seat all passengers. Setups and hors d'oeuvres are served in the lounge at cocktail time, when passengers bring their own bottles. The meals are prepared by world-class chefs but served family-style around round tables seating six guests each.

The *Caribbean Prince* cruises in the Caribbean from mid-November to mid-April on a series of 12-day itineraries featuring Belize, Glovers barrier reef, and the Rio Dulce river of Guatemala (which Luther Blount explored personally in a dugout canoe to discover if his small ship had the correct draft). It's a fascinating route that includes plenty of unusual flora and fauna, time for beaching and snorkeling as well as visiting two famous Mayan ruins—Altun Ha and Quiriqua—plus a side trip to Tikal before or after the cruise. Nine such sailings were offered in 1990, and they are expected to continue through the early decade— or at least until Captain Blount, owner and guiding spirit of American Canadian Caribbean Line, decides that all his passengers have enjoyed the area and must be stimulated with yet another new itinerary. ACCL passengers fly to and from Cancun to catch this cruise, and snorkelers will be in a little bit of heaven off the large barrier reef of Belize.

In early May, the *Caribbean Prince* sails up the eastern seaboard on a 15-day cruise to Warren, Rhode Island, for the summer season. The popular 12-day, one-way Saguenay River cruises are scheduled all summer, followed by two 12-day Fall Foliage sailings between Rhode Island and Montreal. These summer cruises offer a wonderful itinerary through Narragansett Bay and Long Island Sound to South Street Seaport in New York City, up the Husdon River to the Erie Canal, along the St. Lawrence Seaway through the Thousand Islands and into the Saguenay as far as Cape Trinity and the Bay of Eternity (for a Bow Landing!). The cruise ends in Montreal, from whence passengers return to Rhode Island by bus (or vice versa).

More fall foliage can be enjoyed on the 15-day repositioning cruise from Rhode Island down to West Palm Beach in November.

★★CARIBE I

Commodore Cruise Line; Panamanian registry; European officers and international crew; originally built in 1953 and commissioned Olympia *for Greek Line; refitted in 1983; 23,000 tons; 612 feet long; 80 feet at beam; 875 passengers; crew of about 370; cruising speed of 17 knots; 8 passenger decks.*

When the *Caribe I* finally arrived in Miami in July 1983, after many delays, there were sighs of relief. For this 32-year-old vessel has already enjoyed a colorful career and some wondered if a new life was in order. The *Caribe I* was built in Glasgow just after the second world war as the flagship for Greek Line. In fact, her original name was to be the *Frederica,* after Greece's queen, but the name was changed to *Olympia* to avoid dispute. For two decades the vessel crossed the Atlantic and Mediterranean between New York and Greece and made some winter cruises to the Caribbean from New York. She was also known as a party ship—for cruises to nowhere over weekends!

However, Greek Line was on the verge of collapse in 1974 and one dark and steamy night the *Olympia* slipped from her berth in New York harbor and went home. People in the cruise industry still discuss it in amazement. There she was; there she wasn't—leaving behind a mountain of unpaid bills, disappointed passengers, and infuriated travel agents. She was laid up several years near Piraeus until Commodore Cruise Line decided to refit and recommission the vessel for weekly cruises from Miami to the eastern Caribbean.

The vessel is very comfortable, has a decidedly old-world atmosphere, and sits in the water like a battleship. There are eight passenger decks and plenty of outdoor spaces to sun in small or large groupings. Sun Deck boasts several suites and deluxe cabins as well as the former first-class swimming pool, the Out Island Club, and the Out Island disco. The other outdoor pool is on Promenade Deck, near the Atlantic Bar's large sunning area. There are also cabins, the Atlantic Night Club, and theater balcony on this deck. The modern-looking Grand Lounge is on Upper Deck and the large Caribbean dining room can be found on Restaurant Deck, along with some gift shops and the Monte Carlo casino. There is also a small library on Promenade Deck. Passengers realize quickly that the *Caribe I* was a two-class transatlantic vessel. Public areas do not flow one into another, as on modern cruise ships, so it is a bit difficult to find one's way about.

The service crew, mainly from the islands, is friendly and helpful and the food service is considered of high quality. Commodore long ago announced that it does not hire a catering service and pays special attention to the dining room. The evening meals are varied by different themes, including the Captain's Welcome Aboard and Farewell. In fact, Captain Rolf Bassenberg himself is one of the highlights of this cruise ship and a charming person.

The *Caribe I* sails every Saturday afternoon from Miami for Puerto Plata, San Juan, St. John, and St. Thomas. There are three full days at sea, and cruise rates are very reasonable for this mix of the old world and the new.

★★★ + CARLACOSTA

Costa Line; Italian registry and crew; originally built in 1952 and formerly named the Flandre; *refurbished in 1976; 20,477 tons; 600 feet long; 80 feet at beam; 748 passengers; crew of 370; cruising speed of 22 knots; 8 passenger decks.*

The *CarlaCosta* is an old favorite of many Costa passengers, and the grand old lady of the fleet in North America. Following some refurbishing and the addition of some attractive stewardesses, the vessel has been getting high marks for cruises in the lower Caribbean. Every Saturday year-round, the *CarlaCosta* departs San Juan at midnight to offer "Cruising Italian Style" with an Italian midnight buffet to start.

All day Sunday is spent at sea, relaxing and then meeting the captain at his weekly Welcome Aboard cocktail party and dinner. The vessel calls at Curacao on Monday, and that evening a French dinner is served. Tuesday is La Guaria (for Caracas), Wednesday is Grenada, Thursday is Martinique and Friday is St. Thomas (where else?). Again, passengers should burn the midnight oil as sailing from St. Thomas is a lovely sight. The *Carla C.* returns to San Juan at 8 a.m. every Saturday.

Cabins aboard the *Carla C.* are spacious, befitting an older vessel. There are 191 outside and a staggering 183 inside cabins, most with additional berths. The deluxe cabins, suites and apartments do have bathtubs—which are definitely becoming of the other world, these days! Food on board is very Italian, with plenty of homemade pastas and pastries—pizza and gelatti.

Public areas include the Observation Lounge, Casino, Grand Salon, pool area, library and card rooms, theater and dining room on Continental Deck. There are two seatings for all meals. The *CarlaCosta* (I prefer her original name—*Carla C.*) was refurbished recently, and the multimillion-dollar decor restored her art deco ambience. Public areas were fitted with floral carpeting and matching drapes in subtle pastel shades. The ship's casino was opened on the starboard side, and the Promenade Deck lobby was restored. A new Al Fresco Cafe appeared above the pool, for breakfast and lunch buffets with sea views. Approximately 50% of the cabins and all suites were redecorated. The *CarlaCosta* is a popular vessel in the Caribbean, with excellent service and a family-type feeling on board. Rates are good value, and cruises combined with *Daphne* during the winter months are available.

★★★ CARNIVALE

Carnival Cruise Lines; Bahamian registry; Italian officers and international crew; originally built in 1956 and entered service as the Empress of Britain; *also cruised as* Queen Anna Maria; *last refurbished in 1989; 27,250 tons; 640 feet long; 87 feet at beam; 950 passengers; crew of 550; cruising speed of 21 knots; 9 passenger decks.*

The *Carnivale* entered service as a Caribbean cruise ship in 1976, and was the first vessel on which interior designer Joe Farcus of Miami worked. In fact, this began Farcus's long-standing association with Carnival Cruise Lines. Cabins aboard the *Carnivale* are similar to the *Mardi Gras,* her sister ship. They are larger than the "Caribbean style" of other 7-day vessels, and all now have 110 AC current to coincide with what passengers find on land.

There are a large complement of inside cabins—approximately 265— to 217 outside cabins. Many have double and king-size beds, and there are a large percentage of four-person cabins for singles and couples with children. But passengers are not expected to spend much time in their cabins anyway! The Riverboat Club Casino and Lounge is placed prominently in the center of Promenade Deck. In fact, no one is supposed to miss it!

Forward of the casino are the Mardi Gras Night Club and the Fly Aweigh Discotheque, with a library in between. Aft is the cinema and Showplace Lounge as well as children's playroom and shops. There are three separate outdoor pools—plus a children's wading pool—on Sun Deck and an indoor pool/gymnasium down on Riviera Deck. The International dining room is located down on Main Deck. Three full meals, two evening buffets and several daytime snacks are the quantity—if not the quality—of food served aboard.

A much-needed $10-million refurbishment improved the cabin areas and hallways, the Showplace Lounge, Promenade, Mardi Gras Lounge, International dining room, Lido Bar, Sun Deck (which received a 16-person-capacity whirlpool), and Children's Playroom. The general ambience of the vessel received a more Caribbean look, and the old-world decor was replaced—from necessity—in most areas. The refurbishment took place just prior to *Carnivale*'s reposition to Port Canaveral for Thursday and Sunday sailings to the Bahamas that can be combined with central Florida attractions and complete air-sea programs.

★★★ + CELEBRATION

Carnival Cruise Lines; Liberian registry; Italian officers and international crew; built in Malmo, Sweden, and entered service March 1987; 48,000 tons; 733 feet long; 92 feet at beam; 1486 passengers; crew of 670; cruising speed of 21 knots; 9 passenger decks.

The *Celebration* is the final of three superliners built especially for Carnival Cruise Lines in Malmo, Sweden. She is sister ship to the *Hol-*

iday and *Jubilee*. While the *Holiday* has a fantasy theme and the *Jubilee* a nostalgia theme, the *Celebration* has a futuristic theme.

Cabin configuration and suites are identical to the other two vessels as are all public areas. Only the names have changed. The main show-place is the Astoria Lounge. The dining rooms are named Vista and Horizon. The piano bar is the Red Hot and across the way is Admiralty Library. Instead of a Bus Stop or Gazebo, there is now a Trolley. The casino is known as the Rainbow Club; the disco is Galax Z; and the Lido deck restaurant is Wheelhouse Bar & Grill. People places are Holiday Square, Mardi Gras Square, and Bourbon Street. The coffee area is the Bistro and the aft showroom for late-night cabaret is Islands in the Sun.

The public areas are Joe Farcus (the architect/designer who does all Carnival products) glitzy, but that is what Carnival is all about and it works for them. Very well. Effort has been made, however, to present a dining room that is restful and pleasant. The food gets mixed reviews, however, more so than on any other ship line.

There are two outdoor adult swimming pools and one wading pool, and plenty of deck area for bikini watching or other sporting events. The vessel boasts a health spa with whirlpool as well as plenty of shops and people-watching along the promenade area—Bourbon Street, Holiday Square, Mardi Gras Square. Cabin size is good (for the price) and all twin beds are convertible to queen-size. Bathrooms are modular-standard and on the small side—strictly one person at a time, and it helps if you are a midget.

The *Celebration* sails every Saturday from Miami at 4 p.m. and spends Sunday and most of Monday at sea. The vessel arrives in San Juan at 6 p.m. on Monday for just the evening; she arrives in St. Thomas at 8 a.m. on Tuesday, spends Wednesday in St. Maarten, and the next two days at sea. This is definitely a cruise for people who like to sun on deck, gamble, and drink things that come in different-colored liquids on a tray.

★★★CONSTITUTION

American Hawaii Cruises; American registry (returned) and mostly Hawaiian crew; originally built in the U.S. in 1951 and named the Constitution; *previously owned by the C. Y. Tung conglomerate but placed under American custody for cruising in Hawaiian waters; now owned and operated by Peter Huang, Chinese-American businessman; 30,090 tons; 682 feet long; 89 feet at beam; 800 passengers; crew of 320; cruising speed of 20 knots; 9 passenger decks.*

A true sister ship to the *Independence,* an identical twin as it were, the *Constitution* was built at Bethlehem Steel Corp.'s Ford River Shipyard in Quincy, Massachusetts. The vessel made a 23-port gala 60-day maiden voyage to the Mediterranean in April 1951. The ship was built for express liner three-class service between New York and Italy, with calls at Gibraltar and Cannes. Quickly popular with the celebrity set, the American Export Line vessel was among the fastest and safest U.S. flags afloat. First-class passengers included politicians, diplomats, and film personalities, which explains why Grace Kelly chose to sail aboard the *Constitution* with her wedding party in 1956 to become a princess in Monaco.

When American Export Isbrandtsen Lines ended transatlantic service in 1967, the *Constitution* was laid up at Jacksonville, Florida until purchased (jointly with the *Independence*) by the C.Y. Tung Group of Hong Kong in 1974. She joined the Hawaiian Islands itinerary in June 1982, following a complete refit and refurbishment in Taiwan—where she was also rechristened by Princess Grace of Monaco. The *Constitution* is the only American-flag vessel to receive royal (even minor as it is) sponsorship. As a remembrance of the late princess, a beautiful writing room on board has been dedicated to her memory.

The *Constitution* is a comfortable vessel—one that offers passengers a feeling of safety. Although constructed in 1950–51, she is extremely modern in design and decor and one of the first to boast air conditioning throughout! A recent multimillion dollar refurbishment scheme has added a tone and color scheme more suitable to cruising in the Hawaiian Islands. Among the vessel's refurbishments is the addition of a two-room Owner's Suite with deluxe amenities and adjoining two-berth inside cabin for children/nanny, etc. A full-size gymnasium has been installed in the former Starlight Lounge on Sports Deck, there is a new phone system on board, and the public restrooms have been redecorated. The cabins are spacious and well planned for the early 50s, but only the few suites aboard have full bathrooms with tubs. Even in the deluxe cabins, which have plenty of closet and moving-about space, it is just possible to turn around in the bathroom. And if you drop that sliver of soap in the shower, forget it!

Public rooms aboard the *Constitution* are attractive and spacious, especially the Constitution Lounge with the smaller Princess Grace memorial room aft portside and the Friendship Lounge on the starboard side. Captain Harry T. Y. Wu, the master of the vessel, welcomes passengers in the Tropicana Showplace where the nightly shows are also performed. Behind the nightclub is a pleasant bar with good sea views, called Tradewinds Terrace. Below, on Upper Deck, are the shopping and photo arcades as well as some electronic games set up. There is a spacious Lahaina Landing lounge with plenty of outdoor tables, and lounges around the swimming pool. This is where most of the daytime action occurs, from a sumptuous buffet breakfast (7–9 a.m.) to refreshing scoops of sherbet served at 11 a.m., and a deck buffet luncheon (11:45 a.m.–1 p.m.).

If you prefer a quieter area, ascend two flights to Sun Deck and the Beachcomber Bar. This is the former first-class swimming pool and outdoor bar, and it seems to catch the best rays of sun. There is a large Conference Center aft on Main Deck, very suitable for the many seminars aboard, and two dining rooms on Aloha Deck. The captain, hotel manager, and chief engineer dine in the Hibiscus, while other officers have tables in the Bird of Paradise room. The food is excellent, especially if you like plenty of fresh fruits, seafood, and steak, and home-made ice creams. Service has come "full circle" since the cruise was inaugurated and is quite suitable to the type of clientele the vessel attracts. As one passenger said, "Food and service aboard the *Constitution* are equal to the best of ships sailing from Miami." And if you are interested in ship history, contact Greg Abbott, the chief purser.

Captain Wu is a charming fellow who definitely enjoys his work. He is more visible than many other captains and holds a series of small champagne parties for selected passengers throughout the cruise. He also invites a different group to his dinner table each night. Despite the social schedule, Captain Wu is known for running a very tight ship, indeed. His safety standards are very high, evident from the detail of the lifeboat drill.

The all-American crew is hired in Honolulu; hence they are mainly "islanders." They are a young and energetic group who seem eager to please.

However, under Peter Huang's management style, both vessels have been upgraded and a great deal of money has been spent on them. Menus are better, the dining room is more attractive, and the service crew have new uniforms. This refurbishment program does not detract from the American/casual atmosphere on board; rather, it is enhanced. (It also helps when competition is arriving in the form of another ship.) More attention has also been focused on local Hawaiian talent in decor and entertainment.

In order to broaden the market—i.e., attract a younger and more energetic group of passengers—American Hawaii introduced 3- and 4-day cruises aboard the *Constitution* a few years ago, with the rest of the week spent at a resort on the "big island" of Hawaii or Oahu featuring golf and tennis facilities. Introductory packages also included a rental car for the land portion. The response was so spectacular that the idea is available year-round on both vessels. And, during the summer months, children travel free (in the same cabin) with two full-fare adults. The one-week, four-island itinerary of the *Constitution* departs Aloha Tower at 9 p.m. on Saturday, cruises all day Sunday, calls at Maui on Monday, Hilo and Kona on Hawaii (Tuesday and Wednesday), Nawiliwili

(Kauai) on Thursday and Friday, and returns to Honolulu Saturday at 7:15 a.m.

★★★★COSTAMARINA

Costa Cruises; Italian registry; Italian officers and Italian/international crew; $120-million-reconverted vessel in Mariotti shipyard, Genoa, for spring 1990 delivery; 25,000 tons; 572 feet long; 84 feet at beam; 770 passengers; crew of 385; cruising speed of 21 knots; 8 passenger decks.

The glamorous new *CostaMarina* began her cruise career from Genoa during the 1990 summer season to great success. Her western Mediterranean itinerary featured Spain/Tunisia or Spain/Morroco—the only vessel to offer such exotic ports at this time of year (it can be beastly hot then in North Africa). However, the scenery is exciting, and passengers aboard *CostaMarina* can enjoy it while dining in the seaview Crystal Restaurant.

Contrary to most new building, *CostaMarina* has more inside (201) cabins than outside (181 plus 8 mini-suites), which boast oversize portholes—no picture windows here—but telephones and stereo systems are standard. Public areas feature an atrium three decks high, a glass-housed fitness center, and a transparent dome over the Galaxy nightclub. Other amenities aboard ship are Harry's Bar, the Marina Lounge, Tropicana Showroom, and Yacht Club/casino (not open when the vessel sails from Genoa). The outdoor swimming pool on Laguna Deck has Jacuzzis and an adjacent bar. During the winter season, *CostaMarina* sails on Sundays from Port Everglades, alternating east and west Caribbean itineraries.

★★★★COSTARIVIERA

Costa Cruises; Italian registry and crew; built in Italy in 1963 and originally named the Guglielmo Marconi; *purchased by Costa Armatori in 1983, refitted and renamed* CostaRiviera; *refurbished in 1988; 31,500 tons; 700 feet long; 93 feet at beam; 984 passengers; crew of 500; cruising speed of 20 knots; 8 passenger decks.*

The *CostaRiviera,* reconstructed in Italy from the former *Guglielmo Marconi,* arrived in Port Everglades in December 1985 to become the flagship of the company's Caribbean fleet. The 1000-passenger vessel has received very good reviews from the public and, indeed, is very impressive in all respects. The vessel is themed around Italy's famous vacation spots, with decks named Amalfi, Riviera, Portofino, Capri, Sorrento and Venice. The shopping area is called, of course, Via Veneto, and it displays some of the glamorous names in Italian fashion.

Both public rooms and cabins, decorated entirely in Italy of Italian furnishings and fabrics, are attractive and cheerful. Of a total of 492 cabins, only 60% are outside and approximately 50 have full double beds. The average cabin size is decent—especially for a Caribbean-style vessel—and some splendid toiletries as well as fruit baskets are placed in all categories. The deluxe cabins look a little bare—and need a few more amenities, including TV. Alas, bathrooms are standard in all categories and among the smallest afloat—especially for these prices. Watch the showers—anyone more than three feet tall can only wash one side at a time. The only saving grace here is a decent bar of soap—that Costa does provide.

The Portofino dining room on Portofino deck is reachable *only* by two forward stairwells—which tends to be most confusing the first day out. However, the discovery is well worth the effort as the restaurant is attractively decorated in blues, deep red and Mediterranean green to match the mural suggesting Portofino itself. In addition to tables for four, five and six, there are 23 banquettes lining both sides of the room that seat just two. On French night, especially, the setting is romantic—with candles on each table and live music for dancing.

The food is strictly Italian, with plenty of antipasto and freshly made pasta. There is a good wine list with Italian, French, Spanish and domestic brands available at reasonable prices. In addition to French night, at which the shrimp were superb, there is Carnival Night (come as your favorite pirate), Western Night (jeans and paraphernalia) and a Roman Bacchanal night (time for togas). There are two formal evenings on board—the captain's welcome on Sunday and the captain's farewell on Thursday. Food presentation and service is excellent, the taste certainly above average.

Public areas include La Scala and Riviera lounges (forward and aft), the Monte Carlo casino, Grand Prix bar and lounge, several excellent meeting rooms, a pizzeria, and a small bar midships where gelatti is served every afternoon. Capuccino and espresso are available at all the bars throughout the day, and there is a nominal charge per cup. La Dolce Vita cafe on Lido Deck serves buffet breakfast and lunch around the pool, and there are three Jacuzzis up on Sports Deck along with a jogging track, fitness center, sauna and showers, and large youth center. The theater is located on Sorrento and Capri decks.

During a recent drydocking the vessel was spruced up a bit and received new carpeting in the Portofino restaurant, a new marble dance floor in the Grand Prix Bar, and an improved layout in the Rendezvous Bar. On deck, the Jacuzzis received windbreakers as well as wooden steps, and fresh-water showers were installed. Some of the cabins also received new carpeting, and the photo display area was much improved.

There are plenty of on-board activities for all interests during the days at sea—wine tasting, Italian language classes, a cooking demonstration, a parade of the au courrant fashions in the Via Veneto shops, fitness classes, knobby knees and pretty legs contest, etc. Something for everyone. Two young working women in their late 20s had a wonderful time with the Italian officers in the disco—and spent their daylight hours catching up on sleep by the pool! The ship is full of vacationers looking for fun, especially those with Club Perillo, who pay an all-inclusive price for everything (including tips).

Costa Cruises has instituted a new health/fitness program called SpaCosta aboard the *CostaRiviera,* to offer exercise, pampering, and diet programs at a price. Passengers can sign up for one full week or day by day at per diems that are over $150 per person. The programs feature fat analysis, personalized strength and stretch, massages, facials, manicures/pedicures, and sauna. During the summer months, it is a good way to keep parents occupied while their children are having a good time!

The *CostaRivera* departs every Saturday from Fort Lauderdale (Port Everglades) on alternate routes: St. Thomas, St. Croix, and Nassau; or Ocho Rios, Grand Cayman, Cozumel, and Playa del Carmen. Passengers who love the ship and "Cruising Italian Style" are encouraged to return for the other itinerary—or stay aboard and enjoy both!

★★★+CROWN DEL MAR

Crown Cruise Line; Panamanian registry and Norwegian officers; Filipino/international crew; built in 1967 as Las Palmas de Gran Canarias; *rebuilt 1988 and renamed* Crown del Mar; *10,000 tons; 429 feet long; 63 feet at beam; 444 passengers; crew of 195; cruising speed of 16 knots; 5 passenger decks.*

Crown del Mar sails from the new passenger ship terminal of the Port of Palm Beach on Friday afternoons at 5 p.m. to Nassau (8 a.m.– 6 p.m. Saturday) and on Sunday afternoons at 5 p.m. for a day at sea (Monday) and then calls at Cozumel (Tuesday), Cancun (Wednesday), and Key West (Thursday). The vessel, refurbished in Spain, has 138 outside cabins (86 inside) that feature private facillities, color TV, telephones, hair dryers, and personal toiletries kit. There is ample deck space for passengers who prefer outdoor activities and plenty of excitement for those who prefer inside games. Entertainment includes cabaret in the two-tiered Club Tropicana, piano bar at Oh Gee's, and blackjack in the Casino Royale. The main dining room is Las Palmas Restaurant, with informal buffets in Las Brisas Bar and Grill. Crown Cruise Line has launched its own "Crowncierge Service," which features complimentary food and beverage service around the clock in all cabins, complimentary "Crown Crest" champagne upon arrival, and fresh fruit basket.

Add-on air fares and Magic Touch vacations in the Orlando (Disney/MGM) area are also available through Crown Cruise Line.

★★★ + CROWN MONARCH

Crown Cruise Line; built in Valencia, Spain, for late 1990 delivery; Bahamian registry; Norwegian officers and Filipino/international crew; 16,000 tons; 500 feet long; 66 feet at beam; 560 passengers; crew of 210; cruising speed of 18 knots; 7 passenger decks.

Crown Cruise Line's long awaited new building, the 560-passenger *Crown Monarch,* is still a bit of a phantom at this writing. However, the vessel is projected to be on a one-week eastern Caribbean cruise schedule from Palm Beach's brand-new port facilities.

The vessel boasts several attractive lounges: Sensations Nightclub, Casino Royale, Crown Cabaret, and Visions Lounge. The plan also calls for a Splash Bar next to the pool, Captain Nemo's Video Arcade (for children, I presume), the Boardroom library, Palm Dining Room, and SeaFit Sports Center. Cabin configuration has not yet been released.

★★★★★CROWN ODYSSEY

Royal Cruise Line; Bahamian registry and Greek crew; built in Papenburg, Germany, and began service in June 1988; 40,000 tons; 614 feet long; 92 feet at beam; 990/1052 passengers; crew of 470; cruising speed of 22 knots; 10 passenger decks.

Royal Cruise Line's first new ship since 1974 *(Golden Odyssey)* is a blend of art deco interior design with state-of-the-art conveniences. Constructed in Papenburg, Germany, but designed by a team of architects, the vessel was the pride of Royal Cruise Line. In fact, Mr. Panagapoulos (founder and chairman of Royal Cruise Line), loved *Crown Odyssey* so much, he sold her and *Golden Odyssey* to Kloster Cruise Line, Inc., which owns the world-class Royal Viking Line. Kloster claims it will not tamper with Royal Cruise Line or the vessels that so many loyal passengers love and return to several times a year!

Among the design statements aboard *Crown Odyssey* are bay windows (with computerized shades) complementing all Superior Deluxe cabins on Riviera Deck. One deck above, the Penthouse Apartments boast large terraces, separate sitting rooms, and whirlpool tubs. These accommodations are very spacious, and each one features a different decorative theme—from tartan to contemporary to oriental (I presume that passengers can specify the desired decor if booked well in advance). In all, there are 18 categories of accommodations—most with large windows rather than portholes. Public rooms include: the Penthouse Bar and Grill off one of the two outdoor pool areas; two-tiered Coronet theater adjacent to lounge areas (for incentive groups and private meetings); the Odyssey Show Lounge with movable dance floor; an intimate bar called Theo's (after everyone's favorite bartender on the *Golden Odyssey*); the Monte Carlo Court—patterned after lobby areas of the world's traditional hotels—Casino and Yacht Club (where buffet breakfasts and lunches are served and the work of leading yacht photographers are displayed). The Yacht Club is a very pleasant space and is never crowded—even at the lunch hour.

On the very top deck, Horizon, is the Top of the Crown lounge— an oval-shaped structure offering panoramic views by day and disco at night. The two-seating Seven Continents Restaurant on Marina Deck also has sea views and piano music at dinner. This restaurant is one of the most refined rooms on board *Crown Odyssey,* and attractive and imaginative wall hangings change its ambience for certain evenings. Contrary to the buffets in the Yacht Club, which are rather standard shipboard fare, the menu and presentation in Seven Continents Restaurant is outstanding. And, there is always something on the menu to please the palate—meat aficionados will love the beef; vegetarians may order their favorite pastas and steamed veggies; or you can subscribe to the suggestion of the American Heart Association and dine on freshly grilled fish that melts in your mouth. And all is served with great efficiency and care. Royal Cruise Line is known for its excellent service and its warm care of passengers. Sports facilities on board include two outdoor pools, a golf driving range, indoor pool with whirlpools, juice bar, sauna, gymnasium, massage room, and hair salon.

However, *Crown Odyssey* would be just another vessel except for the return of Fernando Oliveira (plus seven, because he has several other Christian names) who has returned to Royal Cruise Line after a brief hiatus elsewhere. Fernando is not just another cruise director—he speaks several languages and remembers *everyone* on first meeting. It is great fun to take a cruise when Fernando is on board, and I hope that all who read this book will enjoy such an experience!

Crown Odyssey has been a fully booked success since her first cruise—for all the above reasons—as well as an excellent support group in San Francisco headquarters. During the winter season she is a busy lady, with cruises to the Mexican Riviera from Los Angeles as well as a repeat of the popular 10-day Pacific Hawaiian Odyssey sailings between Ensenada and Honolulu. A Panama Canal transit and a South American Odyssey complete the winter season, before *Crown Odyssey* sails for Europe from Buenos Aires.

Crown Odyssey's European cruises include six Mediterranean Highlights in spring and fall between Lisbon and Venice, and ten Great Capitals of Europe, as well as eight departures of Scandinavian Capitals and Russia. She concludes her European summer with a Gala Mediterranean cruise and then offers a three-week Magnificent Odyssey from Piraeus to San Juan for the 1992 winter in the Western Hemisphere.

A congenial Host Program, providing appropriate-age gentlemen for dancing, dining, and bridge/backgammon as well as a New Beginnings program of motivational guest lecturers make *Crown Odyssey* a very special cruise ship, indeed.

★★★★★CROWN PRINCESS/REGAL PRINCESS

Princess Cruises; Italian registry; Italian officers and European crew; constructed in Monfalcone, Italy, for July 1990 and Summer 1991 delivery; 70,000 tons; 804 feet long; 115 feet at beam; 1590 passengers; crew of 630; cruising speed of 19.5 knots; 12 decks.

These two distinctive vessels were designed by the very *in* Italian architect Renzo Piano, whose passion for the sea (like any good Genoese) led him to create a dolphinesque profile for the bow and a "crown" that represents the dolphin's head. The result is a sleeker but softer hull with a smokestack aiming straight up to the stars!—quite different from the present container ship–style of most large passenger vessels constructed today. Piano's other credits include the popular Georges Pompidou Cultural Center at Beaubourg in Paris, a space-age soccer stadium in Bari (Italy), and the largest airport in the world (Osaka, Japan).

On a recent visit to Fincantieri Shipyard in Monfalcone, Italy, my first view of *Crown Princess* was through the masts of several dozen small boats bobbing in the harbor—no doubt, awaiting their owners for a weekend sail. Although 70,000 tons, *Crown Princess* boasted a sense of belonging to the serenity of the scene and, indeed, offered the illusion of a dolphin moving through the water. In the opposite berth (but out of view), *Regal Princess* was already quite advanced in her construction. The two are sister ships for delivery in July 1990 *(Crown Princess)* and July 1991 *(Regal Princess)*. Both vessels have been scheduled to spend the summer months in the Mediterranean before arrival in the Caribbean.

While Renzo Piano created the master plan for these two vessels and was responsible for the two top decks, many others filled in the details with great skill. The interiors were designed by a Baltimore company (and executed by a charming executive named Fabio of the Sitmar/ Princess marriage) whose use of light coral, blue, and aqua colors is reflected in the carpeting, furnishings, and fabrics. Carrara marble lines the bathrooms of the suites (14) and mini-suites (36), which boast private verandas and are among the most attractive accommodations afloat. The lamps were commissioned in Venice and the chairs of the vanity are a soft, supple leather. Standard cabins with verandas (134), inside (159), or outside with large picture windows (442), are spacious and welcoming. All feature refrigerator, guest safe, card key access, walk-in closets, music/TV, and convertible beds. There are a total of 10 wheelchair accessible cabins, and provisions for wheelchairs have been made throughout the ship—most notably in the entertainment areas, where the back of the lounges have plenty of room and good sightlines for the handicapped. A wonderful addition that, hopefully, more ship lines will utilize!

Among the public spaces, the Dome on Sun Deck is the most spectacular, with its burgundy-colored leather seating around the perimeter for seaviews, a bar, a romantic dance floor, and banquettes on the starboard side and an interior casino. Areas are sectioned by low glass walls and planting. Passengers should also note the "spine" of the dome—a specially hand-crafted white lacquered cement that took many months to construct and is reminiscent of a Renaissance cathedral. Lido Deck below features two swimming pools, one with Flipper's Bar, Jacuzzis, Presto pizzeria, Characters specialty bar, and the self-service Cabana Cafe for buffet breakfast and lunch. The Stage Door nightclub, with its romantic banquettes, and the upper tier of the International Show Lounge are forward on Dolphin Deck.

Promenade Deck features the two-seating Crown Court restaurant, with aqua and coral chairs that fit the body. The affable Captain Nicola Di Stefano, veteran of three Sitmar ships, has a table for ten here where he can watch the action (and check the menu). Among other things, Di Stefano is adamant that only Romaine lettuce be used in Caesar Salad! Two spacious bar areas are also located on Promenade Deck—Intermezzo and Kipling's. Undoubtedly, a bit of nostalgia from the colonial days of P & O Line (parent company of Princess Cruises), Kipling's is a delightful spot with ceiling fans, rattan chairs, latticework carpeting, and a wooden dance floor. A wonderful place for a Singapore sling and all that! Just forward of Kipling's is the Chianti wine bar—for a change of pace and caviar tastings. The most attractive International Show lounge, with comfortable sofas and armchairs and good sighting, is located at the very forward of Promenade Deck.

Other amenities include a proper theater (with two-by-two red seating) on Emerald Deck, several shops, and the Plaza, with its purser's office on starboard side and Patisserie (for calories and designer coffees) on port side. Down on Holiday Deck are Jammers disco, Images beauty center, and the health spa, with aerobics, gym, sauna, and steam areas. *Crown* and *Regal Princess* are well-designed vessels, and finding one's way about is a snap! They similar to *Star Princess,* but more refined and elegant.

As on *Star Princess,* the contemporary art collection has been curated by Charles Mitchell, president of Creative Galleries in Los Angeles, and it is magnificent. Each piece has been chosen very carefully for the space, and passengers should take special care to enjoy the artwork.

Most dramatic on *Crown Princess* (as *Regal Princess* is not completed at this writing) is Eric Orr's *Prime Matter* water sculpture in the Plaza at entry level and Richard Estes' contribution in the main staircase. Other names that might be familiar are David Hockney, Helen Frankenthaler, and Robert Motherwell (with six pieces). An Italian contemporary is Sandro Chia, in one of the main stairways. All the artworks are documented with name, title, and a bit of background. Princess is proud of its $5-plus million collection of contemporary paintings in the fleet, and rightly so!

Crown Princess made her debut in the Mediterranean before sailing to New York City for five days of festivities, culminating with a christening by Sophia Loren—first lady of the Italian screen. The vessel is based year-round in Port Everglades for 7-day cruises that alternate from eastern to western Caribbean. Ports of call for eastern are St. Thomas, San Juan, and Nassau; the western itinerary is Nassau, Montego Bay, Grand Cayman, and Playa del Carmen/Cozumel. *Regal Princess* sailings begin November 9, 1991, on a similar program.

★★★★★CRYSTAL HARMONY

Crystal Cruises; Bahamian registry; Norwegian and Japanese officers; European hotel staff; Filipino engine; built in Nagasaki, Japan, for delivery July 1990; 49,400 tons; 787 feet long; 97 feet at beam; 960 passengers; crew of 480; cruising speed of 23 knots; 8 passenger decks.

Crystal Harmony seems to be a splendid vessel and reminds me very much of *Royal Viking Sun* with its stateroom amenities, seaview spa, swim-up bar, golf simulator, penthouse suites with butler service, etc. *Crystal Harmony* has a higher percentage of veranda staterooms, more and bigger penthouses, and just a slight edge on passenger space ratio—51.5 versus 51.35 gross tons—over *Royal Viking Sun,* but otherwise the two vessels are quite similar. Walk-in closets, refrigerator/mini bar, TV/VCR, bathroom goodies and hair dryers, terry-cloth robes, and more are standard amenities on top-rated vessels, at the very least in top-rated accommodations. So, the secret of *Crystal Harmony*'s ability to surpass all other cruise ships in elegance and luxury is still a mystery.

In checking the deck plans of *Crystal Harmony,* one surmises that the on-board lifts (elevators) might be very, very busy at certain hours because the public areas are four decks apart and the dining areas are even farther. The Crystal Dining Room has two seatings (6 p.m. and 8 p.m. for dinner); however, there are two smaller specialty restaurants (6–11 p.m.) at which passengers can book tables (at no extra charge). They are Kyoto, for oriental specialties, and Prego, for fresh pastas and other Italian dishes. The Lido Cafe, off Neptune Pool on Lido deck, offers buffet breakfast and lunch; and dinner service is also available in staterooms and penthouses. Michel Blanchet of Los Angeles has been named culinary adviser for Crystal Cruises, and a Japanese-designed Fine Tuned Cooling System enables the ship to keep food products and flowers fresh.

Other on-board amenities include a 3000-square-foot Crystal Spa and Salon, a 3000-square-foot Avenue of the Stars shopping area, and the Caesars Palace at Sea casino designed to resemble a Roman forum, a 270-seat Hollywood Theatre, and several intimate bars and lounges. For viewing the impressive scenery of Alaska, the domed, forward Vista Observation Lounge—tri-level seating and a 270-degree view—is the place to be. Cabaret will be offered twice nightly (to accommodate the two-seating dining), while more ambitious entertainment occurs in the Galaxy Show Lounge. Crystal has also signed up Cable News Network (CNN), the 24-hour news channel, to be available around the clock in all accommodations.

Crystal Harmony spent her inaugural season in Alaska/Canada from San Francisco on 12-day round-trip sailings. During the 1990/1991 winter season, the vessel makes trans–Panama Canal cruises from Acapulco to San Juan (or vice versa). During the summer of 1991 *Crystal Harmony* will offer 16 cruises in Europe ranging from 12 to 14 days each from the Mediterranean to the Baltic—calling at every port possible along the way!

★★★+CUNARD COUNTESS

Cunard Line; Bahamian registry and British officers, international crew; built in Denmark and outfitted; christened in 1976; 17,600 tons; 537 feet long; 75 feet at beam; 796 passengers; crew of 350; cruising speed of 18.5 knots; 8 passenger decks.

One of two sister ships especially designed for short, warm-weather cruises and high passenger capacity, the *Countess* was christened in San Juan in August 1976 by Janet Armstrong, wife of former U.S. astronaut Neil Armstrong, who was the first man to walk upon the moon. Although all Cunard vessels have been christened by prominent women, most of the ships extended the honor to British subjects and members of the royal family. The decision to invite Mrs. Armstrong was prompted by America's 1976 bicentennial celebration and was in keeping with the contemporary concept of the vessel and the astro-theme interior. Not to mention the fact that Cunard predicted (accurately) that the majority of *Countess* passengers would be Americans. Huge photos taken from space decorate the Splashdown Bar on Sun Deck (adjacent to the swimming pool) as well as other sections. (At least two of these photos were taken by Neil Armstrong.) The ship also has the Gemini Dining Room; Nova

Suite, a theater/conference center; Galaxy Lounge and Club Aquarius; and Starlight Lounge, which is adjacent to the casino.

Like the *Princess,* the *Countess* has 259 outside and 121 inside cabins, all with private facilities and all very small. The beds fold over to make sofas by day, but this doesn't help the lack of space very much. I found the cabins very "plastic" and "pre-fab," so be rather careful about slamming dresser drawers and such, or you may jolt your next-door neighbor right out of bed (this happened to me)! However, the deluxe cabins have now been fitted with twin beds that make up into a huge king-size version—wonderful! But there is plenty of public space, both in the lounges and on deck. In addition to using the swimming pool/Splashdown Bar area on Sun Deck, you can shape up at the putting green/driving range and on the paddle tennis court.

The calls for the two seatings in the dining room are harbingers of food that could be improved. Expect to have one Medieval night. The English breakfasts include kippered herrings, Nova Scotia salmon, steamed finnan haddie, and even French onion soup—a quick antidote for the morning after. Or you can breakfast alfresco at the charming cafe on Five Deck, which also serves hamburgers at lunchtime. The food is generally below par, no matter how often passengers complain about it.

A $7.5 million refurbishment project was completed aboard the *Countess* a few years ago and the ship looks great! A new indoor/outdoor theater-in-the-round-plus-disco was executed in the nightclub area. This is also where the captain holds his Welcome Aboard party and the setting is very impressive. The remodeled pool area features a Jacuzzi whirlpool, and there is an enlarged gymnasium aboard. The new "Milky Way" video arcade is for the youth (but expect to find parents there, too). All decks were reteaked, and the outdoor cafe was redone with Casablanca-type fans. The Meridian restaurant was completely redecorated and looks lovely in subtle beige and complementary colors. Other public areas and passenger cabins were also recarpeted and furnished more appropriately to the warm-weather cruising areas. The ship also offers a new Vitality Shipshape health and fitness program. The vessel was refurbished in Malta and the Maltese offered some very charming knights in armor as dramatic accessories to the public areas. I also like the new Cinema/meeting room, which can be expanded to include the Potpourri Room for larger conventions/seminars.

The Cunard *Countess* operates on two alternating itineraries year-round from San Juan. Every Saturday, the vessel sails for either Seven Plus (Tortola, St. Maarten, Guadeloupe, St. Lucia, Antigua, and St. Thomas) or the Caribbean Capitals (Grenada, Trinidad, Barbados, Martinique, and St. Thomas/St. John). A two-week *La Grande Caribbean* is available, which combines both cruises. Or, passengers may opt for the Sail 'n Stay packages that feature a week at sea, plus a week at either the Cunard Paradise Beach Hotel and Club in Barbados or the

372 · · · THE SHIPS

Cunard La Toc & Le Toc Suites in St. Lucia. Both resorts have been refurbished in the past few years. Paradise Beach is the more casual, and there seems like more to do on Barbados. La Toc is very elegant, but there's really nothing happening outside its doors.

★★★+ CUNARD PRINCESS

Cunard Line; Bahamian registry, British officers, and international crew; built in Denmark and outfitted in Italy; christened in March 1977; 17,600 tons; 537 feet long; 75 feet at beam; 802 passengers; crew of 370; cruising speed of 18.5 knots; 8 passenger decks.

The Cunard *Princess* had the distinction of being the only passenger vessel ever christened in New York harbor. (Until NCL's *Seaward* was christened in New York harbor on May 26, 1988, by Norwegian marathoner Greta Weitz and Princess Cruises' 70,000-ton *Crown Princess* by Academy Award–winning film star Sophia Loren, on September 26, 1990.) The late Princess Grace of Monaco did the honors in 1977, and a lovely portrait of the former actress hangs in the main stairwell of the vessel. The *Princess* is identical to the *Countess,* with private facilities in all 259 outside and 121 inside cabins. Be careful about engaging in loud conversations or slamming drawers in your cabin, as everything can be heard next door (see Cunard *Countess*)! Your sleeping quarters become sitting rooms by day, with beds that make up into sofas, but as on the *Countess* you won't want to spend much time here since the spaces are rather small. There are some nice outside deluxe cabins, with bathtubs, color TVs that receive the films, and side-by-side twin beds that can—with a little imagination—be considered king-size! They are excellent value and definitely for those passengers who enjoy being alone!

Passengers aboard the *Princess* are now well acquainted with an extensive refit that included a new indoor/outdoor center, refurbished cabins, Jacuzzis up by the pool, redecorated Meridien restaurant, Outrigger cafe (for buffet breakfasts and lunches), and Topsail lounge. The casino was enlarged behind the Indoor/Outdoor cafe, and the shopping arcade was improved—although the goods in the shops were not. (Can you believe—I couldn't find anything to buy!) The theater was refurbished and is located just behind the Outrigger and between the card rooms. There are two seatings in the attractive restaurant, and the food is the same as aboard *Countess*—below par.

The atmosphere on board *Cunard Princess* seems to be far friendlier than her sister ship, primarily because her Bahamian flag has allowed management to staff the vessel as it feels best. There are several Costa Ricans among the crew, who are like Filippinos and Indonesians in their helpful and caring attitude. Unfortunately, many of the staff

who ran the vessel so well are no longer on board, having been pro-
moted to loftier positions, but Ron Warwick is one of the captains, and
he is one of the nicest fellows with four gold bars afloat! Warwick's
father was the first master of the *QE2* and later commodore of the Cunard fleet; and Ron has written an interesting and sensitive book on the
QE2.

Having sailed all over the map looking for cruise passengers, *Cunard Princess* is now stationed in Europe, where we hope she will find
a deserved happy home. From mid-November to mid-March, she sails
among the Canary Islands on 14-day cruises round trip from Malaga to
Casablanca, Madeira, Las Palmas, La Palma, Tenerife (7-day passengers may disembark/embark here), Lanzarote, Agadir, Madeira, Tangier, and Gibralter. Sail and stays are available in London or Malaga,
and the air fare is most likely included in the cruise price—it's difficult
to decipher the brochure.

During the summer season, *Cunard Princess* sails between Venice
and Piraeus (Athens) on 14-day cruises that feature the Black Sea, Mediterranean Escape, and Classic or Ancient Mediterranean. Turnabout for
7-day passengers is either Limassol (Cyprus), Istanbul (Turkey), or Alexandria (Egypt). Sail and stay packages are available for Athens or
Venice, and air fare is either free or low cost. These itineraries are very
exciting for a vessel that has taken more than a full decade to find
herself. Bon voyage and bonne chance!

★★★★DANAE/DAPHNE

*Costa Cruises; Liberian registry; Italian officers; international crew;
originally built in 1956 and 1955, respectively, as refrigerated cargo
ships for Port Line of Great Britain; purchased by Costas Carras for
Delian Cruises and rebuilt in 1976/75, respectively, in Greece for luxury cruising; 15,560/16,330 tons; 532 feet long; 74 feet at beam; 404/
406 passengers; crew of 250; cruising speed of 21 knots; 7 passenger
decks.*

These two vessels, originally built as refrigerated cargo ships for
Port Line of Great Britain, were completely refitted and beautifully designed as luxury cruisers by John Carras, a wealthy and proud Greek
shipping magnate. Unfortunately, Carras and his Delian Cruises, with
interesting itineraries and on-board lecturers, good food and spacious
accommodations, and printed brochures that were works of art, were a
bit in advance of what the public wanted and the ships were chartered—
due to loss of money.

The *Danae* is one of my favorite ships afloat. I have the fondest
memories of cruising aboard her from Bangkok to Hong Kong (including a four-day storm on the South China Sea), and then sailing up the

Pearl River in the dark of night to Whampoa (Huang-pu). It was February 1977, and the *Danae* made cruise history as the first Western passenger vessel to dock in a mainland Chinese port since 1948. It was an exciting voyage for her passengers and crew, and although there were some minor mishaps, the *Danae* sailed through the choppy waters as smoothly as possible. I think of her on this cruise with memories of impeccable service, delicious food (you could order anything you wanted, even if not on the menu), and top-class entertainment. I especially remember a hot, foamy bath that I slipped into upon my return from dusty Canton—simply glorious!

Accommodations aboard the *Danae* are splendid, no matter what category. There are 161 outside cabins with two lower beds, plus 21 deluxe suites. In addition, on Amalfi Deck, six super suites have a balcony, king-size beds, separate sitting rooms, and enormous bathrooms. The suites also have color TVs, refrigerator/bars, and bidets. All cabins have full bathrooms with tubs, even the 19 inside cabins aboard *Danae* and 22 inside cabins aboard *Daphne*. The same attention has been paid to all accommodations, and the recently refurbished decor features original artwork and hand-woven curtains and bedspreads. The public rooms are also attractive. The Riviera Lounge, spacious and elegant, features a small bar area in the rear that opens onto the deck in good weather. The very pleasant Trevi Restaurant accommodates (on most cruises) all passengers at one seating—one of the criteria for a truly first-class vessel. The food is excellent in true Costa tradition, with plenty of Italian specialties featured on every menu. And Friday nights are Roman Bacchanal evenings with billowing togas (bed sheets from the stewards, if you please) and a decadent feast. A card room and library as well as shopping arcade and the Monte Carlo Casino are situated between the lounge and dining area.

Other facilities include a comfortable theater with a bar, a small Yacht Club lounge/late-night disco, a pizzeria and a gelerateria all located adjacent to the swimming pool and Lido area. There are also a well-equipped gym and sauna. Everything was planned with great care, and the vessel is a good size for getting around easily.

From spring through fall, the *Danae* cruises in the eastern Mediterranean round trip from Venice. The 11-day itineraries vary to feature Israel/Egypt and Yugoslavia, Greece/Turkey, or Greece/Turkey and Yugoslavia. The vessel is primarily European, and some Americans have complained to me that announcements and explanations in English were not sufficient. During the winter months the *Danae* makes a long cruise of about three months from Genoa, either around the world or to the Orient. Brush up on your Italian for this one!

The *Daphne* summers in Alaska, sailing round trip from Vancouver from mid-May through September. The vessel departs Vancouver on Friday at 4:30 p.m., sails the Inside Passage on Saturday, calls at

Ketchikan Sunday, and cruises Endicott Arm Monday morning before calling at Juneau in the afternoon. Tuesday is spent in Skagway as well as Davidson and Rainbow glaciers. Wednesday is Wrangell. Thursday is a sea day, and the *Daphne* returns to Vancouver at 8:30 a.m. on Friday. Two 17-day trans-Panama Canal cruises between Los Angeles and Fort Lauderdale are available spring and fall, with fly free from more than 100 gateway cities.

During the winter season, the *Daphne* sails from San Juan at midnight on Saturdays for St. Maarten, Martinique, Barbados, St. Lucia, Antigua and St. Thomas—an island a day. Costa calls this itinerary "resort cruising" as passengers can have a taste of several resorts during the week. They are: Puerto Rico's Dorado and Cerromar Beach resorts, Cariblue and Halcyon Cove on St. Lucia and Antigua, Sam Lord's Castle on Barbados, the Meridien and Frantel resorts on Martinique, Mullet Bay on St. Maarten and Mahogany Run on St. Thomas. Passengers are encouraged to play golf, tennis, ride, snorkel, fish or sail at these resorts. Is there an extra charge for using these facilities? You bet!

★★★★+DAWN PRINCESS/FAIR PRINCESS

Princess Cruises; Liberian registry; Italian officers and European crew; originally built as Fairwind *and* Fairsea, *respectively, in 1971; renamed by Princess Cruises in 1988 and refurbished in 1989; 25,000 tons; 608 feet long; 80 feet at beam; 890 passengers; crew of 430 cruising speed of 19 knots; 11 passenger decks.*

These very fine sister ships, formerly operated by Sitmar Cruises in North American waters, were acquired by Princess Cruises in 1988 when Princess Cruises bought Sitmar. They have a homey and friendly reputation and a loyal following. Princess spent considerable millions redecorating them, using the same design firm that was responsible for the ship line's new *Star Princess*.

The public areas received special attention on both vessels, including the nightclubs and the South Pacific and Caribbean lounges, where new sound and lighting systems were added. New furniture and drapes are featured in the dining rooms (Lancaster and Ritz on *Dawn Princess,* Grosvenor/Lancaster on *Fair Princess*) and the shopping areas were remodeled to reflect the architectural and design features of each vessel. Cabins also received attention and were rewired with 110 volt current to allow for the use of passengers' hair dryers and other small appliances (formerly, one was obliged to visit the "hair dryer room" on each deck). Computer and satellite systems were also added on board to offer passengers more options on the televisions in the four suites and 26 mini-suites.

Of the total 503 cabins, there are 238 outside and 235 inside—a high ratio of inside cabins—which reflects the age of these vessels (originally built in 1956 by the famous John Brown shipyard on the River Clyde in Scotland). In addition to a library, casino, lounges, and three outdoor swimming pools, each vessel boasts a youth center and the popular pizzeria, where authentic Italian chefs tempt passengers of all ages. These have become family-oriented vessels and children have a wonderful time.

During the summer season, *Dawn Princess* and *Fair Princess* can be found in Alaskan waters offering one-week cruises between Vancouver and Whittier (for Anchorage). Both ships spend the winter on the Mexican Riviera, sailing round trip from Los Angeles on 7- and 10-day cruises to Cabo San Lucas, Mazatlan, and Puerto Vallarta, with Zihuatanejo/Ixtapa and Acapulco added on the longer voyages.

★★★★DELTA QUEEN

Delta Queen Steamboat Company; American crew and registry; built in 1926; most recently refurbished 1986; 1650 tons; 285 feet long; 58 feet at beam; 176 passengers; crew of 74; 12 miles per hour maximum speed; 4 passenger decks; listed in the National Register of Historic Places.

Prior to becoming one of two official steamboats of the Louisiana World Exposition a few years ago, the *Delta Queen* had an interior facelift that made 14 new deluxe staterooms and two superior staterooms on Cabin Deck. The spacious new accommodations are all outside, with large picture windows, and furnished with Governor Winthrop desks, Chippendale armchairs, and Goddard chests. Cotton-sateen drapes blend with the emerald green or spiced rose Saxony carpeting. The windows have stained-glass inserts and the mirrors are of beveled glass. There are Stobard prints of great steamboats of the past on the walls, and brass headboards with porcelain spinnings.

The Orleans Room, the dining and entertainment area aboard the old *Queen,* has also been refurbished. Old New Orleans brass finials support silk-screened linen draperies, and the dining chairs are upholstered in a margaux-colored velvet. The Siamese bark floor, known as iron wood for its strength and durability, has been polished and returned to its natural color.

The Forward Cabin and Texas lounges were refurbished a few years ago, and the air conditioning throughout was upgraded to compensate for those lazy, hazy summer days along the river.

With so much history and with a cozy passenger capacity, the *Delta Queen* is an intimate paddle-wheeler. Not many minutes will pass by after you board before old friends are reacquainted and new ones made.

Since the *Delta Queen* began steamboating life on the rivers of

America in 1927, this carefully preserved and beloved antique entered into the National Register of Historic Places in 1970, has cruised more than 30,000 miles annually, and has visited more than 14 states from her home port in New Orleans. While watching the banks drift by is still the favored pastime, passengers can also enjoy spontaneous sing-alongs, kite flying over the paddlewheel, calliope-playing contests, locking through on the Upper Mississippi and Ohio rivers, first-run films in the lounge, lectures by staff members and visiting guests on river history and commerce, and boat tours.

The *Delta Queen* sails from New Orleans, Cincinnati, St. Louis, Pittsburgh, Memphis and St. Paul on 3- to 12-night cruises along the Mississippi and Ohio rivers. The cruises emphasize a Heart of Dixie, Show Me Showboatin', Kentucky Derby, Ohio Valley, Steamboatin' Sampler, White Lightning, Yankee Steamer, Frontier Adventure, Mississippi Explorer, Great Steamboat Race, New Orleans Express and Heart of America. Steamboatin' Plus Touring, Air Travel and Drivin' are available.

★★★DOLPHIN IV

Dolphin Cruise Line; Bahamian registry, Greek officers, and international crew; originally built in 1956 and formerly named Ithaca; *13,007 tons; 501 feet long; 65 feet at beam; 586 passengers; crew of 280; cruising speed of 17 knots; 6 passenger decks.*

Following a five-year renovation project, the *Dophin IV* looks very spiffy, indeed, and passengers are raving about their experiences on board! The *Dolphin IV* has been transformed into a very charming vessel, and the cruise line is boasting good revenues and satisfied customers from all over the country, with California being its second strongest market after Florida. Dolphin has excellent air-sea programs (claims it was the first to offer free air for short cruises) and good land packages to complete the week's vacation.

The multimillion dollar refurbishment included some new cabins as well as major change of decor in all public rooms. The Monte Carlo Casino has been opened up and several new slot machines added. The Barbizon Restaurant has been lightened up with white interiors and a grand piano for dinner music. Complimentary wine is served with the evening meal. A video-library/card room is attractive in beiges, and just off the very impressive Rendez Vous Lounge. The Miramar Cafe night-club is attractive in red and gray, and the Disco is down below on Dixie Deck.

In addition, attention was also paid to the shopping arcade, now in glass and chrome and called Windows From the World, and the Lido area, where sliding glass doors help passengers through with their breakfast and lunch trays. The food gets good marks and passengers certainly feel that they are getting more than they bargained for aboard *Dophin IV*. This is a cozy vessel, and should appeal to both honeymooners and Golden Anniversary types.

Every Friday afternoon *Dolphin IV* departs Miami for Nassau and Blue Lagoon Island; every Monday, the vessel sails from Miami for Freeport, Nassau, and Blue Lagoon Island. Walt Disney, Golf, and Honeymoon packages are available. *Dolphin IV* is also trying some one-week cruises during Christmas week—to test the waters, so to speak.

★★★★ECSTASY

Carnival Cruise Lines; Bahamian registry; Italian officers and international crew; built at Wartsila/Masa Shipyard in Finland and inaugurated spring 1991; 70,367 tons; 855 feet long; 104 feet at beam; 2044–2600 passengers; crew of 920; cruising speed of 21 knots; 9 passenger decks.

Like the *Fantasy* and *Sensation, Ecstasy* has been designed by Carnival's own Joe Farcus, and the interiors are in themselves fantastic, ecstatic, and sensational! There is a six-deck-high atrium, an elaborate health and fitness facility, the Crystal Palace Casino (namesake of Carnival's very own casino/resort in the Bahamas), Rolls Royce Cafe, Stripes Discotheque, Society Bar, Panorama Bar & Grill (for light meals), Blue Sapphire (state-of-the-art) Show Lounge, Teen Club Disco, Neon Bar, and Explorer's Club, to name a few of the public areas. The two dining rooms have been named Wind Star and Wind Song after the ship line Carnival acquired along with Holland America Cruises.

The itinerary of Carnival's latest superliner, *Ecstasy,* will be Nassau, San Juan, and St. Thomas on weekly Sunday departures from Miami. The ship replaces the *Jubilee,* which has been repositioned to Los Angeles to replace the *Tropicale* on her Mexican Riviera run. Just for the record, the *Tropicale* has moved to San Juan to join the *Festivale* in serving the lower Caribbean

This is the sister ship of *Fantasy,* one of three vessels ordered from Wartsila Shipyard in Finland. The third, *Sensation,* has been more delayed than the first two because of the bankruptcy of the yard—which Carnival and the Finnish government have saved for the time being. In fact, the new name of the yard is Masa, and the $275-million *Ecstasy* is the first vessel constructed under the reorganization.

★★★EMERALD SEAS

Admiral Cruises; Liberian registry and international crew; originally built in 1944 and once called the President Roosevelt; *last refurbished*

in 1988; 24,458 tons; 622 feet long; 75 feet at beam; 782 passengers; crew of 400; cruising speed of 18 knots; 9 passenger decks.

The big white superliner *Emerald Seas* is considered the grande dame of the south Florida to Bahama Islands run, since she has been sailing every Monday and Friday since December 8, 1972, from Miami. The *Emerald Seas* was repositioned to Port Everglades on May 20, 1990, for a Thursday and Sunday departure schedule. In addition to being spacious and comfortable, the ship is one of the oldest afloat. She was built in 1944 by the U.S. government to carry troops and has been known by several names: *General Richardson, Leilani, La Guardia, President Roosevelt,* and *Atlantis.* She was rebuilt for cruising in 1970 by Perama Shipyards in Greece and is now operated by Admiral Cruises, a combination of Eastern and Western Cruise Lines and sister ship line to Royal Caribbean Cruise Line.

Refurbished a few years ago, the *Emerald Seas* looks better than ever, with larger than average cabins ranging from Lanai suites with picture windows to the smaller lower-deck accommodations with berths. All are clean and comfortable, with contemporary patterns in drapes and upholstery. The Rendezvous Bar and Casino, Aquarius Club (a favorite area), and Mayfair Ballroom have all received facelifts. So have the Islander Lounge and double-tiered French cafe, where the noon buffet is served overlooking the pool. The Palm dining room on Ruby Deck is very attractive, has a full service bar, and two seatings for all meals.

Admiral Cruises has also altered the itinerary of the *Emerald Seas* to include a full day at CocoCay (formerly known as Little Stirrup Cay), Royal Caribbean's 140-acre out island, located in the Berry Islands between Freeport and Nassau. Passengers can enjoy miles of sparkling beaches, Emerald Cove, coral reefs, and underwater caves for snorkeling. There are changing facilities and a sumptuous picnic/barbecue available. CocoCay, which has just received a $7-million renovation that includes new double-deck tenders, the CocoCay Boathouse and Mercantile Company (souvenir shops), and several spots to eat and drink, has been added to both Sunday and Thursday sailings to spectacular success. First and second passengers (in a cabin) fly free from selected gateways nationwide. Five- and six-night Supercruise Vacations available at excellent rates.

★★★EUGENIO COSTA

Costa Cruises; Italian registry and crew; originally built in Italy in 1966; refurbished last in 1987; 30,000 tons; 713 feet long; 96 feet at beam; 1100 passengers; crew of 475; cruising capacity of 27 knots; 9 passenger decks.

Flagship and pride of the Costa fleet in the Mediterranean, the *Eugenio Costa* is the largest vessel the Costa group has ever constructed from scratch. This is also one of the most luxurious ships available on the Mediterranean to South America run. The vessel has a total of 638 outside cabins, and 184 inside (although some 157 do not have private facilities).

This is definitely a three-class vessel—a thing of the past to which Americans are not accustomed. However, an $18 million refurbishment program recently has resulted in a very pleasing vessel, although Americans should take note that Italian is the official language on board— neither fellow passengers nor crew speak much else! The public areas of the *Eugenio C.* are spacious and full of surprises with many full-length windows to offer sea views from lounge areas. Built in the mid-1960s, the vessel evokes an Old World atmosphere no matter how many times the furniture gets redecorated.

New on board the vessel are: a bow thruster; a number of cabins rebuilt; an Italian Piazza on Lounge Deck with fountains, boutiques, a pizzeria and gellateria; a sports center on the top deck; the 600-seat La Scala Showroom on Lounge Deck; Trattoria del Mare indoor/outdoor restaurant between the two swimming pools; and new purser's reception area on Venice Deck. In addition, there are a variety of large and small lounges on Lounge Deck in which to sit and relax. There is also plenty of deck space outdoors with attractive teak.

During the summer season the *Eugenio C.* sails from Genoa to the Eastern and Western Mediterranean as well as on a long cruise to the Western Hemisphere that does call in various American ports. During the winter months, the vessel can be seen in South American ports, as its original itinerary was between Genoa and Buenos Aires.

★★★★EUROPA

Hapag Lloyd; German registry and crew; built in Bremerhaven and commissioned in 1982; 34,000 tons; 650 feet long; 95 feet at beam; 600 plus passengers; crew of 320; cruising speed of 21 knots; 9 passenger decks.

Hapag Lloyd's new flagship *Europa* is an impressively designed and spacious vessel. With 12 passenger decks and some 12,000 square feet of outdoor space, there is plenty of room for the 600-plus passengers. Cabins are larger than average (especially for new ships) and are reported to be noiseless, as all are situated in the forward and central section of the vessel. There are some beautiful suites on Sun Deck forward, named after famous composers (Haydn, Wagner, Mozart, Beethoven, Handel, and Schubert). The *Europa* has two outdoor swimming pools, several bars and nightspots, a large health center, theater, casino, spacious restaurant, and Europa Salon (the main lounge). German-speaking readers will certainly enjoy this exciting vessel for worldwide cruises.

A tour of this vessel on her call in New York harbor last year was very exciting. The decor and feeling of spaciousness throughout was a treat, considering what passes these days for a modern cruise vessel. Although the majority of passengers were away on tours of Philadelphia, Niagara Falls, and Washington, DC, those who preferred to stay behind were of all ages . . . from a toddler to grandparents!

The dining room, indoor swimming pool and spa, and the many lounges are very comfortable and inviting. This is a very fine vessel, but cannot be recommended to Americans because of the language problem. *Everything* is in German. Unless you are German-born or bred, you will not appreciate the atmosphere aboard this cruise ship.

Nonetheless, the *Europa* follows the sun around the world, to the South Pacific, South Africa, the Caribbean, Mediterranean, and Scandinavia (during the summer months). There is not a major cruising area where the *Europa* does not call.

During the summer of 1988, *Europa* scheduled more than usual transatlantic sailings and attempted to appeal to the American market. I suspect they were more successful with Germans arriving in the U.S. to spend their cheap dollars. I have not checked *Europa* prices for 1989, but I would doubt they are competitive with U.S.-based ships because of the weak dollar. The *Europa* is a very nice vessel; I have seen her in innumerable ports around the world; but unless you are a very serious Deutschland-phile, love the food, and are fluent in the language, this is not a good choice for the cruise experience. Germans love it, of course, but *Europa* does not attract the *Vistafjord* mix of 50/50 German and English-speaking—especially in Europe.

★★★★FANTASY

Carnival Cruise Lines; Bahamian registry and international crew; designed and built in Wartsila shipyard, Finland, entered service in March 1990; 70,000 tons; 855 feet long; 104 at beam; 2050 passengers; crew of 1000; cruising speed of 21 knots, 14 passenger decks.

Fantasy is the first of a new generation of superliners to join the extensive Carnival Cruise Lines family; already contracted and named, to be built by the same shipyard, are *Ecstasy* and *Sensation*. (Needless to say, these names have caused a "sensation" in the cruise industry.) Interior design on the $200-plus-million-a-piece superliners is being executed by Carnival's in-house architect, Joe Farcus, whose technique is already evident aboard the *Holiday, Jubilee,* and *Celebration.*

The first impression of *Fantasy* is sheer size; this is a huge vessel and, if filled to capacity, could accommodate 2600 passengers having nothing but *fun!* The core of the ship is the Grand Spectrum, and here designer Joe Farcus had his fun with some 12 miles of neon lights that change colors ever so discreetly throughout the day (and night). The Grand Spectrum is also six decks high and covered by the largest glass dome ever constructed for a ship. And if that doesn't strike your fantasy, try the Universe Lounge, meant to showcase glittery Vegas-style revues on a moveable stage. The floor of Universe Lounge also serves for dancing and is black marble with a ceiling of stars overhead. Entry to the lounge is as dramatic as the space itself, and those neon strips (they encompass all public areas) will change color as you watch.

Other not-to-be-missed attractions aboard the *Fantasy* are a 20-foot-tall kinetic sculpture, a 12,000-square-foot Nautica Spa and jogging track, Electricity Discotheque, Cats nightclub, entered through milk cans and decorated with food containers, Cleopatra's Bar, and Club 21 Casino. The Majestic Bar descends to Jubilee and Celebration dining rooms, which also boast dramatic entrances and sea views. In keeping with the new "generation" for Carnival, new menus have been devised that promise more health-conscious meals and circular salad bars. Cabins aboard the *Fantasy* are far more spacious than on other new vessels, and suites boast plenty of space plus whirlpools. Cabins have TVs as well as wall safes (so sensible, because the boxes in the purser's office have become so far away).

The *Fantasy* brings a new dimension to the 3- and 4-day Bahamas market from Miami. The vessel departs on Friday and Monday weekly, and passengers have the opportunity to experience another "fantasy/sensation" at Carnival's own Crystal Palace resort and casino in Nassau. The $250-million mega-resort has a 30,000-foot casino and will have 1500 rooms when completed. Pre- and post-cruise packages here are available, as well as organized shore excursions from the *Fantasy, Carnivale,* and *Mardi Gras.* Let's keep the casino money in the family! And, if you don't gamble (good grief), there are beaches, golf course, tennis courts, and many restaurants and bars in which to spend the time ashore.

★★★FESTIVALE

Carnival Cruise Line; Bahamian registry, Italian officers, and international crew; originally built in 1961 and formerly named the S.A. Vaal; *refurbished in 1978 and launched as the* Festivale; *38,175 tons; 760 feet long; 90 feet at beam; 1146 passengers; crew of 612; cruising speed of 22 knots; 9 passenger decks.*

When Carnival Cruise Lines bought the S.A. *VAAL,* which had transported passengers between Southampton and South Africa, she became the third and largest of the fleet. The 38,000-ton vessel was transformed into a Caribbean cruiser through a $30 million refit in a Japanese shipyard under the direction of architect Joe Farcus. The vessel entered Caribbean service in 1978 and, at the time, was both the largest and fastest vessel sailing weekly from Miami.

No doubt due to the lucrative South Africa trade, the *Festivale* boasts a top deck of some splendid old-world cabins—with full bathrooms, sitting areas and some 10 with verandas. The remaining 272 outside and 309 inside cabins are located on Empress, Upper, Main and Riviera decks and more spacious than average on the Caribbean run but less than elegant.

The *Festivale* has two outdoor pools for adults and a wading pool for children. She also has a children's playroom, health/massage center, Fanta-Z discotheque, Le Cabaret nightclub, Carnivale lounge and bar, Tradewinds Club, Copacabana lounge and—of course—the Glasslight Club Casino and Saloon located smack center on Promenade Deck. Don't miss it, folks—this is Carnival's profit center! The unwindowed Continental restaurant is located down on Main Deck and seats 700 people in each of two meal services.

The *Festivale* was the first of Carnival's fleet to be repositioned in San Juan for Sunday (10 p.m.) sailings to St. Thomas, St. Maarten, Barbados, and Martinique—and the first Carnival vessel to offer passengers four port calls. Full sea days are Wednesday and Saturday. Cruise rates include free round-trip air fare from over 95 continental U.S. cities to San Juan. Pre- and post-cruise packages are available at the El San Juan Hotel (boasting the largest casino in the Caribbean) or the Clarion Hotel & Casino.

★★★★★FRONTIER SPIRIT

Salen Lindblad Cruising/Frontier Cruises; Bahamian registry; Northern European/Japanese officers and crew; built in Kobe, Japan, for service November 1990; 6700 tons; 365 feet long; 56 feet at beam; 164 passengers; crew of 82; cruising speed of 15.5 knots; 5 passenger decks.

Frontier Spirit was built by Mitsubishi Heavy Industries in Kobe, Japan, and is a joint venture of NYK Line, Mitsubishi Corporation, the shipyard, Hapag-Lloyd, and Salen Lindblad Cruising. The ship is essentially the first arrival of a new line called Frontier Cruises but marketed primarily by Salen Lindblad Cruising (SLC). The vessel is considered the first "environment friendly" one afloat, and the first expedition ship built since 1974 (others are coming along quickly, however). She has been designed to safeguard the delicate ecosystems through which the expeditions will pass—including the Arctic Circle, the Northwest Passage, and Antarctica. Another environment friendly feature is the storage and disposal of on-board garbage.

Cabins on board *Frontier Spirit* are spacious all-outside, and some boast terraces. There are two suites, as well as a small swimming pool and spa with sauna, main lounge, single-seating dining room, a fleet of Zodiacs on Deck 6, and a helipad on Deck 8! Food is "continental," and thus far, there are no plans for a Japanese chef on board—pity, because the sushi from some of the *Spirit*'s cruising areas would be spectacular!

Inaugural voyages for *Frontier Spirit* include a South Pacific Trilogy, as well as Australasia, Antarctica, New Zealand, Tasmania, Alaska and the Northwest Passage, Australia's Great Barrier Reef, Indonesia/Bali, and the Amazon and Orinoco rivers. Cruises range from 10 to 31 days (the latter for the Northwest Passage), but most average a reasonable two weeks.

★★★★★GOLDEN ODYSSEY

Royal Cruise Line; Bahamian registry and Greek crew; built in Elsinore, Denmark, in 1974 especially for the American cruise market; extensively refurbished in 1987; 10,500 tons; 427 feet long; 63 feet at beam; 460 passengers; crew of 215; 22.5 knots maximum speed; 7 passenger decks.

Golden Odyssey is a gem of a vessel and something of an anomaly in the present cruise industry. She carries under 500 passengers in a familylike ambience and is one of the great success stories of all times. Before air-sea programs became commonplace, other cruise lines were in awe and envy of *Golden Odyssey* because the ship was filled by the plane! This is a vessel on which you return again and again to see your favorite crew members waiting for you! My husband will never forget the dramatic passage through the Corinth Canal aboard *Golden Odyssey* and I will never forget a gondola ride in Venice and a tour of Ravenna! A *Golden Odyssey* cruise is an experience to be savored forever.

The *Golden Odyssey* has 234 staterooms, of which 183 are outside doubles, 43 are inside, and eight are deluxe suites. Some cabins accommodate three and four persons and some connect. The cabins are all decorated in bright, Mediterranean colors with reproductions of Greek embroideries from the Benaki Museum in Athens on the walls. Each has two lower beds in a parallel or "L" arrangement that are made up to look like sofas by day. All cabins have wall-to-wall carpeting, individual air-conditioning control, three-channel music, rosewood furniture, vanities, three closets, and tiled bathrooms with showers. Full bathtubs are found in the deluxe suites on Riviera Deck; and in rooms 703, 704, and 710; and in rooms 536–553, 436–453, and 327–343 (not including inside rooms). Continental breakfast and snacks on a 24-hour basis are served in the cabins. Cabins are on the small size, but then this is a smaller than average vessel. Just beware that your husband may be not able to stand up in the shower.

The Lotus Restaurant on Odyssey Deck seats about 250 passengers at a time in tables of two to eight persons. Breakfast is open seating, while luncheon is served from noon (main) and 1:30 p.m. (late). Dinner hours are 6:45 p.m. (main) and 8:30 p.m. (late). Next to the Lotus dining room is a small, private room for cocktail parties. Among the five bars on board, one is on the swimming pool deck where an outdoor buffet is served at lunchtime. The main public area, the Ulysses Lounge, accommodates the full passenger list for afternoon lectures, classes, evening cabaret (an English theatrical group performs scenes from popular musicals), folkloric shows, and Greek night performances as well as dancing. For night owls, the Calypso Lounge on Riviera Deck becomes the late-night disco. And for those who have not had enough to eat, the Midnight Buffet begins at 11:30 p.m. in the Lotus Restaurant (again!). The *Golden Odyssey* also has a library/writing room, card room, gym with saunas, beauty salon, and hospital.

The *Golden Odyssey* received a smashing $10 million refit in late 1987 with interiors of hunter green, deep blue, and cranberry hues. New and stylish are the Rendezvous Foyer/embarkation lounge on Odyssey Deck as well as the popular Wooden Horse Bar, which now boasts a painting of horses by a modern Chinese artist. The Greek design team of A. and M. Katzourakis retained many of the original ship interiors, but enhanced them with brighter colors. The Lotus restaurant combines coordinated shades of blue with lotus-flowered prints on the modern Scandinavian furniture. The Calypso Lounge is a blend of salmon and blue chairs, with cozy banquettes and couches. Staterooms also received their due, with new furniture, original prints by Chinese and Japanese artists, a pull-out table, and state-of-the-art telephone system.

During the winter season *Golden Odyssey* sails from Curacao and San Juan on 7-day cruises that can be combined to two weeks each. Transatlantic sailings are very popular in spring and fall. From May through November the yachtlike vessel cruises the Mediterranean, Aegean, and Black seas on 12-day programs. In addition to its popular Sea of Ulysses and the Black Sea program, Royal Cruise Line has introduced a Greek Islands and Ancient Civilizations program that is new to past passengers. *Golden Odyssey* is a wonderful size for cruising both the Aegean/eastern Mediterranean and Caribbean, and one of a fast-fading breed.

★★★★HOLIDAY

Carnival Cruise Lines; Bahamian registry; Italian officers and international crew; built in Aalborg, Denmark, for Carnival and entered

Caribbean service July 13, 1985; 46,052 tons; 728 feet long; 92 feet at beam; 1452 passengers; crew of 660; cruising speed of 21 knots; 9 passenger decks.

The *Holiday* was the first of three "superliners" constructed for Carnival Cruise Lines Scandinavia. When all three *(Holiday, Jubilee, Celebration)* were in place at the end of 1987, Carnival became the largest of the worldwide cruise lines (at least for a while) and boasted over a half million annual passengers. The *Holiday* is a definite departure in design attitude and on-board atmosphere for Carnival, and the vessel presents a new image for the rest of the Carnival fleet.

Cabins are more or less the same, however, with more spaciousness than usual in the standard categories and all L-shaped twin configuration convertible to "togetherness" sleeping arrangements. There are 10 veranda suites that feature bathtub Jacuzzis; 431 outside twins and 252 inside twins. There are six outside and 27 inside upper/lower berth cabins.

One startling design departure for Carnival on the *Holiday* is formal meal service, featuring two separate windowed (at last!) restaurants, the Seven Seas and the Four Winds. Both are located on America Deck but reachable by separate stairwells. Both are very attractive, with tables for eight, six, four and (a very few) two dressed in pink. Chairs in the Four Winds are upholstered in a copper-colored basket-weave velvet pattern, those in the Seven Seas are in burgundy velvet. The decor certainly enhances the setting, but meal presentation needs a lot of work. The Seven Seas restaurant is also the site of the gala Midnight Buffet.

My favorite room on board the *Holiday* is the Carnegie Library, which has been endowed with a classical decor and really does have some books. Large glass doors can enclose the space during the day for quietude or private parties; in the evening, music from Rick's American Cafe across the corridor turns the library into a pleasant cocktail lounge— the only intimate space aboard. Rick's is a 90-seat piano bar (passengers are encouraged to pretend they are in Casablanca) connected to the casino by a spiral red staircase. Of course.

The Gaming Club casino seats 250 and is supposed to be the largest afloat (at this time). There are 21 blackjack and two roulette tables, three for craps, and a wheel of fortune. Add to this more than 100 electronic slot machines. Starboard of the casino is the Bus Stop cafe, through which the 1:30 a.m. mini-buffet is served. It is a renovated 1930s vintage bus, with a bar/cafe adjacent to satisfy the late-night crowd.

Forward of Bus Stop is Times Square, a full-width-of-the-ship area featuring sculptured figures in stainless steel and acrylic to represent performing artists. Times Square flows into the top section of the enormous Americana Lounge, which spans two decks and accommodates over 900 passengers. With a stars-and-stripes motif, this lounge is the site of full theatrical and cabaret presentations.

Broadway is another enclosed promenade space—with a simulated brick sidewalk that takes passengers into the Bus Stop area. Broadway also has Capuccino's, where special coffees and sweets can be bought. Behind the coffee house on port side is the Tahiti lounge, decorated in Polynesian style. The 78 hand-carved mahogany totems that line the walls were, however, carved by a Bahamanian named Henry Fernander. The room also served as a small meeting area, and is equipped with a movie screen concealed in the ceiling.

Reflections Disco functions as a meeting room by day and a swinging disco place at night. The aft Blue Lagoon lounge is the second showroom aboard the *Holiday* and features a midnight special every evening as well as cocktails and dancing before and after dinner. The decor of the room suggests an undersea grotto and is obviously an acquired taste. Directly above Promenade Deck is the Wharf bar and grill, which serves buffet breakfast and lunch. It happens to be the "mechanical room" of the vessel, but ducts and such are concealed behind a tugboat called Sweetness and the usual paraphernalia one expects on a wharf.

Forward of the two restaurants, Carnegie Library and Rick's Cafe on America Deck, is Union Square—another enclosed promenade with seats of rattan on the port side, easy chairs on the starboard. The Galleria shops adjacent offer gifts and sundry items, a boutique and duty-free liquor store. Artworks throughout the vessel are indicative of the media in which Americans are working. A six-foot fountain created by San Francisco artist Helen Webber, with 400 sculptured titles and a sea fantasy theme, is located in the Purser's Lobby so passengers pass by at least twice per cruise.

The *Holiday* also has a children's playroom, a game room, a large health club with whirlpool, massage and gym on Veranda Deck, and two adult swimming pools. On a hot day at sea, these pools are hardly adequate for the full passenger complement. It was people to people the last time I looked out at the very crowded pool aft on Lido Deck!

The *Holiday* sails every Saturday at 4 p.m. from Miami for Sunday at sea, Monday at Cozumel/Playa del Carmen, Tuesday at sea, Wednesday at Grand Cayman, Thursday at Ocho Rios, Friday at sea, and return to Miami at 8 a.m. on Saturday. The itinerary may be reversed on certain sailings. Cruise rates include free round-trip air fare from over 165 cities to Miami. Pre- and post-cruise packages are also available.

★★★★HORIZON

Celebrity Cruises; Liberian registry; Greek officers; international crew; built in Papenburg, Germany, for delivery in May 1990; 46,000 tons;

682 feet long; 95 feet at beam; 1354 passengers; crew of 642; cruising speed of 21.5 knots; 9 passenger decks.

The *Horizon* is a wonderful surprise, and Chandris can be justly proud of its first "new" vessel in the Celebrity Cruises line! She is a beauty with her futuristic exterior and space-age smokestack emblazoned with the new Chandris logo—an *X* riding the waves. Indeed, the white and blue–hulled vessel has an outward character quite apart from the boxlike designs that seem to appear with such regularity these days. The *Horizon* is sleek and understated—a refreshing delight.

The interior of the vessel is also understated and in excellent taste. Four international design firms shared the responsibility for the interiors, including the famed husband-and-wife Katzourakis team of Greece, who must have conceived the Horizon Lobby (entry hall), as it reminds me of the Agora, the marketplace of Athens in classical times. While the pastel colors were a bit of a shock at first sight, but one becomes quite enamoured with this busy area, and the doric-style columns above add a certain stability and peace.

While the ship is fairly large and will most likely always be filled to capacity, there is plenty of space for everyone. Fantasy and Galaxy decks provide the public areas, although the America's Cup Club with panoramic views on Marina Deck seems to be the most popular preprandial meeting place. Fantasy Deck features the Zodiac Club/Gemini Disco aft, with the Casino Royal/Plaza Bar and Mall shops (where merchandise could be more worthy of the prices) midships, and the second tier of the Palladium Show Lounge forward. Along the Panorama Gallery on Fantasy Deck are display cases featuring reproductions of ancient Cycladic artifacts—no doubt, a Chandris family personal touch. Other artwork on the *Horizon* is contemporary, and complements very well the decor throughout the ship.

Galaxy Deck boasts the large Palladium show lounge forward, a cozy Rendezvous Lounge/piano bar midships (with a library and card room portside), and the Starlight restaurant where the menus are under the direction of noted French chef Michel Roux (who has earned a few Michelin stars from two restaurants in the London area). Food and service in the dining room are certainly well above "cruise fare," and passengers do not seem to be streamlined through the two seatings. The menu and wine list offer plenty of variety, and compliments were heard all around.

The breakfast and luncheon buffets in the Coral Seas Cafe are also well presented (I was impressed that "real" china was utilized), and there were many fine comments about the plentiful supply of coffee and tea throughout the afternoon. In between meals, there are two lovely pools and plenty of lounge chairs on Marina Deck as well as a whirlpool, jogging track, Fantasia (teen room), Olympic Health Club, and small Mast bar up on Sun Deck. Children have their own playroom down on Florida Deck next to the Steiner beauty salon (where complimentary facials were offered on Friday). And if there is an organized tour of the Bridge, take it—it's quite "unique," as Captain Iakovos Korres likes to boast, with its fantastic four-color radar equipment and enclosed "wings"!

Cabins aboard *Horizon* are spacious and feature radio and TV (with feature films). There are two Presidential suites and 18 Horizon suites, 40 double-bed cabins, and 469 twins (all outside); inside cabins number 32 double-bed and 112 twins. There are also two cabins set aside for wheelchair passengers. The pastel colors in all accommodations are pleasant and restful. Cabin service is excellent, with European stewardesses in the higher categories. Fresh linens, ice, and water need never be requested. Room service is also impressive—and very swift. All this— and we were only on the second cruise *Horizon* ever offered!

During the summer season *Horizon* is one of just four cruise ships allowed regular calls in Bermuda. She sails every Saturday from New York for Hamilton and then St. George's from April through October. Be on deck to watch the delicate maneuvering of the vessel through the narrow St. George's channel. And while in this charming town, do not miss a bowl of the best fish chowder on the island—at the nearby White Horse Tavern. Spicy it is! From November to April, *Horizon* is based in San Juan for one-week cruises every Saturday to Martinique, Barbados, St. Lucia, Antigua, and St. Thomas.

★★★★★ILLIRIA

Classical Cruises; Liberian registry and Greek-Filipino crew; built in Italy in 1962; refurbished in 1981, 1986, and 1990; 4000 tons; 333 feet long; 48 feet at beam; 140 passengers; crew of 89; cruising speed of 16 knots; 5 passenger decks.

The *Illiria* is no stranger in refined circles—among travelers who have cruised aboard through their museum, alumni, and garden club/national trust affiliations since 1982 through Travel Dynamics (which will continue to sell some cabins). Now that the vessel is being marketed to the general public through Classical Cruises, even more aficionados will be found; the *Illiria* is a gem of a vessel. Cabins are very comfortable (they have just been redecorated) and range from cozy singles to very spacious suites. The public areas are warm and inviting for talks, tea, or cocktails at the bar.

Fellow passengers are active and eager—they wouldn't be aboard if they were not—and it is easy to find topics of similar interest. I sailed aboard *Illiria* up the Hudson River with one group from the National Trust, another from a California garden club. They came to see the fall foliage and historic properties, especially West Point, and the organized tours were very well received. Classical Cruises' programs from April through October in Turkey, the Greek Islands, and the Black Sea are perfect for the *Illiria;* they complement the deck space for viewing, a splendid wood-paneled library full of wonderful books, and a museum-quality art collection throughout the ship.

The dining-room seats all passengers at tables of choice—nothing is assigned but single travelers need not worry here, because everyone is so friendly. Food is under the direction of chefs from the Culinary Institute of America and complimentary house wines are served at lunch and dinner. Buffet breakfasts and lunch are also served by the small pool, weather permitting. There is plenty of deck space on which to relax and read, as well as a small gymnasium adjacent to an even smaller boutique/beauty parlor. Oh well, this is a ship on which to stretch the mind.

During the inaugural season of Classical Cruises from Istanbul, there was a choice of five different programs including the week's cruise to Kusadasi (Ephesus), Rhodes, Crete (Aghios Nicolaos), Santorini, Mykonos, Piraeus (Athens), and Lesbos (Methymna). In addition to expert lecturers on board, special shore features include Cretan dances in Aghios Nicolaos, wine tasting in Santorini, and a traditional island "glendi," or feast, at a taverna in Methymna.

During the 1991 season a much longer visit to Kusadasi has been scheduled and Piraeus dropped in honor of Patmos and Bodrum visits. And from mid-June to early September the *Illiria* is offering one-week Black Sea cruises from Istanbul—the vessel's home port. Sailing weekly from Istanbul on Mondays allows passengers to arrive early in Istanbul and have ample opportunity to explore this fascinating city at the crossroads of eastern and western cultures.

During the winter months, the *Illiria* is scheduled to cruise in Antarctica.

★★★INDEPENDENCE

American Hawaii Cruises; American registry and crew; originally built in the U.S. in 1951 and named the Independence; *extensively refurbished in 1989; 30,090 tons; 682 feet long; 89 feet at beam; 800+ passengers; crew of 320; cruising speed of 20 knots; 9 passenger decks.*

Former flagship of American Export Lines, the *Independence* was a three-class vessel carrying some 1000 passengers across the Atlantic and on long cruises throughout the world. She was retired in 1967 when travel by ship became outmoded, and was laid up near Baltimore, Maryland. The vessel was purchased by Atlantic Far East Lines, a subsidiary of the C. Y. Tung group of Hong Kong in 1974 and placed into service as the *Oceanic Independence.* Five years later, the vessel was transferred to American Global Lines (another subisidiary of the C. Y. Tung group) and once again flew the U.S. flag—by act of Congress. She began operating weekly cruises from Honolulu around the Hawaiian Islands on June 21, 1980.

Like the *Constitution,* this vessel is now owned by Peter Huang, who took over control of American Hawaii Cruises a few years ago. The ship is under the excellent care of Captain Larry Kelley of West Roxbury, Massachusetts. A former naval officer, Kelley spent his childhood near Bethlehem Steel's Quincy yard, where the *Independence* was built and launched.

The *Independence* began 1988 with a glamorous multimillion-dollar refurbishment designed by a Honolulu firm that features wall prints by Hawaiian artist Pegge Hopper. Throughout the vessel are new carpets, wall coverings, upholstery and draperies, decking, retiling of the two swimming pools, as well as refinishing of all the lovely woods on board. In addition to the cosmetic changes, the mechanical plant of the vessel was thoroughly inspected and upgraded to comply with new U.S. Coast Guard requirements. The dining room was gutted and redecorated, new menus and new uniforms were instituted, and a new director of Passenger Services/concierge is on board to help passengers with personal requests and travel plans. Other popular innovations are a weekly ice cream social as well as hot dogs/hamburgers out on deck every afternoon from 2 to 4 p.m. Sounds so American!

The *Independence* has 20 suites (including a two-bedroom owner's suite), 27 deluxe cabins, 107 outside cabins with two lower beds, 8 outside with double beds, and 6 outside with upper/lower berths. There are 141 inside cabins with 2 lower beds, 17 inside with double beds, 60 inside doubles with upper/lower berths, and 11 inside singles with lower berths. All cabins have private facilities and are definitely larger than average for cruise space. On-board facilities include two outdoor swimming pools, a full Sports Deck, Barefoot Bar overlooking the Sun Deck pool, and Latitude 20° with a glass wall over the Upper Deck pool. The Palms dining room, down on Aloha Deck, does not have sea views but is divided into smoking and nonsmoking sections. What was once another dining room on Main Deck is now a conference center, booked in advance on many cruises for groups who wish to combine business with pleasure. Midships on Promenade Deck is the Independence Lounge, while the huge Pacific Showplace (for evening entertainment) and the Commodore's Terrace are aft. The Hunt breakfast is served on deck, and morning sherbet and afternoon tea are available in the Parisian-style Sidewalk Cafe on Upper Deck, which also houses shops and the children's playroom. A cinema is down on Coral Deck.

There is plenty to do aboard the *Independence* when not just drinking in the magnificent scenery, and a long list of celebrities from stage, screen, and television are willing to sing for their supper. Rosemary Clooney was entertaining aboard the *Independence* last spring, and packed them in in the Pacific Showplace. There is a popular Youth Recreation Center, with jukebox, dance floor, and soda fountain aboard the vessel and it is rumored that Captain Kelley stops by nightly for his favorite flavor of ice cream. Kaui Barrett, the social hostess, divides her time between the *Constitution* and *Independence,* teaching the hula dance or lei making or giving ukulele lessons (when she is not aboard, someone else fills in), and there are excellent local shows of traditional Hawaiian music and song.

During the summer season, when a more youthful set of passengers is aboard, underwater sports are popular, and there are excellent scuba and snorkeling tours planned. All this, plus tax-deductible seminars at sea make these cruises something to consider. The itinerary is so marvelous and the atmosphere so infectious that just about *everyone* ends up buying an Aloha shirt or a Muumuu, the native dress.

The *Independence* sails every Saturday at 9 p.m. from Aloha Tower in Honolulu, along with the *Constitution.* Sundays are spent at sea, cruising among the islands. On Monday at sunrise, the *Independence* arrives at Nawiliwili, Kauai; Tuesday is spent at Kona and Wednesday at Hilo, both on the "big island" of Hawaii; Thursday morning to Friday evening is at Kahului, Maui (everyone's favorite), and on Saturday morning the *Independence* sails in tandem with the *Constitution* back to Aloha Tower in Honolulu. Three- and 4-day mini-cruises are also available, with the rest of the week spent at a Hawaiian resort. Golf packages and kids free (in same cabin with two full-fare adults) during the summer vacation months are standard American Hawaii Cruises offerings.

★★★★★ISLAND EXPLORER

Spice Island Cruises; Indonesian flag and crew; designed in Norway 1985; 859 tons; 134 feet long; 42 feet at beam; 36 passengers; crew of 25; cruising speed of 16 knots; 3 passenger decks.

The *Island Explorer* was designed by Westamarin of Norway and is the first jet-driven expedition vessel. The vessel utilizes two 1300 horsepower engines and water jetted from the stern that propels without need of shaft or propeller. The twin-hulled vessel has satellite telex and phones, three desalinators and three inflatable landing craft for excursions.

There are 18 all-outside cabins with large windows, telephones, sound and shortwave systems and private facilities. Six are suites and all were Italian designed. All cabins offer the ambience of being in Indonesia, with hardwoods and antique batiks and tapestries. Facilities include a glass-enclosed dining room and lounge, a covered patio adjacent to open area up on Sun Deck. Sports facilities on board include water skis, wind surfers, glass-bottom boat, deep sea fishing equipment, snorkeling and scuba diving equipment.

Abercrombie and Kent is the general U.S. sales agent for *Island Explorer,* but P & O Australia supervises technical and operational management of Spice Island Cruises, owner of the vessel, and is apparently considering expansion of the fleet. The vessel has enjoyed success in cruising among the so-called Spice Islands, and cruise/land tours from 7 to 17 days are available. With almost the highest crew/passenger ratio afloat, one can be assured of wonderful service from smiling people. It is the perfect way to see Indonesia, especially the remote areas, with the *Island Explorer* your comfortable home at every call!

The *Island Explorer* cruises among the Indonesian archipelago most of the year (A & K does not offer programs during the summer months). The adventures are called Sandalwood and Dragons (Bali, Komodo, and the Lesser Sundas of 8 or 14 days); Dance of Welcome (westbound from Kupang to Bali for 7 or 14 days); Volcanos and Wildlife (exploring the wildlife reserves, tropical beaches, and great volcano of the Sunda Straits); and Spice Islands Exploration (an 8-day cruise with additional visits to Singapore and Hong Kong).

While on board *Island Explorer,* you will enjoy more than your share of Gado Gado salad, which can be made of any vegetables as well as bean curd and boiled eggs. Below is a recipe for the famous peanut sauce that accompanies it:

$^1/_2$ lb. unsalted peanuts
vegetable oil
4–5 shallots
3 cloves garlic
3 red chilis
1 piece ginger root smashed
bunch lemon grass
juice of one lime
1–2 Tbsps. brown sugar
pinch of salt

Fry peanuts in some vegetable oil. Add shallots, garlic, chilis, lemon grass, and ginger root to soften. Place in blender and reduce to liquid paste. Enjoy!

★★★★★ISLAND PRINCESS/PACIFIC PRINCESS

Princess Cruises; British registry and crew (with Italian dining room personnel); sister ships built in West Germany and launched in 1970 (Pacific Princess) *and 1972* (Island Princess); *20,000 tons; 553 feet long;*

82 feet at beam; 610 passengers; crew of 350; cruising speed of 19 knots; 7 passenger decks.

The *Island* and *Pacific Princess* rank high in the most attractive cruise ship category; with the distinctive Princess Cruises logo atop their smokestacks, both are among the luxurious vessels in the P & O family. Although identical in design and ambience, they differ somewhat in decor. However, once you find your way around one of these *Princesses*, you'll feel right at home aboard the twin. You'll also be very pleased with your choice of vessels!

Although Princess has expanded its fleet in recent years with such glamorous attractions as *Royal Princess, Star Princess,* and *Crown Princess* (not to forget *Regal Princess*, in the shipyard), many loyal passengers still prefer what they now consider the "babies" of the family; they love the intimacy of the smaller vessels and the fact that meeting and making new friends is so much easier here than on the 1200–1500-passenger newer ships. Both *Island Princess* and *Pacific Princess* are justly famous as they were featured in the *Love Boat* series, which is still enjoyed by millions of viewers worldwide (in syndication).

With a total of 13 different public rooms you feel the spaciousness aboard these vessels—from the gracious Purser's Lobby, with its dramatic staircase and galley to the romantic Starlight Lounge in the forward section of Sun Deck. This lovely hideaway has wraparound windows that allow wonderful views of the sea and sky. On Riviera Deck the Carib/Pacific lounge, bar, and club; the Princess Theater; and the Carousel lounge and bar offer a variety of entertainment. And if you're a night owl, the Skal Bar turns into a disco at midnight. For games and more serious pursuits, you can seek out the Bridge and International lounges or the library/writing room one deck below. Both vessels have the Coral Dining Room (located on Coral Deck) with two sittings for luncheon and dinner, and two swimming pools. The Crystal Pool on Sun Deck is the most glamorous, with its Sun Dome for inclement weather (of course, it is rarely needed).

Accommodations aboard both these Princess vessels are splendid. The deluxe suites are spacious and delightful. The sitting areas are perfect for private gatherings, and you can find large beds in cabins 346, 348, 349, and 350. The deluxe outside twin cabins are as large as mini-suites, and the standard twin gains space by day with one bed that folds into the wall while the other becomes a sofa. The crew aboard both vessels is friendly, attractive, and helpful; and the British officers are stunning in their short white uniforms and knee socks! In the dining room the Italian chef and stewards dish up a cuisine that has both a fine reputation and sex appeal. Needless to say, the food is another outstanding feature on these two vessels, so plan to enjoy yourself and forget about calories.

During the summer season both vessels can be found in Alaskan waters, sailing between Vancouver and Whittier (Anchorage) on 7-day cruises. Princess is one of the major ship lines in Alaska and offers many interesting programs and land tours. Following some Caribbean sailings, the *Island Princess* offers 11- and 14-day cruises in South America—primarily along the Amazon River between Manaus and San Juan, as well as two special Rio de Janeiro programs. During the winter season *Pacific Princess* sails in the South Pacific and Polynesian Islands, departing from Sydney, Papeete, Auckland, and Honolulu, on 11- and 14-day cruises.

★★★JASON

Epirotiki Lines; Greek crew and registry; built in Italy in 1965; refurbished and launched as Jason *in April 1968; 5250 tons; 346 feet long, 61 feet at beam; 268 passengers; crew of 112; cruising speed of 15 knots; 6 passenger decks.*

The *Jason* is one of the most charming of the Epirotiki fleet; the vessel has a pleasant ambience and is a good size for those who prefer the smaller ships. The vessel has 134 cabins situated among four decks, and all but 30 have outside views. All have private facilities with stall showers. The only full baths found on the ship are in suites A1 through A6 on Apollo deck. The cabins, small but very pleasant, have fold-over sofa arrangements for day. Large murals reminiscent of the island of Thira and curtain designs that feature shields of ancient Greek heroes make the rooms even more pleasant.

The *Jason* is justifiably proud of the many fine artworks on board, which add to her appeal as a cruise vessel. Up on Jupiter Deck an unusual fountain supplies fresh seawater to the Argo Pool, while the mosaic tabletops in the adjoining Argonaut Bar reflect the designs of ancient warrior shields. Below, in the Orpheus Nightclub (a disco after 10 p.m.), a life-size bronze and copper figure of Orpheus plays his lyre. On Dionysos Deck (also called Main Deck), the Jason Bar stands out with its tapestry of Jason yoking the wild bulls in the sacred field of Ares, and the corridor to the Golden Fleece Lounge boasts a monumental brass sculpture, *Sunburst,* which is said to be the largest bronze work cast in Greece since the classical age. It's impossible to sail aboard this vessel and not become interested in Greek mythology.

Some lovely tapestries inside and around the Eros Dining Room deck the cheerful restaurant that seats the entire complement of passengers at one time. The gold and orange room has large, bright windows to constantly remind you of the excitement of the sea. The food and service are reported to be good, especially the Greek dishes and fine selection of local wines. Epirotiki has concocted a special drink for each ship, and this one is known as Jason Night; it consists of one ounce of gin, two ounces fresh lemon juice, syrup, and a splash of apricot brandy. It sounds as though it would burn beautifully!

The *Jason* is a popular vessel and well suited for one-week cruises from Piraeus. The vessel's most recent itinerary featured ports in Turkey, Egypt, and Israel, as well as the Greek Islands of Rhodes and Patmos. The ship can also be found on charter in the Caribbean during the winter season.

★★★+JUBILEE

Carnival Cruise Lines; Liberian registry; Italian officers and international crew; built in Malmo, Sweden, and entered service in July 1986; 48,000 tons; 733 feet long; 92 feet at beam; 1486 passengers; crew of 670; cruising speed of 21 knots; 9 passenger decks.

The *Jubilee* called at New York en route to homeport of Miami and made a terrific impression on all who stopped by to visit. For starters, the *Jubilee* completely dwarfed two other ships in port—the *Nordic Prince* and *Stella Solaris*—as the second of three superliners to join the Carnival fleet within an 18-month period. With the arrival of the *Celebration* in March 1987, all three superliner sister ships are in place for Carnival and the ship line is looking forward to its new generations of superliners—*Fantasy* (which arrived in Miami in February 1990), *Ecstasy* (spring 1991), and *Sensation* (under registration at this writing, but very much on the drawing board). Life keeps sailing ahead at this company!

The *Jubilee* is identical to the *Holiday* but rather more subdued and sophisticated in its interior. While the *Holiday* design jumps out and is themed to suggest throngs of people—Union Square, Broadway, Bus Stop, Times Square—and the *Jubilee* does have Trafalgar Square, Park Lane and Tivoli Square—the art work is not so three-dimensional and always getting in one's way. Colors are also better in most of the public areas.

Cabins are standardized and spacious for new construction in the 7-day market. Large picture windows dominate in the outside accommodations, and the L-shaped bed configuration can be changed in all cabins to simulate the king-size variety. Bathrooms are still small, but subdued tilework has been added, to give a more homey feeling. Ten suites on Veranda Deck have terraces and are attractively decorated with TV/bar console, walk-in closets with small safe, and bathtubs.

A small gymnasium/fitness center is also on Veranda Deck and overlooks a Lido Deck pool—so watch out, girls! There are two pools on Lido Deck, with the air-conditioned Funnel Bar and Grill between. This is a most attractive room for buffet breakfasts, lunch, and afternoon snacks, with tables for six on which there are posters of old liners and now extinct steamship companies. Funnels line the bulkheads and the whole area looks as though it works well.

The Burgundy and Bordeaux dining rooms on Atlantic Deck are joined by a common galley and replicas of the *Holiday* restaurants. Both are very attractive, with pink tablecloths, a raised center, some booths, and both round and rectangular tables. I did not stay for lunch aboard the *Jubilee* in New York, but the hors d'oeuvres were quite good. Carnival does not promise gourmet food, but is making an attempt to make dining more memorable. The dining-room staff wears white gloves on special occasions, which is supposed to make it taste better!

Adjacent to the Burgundy dining room is Churchill's Library and the Speakeasy Lounge—the most incongruous combination one can imagine, but it works in the evening because cocktail service is available in the library, away from the piano bar. Neither room is quite so attractive as respective counterparts on the *Holiday*. Forward is Trafalgar Square, the shopping area, children's video game room and the lower level of the large Atlantic Lounge.

Promenade Deck is total public space, with a children's pool aft (the children's playroom is one deck below). There are: Terraces in the Grove Lounge, with a dance floor that can become a raised stage; the Oz discotheque; Smuggler's Lounge, decorated with sidings from an old barn in Sweden; the Espresso's Cafe, where exotic coffee drinks can be purchased; the vast Sporting Club Casino; the Gazebo with bar; Tivoli Square and the upper section of the Atlantis Lounge.

The *Jubilee* was constructed of some 23 different prefabricated sections and boasts a massive red, white and blue winged stack. Interior architect Joe Farcus tried to create an overall feeling of nostalgia, and created many, many spaces in which 1500 to 1900 passengers can play. As one visitor said, "Carnival is not so much in the cruise business as in the vertical integration business." Whatever that means.

The *Jubilee* was repositioned from Miami to Los Angeles in April 1990 to assume *Tropicale*'s itinerary but offer a 50% passenger capacity to the route. *Jubilee* departs the west coast every Sunday afternoon for Puerto Vallarta, Mazatlan, and Cabo San Lucas.

★★★STAR/SHIP MAJESTIC

Premier Cruise Lines; Bahamian flag and international crew; originally built 1972 as Sun Princess; *acquired by Premier in 1989 and refurbished; 17,750 tons; 535 feet long; 75 feet at beam; 768 passengers; crew of 370; cruising speed of 21 knots; 7 passenger decks.*

Star/Ship *Majestic* is a high-density vessel—many passengers for the space allowed—and from fresh reports, there is not much space on deck during the day at sea on 4-night cruises. However, this vessel has an unusual itinerary from Port Canaveral. Called Abacodabra by Premier Cruise Lines, the *Majestic* visits the Abacos—a cluster of out islands in the Bahamas chain that vary from the 125-mile-long Abaco Island to others that are just isolated islets.

Among the islands visited by Star/Ship *Majestic* are Green Turtle Cay, Great Guana Cay, Man O-War Cay, and Treasure Cay. Windsurfing, sailing, pedal-boating, snorkeling, and swimming on the spectacular, white powdery sand beaches are highlights of daytime activities. In the evening on Treasure Cay, there is an outdoor Caribbean show, dancing, and midnight buffet.

Star/Ship *Majestic* sails from Port Canaveral every Thursday and Sunday for the Abacos out islands. All cruises of 3 or 4 nights include an entire week—visits to the Magic Kingdom Park, EPCOT Center, and the new Disney-MGM Studios Theme Park as well as tours to NASA's famous Spaceport USA at Kennedy Space Center.

★★★MARDI GRAS

Carnival Cruise Lines; Bahamian registry; Italian officers and international crew; originally built in 1962 and entered service as the Empress of Canada; *last refurbished in 1985; 27,250 tons; 650 feet long; 87 feet at beam; 906 passengers; crew of 508; cruising speed of 21 knots; 9 passenger decks.*

The *Mardi Gras* was the first launched of the present super fleet of Carnival Cruise Lines. The vessel entered year-round Caribbean service in 1972 on 1-week cruises from Miami. The *Mardi Gras* has an old-world ambience, and the continued use of so much original wood and brass contributes to the feeling of a past grandeur. The enclosed promenades add to the reality that this ship began life sailing across the cold Atlantic.

Cabins on board the *Mardi Gras* are certainly larger than what one would call "Caribbean style," and there is a high complement of inside cabins, which keeps the average rate at a low level. Double and king-size beds have been placed in many of the cabins to attract honeymoons on the Sunday sailings. Many cabins can accommodate four singles in adequate comfort. Carnival recently installed 110 AC power in all of the vessel's 457 cabins to standardize them with what passengers can expect on land.

The Grand Ballroom is balconied, a trait of many older vessels. There are several lounges/bars, including the Showboat, Carousel—recently expanded into the port-side promenade, with a larger bar and additional seating. The Showboat Club Casino—hottest spot on the ship— has been enlarged into the El Patio Grande area. Other public rooms are the Point After discotheque, the Den/Lido bar with audio equipment for on deck dancing, and the Seaview Snack Bar on Sports Deck for after- noon on deck food service. The non-windowed Flamingo dining room on Riviera Deck is not the most cheerful afloat. There are outdoor and indoor swimming pools, a full cinema, exercise room/sauna, and duty- free shops for gifts, sundries and liquor.

As on all Carnival ships, there is plentiful food of average quality. In addition to three full meals a day, there is a midnight buffet as well as a late-night buffet, and snacks available during the daylight hours. To work off all the calories, decks sports include trapshooting (extra charge), table tennis, shuffleboard and golf driving.

The *Mardi Gras* sails from Port Everglades (Fort Lauderdale) on Thursdays for Nassau, arriving at 9 a.m. every Friday. Shore excursions feature Carnival's own Crystal Palace Casino/Hotel and nightclub show. The vessel departs Nassau on Saturday at 6 a.m. for a day at sea before returning to Port Everglades at 7 a.m. on Sunday. The 4-day Bahamas cruise departs Port Everglades on Sundays at 5:30 p.m. The vessel spends Mondays in Freeport (for gambling) and Tuesdays in Nassau (same ex- cursion as above). The *Mardi Gras* returns to Port Everglades at 7 a.m. on Thursday. Fly Aweigh add-ons and pre- or post-cruise tours in Flor- ida are available.

★★★★MERIDIAN

Celebrity Cruises; Bahamian registry; Greek officers and international crew; originally built in 1963 in Trieste and known as Galileo Galilei *of Lloyd Triestino Line; sailed as* Galileo *for Chandris Fantasy Cruises; completely refitted in 1989 and relaunched as* Meridian *for Celebrity Cruises in April 1990; 30,440 tons; 700 feet long; 94 feet at beam; 1106 passengers; crew of 500; cruising speed of 24.5 knots; 8 passen- ger decks.*

Chandris spent $55 million on the former *Galileo* to bring the ves- sel into the Celebrity Cruises fleet, and the results are very fine, indeed. Without disturbing the traditional lines of the exterior, the moderniza- tion has given new life to a ship so familiar in ports around the world. The new blue-and-white hull is topped with the now trademark Celeb- rity Cruises smokestack on which the *X* of Chandris is riding the waves.

The *Galileo* accommodated 1074 passengers; the *Meridian* has a passenger complement of 1106 in 553 cabins, of which 258 are on the inside. Of the 295 outside cabins, there are eight large suites on Cap- tain's Deck (just aft of the Bridge) that feature picture windows as well as skylights! There are 47 deluxe cabins with separate seating areas on Atlantic Deck, and the outside cabins on Horizon Deck boast seaviews from "floor to ceiling" windows. Two cabins have been adapted for wheelchair passengers. All accommodations have radios and telephones but no TV, refrigerator, or mini-safe—even in the suites.

Among the structural changes on the *Meridian* are an entirely new sun deck area with three whirlpools, plenty of lounge seating, and a bar. Below on Lido Deck is a new swimming pool as well as the Marina Cafe, serving buffet breakfast and lunch plus tasty barbecues. At night, the interior of the cafe becomes the Marina Disco fantasyland through the use of hundreds of twinkling lights and appropriate music. The main public rooms are located on Horizon Deck: the Zodiac Club, intimate Interlude Bar, Monte Carlo Casino, Rendezvous Lounge with piano bar, and Celebrity Showroom. Along the sides are shops and card room as well as the refurbished Palm Court and Promenade—reminiscent of the "good old" transatlantic days.

The Four Seasons restaurant on Bermuda Deck (with exposed Wine Cellar) is under consultancy of Michel Roux, a renowned French chef who has earned several Michelin stars for restaurants in the London area. Roux's role is to create some special recipes, design menus, and train restaurant staff. Although I only visited the *Meridian* in Bermuda and have not yet had the opportunity to sail aboard, everything seemed to be in fine order. A two-level cinema and a small chapel—both retained from the original vessel—complete the public spaces.

During the summer season the *Meridian* sails Sundays from New York for Somerset, Bermuda, where the new West End Pier, King's Wharf, has been constructed. Here, passengers may explore the nearby Maritime Museum, ferry or bus into Hamilton, or rent mopeds for independent touring. The winter months find *Meridian* in Port Everglades for Sunday sailings to Antigua, St. Thomas, and Nassau. Captain Andrianatos, formerly of the *Amerikanis,* is master of the *Meridian*.

★★★ + MERMOZ

Paquet French Cruises; Bahamian flag; French officers and international crew; originally built in 1956 as Jean Mermoz; *relaunched in 1970 as* Mermoz; *last refurbished 1984; 13,800 tons; 491 feet long; 61 feet at beam; 530 passengers; crew of 320; cruising speed of 16 knots; 5 passenger decks.*

The *Mermoz* is a compact vessel on which cuisine, under the direction of head chef Jean Abauzit, is very important; the French definitely have a flair for such things. For such a small vessel, the *Mermoz* boasts an assemblage of 52 chefs, cooks, pastry chefs, and bakers—not to mention all those who do the washing up! There is one sitting for all meals (dinner begins at 8 p.m.) either in the Restaurant Massilia (cabin category 7 to 15) on Delos Deck or the Renaissance Grill (cabin category 1 to 6) overlooking the Roman Bath pool. There is also a self-service buffet in the Lido Ancerville, adjacent to the sun deck pool.

Other amenities include four bars, the Gibraltar Cinema (showing both French and English films) on Gibraltar Deck, Galapagos Club/Disco on Galapagos Deck, the Grand Salon Mermoz, a small casino, complete health club with hydrotherapy/sauna/massage, and small but classy boutique. There are 15 different cabin categories, including 17 cabins available for single passengers only.

The *Mermoz* sails the world—around South America, Easter Island, Galapagos/Panama/Florida, Florida/Antilles, the Caribbean, transatlantic from Guadeloupe to Rouen, France (during the 15-day crossing, Berlitz will immerse you in the French language for a few hundred dollars extra); the Baltic, Fjords of Norway and Spitsbergen, Iberian Shores (from Le Havre to Toulon), Music Festival at Sea (Toulon/Toulon) now entering its 35th and 36th years, Mediterranean Shores, Greece/Cappadocia, en route to Yemen (Heraklion, Crete to Djibouti), India/Ceylon (Djibouti to Port Victoria, Seychelles), and Seychelles to South Islands (Mauritius). All this, and a plethora of shore excursions and cruise land-extensions!

★★★★MISSISSIPPI QUEEN

Delta Queen Steamboat Company; American crew and registry; built by Jeffboat in Jeffersonville, Indiana; launched July 1976; refurbished in 1984 and 1989; 4500 tons; 382 feet long; 68 feet at beam; 398 passengers; crew of 150; 8 miles per hour maximum speed; 7 passenger decks.

When the *Mississippi Queen* was commissioned on July 25, 1976, in Cincinnati, Ohio, it was the culmination of a ten-year project that cost $27 million and involved the craftsmen of both England and America. This *Queen* was the largest and most spectacular riverboat ever built, and special arrangements were made for her to be constructed in Jeffersonville, Indiana, where nearly 5000 steamboats had been born during the 19th century.

The *MQ* is over 100 feet longer, ten feet wider at beam, and almost 3000 tons larger than her venerable sister, the *Delta Queen*. She also carries twice the passenger and crew capacity. Her exterior was devised by James Gardner of London, who also participated in the design of Cunard Line's flagship, the *Queen Elizabeth 2*. The exterior was somewhat altered during the 1989 refurbishment program. Fluted twin smoke stacks appeared, along with filigree and wrought-iron trim around open decks and the pilot house. At the stern of the vessel, the great paddle wheel was painted a brilliant red, and the two-story glass windows behind it outlined in stark white. The interior of the vessel has been conceived very carefully to offer every nuance of the ambience of 19th-century river life, without breaking the Safety at Sea Law that states all materials must be as nonflammable as possible. Although none of the fine old polished woods of the *DQ* are possible here, the moldings, mirrors, highly polished steel and brass everywhere, and the plush carpeting throughout the public areas certainly recall the opulence of the great steamboat era.

The *MQ* has 145 outside cabins, of which 94 have private verandas just like the good old days. The cabins are well-designed, some with pullman-type berths, and 79 are on the inside. All cabins-staterooms now have names and have been redecorated, including the 14 deluxe suites with large picture windows and private verandas added to Promenade Deck. All are extremely spacious, with king-size beds, full baths, and sitting areas, and the forward two suites have the same wonderful view as the captain's! Nothing was spared in decorating these accommodations, from silk draperies and custom-sculpted carpets to hand-crewel bedspreads, black iron and brass beds, ebony-colored dressers, Stobart prints of old steamboats on the walls, and other brass-and-glass furnishings.

Public areas of the *MQ* have also been refurbished, and the prominent colors are ruby, lapis, emerald, and gold tones. The Grand Saloon has lapis upholstery on the banquettes; the Library has deep emerald and lighted bookcases of glass-and-brass; the Center Bar has lapis and almond hues in upholstery; the Gift Shop has emerald walls and carpeting and brass-and-glass cases; the dining room has new carpeting and window shades in all the colors. Even the two Paddlewheel Lounges, upper and lower, have lapis, emerald, and ruby accents now.

At the other end of the Observation Deck is the Dining Saloon, with windows so large the river is always at your elbow. There are two sittings for all meals, the only awkward aspect of the entire program. The Dining Saloon opens onto the Upper Paddlewheel Lounge, overlooking a double-tiered space sheathed in glass just forward of that ever-churning red paddlewheel. The lounge is where the day's fun usually begins and ends: Dixieland, barbershop quartet, and jazz are all live continually as the libations flow on. You will always meet new friends in this lounge—and find old ones!

Promenade Deck aft is the location of the famous Calliope (claimed to be the largest in the world) and the Calliope Bar. Passengers try their talent on the "steam pianna" throughout the cruise, and it's even computerized so sour notes can be heard again. Midship on Promenade Deck is a small Jacuzzi pool, open year-round and heated to suit the temperatures of the day, as well as a small gym, massage areas, and sauna. A library is the most recent additon to Observation Deck, and history lovers will enjoy the many books covering "steamboating" and the Old South. The library provides quiet and relaxation; next to it on the port side is an expanded Steamboatique, with over 400 selections of gifts and souvenirs from porcelain dolls to riverboat gambler sets. The main body of the Paddlewheel Lounge is located aft on Texas Deck. The Purser's Office, Forward Lounge, and embarkation/disembarkation areas are forward on Cabin Deck and boast new carpeting, softer lighting, and new valances on the floor-to-ceiling windows. The theater and beauty shop have gone, but two elevators still remain and have been rebuilt with Victorian mahogany walls and brass handrails.

The *MQ* has a loyal following and attracts a more active and energetic crowd than those devoted to her elder sister. The captain and his fine American crew are young and enthusiastic and make the voyages very special for all on board as the paddlewheeler transverses the heart of America. Life aboard ship revolves a great deal around the Paddlewheel Lounge, and there is plenty of local entertainment in the Grand Saloon or up in the Calliope Bar. Kite flying, exercise sessions, riverboat bingo, calliope contests, lectures, shore gazing, pilot house turns, locking through the Upper Mississippi, and eating well are all part of on-board life.

The *Mississippi Queen* sails from New Orleans, Memphis, St. Louis, Chattanooga, and St. Paul on a series of cruises from 3 to 11 nights. Highlight of the summer schedule is the annual Great Steamboat Race from New Orleans to St. Louis. The *Mississippi Queen* has been a part of the river for a full decade now, offering such enticing-sounding steamboat adventures as Mississippi Explorer, Heart of Dixie, The Tom Sawyer, Yankee Steamer, Frontier Adventure, Southern Comfort and Mississippi River. Throughout the year there are also special theme vacations on board—Big Band Cruises, Southern Celebration, Civil War, Mark Twain Celebrations, Fall Foliage, Dixiefest, and Old Fashioned Holidays. Pre- and post-cruise tours in Cajun Country are also available.

★★★NEPTUNE

Epirotiki Lines; Greek crew and registry; built in 1955 in Denmark; refurbished and relaunched as Neptune *in April 1972; 4000 tons; 300 feet long; 45 feet at beam; 190 passengers; crew of 97; cruising speed of 14 knots; 6 passenger decks.*

The *Neptune* is the smallest of the Epirotiki fleet, even smaller than the "private yacht" *Argonaut*. The vessel has only 96 cabins (of which 24 are inside), all with private facilities and a fold-over sofa arrangement for daytime use. You will find full baths in only three Special

Staterooms (HS, HS1, HS2) located on Hera Deck, just inside the observation area. The cabin decor features murals depicting the underwater Palace of Poseidon (Neptune), with curtains on which "happy waves" seem to play in blues and greens or gold and brown tones. As on all Epirotiki vessels, interior designer Maurice Bailey and artists Arminio Lozzo and Russel Holmes have integrated the mythological tales of the ship's namesake throughout.

The vessel has *Poseidon* painted in Greek on the stern, but *Neptune* in Roman characters on the bow (for the American passengers, no doubt). However one calls this fellow, he was Lord of the Sea; and this ship's tapestries, mosaics, brass sculptures, and other artworks indicate this. The Lounge of the Tritons, the main public area, has three large tapestries of Neptune with his trident. Next door in the Poseidon Bar, a large, swirled mosaic made me think of the *Poseidon Adventure* (which I doubt was the intention). In the passageways handmade brass lamps represent the house of Poseidon, and more tapestries hang in the Dining Room of the Sirens, a cheerful restaurant in purples and pinks that seats the full complement of passengers. The large viewing windows also add to the pleasant effect.

Another nice spot is up on Hera Deck in the solarium, located between the swimming pool and the Mermaid Bar. Here you can catch a bit of the sun, enjoy the excitement of the sea, and appreciate the highlight of this floating art gallery—the magnificent mosaic by the swimming pool. And while you're up here, try a Neptune Wave, the ship's specialty that consists of one ounce tequila, two ounces fresh orange juice, and one-quarter ounce Grenadine. I know that it's served with a smile!

The *Neptune* is often positioned on the 3- and 4-day Glorious Greek Islands itinerary, departing Piraeus every Friday for Mykonos, Rhodes, Kusadasi (for Ephesus), and Patmos. Every Monday the vessel sails for all of the above—plus Santorini and Heraklion (Crete).

★★★+NEW SHOREHAM II

American Canadian Caribbean Line; American registry and crew; built in Warren, Rhode Island, and commissioned in 1979; 100 tons; 150 feet long; 32 feet at beam; 72/90 passengers; crew of 15; cruising speed of 12 knots; 3 passenger decks.

The tiny coastal cruiser *New Shoreham II* was designed and built by Luther Blount at his very own shipyard in Warren, Rhode Island. Mr. Blount also owns and operates American Canadian Caribbean Line, and he designed this vessel with a shallow draft so she could cruise right up on the shore. In fact, the front section of the bow opens to disembark passengers. The *New Shoreham II* has just 36 cabins, some of which will accommodate third persons, but the quarters could be rather close. Most cabins have large seaview windows and private facilities. Those in the thrifty category are inside, with facilities across the hall. The vessel has one lounge and a dining room on Atlantic Deck. There is no commercial bar, so passengers are encouraged to bring along their own favored beverage (soft drinks are complimentary) for the cruise.

Life aboard the *New Shoreham II* and the itineraries are for the agile and young at heart. The *New Shoreham II* begins her winter season with a 12-day Virgin Islands cruise from St. Thomas, interspersed with new itineraries that follow the footsteps of Christopher Columbus (in honor of the impending 500th anniversary of his arrival in the New World in 1992). Columbus Discovery Part I features the U.S. Caribbean islands between St. Thomas and San Juan. Part II highlights the Caicos, San Salvador, and Nassau, and the multitude of cays along the route. Both discoveries offer non-stop fascination—especially as Columbus did not have a ship with a bow that extends onto the beach!

In early May, the *New Shoreham II* departs from West Palm Beach, Florida, for a 15-day sailing up the eastern seaboard to summer homeport in Warren, Connecticut. From the Blount dock on the Warren River, *New Shoreham II* sails through Narragansett Bay, past Newport (Rhode Island) to South Street Seaport in New York, then up the Hudson River to the Erie Canal. As Blount boats are the largest to traverse the Erie Canal (the retractable pilot house allows passage under low bridges), this is a highlight of the cruise. The vessel (along with *Caribbean Prince*) continues to Lake Ontario, the Thousand Islands, and into the St. Lawrence Seaway to Montreal and Quebec. Passengers spend two nights on board their small vessel in each city and then visit the real highlight— the Saguenay River, where they disembark directly, via bow ramp, onto the shore of the Bay of Eternity. Back to Rhode Island by bus (or vice versa).

Two Fall Foliage cruises between Warren and Montreal in October, are followed by the 15-day sailing down the eastern seaboard to West Palm Beach.

★★★★★NEWPORT CLIPPER/NANTUCKET CLIPPER/YORKTOWN CLIPPER

Clipper Cruise Line; American registry and crew; ships built at Jeffboat Inc. in Jeffersonville, Indiana; October 1983, December 1984, June 1988; 100 tons each; 207 feet long; 37 feet at beam; 100 passengers in lower beds; 138 passengers on Yorktown; *crew of 28; cruising speed of 10 statute miles per hour; 4 passenger decks.*

These charming yachtlike vessels, *Newport* and *Nantucket Clipper*, are twins with 51 outside cabins (the new *Yorktown Clipper* boasts cabins for 138 passengers on a slightly larger ship) that feature large picture windows, plenty of closet space, a pleasant light wood decor, and just-average bathrooms. Other cabin amenities include lockable drawers, individual heating and air-conditioning controls, some chairs and a built-in corner table, and a dressing table with large lighted mirror.

The ships have no elevators between decks and there are no separate activity areas for children. There is also no doctor aboard, since the vessels do not sail farther than 20 miles from a safe harbor. There is also no casino, disco, nightclub, midnight buffet, or other nonparticipatory type of entertainment. Instead, the atmosphere is rather like visiting Grandmother—with plenty of cards, puzzles, quiet conversation, and books. First-run movies via VHS cassettes are shown in the dining room, following a good day of sailing and touring.

The interior of the vessels, with pale woods and gentle colors, are soothing to the soul, and the ambience on board is similar to that found on the luxury hotel barges and riverboats of Europe. There is just one dining room that seats all passengers, and one main lounge with a bar and piano. Meals are very tasty American-style cuisine, and the American-trained chefs are eager to please and be praised. There is no room service, but in-between snacks are available. There are also no telephones and only bird calls available, if you must be awakened artificially!

A note from my friend, inveterate traveler "Mary B," who pays a premium on most cruise ships because she has a single cabin. As a mature woman alone (let's face it, she's a grandmother), Mary B found the ambience of the vessel to be "laid-back, sunny, and warm" with both passengers and crew friendly and helpful. Mary B likes good food and found the meals aboard the best she has ever enjoyed afloat—especially the special recipe Toll House cookies that appear every afternoon at teatime. The chefs are trained at the Culinary Institute of America and pay special attention to the latest trends in food—lots of fresh fish and lighter dishes—excluding the cookies, of course! In fact the Clipper Chocolate Chippers are so unusual that I know the chef will not mind my sharing his recipe with readers—make them for your friends and then take a Clipper cruise and compare!

(Preheat oven to 350 degrees)

1 cup dark brown sugar
1 cup granulated sugar
1 cup butter
1½ Tblsp. baking soda
¼ cup Frangelico liqueur
¼ cup Tia Maria liqueur
1 Tblsp. salt
4 eggs
5 cups all purpose flour

2 lbs. chocolate chips
4 oz. pecans (chopped)
4 oz. walnuts (chopped)

Cream together sugars, butter, baking soda, and salt until light and creamy. Add eggs and liqueurs a bit at a time until blended. Add flour, chips, and nuts; mix well. Place in dollops on greased cookie sheet and bake until golden. Makes approximately 48 two-ounce cookies. Serve warm if possible.

The crew on board these clipper ships must be having a wonderful time because they are attractive, friendly, and always ready to serve. Cabin and dining room staff are the same, so they work hard too! Special mention should be made of the cruise staff, which acts as purser, shore excursion manager, etc. They are super helpful and cheerful—no matter what the hour and how delayed your plane happens to be!

The *Newport Clipper* is on charter until 1991 and returns to service during the summer season in eastern Canada, while *Nantucket Clipper* cruises the northeast from Boston, as well as up and down the historic eastern seaboard. During the winter both vessels cruise in the Caribbean, from St. Thomas to the Virgin Islands, as well as through the Windward and Leeward Islands on 7-day sailings. The *Yorktown Clipper* is off on another adventure during the winter season, discovering the natural treasures of the Orinoco River as well as the delightful Central American country of Costa Rica—a naturalist's paradise—and the Panama Canal/San Blas Islands. In spring *Yorktown Clipper* makes her way up the western coastline, stopping en route to enjoy Mexico's Pacific coast and whale watching in the Sea of Cortez, to Alaska for summer cruises through the Inside Passage. The small size of the vessels offer a different perspective to these cruises.

Clipper Cruise Line is also aware that its clientele—of 50ish and older—are golfers; they have added some specially designed one-week cruises that feature famous south Florida courses during the spring and fall season. Since Clipper ships are always so in tune with coastlines, it is possible to bring those clubs aboard and hope for a chance to hit the links!

★★★★★NIEUW AMSTERDAM/NOORDAM

Holland America Line; Netherlands Antilles registry; Dutch officers and Indonesian-Filipino crew; both built at St. Nazaire in France; Nieuw Amsterdam *commissioned July 1983,* Noordam *April 1984; 33,900 tons; 704 feet; 90 feet at beam; 1212 passengers; crew of 542; cruising speed of 22 knots; 11 passenger decks.*

These two $150/$160 million vessels designed and built by Holland America Line were planned to return passengers to the old "ocean liner" philosophy of the good old days. Both public rooms and staterooms have "old world" touches that are obvious even to the neo-phythe. A great deal of thought and good taste was applied, and money was spent on good materials and craftsmanship. Polished rosewood, teak, and other high-quality woods are used on the interior and decks and beveled corners are impressive—even to the experienced eye. There is a comforting lack of chrome, plastic, vinyl, and bright colors.

Public areas are expansive without being overwhelming, and state-rooms are far more spacious than one would anticipate on a cruise ship built in the 80s. Every cabin has touches of grained-wood paneling and dressers. Even the mirrors are trimmed in wood. There is plenty of counter and storage space, and every cabin boasts a color TV. The modular bathrooms seem to be the only bow to the modern age; they are smallish but cheerful and well lit, and the deluxe cabins have good-size bathtubs.

Each vessel has 194 spacious inside cabins; the *Nieuw Amsterdam* has 411 outside staterooms and suites, the *Noordam* two more with 413. The most luxurious accommodations are 20 suites in a special area on Navigation and Boat decks, with large picture windows and king-size beds. (As on many ships, watch out for accommodations on these decks because of partially obstructed views due to the lifeboats.) Nonetheless, for those who prefer the ultimate in privacy, it is rather difficult to find these cabins. But these are two vessels where even the inside twin cabins are pleasant, according to a travel agent friend who found himself in one. And, as a result of restoration during a recent drydocking, both vessels now boast four staterooms with bathrooms accessible by wheel-chair. These are Category C—#100, 101, 102, 103—on Boat Deck of both vessels.

The *Nieuw Amsterdam* and *Noordam* are indeed sister ships, with identical exteriors and layout. But the interior of each has been planned with a difference. The *Nieuw Amsterdam* is "themed" to reflect the Dutch influence in the New World. It has the Manhattan dining room (two seatings), Stuyvesant Lounge and Minnewit Terrace, Hudson and Explorers lounges, Peartree Club and Partridge Bar, The Big Apple disco, The Wampun casino, and Perel Straet shopping area. There is a fine collection of antiques and paintings aboard that recall the 17th and 18th centuries, when Holland was so prominent in the New World. Accord-ing to HAL, a leading Dutch historian and an antique dealer spent two years seeking the appropriate items throughout Europe and the United States and most of the purchases are of museum quality. Certainly, the artworks are an integral part of the overall ambience of the vessel.

The theme of the *Noordam* is also the 17th and 18th centuries, but expanded to reflect the influence of the Dutch East India Company throughout the world. Established in Amsterdam in 1603, the company was one of the premier traders in both the East and West. Hence, the *Noordam* has the Amsterdam dining room, Admiral's Lounge, Tasman

Terrace, Piet Heyn (well-known admiral), Explorers Lounge, Horn Pipe Club, Shanty Bar, Big Dipper, De Halve Maen (name of the ship Henry Hudson sailed up the Hudson River in 1609), and Canael Straet shopping area.

Both vessels have the Crow's Nest late-night lookout on Sun Deck, a fabulous Ocean Spa, supervised by the Sheraton Bonaventure Resort & Spa of Fort Lauderdale, for exercise and sports, two outdoor swimming pools as well as a heated whirlpool, a card room and a library, and the Lido Restaurant, where buffet breakfasts and lunch are served. There are a myriad of activities and entertainment available day and night, beauty/barber shop, attractive boutiques and round-the-clock food. Communications with the outside world are excellent, plus daily news/ stock quotations via UPI. All the 80s and 90s vessels are claiming the latest in navigation facilities, and the *Nieuw Amsterdam/Noordam* system is known as INMARSAT, established by the International Maritime Satellite Organization.

Officers are Dutch; the service crew is Indonesian-Filipino and some of the friendliest and most helpful afloat. While there are occasional "language" problems, their eagerness to please is quite overwhelming and no one disembarks a Holland America vessel without the memory of a warm and caring atmosphere. The "No Tipping Necessary" policy works, and although passengers do wish to offer gratuities, none of the cruise staff suggests a daily amount. As a result, there is a friendly hole in one's pocket at the end of the cruise—and everyone is happy!

Food service aboard both vessels is excellent and there are plenty of places to consume calories! The self-service Lido restaurant offers buffet breakfast and lunch as well as 24-hour coffee and its own ice cream section. Hamburgers and hot dogs are prepared on deck at noon for the fast-food crowd. Dinner in the two-seating dining rooms is gracious, and the tables are placed so there is considerable privacy and quietude between passengers. The company instigated a "lighter" menu recently and it works well. Just in case anyone thinks he is going to *lose* weight, special desserts can be prepared at table at least once during the cruise.

During the summer season, *Nieuw Amsterdam* and *Noordam* join the rest of the fleet *(Rotterdam* and *Westerdam)* in Alaskan waters for a series of some 50-plus sailings from Vancouver through the Inside Passage. Ports of call are Ketchikan, Juneau, Glacier Bay, and Sitka, as well as cruising in Glacier Bay during the one-week round-trip sailings. The cruises are available in conjunction with Westours motorcoach land arrangements of Alaska's interior and stays at Westmark Hotels throughout the state. Both Westours and Westmark are subsidiaries of Holland America Line, a formidable presence in our 49th state.

Panama Canal transits are another important feature of both these vessels, especially as spring and fall repositioning cruises—both excellent times to be cruising between the west coast and south Florida. During the winter months *Nieuw Amsterdam* and *Noordam* are in the Caribbean on warm-weather programs.

The *Nieuw Amsterdam* sails from Tampa on weekly Discovery Cruises to the western Caribbean called Four-Port-Plus, calling at Key West, Playa del Carmen, Ocho Rios, and Grand Cayman. The *Noordam* sails from Fort Lauderdale (Port Everglades) on 10-day Seafarer/Wayfarer itineraries that feature Big Band names from the Swing era as a popular theme during the fall cruises. Early spring finds the *Noordam* sailing round-trip from Los Angeles to the Mexican Riviera before pointing her bow north and Alaska!

★★★★NORDIC EMPRESS

Royal Caribbean Cruise Line; Liberian registry; Norwegian officers and international crew; constructed at Chantiers de l'Atlantique shipyard, St. Nazaire, France, for June 1990 delivery; 45,000 tons; 673 feet long; 100 feet at beam; 1610 passengers; crew of 640; cruising speed of 19.5 knots; 12 passenger decks.

This vessel was originally ordered for Royal Admiral Cruises, the parent company of Royal Caribbean Cruise Line, as the *Future Seas* and expected to replace the time-honored *Emerald Seas* on the 3- and 4-day Bahamas run. However, RCCL decided to enter into competition with its Miami-based neighbors (Norwegian Cruise Line and Carnival Cruise Line) and offer this vessel as the newest and most luxurious in the short cruise market.

Indeed, *Nordic Empress* is the most sophisticated of the cruise vessels sailing from south Florida to the Bahamas with her European-designed interiors. Focal point of the ship is the nine-deck-high Centrum whose designer—a Norwegian named Njal Eide—also created the five-deck-high Centrum aboard *Sovereign of the Seas*. Eide is also responsible for the spectacular Carmen Dining Room on *Nordic Empress,* which is wrapped in a semicircle of glass spanning two decks and overlooking the aft section of the vessel.

Overlooking the bow is Eide's glass-domed Windjammer Indoor/Outdoor Cafe for buffets in an informal atmosphere. After-dinner entertainment can be found Las Vegas-style in the snazzy Strike Up the Band show lounge. Or passengers can entertain themselves in the tri-level Casino Royale located midships—so that only the very clever can pass by instead of passing through! Other public areas are the familiar Viking Crown Lounge, a Fortune 500 conference center, the themed Carousel Lounge with sailcloth-tented ceiling, and the art-deco High Society lounge.

As *Nordic Empress* passengers spend their days in port, Sun Deck has been designed with romantic evening activities in mind—dancing under the stars! There is plenty of outdoor deck space and two swimming pools (one for children). There are also a ShipShape Fitness Center, Golf Ahoy Center, and Kid/Teen Center, as well as a video game room.

Only 60% of *Nordic Empress'* 805 cabins are outside, with large windows, and the 71 deluxe variety boast terraces. All feature two convertible lower beds, color TV, radio, telephone, temperature controls, and private facilities. All cabins have been decorated in soft and restful colors, and they are slightly more spacious than the RCCL norm.

Nordic Empress sails on 3- and 4-night cruises from Miami to the Bahamas, calling at Nassau and CocoCay (the ship line's private out island). The 4-night cruises also include Freeport. Two- and 3-night stays at resort hotels in the Florida keys and Key West are also available.

★★★★NORDIC PRINCE

Royal Caribbean Cruise Line; Norwegian registry and officers, international crew; built in Wartsila shipyard in Helsinki and originally launched in 1971; refitted and lengthened in 1980; 23,000 tons; 635 feet long; 80 feet at beam; 1012 passengers; crew of 400; cruising speed of 16 knots; 8 passenger decks.

Second of the famed RCCL fleet to be stretched, the *Nordic Prince* gained 85 feet and 4500 tons, allowing space for 310 more passengers and 80 additional crew. As a result of this process, the ship now has 339 outside and 180 inside cabins, all with private facilities. The size of the cabins has not changed—there are just many more of them. However, the dimensions of the public areas are much larger, especially the Camelot dining room, the Showboat Lounge (and theater), and the Carousel Lounge. In addition, the Midsummer's Night Lounge on Promenade Deck and the pool area with a new pool cafe for luncheon buffets have both increased considerably in size. Food and service aboard the *Nordic Prince* is on par with the other RCCL vessels, and the entertainment is exactly the same. Royal Caribbean uses the same nightclub attractions on all its ships and flies them from port to port, so you see each act only once. In short, this vessel is another fine RCCL product—the only differences are the names of the public areas and the ports of call, which are generally in Caribbean and southeastern coastal waters.

During the summer season the *Nordic Prince* can be sighted sailing in and out of New York harbor every Sunday on the Bermuda run. The vessel calls at St. George's on Tuesday and then moves to Hamilton for the rest of the week. The vessel departs Bermuda on Friday afternoon for a day and a half at sea en route to the Sunday morning return to the Big Apple. When *Nordic Prince* returns to the Caribbean the vessel is on a series of 8- and 10-day programs. The 8-day itineraries depart Miami on Saturday for the eastern Caribbean, featuring Nassau, San Juan, St. Thomas, and St. Maarten, with two full days of cruising before returning to Miami. The 10-day Caribbean itinerary features St. Thomas, Antigua, Barbados, Martinique, and St. Maarten; called the Antilles Vacation, this cruise has the same itinerary as *Song of Norway* but offers four extra nights at sea to enjoy the facilities of the *Nordic Prince*.

★★★★+NORWAY

Norwegian Cruise Lines; Bahamian registry and Norwegian officers, international crew; originally built in France in 1962 and launched as the flagship of French Line; relaunched in 1980 as the Norway; *$40-million refurbishment in 1990; 75,000 tons; 1035 feet long; 110 feet at beam; 2044 passengers; crew of 900; cruising capacity of 18 knots; 9 passenger decks.*

Knut Kloster, whose family owns Norwegian Cruise Lines, says he bought the former SS *France* because she smiled down at him from her forlorn dock in Le Havre (where the vessel had been tied since being ignominiously pulled from service in 1974), and he wanted to see her smiling for the next 20 or so years. As the rest of the industry looked upon the project with great skepticism, Kloster plunked down $18 million for the vessel, once considered the best French restaurant in the world, and transformed her three cold-weather classes into a one-class floating Caribbean resort. Several million dollars and a decade of service later, no one who sees this beautiful blue and white vessel docked in Miami can help but be overwhelmed, for she looks ten blocks long, and she certainly is smiling!

Danish naval architect Tage Wandborg, who has more than 30 modern cruise ships and more than 100 conversions to his credit, supervised the reincarnation and left behind his distinctive and stylish trademark. For the decoration of the public areas, Kloster hired the late interior designer Angelo Donghia of New York, who had some famous clients and was a familiar figure in the new hotel and nightclub circuit. Donghia and his staff of 80 came up with the decor of 74 suites, 871 other staterooms and cabins, and 14 public rooms, among others. Some of Donghia's achievements are the disco, "A Club Called Dazzles," with portholes into a lighted swimming pool and a glass dance floor that reflects the discotheque lighting; the cabaret, "Checkers," with red and black decor and a rug that looks like a checkerboard; the "Windjammer Bar," small and nautical; and the "Monte Carlo Room," with a carpet of kings and queens. By far, everyone's favorite room aboard is the

"Club Internationale" in which he kept the glamorous and elegant days of transatlantic crossings. This room, by day or night, is subdued and very romantic in an Art Deco manner. The 1800 pieces of art worth nearly $1 million were commissioned and placed under the supervision of a husband and wife team from Oslo who dealt primarily with Scandinavian artists. The *Norway*'s largest public room is the North Cape Lounge, located aft on Pool Deck, which can accommodate a mere 650 passengers.

The *Norway* has two most attractive dining rooms, both decorated in soft browns and beiges, and there are two seatings for all meals. Passengers in the aft section of the vessel dine in the double-deck Leeward, while those in the forward section use the Windward dining room. Many other places to eat include the Great Outdoor Restaurant and the Cafe de Paris, or Svens, where you can buy gooey ice cream concoctions. Add to this some 13 bars, manned by a staff of 75, so passengers can hop to their hearts' content without being seen in the same place too often!

Aside from eating and watering, activities abound on board this floating resort—two outdoor pools and an indoor pool/gymnasium/sauna complex, a full casino, cinema (with feature films), exercise classes, lectures, fashion shows, two "streets" lined with elegant shops (Champs Elysses and Fifth Avenue), bridge and backgammon tournaments, and a very pleasant library. You don't even have to leave your cabin for much of this, because a full closed-circuit television service begins each morning at nine. In the evening, in the 541-seat Saga Theater are presented super-duper productions of NCL's own dance revue, *Sea Legs Goes Hollywood,* and a lavish Broadway musical, in addition to any number of guest entertainers who play throughout the lounges and nightclubs. On a recent cruise, we loved *Barnum!* and the Fifth Dimension show in the Saga Theatre was riveting. Phyllis Diller, in the North Cape lounge, was not so well received. Also on board were several well-known football stars—with NFL films and "plays"—very, very popular! NCL always has something for everyone!

The *Norway* offers 23 different categories of cabins as befits a ship of her great size. These range from Grand Deluxe Suites on Viking Deck (with two bedrooms, sitting room, and private dining room) that are available on request only and cost over $10,000 for the week to an Inside Stateroom (upper and lower berths) that are available for much less. Even the inside cabins are spacious with the high ceilings of yesteryears. Many cabins still have the old wall fans from transatlantic days, and all the former first-class cabins have large bathtubs and bidets, along with roomy wardrobe space. The ship line added several new cabins in the conversion, including some minisuites on Pool Deck that are small but special and very pleasant. These Pool Deck Suites have unusual, super-large windows that were once part of an enclosed promenade area. Since the suites are several stories up, you never need to close the drapes—ah, moonlight!

The *Norway*'s most recent $40-million refurbishment (she returned to service on October 20, 1990) involved an addition of two glass-enclosed decks named Sun and Star, some 5000 gross registered tons, a 6000-square-foot Roman Spa, an elegant new supper club, a new health and fitness center, and 135 new staterooms, of which the owner's and grand deluxe suites (760 and 600 square feet, respectively) feature floor-to-ceiling windows, Jacuzzi, and wrap terraces and are among the largest afloat. Of the 135 new staterooms, 40% have balconies and 20% of the total accommodations are now suites. As another bonus for many travelers, several existing cabins have been converted into single categories.

The Roman Spa is unlike anything else afloat! The complex boasts 14 treatment rooms (including the first hydrotherapy baths at sea), herbal wraps, state-of-the-art computerized cardiovascular fitness equipment, and an aquacise pool. Complementing the new facility are a 360-degree jogging track and 12-person Jacuzzi. Half to 6-day packages, as well as individual treatments, are available for purchase on board. Calorie-controlled meals are also on the program.

Attention has been paid to dining and food service. The Leeward dining room has become a two-tiered area, with seating for 150 passengers on the upper level. The Lido Lounge was enlarged into an a la carte supper club for reservation dinner and dancing by night, a poolside social room by day. Buffets in the Great Outdoor restaurant still remain popular, with over 135 chefs and cooks preparing the abundance of food throughout the vessel. Breakfast and snacks in the cabin are still limited, and there is now a service charge (!), which sets a shocking precedent for a ship line attempting to increase on-board revenue.

Kids have a wonderful time on the *Norway,* with plenty of space in which to play. They have their own *Cruise News* daily, their own activities area (Trolland), that wonderful ice cream parlor, and even special shore excursions. When the vessel calls at NCL's Pleasure Island, treasure hunts and relay races are arranged and, of course, there are nonstop hamburgers at lunchtime! Grown-ups go for these as well, I noticed.

The *Norway* sails every Saturday from Miami for two days at sea, and calls at St. Maarten, St. John, St. Thomas, and NCL's Pleasure Island (Friday from noon to 7 p.m.), where the ship line delivers a cook-out, limbo contest, Calypso band, and treasure hunts. Passengers may take advantage of the fine Dive-In program here, which includes snorkeling equipment and instruction on the ship and a special underwater trail off the island.

The only serious complaint I heard aboard the *Norway* concerned the amount of walking necessary from one section to the other. As the vessel is over 1000 feet long, it is not a good choice for the less than agile (wheelchair users fare very well, however). The size of the *Norway* also prevents her coming alongside in port, and passengers must use 88-foot tenders that hold about 400 persons. The *Norway* carries two of these 55-ton open boats in the forward section of Pool Deck, and they are lowered by cranes when needed. The system works quite efficiently because the crew and staff have been well trained.

★★★★OCEAN PEARL

Pearl Cruises; Bahamian registry; Scandinavian and American officers; European hotel management; Filipino crew; originally built in 1967 in Finland and named Finnstar; *rebuilt in 1982 and rechristened the* Pearl of Scandinavia; *extensively refurbished in 1988 and rechristened* Ocean Pearl; *12,400 tons; 514 feet long; 66 feet at beam; 500 passengers; crew of 225; cruising speed of 20 knots; 9 passenger decks.*

The former *Pearl of Scandinavia* was acquired by Ocean Cruise Lines in the spring of 1987 and, following a multimillion-dollar refit, was rechristened *Ocean Pearl.* Her passenger complement has been raised to 500, in 11 different cabin categories. Public rooms have been redecorated in oriental motifs, two new bars have been added as well as a fitness center and 24 more cabins (two inside cabins included). Several public rooms have been renamed: the Orchid Room restaurant (now overlooking the bow area and sea); Raffles Cafe and Discotheque (including outdoor buffet and barbecue); and the aft decks have been re-teaked. A popular Piano Bar is in the former restaurant space, and the main Marco Polo Lounge and Explorers Bar is much improved and very impressive. There is also a Skylight Lounge and Card Room located on Sky Deck (just aft of the bridge), which has a quiet atmosphere, sea views, and Singapore-style rattan decor that offers the nuance of colonial times.

The ship is bright and clean, with service both helpful and friendly. The Filipino stewards get high marks, and everyone *adores* the darling bar hostesses. This is one vessel where the lounge stewards do not ignore passengers' thirsts! Port material and briefings are very important on this type of cruise, and passengers are pleased by the comprehensive material that awaits them in the cabin. Cruise staff on board is especially helpful in answering questionss and well experienced in the whys and ways of the Far East. This is not a vessel where evening entertainment is that important, because the land tours are so thrilling that retiring early is sensible.

Ocean Pearl sails year-round in the Far East on two-week cruises. China Dynasty sailings have been cut to a minimum and substituted with new and exciting itineraries between Singapore and Bombay (Jewels of India) and Bombay and Mombasa (Passage to India). These are in addition to the popular Spice Islands (round-trip from Singapore), Great Cities of Asia (Singapore/Hong Kong) and Bangkok/Bali & Beyond (Singapore/Bangkok). The China Dynasty cruises are of 10 days' duration and sail between Hong Kong and Tianjin (for Beijing). The cruise programs include pre-sailing hotel stays where necessary and optional post-cruise tours in ports of choice.

★★★★OCEAN PRINCESS

Ocean Cruise Lines; Bahamian registry; Greek officers and international crew; originally built in 1967 and known as Italia *or* Princess Italia; *rebuilt in 1984 and rechristened* Ocean Princess; *12,200 tons; 492 feet long; 71 feet at beam; 460 passengers; crew of 250; cruising speed of 19 knots; 8 passenger decks.*

Ocean Princess decor is strictly contemporary, with a Scandinavian look to the cabins. Public areas include Harry's Bar, the Monte Carlo Casino, Four Seasons Restaurant in peach and gray tones, Marco Polo Lounge for dancing and nightclublike entertainment, an intimate Piano Bar, Raffles Discotheque, and a 175-seat Princess theater. There is a heated outdoor swimming pool, plenty of deck space for sunning, the Cafe de Paris for buffet lunches and The Health Club for exercise or Finnish-style sauna. The vessel also has Rendezvous Square, with its high fashion boutique, beauty salon, and massage.

There are 17 deluxe, 114 outside, and 129 inside cabins, all with tiled shower/bathrooms aboard the *Ocean Princess* (the deluxe cabins have tubs). That is just about 50% inside cabins—a very high ratio for a cruise vessel that wants to position itself in the marketplace as "four star." Reports are that service has to be improved as it is more than noticeable on small ships like this, especially those that want to attract top clientele.

During the summer season *Ocean Princess* sails from Copenhagen on 7-day Fjords and Fairy Tale cruises to Flam, Gudvangen, Hellesylt, Geiranger Fjord, Bergen, Oslo, and Frederica. In high summer, two-week sailings to North Cape/Spitsbergen are offered. An alternate itinerary from Copenhagen visits Scandinavian capitals and Russia, calling at Kalmar, Stockholm, Leningrad, Helsinki, and Visby. Longer cruise/tours are available. Ocean Cruise Lines is offering more extensive cruises in the Southern Hemisphere in conjunction with travel pioneer Lars Eric Lindblad. Called Limited Editions, the cruises include Antarctica, the Falkland Islands, and the glaciers of Patagonia, as well as the tributaries of the Amazon River. The South American programs feature: Expedition Antarctica (round-trip sailing from Buenos Aires);

Antarctica, The Falklands, and Patagonia; Carnival in Rio (Buenos Aires to Rio or reverse); Grand South America (Buenos Aires to Manaus or vice versa); and Amazon Adventure (Manaus to Barbados).

★★★★STAR/SHIP OCEANIC

Premier Cruise Lines; Panamanian registry; Greek officers; international crew; built in Trieste in 1965; refurbished 1986 and rechristened by Minnie Mouse; 40,000 tons; 671 feet long; 96 feet at beam; 1180 passengers; crew of 550; cruising speed of 26 knots; 8 passenger decks.

Premier bought the *Oceanic* from Home Lines for $20 million in the fall of 1985 and spent another $10 million in refurbishing the public areas. The result, under the direction of Agni and Michael Katzourakis, is very impressive. This renowned husband-and-wife team from Athens did not tamper with the existing design of the vessel—which has worn well over two decades as both classic and modern—but concentrated on brighter colors and an effective use of mirrors to lighten the interior. Over 30,000 square yards of carpet was woven in England especially for the vessel's eight passenger decks. Furnishings and what new beds were brought in (there are now 167 double beds) are from Finland, the chairs are Italian, and the new deck teaking is from Nigeria. The refurbishing was completed in this country.

The Katzourakis team did not tamper with the sculptures in the stairwells, which are essential to feeling at home in the *Oceanic*. They did change the entire atmosphere of the magradomed pool area, however, with the use of striped yellow awnings, white furniture, yellow lamps a la Bourbon Street and plenty of foliage. All other areas—the Satellite cafe, Galaxy disco, Starlight Cabaret, Tropicana Club, Mars Bar, Lucky Star Casino, Heroes & Legends Pub (resembling a British pub and the only dark area on the ship) and Seven Continents restaurant—are attractive and cheerful.

The Broadway Showman has very uncomfortable seating arrangements, but Premier promises all kinds of scintillating entertainment here. It's a splendid idea, especially after the children are fast asleep and dreaming of Mickey, Minnie, Goofy, and lots of ice cream cones!

Children's facilities on board are excellent—this is truly a ship for the whole family. There is a spacious Teen Activity Center and a large Children's Recreation Center with arts and crafts room, splash pool and outdoor supervised activities for ages 2 through 12. Adult playrooms include the Seasport Fitness Center, complete with gym and eight-lap jogging track, and Lucky Star Casino, conveniently adjacent to a beautiful shopping arcade.

The hull is now Premier red and (bravo) the great lady is back in service and looking better than ever! As Minnie Mouse said at the re-christening, "We wish her well and all those who sail with her!" The *Oceanic* departs Port Canaveral every Monday and Friday for Nassau and Salt Cay, an Out Island. Fantastic one-week packages that include the cruise, hotel accommodations and unlimited entries to Disney World and EPCOT Center, a tour of the Space Center and rental car are available. Hurry!

★★★★ + OCEANIC GRACE

Oceanic Cruises; Japanese flag and crew; constructed in Japan and launched in April 1989; 5050 tons; 336 feet long; 50 feet at beam; 118 passengers; crew of 70; cruising speed of 19.6 knots; 5 passenger decks.

Designed in Holland and constructed in Japan, *Oceanic Grace* is the oriental version of Sea Goddess Cruises. The 59 all-suite vessel features accommodations that are approximately 185 square feet with twin or queen-size beds and large windows. All cabins are located midship and are nicely decorated. For western tastes, the beds are rather hard and the bathtubs are somewhat on the short side, but these are minor complaints (take showers). There is one wheelchair-access stateroom. Other amenities include phone, radio/TV/VCR, refrigerator and mini-bar, personal safe, toiletries, and hair dryer. Athletic and health features on board are a jogging track, gym, saunas, fresh-water pool, and Jacuzzi, as well as watersports equipment in the "marina," or water-level platform for skiing, snorkeling, para-sailing, windsurfing, and scuba diving offered on a complimentary basis. The company hopes to have real diver enthusiasts on board and will furnish as many as six trained and certified instructors/buddies.

Food on board *Oceanic Grace* is considered some of the best afloat as the chefs were trained at the famed Palace Hotel in Tokyo, and Japanese-style dishes are designed from the freshest ingredients possible and presented to the diner as works of art. Breakfast and lunch are served buffet style in the Day Lounge or by the swimming pool and feature both western and oriental items. Dinner is served from 7 to 10 p.m. in the Main Restaurant, where seating is not assigned. Many shore excursions suggest local restaurants where passengers can enjoy specialties of the region for a price (!). Wine and drinks are expensive on board (and ashore), but beer is complimentary during the day and sake is reasonable by the bottle.

In addition to the Day Lounge on pool deck, there is the Main Lounge one deck below, which is very attractively decorated and utilized for musical entertainment. As on Sea Goddess and Seabourn Cruises, there is no formal entertainment on *Oceanic Grace,* as passengers are expected to relax and entertain themselves. The ship attracts sophisticated and educated Japanese executive couples who speak English and enjoy meeting and conversing with westerners. In fact, Oceanic Cruises would like to have about 30% Americans/westerns on every cruise to offer a good "mix."

The one-week cruises (some of which can be embarked for only 3 or 4 days) sail from Yokohama, Nagasaki, Tokyo, Kobe, Hakodate, and Guam. The Guam/Marshall Islands/Micronesia itinerary is new in 1991 and features calls at Palau, Rota, Saipan, Truk Lagoon, Ulithi, Woleai, and Yap. A one-week cruise for an American couple, including air fare, is approximately $10,000, but the good news is—there is no tipping on board *Oceanic Grace,* and even the photographs are free!

★★★OCEANOS

Epirotiki Lines; Greek registry and crew; formerly known as Ancona; *rebuilt in 1978 and relaunched as* Oceanos; *14,000 tons; 488 feet long; 65 feet at beam; 516 passengers; crew of 250; cruising speed of 15 knots; 6 passenger decks.*

The *Oceanos* is another Epirotiki acquisition completely refurbished for her rebirth by the line's favorite architect/interior designer, Maurice Bailey. The new design includes artworks that reflect the name of the vessel. Bailey has made what I consider a pleasant but not deluxe ship, with 188 outside and 68 inside cabins, all with private facilities and fold-over beds for use as daytime sofas. The public areas, which I consider limited, include only one large lounge, the Modern Odyssey Lounge, on Apollo Deck. A smaller gathering place, situated one deck above, on Jupiter, is called the Old Athens Club, and lies adjacent to a bar and the Selene Discotheque as well as to a shopping gallery. Outside on deck is a small swimming pool. The Byzantine Dining Room, located on Dionysus Deck, has two seatings for all the Greek/European meals.

During the summer season *Oceanos* offers 3- and 4-day Aegean cruises from Piraeus, departing Monday (Aegean Byzantine) and Friday (Aegean Minoan). A one-week combination is known as the Homeric. These cruises are offered through October—a high-season travel month for Americans, according to Epirotiki.

★★★ODYSSEUS

Epirotiki Lines; Greek registry and crew; formerly known as Aquamarine; *acquired by Epirotiki in early 1988 and extensively refurbished; 12,000 tons; 483 feet long; 61 feet at beam; 452 passengers; crew of 190; cruising speed of 18.5 knots; 7 passenger decks.*

When last seen this vessel was languishing in Hong Kong harbor, while Greek banking interests searched for a new owner. As the *Aqua-*

marine, this vessel was operated by a member of the Kavounides family (the now defunct K-Lines) on China cruises between Hong Kong and Kobe in 1978/79. It was a great idea, but badly operated, and the program went bankrupt.

Epirotiki acquired and renamed this vessel *Odysseus* in early 1988 and hired Italian/American designer Armenio Lozzi for the interior decor. Deck names are now standard with all Epirotiki ships—Apollo, Jupiter, Dionysus, Poseidon, Hera, Venus, and Chronos—while public rooms are named after the adventures in the *Odyssey.* Sirens, Circe, Naussica, Aeolian Winds, Penelope, Lotus-eaters, and Ithaca will all be found on board. The public areas include a grand salon, a second lounge/bar, a writing room, reading veranda, disco, boutique, casino, dining room, and taverna, as well as swimming pool and Lido area. A gym/sauna and movie projection area have also been added.

Cabins are large on this vessel, approximately 90% have an outside configuration, and almost all have a separate seating area. All cabins feature private facilities (albeit very old-fashioned ones), plus plenty of wardrobe and drawer space. There are some very pleasant cabins aft on the top deck, as I recall. Odysseus is well suited to Epirotiki's Seven Seas two-week programs between Venice and Genoa that cruise the Adriatic, Ionian, Aegean, Black, Tyrrhenian, and Ligurian seas, as well as the Sea of Marmara. The mid-May through October cruises feature enrichment programs and classical music performances on board. Complete air, land, and sea packages are available. During the winter season *Odysseus* is a familiar sight in the Caribbean on an interesting cruise itinerary from Trinidad.

★★★ORIENT EXPRESS/EUROSUN

Europe Cruise Line; Bermuda registry and British/international crew; built in 1975 for the Baltic as the Silja Star *passenger/car ferry; began service as* Orient Express *May 1986; 12,500 tons; 500 feet long; 70 feet at beam; carries 240 cars; 670 passengers; crew of 225; cruising speed of 20 knots; 6 passenger decks.*

This vessel has changed hands recently and is now owned by Europe Cruise Line, a subsidiary of Rederi EffJohn of Finland, which operates 14 ferries in Europe under the names of Sally Line and Silja Line and now also owns two American-based cruise companies—Commodore Cruise Line of Miami and B.S.L. Cruises (formerly known as Bermuda Star Line) in New Jersey. Europe Cruise Line purchased the *Orient Express*—which it calls the *Eurosun*—in late 1989 for a reported $40 million. The cruise line had been chartering the vessel from November to April on one-week programs to the Canary Islands, Madeira, and Morocco, which were promoted in North America through Commodore Cruise Line. Plans are to continue this series during the winter season. Meanwhile, through an agreement with Orient Express Hotels, the ship will be an *Orient Express* for the summer months and sail every Saturday from Piraeus, Istanbul, Kusadasi, Patmos, and Katakolon. At least for now.

The *Orient Express* was formerly operated in the Baltic as a passenger/car ferry and still has the capacity to carry 240 vehicles. Among the cabin complement are 14 super-deluxe staterooms with two lower beds (the rest of upper and lower berths vis-a-vis a train)—all bestowed with names from the famed Pullman cars of the Orient Express train. Services and amenities aboard include indoor and outdoor swimming pools, health club/sauna, boutique, nightclub and disco, cinema, beauty/barber shops, children's playroom/attended nursery, full casino, and concierge. There is no in-cabin service.

There are many grades of cabins on board, and the top is called Pullman Class, with just 28 passengers who enjoy their own bar, sun deck, and swimming pool, plus lovely views from their all-amenity cabins. They even boast 24-hour room service. Pullman Class travelers dine in the Venice-Simplon-Orient-Express (VSOE) restaurant, which accommodates just 60 persons, with table d'hote included in the fare or a la carte, open seating, and excellent service. The "others" take their meals in the Savini restaurant, which has two seatings and splendid sea views. There are also several bars on board, including a new one called Raffles. The *Orient Express* is a good value, and several all-inclusive packages are available during the summer itinerary, including ones that feature the Cipriani Hotel in Venice (an Orient Express hotel) and the famous train back to London.

One doubts, however, that Europe Cruise Line will continue the *Orient Express* name and theme of this vessel much longer, so watch for more and more information concerning *Eurosun*. Also watch for Europe Cruise Line, which plans to have at least three vessels in the next few years.

★★★ + ORPHEUS

Epirotiki Lines; on long-term charter to Swan Hellenic Cruises; Greek flag and crew; originally built in 1952 as the Munster; *rebuilt in Greece in 1969 and renamed the* Orpheus; *refurbished in 1983; 5,000 tons; 353 feet long; 51 feet at beam; 300 passengers; crew of 139; cruising speed of 15 knots; 6 passenger decks.*

The *Orpheus* is a comfortable Greek vessel that has learned to speak English, according to the Swan Hellenic company that has chartered the ship from Epirotiki for several seasons. Swan carries less than the 300 passenger complement in a less-than-ritzy but very sociable atmosphere.

There are no fixed seating arrangements in the cozy Dionysus restaurant, and there is light evening music in the Lounge of the Muses. Other public areas include the Apollo Lounge and the Jason Taverna, where buffet lunches are served at sea. There is a small shop aboard, a British registered doctor, a hairdresser, and laundry. There is also a superb reference library because these cruises are for those who enjoy intellectual stimulation.

Swan Hellenic Cruises is renowned for having excellent lecturers, British historians, archaeologists, and artists on board to share their enthusiasm with fellow passengers. Every cabin also has a copy of the Swan Hellenic Handbook, considered the bible of every cruise. All sailings are approximately two weeks air-sea from Gatwick, England. For a real primer of the Hellenistic World one can never beat Swan Hellenic cruises around the Mediterranean, Aegean, Black Sea, and Adriatic.

A few of the enticing programs each year: Red Sea; In the Steps of St. Paul; Wonders of the Ancient World; Richard the Lion Heart and the Crusades; Jason and the Argonauts; From the Adriatic to the Aegean; Around Turkey; A Greek Odyssey; Venetians and Ottomans, Battle for the Mediterranean; Black Sea; Troy and the Trojan Wars; Renaissance and pre-Renaissance Italy; Western Mediterranean; Moroccan and Moorish; With Vulcan to Byzantium; Egypt and the Holy Land. Call Swan's U.S. representative, Esplanade Tours (1–800–426–5492) for brochure.

★★★PEGASUS

Epirotiki Lines; Greek registry; Greek crew; built in Scandinavia in 1975 as Sven Corona; *refurbished and renamed* Sundancer *in 1985; acquired by Epirotiki in 1985; 14,000 tons; 473 feet long; 66 feet at beam; 832 passengers; crew of about 350; cruising speed of 21 knots; 9 passenger decks.*

Just before a May 1986 inaugural, the former *Sundancer* received a $10 million refurbishment and was renamed *Pegasus* by Epirotiki Lines. The Dionysus dining room accommodates 350 passengers at a sitting, as does the Argonaut Grand Salon. The vessel also boasts seven bars, a library, card room, disco, casino, veranda, two swimming pools, Jacuzzis, and two cinemas.

During the summer season, *Pegasus* can be found cruising the Glorious Greek Isles on 3- and 4-day sailings from Piraeus. The Friday departures call at Mykonos, Rhodes, Kusadasi, and Patmos; the Monday sailings add Santorini and Heraklion. During the winter months *Pegasus* could be found showing the Epirotiki flag in South America or the Caribbean.

★★★★POLARIS

Special Expeditions; Bahamian registry and Scandinavian officers; international crew; built in Denmark in 1960 as overnight ferry; rebuilt 1982 as Lindblad Polaris; *became simply* Polaris *in 1988; 2214 tons; 238 feet long; 43 feet at beam; 80 passengers; crew of 40; cruising speed of 16 knots; 4 passenger decks.*

Polaris is an unpretentious but comfortable vessel that Lars-Eric Lindblad utilized on two separate lengthy occasions for his programs and now is utilized by his son, Sven Olof, who operates Special Expeditions. Accommodations and public areas are very pleasant, with a Scandinavian flair. Cabins are small and the private facilities merely functional, but they are there. There are some larger cabins available. Public space is minimal, and if you do not wish to sit in the bar/lounge, there is a delightful and well-stocked library.

The Dining Room (formerly called Wasa Restaurant) seats all passengers together and offers panoramic seaviews from three sides. On two separate cruises—one in the Baltic, the other along the west coast of Africa—the cuisine was decidedly Scandinavian/European. Swedish smorgasbord-type buffets were served at breakfast and lunch (great fun) with a four-course sit-down meal in the evening. There is an extensive wine list, and the lounge bar is always busy. *Polaris* also boasts a sauna, beauty shop, and small boutique.

Special Expeditions and *Polaris* cruises are for travelers who are "environmental friendly" and wish to learn about their surroundings. There are always specialists on board to talk about flora, fauna, birds, fish, etc. In addition to a fleet of Zodiacs, the *Polaris* carries a glass-bottom boat so 20 passengers at a time can observe in comfort the brilliant underwater world. Shore tours generally begin early (often before breakfast), so there is no night life on board *Polaris,* other than an after-dinner lecture or slide show. The expedition and your fellow passengers are the main event on this cruise.

Sailing areas for the *Polaris* are Central America (especially Costa Rica), the Panama Canal, Coastal Iberia and France, an annual circumnavigation of the British Isles, the North Cape and the Arctic, Canada's Maritime Provinces and the Bay of Fundy, Atlantic Seaboard, A Thousand Miles up the Amazon, the Orinoco River and lower Caribbean islands, and from the Caribbean to the Pacific Ocean. Antarctica on special charters is also a possibility. Apply for a copy of the *Special Expeditions Traveler* (newsletter) for a taste of what this company has to offer each year.

★★★★ to ★★★★★+QUEEN ELIZABETH 2

Cunard Line; British registry and crew; built on the River Clyde and launched in 1967; christened by Her Majesty the Queen; maiden voyage in 1969; last major refit 1987; 67,139 tons; 963 feet long; 105 feet at beam; 1864 passengers; crew of 1025; cruising speed of 32.5 knots; 13 passenger decks.

From December 1986 to the end of April 1987, the *Queen Elizabeth 2* was in a Bremerhaven drydock experiencing a $165-million refit. Much of the money was spent in the engine room, where the largest diesel electric plant found in a passenger vessel was installed. Cunard took advantage of this extensive drydock period to add another set of penthouse suites as well as redo most of the cabins and public spaces. The result is spectacular—one wonders how we ever tolerated her former decor. Let us hope that Cunard continues the refurbishment in top form as we enter the 1990s and a world of many new and extravagant cruise vessels. While the *QE2* remains in a class by herself, she is no longer the only "city at sea" afloat with enough amenities to keep passengers busy for months. Other ships have been inaugurated and there is fierce competition afloat!

Gone is the drab British-style decoration that overwhelmed so much of the vessel. The most striking examples are the shopping area, which has been transformed into a glamorous profusion of name designer boutiques and souvenir shops, and the former Double-Down Room, which has become a splendid Grande Lounge with tiered seating and a state-of-the-art entertainment center. It is a large room, but it has none of the cold glitz associated with other spacious showrooms afloat. As an added bonus, those upstairs buying Gucci and Pucci or renting a black-tie for certain transatlantic nights, can watch the shows or other activities. Behind the Grande Lounge, in the former Double-Down bar area, is the bright and airy Yacht Club, which overlooks paddle tennis/volleyball court by day and is properly romantic at night with a Lucite-covered baby grand piano/and bar. Adult, teenage, and children's games rooms are off the Yacht Club so the various generations can keep track of each other.

The Queens Room, considered the first-class showroom, looks handsome with plush leather seating and flows into the Lido area aft, where buffet breakfasts and lunches are served around the magrodome-enclosed swimming pool. The Lido can become beastly hot, whether the magrodome is open or not, and many diners break the rules and escape with their trays into the air-conditioned comfort of the Queens Room—even down to the Midships Bar, which has escaped any new ideas and remains the same nondescript green along seaview windows (and whatever is inside; it's so dark and dreary, who can tell?). The library and card rooms on the portside are also spruced up and, for some reason, deck chairs remain as usual in this area.

Midships portside on Boat Deck, in the space formerly occupied by the first-class writing room/then computer center, is an attractive boardroom, which can be used for business meetings, private parties, seminars, etc. It is a very nice addition except during a transatlantic storm—when I would suggest seminars be transferred below to the Golden Door Spa at Sea! The theater remains among the best afloat, with comfortable seating, a balcony section, and a convenient location (how many times have you scratched a good program because the theater was several decks down?).

The Casino and Theatre Bar look more or less the same, but the Children's Playroom, complete with nannies, received a new coat of paint and the young ones have a wonderful time up there. The Computer Learning Center, among the first afloat, has been relocated forward on Two Deck in a larger space. This is one of the most popular facilities aboard, and trained instructors offer several classes daily (arrive early if you want a seat). Other intellectual pursuits on board are a series of lectures—generally, something for everyone—classical and popular concerts, the *QE2* Network, or view from the bridge on television in every cabin (VCRs in first-class and above accommodations), a mini-version of the *International Herald Tribune* delivered beneath your door, and newfangled telephones that wake you up (when they work) and will get you anywhere on earth or above.

The *QE2*'s four elegant restaurants received some attention and the results are quite evident. The economy/transatlantic dining room looks truly lovely now (another former decor disaster) with what looks like Aztec art deco and carefully dressed seaview windows. Now called the Mauretania restaurant, after a former Cunard vessel, the place is very cheerful and the staff tries to please. Dinner dancing is available on select evenings, and an International Food Bazaar has allegedly been instituted on special nights. Open to all *QE2* passengers, the event features four themed buffet tables (with foods from Europe, America, British Isles, and the Orient) and appropriate regional drinks. Each table will offer a choice of 20 different dishes as well as breads, cheese, and desserts. Cunard has been promising this special feature since the refit; let us hope the logistics of managing passengers' requests for seating is successful. Don't think I am not aware of the criticism of the food in this restaurant, which British people call "ghastly" and Americans "just plain awful."

The first-class Columbia restaurant still boasts the sterling silver loving cup presented to Samuel Cunard in 1840 by the citizens of Boston. It also has a new center floor where dinner dancing is offered twice weekly, and the menu is the same as in Mauretania. (This restaurant receives more criticism than any restaurant afloat; people expect Super

Class meals and attention here and it will never happen.)

Super class on the *QE2* means the Princess Lounge and Grill for Category D (Ultra Deluxe) passengers and the Queens Lounge and Grill for Category C to AA (Ultra Deluxe and Luxury) passengers. These are both wonderful restaurants that deserve every kudo offered. Meals are cooked to order (ask for your favorite dishes at lunchtime and you will receive them at dinner), service is usually impeccable, and people watching is terrific in both dining rooms! The Princess Grill is more cozy and romantic, but the Queens Grill is where the high-rolling action takes place and its manager takes very good care of his clientele. The Queens Grill Lounge is also the place to be seen for drinks at lunchtime, tea, and the congenial cocktail hour that begins about 8 p.m. The *QE2* uses about 150 pounds of caviar on each 5-day transatlantic crossing, and the grill rooms are where most of it is served. (If you ask for it in your stateroom, you are charged accordingly.) The 20,000-bottle wine cellar is superb, and the ice cream is unrivaled.

If all this glorious food makes you nervous, the *QE2* boasts the famous Golden Door Spa at Sea with two locations, and several other sporting facilities including a computerized golf range. A popular jogging track can be found on Boat Deck; there is weight training equipment and four Jacuzzis, as well as saunas and trained masseuses. Most everything is complimentary, except the massage and hair and beauty treatments in the excellent Steiner/Elizabeth Arden salon.

Accommodations on board the *QE2* range from Super Class suites to inside cabins with upper and lower berths, and your dining experience depends upon the category you choose. The 8000 category suites are lovely in good weather, but all that glass looking out on a nasty, gray sea can be gloomy—especially if you are traveling alone. On transatlantic crossings the B category accommodations offer the traditional sea-going ambience and retain their coziness even when the north Atlantic acts up. However, passengers who choose the lower categories have just as much fun as everyone else—provided they do not expect to be pampered. For the ship is a floating city and there are so many daily activities available, there is little time to dream up a list of complaints (although a certain percentage manage to do so on every sailing).

Several years ago Cunard created the ultimate travel experience by offering "SS-ST"—superliner/supersonic between the U.S. and London as well as other major world ports. The result is that Cunard has become the largest charterer of British Airways Concorde service and offers the sea/air packages at hefty but decent rates. And it's a great way to go! During the scheduled transatlantic crossings between April and December Cunard offers a series of escorted European tours as well as discounts at Trafalgar House properties—the Ritz and Stafford in London, and the Bellevue Stratford in Philadelphia. Whatever you choose, Cunard has the facility to arrange a complete vacation program—as long as you do not expect the same courtesy and coddling prior to embarkation that other ship lines delight in offering. Alas, that is not Cunard's style—perhaps someday it will be.

During the past two years, the *QE2* spent part of the winter months in Japan on lucrative charters, but she is now back on schedule and celebrated the 150th anniversary of Samuel Cunard's transatlantic vision during the appropriate 1990 period. A five-continent world cruise in 1991 for the *QE2* includes ports in the Mediterranean for the first time in seven years. Scheduled transatlantic crossings will occur during the "season," as well as shorter cruises to Bermuda/Caribbean or around England.

★★★QUEEN OF BERMUDA

B.S.L. Cruises; Panamanian registry and international crew; originally built in Mississippi in 1958 and named Brazil, Volendam, Monarch Sun, Volendam; *rebuilt 1985 and rechristened* Liberte, *then* Canada Star; *23,500 tons; 617 feet long; 84 feet at beam; 725 passengers; crew of 350; cruising speed of 18 knots; 9 passenger decks.*

This vessel has enjoyed a colorful history in the past three decades! Holland America operated her as *Volendam,* then chartered the ship to the short-lived Monarch Cruise Lines, and reclaimed her briefly as *Volendam* before passing her on to American Hawaii Cruises. Following an extensive and very cheerful refit, the vessel became *Liberte* for short-lived around-Tahiti cruises. Several million dollars later, the vessel was leased by Bermuda Star Line, who called her *Canada Star* for summer sailings each week between New York and Montreal. However, Bermuda Star Line discovered that this ship was more suited to the Bermuda run, and renamed her *Queen of Bermuda* in May 1988—in honor of a famous passenger liner of the past. As quality/value cruises on the New York to Bermuda run are quite competitive, a renaming like this is a good ploy.

The $25-million refit of this 725-passenger vessel in 1985 was very successful, as accommodations were redecorated and redesigned to feature some 80% in outside configuration. The Polynesian theme of the vessel has been retained (it's cheaper that way), but it somehow does not detract from the itinerary. Cabins are very attractive, and all now boast color TVs. A second swimming pool was added as well as a youth recreation center and Le Club nightclub/disco aft on Boat Deck. Other public areas include the spacious Discovery Bay casino, library, and card room, Polynesian Showplace, Reef restaurant and lounge off the swimming area (for buffet breakfasts and lunches), and a nice shopping arcade. The lounge on Observation Deck is a favorite spot, and the dining room on Main Deck is now very attractive. There are also a launderette, theater, and fitness center.

Service on board is primarily rendered by Koreans, who aim to please, and the food is good quality for the money. Cruises aboard this vessel are good value, especially considering the size and configuration of the cabins. During the summer season *Queen of Bermuda* sails from New York on 10-day cruises to the Caribbean calling at San Juan, St. John, St. Thomas, St. Maarten, and (occasionally) Bermuda. The vessel also offers some New England/Canada fall foliage cruises between New York and Montreal during the month of September. From November to May *Queen of Bermuda* sails every Saturday from New Orleans to the Yucatan, calling at Key West, Playa del Carmen, and Cozumel. Air-sea programs and some shorter holiday cruises are also available.

★★★REGENT SEA

Regency Cruises; Bahamian registry; Greek officers and international crew; European service crew; originally built in 1957 and sailed as Gripsholm *for Swedish America Line; refurbished in 1975 and renamed* Navarino *for Mediterranean cruises; refurbished in 1985 and renamed* Regent Sea; *22,000 tons; 631 feet long; 83 feet at beam; 722 passengers; crew of 365; cruising speed of 19.5 knots; 9 passenger decks.*

Since the former *Navarino/Gripsholm* rebirth as *Regent Sea,* all reports have been excellent for on-board services and food and itineraries. As a vessel, she is one of the most comfortable afloat, with old-world spaciousness in accommodations and public areas and a feeling of stability. Karageorgis (a wealthy Greek shipper and the former owner) transformed the ship into a cruise-style vessel, added a theater and some suites (I understand from a former *Gripsholm* purser that his ex-cabin is now a top-grade accommodation—which says something about the treatment of officers on Swedish America Line!).

The ship was designed with all outside cabins, so the 23 inside variety are courtesy of Karageorgis—prefab and small. The rest of the accommodations are so spacious that passengers are immediately impressed by the fact that they do not run into each other—or themselves—in the bathroom. Many have double beds and most boast bathtub as well as shower. Single travelers are matched with a colleague (of the same sex) and even upgraded if necessary.

Public areas on board *Regent Sea* are attractive, and all paths lead midships on Verandah Deck to the Regency Lounge. Forward of the main lounge is a shopping arcade, card room, Casino Royale, the lime green/white rattan Riviera Verandah, romantic Rendezvous Lounge with live mood music, popular computer room, and Ruby Lounge (where video cassettes can be seen). Aft of the main lounge is the Lido Cafe/

Verandah/Disco where food, music and dance action takes place from buffet breakfasts until sandwiches and pizza in the wee hours of the next day. A lovely swimming pool is aft on Verandah Deck, with an indoor pool/fitness center/spa area located down on Dorado Deck.

The Caravelle dining room on Allegro Deck is a place of great enjoyment for *Regent Sea* passengers, not only for its pleasing decor, but for the pleasing menus provided by top-notch caterers. Here, as elsewhere on the vessel, the European-style service is apparent and enjoyed by the well-cruised clientele. For it is the experienced set that Regency appeals to, at prices that everyone can afford but hardly believe! A very comfortable theater is located forward of the dining room.

The *Regent Sea* spends the summer in Alaska and winters in the Caribbean, cruising every Sunday from San Juan on an Islands in the Sun program. The itinerary features St. Barts, Trinidad, St. Lucia, St. Maarten, and St. Thomas—an interesting mix of what the islands have to offer. Special packages include Family Reunion or Honeymoon. A Sea Safari program for beginning to advanced scuba divers is also available.

During the summer, *Regent Sea* can be found in Alaska sailing every Sunday from either Vancouver or Whittier (Anchorage) for College Fjord/Columbia Glacier, Sitka, Lynn Canal, Skagway, Juneau, Ketchikan, and all-day cruising the Inside Passage. A popular 5-day Jazz Festival at Sea takes place between Vancouver and Los Angeles in September, with many celebrity guests as well as passenger participation encouraged!

★★★REGENT STAR

Regency Cruises; Bahamian registry and international crew; built in Holland in 1957 and sailed as Statendam *until 1982; refurbished and renamed* Rhapsody *by Paquet; 24,500 tons; 642 feet long; 79 feet at beam; 950 passengers; crew of 450; cruising speed of 19 knots; 9 passenger decks.*

With the rebirth of the *Statendam* as *Regent Star,* the vessel gained some new diesel engines and improved maneuverability via a bow thruster. The *Star* is another traditional vessel, with plenty of space for passengers. Regency did not change much of the decor when it assumed operation during the summer of 1987, as Paquet has already spent money on that. The vesssel has 487 spacious accommodations, of which 187 are inside.

The main public rooms are located on Promenade Deck, with its Regency Lounge, Lido cafe and bar that opens onto the outdoor swimming pool area, the Starlight lounge/disco, Casino Royale, computer room, library/card room. The Cordon Bleu dining room is located on

Bolero Deck, a theater on Concerto Deck, and indoor pool/fitness center on Domino Deck. Rather far down, but that is the way these vessels were built in the good old days.

The *Regent Star* is a solid and comfortable vessel that offers good value, without being so elegant as others in the Regency fleet. During the winter months she is based in Montego Bay for Sunday departures on the original Regency schedule. The one-week cruises feature Ocho Rios, a day at sea, a partial transit of the Panama Canal through Gatun Lock to Gaton Lake, Puerto Moin (Costa Rica), another day at sea, and Grand Cayman. From late June to mid-October, the *Regent Star* sails between Montreal and New York, offering an exciting and varied itinerary in New England and Canada. The northbound sailings call at Newport (Rhode Island), cruise the Cape Cod Canal, and visit Bar Harbor (Maine) and Halifax (Nova Scotia). A highlight is cruising Saguenay Fjord before arrival at Quebec City and then Montreal. Southbound ports are Quebec City, cruising Perce Rock, Charlottetown (Prince Edward Island), Portland (Maine), Provincetown (Massachusetts), through the Cape Cod Canal to New York City! Special repositioning cruises to and from Montego Bay are also available.

★★★REGENT SUN

Regency Cruises; Bahamian registry and international crew; originally built in 1964 and former names were Hanseatic, Shalom, *and most recently* Doric *and* Royal Odyssey; *last refurbished in 1982; 25,500 tons; 627 feet long; 81 feet at beam; 836 passengers; crew of 390; cruising speed of 19 knots; 9 passenger decks.*

The 816-passenger *Regent Sun* enjoyed a very happy life as the *Doric* for Home Lines. When she was sold to Royal Cruise Line in 1982 and became *Royal Odyssey,* the vessel underwent an extensive refit under the loving care of interior designers A. and M. Katzourakis, who created colorful schemes throughout. In fact, practically nothing was left of the former *Doric*. A great deal of money was spent and the result was quite impressive. Regency Cruises acquired a "ready to sail" vessel and has made her its flagship.

The multitiered Odyssey Lounge, where theatrical entertainment occurs in the evening, has an Italian parquet dance floor designed by David Legno, as well as reportedly spectacular lighting system. Both indoor and outdoor pools have been refurbished and tiled with French Briare ceramics. The Ambrosia Dining Room has been opened up, with windows to the sea, and Greek-designed tapestries and mirrored abstracts grace landings and corridors. All staterooms are accented with silkscreen panels, and even the Ice Cream Parlor has been brightened.

The *Regent Sun* boasts a total of 409 cabins: 22 superior deluxe suites; 33 junior suites; 280 outside cabins; and 73 inside cabins. Bathrooms have been modernized and many have tubs as well as showers. All cabins have individual air conditioning, American electrical outlets, twin beds, full vanities with long mirror, music, and telephone for 24-hour room service. In addition to the four lounges, the vessel is equipped with five bars, card-room casino, library and writing room, theater, gymnasium, sauna, and hairdresser. She is well organized and spacious enough for the full complement of passengers.

During the summer season *Regent Sun* is in Alaskan waters on Friday departures every week from June through September between Vancouver and Whittier (for Anchorage). From October through April, the vessel is based in San Juan for Sunday departures to Gems of the Caribbean. The itinerary calls at Grenada, Barbados, Martinique, Marie Galante for a private beach party, and St. Thomas. Special packages are available with stopovers in San Juan. Or, satisfied passengers can embark the *Regent Sea* for another one-week cruise from San Juan!

★★★★★ + RENAISSANCE I–VIII

Renaissance Cruises; Italian registry; Italian officers and European crew; all eight ships built in La Spezia, Italy, 1989–91; 4500 tons; 290/297 feet long; 50 feet at beam; 100/114 passengers; crew of 67/72; cruising speed of 15 knots; 6 passenger decks.

These eight vessels are identical except for a few modifications as noted above. Some of the Renaissance ships will carry another 14 passengers, 5 more crew members, and be some seven feet longer—hardly noticeable even among the experts! The vessels feature all-outside suites (four Renaissance with private balconies, 39/40-plus Deluxe with three seaview windows, 7/12 Superior with portholes) ranging in size from 220 to 290 square feet, with queen- or twin-size beds (convertible), color TV/VCR (remote controlled if you can figure it out), bar/refrigerator, which has been stocked to your preference, security lockdrawer, etc. The decor is refined with good use of dark wood panels and mirrors that offer a yachtlike ambience. The sitting area furniture is covered in suede. The teak-floored bathrooms have stall showers with a seat, marble vanity, plush towels, terry-cloth robes, built-in hair dryer, and designer toiletries. Starboard cabins are for non-smokers; portside for those still with the habit. Suite stewardesses are Scandinavian.

On-board amenities include the Lounge, Club with piano bar and small casino, Library, Boutique, outdoor pool and spa with Jacuzzi, sauna, and beauty salon, and a sports platform with Zodiacs, sunfish, and snorkeling equipment. As on Sea Goddess and Seabourn Cruises, life on board Renaissance is low-key, with planned activities—other than enrichment lectures—a rarity. Dress is comfortable elegance and passengers are sophisticated travelers who know what to expect. The Restaurant offers tables from two to eight and guests are free to dine as they wish, from 7:30 to 10 p.m. Breakfast and lunch are informal and served buffet style al fresco, with hot items cooked to order. Continental breakfast and an international menu are available in the suites.

Destinations are the primary focus of these chic small vessels, with an emphasis on itineraries that other ship lines have not yet "discovered." For example, some 25 mainly one-week cruises have been planned through 1991 aboard the first six ships. The itineraries feature 180 different port calls (many of them exclusive to Renaissance Cruises) in 50 countries and on four continents. The published cruising areas are: Far East, Mediterranean, Europe, Scandinavia, Black Sea, Red Sea, around Africa, South America, and Caribbean. Each itinerary is called a "collection," and the compendium of Renaissance Cruises Collections is a work of art. Call for a copy and dream!

★★★ROMANZA

Chandris Cruises; Panamanian registry; Greek officers and international crew; built in 1939 and named Aurelia; *refurbished in 1971 as* Romanza; *11,000 tons; 488 feet long; 60 feet at beam; 562 passengers; crew of 230; cruising speed of 15.5 knots.*

The *Romanza* is the charmer of the Chandris family and popular with young Europeans; Americans looking for a value cruise in the Greek Islands that can be combined with a stay at one of Chandris' five resort hotels will enjoy this vessel. She sails Saturdays from Venice to Dubrovnik, Corfu, Heraklion, Rhodes and Piraeus, passing through the historic Corinth Canal on the return to Venice. Passengers may embark in either Venice or Piraeus (Thursdays).

The ship has 137 outside and 160 inside cabins, all with private facilities (shower and toilet). Most of the accommodations are designed for two berths; only 15 inside cabins are sold as four-berth, and 35 others on Capri Deck can accommodate a third or fourth person. The public areas feature four bars, a large lounge, card room, casino, discotheque, theater, children's playroom, swimming pool, and dining room (for two seatings at all meals). The atmosphere and crew throughout the vessel are all Greek, with the exception of Indian stewards in the cabins.

The *Romanza* is not under the Chandris Fantasy Cruises umbrella but is marketed through the same offices in New York, Miami and Beverly Hills. For an interesting Cruise and Stay vacation in Greece at value prices, the *Romanza* should be considered especially for honeymooners ($100 discount just for being married!) and senior citizens.

★★★★★ROTTERDAM

Holland America Line; Netherland Antilles registry, Dutch officers, and Indonesian crew; originally built in the Netherlands in 1959 and christened by former Queen Juliana; last refurbished 1989; 38,000 tons; 748 feet long; 94 feet at beam; 1070 passengers; crew of 603; cruising speed of 21 knots; 10 passenger decks.

They don't build ships like the *Rotterdam* anymore. Her sleek black and white hull exudes confidence and comfort and a seaworthiness that is hard to find these days. She has an old-world charm that grew on me, even though I thought she got left behind in the beauty and glamour department. However, this vessel has some very fine features and a very loyal following. Among the ship's finest assets are her interior woods, many of which are rare today, the artistry of which has been lost forever. This and the spaciousness throughout offer a certain grace that can never be repeated on most of the newer vessels.

The *Rotterdam* has some wonderful public areas, and you can get rather lost from forward to aft. You enter the vessel via Main Deck, near the front office and beauty parlor. Two flights up is Promenade Deck, which extends from the vast swimming pool area to the 450-seat theater in the forward section. In between are the pleasant Lido Terrace, a large Lido Restaurant for breakfast and buffet luncheons, a card/game room, the Lynbaan shopping center, the Ocean Bar, and the Queens Lounge with a bust of Juliana surveying all those who enter. One deck up are two nightclubs, the Ambassador Room and the Ritz Carlton, the latter of which has an elegant winding staircase up to a terrace and open deck area. But one cannot bypass the smoking room, the Tropic Bar, more shops, and a pleasant theater balcony that seats 160 passengers. The dining rooms down on B Deck are called Odyssey and La Fontaine. In the tradition of vessels designed for the transatlantic run, these dining rooms do not have a sea view, but they are very well planned and comfortable. The vessel also has indoor swimming pool/sauna/massage areas, casino, and self-service laundry and ironing facilities.

During her most recent refurbishment, a $15-million renovation completed in 1989 in Portland, Oregon, back-of-the-house equipment as well as passenger amenities received attention. The public rooms—especially the Sky Room, Ritz Carlton Lounge, Ambassador Lounge, Queens Lounge, Library, and both Ocean and Tropic bars were freshened. The Lido area (restaurant and deck) received a face-lift and Upper Promenade Deck was extended. All staterooms boast new decor, as well as some bathrooms. Even the Casino was on the list—with an additional 31 slot machines and two blackjack tables!

The *Rotterdam* has 304 outside cabins and 246 inside, all with private facilities. While not glamorous by my standards, the accommodations are sturdy, functional, and spacious—nothing tacky nor prefab about them. The crew is eager to please, friendly, and forever smiling, offering gracious service. Holland America runs its own training school in Djakarta for crew aboard three of its vessels, and does a fine job. There is a No Tipping Required policy on board, which does not mean that some gratuities aren't rendered—but the crew does not go around with palms extended, a refreshing change from most cruise ships.

During the summer season the *Rotterdam* joins the Holland America fleet sailing weekly from Vancouver. The Thursday departures call at Ketchikan, Juneau, Sitka and cruise Glacier Bay. There are two beautiful days at sea through the Inside Passage. During the fall and early winter the *Rotterdam* is returning to the longer voyage—for which she was designed and is so beloved by a loyal HAL following. A 47-day Around South America sailing is followed by an Around Hawaii from the west coast. The vessel makes a series of 10-day southern Caribbean cruises from Fort Lauderdale before repositioning through the Panama Canal to Alaska for another summer!

★★★★★ROYAL PRINCESS

Princess Cruises; British registry and officers; European/British crew; completed in November 1984 in Wartsila Shipyard, Helsinki; christened in Southampton by HRH the Princess of Wales; 45,000 tons; 757 feet long; 106 feet at beam; 1200 passengers; crew of approximately 500; cruising speed of 20 knots; 9 passenger decks.

The *Royal Princess* is very royal indeed and a real beauty. Designed and constructed at the famous Wartsila shipyard in Helsinki, the $150 million vessel has all outside cabins and a passenger complement of 1200. All 600 cabins have nice picture windows, twin beds that convert to doubles, queens or kings, spacious bathrooms with both tub and shower, individual climate control, refrigerators and color TV. Fire-resistant woods have been used in the cabinets and closet areas. Suites, deluxe cabins and some standard cabins have private terraces.

A cruise aboard the *Royal Princess* is a real experience. The ship is large and boasts a variety of places to play. The Lido pool area with its Jacuzzis is a pleasant spot in which to sun and read. There is another outdoor pool above. The ship has a total of ten decks, four swimming pools, a Promenade Deck for joggers, and a full health spa with massage and sauna, just for starters. The Horizon lounge on Sun Deck is perfect for sunsets and early evening, but gets very busy as the night moves along.

Because the cabins are on the upper decks, one goes "down" to public areas. The Crown Casino, Riviera club, Terrace Room, Princess

Court, library, theater, bridge room and International lounge are all located on Riviera Deck. Below on Plaza Deck are the Continental dining room, Purser's Lobby, and beauty salon. The dramatic Princess Court, a two-story space winding down by spiral staircase to the Plaza entrance hall, is the focal point of the vessel. Public rooms are spacious but leave one a bit cold; the designers seem to have overlooked the need for quiet little hideaways (with or without bar) that are so important to a ship of this size. The artwork is impressive, as it is on all Princess vessels. The largest and most dramatic piece is ''Spendthrift'' by British artist David Norris. With a height of more than 11 feet, it features three groups of gray-green bronze seagulls in flight and is located in the Plaza—heart of the ship. There are enamel and ceramic murals as well as a tapestry wall hanging in the public rooms. Staterooms have seven original lithographs, commissioned for *Royal Princess* from artists Paul Hogarth, Chris Corr, Alistair Crawford, and Paul Benjamin.

Breakfast on your own terrace is a must; buffet luncheons are popular on Lido Deck, with the usual hamburgers, salads, fruit and pastries; dinner is a formal affair in the two-sitting Continental dining room. The Italian chefs and stewards enjoy making special pastas as well as flaming desserts for passengers, and are well rewarded for their services. There is 24-hour cabin service, and with your own small refrigerator in which to keep snacks, no one is likely to ever experience hunger pains aboard!

Officers and hotel crew are British and very charming. I was impressed that the staff captain stopped by to explain lifeboat procedures personally (as we had embarked after the cruise had begun). Captain Young enjoys his vessel, with good reason, and everything works well. This is a vessel on which a longer cruise is a ''must,'' so plan to take at least two sailings back-to-back for three weeks or so!

In response to consumer demand, the *Royal Princess* is spending her summers in Europe, with 12- and 14-day sailings from Barcelona, Venice, London, and Naples—ah romance. The *Royal* leaves her spring trans-canal program early to go transatlantic, stays in Europe into November, then returns to the Panama Canal scene between San Juan and Acapulco. Ports of call on the 11-night sailings from San Juan are St. Thomas, St. Maarten, Martinique, Curacao, and through the Panama Canal to Acapulco. From Acapulco, the 10-night cruises call at Puerto Caldera (Costa Rica) through the Panama Canal to Curacao, St. Croix, and St. Thomas to San Juan. On any cruise, life aboard this vessel is a splendid sojourn.

★★★★★ROYAL VIKING SEA/SKY/STAR

Royal Viking Line; Bahamian registry, Norwegian officers, and European crew; 28,000 tons each; built in Helsinki in 1972/3; all rebuilt in

*Bremerhaven and stretched with a 93-foot midsection from 1981–3; 710
passengers; crew of 410; 676 feet long; 83 feet at beam; cruising speed
of 21 knots; 8 passenger decks.*

All three vessels are truly elegant and offer a lovely cruise experience. The ships have recently been re-refurbished, and the new look
adds contemporary colors that highlight the vessel's distinctive Scandinavian ambience. Some public rooms have been changed around—most
notably the Casino—and a new health club with expanded facilities has
been added! The Casino has been moved to a more accessible location
on Promenade Deck beside the refurbished aft bar (the nightclub). Elsewhere, all interior decor has been brightened, as well as plumbing and
galleys modernized. The outside deck space has also been renovated,
with attractive white-frame seating crowned by blue and white–striped
cushions. The result: very plush!

The much publicized stretch of the three vessels added several spacious penthouse suites as well as a new outdoor pool and Lido bar on
Sky Deck. The elegant Discovery/Windjammer rooms, with their plush
seating and dramatic views of the ocean or port, remain the same in the
forward section of each vessel. All suites have separate sitting areas,
partitioned bed and vanity rooms, two bathrooms, refrigerator, and closed-
circuit television. The Scandinavia Deck dining rooms, with their over-
sized windows on the sea, have been enlarged to still offer one-seating
meals (which I consider the true sign of a first-class vessel). Other features include a small chapel, a private room off the dining room for
cocktail parties, and enlarged reception and shopping areas.

Closetspace is plentiful in all cabin categories and most bathrooms
have full tubs, if that is important to you. Cabin service is excellent,
and surfaces are spotless at all times. The Scandinavian stewardesses
(who master a 14-chapter instruction book) are the epitome of efficiency—if a bit on the ''bossy'' side. In short, keep your belongings in
shipshape order! Standard cabins tend to be on the small side for such
an elegant vessel, but this was the beginning of modular construction,
and most are of the same size and configuration, with two portholes.

There are plenty of activities offered daily aboard all three vessels,
although bingo always seems to be the most popular. Occasional speakers, self-acclaimed experts in their fields, offer enrichment lectures on
many cruises. Expect to find authors touting their own works, although
few of them push the product. If you buy the shore excursions, well-
written briefs on each port will be presented. Otherwise, ask the librar-
ian (if you can find same) for some good background material, or bring
along your own as I always do.

Other features on all three vessels include a Casino Royale on Bridge
Deck with blackjack and roulette, slot machines, and a small bar. A
new lounge on Sky Deck seats about 200 people for live shows and

dancing and acts as a Supper Club for about 60 passengers on selected evenings at sea. A special menu and entertainment/dancing throughout the dinner service is featured here. The penthouse suites have a "butler" for anything passengers may need (parties, baby sitting, room service, etc.). All passengers will find a concierge in the reception area to handle their queries on a myriad of subjects. At least three spoken languages are required of all who act as concierges.

All three vessels also boast a fine theater on Mediterranean Deck for first-run films, a small chapel on Pacific Deck, beauty/barber shops, a hospital, launderette, large reception area and shops, saunas and some masseuse/eurs. Luncheons are served by the pool on sea days (full breakfasts are served in cabins/suites), and midnight snacks are available in one of the lounges, although no one really needs it because the ship line has instituted "nouvelle" cuisine and the results are very pleasing.

Royal Viking Line is proud to be the only cruise line named a member of the prestigious Les Toques Blanches culinary society. The line was also named to the Master Chefs Institute. Guest chefs appearing on board in the past few years have included Andre Soltner of Lutece in New York City and Joyce Goldstein of Square One restaurant in San Francisco. When the *Star* is on her Bermuda run during the summer, a number of New York–area chefs love to come aboard and show off their culinary art! A new spa cuisine menu was introduced last year, and musicians now stroll through the dining room.

Royal Viking vessels roam the world, and passengers can luxuriate on board for a few days or take back-to-back itineraries for as long as several months! One vessel spends the summer season in Alaska/Canada, sailing between San Francisco and Vancouver or round-trip from Vancouver. A series of Canada/New England cruises are now also popular for one week between New York and Montreal or round-trip for 14 days from either port-city. Two-week cruises cover Southeast Asia between Hong Kong and Singapore, or the South Seas between Sydney, Australia, and Auckland, New Zealand, as well as combinations of the above. Longer sailings from San Francisco/Los Angeles visit the Hawaiian and French Polynesian islands.

Royal Viking vessels are also a familiar and very welcome sight in European ports of call, from the Mediterranean to the Land of the Midnight Sun to the great capitals of the Baltic and the British Isles. Add to this a full program around the west coast of South America, from the Amazon River to the Strait of Magellan in the spring and fall, as well as Panama Canal sailings between the west coast and Acapulco, San Juan, and Port Everglades. The *Star* offers the Connoisseur's Guide to the Caribbean (winter) and Bermuda (summer) and the Explorer Series aboard the *Sea* features calls at exotic ports in the Orient and Indian Ocean.

Royal Viking Line has established a complementary tour company that operates independently of the cruises, but passengers should be interested in their quality and emphasis on unusual experiences. Some of the areas covered this past year have been China and Tibet, Thailand and Burma, India and Nepal, Kenya, castles and chateaux of France and Germany, manor houses of the British Isles, and ancient cultures of Ecuador, Peru, and the Galapagos Islands. Some of the Royal Viking tours offerings have been added to the Cruise Atlas.

★★★★★ + ROYAL VIKING SUN

Royal Viking Line; Bahamian registry and European crew; 38,000 tons; built by Wartsila Marine Industries in Finland for service entry December 1988; 740 passengers; crew of 460; 673 feet long; 95 feet at beam; cruising speed of 21 knots; 8 passenger decks.

The *Royal Viking Sun* is one-third larger than existing RVL vessels, yet only carries 4% more passengers. The $125-million ship boasts more space per passenger than almost any cruise vessel ever built (51.35) except *Crystal Harmony*. The 370 staterooms all have walk-in closets and average about 200 square feet, with 96% outside and 39% of these with private verandas. In addition, accommodations offer TV/videos, convertible beds, and refrigerator/bars. There are 18 penthouse suites named for explorers (Cook, Amundsen, Columbus, Nansen, Tasman, Eriksson, Drake, and Magellan) and an ultra-luxurious Owner's Suite on Sky Deck, all with convertible king-size beds, private verandas, and Jacuzzi baths, as well as exclusive butler service. Also on Sky Deck is the Stella Polaris Room, an observation lounge forward.

Another set of penthouse suites is located on Bridge Deck (Vasco da Gama, Bougainville, Palmer, Heyerdahl, Cartier, Cabot, Bering, Amerigo Vespucci, Vancouver, and Balboa). The Garden Lounge and Garden Cafe (informal dining during the day) are located on Bridge Deck, as is the Royal Grill a la carte restaurant seating 60 persons (with advance reservations) and offering both continental and nouvelle cuisine in an intimate ambience. The supperclublike setting features live music, and the menu will be prepared by the world's best visiting chefs on a rotating basis. Paul Bocuse, who has become a mini-corporation, is the consulting chef for Royal Grill and has planned its menus.

Other public-area amenities are the Oak Room wood-paneled lounge with fireplace (reminiscent of the former Smoking Room men-only lounges on such glamorous vessels as the *Normandie*), two swimming pools (one with a swim-up bar), Royal Viking Spa with sea views, located near the lap pool, Norway Lounge with state-of-the-art sound/light equipment, multipurpose Starlight theater with flexible seating, card room, Compass Rose Wine Bar and piano lounge, the Casino and Midnight

Sun Lounge (the ship's nightclub). Most of the public rooms are on Norway Deck, including the Dickens Library and Royal Arcade shopping area.

The single-seating Royal Viking dining room is surrounded by large picture windows and divided into three sections to maximize the sea views. Alternate dining is available in the Garden Cafe and Royal Grill. There are eight passenger decks in all, with deluxe cabins on Discovery Deck and other accommodations on Scandinavia, Atlantic, and Pacific decks.

Other interesting features of the vessel include rubber-mountain engines, automatic window-washing equipment, excellent soundproofing in all cabins, an open Promenade Deck, custom-designed tenders, and a croquet court! This is definitely a first for cruise ships and although a scaled-down version of a professional croquet court (not the backyard variety), it has proved to be very popular. Already, there have been several "croquet cruises" of note.

Royal Viking Sun has earned a most glamorous reputation since her christening in San Francisco by Mr. and Mrs. James Stewart (yes, the actor) in January 1989. Her annual world cruise is the most prestigious afloat—with many interesting segments and Royal Viking Tours programs available. She also visits South American port cities and spends the summer season in the Mediterranean/Adriatic/Black Sea/western Europe/North Cape, and Baltic capitals. A busy lady and all who know her are enamored!

During a recent dinner with a colleague I mentioned that an occasional recipe would find its way into the ship guide. We both agreed that the Creme Brulee from *Royal Viking Sun* should be one of the favored due to so many rave reviews! However, please note that the following recipe arrived straight from the RV *Sun* kitchen and should be modified to personal taste:

 8 cups heavy cream
 3 vanilla beans
 16 egg yolks
 2 cups fine sugar

Place vanilla beans and heavy cream in saucepan on stove; scald and remove from heat. Gradually add sugar to beaten egg yolks until light and fluffy. Remove vanilla beans and add warm cream slowly to egg mixture. Pour into individual oven-proof dishes and bake at 300° until set. Cool. Just before serving, sprinkle each dish with a layer of sieved light-brown sugar and place under grill until sugar forms a thin caramel glaze. (Do not burn!) Serves 16 individual portions.

440 · · · THE SHIPS

★★★★★ + SAGAFJORD

Cunard/Nac; Bahamian registry; Scandinavian officers and European crew; launched in 1965; refitted in 1979 and 1984; 24,500 tons; 620 feet long; 80 feet at beam; 618 passengers; crew of 320; cruising speed of 20 knots; 7 passenger decks.

The *Sagafjord* became a quarter of a century old in 1990! Her age enhances, rather than detracts from, the quality of cruise life one finds aboard. The vessel was built for Norwegian America Line at a time when sailings were still great happenings—with lots of flowers, champagne and steamer trunks. Hence, cabins are large (no locked knees when you sit down on these beds) and there is plenty of closet space. There are also a record 54 singles, for those traveling alone. Pampering begins at once, with such cabin amenities as terry-cloth robes and smelly soaps. Men get a *Sagafjord* cap, while ladies receive a tote bag that is light and very useful both on board and ashore. From time to time, other remembrances appear in your cabin—it's all part of the process of being pampered.

The *Sagafjord* remains everyone's favorite vessel afloat and Cunard can be proud of its additions—Golden Door Spa, two-tiered nightclub, double-height windows in the dining room, and some two dozen suites—which are now several years old and have become part of the furniture! While other vessels now boast state-of-the-art this and that—even five-story glass elevators—the *Sagafjord* remains a true seagoing vessel with traditional values. She truly is a home away from home for all who sail on her, with a warm and caring ambience that is unsurpassed. The *Vistafjord* may be a touch prettier, and you may find more caviar on the *Sea Goddess* ships, but the cruise experience aboard *Sagafjord* is untouchable—especially when Ingvar and Meredith and Captain Berntsen are there to take care of you (not to forget the charming stewards, captains, and chiefs)!

Although the average age on board is still "retired," there is a nice complement of attractive and interesting passengers in their 40s and 50s and everyone mixes very well. One couple from Boston had been told about the *Sagafjord* by their son and daughter-in-law, who had honeymooned aboard last summer in Alaska. Another couple (very retired) from Texas had enjoyed their first two weeks aboard (from Galvaston to L.A.) so much, they decided to make the return through the Canal immediately.

Although the ship's registry is now in the Bahamas, officers remain Scandinavian and the crew is Northern European (with some charming western Canadians added to the cabin stewardess roster). The hotel manager is a jolly Swede named Ingvar Torstensson, upon whose stout shoulders fall *everything* a passenger sees and does (with the exception of the lifeboat drill). Ingvar's favorite expression is "No Problem!" and the total spirit of the crew is generated from this one personality and his messy little office!

By day, life aboard the *Sagafjord* is not "casual chic," it's just plain casual and do as you please. But every evening is an event—from (black tie) formal to dress-up for an elegant restaurant. The food is worth your primping. If passengers have any complaint, it's the dinner menu, which is too bountiful and the food too beautifully presented to resist. (To the Golden Door Spa every morning for exercise!)

However, what can compete in one's memory with the sight of those handsome officers in dress uniforms walking down the double staircase into the dining room? Only the parade of 50 stewards on the same staircase with platters of flaming Norwegian Surprise!

Rudi Sodamin, executive chef for Cunard Line, suggests Flamed Shrimp as a party recipe that can be created at table (the flaming part) or in the kitchen:

3 Tbsps. butter
1 small onion, chopped
1 medium tomato, peeled & coarsely chopped
½ cup fresh, sliced mushrooms
½ heavy cream
3 garlic cloves, minced
2 Tbsps. chopped parsley
1 lb. raw, deveined, cleaned shrimp
salt & freshly ground pepper
¼ cup cognac
1 Tbsps. slivered almonds

Melt half butter in skillet and lightly brown onions. Add tomato and mushrooms. Simmer and stir in cream. Remove from heat. Mix in garlic & parsley and set aside. Sprinkle shrimp with salt and pepper. Heat remaining butter in another skillet and saute shrimp until they turn pink. Heat cognac, add to shrimp, and flame. When flames die out, stir in tomato-mushroom sauce and heat through. Sprinkle with almonds and serve. Voila!

The *Sagafjord* begins every year with a global or long voyage that always departs from Port Everglades and is full of many loyal passengers who wouldn't dream of spending their winter months anywhere else! If it's not a four-continent world cruise, then it is a 36-port Polynesian and Oriental Mystique that returns to North America in early April. No matter where the ship sails, a good time is always enjoyed by all aboard.

During the spring and fall, the *Sagafjord* sails between Port Everglades and Los Angeles on 2-week transcanal cruises, then repositions in Alaska for 10- and 11-day sailings through the famous Inside Passage. As the premier vessel in Alaska, the *Sagafjord* sails northbound from Vancouver (11 days) visiting Ketchikan, Juneau, Skagway, Sitka, Valdez, Seward, Nome, and Anchorage, while cruising by Endicott Arm, Hubbard Glacier, Columbia Glacier, College Fjord, Kenai Fjord National Park, Cook Inlet, and Kachemak Bay. During the latest Alaska sailings *Sagafjord* was granted permission to enter Glacier Bay National Park and Preserve for five full-day calls. These calls were made by special permits of the National Park Service of Alaska, and a naturalist from the park service was on board to lecture on the rapid deglaciaton process that has been taking place in Glacier Bay over the past two centuries (at least, since anyone noticed). The southbound journey (10 days) is similar, with the exception of King's Bay and Port Nellie Juan. Deluxe tours of the interior of Alaska are available as well as pre- and post-cruise stays in Vancouver.

★★★SANTA CRUZ

Galapagos Cruises of Quito, Ecuador; Ecuadorean crew and registry; designed and built in Spain exclusively for Galapagos cruises; launched December 1979; 1,500 tons; 230 feet long; 90 passengers; crew of 35; cruising speed of 15 knots; 4 passenger decks; American Bureau of Shipping highest international safety classification.

The *Santa Cruz* is a first-class ship accommodating 90 passengers in 45 cabins, far superior to anything before found in the Galapagos Islands. All twin and triple cabins are outside, and five single, inside cabins are on Main and Upper deck. All cabins have private facilities and are well designed with comfortable beds and a feeling of spaciousness. The vessel has a large sundeck, a pleasant one-seating dining room, and an attractive lounge area with bar. The bar hours are flexible to passengers' wishes, and bartender Pepe makes terrific Pisco Sours—the local cocktail. Mixed drinks are rather expensive since most supplies are imported by air, and wine can run to $20 per bottle. Beer and cigarettes cost about $2 each. The food on board is good, but not gourmet to my taste. Breakfasts are wonderful (omelets, pancakes, fruit, and fresh juices), but my coffee was powdered Nescafe. The dinners of fresh fish and fresh lobster tails are superb.

Life on board the *Santa Cruz* is decidedly casual, as each passenger is restricted to 20 pounds of luggage. Men are required to wear nothing more formal than a short-sleeved pullover, while woman may want a more dressy outfit for the evening. After all, the charming Carlos, captain of the *Santa Cruz,* may invite you to dine at his table!

★★★★SEA BIRD/SEA LION

Special Expeditions (on long-term charter); American registry and crew; built near Seattle, Washington, in 1982; formerly known as Majestic Explorer *and* Great Rivers Explorer, *respectively; refurbished and renamed in 1990; 100 tons; 152 feet long; 31 feet at beam; 70 passengers; crew of 25; cruising speed of 12 knots; 4 passenger decks.*

These two vessels are well suited to Special Expeditions cruises and one (or both) have been chartered by Sven Olof Lindblad previously for his programs. They are now on long-term charter to his company and have been nicely refurbished to carry just 70 passengers in all-outside cabins with lower beds, private facilities, and individual climate controls. Most accommodations also feature a large picture window.

The vessels have a shallow draft of eight feet and bow thrusters that provide maximum maneuverability into small coves and access to unreachable waterways. A fleet of rubber landing craft are also on board. These are "expedition" vessels, and life on board reflects this. There is a bar/lounge, dining room, and sun deck. The vessels can be found on the Columbia and Snake rivers (in the wake of Lewis and Clark), exploring Alaska's coastal wilderness, and voyaging to the Sea of Cortez around Baja, California, to observe migrations of whales and other animals. All expeditions are led by naturalists.

★★★★★+SEA GODDESS I AND II

Cunard/Sea Goddess; Norwegian registry; Norwegian officers; European/American crew; custom built in Wartsila Shipyard, Helsinki; inaugurated April 1984 and May 1985, respectively; 4250 tons; 344 feet long; 48 feet at beam; 118 passengers; crew of 89; cruising speed of 17.5 knots; 5 passenger decks.

Sea Goddess I and *II* both arrived as scheduled and were christened by Princess Caroline of Monaco. The 118-passenger vessels do, indeed, have the ambience of a private club. The all-suite accommodations are 205 square feet (including full bathroom) and decorated in top-quality pastel fabrics. Many have convertible twin/double beds. The wall units of white oak contain a superlative stereo/video system as well as a well-stocked complimentary bar (replenished daily). Frankly, the cabins are quite small (the ship was designed by a fellow who only knew yachts) and the bathrooms were unfortunately made for midgets. Since the only complaints about the vessel deal with the size of accommodations, Cunard has opened up several cabins into connecting suites, and the result is spectacular. However, cabin amenities are lovely—fresh flowers and fruit, ice, and your choice of drinks in the refrigerator, and a programmable wall safe—hurray! (I presume that anyone gauche enough to demand caviar daily would receive it.) Bathroom amenities include lovely terry-cloth robes, smelly soaps, shampoo/conditioner, and both pre- and post-tanning lotions. Closet space is quite adequate (except the hangers are too big) and there are plenty of full-length mirrors. The ship line also offers playing cards and a few books to peruse in the cabin.

Public areas on these charming vessels include a large sport deck, off which an aft platform into the water is used for water skiing, wind surfing, snorkeling, etc. (My husband discovered jet skis and a new fan was made.) There is also a health center, attractive outdoor pool with hot tub, tropical greenhouse, and outdoor cafe for alfresco buffet breakfasts and lunches. A spacious library/card room is for passengers who prefer some quiet time. The library has a good assortment of books as well as a few hundred video tapes for viewing in the privacy of your cabin (sorry, I did not notice any X rated).

Throughout both *Sea Goddess I* and *II* are beautiful floral bouquets and elegant touches in brass and wood. The dining salon on 2 Deck has the atmosphere of a fine restaurant, with flowers and crystal and leatherbound menus. Passengers are encouraged to dine as they like between 8 and 10 p.m. and order their fancy, with complimentary Russian caviar and complimentary wines especially selected for that particular menu. Tables are not assigned, so couples may mix and match, or ask to sit by themselves. Soft piano music is played throughout the meal. Dinner means coat or jacket every evening, with black tie suggested at Welcome and Farewell parties.

Breakfast and lunch on deck are very, very lovely on board *Sea Goddess* because they are personal and no one has to stand in line with a tray and plastic fixtures. The blue-rimmed Villeroy & Boch china is a splendid way to enjoy one's repast in the fresh air. Breakfast and lunch are also served in the restaurant for those who require formal service. The food on board is excellent (but not outrageously delicious) and there is definitely an overabundance of caviar available. I believe that Dirk Pons, chief steward on *Sea Goddess II,* said that passengers consumed several kilo of Beluga Caviar each week. Dirk's attention to detail on board is quite overwhelming; my impression is that he delivers to passengers more than many can appreciate. These are very special ships and people should go on with a group of very dear friends.

Evening entertainment features a casino as well as dancing in the Main Salon. More intimate is the Piano Bar or Club Salon. Passengers enjoy such thoughtful details as subdued lighting in all public areas after dark. But the most relaxing aspect of *Sea Goddess I* and *II* is the lack of planned activities. Passengers do not feel obliged to be somewhere at a certain time—which often makes a cruise more tiring than staying at home! We enjoyed a fine Scottish singer on our *Sea Goddess II* cruise and he entertained just enough to be delightful—but never overpowering in such a small space.

Both *Sea Goddess* vessels spend the posh summer "season" in the Mediterranean, where they definitely belong, because the kitchen can stock good stores and the ability of being yachtlike in ports of call enhances the on-board ambience. The sports platform is a fabulous feature in the beautiful waters of the Mediterranean Sea and Greek Islands. (Those who do not do well on small vessels should avoid transatlantic crossings, however.) During the winter months *Sea Goddess I* cruises in the Caribbean between St. Thomas and Barbados, calling at such places as Palm Island, Mustique, Antigua, Virgin Gorda, St. Barts, and St. John in one week. Longer holiday sailings are available.

Sea Goddess II embarks upon a series of Orient experiences during the winter season, sailing from Haifa through the Red Sea to Bombay, from Bombay to Singapore, with several two-week departures from Singapore. The vessel reverses her itinerary in the spring and returns to Haifa by mid-April for Mediterranean cruises all summer.

For the decade of the 1990s, Cunard has devised something called Connoisseur Cruises, which means that selected sailings are to be enhanced by special hosts or hostesses, expert in the art of entertaining, fine wines, gourmet food, etc. Four of the Caribbean cruises featured famous hostess Simone Levitt—a veteran entertainer on her own yacht, La Belle Simone. The Epicurean sailings have highlighted top American chefs (chosen at a cook-out in Aspen, Colorado) and some vintners who showed their wares. It was a brilliant scheme to increase passenger levels for what is sometimes a lackluster Caribbean season—because of the competition.

★★★★+SEA PRINCESS

Princess Cruises/P&O Lines; British flag and officers; Goanese and European crew; built by John Brown on the River Clyde in 1966 and launched as Kungsholm *of Swedish America Line; refitted and relaunched in 1979 as* Sea Princess; *last refurbished in 1986; 28,000 tons; 660 feet long; 87 feet at beam; 710 passengers; crew of 350; cruising speed of 20 knots; 6 passenger decks.*

P & O Lines has good judgment; it has refurbished the lovely *Sea Princess* (former *Kungsholm*) and sent her into the Caribbean under the aegis of Princess Cruises. The multimillion-dollar refurbishing project included teak decking, health club and spa, new Crown Casino, redecorated Starlight lounge, six new suites with private spas (Nos. 29, 31, 35, 39, 43 and 47 on Aloha Deck), indoor/outdoor bar in the Carib lounge and redecorated and renamed Coral dining room. The International lounge has also been refurbished and fitted with state-of-the-art lighting and sound equipment. Money well spent to return a traditional lady into the elegant one she deserves to be.

The elegant *Sea Princess* boasts a traditional ambience, as befitting an all first-class vessel that was built for Swedish America Line. She has two swimming pools, two lounges, and a casino on Lido Deck, with a health spa/gymnasium down on Emerald Deck. The main showroom, theater, and Riviera Bar are located on Riviera Deck forward, with the Coral dining room down on Coral Deck.

The *Sea Princess* has handsome British officers and hotel staff, and an international service crew. P & O added some 86 inside cabins in 1979, but *Sea Princess* remains the superior quality vessel she always was. P & O has taken good care of the lady, even polishing the beautiful teak paneling daily!

During the summer *Sea Princess* joins much of the other fleet in Alaska, sailing between Vancouver and Anchorage every week. Following the season *Sea Princess* returns to the Orient for cruises from Hong Kong and Singapore and spends the winter in the South Pacific, sailing round trip from Sydney as well as from Hong Kong and Singapore on two-week cruises. Beginning in Spring 1991, *Sea Princess* returns to Southampton, England, and the P & O family—by popular demand. She will sail through the late autumn from Southampton on cruises to the Mediterranean, Greek Islands, Black Sea, and Canary Islands before following the sun to the South Pacific. We wish her well in her newest venture!

★★★★★+SEABOURN PRIDE/SEABOURN SPIRIT

Seabourn Cruise Line; Norwegian registry and officers; European hotel staff; built in Bremerhaven for December 1988 and 1989 service, respectively; 10,000 tons; 439 feet long; 63 feet at beam; 212 passengers; crew of 140; cruising speed of 18 knots; 6 passenger decks.

The $50-million (each) *Seabourn Pride* and *Seabourn Spirit* are successfully defending their reputation for providing a new standard of excellence on the high seas! The ships are beautiful to behold, the interiors spacious and comfortable. Both *Pride* and *Spirit* feature all-suite accommodations that measure approximately 10 feet by 27 feet, with a walk-in closet and a large bathroom with marble vanity and two sinks! Next to the three-by-five-foot picture window is a lovely sitting area, with sofa and two chairs plus a coffee table that raises to become a dining table for breakfast, lunch, or dinner. Other in-suite amenities include convertible twin beds (to queen), TV/VCR, hairdryer, plentiful fluffy towels and terry robes, designer soaps and other toiletries, a sewing kit with threaded needles, personalized stationery, (programmable) private safe, and electronic windowshade (which took me a few days to master).

Each suite (there are 100 of the same configuration, including four oriented for wheelchairs, plus six of the "regal" variety) also features a small refrigerator/bar stocked with sodas and beer (no charge) and replenished daily. The ship line also offers a Bon Voyage champagne and personal liquor if you desire it. Passengers are cared for by hard-working Scandinavian stewardesses who keep the suites immaculate, deliver fresh fruit daily, and turn down beds with chocolates and a full breakfast menu on the pillow. Meals en suite are served with considerable flair—dinner is course by course, as busy as the stewards are—and the food is as spectacular as the presentation.

Menus for the Restaurant—where there is unassigned seating between the hours of 7:30 and 10 p.m.—were developed by Stefan Hamrin of Sweden, whose talent aboard ships and ashore in Europe is renowned. Table settings feature Norwegian crystal by Hadeland, silver flatware by Germany's Robbe and Birking, and Wedgwood china designed especially for Seabourn. Service is formal and can be a bit slow on evenings when everyone decides to dine simultaneously—but relax and enjoy! Ordering off the menu is just fine, and the most requested dishes are broiled chicken, steak, and a simple pasta dish, according to the maitre d'hotel, who personally seats all passengers in the Restaurant.

One evening I tasted the crabmeat cakes with mustard sauce as an appetizer and they were simply heavenly. A request for the recipe was honored—albeit a bit sketchily—so we must improvise a little, but you will not be disappointed:

1 lb. crabmeat (picked over)
½ lb. combination chopped fresh salmon, seabass, St. Pierre
dash tabasco, chili sauce, soy sauce, salt & pepper
1 cup finely chopped vegetables (celery, carrots, peppers, etc.)
5 pieces chopped shallots
2 cloves chopped garlic
4 eggs
1 cup fine bread crumbs

Combine all ingredients; pat into small cakes and fry *very lightly* in Teflon pan; serve with sauce of 2 chopped shallots, ½ cup white wine (reduced), ½ cup cream (preferably half and half) and Dijon mustard to taste (2 to 4 Tbsps.). Serves four.

As an alternative to the formality of the Restaurant, where jackets and ties are required and dinner dancing takes place on occasional evenings, the Veranda Cafe serves buffet breakfast and lunch (with hot items to order) as well as sit-down dinners with a limited but tasty menu (and if you just fancy a simple hamburger—that's fine). Some passengers have found themselves at dinner in the Veranda Cafe at least twice on a week's cruise—just to get away from it all! These vessels were designed for travelers with the sophistication to "do their own thing," and life on board is very conducive to this.

Public rooms include the Magellan/Amundsen lounges for large parties and evening entertainment, The Club for cabaret (a wonderful pianist/songster was here last year), and the Constellation/Horizon lounges on top deck for early morning coffee, afternoon tea, and cocktails. These spaces have panoramic views and are really lovely. The bar extends to the outdoor Sky Bar overlooking the pool/Jacuzzi area. Continuing the theme of spaciousness on board *Seabourn Pride* and *Seabourn Spirit* is the spa/gymnasium/beauty salon area, which has large seaview windows and a wonderful staff. A "marina" area extending from the stern of each vessel offers complimentary watersports (as well as another swimming pool) when at anchor and appropriate. A small casino (many complaints about the unpleasant croupiers—who we hope have been replaced) and a library that needs some more current videos complete the indoor picture.

Seabourn Pride and *Seabourn Spirit* cruise the Mediterranean, in northern Europe, transatlantic, New England/Canada, in the Caribbean, around South America, through the Panama Canal, and along the Mexican Riviera. The brochure is simple, elegant, and memorable—just like a Seabourn Cruise!

★★★SEABREEZE

Dolphin Cruise Line; Bahamian registry; Greek officers and international crew; originally built in 1958 as Federico C. *for Costa Line; refitted and rechristened in 1983 as* Starship Royale *for Premier Cruise Line; refurbished in 1988 and renamed* SeaBreeze; *21,000 tons; 606 feet long; 74 feet at beam; 840 passengers; crew of 350; cruising speed of 22 knots; 8 passenger decks.*

You wouldn't recognize this vessel from her sailing days as *Starship Royale* for Premier Cruise Line. Replacing the startling red hull is a temperate white with attractive blue stripes, a charming SeaBreeze painted in script on the prow, and a playful Dolphin on the smokestack. Over $5.5 million was spent by Dolphin Cruise Line to refurbished the ship, much of it in the cabin areas, where radio and telephone were installed; some lower deck cabins were gutted and rebuilt.

The names of the decks have been changed and reflect everyone's favorite operas (or characters in them)—Aida, La Boheme, Carmen, Daphne, Electra, Fidelio, La Gioconda, Isolde, and Juliet (note that the names of the decks correspond to their letters). Public rooms have received the low-key treatment, with blue Dolphin logo carpeting. Facilities on board include the Four Seasons Observatory, Water Music

Whirlpool and Prelude Bar, Royal Fireworks Lounge (which should temper the works because it is surrounded by deluxe cabins), "surprise" Casino, Carmen Lounge, and Pastorale Cafe (buffet breakfast and lunch served here), La Mer pool, Slim Gym Center, Serenade Bar, and the Bacchanalia Restaurant. There is also a small children's corner/recreational area, Intermezzo Theater, and Agitato Disco. Food and service are on a par with a three-star vessel.

The *SeaBreeze* sails every Sunday from Miami at 4 p.m. to Grand Cayman (Tuesday), Montego Bay (Wednesday), and Playa del Carmen/ Cozumel (Friday). The Sunday departures are convenient to honeymooners as well as young families. The ship is popular with both groups, especially during the summer months.

★★★★SEAWARD

Norwegian Cruise Line; Bahamian registry, Norwegian officers, and international crew; built in Finland for service June 1988; 42,000 tons; 700 feet long; 96 feet at beam; 1534 passengers; crew of 624; cruising speed of 21.5 knots; 10 passenger decks.

The $120-million *Seaward* was christened in New York harbor by Greta Waitz, famed marathoner and Olympic champion, in a ceremony that raised money for the U.S. Olympic Team. Mrs. Waitz is a Norwegian citizen but seems to spend some time in North America—mainly winning the women's division of marathons in New York City.

Seaward has 767 cabins, of which 67% are in the outside configuration. According to the published rate list, there are 13 different cabin categories ranging from deluxe suites on Norway Deck to standard inside with upper and lower berths on Atlantic/Biscayne decks. At this writing rates range from just under $300 a day per person down to just over $200 a day per person.

Facilities on board include diversified dining in two dining rooms— Seven Seas and Four Seasons with strolling musicians, plus a 92-seat Palm Tree Restaurant that offers a more intimate atmosphere, an a la carte menu, white-glove service, sea views, and a $35+ charge. The Palm Tree is by reservation only. Less formal meals can be enjoyed in the Big Apple Cafe and East/West Side Patios, which serve from breakfast to midnight buffets. There is also an ice cream parlor on board called Lickety Splits.

International Deck is the main public area, with its Cabaret Lounge, Stardust Lounge, Everything Under the Sun shopping arcade, Oscar's Piano bar, Monte Carlo Casino, photo shop, and card room. Boomer's Nightclub is located on Norway Deck. Pool Deck features the Indoor/ Outdoor cafe, bar, and ice cream parlor. Sun Deck boasts the Palm Tree restaurant as well as Gatsby's wine bar, an observatory lounge, fitness center, and Coconut Willy's forward outdoor bar.

Captain of the *Seaward* is Torbjon Hauge, formerly of the *Norway*. The ship features fabulous Broadway-type entertainment and the well-known NCL Dive-In Program, and sails from Miami every Sunday afternoon for NCL's Pleasure Island, Ocho Rios, Grand Cayman, and Cozumel. Two double-deck, catamaran-style tenders (embarked from #1 Deck) will carry passengers to shore when docking facilities are not available.

★★★★+SKY PRINCESS

Princess Cruises; Liberian registry; Italian officers and European crew; built in France in 1984 as Fairsky *for Sitmar Cruises; renamed in 1988 by Princess Cruises and refurbished in 1989; 46,000 tons; 789 feet long; 98 feet at beam; 1200 passengers; crew of 535; cruising speed of 19 knots; 11 passenger decks.*

The newer of the three vessels in the Sitmar fleet, which Princess Cruises acquired in 1988, the now-named *Sky Princess* began her $150-million life in Alaska in May 1984 to great success—despite what we all considered her overwhelming size (how times change)! *Sky Princess* is now considered "mid-size" and a very attractive vessel, but thank goodness Princess Cruises decided on some refurbishment; the original decor was divided among four different firms from four different countries and the result was total confusion!

More than a million dollars was spent on the Showroom aboard *Sky Princess,* which included a new stage, intimate bar area adjacent with full view of the entertainment, multi-tiered seating, and new furnishings. The Starlight Disco, Veranda Lounge, and Promenade Lounge also received attention, and small personal safes were installed in all cabins. *Sky Princess* has some splendid facilities, including a large library, card rooms, greatly expanded casino, Rainbow Bar, and the glass-encased Horizon Lounge forward on Riviera Deck. Aft on Riviera Deck is the Starlight Disco, reachable only from the aft stairway on Promenade Deck.

Although the public areas on Promenade Deck flow well, attempting to reach your dining room—Regency or Savoy—on Aloha Deck is a major problem the first few days on board. This vessel is a challenge to even the best of scouts! There are also two swimming pools, a spacious spa with whirlpool and gymnasium on Sun Deck, and a large area for children and teens aft on Aloha Deck. The ever-popular Pizzeria is conveniently located midships on Promenade Deck. There is also a proper two-tiered theater for movies and meetings.

The 606 cabins aboard *Sky Princess* are spacious, with 388 outside (including 10 veranda suites and 28 mini-suites). All cabins boast color

TV, plenty of storage space, and showers that one can turn around in! However, as on other former Sitmar vessels, there is a high percentage of inside cabins.

Sky Princess is one of Princess Cruises' four "superships" making a major presence in the Caribbean in the 1990s. (The other three are *Star Princess, Crown Princess,* and *Regal Princess*). The vessel sails from either San Juan or Fort Lauderdale on 7- and 10-day cruises with three different itineraries covering the eastern, western, or southern islands of the Caribbean. During the summer season *Sky Princess* returns to Alaska, where Princess Cruises is another major presence!

★★★SKYWARD

Norwegian Caribbean Lines; Bahamian registry and Norwegian officers, international crew; originally built and launched in 1970; refurbished 1985; 16,250 tons; 525 feet long; 75 feet at beam; 730 passengers; crew of 330; cruising speed of 18 knots; 7 passenger decks.

The *Skyward* is similar to the *Southward* in plan and many of her public rooms have been renamed in the recent refurbishment. On Cabaret Deck aft is now the Ports of Call restaurant, with an attractive subdued decor of gray, blue and soft reds that make the space bright by day and romantic in the evening. Diners have nice sea views from windows port and starboard. The restaurant flows into Shuffles card room, the Monte Carlo Casino and Connections lounge midships. Forward is Tivoli Cabaret, with maroon and gold furnishings. The Captain's Bar on portside has nautical motif and paintings.

All 221 outside and 141 inside cabins aboard the *Skyward* also received new furnishings and are very attractive, with blue bedspreads, bright curtains and brass lamps. Above on Boat Deck is the Quarter Deck Cafe for buffet breakfast and lunch overlooking the swimming pool. The Upper Deck Bar has rattan furniture and a quiet atmosphere.

In April 1989 the *Skyward* joined the *Starward* in San Juan for a series of cruises to Barbados, St. Lucia, Guadeloupe, St. Thomas, and St. Maarten. The sailings depart every Saturday year-round at 10 p.m.

★★★★★SOCIETY EXPLORER

Society Expeditions Cruises; Bahamian registry; European officers and European/Filipino crew; built in Finland in 1969 and originally named Lindblad Explorer; *refitted and rechristened May 1985; 2500 tons; 238 feet long; 45 feet at beam; cruising speed of 13 knots; 6000 mile cruising range; 96 passengers; crew of 60; 6 passenger decks.*

The *Society Explorer* has long been famous as an "expedition" vessel, carrying passengers to exotic places around the world as the

Lindblad Explorer. Contrary to what we were led to believe, the *Society Explorer* was always owned by Heiko Klein of Bremen, West Germany, who assumed control of the ship and the company in July 1987. Klein owns and operates both vessels (including *World Discoverer*) that have sailed under the Society Expeditions banner. Klein is not only a sympathetic traveler but an excellent businessman, and future passengers can be feel happy that the "new" *Society Explorer* will offer a memorable expedition/cruise experience.

The *Explorer* has 50 outside cabins with two lower beds and private facilities. The cabins are small but adequate and nicely redecorated. Don't pack an extensive wardrobe as space is limited and life on board quite casual, unpretentious, and family-like (expect to have your smallest wish delivered). Fellow passengers are flexible and welcome the new experiences offered by Society Expeditions Cruises—so leave the jewels at home and enjoy! Although the vessel was not "stretched" as intended, a health club/sauna and sun deck were added, the dining room enlarged and the lounges made a bit more luxurious. On board are naturalists, art specialists, botanists, marine biologists and anyone else in the area—who all seem to add to the "fun" of the expeditions. A small laboratory is kept busy at all times.

The vessel is equipped with special gear and design features such as ice-strengthened hulls, bow thrusters, shallow drafts, and inflatable Zodiac landing craft to explore otherwise inaccessible areas. Officers are efficient German/Austrian, with Swiss chefs and Filipino/Indonesian crew. A new club for past passengers, inaugurated by my friend Kirk Kirkpatrick who was called in as company doctor, is named Discoverers Society and is very popular.

As on all Society Expeditions Cruises, advance booking means plentiful goodies by mail—reading lists, name tags, flight bag, notebook, maps, backpack, and parkas (for Antarctica). A full log of the expedition (in case you missed something) arrives a few weeks after your expedition, and your name is placed on the list for *Adventures*—the newsletter. *Society Explorer* project calendar for the future features Antarctica as well as South America and the Far North. The vessel is never idle and waiting for the adventuresome traveler!

★★★★SONG OF AMERICA

Royal Caribbean Cruise Line; Norwegian registry and international crew; built in Wartsila Yard in Helsinki and launched in 1982; 37,500 tons; 705 feet long; 93 feet at beam; 1390 passengers; crew of 500; cruising speed of 16 knots; 12 passenger decks.

With the inaugural service of the *Song of America* on December 5, 1982, and christened by opera star Beverly Sills (also known as "Bubbles''), Royal Caribbean Cruise Line became a four-fleet company, but not for long. (At this writing, RCCL boasts seven vessels, with two more on order!) The new vessel was three years in the planning and over a year in the construction, at a final cost of approximately $140 million. Interior design of the vessel has been executed by two of Scandinavia's best: Mogens Hammer of Denmark and Finn Nilsson of Norway. The ship has a total of 707 cabins plus 21 deluxe staterooms and one super suite, all with pleasing Scandinavian decor and complementary Caribbean colors. The walls are off-white and natural tones. All cabins have 100-volt current for American-made hair dryers, curlers, and electric shavers, in addition to modular bathrooms with showers.

The *Song of America* boasts the well-recognized RCCL trademark, the cantilevered Viking Crown Lounge. However, this one encircles the funnel stack some 12 decks above sea level and offers a complete 360 degree panorama. On a clear day, you can see some 20 miles (so they say). The lounge also holds about 140 passengers comfortably, almost three times more than those above the rest of a fleet, and an elevator whisks you into the center with nary a hair out of place! This is a popular spot when the *Song of America* sails away from port as the panoramic views from the Viking Crown Lounge at any hour looking back to land are both spectacular and romantic! The vessel also has a proper theater for first-run films on Cabaret Deck. Other public areas include the Can Can and Oklahoma lounges on Cabaret Deck, and the main dining room on Main Deck. This large facility is divided into the Madame Butterfly restaurant, the Ambassador Room, and the Oriental Terrace, all of which will change settings and specialties at each dinner service. In addition to the Welcome Aboard dinner, there is French Night, Italian Night, a Spanish dinner and a Caribbean dinner. The Captain's Gala Dinner on Friday is followed by America the Beautiful night, and don't forget the impressive looking Midnight Buffet! The late-night spot can be found in the Guys and Dolls Lounge on Promenade Deck. Sun-seekers will love the two huge pools, with bar and outdoor Verandah Cafe on Sun Deck, and fitness buffs should not miss the gymnasium and saunas on Bridge Deck. The Mast Bar and Sun Walk are located up on Compass Deck.

The *Song of America* sails every Sunday from Miami for Playa del Carmen, Cozumel, Grand Cayman, Ocho Rios, and Labadee. RCCL has excellent air-sea programs, and it is never a surprise to find the huge California contingent already on board and enjoying a light lunch soon after their Miami arrivals.

★★★★★+SONG OF FLOWER

Seven Seas Cruise Line Ltd.; Norwegian registry; Norwegian and Japanese officers; European crew; built in West Germany in 1986; formerly named Explorer Starship; *8282 tons; 407 feet long; 52 feet at beam; 216 passengers; crew of 144; cruising speed of 17 knots; 8 passenger decks.*

This vessel, formerly owned by the Scandinavian firm of Fenly and Eager and leased to (the now bankrupt) Exploration Cruise Lines of Seattle, Washington, was top of the line for the small ship company. Sold in 1989 to Tomoko Uenaka of Japan (whose fortune comes from the lucrative wedding industry), *Song of Flower* now sails for Seven Seas Cruise Line Ltd.—a joint venture of Japan's K Line and the Meiyo Corporation of Japan. According to an enthusiastic report from my colleague, George Devol, who publishes *Ocean and Cruise News,* the vessel is even *more* top of the line with the marriage of Ms. Uenaka's good taste and experienced cruise professionals who manage the operating company. Staff comes from other 5-plus star vessels, and the decor was redone by the same company that made Sea Goddess and Seabourn cruise ships so glamorous.

Song of Flower features all-outside staterooms with TV/video, computerized telephones, well-stocked complimentary mini bars and refrigerators, individual a/c and deluxe bathrooms with hair dryers and designer toiletries. There are several categories of staterooms, all with large sea-view windows and ample closet space. A series of 10 new suites on Main Deck has reduced the passenger capacity, which Ms. Uenaka prefers to keep under a manageable and friendly 200 persons.

Public rooms include the Observation Lounge, Main Lounge, Nightclub/Disco, and well-appointed Galaxy dining room that now features one seating at un-assigned tables. The food is prepared by an Austrian chef, and the European service is gracious. Drinks and wine are included in the cruise fare; there is no tipping and no pressure from the staff other than to be pampered.

Other amenities are a boutique, library, casino, sports deck, large sun deck with swimming pool and Jacuzzi, health club/sauna, and veranda cafe. A watersports platform is used when at anchor, and a 120-passenger *Tiny Flower* excursion vessel takes passengers into little coves and inlets. While these cruises are at present marketed primarily in Japan, on-board ambience is very friendly between the Japanese and western passengers. Menus and daily programs are in English. Watch for more news of this spectacular "new" vessel (as well as additions to the fleet), which summers in Alaska on one-week cruises from Vancouver to Misty Fjord, Ketchikan, Sitka, Tracy Arm, Juneau, and Wrangall Narrows. *Song of Flower* winters in the Far East from Singapore to Pangkor, Penang, Phuket, Pualu Seribu, Semarang, Jakarta, and Bali, as well as between Hong Kong and Kobe. A most attractive brochure in English can be obtained from Seven Seas Cruise Line, Ltd., at 1–800–661–5541. Rates are a "steal" for such a top-quality product!

★★★★SONG OF NORWAY

Royal Caribbean Cruise Line; Norwegian registry and officers, international crew; built in Wartsila shipyard, Helsinki, and originally launched in 1970; refitted and lengthened by 85 feet in 1978; 23,005 tons; 635 feet long; 80 feet at beam; 1040 passengers; crew of 400; cruising speed of 16 knots; 7 passenger decks.

The *Song of Norway* was the first-born of the RCCL fleet and she remains one of the most popular. For the second time (1986/1990), *Song of Norway* was awarded Ship of the Year status from the prestigious World Ocean and Cruise Liner Society—a group of aficionados who remit "report cards" on the ships they have traveled the past year. So, popular she certainly is! Following eight years of success, the vessel was returned to Wartsila shipyard in Helsinki for a "stretching," which added 85 feet to her midsection and increased her passenger complement by 30%. Public rooms were also increased in size, and the vessel has one of the most beautiful sun-and-pool areas afloat.

Like all RCCL vessels, the *Song*'s public rooms have been named after hit Broadway musicals. There is the *King and I* dining room, the *My Fair Lady* forward lounge, the *South Pacific* aft lounge. The famous cantilevered Viking Crown Lounge on the funnel stack still accommodates only 67 passengers comfortably, and the panorama is impressive. The Lounge of the Midnight Sun nightclub was enlarged and has simultaneous slide shows happening on several wall areas, so it's best to stay sober and enjoy! Entertainment quality is very high, as on all RCCL ships, and passengers never see the same nighttime attraction twice. The dining service is themed each night, with costumes for the waiters and different table settings as well as menu offerings.

The *Song of Norway* has a total of 535 cabins, most of them rather small but compact. Third and fourth persons in them make it very cozy, indeed. The stretching of the vessel, however, allowed for several new outside deluxe and larger cabins (13 even have bathtubs). On-board anemities are excellent, and the ship has a reputation for being beautifully managed and maintained. There is plenty to occupy the days at sea, and plenty of space in which to be active.

The *Song of Norway* sails every Sunday from San Juan, Puerto Rico, at 10 p.m. for a day at sea, followed by Martinique, Barbados, Antigua, St. Maarten, and St. Thomas. She returns to San Juan at 8:30 a.m. the following Sunday, so there should be time at either end of the cruise to explore the delightful old city of San Juan, with its many shops, museums, and art galleries.

★★★SOUTHWARD

Norwegian Cruise Lines; Norwegian registry and officers, international crew; originally built and launched in 1971; refurbished in 1984 and 1987; 16,607 tons; 541 feet long; 75 feet at beam; 754 passengers; crew of 320; cruising speed of 16 knots; 9 passenger decks.

When the *Southward* was placed into service in 1972, she was the first cruise vessel to sail on a 14-day itinerary from Miami. She did so until 1975 when the growing appeal of shorter cruises dictated the change. However, this vessel has retained something of her longer cruise atmosphere, and is considered by many to be the most regal of the three Norwegian Caribbean 7-day vessels. The *Southward* has 259 outside and 111 inside cabins, all with private facilities and all of the same Caribbean-size. Ten very pleasant, deluxe outside staterooms with separate sitting area and full bath are on Boat Deck, just forward of the El Dorado Dining Room. The main public areas are located on Mayflower Deck: the lovely Clipper Lounge, the health center, casino, library and card room, art gallery, and cocktail lounges. The swimming pool and Lido bar comprise Beach Deck, and the Crow's Nest nightclub can be found up on Tropicana Deck. A game room and shops are down on Atlantic Deck, and the two-tiered theater is between Biscayne and Caribbean decks. It's a simple ship on which to get around, and it has a cozy ambience despite its more than 700-passenger capacity. Food, service, and housekeeping amenities are as on all NCL vessels. Coffee, tea, and juice are available in the cabin around-the-clock. Finger sandwiches are available from 7 a.m. to 11 p.m. Continental breakfast service only.

The *Southward* looks sparkly and very clean since refurbishment. She departs Los Angeles every Monday and Friday for 3- and 4-day cruises to Catalina, Ensenada, and San Diego (on the 4-day itinerary).

★★★★SOVEREIGN OF THE SEAS

Royal Caribbean Cruise Line; Liberian registry; Norwegian officers and international crew; built at Chantiers de L'Atlantique, St. Nazaire; maiden voyage January 1988; 74,000 tons; 880 feet long; 106 at beam; 2282 passengers; crew of 750; cruising speed of 16 knots; 14 passenger decks.

The world's largest cruise vessel arrived in Miami on schedule for viewing by a cast of thousands and christening by former First Lady Rosalynn Carter. It seems that the Carters have enjoyed one or two RCCL cruises since their abdication, and the ship line thought it would be a nice gesture to invite Rosalyn as "godmother." In return, RCCL made a $25,000 donation to the Carter Library in Atlanta and invited over a dozen family members as well as the Secret Service to the festivities held dockside and then afloat for a week.

It is quite awesome to sail aboard this $185-million-dollar vessel— the largest yet designed, built, and afloat! *Sovereign of the Seas* is a big ship; there is no doubt about it, and it represents a departure from what has become the "traditional" cruise vessel. Upon entry, the familiar "purser's square" has become an overwhelming Centrum with multi-level sweeping staircases and glass elevators that go up and down five stories. Is this a cruise ship or have we turned the wrong corner into a Hyatt Regency Hotel?—is the primary reaction of most passengers. In the Centrum is, indeed, the purser's office, as well as shore excursion office and entrance to the Kismet dining room. The duplicate Gigi dining room is located one level below—on Main Deck—where serenaders perform during the cocktail hour. One deck below Main, if you can find them, are Cinema I and II (they were offering some tempting feature films when I was on board, but it seemed like too much of a struggle to make the show! It seems outdated to place theaters on the lowest deck possible—especially when ship lines are expecting to entice meetings and conventions on board).

The design of the vessel features most cabins forward and public rooms aft. Of the 1141 cabins, 722 are outside configuration and a staggering 419 are inside. There are 124 three-berth and 88 four-berth cabins. All are standard RCCL small, with the exception of those located on Bridge Deck, which are considered deluxe staterooms and suites. Aft on Bridge Deck, by the way, is a large and impressive health center with gymnasium and sauna and Jacuzzi. It should become one of the most popular places on board.

Public areas are enormous, and passengers do feel at times that they are not afloat but in New York City's convention center. The Folies, Finian's Rainbow, and Music Man lounges are huge; so is the Casino Royale and Anything Goes Discotheque. However, there are a few little hideaways for people who prefer more intimate settings. The Champagne Bar is an oasis in the midst of activity, nestled between the handsome library and card room/conference center. The Champagne Bar was not offering the bubbly when I was aboard, but on display was a "sovereign" of Taittinger champagne—the largest bottle ever made and offered by the wine firm for the christening of the *Sovereign*. Also offering some quietude is the 360-degree Viking Crown Lounge, which features nice ship and sea views from high above, but why doesn't it turn? The lounge overlooks the swimming pool area, which will certainly resemble a so-called "meat market" when the sun is shining high. The pool area flows into the Windjammer cafe forward, where breakfast and lunch buffets are served; aft of the pool area is a kids/teen/video games hideout.

There is plenty to see and do on board *Sovereign of the Seas* from sunrise stretch classes at 7 a.m. down through dance music in the Music Man Lounge until 1:30 a.m. Evening entertainment in the many lounges is quality stuff—if you like theatrical glitz. You can also walk the four miles of corridors, ride the 18 elevators on board or play every one of the 170 slot machines. The vessel is as high as the Statue of Liberty (171 feet) and its four giant engines are "floated" on rubber mountings to ensure smoother sailing. Captain Stangeland calls the vessel "surprisingly easy" to handle and a "dream come true."

Sovereign of the Seas sails every Saturday from Miami to Labadee, Haiti, San Juan, and St. Thomas. Upfront discounts are offered on certain sailings; all rates include airfare. Despite all the comments about this "behemoth" of a vessel, *Sovereign of the Seas* has proved to be so successful that RCCL has ordered two more! *Sovereign II* is scheduled for San Juan sailings in late 1991 and *Sovereign III* (home port yet to be determined) will arrive in 1992.

★★★★STAR CLIPPER/STAR FLYER

Star Clippers Inc; Belgium/Luxembourg flag; European officers and crew; constructed in Belgium for late 1991 and 1992 delivery; four-masted sailing ships; 357 feet long; 208 feet high; 48 feet at beam; 180 passengers; crew of 60; sailing speed of 17 knots; 4 passenger decks.

The president of this new ship line, Mikael Krafft, says that it has been his dream to build and operate a fleet of clipper ships—so, he is realizing his dream with the first two commercial sailing ships classified by Lloyd's Registry of Shipping since the 1900s. And, at 208 feet high, these spectacular clippers are the tallest of the tall ships! Inspiration for the vessels is attributed to Donald McKay, a Scottish American naval architect of the mid-1800s, who created some of the world's great clippers.

Star Clipper (late 1991) and *Star Flyer* (1992) each have been designed with some 17 sails that will speed the vessels 17 knots under full sail; however, a diesel engine will power the ships when winds are not favorable. They will also have anti-roll stabilizing tanks so that no more than five to seven degrees heeling will occur under sail or at anchor. All but 11 of the 90 cabins are outside and feature marble-lined bathrooms. In-cabin amenities include hair dryers and TV/VCRs as well as convertible lower berths.

The public areas of these so-called clipper ships are plushly designed with an abundance of polished woods and brass. The dining room seats all passengers at unassigned tables, and gentlemen are asked to wear shirts with sleeves and collars (jackets are optional). The food will be fresh and healthy and fill the plate! Each Clipper Dining Room can double as a meeting/conference area, with audio and visual equipment in place. Public space is less than on the Windstar vessels, with just a Piano Bar/Lounge/Tropical bar and a wood-panelled library with fireplace and overstuffed furniture. After-dinner entertainment will be lowkey.

Sports facilities on board the clippers include two Jacuzzis, a vitacourse on which to work off excess nourishment, and equipment for use at out-of-the-way beaches. The vessels will also carry 10 Zodiacs and four 60-person tenders. *Star Clipper* will be home ported in St. Maarten for weekly sailings to the Virgin Islands, alternating with the Leeward Islands. The Virgin Islands itinerary includes Virgin Gorda, St. Thomas, St. John, Tortola, Jobst Van Dyke, Anguilla, and Peter Island. The Leeward Islands feature St. Barts, St. Kitts, Montserrat, Antigua, Nevis, Statia, Saba, and Barbuda. *Star Flyer* will sail on the same itinerary— in reverse order—during the winter season, and from Monaco for ports in the Mediterranean during the summer months.

★★★★+STAR PRINCESS

Princess Cruises; Liberian registry; Italian officers and European crew; built in Chantiers de l'Atlantique at St. Nazaire, France, for March 1989 service; 63,524 tons; 805 feet long; 105 feet at beam; 1470 passengers; crew of 563; cruising speed of 19.5 knots; 13 passenger decks.

The first of three new "superships" to join the Princess fleet (*Star Princess* 1989; *Crown Princess* 1990; *Regal Princess* 1991), *Star Princess* was christened in Fort Lauderdale, Florida, in March 1989 by a "princess" of the screen set—the beloved Audrey Hepburn—in the presence of many dignitaries, including the chairman of P & O (the parent company of Princess Cruises). The vessel began her career with a Caribbean cruise and spent her inaugural summer in Alaska.

The *Star* features a total of 735 spacious passenger cabins. Standard outside (510) and inside (165) cabins are 180 square feet, while the 14 suites with terraces are 530 square feet and the mini-suites with terraces are 370 square feet. There are 10 wheelchair-accessible cabins of 240 square feet each. All accommodations have such amenities as refrigerators, programmable safes, dressing areas, and plenty of closet space. The teak-floor bathrooms are well designed, and complimentary toiletries are available in the higher categories, as well as built-in hair dryers and terry-cloth robes (in the suites).

Although very large and somewhat boxy in design, the vessel handles like an "angel," according to Captain Lagomarsini, and watching the entrance into Nassau harbor was quite a remarkable performance! Captain Lagomarsini, who joined Princess Cruises with the 1988 Sitmar merger, is an unusual fellow who allows no detail on board to pass him by, and both crew and passengers seem to appreciate this. The support staff in the purser's office also deserve special mention for their most pleasant personalities.

While *Star Princess* does not have the glamour of the *Royal Princess,* there was some time after the Sitmar acquisition for Princess Cruises to put its imprint on the vessel, including a contemporary art collection of note. Among the major works is a 20-foot stainless-steel kinetic sculpture entitled "Suspended Forms" by artist George Baker for the Plaza, the three-story atrium foyer that passengers first encounter upon entry and where the captain's receptions are held. The Plaza is a focal point for meeting, enjoying designer coffees ($3 each), traditional cocktails and some creative calories at La Patisserie, or listening to dance music in the evening. A dramatic staircase connects the area to Emerald deck.

Additional artworks adorn other public areas and all cabins, from standard to suites. Next to each piece is a plaque with title, a mini-description, and the name of the artist. This is a wonderful monument to the contemporary scene—especially with such names as David Hockney, Ellsworth Kelly, and Sam Francis.

One deck above the Plaza are the Galleria duty-free shops (save your money) and the Vineyard wine bar, where a selection of caviars ($3–15 per ounce) are served with appropriate libations (at appropriate prices). A popular spot, open at odd hours, that deserves better treatment. The noise level here is high, as it is throughout the ship—a definite distraction to tete-a-tetes!

Most public rooms are located on Promenade Deck, with the two-deck Starlight Lounge forward and the Fountain Court restaurant aft. The dining room accommodates a total of 800 passengers at two sittings, and the noise level is almost impossible and must be corrected. The food needs considerable work as well—even first-time cruisers made comments. Midships on Promenade Deck is Le Grand Casino and adjoining Entre Nous Bar.

A well-appointed Youth and Teen Center is located on Aloha Deck just below Lido Deck with its two swimming pools, hot tubs, Cafe Cornucopia for indoor/outdoor buffets, Characters crazy bar, and Pronto Pizzeria. I never tried Characters but was astounded by the amount of pizza served from Pronto (11 a.m. to 7 p.m.; 9 p.m. to 1:30 a.m.)! Above Sun Deck forward is the lovely Windows to the World, offering a 270-degree view of the sea in gracious surroundings. Afternoon tea is served here, as well as scarf-folding classes and the captain's repeaters party. It is a very nice space, but a wee bit difficult to locate; much easier is the beauty salon and gymnasium down on Holiday Deck.

Star Princess joins the Princess fleet of six vessels in Alaska during the summer season. She is one of the line's four "superships" in the Caribbean all winter on 7- and 10-day cruises from San Juan and Fort Lauderdale, calling at islands in the southern and eastern regions.

★★★ + STARWARD

Norwegian Cruise Lines; Bahamian registry and Norwegian officers, international crew; built and launched in 1968; refurbished in 1985; 16,100 tons; 525 feet long; 75 feet at beam; 758 passengers; crew of 315; crusing speed of 19 knots; 7 passenger decks.

The *Starward* is a proud vessel, with the completion of extensive refurbishing that not only included cabin furnishings but a redesign of the public areas as well. The former Galaxy Deck is now called the Cabaret Deck, with a glamorous new Windows on the Sea restaurant aft. Decorated in shades of violet, blue, pink and mauve, with art nouveau glass panels and woven murals of seascapes, the restaurant is a most pleasant space with panoramic views from large picture windows on three sides. Midships on Cabaret Deck are the Monte Carlo Casino and Reflections lounge. Forward is the Starlight Cabaret, which explains the name of this deck, with padded leather lounge chairs and soft color tones. The cabaret was expanded with new decking at the bow, and now boasts a sophisticated audio-visual setup for the shows.

Above on Boat Deck is Signals cafe, where buffet breakfast and lunch are served daily overlooking the swimming pool. The table and bar area is now an indoor/outdoor concept, with a signal flag decor and spiral staircase up to the Sun Deck pool. Above on Compass Deck is the Topsiders bar/hideaway—a good place for private parties and quiet conversation.

Although most of the refurbishment was cosmetic, the *Starward* also received a 400-square-foot, 50-ton ducktailed stern to provide smoother sailing in turbulent seas. The new stern also makes the vessel more fuel-efficient, by at least 10%. The *Starward* sails every Sunday from San Juan for Barbados, Martinique, St. Maarten, Antigua, and St. Thomas. Dive-In, pre- and post-cruise tours and air-sea packages are all available.

★★★★ + STELLA MARIS

Sun Line; Greek registry and crew; originally built in 1960; rebuilt in 1966; 4000 tons; 300 feet long; 45 feet at beam; 180 passengers; crew of 110; cruising speed of 16 knots; 4 passenger decks.

The *Stella Maris* is a little gem, one of the most charming vessels around. She really is "yachtlike" with an intimate feeling throughout and a very special ambience. The ship has 80 outside cabins and 13 inside, all with private facilities and all with a decor of cool colors. The 16 deluxe cabins are done in beige with either blue or red velvet chairs and accents. The public areas are also decorated in cool velvets: the

Salon Athinai and Belvedere lounges on Sun Deck and a small swimming pool aft, and the small and friendly Poseidon Restaurant on Aegean Deck with bright-blue chairs and green tablecloths. Life aboard the *Stella Maris* has a style all of its own. Service is superb because the crew cares a great deal. Bartenders (like Stavros, everyone's best friend!) learn passengers' preferences by the second day, and stewards are always waiting with a smile to pull out a chair or arrange a table for newfound friends. Captain Aslanis runs a happy ship, but departs on schedule no matter who is still ashore (we observed a couple board the vessel from a tugboat in Dubrovnik harbor because they were late)! The captain can also tell you precisely when (rare) choppy waters will end; and they do! The *Stella Maris* is a great favorite of mine, and one of the most delightful cruise ships afloat. I recommend her with all my heart, especially for travelers who feel intimidated by larger vessels. There is just one seating in the dining room (around 8 p.m.) and everyone seems to get the same royal attention. (Note: There is no lift between decks; however, this does not seem to deter those who need aid in walking as distances are small and the crew always attentive.)

During the summer season the *Stella Maris* cruises between Venice and Nice. The one-week itineraries are exceptionally well planned to offer the best possible shore experiences in this central part of the Mediterranean. The Saturday departures from Venice to Nice call at Dubrovnik, Corfu, Valletta, Messina, Capri, Elba, and Portofino (weather permitting, because tenders are employed). On alternate Saturdays the *Maris* sails from Nice to Venice, calling at Portofino, Elba, Sorrento, Messina, Katakolon, Corfu, and Dubrovnik. Air France is offering good air-sea programs between the U.S. and France for these cruises. And to be really chic, you can take the Simplon Orient-Express between Paris and Venice at the beginning or end of your cruise. It is a terrific complement to the *Stella Maris* itinerary! But, if you do, be sure to pack some 1920s gear for dinner aboard—feathers and spats and such. It's great fun to "dress" in the evening as you ride the rails from Italy to Switzerland and France. In the spring and fall the *Stella Maris* sails every Friday from Piraeus to Istanbul, Kusadasi, and Bodrum in Turkey, Rhodes, Heraklion (Crete), Santorini and Delos (weather permitting), and Mykonos. These cruises are offered in April and May, September and October—perfect times of the year for such an event. The *Stella Maris* is my baby—I love her!

★★★+STELLA OCEANIS

Sun Line; Greek registry and crew; originally built in 1965 and formerly named the Aphrodite; *rebuilt in 1967 and relaunched; 6000 tons; 350 feet long; 53 feet at beam; 280 passengers; crew of 140; cruising speed of 17 knots; 6 passenger decks.*

The *Stella Oceanis,* with 300 passengers and 6000 tons, is the middle member of the Sun Line fleet. This is a very pleasant vessel, but it lacks the class of the *Solaris* or the unique charm of the *Maris II.* The *Oceanis* has a total of 159 cabins, of which 113 are on the outside. All have private facilities. There are 20 deluxe accommodations—many of them are connecting—and six deluxe suites. The public rooms are few but more than adequate for the size of the vessel. With the exception of the Plaka Taverna, a terrific room on Lido Deck that becomes the late-night disco and is available for movies or private parties, the public space is centered on Oceanis Deck. Here the Salon Minos with gold carpets and velvet chairs seats the entire ship complement amid the murals of Minos the Bull. The main lounge has a pleasant bar and a small club in the aft for private gatherings. A boutique and casino lead the way to the Aphrodite Restaurant, also designed with gold and blue accents, with pleasant ocean-view windows. There are two meal seatings.

During the summer season, from early April through October, the *Stella Oceanis* is at home in Piraeus for cruises to the Greek Islands and Turkey. The four-day sailings departing Monday evenings call at Hydra, Thira (weather permitting), Heraklion, Rhodes, Kusadasi, and Mykonos. The Friday morning sailings of three days visit Mykonos, Rhodes, Kusadasi, and Patmos. These popular cruises are available from the first week in April through October. A pity, but *Stella Oceanis* does not cross to the Western Hemisphere for the winter season any longer.

★★★★★STELLA SOLARIS

Sun Line; Greek registry and crew; originally built in 1953 and formerly named the Camboge; *rebuilt in 1973 and launched as the* Stella Solaris; *18,000 tons; 550 feet long; 72 feet at beam; 620 passengers; crew of 310; cruising speed of 20 knots; 8 passenger decks.*

Flagship of the Sun Line fleet, the *Stella Solaris* is a gracious and well-maintained vessel with excellent service. The all-Greek crew is friendly and attentive and most of the cruise staff outstanding (everyone's favorite is a charming young lady from Mexico named Beatrice). The *Stella Solaris* is Mrs. K's pride and joy, and her tender, loving care is most apparent.

I have sailed three times aboard *Stella Solaris,* and each sojourn has been just splendid. We are not discussing here a glitzy vessel with state-of-the-art amenities; rather, a very comfortable and homey ship that relaxes and refreshes the soul from the beginning of the cruise to the end. In the Greek Islands and Turkey, the *Stella Solaris* is like taking one's home around on the back because the ship is such an extension of the ports. In the Black Sea, the ship was a haven from all the dust and depression found in Russian ports—the Romanian port of Constanza was a more pleasant experience.

During the winter seaon *Stella Solaris* is known for her pioneering Amazon River cruises, led by renowned lecturer Captain Loren McIntyre, who has climbed the Andes to the source of the river and canoed its many tributaries. McIntyre is a great addition to these Amazon River cruises, which Sun Line has now extended. New are sailing from Buenos Aires to Valparaiso, which feature a passage through the Straits of Magellan and optional fly-overs of Antarctica and Cape Horn. It is a very exciting winter program that does not include (thank the dear Lord) Carnival in Rio!

The *Stella Solaris* has a total of 329 cabins with private facilities, of which 250 cabins are on the outside (218 have full bathtubs). Of the 66 deluxe staterooms, 28 suites on Boat Deck can accommodate a third person on the sofa bed. These suites are very comfortable, but passengers should note that joggers begin making their miles around Boat Deck about 7 a.m. Frankly, I found this a wonderful breakfast-in-bed diversion, but others may prefer lower-based cabins for more quietude. All the cabins are nicely furnished. I would avoid cabins called "outside communicating rooms," which I think are badly designed with partitions that are too thin to afford adequate privacy. The public spaces are very pleasant. The main lounge is the center of activity for briefings and entertainment, although the Piano Bar is more popular with those who like cocktails at sunset or sailing away. Other public areas are the Monte Carlo Room and bar/grill (mainly for drinks) on Solaris Deck, a card room on Boat Deck (aft of the deluxe cabins), and the Lido bar and swimming pool on Lido Deck (where a fine buffet luncheon is served). The vessel also has a small gymansium/massage/sauna and a children's room on Golden Deck, a lovely theater on Sapphire Deck, and a disco way down on Main Deck (if you can ever find it).

The dining room is conveniently located on Solaris Deck and, if you insist, it is possible to have a table for two. Service is excellent and the Greek specialties are definitely the best. Upon request, you will receive more wonderful Greek dishes than appear on the menu. The luncheon buffets in the Lido are *very* popular, with an overwhelming variety of cold salads. If you are a feta cheese fan (the ship stocks approximately two tons per season), you will love the Greek salads! The kitchens are spotless and wonderful soups are simmering around the clock. In the Solaris Deck bars, fresh daily made potato chips are the nemesis of all passengers—but well worth every nasty calorie!

Among the many wonderful appetizers in the Greek recipe books is one that Sun Line does especially well—Taramasalata (red fish roe puree): Place one jar of Tarama in blender at low speed until creamy. Add 4 Tbsps. grated onions, 7 slices white bread (crusts trimmed) that was soaked in water and squeezed dry. Blend. Add slowly 1 cup olive oil, juice of two lemons until mixture is white and creamy. Garnish with parsley and Greek olives. Serve as dip or on crackers. Wonderful, but where is the garlic? (I would add at least one minced clove.)

During the season in the Aegean *Stella Solaris* sails on Mondays from Piraeus on two separate itineraries. The Greek Islands and Turkey visits Dikili, Istanbul, Kusadasi, Rhodes, Heraklion, Santorini and Delos (weather permitting), and Mykonos. The Greek Islands, Egypt, Israel, and Turkey calls at Rhodes, Alexandria, Port Said, Ashdod, Samos, and Kusadasi. The cruises are offered from late April through October and are combinable for a wonderful two-week sailing.

The annual Primavera eastbound transatlantic sailing of the *Stella Solaris* departs south Florida at the end of March for approximately three weeks to Piraeus, calling at Madeira, Lisbon, Cadiz, Tangier, Gibraltar, Barcelona, Palma de Mallorca, Villefranche, Livorno, Civitavecchia, Capri, Messina, and Katakolon. The eastbound sailing to Fort Lauderdale takes place in mid-September.

★★★★SUN VIKING

Royal Caribbean Cruise Line; Norwegian registry and officers, international crew; built in Wartsila shipyard, Helsinki and launched in 1972; 18,559 tons; 563 feet long; 80 feet at beam; 726 passengers; crew of 320; cruising speed of 16 knots; 8 passenger decks.

The *Sun Viking* is the last of the Royal Caribbean vessels of her original size and configuration. Last to be launched in the cruise market, the *Sun Viking* was never stretched because the *Song of America* was ordered, so she now looks small compared with her companions, especially if you are standing in the main entrance hall and looking fore and aft along Karl Johans Gate (where Information, cruise director's office, and gift shops are located). Like her sisters, the *Sun Viking*'s public areas are named after Broadway hit musicals. Located on Restaurant Deck are the HMS Pinafore Dining Room, the Merry Widow Lounge, and the Annie Get Your Gun Lounge (with its Sitting Bull Bar over to the side). But my favorite place on this and other Royal Caribbean ships is the circular, cantilevered Viking Crown Lounge ten stories above the sea and reachable only by outside staircase. This lounge is intimate, for it holds just 60 persons, whether for a predinner cocktail or quiet, romantic evening drink. The second most attractive lounge on the vessel is the nightclub/disco, Lounge of the Northern Lights, which features on-the-wall entertainment, a travelogue picture story with slides taken by RCCL's own photographer, who travels the globe in search of this material. There is no cinema/theater on board, so feature films are shown in the Annie Get Your Gun lounge when convenient. (This lounge was refurbished during a recent wet-docking of the vessel.) Live, late-night entertainment can be found in the Lounge of the Northern Lights, after which disco music continues until about 3 a.m. The *Sun Viking* tends to attract a livelier clientele than most cruise ships in the area. These passengers also enjoy the ShipShape program, especially the reward of a free T-shirt if they work hard enough.

The *Sun Viking* has 266 outside and 114 inside cabins, all with private facilities. They are not the most spacious afloat, but are beautifully serviced. The vessel features the same food service and entertainment features as the *Song of Norway,* plus a sauna/massage center adjacent to the topside midships swimming pool.

The *Sun Viking* was named Ship of the Year in 1982 by the prestigious World Ocean and Cruise Liner Society, whose members "rate" the vessels they have experienced. There is nothing like contented passengers—and the *Sun Viking* is known for making people happy. One reason is sure to be the managable size of the vessel; "stretching" has not proved to be such a great idea for many cruise passengers. Still, RCCL receives excellent marks from a contented clientele who are happy with a pleasant cruise experience on well-run vessels. Everything on board occurs with the precision of a Swiss watch; in fact, door-to-door service is among the best.

During the winter months *Sun Viking* sails from San Juan every Sunday evening for Barbados, St. Lucia, Guadeloupe, St. Barts, and St. Thomas. During the summer of 1990 she became the first RCCL vessel to offer European cruises with 12-day sailings from Lisbon to the Mediterranean, from London to ports in the Baltic, and from Lisbon to Northern European cities. This was an exciting breakthrough for *Sun Viking* and RCCL, and the company expects to be even more "global" with its ships in the future.

★★★SUNWARD II

Norwegian Caribbean Lines; Bahamian registry and Norwegian officers, international crew; originally built in 1971 and formerly named the Cunard Adventurer; *rebuilt and relaunched in 1977 as the* Sunward II; *refurbished 1985; 14,100 tons; 492 feet long; 70.5 feet at beam; 670 passengers; crew of 315; cruising speed of 16 knots; 7 passenger decks.*

The *Sunward II* is yet another Norwegian Caribbean Lines success story. This vessel was the former ailing Cunard *Adventurer* that some travelers said was on her last legs and no longer seaworthy (even though not even five years old). But NCL bought the vessel and transformed her into a fun-filled and sunny ship for three- and four-day cruises to the Bahamas. NCL scheduled the usual ports of Nassau and Freeport, but added an Out Island just for sunning, snorkeling, and swimming. It has worked so well that many passengers choose this cruise just for the beautiful "Bahamarana" beach party at NCL's Pleasure Island. The ship has about 50 Sunfish, rental equipment for snorkeling, and five instructors on board for the beach call. Cabanas have been built past the sand dunes, and the ship's band plays on while you play and party (food and drink are brought ashore). The Dive-In program is Number One here.

A very elegant "retired" gentleman we know won a cruise aboard the *Sunward II*. He upgraded himself to a suite, took along a lady friend, and had a wonderful time. He said he was impressed by the number of incentive groups on board and the good mix of ages. It was not a rah-rah crowd as one might think, but a nice complement of business executives, young couples and families.

The *Sunward II* has 238 outside and 121 inside cabins, all with private facilities. The accommodations are standard but well designed, and there are plenty of suites and larger-than-average outside staterooms. This vessel was refurbished with a few days of good fun in mind, and that is the feeling projected throughout the public areas: the split-level Sunburst Dining Room, the Bahamarana Lounge on Boat Deck where the on-board Las Vegas–style revues are staged, the Crow's Nest Nightclub, the Buccaneer bar with outdoor stage, and the Lido Cafe/Disco. In addition, there is an enlarged casino with bar as well as enclosed cinema on Bridge Deck, and a large swimming pool area with sauna and massage rooms aft on Bahamas Deck. There are a few shops on Atlantic Deck and a beauty salon down on Caribbean Deck.

Every Friday the *Sunward II* departs Miami for Nassau and one of the Bahamas' most beautiful atolls in the Berry Islands. The vessel returns to Miami on Monday morning. Every Monday afternoon the *Sunward II* sails for Nassau, NCL's Pleasure Island, and Freeport. The vessel returns to Miami on Friday morning.

★★★ + TROPICALE

Carnival Cruise Lines; Liberian registry; Italian officers and international crew; built in Aalborg, Denmark, especially for Carnival Cruise Lines; commissioned in January 1982; refurbished in 1989; 36,674 tons; 660 feet long; 85 feet at beam; 1022 passengers; crew of 550; cruising speed of 22 knots; 10 passenger decks.

The $100-million *Tropicale* made her debut in January 1982, and Carnival Cruise Lines called its new vessel the eighth largest cruise ship afloat (at the time). Certainly, she was the first of several new ships scheduled to make waves during the decade of the 80s. The 1200-passenger *Tropicale* has a distinctive outward appearance, with a winglike funnel that was originally planned for aesthetics' sake but has proved to be effective in moving the smoke outward. Other innovative features include a below-water bulbous bow for fuel efficiency (makes the vessel appear to be on water skis), and computerized engine room and bridge. A satellite reception dish brings TV signals into the cabins but does not seem too successful more than several miles from shore. The vessel is energy-efficient and even recycles about 80 tons of nonpotable water each day for maintenance functions. A squared-off stern was apparently designed for economy in building the accommodations section.

The 511 passenger cabins were installed fabricated; even the lavatories were constructed as entire units. Cabin size is unusually spacious for a modern-day vessel, and the majority have large seaview windows as well as twin beds that can be converted to king-size configuration. Wardrobe and storage spaces are both plentiful (beds are built high enough for suitcases to slide easily under them), and all cabins are card-coded, which means you can never forget your number. Closed-circuit televisions overhead bring feature films several times daily, and 24-hour room service is also available. Keep it simple on the room service order, and expect plastic dishes—which is far better than the paper plates that arrived on the inaugural sailing! If plastic in the cabin is offensive, take the stairs to the Boiler Room where your scrambled eggs will be still hot and eaten on deck—on plastic plates.

The Boiler Room, aft on Lido Deck, is also the scene of hot dogs and hamburgers at lunchtime and afternoon tea with cakes. There is plenty of deck space on the *Tropicale,* although even three (albeit small) swimming pools are inadequate for the size of the passenger complement. Popular on tropical evenings is the Patio Bar, which remains open until an unorthodox 6 a.m., where a calypso band plays for dancing and fountains take over in the main pool. The Grand Midnight Buffet is also served here. Otherwise, passengers flock to the Tropicana Lounge where extravaganzas are offered nightly after dinner, or to the Islands in the Sun lounge on deck above, which appears to be a bit more cozy (but is actually huge)! The late-night set frequents the Extra-Z Disco or the casino, both of which close only when the last group goes.

The 658-capacity Palm Restaurant, surprisingly, is located down on Riviera deck (the current trend is to enjoy sea views). Meal presentation is fine and the dinner menus quite a departure from the usual Carnival fare. Special theme nights break the monotony. All beef dishes are excellent and obvious care is used in the selection of top-grade meat. A special wine list selected by Vice-President Bob Dickinson is for those willing to pay a little more.

The *Tropicale* boasts 12 suites up on Verandah Deck, with their own sea-view balconies, bars, and bathtubs plus separate conversation areas. The suites are pleasant, although the sitting areas seem less bright and cheerful than the average cabin. The *Tropicale* was refurbished in late 1989 under the direction of Carnival's in-house architect Joe Farcus, who designed the vessel. The main showroom, Tropicana Lounge, was redone with new stage and banquettes. Other public rooms with new interiors are Islands in the Sun lounge, Paradise Club casino, and Chopsticks piano bar—converted from the card and video room. The dual promenades and cabins also received attention.

Since January 1990 the *Tropicale* has sailed from San Juan, joining the *Festivale,* on cruises to the lower Caribbean. The *Tropicale* departs every Saturday at 10 p.m. for St. Thomas, Guadeloupe, Grenada, La Guaira/Caracas, and Aruba. Friday is spent at sea before the ship's return to San Juan on Saturday morning. Air-sea plus pre- and post-cruise packages are available.

★★★UNIVERSE

World Explorer Cruises; Liberian registry; Chinese and international crew; originally built in U.S. in 1953 and formerly called the Badger Mariner, Atlantic, *and* Universe Campus*; rebuilt in 1957 and refurbished in 1990; 18,100 tons; 564 feet long; 76 feet at beam; 550 passengers; crew of 220; cruising speed of 15 knots; 6 passenger decks.*

The 550-passenger *Universe* provides a different type of cruise experience. The atmosphere on board is casual and friendly and the accommodations all have private facilities, but they have a dormitory feel. Cruise emphasis here is on learning, and the *Universe* makes two around-the-world cruises each year (September and January). This Semester at Sea program can accommodate about 500 students, who do their research and field trips in worldwide ports of call.

From mid-May through August, the learning process is open to the general public as the *Universe* makes 14-day cruises from Vancouver to Wrangell, Juneau, Skagway, Glacier Bay, Columbia Glacier/Valdez, Anchorage (Whittier), Sitka, Ketchikan and Victoria. The vessel offers culture without glitz—seminars on arts, customs, history, and geology of the ports visited in both slide presentations and lectures. For further research, there is an 12,000-volume library on board.

Lecturers include political scientists, naturalists, historians, anthropologists and geologists—many of them college professors. The cruise manager, Ron Valentine, who teaches advanced law and history when not on aboard, coordinates the ship's classical entertainment program. Past sailings have featured chamber ensembles, string quartets and light opera.

Black tie and fancy dress are to be left behind on this cruise as there is neither glitz nor glitter of the Las Vegas–type of entertainment on this vessel. Instead, there is plenty of good conversation and even some gentlemen hosts for ladies' companionship while dining, dancing, and all ship and shore activities. This is a cruise on which real friends are found and kept, according to so many previous passengers.

There are a few better cabins on Boat Deck, but most are standard and can accommodate third and fourth persons. A few single cabins are available and not overly priced. There are four lounges—the Commodore, Mandarin, Denali, Alyeska (the Aleute word for Alaska)—the North Star nightclub, a full theater, youth center, meeting room, exercise room, full laundry, swimming pool, gift shop and glass-enclosed promenade (one side is non-smoking). The dining room is located on Main Deck.

World Explorer Cruises has instituted a convenient on-board credit system, so passengers can sign and settle at the end—just like the more glamorous ships. Rates are extremely reasonable for such a fascinating experience, and pre- or post-cruise stays are available in Vancouver or Seattle.

★★★VICTORIA

Chandris Fantasy Cruises; Panamanian registry; Greek officers and international crew; built in 1936 as Dunnottar Castle; *rebuilt in 1958; last refurbished in 1990; 19,000 tons; 573 feet long; 72 feet at beam; 550 passengers; crew of 330; cruising speed of 16 knots; 7 passengers decks.*

The *Victoria* has been another favorite of the Fantasy fleet for many loyal Chandris passengers; the interior of the vessel is old-world and still very impressive. The woods and the size of the public areas are wonderful! Following a drydocking in early 1990, the *Victoria* began a new life offering Baltic Sea and North Cape cruises from late May through mid-September and then Canary Islands cruises from Genoa. The *Victoria* is well suited to these itineraries, and they should be very popular with both North Americans and Europeans.

The *Victoria* has a total of 279 cabins, of which only 63 are inside configuration. More than half the cabins are 180 square feet, and the suites are approximately 290 square feet. Ten top cabins were installed on Pearl Deck some years ago, where the gym/sauna is also located (near the children's playroom). Below on Rendezvous Deck are the main public rooms—Riviera ballroom, El Patio lounge, a small casino and several slots, shopping center and the enclosed promenade flowing into a Winter Garden area. Two swimming pools aft are surrounded by a spacious Lido Deck. A double-tiered theater is located on Sapphire and Emerald decks, and the Roman dining room is on Coral Deck.

During the winter season the *Victoria* sails at 11:45 p.m. every Monday from San Juan for St. Thomas, Martinique, Grenada, La Guaria (for Caracas) and Curacao. Sunday is a sea day and the vessel returns to San Juan at 8 a.m. on Monday. A special two-week sailing takes place in early January.

★★★+ VIKING SERENADE

Royal Caribbean Cruise Line; Bahamian registry; Scandinavian officers; international crew; built in France in 1982 as Scandinavia; *refurbished in 1985 as* Star Dancer; *refurbished in 1989 and renamed* Viking Serenade; *27,000 tons; 608 feet long; 87 feet at beam; 976 passengers; crew of 480; cruising speed of 21 knots; 7 passenger decks.*

For such a young vessel, *Viking Serenade* seems to have already enjoyed a very full life. Designed to carry vehicles (cars and RVs) as well as passengers, she first sailed from New York to the Bahamas, but not with great success. Most recently sailing as *Star Dancer* for Admiral Cruises, she was brought into the Royal Caribbean fleet in January 1990 to inaugurate the company's presence in Alaska and Mexico, but not before the distinctive Crown and Anchor logo appeared on her stack and the traditional royal blue stripe around her white hull.

Other decorative changes consistent with RCCL style include artwork from Mayan images to Alaskan landscapes in the public rooms, a lobby embellished with brass and bronze, and tasteful color schemes in cabins and lounges. The updated Starlight Lounge now features Las Vegas–style revues and cruise staff shows in the evening. Other onboard amenities are Stanley's Pub, casino, disco, library/card room, Sundown lounge, Lido bar/grill, health club/spa, outdoor swimming pool, and Windows of the World dining room—although I expect Royal Caribbean to change the names to suit its Broadway musical theme.

There are 284 outside cabins with large picture windows and 200 inside cabins, all with two lower beds (some of which are convertible). Some cabins can accommodate third and fourth persons, and some can be combined into suites. There is one handicap-equipped cabin on board.

Every Sunday from the end of May to mid-September, *Viking Serenade* departs Vancouver to the Inside Passage, Tracy Arm, Skagway, Haines, Juneau, Ketchikan, Misty Fjord, and through the Inside Passage back to Vancouver. Her winter program sails from Los Angeles on Saturdays to Puerto Vallarta, Mazatlan, Cabo San Lucas, and cruising the Baja Peninsula.

★★★★★+ VISTAFJORD

Cunard/NAC; Bahamian registry and northern European crew; launched in 1973; refitted in 1983; 24,500 tons; 628 feet long; 82 at beam; 749 passengers; crew of 390; cruising speed of 20 knots; 8 passenger decks.

The *Vistafjord* is a happy ship and settled splendidly into the Cunard family. In the past few years, the vessel has been refurbished and rejuvenated to such an extent that she is one of the finest afloat. Cunard's additions work well—the two-level indoor/outdoor Club Viking, the Golden Door Spa at Sea, an enlarged casino, a room full of IBM computers with an excellent team of instructors, and the two dozen modular cabins (some of which can be opened into spacious suites). The public rooms are sparkling and the Lido Cafe overlooking the swimming pool area is a charming spot from early riser coffee to buffet luncheons, tea with cakes and cocktails.

The modular cabins (set in where shuffleboard used to be) are spacious and bright, furnished with light woods and fabrics and boasting plenty of mirrors and closet space. The only wrinkle is that one must be quite slim to turn around in the bathroom. Twin beds are placed side by side, so couples can get cozy. Cabins on the top of the module have private terraces and sea views between lifeboats. Those on the deck below have sliding glass doors and a view of the action on the Promenade.

Although the *Vistafjord* was designed in the early 1970s, she has that old-world elegance suited to long and leisurely cruises because she is a replica of sistership *Sagafjord*. Hence, the passenger/space ratio is superior both in original accommodations and public rooms. In contrast to the *Sagafjord,* which caters primarily to Americans, the *Vistafjord* is European in ambience and attitude. She is very popular with the well-heeled German-speaking segment and attracts a good percentage on the European itineraries. Some tend to be very, very pushy and create chaos (especially when there is food around); there are also a sprinkling of British, French, Spanish, and Italian passengers, so the mix is interesting.

Food, glorious food is what the *Vistafjord* is all about although not so brilliant as it once was because Chef Rudi Sodamin was brought ashore by Cunard to mastermind the menus aboard its five luxury vessels. Still, it is among the best afloat, especially the abundance of fresh seafood at luncheon buffets! With such a European ambience on board the *Vistafjord,* dishes tend to cater to the German palate; however, health-conscious Americans have the option of bypassing the heavy sauces at every meal. The dishes are beautifully presented and dining-room service is warm and personal. The young European stewards are, for the most part, in training for their own (or family-owned) restaurants and very eager to please.

Amenities on board the *Vistafjord* are superior to other vessels and equal to the *Sagafjord.* Every passenger receives a terry-cloth robe (fresh daily), as well as a hat (men) and bag (women), a daily edition of the *Herald Tribune* (sent by satellite), perfumed soaps (bad for the skin but terrific for washing undies), complimentary skeetshooting and launderette, a staff that remembers each passenger's name and preferences in food and drink, and various other cabin gifts including the traditional ashtray enscribed with itinerary. It is a pleasure to accept such "amenities'' as normal; it is difficult for most passengers to return to the real world. Undoubtedly, these subtle details result in a repeat factor as high as 60% on many *Vistafjord* cruises. (Which does not mean that first-time passengers are discriminated against—they, too, get hooked!)

The *Vistafjord* spends April through November in Europe, offering a series of sailings that range from the fjords of Scandinavia to the Baltic, around western Europe and Italy, the Holy Land, and the Black Sea. The *Vistafjord* is also fond of the Canary Islands and parts of northwest Africa. A special Holy Land cruise in spring 1990 featured Music and Theatre Festivals at Sea, which we hope will be repeated in ensuing seasons. Following a transatlantic crossing to the Western Hemisphere, *Vistafjord* offers some Caribbean cruises before sailing for the South Pacific. The winter season of *Vistafjord* is a mixed bag as she fills in on world cruises when *QE2* is unavailable, so if you are a fan of this vessel, check in advance on her winter schedule. This is a ship that must be booked well in advance if you want a particular cabin category (and a sea view, as many cabins look into lifeboats).

★★★★★WESTERDAM

Holland America Line; Bahamian registry; Dutch officers; Indonesian/ Filipino crew; built 1986 in Papenburg, West Germany, for Home Lines; stretched in 1989 by HAL; 52,000 tons; 798 feet long; 95 feet at beam; 1476 passengers; crew of 700; cruising speed of 21 knots; 8 passenger decks.

The *Westerdam*, originally constructed as the *Homeric* for Home Lines and delivered in 1986, became a member of the Holland America family in November 1988. A year later the vessel was returned to the West German yard for a $65-million refit featuring the placement of a 130-foot section mid-ship. This section, which was part of the original design, added 10,000 gross tons, 247 new cabins, several attractive public rooms, and an expansion of outdoor facilities. The 1476-passenger *Westerdam* is now the largest vessel in the Holland America fleet.

Among the cabin additions are four especially equipped for the handicapped (002 and 021 on Navigation Deck; 068 and 087 on Upper Promenade Deck). Highlight of the refit is the two-level, 800-seat Admiral's (show) Lounge, converted from two lounges on separate decks. Adjacent to the show lounge is a series of new spaces—the Bookchest (library), Explorers Lounge (afternoon tea is served here), Ocean Bar (where all the action begins about 11 a.m.), some meeting and card rooms, and boutiques. Aft of the new area is the Big Apple teen club, Peartree saloon and disco, and Casino.

The restaurants aboard *Westerdam* received great attention. The Amsterdam dining room increased from 520 to 875 seats, and the Lido

buffet—a Holland America trademark—was expanded. A second buffet, the Verandah Restaurant, adjacent to the magra-domed Verandah
Pool on Sun Deck is also new—as well as additional seating and two
whirlpools. More seating and a tennis court were also added to what is
now known as Sports Deck.

With the $1 million of 17th- and 18th-century Dutch artifacts (in-
cluding a cannon brought from the deep by a French fisherman) around
the ship, the *Westerdam* has truly become a Holland America family
member. She has become a mega-ship, however, and the length of her
corridors can seem endless. Plan extra time for finding the Amsterdam
dining room!

The *Westerdam*'s re-entry in Spring 1990 was a series of sold-out
10-day cruises to the Caribbean and Bermuda from New York City.
Since the company has not offered sailings from New York harbor since
headquarters were transferred to Seattle, it was a nostalgic time for many
loyal Holland America passengers. Following a 22-day repositioning
cruise to Alaska, the *Westerdam* joins the HAL fleet until October and
one-week sailings from Fort Lauderdale called Four-Port-Plus. This eastern
Caribbean itinerary features San Juan, St. Thomas, Nassau, and Tortola
(with an excursion to Virgin Gorda).

★★★★★WIND STAR/WIND SONG/WIND SPIRIT

*Windstar Sail Cruises; Bahamian registry; European officers and
service crew; built in Le Havre and launched 1986, 1987, 1988; sail
cruisers; 5350 tons; 440 feet long; 52 feet at beam; 4 masts with 6
computer-controlled sails; 150 passengers; crew of 84; 4 passenger decks.*

These three sailing vessels offer the most unique and delightful
cruise experience afloat! They are beautiful to behold from both near
and far. Their sleek exterior is breathtaking, especially when under full
sail. When passengers are ashore and view the vessel at anchor they
take great pride in saying "That's my ship!" A great deal of hard work
and thoughtful design in the making of these vessels has resulted in
ships of great style. Everything about them is pleasing to the eye and
senses, although they are not for everyone. Windstar was designed for
people who enjoy the elements—who like to sit on polished teak decks
and watch the wake, converse with fellow passengers, revel in the wind
flirting with sails, or enjoy a book from the well-stocked library on
board. There is no razmataz as the ambience is truly "casual chic."
Dress accordingly, and do your own thing.

The compact cabins were thoughtfully conceived, with two round
portholes, twin beds that convert to queen size, a welcome refrigerator/
mini-bar, state-of-the-art telephone, small wall safe, TV/video (a selection of tapes is available at the purser's office), and plenty of storage

space. The teak-floored bathrooms are the best afloat, designed in a cloverleaf with super shower, hairdryer, terry-cloth robes to match the towels, lovely soaps, shampoo, and Evian water spray (for touring in hot climates). All cabins are equal, although a few can accommodate a third person. They are truly a pleasure in which to spend a week—and they are kept spotless by a bevy of attractive young ladies in white shorts. A floral arrangement, a basket of fruit replenished daily, and nighttime chocolates complete the picture. Continental breakfast and snacks are available in the cabin around the clock.

The public spaces on the Windstar vessels are beautiful. The sky-lighted main lounge is pleasant by day or night; the dining room is like an elegant restaurant. The top-deck veranda restaurant serves the best buffet breakfasts and lunches ever encountered for dining inside or under umbrellas. The aft deck boasts a small swimming pool and hottub where early bird coffee is served and where the bar is a popular watering hole. A resident pianist tinkles the keys of a small piano in the late afternoon.

Also popular is the aft sports platform one deck below, where inflatable motor launches offer waterskiing. Snorkeling and scuba equipment and windsurfing boards are also complimentary, or you can use the platform for a dip in the sea. There is a small gymnasium adjacent with sauna, just big enough for a loving couple. Other facilities include a beauty salon, medical office, and two shops (full of chic but pricey items—the Windstar watches are most tempting), and a compact but very lively and popular casino. At night, the veranda restaurant becomes a disco, but it has not proved to be overwhelmingly popular as passengers prefer to retire early after a full day of watersports, sun, and the sea.

These vessels are not for the single traveler unless in a congenial group. There is no arranged seating in the dining room, so couples tend to sit with new (or old) friends, and there is a full program of activities available daily, but nothing that resembles the normal cruise-ship routine. With approximately 150 passengers on board, the ships are perfect for small groups, and there is pleasant interaction between them. Food is nouvelle whatever and the menu varies according to cruising region—fantastic tropical fruits around Tahiti, more emphasis on presentation in the Mediterranean. The dining room is always a pleasure, and it's fun to dress up a bit in the evening, although ties are not necessary.

As so many passengers become fascinated with the mechanics of sailing the ship, the bridge is always open and the captain or his first officer always willing to explain the instruments and computers. It is especially interesting in the South Seas, where the fantastic vistas hide coral reefs and the vessel must be carefully maneuvered between them. Here, Frenchman Jean-Marie Guillou, captain of *Wind Song,* delights in entertaining his passengers with his knowledge of French Polynesia.

Guillou is just one of the charming and personable staff on board—but he leads the pack!

Wind Star and *Wind Spirit* both winter in the Caribbean and separate for the summer season. *Wind Star* sails weekly from Antigua to St. Barthelemy, Rendezvous Island, St. Martin, St. Kitts, Barbuda, and Ille des Saintes from late October until April 1. *Wind Spirit* departs from either St. Thomas or Barbados on one-week cruises with unusual port calls. Her St. Thomas itinerary features St. John, St. Martin, Rendezvous Island, St. Barthelemy, Virgin Gorda, and Jost van Dyke. From Barbados, she visits Soufriere, Bequia, Mustique, Tobago Cays and Pigeon Pt., Grenada, and Palm Island.

From May through September, *Wind Star* offers one-week cruises from Monte Carlo, Venice, and Rome (Civitavecchia), with many calls at the fashionable ports along the Italian Riviera. New for *Wind Spirit* in 1990 was a season in Alaska, sailing between Prince Rupert and Juneau. She must have been quite a sight among the glaciers and forests, as she visited Ketchikan, Misty Fjords, Petersburg, Tracy Arm, Sitka, and Skagway! Repositioning cruises included a transit of the Panama Canal.

Meanwhile, *Wind Song* continues her very successful year-round Saturday-to-Saturday cruises from Papeete, Tahiti, to Huahine, Raiatea, Bora Bora, and Moorea. This is a wonderful way to see the Society Islands—which are very beautiful but very, very expensive ashore. Also, the natives are not overly friendly, so *Wind Song* serves as a wonderful cocoon from which to enjoy Polynesia. Two 14-day cruises through the Marquesas are also available in June and October. *Wind Song* is popular with West Coast cruise passengers because getting to Tahiti from there is just a skip and a jump—it's much more difficult from the East!

★★★★★WORLD DISCOVERER

Society Expeditions Cruises; Liberian registry; West German officers; Filipino crew; built in 1974 in Germany; refurbished 1984; 3150 tons; 285 feet long; 50 feet at beam; 140 passengers; crew of 75; cruising speed of 12.5 knots; 6 passenger decks.

The *World Discoverer* was designed and constructed as a specialist cruise ship, with a shallow draft, easy maneuverability, and a strengthened hull to navigate around icebergs. In addition, her equipment on the bridge is among the most sophisticated possible, and the vessel carries super-launches and inflatable Zodiacs for exploring narrow and otherwise impassable waters.

The *Discoverer* was refurbished a few years ago by society decorator Carlton Varney, but toned down to a more normal ambience by owner Heiko Klein, who wisely realized that his passengers preferred a less dramatic atmosphere. The compact vessel accommodates 140 passengers in attractive outside lower-berth cabins with ample storage, private facilities, music system, and air conditioning. Klein has also lowered prices since taking over the company and has made a distinguished effort to work through travel agents.

The Lido lounge is gracious in quiet blues, while the Main Salon has an oriental theme with brass palm trees and a black/white postage-stamp dance floor. The Marco Polo dining room is all pink with large seaview windows, lovely china and crystal, and covered chairs for open-seating service. Food is in the hands of the Swiss and Austrians, with a focus on European cuisine and served with a flair. A small swimming pool aft of the Lido lounge has teak benches, with two spacious sunning decks above. A lecture room/cinema is located on Observation Deck; the library and a small shop are inside the promenade area on Boat Deck, and the beauty/fitness center are down on Spa Deck.

The *World Discoverer* explores the whole wonderful world! In true expedition style, she was the first vessel to cruise New Guinea's Sepik River, as well as land on Peter I Island—usually unapproachable because of heavy Antarctic pack ice (1982). In 1985 *World Discoverer* made the first crossing by a passenger cruise ship from the Pacific to the Atlantic—west to east through the Northwest Passage. And in the Crystal Jubilee (1989) Year of Society Expeditions Cruises, *Discoverer* became the first non-Ecuadorian vessel allowed to visit the Galapagos Islands. In tandem with those of the *Society Explorer,* programs of the *World Discoverer* have been standardized so passengers can plan their expeditions well in advance. The programs include Greenland/St. Lawrence River, Amazon, Northern Europe, Antarctica, South America west coast, West Africa, Norwegian Fjords, and the Canadian Arctic. Many combinations of the above are available.

To penetrate the coastlines and feel a participation in these "projects," passengers use European rubber Zodiacs as well as two super-launches for transportation ship to shore. Plan, however, on as many "wet" (up to your knees in water) landings as dry ones. The result is "feeling" like an explorer but never missing the comforts of home!

★★★ + WORLD RENAISSANCE

Epirotiki Lines; Greek registry and crew; originally built in 1966 and named Renaissance; *12,000 tons; 492 feet long; 69 feet at beam; 450 passengers; crew of 235; cruising speed of 18.5 knots; 8 passenger decks.*

This charming vessel was the flagship and pride of Paquet French Cruises but was sold in an economy measure to Epirotiki Lines in 1977.

Epirotiki changed her registry and crew to Greek and renamed her *World Renaissance*.

The *World Renaissance* is a very charming small vessel, with just 173 outside cabins and 40 inside. Decks and public rooms have been renamed to reflect Greek ownership. The El Greco grand salon is one of the pleasantest small lounges afloat, and the Lido/swimming pool area is perfect for those itsy-bitsy bikinis that Europeans love. In fact, there are two heated pools on board, the other by the Xenia discotheque/ bar. The Pelagos dining room seats 400 and the lounge/grill another 60, so if there is not a crowd, everyone can dine at the same time. The vessel also boasts a gymnasium/sauna and a small theater. The card room is perfect for small cocktail parties, and there is a small casino. A very nice little cruise ship.

During the official Aegean/Mediterranean season *World Renaissance* offers lovely cruises either on a 7- or 14-day schedule. Her one-week sailings may be the Golden Fleece (Greek Islands and Turkey) or the exciting Seven Seas. During the winter months *World Renaissance* respresents Epirotiki in the Caribbean or South America.

PORTS OF EMBARKATION

In all the excitement of sailing, the port where you board or leave the ship sometimes gets lost in the shuffle. Many cruise lines offer pre- and post-cruise vacation packages, but even if you have only a few hours while waiting for the ship to leave or the flight home after the cruise, there may be time to get a feel for the place—to enjoy the local color, sample traditional foods, even do some shopping. In many ports of embarkation, the most interesting sights, tastes, and bargains are virtually dockside.

THE CARIBBEAN/BAHAMAS

Bridgetown, Barbados is the capital of an island noted for its beaches and resorts rather than spectacular sightseeing or shopping bargains. The port, often filled with the British Navy, is a warm, 10-minute walk or quick cab ride from the center of town; a longish cab ride from the airport at the southern tip of the island ($10–15). Agree on the fare in advance.

Trafalgar Square is the center of political life . . . St. Michael's Cathedral was visited by George Washington . . . the Barbados Museum contains maritime, local, and Indian artifacts and memorabilia . . . Andromeda Gardens is a refreshing taste of Caribbean flora . . . Farley Hill National Park overlooks the island's Scotland District, and Queen's Park combines plant life with historical buildings. The best way to get around is by taxi, and the beaches and resorts along Barbados' Platinum Coast are only minutes away from town.

Pelican Village and Temple Yard, both only minutes on foot from the dock, are good places to buy arts and crafts, and most duty-free shopping is located on Broad Street. Local menu favorites include flying fish, lobster, curries, and spicy, thick soups. Restaurants are plentiful in all price ranges . . . hotel buffets are a good way to sample the best of island cuisine . . . don't forget the famous Barbados Mount Gay rum.

Fort-de-France, Martinique, is a delightful blend of the tropics and Paris as it was maybe 30 years ago. The port is within walking distance of shops selling the latest in French perfumes and clothing as well as outdoor cafes, restaurants, and markets. The airport is only 5 miles from town, and taxi fares are government-controlled.

Musee Departemental de la Martinique features Caribbean Indian and colonial historical objects . . Musee de la Pagerie contains memorabilia of Napoleon's Empress Josephine, who was born here . . . Gaugin, the painter, spent time here as well, and there is a museum in his honor . . . and a collection of rum-making equipment and tools at the Musee du Rhum.

Rue Victor Hugo, rue Schoelcher, and the narrow streets around them comprise the main shopping district where French goods, particularly luxury items, clothing, shoes, and perfumes, can be a bargain. The many sidewalk cafes and snack trucks at La Savane, the main square, are two ways of sampling the local refreshments . . . crayfish, langouste, blood sausage, and hot, creole dishes are among the best . . . French wines are plentiful, as is the local concoction, a white rum with lime punch.

Montego Bay, Jamaica, is one of the island's major resort areas; the port is easily accessible to beaches as well as sightseeing attractions. The airport is less than 5 miles from the port area, and most taxis charge flat fees between points.

One of the island's 200 beaches is Doctor's Cave Beach, a good spot to see Jamaica in action; others tend to be more secluded . . . Rose Hall Great House is a fine example of 18th-century Caribbean architecture . . . Greenwood was home to Elizabeth Barrett Browning . . . the Governor's Coach tour, by diesel rail car, provides a quick glimpse of plantations, coffee groves, and villages outside the city . . . Jamaica's famous rafting is available nearby on the Martha Brae River.

Fabrics, embroidery, resort wear, artwork, and rum are among the local products worth investigating . . . duty-free imports include watches, porcelain, jewelry, cameras, and recording equipment . . . the Jamaican Crafts Market is a good place for local handiwork. Pepperpot soup is just one of many local favorites that have made Jamaican cooking popular with visitors . . . rice and peas, curried goat, saltfish, patties (meat and spice-filled pastries), and local fruit-flavored ice creams are not to be missed either.

Philipsburg, St. Maarten, is the Dutch end of an island whose flip side is French. Philipsburg is noted for shopping bargains while many of the best beaches are near Marigot, the French capital, and only a few minutes away by taxi or local bus. The airport is halfway between the towns and all but the very smallest cruise ships anchor off Philipsburg.

There is very little in the way of historical landmarks or museums; people come here to shop and sun . . . the entire island can be circled in less than four hours and, for the very brave, mopeds are available for hire . . . beaches are beautiful, often topless on the French side, and within walking distance of the pier in Philipsburg.

St. Maarten has the reputation of being one of the Caribbean's best shopping areas for bargains on imported goods of all kinds, including gold jewelry, and Philipsburg is little more than a hectic collection of dozens of shops along the town harbor. Between shopping sprees or a plunge in the ocean, try one of the numerous seaside, open-air restaurants along the harbor.

St. Johns, Antigua, is a sleepy little town on an island noted for very glamorous resorts. The port itself is isolated from everything except a small crafts market and a few shops selling local products. The short trip from the airport will cost about $7 and taxis are available at the pier for trips to town or other attractions.

St. Johns itself is not why people come to Antigua, although the botanical gardens, the museum in the Old Court House, St. John the Divine cathedral, and many of the restored colonial buildings have an understated appeal . . . English Harbour, with its handsomely restored Nelson's Dockyard and once home to Horatio Nelson's British fleet in the late 1700s, is well worth a visit . . . and there are 365 beaches to choose from.

Local products include printed fabrics and clothing, pottery, straw work, and Antigua rum . . . duty-free goods include liquor, perfume, and jewelry . . . Redcliffe Quay and St. Mary's Street are the main shopping areas in St. Johns. Fresh fish, lobster, and native pineapple are among the local favorites . . . English Harbour is a particularly pleasant place for an outdoor lunch.

San Juan, Puerto Rico, one of the biggest cities in the Caribbean, offers a variety of attractions and amusements found nowhere else in the region. Allowing for chaotic driving, a taxi ride from the airport 10 miles away takes approximately 30 minutes ($12). The port in Old San Juan is within walking distance of the historic landmarks, shopping, and restaurants of a beautifully restored old city.

Old San Juan is a six-block-square area of narrow streets, squares, monuments, and museums . . . El Morro Castle, at one end, protected the city for 500 years . . . San Juan Cathedral, La Fortaleza (the oldest governor's mansion in the New World), and a number of museums dedicated to such things as books, glass, the Puerto Rican family, Indians, and Pablo Casals, are other attractions within walking distance . . . seaside resorts with casinos and floor shows to rival Las Vegas are found in the Condado area close to the airport . . . across the bay from the cruise terminal is the Bacardi Rum factory.

The streets of Old San Juan are filled with shops of every description . . . jewelry, crafts, and fashion boutiques are good buys, as well as cigars, rum, religious carvings, and musical instruments. The old city also has plenty of breezy cafes, bars, and restaurants, many of them on the second floor to catch the sea air . . . One is across the street from the cruise terminal.

St. Thomas and St. Croix are the major ports of the U.S. Virgin Islands. The piers, depending on where your ship is anchored, are within minutes of shops and eating places; some may be dockside. A taxi from the airport will cost about $4 on St. Thomas, $8 on St. Croix. Major shopping areas and beaches are easily accessible by taxi from the pier in both ports.

No one goes to St. Thomas for sightseeing; they go to shop and, although prices are not what they used to be, there is certainly a larger selection here than anywhere else in the Caribbean . . . there are also beautiful beaches on St. Thomas, and Magen's Bay, about 30 minutes away from the ship, is the best . . . Coral World Marine Park provides safe underwater viewing. The nearby island of St. John, home to Caneel Bay resort and the Virgin Islands National Park, is a must if you have a day to spare. On St. Croix, Buck Island Reef is the only U.S. underwater national monument . . . Whim Greathouse, built in the 1700s, and Fort Christianvaern, a remnant of the islands' Danish heritage, are also worth visiting.

Items of every description are available in small shops and huge, frenzied warehouses . . . Most large stores will deliver to the ship . . . but does it really make sense to save a dollar or two on a bottle of whiskey if you have to schlep it all the way home?

EUROPE

Barcelona, Spain's second largest city, is cosmopolitan, gracious, and busy. The port is in the heart of the city, close to museums, historic neighborhoods, and dozens of seafood restaurants, and a $15 cab ride from the airport.

In the port area are the Picasso Museum, Plaza Puerto de la Paz with a bronze statue of Columbus, a replica of Columbus's flagship Santa Maria, and a Maritime Museum . . . Barcelona's Gothic cathedral up from the port is a must . . . the Ramblas is a lively promenade lined with shops, markets, and cafes . . . the Gothic Quarter dates back to the 14th century . . . Ciudadela Park, near the Picasso Museum, contains a zoo and the museums of modern art and natural history . . . Montjuich Park, with its castle overlooking much of the city, contains a cluster of museums, including the Museum of Catalan Art and Ceramics, the Archeology Museum, and the Joan Miro Foundation.

The best area for shopping is Paseo de Gracia and Rambla Catuna, although the best for antiques is around the Cathedral . . . El Encants are Barcelona's lively flea markets. Plaza Real is ideal for outdoor cafes, nearby Calle Escudellers is filled with bars and some of the city's oldest restaurants . . . the otherwise seamy Barcelona neighborhood near the port is a favorite spot for inexpensive, seafood restaurants . . . in addition to seafood, snails and pasta dishes are favorites among local residents.

Copenhagen, capital of Denmark, is one of the most enjoyable cities in Europe. The port itself is about 10 minutes from the city's center and roughly 10 miles; allow 30 minutes by taxi ($15).

Tivoli, the city's non-stop amusement center (during the summer and fall months), is the most famous attraction, featuring classical and jazz concerts, an amusement park, gardens, fireworks displays, and theater . . . among the museums are the Ny Carlsberg Glyptotek (ancient to 19th-century art), Kastellet (a 300-year-old fortress), Dunstindustrimuseet (decorative, European, and Oriental art), and the Kobenhavns Bymuseum (the 800-year history of Copenhagen) . . . City Hall Square and Stroget, a pedestrian mall, are good places to get a taste of city life.

Quality, design and, of course, price are the main ingredients of shopping here, although visitors can take advantage of tax-free shopping . . . silver, clothing, toys, glassware are worth considering.

Dubrovnik, on Yugoslavia's Dalmatian Coast, is a medieval masterpiece guarded by walls 1000 years old and built around an ancient harbor.

The Placa is the main street of the old city, where the port is located . . . the city's walls can be explored for a small fee and within the old city are several churches and Franciscan and Dominican monasteries . . . very near the old port are the Sponza and Rector's palaces dating back to the 12th century . . . museums include the Cathedral Treasury and its collection of gold and silver, the Cultural and Historical Museum in the Rector's Palace, the Ethnographical Museum, Maritime Museum, and the Aquarium.

The best area for shopping is along the Placa in the old city . . . special buys can be found in leather goods, textiles and lace, and wood carvings. The cafes there are the best place for people watching as well as refreshment.

Genoa is huge, noisy, steamy, and exciting, the biggest Italian port. Fortunately for visitors, the docks are located within easy access to the city's center. The maritime terminal is roughly 3 miles from the airport ($10).

One of the best ways of seeing Genoa is by boat tour (an hour's trip) on the harbor . . . Via Garibaldi is a street lined with historic palaces, many of which contain rare works of art, and small museums . . . the Royal Palace on Via Balbi contains works by Van Dyck . . . San Lorenzo Cathedral reflects several hundred years of architecture and art, and Piazza San Matteo is noted for its houses originally belonging to the Andrea Doria family . . . Piazza de Ferrari is modern Genoa's busy center. For a quick and tasty bite to eat, try a tavola calde or coffee bar, where you can stand at the counter with the locals.

Hamburg, almost completely destroyed in World War II, is a modern, fast-moving city, Germany's second largest. The port, 70 miles from the North Sea on the Elbe River, is busy and huge, but the city itself can be seen quickly and easily. Cruise-ship berths are roughly 20 miles from the airport, with a travel time of one hour ($35). The city center is a $15–20 cab ride from the piers.

Most of Hamburg's attractions can be seen on foot from the city center . . . the famous opera house is ultramodern, near the botanical gardens, originally laid out in 1821 . . . the St. Pauli district is noted for its shady evening activities . . . museums include the Kunsthalle (the city's primary art museum), the Hamburg Historical Museum, and a museum for decorative arts and crafts . . . at the harbor itself is the Oevelgonne Museumshafen (the harbor museum).

For quality luxury goods try the stores on Jungfernstieg, Neuer Wall, and Dammtorstrasse . . . there are also a number of arcades and less expensive department stores. Eel soup, pea soup, pig's feet, and herring are favorite dishes among the locals.

Lisbon, capital of Portugal, is a place for strolling and lingering on boulevards and in cafes. The airport is about 7 miles from the docks; allow 30 minutes ($8). The city center is 15 minutes from the port by taxi ($5).

Praca do Rossio is the center of action in the city . . . St. George's Castle has guarded the city since the Middle Ages, and just as old is Largo da Se, the cathedral . . . the section called Alfama is the oldest part of Lisbon, one that reflects the city's strong Moorish influences . . . the Gulbenkian Foundation Museum and the Gulbenkian Modern Art Center feature works by many of the great impressionists . . . the Tower of Belem honors some of the country's most famous explorers, and along the river are museums, a planetarium, and a monastery.

Leather goods, embroidery, clothing, and pottery are among the bargains in Lisbon, to be found in small shops in the downtown section (Chiado and Baixa) . . . Lisbon is famous for its tiles, and you can have your own patterns done if you wish. Essential to any visit to Lisbon is a stop at one of the hundreds of cafes where the population gathers to watch the world go by.

Malaga is the heart of Spain's Costa del Sol, not as attractive as smaller resort areas along the coast but vibrant and growing.

The city's cathedral dates back to the 16th century and contains an interesting art collection . . . a series of parks and gardens lead to the Moorish Alcazaba, site of the city's Archeological Museum . . . the resorts of Torremolinos and Marbella are nearby . . . prehistoric caves can be found on an excursion to Nerja. Try the seafood restaurants along the beach road; the catch is right off the boat.

Monte Carlo hardly needs an introduction. Tiny, elegant, a center for arts and entertainment as well as good living, it is the jewel of the Riviera. The airport at Nice is 12 miles away. By helicopter it's 10 minutes ($60); by taxi allow 45 minutes ($40, $10 by bus). Once at the port you are within walking distance of the entire city, and taxis are also available.

Much of the royal palace is open to visitors, as is the Palace Museum, the Waxworks Museum, and the Oceanographic Museum and Aquarium . . . the cathedral, the ramparts of the city, the Misericorde Chapel, and the Gardens of Saint Martin are also worth a visit . . . and there is the famous casino and opera house. Tours of Monte Carlo are available by helicopter and motorcoach.

Don't look for cut-rate bargains here, but if it's luxury items, such as art, designer clothing, or jewelry you're shopping for, this may be the place.

Naples is a teeming, chaotic Italian city whose reason for existence is shipping, notably passenger shipping. The port is conveniently located within walking distance of much of the best of the city.

For most tourists Naples is, unfortunately, a passing-through place while on the way to Capri, the Amalfi Drive, Pompeii, or Sorrento, but it has a charm worth sampling . . . Near the port is Piazza del Plebiscito, the center of social life, and the galleria at Piazza Trento e Trieste, which houses cafes and shops under four wrought-iron arcades . . . The impressive Castel Nuovo, built in the 13th century, the Royal Palace, and the National Archaeological Museum (containing one of the world's best collections of Greco-Roman antiquities) are well worth a visit . . . The tiny port of Santa Lucia has a song named after it . . . At the Capodimonte Palace, the National Galleries contain works by some of Italy's best-known painters . . . If you have time, excursions on your own or by motorcoach are possible to Pompeii, Herculaneum, Vesuvius, and, of course, the glamorous island of Capri.

Via Roma and Via Chiaia are popular shopping areas among local residents, and tourists will find higher-priced items around Piazza dei Martiri. Try the cafes up from the port in the arcades at Piazza Trento e Trieste . . . For seafood, Santa Lucia offers tiny restaurants built on the edge of the harbor.

Nice lies at the heart of the French Riviera, a bustling city as well as a seaside resort. The airport, four miles away, is approximately 15 minutes from the port area ($15–20) by taxi. The port area is only minutes from the center of city life, which is the beach.

The great French artists Chagall, Matisse, and Renoir are well represented here in museums, but the major attraction, of course, is the waterfront with its bikinis, cafes, and restaurants specializing in the zesty Mediterranean school of cooking, with an emphasis on fish, fresh produce, and Italian influences.

Piraeus is the not terribly attractive port for Athens. A huge center for international shipping it is, thankfully, only about 5 miles from more appealing attractions, such as the Acropolis. The port is about 30 minutes from the Athens airport ($12) and about the same from the pier to the city center. Be sure to agree on the price before setting out.

In addition to the spectacular Acropolis, which perches above the city, there are dozens of archaeological landmarks and museums in the city, all dedicated to 4000 years of Greek history . . . On a more modern note, the Museum of Greek Popular Art contains examples of folk art and culture, and the National Picture Gallery is dominated by the 19th century . . . the National Gardens and the Zapio Gardens provide a green contrast to a city that is overwhelmingly concrete-gray . . . the Maritime Museum is in Piraeus itself.

Two primary shopping areas are located near the famous Syntagma, the hub of modern Athens. Stadiou and Upper Venizelou are for luxury items; Ermou and Monastiraki for less expensive goods, where bargaining is still a way of life in the big city . . . Antiquities are not cheap and come under strict government control. For local color try any of the hundreds of tavernas or cafes. The Plaka is a good spot for the former, which serve relatively inexpensive Greek food; Syntagma and Kolonaki are best for people watching and thick Greek coffee . . . There are also inexpensive, non-touristy seafood restaurants on the waterfront of Piraeus.

Southampton is one of two ports commonly used for cruises embarking in England, the other being Tilbury. Southampton is usually reached by boat train from London, a 1½-hour trip arranged through Britrail or your cruise line.

Although it dates back prior to the Norman Conquest in 1066, much of Southampton was destroyed in World War II and most of what is worth visiting lies outside the city . . . the New Forest is 9000 acres of unspoiled countryside and forest originally the private preserve of William the Conqueror . . . Nearby Beaulieu Abbey is a remarkable country home that was once a Cistercian abbey and today includes one of the most comprehensive automobile museums in the world . . . the Isle of Wight, long a favorite with yachtsmen and writers, is a short ferry ride away. For lunch, try one of two or three remaining historic pubs, which date back to the 14th century.

Tilbury is on the outskirts of Greater London, 40 miles from both Heathrow and Gatwick airports and 25 miles from the city's East End. There is really no reason to spend time in Tilbury with London so close, but the one-hour trip from the city can be made by train or motorcoach.

Venice is, without a doubt, the strangest and sometimes most beautiful, city in Europe. Be prepared to sightsee by water or on foot because all other forms of private transportation are forbidden. And everything is expensive. Depending on which pier your ship is assigned, the trip from Marco Polo International Airport (9 miles) takes roughly 40 minutes ($60) by private water taxi. There are also water buses available between the airport and the Lido or St. Mark's Square. Count on a 15-minute water taxi ride ($20) from the docks to St. Mark's Square.

Piazza San Marco (St. Mark's), the Rialto Bridge, and the Grand Canal are some of the famous sights to walk through . . . Along the way are numerous palazzos, often containing impressive art collections, and dozens of churches . . . St. Mark's, in addition to wonderful cafes, offers St. Mark's Basilica, museums, and the Doges' Palace for sightseeing . . . The Academy of Fine Arts contains a record of Venetian painting since the 14th century . . . The Lido is the playground of Venice, with one of the few casinos in Italy. The secret to eating well in Italy is to sample what's in season . . . Trattorias are the best bet for sampling typically Venetian dishes at moderate prices . . . local favorites include seafood such as squid and prawns and wines from neighboring regions, including Valpolicella and Soave.

FAR EAST/PACIFIC

Auckland is New Zealand's largest city, which is not very large but very enjoyable. The port is about 15 miles from the airport ($20) and right in the downtown shopping district.

Among the attractions are the Auckland War Memorial, which has beautiful examples of Maori art, and the Museum of Transport and Technology, providing a glimpse of curious tools and machines of the past . . . Victoria Park Market is a bustling flea market/arts and crafts show/marketplace . . . One Tree Hill includes one tree, an observatory, and a towering obelisk . . . Mt. Eden provides a view of most of New Zealand, at least it seems that way . . . the Kelly Tarlton Underwater World takes the visitor beneath the sea for a look at local fish and sealife . . . Parnell Rose Garden and Village is a shopping complex in a colonial setting.

Shoppers should visit the greenstone factories around town. The type of jade is a traditional stone used by the Maoris for jewelry . . . and because there are more sheep than people in New Zealand, wool

products are definitely worth investigating . . . as is the pottery turned
out by some 5000 craftsmen in the country. Fish and chips is a popular
snack in Auckland, but try some of the local fruits, cheeses, and fresh
seafood as well. Lamb, of course, is ever present on menus, and tea-
rooms are plentiful . . . if you can find a Maori hangi, or feast, don't
miss it.

Bali is considered by many travelers to be among the world's most
beautiful places. Part of Indonesia, it is 90 miles long and rich in religious traditions.

Among the attractions of Bali is the Denpasar Museum and market,
which includes a museum of Balinese culture . . . the Bat Cave is
creepy but interesting . . . visit the Batur temple and volcanic lake with
over 300 shrines . . . the Celuk gold and silver works are in a small
village near Denpasar . . . the Gunung Kawi is a Hindhu Balinese
sanctuary . . . Kuta Beach is a popular resort, and the Sangeh Monkey
Forest is home for the island's sacred monkeys . . . Pedjeng is considered the center of ancient Balinese dynasties . . . Ubud, with its
painters, galleries, and studios, is essential to any visit.

Food is very important to the Balinese and is used in religious
ceremonies and festivities that are held virtually year-round . . . Among
the local favorites worth trying are suckling pig, sea turtle, rijsttafel,
duck, and fish.

Bangkok, capital of Thailand, is huge, sprawling, chaotic, and a
city of astounding contrasts ranging from the unbelievably serene to
sordid. The main port is some distance from the city (150 miles approximately; a 4-hour trip), but smaller vessels can maneuver the Chao Phraya
River. The airport is 30 minutes from downtown Bangkok.

This is a city of wonderfully gentle, lovely people, over 400 magnificent temples, chaotic shopping bazaars, and pockets of sex clubs and
bars that seem to be terribly exploitative of the Thai people . . . From
the Chao Phraya River you can take in the Grand Palace complex and
the temple of the Emerald Buddha . . . other temples (you can take
half-day and full-day tours of temples only) include those honoring the
Reclining Buddha and the Golden Buddha . . . the National Museum
is one of the biggest in Asia and represents 6000 years of Thai culture
. . . outside Bangkok is the Ancient City, worth a visit if you have the
time . . . as is the Crocodile Farm with its 10,000 inhabitants . . . the
best way to see the city if it's your first time is by an organized tour,
which can be arranged at any of the major hotels.

Thai silk, emeralds, and semi-precious stones are the real shopping
bargains, but some of the shopping bazaars are a must, even if you

don't buy. There are entire streets filled with shops selling nothing but paraphernalia for temples and temple worship, and another section of the city in which shops sell nothing but chains of gold. Thai food is very good, very spicy, and can be very, very hot, so be careful. The seasonings are heavy on garlic, basil, coconut, and lemongrass. Thai buffets at some of the hotels are a good way to sample.

Hong Kong, with its non-stop activity, millions of people, and boats of every description, may be the world's most exciting harbor. A taxi from Kai Tak Airport will cost approximately $3.50. From there, taxis to the downtown area run about the same, but be sure to take the Star Ferry at some point in your visit. The short trip between Kowloon and Hong Kong Island is a unique way to see the city and costs almost nothing.

Tiger Balm Gardens and Sung Dynasty Village, a reconstruction of a complete Chinese town dating back to the Middle Ages, are musts . . . Statue Square and Victoria Park are popular social and recreation areas . . . The Fung Ping Shan Museum contains a collection of porcelain . . . Other museums include the Hong Kong Museum of Art and the Jade Museum at Tiger Balm Gardens.

Hong Kong is best known for two things—shopping and food. Be prepared to bargain for jade, designer clothing and accessories (some are counterfeit), porcelain, ivory, fabrics, antiques, and electronics, but be sure you're getting a good deal; U.S. prices for much of what is now sold in Hong Kong can be competitive. Li Yuen Street, Hollywood Road, and Kansu Street are favorite shopping areas, and the Poor Man's Nightclub near the Macau Ferry, with its massive piles of merchandise and food stalls, is a unique experience any time of day. Cantonese cooking is the predominant cuisine in Hong Kong, but the variety within it is astounding and everything else is possible, from nouvelle cuisine to Indian . . . Dim sum is a chaotic but delicious way to sample a wide variety of dishes.

Honolulu, on the Hawaiian island of Oahu, is known for two things, Waikiki and Pearl Harbor, but there are other reasons for spending some time there. The port is in the downtown section, halfway between the airport and Waikiki (15–20 minutes and $10 either way).

Waikiki is a stretch of beach, resort hotels, shopping centers, and a multitude of restaurants that often surprises first-time visitors by its small size. It's a good introduction to Hawaii, but there are more spectacular beaches . . . Oahu can be circled by public bus or by car, and that's a good way to get a taste of the island . . . the USS *Arizona*

Memorial at Pearl Harbor is a moving tribute to the sailors who died there . . . the Bishop Museum is a fine collection of Hawaiian art and cultural artifacts, and the Honolulu Academy of Arts, built in the Spanish style around courtyards, has dozens of galleries.

For the hungry, the Waikiki restaurants range from fast food to elegant dining, and Restaurant Row is a new area downtown.

Kobe, Japan, is best known in America for its beef, but there are other attractions as well. The port is 20 miles from the Osaka airport (40 minutes by taxi, $70) and only 5 minutes from the city center ($6). It is also possible to reach Kobe by bullet train from Tokyo or Osaka, the latter trip costing about $15.

If you're lucky enough to be in Kobe during the spring, cherry trees will be in bloom . . . Mt. Rokko provides a view of the surrounding region . . . the Ikuta and Minatogawa shrines reflect traditional Japanese life, and the Hakutsuru Art Museum contains a good collection of bronzes, pottery, and ancient art from Japan . . . the Municipal Art Museum reflects the influence of the West on Japan's history . . . There is an underground shopping arcade at Sannomiya. Most of the shopping is in the downtown business area, but the Kobe International House is another option.

Kobe beef, pampered and massaged before it reaches the table, is about the best in the world, and the city is also known for the quality of its sake . . . You might also consider local favorites such as blowfish or fugu soup.

Papeete is the hub for the enchanted islands of French Polynesia, which we tend to lump together as Tahiti. Tahiti is, in fact, the largest of several islands, and Papeete is the capital city. This is a part of the world fantastically rich in legend and myth created by some of the best writers and painters of western civilization. Melville, Robert L. Stevenson, Jack London, and Paul Gaugin are just a few. Captain Cook was not the first to bring these islands to the attention of Europe, but has received most of the attention. The port is in the town center, close to the airport.

Among the sights worth visiting are the Paul Gaugin Museum at the opposite end of the island from Papeete, the Captain Cook Monument outside the town, and numerous waterfalls along the coastal road . . . the major attraction, of course, is the natural beauty of the island itself, particularly the dazzling beaches . . . In Papeete, itself, there is a cathedral, a cultural center, and Bougainville Park, named after a French explorer.

Singapore may be the easiest, and certainly the most curious, city in the Far East to visit. It's a city of gleaming skyscrapers where everything works and efficiency is prized. In the midst of this 21st-century atmosphere, centuries of tradition of at least four cultures are reflected in unexpected places. The port is roughly 30 minutes from the airport ($15) and 5 minutes ($4) from the downtown area.

In Singapore it's a choice of towering shopping centers in which hundreds of tiny shops are connected by escalators or pockets of history . . . Orchard Road is lined with hotels and shopping centers . . . tiny Chinatown has survived the onslaught of skyscrapers . . . Serangoon Road is known as Little India . . . the colonial past is reflected in such buildings as Parliament House, the Victoria Theater, and City Hall . . . Raffles Hotel, a wonderful vestige of Singapore's British past, is, perhaps, the single most interesting experience in the city.

Shopping and eating in Singapore are remarkable adventures and, unlike many other Asian cities, relatively safe and carefree. It would be useless to list the shopping bargains because virtually anything can be bought here. Electronics can be especially good buys. In a city of wonderful Chinese food that little resembles the American equivalents, as well as surprisingly excellent hotel restaurants, one of the taste treats in Singapore is the street food that is, thanks to strict government supervision (the Singapore government is strict about everything and consequently everything works, even if it sometimes seems slightly oppressive), quite safe. And delicious, so don't be afraid to try whatever looks good or strange.

Sydney must rank among the top five port cities in the world. Friendly, sunny, and entertaining, its spirit is invigorating and contagious. The ports, depending on where your ship puts in, are about 10 miles from the airport ($15) and can be literally in the historic district or just minutes away by taxi.

Sydney is a city of villages, neighborhoods, and coves surrounded by water . . . just up from the cruise piers is the Rocks, a restored area originally settled by convicts transported from Britain. It is now a collection of shops, restaurants, and bars, a favorite social spot for residents and tourists alike . . . Dominating the harbor is the world-famous Sydney Opera House. Tours are conducted throughout the day . . . One of the best ways to see the city is by ferry. It doesn't really matter where you go, but Manly, a seaside resort that is a delightful throwback to a simpler age, is wonderful, and the views of the city from the zoo across the bay are spectacular . . . Among the museums are the Australian Museum, for a look at the continent's natural history, the Art Gallery of New South Wales, and an interesting Geological and Mining

Museum . . . there are beaches everywhere, and they're all worth visiting.

Shoppers can find anything and everything, but many look for Australian opals . . . Double Bay is a trendy shopping area, and Paddington is a wonderful neighborhood of small, less expensive shops and art galleries as well as restaurants. Eating is a breeze in Sydney, ranging from coffee and tea shops to the most elegant nouvelle cuisine at the glamorous hotels such as the Regent of Sydney. The Rocks is convenient for eating if time is limited . . . Try the local seafood such as John Dory, prawns, and bugs . . . and don't overlook the Australian wines; they may put you off California for good.

Tokyo is an expensive city to visit on your own. A taxi from Narita Airport to the port is about $150. From the pier, however, you can get to the downtown area for about $10–15. It is also possible to take a bus from Narita to the downtown air terminal for $20. To get around the city itself, consider the subways.

One of the newest museums in Tokyo is the Fukagawa Edo Shiryokan, which includes reconstructions of 19th-century Tokyo, then called Edo . . . the Meji Shrine, and its spectacular grounds, is one of the required items on any city tour . . . the Asakusa district is a good example of old Tokyo, and Shibuya is an example of the new . . . Kiyosumi Garden is worth a visit, and all roads seem to lead to the Imperial Palace . . . Ginza is one of best-known shopping streets in the world . . . among the dozens of museums are the Japan Folk Crafts Museum, the National Museum of Modern Art, the Japanese Sword Museum, and the Tokyo National Museum, which is the largest in Japan.

Beware of shopping in Tokyo: Prices are very high due to the currency exchange, and many items made in Japan, especially electronics, cameras, etc., can be purchased for less money in the United States . . . Silk kimonos can be found for good prices. The International Arcade is a good place to look . . . Local handicrafts such as lacquerware and pottery are also bargains.

NORTH AMERICA

Anchorage is Alaska's "big" city and gateway for the ports of Seward and Whittier as well. The airport is about 7 miles from downtown ($6). Passengers are generally transported by train or bus to the port areas.

Among the historic sights in Anchorage are the Anderson House, one of the earliest homes, which is located in Elderberry Park . . . In Crawford Park is the first schoolhouse built in the city . . . The Anchorage Museum of History and Art has a good collection of Indian and Eskimo artifacts . . . Earthquake Park and the Anchorage Zoo are two of the nature-related activities in town.

Shoppers should look for Native American crafts, including jewelry, totem poles, and baskets . . . Anchorage also is noted for its furs . . . The Alaska Native Arts and Crafts Cooperative is a good place to watch artisans at work and purchase their products.

Baltimore, for a rather small city, is a huge port. Allow 30 minutes from the airport by taxi ($15), and from the Dundalk Marine Terminal to downtown about 20 minutes ($10). There is parking available at the pier.

Harborplace is Baltimore's pride and joy, a gleaming complex of restaurants and shops at the city's inner harbor . . . The National Aquarium features a 17-story shark tank . . . From the World Trade Center, the Top of the World provides a view of the entire city and then some. Other attractions include the U.S. frigate *Constellation,* the Maryland Science Center, and the Davis Planetarium . . . two museums worth visiting are the Baltimore Museum of Art and the Walters Art Gallery, downtown.

The Chesapeake Bay provides some of the city's best meals . . . Be sure to try soft-shelled crabs if in season, or the spicy, hard-shelled variety if they're not . . . Oysters and clams are also indigenous, and Harborplace has several restaurants where you'll find them.

Boston, the gateway to New England, is a relatively small city with a huge, meandering harbor. The Black Falcon Cruise Terminal is about 15 minutes from Logan Airport ($9) by cab or 10 minutes from downtown ($8). Parking is available across the street.

Boston is a pleasing combination of old and new . . . The Freedom Trail takes you past and through many of the most famous sites of the Revolutionary War as well as through the city's lively North End . . . Quincy Market/Faneuil Hall, near the harbor, has been restored and turned into dozens of restaurants and shops . . . the Boston Aquarium across the street is one of the best in the world . . . Beacon Hill and Back Bay are good for wandering through narrow streets, past elegant homes and interesting shops . . . across the Charles River, Cambridge and Harvard University are worth a visit. Museums include the Museum of Fine Arts, one of America's best, the Gardner and the Fogg. Kids will love the Children's Museum, very close to the harbor area.

Shoppers should head for Filene's Basement, a local tradition for bargains, or Copley Place, one of the newest giant shopping complexes in the downtown area. Newbury Street is also a choice spot for small, elegant shops. Food is good everywhere, but the Quincy Market area offers an amazing variety of snacks and quick meals as well as some of the city's oldest and best-known restaurants. Italian North End is a great place for coffee.

Ft. Myers, at one end of Florida's intercoastal waterway, is on the relatively undeveloped Gulf Coast (compared with Miami, at least). The airport is about 30 minutes from the downtown area.

The primary attraction in the Ft. Myers area is the Gulf and its resort areas . . . Sanibel and Captiva islands are definitely worth a visit (the beaches are noted for their huge variety of shells) . . . the Jimmy Connors Tennis Center is nearby . . . Ding Darling is the name of a fascinating wildlife refuge where alligators sometimes hold up traffic . . . the Edison Winter Home and Museum is a charming combination of history and tropical gardens.

Try the local seafood at smaller restaurants, but if you're looking for a fancy meal, a number of resorts on Sanibel and Captiva can provide it, often with spectacular Gulf views.

Jacksonville, close to the Georgia border on Florida's northeast coast, is worth a visit with a car because its attractions tend to be widespread. The airport is roughly 20 miles from the port ($20).

Riverwalk, on the banks of St. John's River, is a complex of shops, restaurants and entertainment venues . . . Saint Augustine, the oldest town in America, is about 30 minutes away, and Annheuser-Busch has a brewery outside of town where visitors can take tours and sample the merchandise . . . the Jacksonville Zoo has 60 acres, including an African veldt display . . . Kathryn Abbey Hanna Park has 450 acres on the ocean for picnics, camping and swimming . . . museums include the Jacksonville Art Museum with a fine collection of Oriental porcelain, and the Museum of Arts and Sciences. Riverwalk is a convenient place for a bite to eat.

Ketchikan, a popular port of call for many cruise ships, also is a port of embarkation for some of the smaller vessels. The airport is a 10-minute ferry ride from downtown ($3).

Ketchikan is one of Alaska's centers for Native American cultures . . . Saxman Totem Park has over 20 totem poles on display, and the Tongass Historical Society is on Dock Street near the port . . . the Totem Heritage Cultural Center has over 30 poles and other artifacts of Indian life . . . the Creek Street Historic District, a winding collection of wooden houses on pilings was, at one time, Ketchikan's rowdy nightlife area; there is even a brothel museum called Dolly's House.

Ketchikan is a good place to buy crafts and the works of local artists.

Los Angeles is a great city with a depressing port 25 miles away from almost everything ($25–35 by cab). There is no parking at the pier, although areas can be found within a mile or two. So do your sightseeing in glitzy L.A. instead.

Disneyland is only one of many amusement parks; Universal Studios and Knotts Berry Farm are others . . . the La Brea tarpits have their own museum next door to the gorgeous Los Angeles County Museum of Art . . . other museums of note include the J. Paul Getty Museum and the newish Museum of Contemporary Art . . . the El Pueblo de Los Angeles State Historical Park is the oldest part of the city.

Shoppers will find whatever they can imagine in the L.A. area . . . Beverly Hills' Rodeo Drive is a must, even if you can only afford to window shop, and Melrose Avenue has things Californian . . . Century City has an enormous shopping mall of chic department stores and boutiques. Whatever you want to eat is here. There's Little Tokyo for Japanese, Mexican is all over town (Melrose is good for Mexican and Italian), there are the "in" spots with big names and prices, and the drive-ins. Public transportation is not Los Angeles' strength; if you're planning extensive sightseeing it would be better to rent a car.

Miami has had an exciting rebirth, complete with a new, glittering skyline, a renaissance of hotels and restaurants, and a new appreciation for its heritage. The port facilities, among the best in the world, are about 20 minutes from the airport ($15–20 by cab) and minutes from Miami Beach and the downtown area. Parking is available at the pier.

With a few hours to spare in Miami there are several options . . . Miami Beach, with its restored art-deco sections, glamorous seaside hotels and chic shopping, is only 15 minutes ($8) away . . . Key Biscayne, a quieter stretch of beach resorts is no farther . . . cultural attractions include the Dade County Art Museum, the Museum of Science, and the Space Transit Planetarium . . . Kids will enjoy Planet Ocean, Seaquarium, and Metrozoo.

Shoppers are in luck because of the close proximity of the port to the downtown shopping districts . . . Miami Beach is another prime location . . . and very close to the piers is a new shopping complex on the waterfront that combines attractive small stores with an entire floor of eateries, offering a taste of everything.

Montreal is a wonderful combination of old and new. The port, on the St. Lawrence River and within walking distance of the city's center, is 40 minutes from Dorval International Airport ($18).

Old Montreal and Notre Dame Cathedral lie at the heart of the city and should not be missed . . . Mont Royal overlooks the area, and the Botanical Gardens are the third largest in the world . . . Benjamin Franklin slept in Chateau Ramezay near Place Royale, the city's oldest landmark . . . museums include the McCord, for Native American artifacts, the Montreal Museum of Fine Arts, and the Saidye Bronfman Centre, noted for its avant-garde exhibits.

Shoppers will be amazed by the city's vast underground (remember the winters are cold) of shops, but Saint Catherine Street is another prime location for spending money. Food is taken seriously here, and the accent is on Quebecois cooking, which tends to be hearty and flavorful. Saint Denis, de la Montagne, and Crescent are lined with restaurants and nightspots.

New Orleans, with its French and Cajun heritage and its traditions of jazz and nightlife, is like no other city in the United States. The cruise piers are minutes from the center of everything, including the French Quarter, and about 40 minutes from the airport ($10 by cab). Parking is available close by.

Two good ways to explore New Orleans are by the CBD shuttle bus or the Charles Avenue Streetcar, a 152-year-old historic treasure . . . The French Quarter is the center of social life and jazz life, while the quieter residential Garden District is lined with 19th-century mansions . . . Audubon Park boasts a highly respected zoo, and the old

Pontchartrain Hotel is worth a walk through just to soak up the atmosphere.

Shoppers flock to Canal Place and its swishy shops and Riverwalk, a spectacular complex of 200 stores and restaurants in what were originally river warehouses . . . The New Orleans Center, another shopping complex, just opened in 1988. Even if your taste doesn't run to blackened redfish, there's bound to be some Cajun cooking to suit your palate or something else to be found at Riverwalk or the Jackson Brewery, a rapidly expanding renovation of an old brewery that now holds shops and eating places . . . and for something really weird, New Orleans has a restaurant that originally perched halfway up the Eiffel Tower in Paris.

New York, the Big Apple, has one of the world's most exciting approaches by water and, despite its size, is remarkably easy to visit for a few hours or a few days. The port is located on the Hudson River at midtown Manhattan, an hour from JFK airport ($30 by cab) and several long blocks from Rockefeller Center ($5 by cab). There is parking at the pier.

A visitor could easily spend weeks in New York, but with only a few hours there are certain musts . . . the top of the Empire State Building or the World Trade Center . . . a stroll down Fifth Avenue . . . the Metropolitan, Modern, Guggenheim, or Whitney art museums . . . Greenwich Village and Little Italy, Chinatown or Soho . . . a tour of Rockefeller Center or Radio City Music Hall . . . if you're overnighting, a Broadway, off-Broadway or off-off-Broadway show or an opera, ballet, or symphony performance at Lincoln Center.

Shoppers have an entire city to choose from . . . the giant department stores such as Saks, Lord & Taylor, and Bloomies, the bargains on Orchard Street . . . the posh shops of Madison Avenue and Columbus Avenue . . . the bargain cameras and electronics in midtown . . . the art galleries and boutiques of Soho and the Village. And for the hungry there's Chinatown, Little Italy, Little India, Hell's Kitchen (closest to the piers), the trendy restaurants of the Upper West Side or the Eastern European eateries on the Lower East Side . . . pasta places are fashionable and affordable, but there are world-famous spots, too . . . and don't ignore New York's street food—just about every nationality and type of snack food is represented.

Philadelphia is an old city that is relatively new to cruising. The port at Penn's Landing is adjacent to some of the city's most historic areas and has its own maritime museum. The trip from the airport will take roughly 30 minutes unless it's rush hour ($20).

Although history has always been Philadelphia's strong point, in recent years it has had a renaissance of hotels and restaurants and its museums, theater, and music can hold their own with most American cities . . . Independence National Historical Park includes Independence Hall and some 40 buildings dating prior to the 1800s . . . the Liberty Bell is also here . . . Society Hill is famous for its architecture, gardens, and courtyards . . . museums include the excellent Philadelphia Museum of Art, the Pennsylvania Academy of Fine Arts (the oldest museum in America), and the Academy of Natural Sciences Museum . . . the Franklin Institute of Science is a favorite with kids of all ages . . . one way to see the city is by horse-drawn carriages, which leave from Walnut Street.

Shoppers can choose department stores, including the well-known John Wanamaker, or chic boutiques on Walnut Street. If you're hungry, try the Reading Terminal Market, where the food stalls and small restaurants mingle with butchers and grocers and where you can get Philadelphia cheese steak . . . there are also great Italian restaurants near the Italian market, including Victor's, where you can sing opera along with your meal. If Mario Lanza, who grew up in the neighborhood could, so can you.

Port Canaveral is about an hour from the Orlando International Airport and 90 minutes from Walt Disney World. There is parking at the pier.

There's little reason to spend much time there except to visit three of America's biggest attractions: Disney World, Epcot Center, and Cape Canaveral, launch site for NASA's space program. The John F. Kennedy Space Center is just north of the port, and taxis are available. Disney World and Epcot each require at least half a day's visit, and that's rushing.

Port Everglades, the port for Fort Lauderdale, which is only minutes away, is rapidly giving Miami a run for its money as busiest cruise port in Florida. The port is only 2 miles from the airport ($5 by cab) and 3 miles from the center of town ($6). Miami is some 60 miles south.

Fort Lauderdale has been called the Venice of America, but its major claim to fame is its welcoming attitude toward millions of college kids who cover its beaches each spring . . . Despite efforts to upgrade its image, the Strip, which runs along the ocean, has a rather appealing seediness, with its inexpensive hotels, restaurants, and bars . . . a more classy impression is created along Las Olas Boulevard, where renovation has resulted in trendy shops and eating places . . . Stranahan House, the oldest building in Fort Lauderdale is now a museum, and there is also a Museum of the Arts . . . If you're traveling by car, Flamingo Gardens and the Everglades Holiday Park are good for a visit . . . Ocean World is right next to the port.

San Diego, in sunny southern California, is just the right size for quick exploration, and many of the attractions are very close to the pier. The port is roughly 5 miles from the airport ($6 and 20 minutes by cab).

The emphasis in San Diego is on rest and relaxation . . . the San Diego Zoo is world famous . . . Sea World has re-created Antarctica for hundreds of penguins . . . The San Diego Wild Animal Park is outside the city in the San Pasqual Valley . . . There are 75 golf courses in the area. Cultural and athletic pursuits can be followed in Balboa Park's 1000 acres of museums, theaters, and sports facilities . . . Among the museums are the San Diego Museum of Art, the Timken Art Gallery, and the Aerospace Museum . . . The Gaslamp Quarter and Seaport Village provide shops and dining in re-created historical settings . . . and Tijuana, Mexico, is less than 20 miles away.

San Francisco collects visitors' hearts for good reason: The vistas are breathtaking, the attractions and amusements rewarding, and there's something about the climate that is invigorating. The port is roughly 20 miles (30 minutes) from San Francisco International Airport ($35 by cab) and 15 minutes from the center of the city ($5). There is also a quick bus service from the airport that delivers to Fisherman's Wharf and the major hotels. There is parking convenient to the port.

Take your walking shoes and climbing sticks or money for cab or cablecar fare; San Francisco is all hills . . . Golden Gate Park, probably the most beautiful park in the U.S., is a must . . . Chinatown is the closest thing to being in China you'll find in North America . . . Nob Hill is luxurious and lovely . . . Fisherman's Wharf and the surrounding arcade/piers are crowded and lively . . . The ferry to Sausalito or a tour by boat of San Francisco Bay is a delight (you can even visit Alcatraz) . . . Museums include the notable DeYoung in Golden Gate Park and, for the kids, the Exploratorium, a touchy-feely place at the Palace of Fine Arts.

Shoppers should head for Union Square, where all the ritzy department stores are located, but nearby Chinatown has more bargains. And the only problem with eating in San Francisco is deciding where and what: North Beach for Italian, Chinatown for obvious reasons, and seafood at cafes and restaurants all over . . . there's good Mexican food in the less affluent Mission district near the convention center and wonderful, informal restaurants on Geary and Haight.

Savannah is Georgia's historic capital on the banks of the Savannah River. The port is about 10 miles, or 15 minutes, from the airport ($15).

Savannah's official Historic District encompasses most of its visitor attractions . . . These include Davenport House, Owens-Thomas House, and the King-Tisdell Cottage, which contains a museum dedicated to black history and the cultures of the Sea Islands . . . The Juliette Gordon Low Scout National Center is where the Girl Scouts were started, and Old Fort Jackson, Fort Pulaski, and Fort Screven commemorate Savannah's role in three wars—the War of 1812, the Civil War, and the Indian Wars.

St. Louis, in the heart of the American Midwest, has been a cruise port since Mark Twain's riverboat days. The modern port is some 15 miles, or 20 minutes, from Lambert St. Louis International Airport ($20 by cab, $6 by airport limo).

Gateway Arch is the most spectacular sight in St. Louis, and it contains the Museum of Westward Expansion, which is what the arch celebrates . . . The Anheuser-Busch Brewery, in art-deco buildings, is a National Historic Landmark . . . The National Museum of Transport focuses, naturally enough, on train travel, and provides hands-on activities . . . other attractions include the Missouri Botanical Gardens, and Grant's Farm and Six Flags Over Mid-America, two amusement areas of particular interest to kids . . . Art enthusiasts will enjoy the Laumeier Sculpture Park, with its 96 acres of gardens and sculptures, and the St. Louis Art Museum.

Shoppers have a choice of several retail complexes: St. Louis Center, West Port Plaza, Plaza Frontenac, and St. Louis Union Station. And if you're hungry, don't forget this is beefsteak country, but the city's restaurants also reflect its varied cultural heritage, and most ethnic varieties are available.

Seattle, gateway to Alaska, has a wonderful combination of adventurousness and sophistication. Sea-Tac Airport is about 30 minutes ($20) from downtown, where the port is located. Parking is available. From the piers much of Seattle's best is within walking distance or a short cab ride.

For a bird's eye view of the city, journey up the Space Needle, originally built for the 1962 World's Fair . . . the waterfront has enough to keep you busy all day, including restaurants and warehouses full of shops. There is also a fascinating aquarium depicting local sealife . . . Pike Place is a bustling market in a historic setting where most of Seattle seems to gather. There are also dozens of shops, restaurants, and cafes high above the harbor . . . The Pioneer District has preserved what was the seamy side of town during Gold Rush days. The southern end of the Klondike Gold Rush National Historical Park is here, the rest being in Alaska. Next door is the city's colorful Chinatown . . . Seattle Center, built for the World's Fair, continues to attract visitors to its theaters, exhibitions, and amusements . . . Museums include the Museum of History and Industry, which details the history of the Northwest, the Seattle Art Museum, and the Charles and Emma Frye Art Museum.

The waterfront, Pike Place, downtown, and the University of Washington area are the best for shopping, and seafood, especially salmon, oysters, and other local catches, are essential ingredients for a good meal.

Tampa/St. Petersburg is the center of Florida's popular Sun Coast. Depending on where your ship is sailing from, the airport is roughly 20 minutes ($15) from the Tampa port area; 35 minutes ($25) from St. Petersburg's port.

Being vacationland, much of Tampa/St. Pete's interests are outdoors . . . Florida Downs is a major race track . . . Busch Gardens' Dark Continent is just outside of Tampa . . . Ybor city is the former Cuban neighborhood . . . In St. Pete are the HMS *Bounty* and Historical Museum, the Sunken Gardens, the Salvador Dali Museum, and the Museum of Fine Arts . . . Along the Gulf coast is the Suncoast Seabird Sanctuary and the Tiki Gardens.

Vancouver is the most northern of the great cities of the Pacific Northwest, a blend of pioneer spirit, cosmopolitan flair, and British tradition. The port is smackdab in the middle of the city, within walking distance to downtown attractions. The airport is 45 minutes away ($15 by taxi).

The best thing about Vancouver is just being there, but there are attractions as well . . . Robson Square, basically a business area, deserves a look for its architecture . . . The Seawall Promenade at Stanley Park provides magnificent views of land and water, and the park itself contains a zoo, the well-known Vancouver Aquarium, a miniature railway, and other amusements . . . In Vanier Park are the MacMillan Planetarium, the Maritime Museum, and the Vancouver Museum . . .

The Museum of Anthropology includes what may be the world's best collection of Indian relics . . . The Sun Yat Sen Garden contains a full-size Chinese garden.

Granville Island is a lively collection of shops, markets, and waterfront restaurants . . . Other shopping can be done in department stores such as Eaton and Hudson's Bay Company or in Gastown, where turn-of-the-century buildings have been converted into shops and restaurants . . . Other shopping/dining areas of interest are Chinatown and Robson Street . . . and for a view, you might consider one of the city's three cloud-high revolving restaurants.

SOUTH AND CENTRAL AMERICA

Acapulco may be Mexico's oldest seaside playground, but it still has a lot of appeal. The port is about 15 miles from the airport ($12) and within walking distance of the city center.

The best thing to do in Acapulco is soak up the sun and the local lifestyle . . . Begin at any of many beaches, including Condesa, Icacos, and El Morro . . . The oldest part of the city is Caleta Beach . . . For cliff divers, go to the Quebrada Cliffs in the early afternoon . . . El Fuerte San Diego, which used to guard the city, now is a museum . . . Kids will like CICI, a combination amusement park and dolphin show, and Parque Papagayo, the zoo . . . There's also a small archaeology museum in town.

You don't have to leave the beach areas for anything in Acapulco. Vendors sell food and merchandise, and the waterfront streets are lined with shops. From Condesa to El Morro is a particularly good area for shopping, and Puerto Marques is packed with food stalls. There are, of course, high-priced restaurants scattered on the hills of the city, and many of the resorts are a good choice for an informal lunch at the beach. Shoppers should look for clothing rather than crafts.

Buenos Aires, the capital of Argentina and the largest city in the southern hemisphere, has been called the Paris of South America because of its European ambience and beauty. The port is almost 50 miles from the airport ($15 by taxi) and only 15 minutes ($2) from the city's center.

In a city the size of Buenos Aires it is difficult to see everything in a few hours . . . Consider the Fine Arts Museum, the largest in Argentina or the pedestrian mall called Florida . . . Historical monuments include the Old Monastery of Recollect Friars and the Cathedral and Mausoleum of the Liberator General . . . The La Boca area is noted for its color, charm, and artists' studios.

Shopping is particularly good for leather products and antiques . . . The antiques bazaar at Plaza Dorrego is open on Sundays . . . Stores along the pedestrian mall are popular with visitors. For taste treats, remember that Argentinians consume more beef than any other nationality in the world . . . Informal steak grills called parrilladas are plentiful and have a cheerful, unpretentious atmosphere . . . and be sure to take advantage of the cafes along the boulevards.

Manaus, hundreds of miles up the mighty Amazon River, is a quaint outpost complete with spectacular 19th-century opera house and orchids growing like dandelions. It's a tiny place, easily explored, and usually at the end or the beginning of an Amazon/Caribbean cruise.

Puerto Montt, Puerto Williams, and **Punta Arenas** are all jumping-off points for Antarctica or South Pacific cruises after long flights from Miami or New York. They are tiny outposts of civilization where the weather is rugged and the rugged people isolated. Fishing is a major industry; the mountains, lakes, and rivers are spectacular.

Rio de Janeiro may be the world's largest tropical playground. The port is about 30 minutes from the airport and 20 minutes from the central beach hotel district.

Beaches, mountain peaks, and more beaches comprise most of what Rio has to offer . . . Copacabana and Ipanema are the best-known beaches to visitors, and they are also the most crowded . . . Barra da Tijuca tends to be deserted by comparison. The beach is central to the lives of those who live here, so be sure to take in the local color . . . Corcovado, with its famous statue of Christ, overlooks the city and can be reached by train . . . Sugarloaf, not as tall but equally stunning, is reached by cable car . . . Museums in Rio include the national Museum of Fine Arts, with a good collection of Brazilian works, and the Museu Chacara do Ceu, which includes works by modern European masters . . . The Botanic Garden, with thousands of species of tropical plants, is near Rio Jockey Club, one of South America's great race tracks.

Shopping as well as eating is good in Ipanema . . . Seafood and beef are local favorites, and much of the dining is done outdoors, in bistros, adegas, and bars . . . churrascarias are the noisy, crowded, and friendly places where beef is the specialty, often all you can eat.

STOP PRESSES

- Windstar Sail Cruises has changed its name to Windstar Cruises.
- Commodore Cruise Line and BSL Cruises will operate as Commodore Cruise Line with *Caribe, Bermuda Star* and *Queen of Bermuda* as well as two new vessels being constructed in Spain. New address of Commodore Cruise Line: 800 Douglas Road, Coral Gables, FLA 33134. Tel: (800) 237–5361 for individual reservations; (800) 529–3000 for executive offices.
- Royal Caribbean Cruise Line's two new 'sovereign-size' ships are named *Monarch of the Seas* (March 1991) and *Majesty of the Seas* (late 1991). *Monarch of the Seas* begins service on May 5, 1991 to the southern Caribbean. The year-round weekly sailings call at Barbados, Martinique, Antigua, St. Maarten and St. Thomas.
- RCCL is also repositioning *Song of Norway,* from San Juan to Mexican Riviera cruises during the winter months and Alaska in summer. A $75 million refurbishment of *Viking Serenade* will add 260 cabins and boost capacity to 1500 passengers. The vessel will not return from Alaska but depart from Los Angeles on 3-night cruises to Catalina Island and Ensenada, adding San Diego on the 4-night sailings.
- Kloster Cruise Ltd. has ordered a 10,000-ton vessel of 212 passengers (Seabourn-Cruise-Line style) for its Royal Viking Line division with delivery expected February 1992. The parent company of RVL and Norwegian Cruise Line is also building two 1200 passenger ships in Europe at a cost of $200 million each.
- Costa Cruises plans to introduce three more cruise vessels by late 1993. The first ship will be a reconstruction similar to *Costa Marina.* Two will be new construction—of 50,000 tons each from a Fincantieri shipyard in Italy—for "Cruising Italian Style".
- Costa Cruises' parent company, Costa Crociere of Genoa, has formed a joint venture with Sovcomflot AKP of Moscow to operate four ships in Europe, the Black Sea, and the Soviet Baltic. Called Prestige Cruises, the four ships will be *Fyodor Dostoyevsky, Maxim Gorky* on the Soviet side and Costa's *Danae* and *Daphne* and market primarily to Europeans—with perhaps 10 to 30 percent of the berths to North Americans. The *Danae* will enter the fleet immediately, with the *Daphne* arriving (after her scheduled Caribbean and Alaska itineraries) mid-1992.
- Clipper Cruise Line has turned the *Newport Clipper* over to its owner, Coastal Cruise Line, and will not re-enter the Clipper fleet as previously announced. Clipper plans to replace the vessel with a small 'expedition' ship for service in 1992.

- Celebrity Cruises' *Zenith* (April 1992), sistership to *Horizon,* sails from Port Everglades on an Eastern/Western Caribbean itinerary on alternating Saturdays. Eastern Caribbean ports are Antigua, St. Thomas, and Nassau; Western Caribbean ports are Nassau, Ocho Rios, Grand Caymen, Playa del Carmen, and Cozumel.

- Crystal Cruises has announced a 60-plus day sailing of *Crystal Harmony* to the South Pacific following her 1991 inaugural cruises in Europe.

- Society Expeditions Cruises' *Society Adventurer* sails on 10- to 20-day segments in Antarctica through early 1992.

QUICK—REFERENCE CHARTS

★★★★★+ A refined and elegant cruise experience; there is none better afloat; it is definitely not like being at home; superb facilities, service, food, and drink; fine attention to detail; ships beautifully maintained; rates run accordingly.

★★★★★ A luxurious cruise experience; ships have two seatings in the dining room (except the smaller vessels), but don't expect kilos of Beluga caviar upon request; greater variety of cabin categories; excellent on-board facilities and memorable services; rates can be very high in the suites.

★★★★ An excellent cruise experience; cabins can be quite small on the newer breed of vessels, large but showing their age on the older ships; food is good and nicely presented though often provided by a catering service; great attention to nighttime entertainment and gambling casinos; ships appeal to all ages and all types; many different cabin categories, and some itineraries are very interesting.

★★★ Good value and good fun on a variety of vessels; ships of all ages and for all types of people; cabins not plush, but comfortable; bathrooms can be old-fashioned; food is bountiful and often quite good; bars not always so good, especially if a concession; mainly older vessels that have been frequently refurbished; all facilities on board (swimming pool, theater, casino, boutiques, entertainment) without extra; highly recommended, especially if itinerary is interesting; rock-bottom rates can be enjoyed!

★★ Ships need work; travelers who are looking for a good deal will enjoy them, especially if itineraries suit them.

Key to rates

O—Outrageous; if you to ask, you can't afford it! ($600 to !!!! per person, per day, plus tips appropriate to the divine service—although these are included on Seabourn and Sea Goddess cruises)

H—High, especially in the top cabin categories (per diems up to $500, plus, plus)

HM—High Moderate (per diems of $200 to $400)

M—Moderate (approximately $150 to $300 a day)

V—Value (under $100 to about $200 for the best cabin, per person, per day)

NOTE · · · The above rates are only an approximation; published cruise prices today have little relevance because of discounting, twofers, and last-minute giveaways. (A full ship is a happy ship, especially for the crew, who depend upon their weekly tips.) See your travel counselor for the true figure, as round-trip economy airfare is usually included. Port taxes, tips, shore excursions, and personal expenses are extra.

Key to ship-line abbreviations:
AHC—American Hawaii Cruises
BSL—Bermuda Star Line
HAL—Holland America Line
NAC—former Norwegian American Cruises
NCL—Norwegian Cruise Line
OCL—Ocean Cruise Line
P&O—Peninsular and Orient Steam Navigation Company
RCCL—Royal Caribbean Cruise Line
RVL—Royal Viking Line

Major Cruise Ships of the World (by size)

Rating	Ship	Cruise Line	Flag	Tonnage	Pass.	Cruising Areas	Rates
★★★★+	Norway	NCL	Bahamas	75,000	2400	Caribbean	M/HM
★★★★	Sovereign of the Seas	RCCL	Liberia	74,000	2300	Caribbean	M/HM
★★★★	Ecstasy	Carnival	Bahamas	70,367	2044	Caribbean	M/HM
★★★★	Fantasy	Carnival	Bahamas	70,000	2000	Bahamas	M
★★★★★	Crown Princess/ Regal Princess	Princess	Italy	70,000	1590	Caribbean	HM/O!
★★★★–	QE2	Cunard	Britain	67,140	1800	worldwide	M–O!
★★★★★+							
★★★★	Star Princess	Princess	Liberia	63,524	1470	Caribbean	HM/H
★★★★+	FairMajesty	Princess	Liberia	62,500	1470	Caribbean	HM/H
★★★★★	Westerdam	HAL	Bahamas	52,000	1500	Alaska/Carib	M/HM
★★★★★–	Crystal Harmony	Crystal	Bahamas	49,400	960	Carib/Europe	HM/O!
★★★★★+							
★★★+	Celebration	Carnival	Liberia	48,000	1500	Caribbean	M
★★★+	Jubilee	Carnival	Liberia	48,000	1500	Caribbean	M
★★★★+	Sky Princess	Princess	Liberia	46,000	1212	Alaska/Mex/Caribbean	M/HM
★★★★	Holiday	Carnival	Bahamas	46,000	1500	Mexico	M
★★★★+	Horizon	Celebrity	Liberia	46,000	1354	Bermuda/Carib	M/HM
★★★+	Canberra	P&O	Britain	45,000	1800	worldwide	M
★★★★★	Royal Princess	Princess	Britain	45,000	1200	worldwide	HM/O!
★★★★	Nordic Empress	RCCL	Liberia	45,000	1610	Bahamas	M/HM

511

Major Cruise Ships of the World (by size) (cont.)

Rating	Ship	Cruise Line	Flag	Tonnage	Pass.	Cruising Areas	Rates
★★★	Seaward	NCL	Bahamas	42,000	1500	Caribbean	M
★★★★★	Crown Odyssey	Royal	Bahamas	40,000	1000	worldwide	HM/H
★★★★	Starship Oceanic	Premier	Panama	40,000	1200	Bahamas	V/M
★★★	Festivale	Carnival	Bahamas	38,000	1200	Caribbean	M
★★★★★	Rotterdam	HAL	Neth. Antill	38,000	1070	World	M
★★★★★+	Royal Viking Sun	RVL	Bahamas	38,000	740	worldwide	HM—O!
★★★★	Song of America	RCCL	Norway	37,500	1414	Mexico	M/HM
★★★+	Tropicale	Carnival	Liberia	36,600	1022	Caribbean	M
★★★+	Starship Atlantic	Premier	Liberia	36,000	1200	Bahamas	V/M
★★★★	Europa	Hapag Lloyd	W. Germany	34,000	605	worldwide	HM/H
★★★★★	Nieuw Amsterdam/ Noordam	HAL	Neth. Antill.	33,900	1200	Alaska/Carib/Mex	M
★★★★	CostaRiviera	Costa	Italy	31,500	1000	Caribbean	M
★★★★	Meridian	Celebrity	Bahamas	30,440	1106	Bermuda/Carib	M
★★★	Constitution/ Independence	AHC	U.S.	30,000	800	Hawaii	V/M
★★★	Eugenio Costa	Costa	Italy	30,000	1100	worldwide	M/HM
★★★★★	Royal Viking Sea/Sky/Star	RVL	Bahamas	28,000	710	worldwide	HM/H
★★★★+	Sea Princess	P&O	Britain	28,000	730	worldwide	M–H
★★★	Mardi Gras	Carnival	Bahamas	27,250	906	Bahamas	V/M

★★★	*Carnivale*	Carnival	Bahamas	27,250	950	Bahamas	V/M
★★★+	*Viking Serenade*	RCCL	Bahamas	27,000	976	Alaska/Mex	M/HM
★★★	*Britanis*	Chandris	Panama	26,000	926	Carib/Mex/S. America	V/M
★★★	*Regent Sun*	Regency	Bahamas	25,000	836	Carib/Alaska	M
★★★★+	*Dawn Princess/Fair Princess*	Princess	Liberia	25,500	809	Alaska/Carib	M/HM
★★★★	*Costa Marina*	Costa	Italy	25,000	770	Europe/Carib	M
★★★★★+	*Sagafjord*	Cunard/NAC	Bahamas	24,500	610	worldwide	HM–O!
★★★	*Regent Star*	Regency	Bahamas	24,500	950	Alaska/Caribbean	M
★★★★★+	*Vistafjord*	Cunard/NAC	Bahamas	24,500	749	Europe/Carib	HM–O!
★★★	*Emerald Seas*	Admiral	Liberia	24,500	782	Bahamas	V/M
★★★	*Bermuda Star*	Commodore	Panama	23,500	725	Canada/Mex	V
★★★	*Queen of Bermuda*	Commodore	Panama	23,500	725	Bermuda/Caribbean	V
★★	*Caribe I*	Commodore	Panama	23,000	875	Caribbean	V
★★★★	*Song of Norway*	RCCL	Norway	23,000	1040	Caribbean	M
★★★★	*Nordic Prince*	RCCL	Norway	23,000	1020	Bermuda/Caribbean	M
★★★	*Regent Sea*	Regency	Bahamas	22,000	722	Alaska/Caribbean	M
★★★	*Azure Seas*	Admiral	Liberia	21,500	756	Mexico	V
★★★	*Sea Breeze*	Dolphin	Bahamas	21,000	840	Caribbean	V/M
★★★+	*Carla Costa*	Costa	Italy	20,500	748	Caribbean	V/M
★★★★★	*Island/Pacific Princess*	Princess	Britain	20,000	610	Worldwide	HM
★★★	*Amerikanis*	Chandris	Panama	20,000	610	Caribbean	V
★★★★	*Americana*	Ivaran	Norway	19,500	88	S. America	H/HM

Major Cruise Ships of the World (by size) (cont.)

Rating	Ship	Cruise Line	Flag	Tonnage	Pass.	Cruising Areas	Rates
★★★	Victoria	Chandris	Panama	19,000	550	Europe/Carib	V
★★★★	Sun Viking	RCCL	Norway	18,500	728	Caribbean/Europe	M
★★★	Universe	World Explorer	Liberia	18,100	550	Alaska	V
★★★★	Stella Solaris	Sun	Greece	18,000	650	E. Med/Carib/S. America	HM
★★★	Starship Majestic	Premier	Bahamas	17,750	768	Bahamas	V
★★★+	Cunard Countess	Cunard	Britain	17,500	800	Caribbean	M
★★★★+	Cunard Princess	Cunard	Bahamas	17,500	800	Europe	M
★★★	Odysseus	Epirotiki	Greece	17,000	550	Greece/Carib	M
★★★	Southward	NCL	Bahamas	16,600	767	Mexico	M
★★★★★	Daphne	Costa	Liberia	16,300	425	Alaska/Caribbean	M
★★★★	Danae	Costa	Liberia	16,300	425	worldwide	M
★★★	Skyward	NCL	Bahamas	16,250	730	Caribbean	M
★★★	Starward	NCL	Bahamas	16,000	788	Caribbean	M
★★★+	Crown Monarch	Crown	Bahamas	16,000	560	Caribbean	M
	Enrico Costa	Costa	Italy	16,000	700	Europe/S. America	V
★★★	Sunward II	NCL	Bahamas	14,100	700	Bahamas	V
★★★	Pegasus	Epirotiki	Greece	14,000	832	E. Med./S. America	V/M
★★★	The Azur	Chandris	Panama	15,000	700	Med/Carib	V/M
★★★+	Mermoz	Paquet	Bahamas	13,800	530	World	M
★★★	Oceanos	Epirotiki	Greece	14,000	516	E. Med.	V

★★★	*Dolphin IV*	Dolphin	Bahamas	13,000	586	Bahamas	V/M
★★★	*Eurosun*	Europe Cruise	Bermuda	12,500	670	Med.	M
★★★★	*Ocean Pearl*	Ocean/Pearl	Bahamas	12,400	500	Orient	M–H
★★★★	*Ocean Princess*	OCL	Bahamas	12,200	460	Europe/S. America	M
★★★+	*World Renaissance*	Epirotiki	Greece	12,000	426	Caribbean/Europe	M
★★★★★	*Golden Odyssey*	Royal	Bahamas	10,500	460	Caribbean	HM/H
★★★	*Romanza*	Chandris	Panama	10,000	562	Med.	V
★★★+	*Crown del Mar*	Crown	Panama	10,000	444	Mexico	M
★★★	*Berlin*	Europ America	W.Germany	9,570	470	Europe/Caribbean	M
★★★★★+	*Seabourn Pride/ Seabourn Spirit*	Seabourn	Norway	10,000	212	worldwide	O!
★★★★★+	*Song of Flower*	Seven Seas	Norway	8,282	216	Alaska/Orient	H/O!
★★★★★	*Frontier Spirit*	Frontier	Bahamas	6,700	164	Antarctica	H/O!
★★★+	*Stella Oceanis*	Sun	Greece	6,000	300	E. Med/Caribbean	M
★★★★★	*Wind Star/Wind Song/ Wind Spirit*	Windstar	Bahamas	5,350	150	Carib/Tahiti/Med.	HM
★★★	*Jason*	Epirotiki	Greece	5,250	268	E. Med.	V
★★★★+	*Oceanic Grace*	Oceanic Cruises	Japan	5,050	118	Orient	H/O!
★★★	*Orpheus*	Swan Hellenic	Greece	5,000	160	Europe	M

Small Cruise Ships of the World (including river ships)

	Ship	Cruise Line	Flag	Passengers	Cruising Areas	Rates
★★★	*Mississippi Queen*	DQ Steamboat	U.S.	405	Mississippi/Ohio	HM/H
★★★★	*Danube Princess*	Exprinter	Germany	215	Danube River	M/HM
★★★	*Neptune*	Epirotiki	Greece	215	Aegean	V
★★★+	*Deutschland/Britannia/ France*	KD German Rhine	Germany	208/202	Rhine/Moselle rivers	M
★★★+	*Austria/Italia/Nederland*	KD German Rhine	Germany	192/190	Rhine/Moselle rivers	M
★★★★	*Delta Queen*	DQ Steamboat	U.S.	180	Mississippi/Ohio rivers	HM
★★★★	*Star Clipper/Star Flyer*	Star Clippers	Belgium	180	Europ/Carib	HM
★★★★	*Anni/Aton/Hotp/Tut*	Sheraton	Egypt	178	Nile River	HM
★★★+	*Helvetia*	KD German Rhine	Germany	176	Rhine/Moselle rivers	M
★★★★	*Stella Maris II*	Sun	Greece	175	Mediterranean	HM
★★★★	*Caledonian Star*	Salem Lindblad Expeditions	Bahamas	156	Alaska/Carib	M
★★★	*Argonaut*	Epirotiki	Greece	150	charter	H
★★★★★	*World Discoverer*	Society Exped	Liberia	140	expeditions	H
★★★★	*Europa*	KD German Rhine	Germany	138	Rhine/Moselle rivers	M
★★★★★	*Illiria*	Classical Cruises	Liberia	140	Med/Antarctica	H
★★★	*Ambassador*	Salen Lindblad	Yugoslavia	120	Adriatic	M
★★★★★+	*Sea Goddess I and II*	Cunard/SG	Norway	100	worldwide	O!
★★★★	*Society Explorer*	Society Expeditions	Bahamas	100	worldwide	H

516

★★★★★	*Nantucket/Yorktown Clipper*	Clipper	U.S.	100/138	Caribbean/East Coast	HM
★★★★★+	*Renaissance I–VIII*	Renaissance	Italy	100/114	Worldwide	H
★★★★	*Isis/Osiris*	Hilton	Egypt	90	Nile River	HM
★★★	*Bucanneer*	Galapagos	Ecuador	90	Galapagos Islands	M
★★★	*Santa Cruz*	Galapagos	Ecuador	90	Galapagos Islands	M
★★★	*Caribbean Prince*	Am Canadian	U.S.	80	Carib/Canada	M
★★★★	*Polaris*	Special Expeditions	Bahamas	80	World	H
★★★+	*New Shoreham II*	Am Canadian	U.S.	72	Carib/Canada	M
★★★★	*Sea Bird/Sea Lion*	Special Expedition	U.S.	70	Alaska/Baja	M
★★★★	*Nile Cruise*	Swan Hellenic	Egypt	68	Nile River	HM
★★★★	*Bashan*	Abercrombie & Kent	China	66	Yangtzse River	H
★★★+	*Glacier Bay*	Exploration	U.S.	60	Alaska	M
★★★★★	*Island Explorer*	Abercrombie & Kent/Spice Islands	Indonesia	36	Indonesia	H

INDEX

519

SHIPS AND SHIP LINES

Ocean Cruise Lines, 314, 415, 416
Oceanic, 8, 11, 417–18
Ocean Islander, 9
Oceanos, 302, 419
Ocean Pearl, 7, 415–16
Ocean Princess, 416–17
Odysseus, 419–20
Orellana, 304
Orient Express, 420–21
Orpheus, 302, 339–40, 421–22
Osiris, 265

P & O Cruises, 2, 317–18
Pegasus, 303 422
Polaris, 335–36
Premier Cruise Lines, 17, 319–20, 417
Princess Cruises, 12, 15, 317, 320–22, 393, 434, 445

Queen Elizabeth 2, 2, 3, 10, 11, 13, 19, 20, 26, 27, 291–94, 424–27
Queen of Bermuda, 278, 427–28

Regency Cruises, 19, 322–23, 428, 429, 430
Regent Sea, 321, 322, 428–29
Regent Star, 321, 322, 429–30
Regent Sun, 321, 430–31
Rhine Cruise Agency, 13
Romanza, 282, 432
Rotterdam, 2, 307, 308, 433–34
Royal Caribbean Cruise Line, 11, 13, 16, 324–27, 410, 452, 455, 456
Royal Cruise Line, 7, 11, 15, 32, 328–30, 365, 384
Royal Princess, 434–35
Royal Viking Line, 2, 7, 12, 15, 16, 22, 27, 330–31, 435, 438

Royal Viking Sea/Royal Viking Sky, Royal Viking Sun, 435–38
Royal Viking Sun, 330, 438–39

Sagafjord, 2, 22, 27, 38, 295, 440–42
Salen Lindblad Cruising, 15, 332
Santa Cruz, 304, 442
Seabourn Cruise Line, 333, 446
Seabourn Pride/Seabourn Spirit, 12, 333, 446–48
Sea Goddess I and II, 20, 22, 295–96, 443–45
Sea Goddess Cruises, Ltd., 12, 19, 22, 295–96, 443–45
Sea Princess, 3, 321, 445–46
Seaward, 313, 449–50
Sheraton Nile Cruises, 268–69
Skyward, 312, 451
Society Expeditions Cruises, 15, 334–35, 451, 476
Society Explorer, 334, 451–52
Song of America, 325, 326, 327, 452–53
Song of Norway, 16, 325, 326, 327, 455–56
Southward, 312, 313, 456
Sovereign of the Seas, 6, 13, 325, 327, 456–58
Special Expeditions, 335–36
Star Clipper/Star Flyer, 458–59
Star Princess, 320, 459–60
Starward, 312, 461
Stella Maris II, 337–38, 461–62
Stella Oceanis, 337–38, 462–65
Stella Solaris, 18, 337–38, 463–64
Sun Boat, 252
Sun Line Cruises, 337–38, 461, 462
Sun Viking, 325, 326, 465–66
Sunward II, 8, 16, 313, 466–67
Swan Hellenic Cruises, 15, 22, 339–40

PORTS OF CALL